ADULT DEVELOPMENT & AGING

BIOPSYCHOSOCIAL PERSPECTIVES

Each generation has its unique needs and aspirations. When Charles Wiley first opened his small printing shop in lower Manhattan in 1807, it was a generation of boundless potential searching for an identity. And we were there, helping to define a new American literary tradition. Over half a century later, in the midst of the Second Industrial Revolution, it was a generation focused on building the future. Once again, we were there, supplying the critical scientific, technical, and engineering knowledge that helped frame the world. Throughout the 20th Century, and into the new millennium, nations began to reach out beyond their own borders and a new international community was born. Wiley was there, expanding its operations around the world to enable a global exchange of ideas, opinions, and know-how.

For 200 years, Wiley has been an integral part of each generation's journey, enabling the flow of information and understanding necessary to meet their needs and fulfill their aspirations. Today, bold new technologies are changing the way we live and learn. Wiley will be there, providing you the must-have knowledge you need to imagine new worlds, new possibilities, and new opportunities.

Generations come and go, but you can always count on Wiley to provide you the knowledge you need, when and where you need it!

PRESIDENT AND CHIEF EXECUTIVE OFFICER　　　　　　　**CHAIRMAN OF THE BOARD**

ADULT DEVELOPMENT & AGING

BIOPSYCHOSOCIAL PERSPECTIVES

Third Edition

Susan Krauss Whitbourne, Ph.D.

University of Massachussetts at Amherst

John Wiley & Sons, Inc.

VICE PRESIDENT AND PUBLISHER	Jay O'Callaghan
EXECUTIVE EDITOR	Christopher Johnson
ASSISTANT EDITOR	Eileen McKeever
PRODUCTION SERVICES MANAGER	Dorothy Sinclair
PRODUCTION EDITOR	Janet Foxman
EXECUTIVE MARKETING MANAGER	Jeffrey Rucker
CREATIVE DIRECTOR	Harry Nolan
DESIGNER	Hope Miller
PHOTO EDITOR	Elle Wagner
EDITORIAL ASSISTANT	Carrie Tupa
MARKETING ASSISTANT	Rachel Cirone
SENIOR MEDIA EDITOR	Lynn Pearlman
PRODUCTION MANAGEMENT	Patty Donovan/Pine Tree Composition, Inc.
BICENTENNIAL LOGO DESIGN	Richard J. Pacifico

COVER ART: Henri Matisse (1869–1954), *L'Escargot*, 1953. Gouache on paper, cut and pasted on paper mounted (2864 × 2870 mm). © 2007 Succession H. Matisse, Paris / Artists Rights Society (ARS), New York. Photograph: © 2007 Tate Gallery, London, England. Reproduced with permission.

This book was set in Berkeley-Book by Laserwords Private Limited, Chennai, India and printed and bound by R.R. Donnelley—Crawfordsville. The cover was printed by Phoenix Color.

The book is printed on acid-free paper. ∞

To order books or for customer service, please call 1-800-CALL WILEY (225-5945).

Library of Congress Cataloging-in-Publication Data:

Printed in the United States of America

10 9 8 7 6 5 4 3 2 1

PREFACE

We are all aging. This very fact should be enough to draw you into the subject matter of this course, whether you are the student or the instructor. Yet, for many of us, it is difficult to imagine what we will be like in the future, be it 50, 40, or even 10 years from now. The goal of this book is to help you imagine your future and the future of your family, your friends, and your society. To do so, I have brought together the scientific enterprise of aging with the more personal approach that will encourage you in this imaginative journey into the future.

In this third edition of *Adult Development: Biopsychosocial Perspectives*, I have based much of the material on the course I teach at the University of Massachusetts Amherst on the Psychology of Aging. When I was asked to revise the text, I decided to incorporate my day-to-day teaching of the course into the text itself. What you will read follows very closely with the way I approach the course and engage my students in the learning process. Examples, self-assessment exercises, figures, and tables, as well as the words in the text, reflect what I have found to be of most interest to my students.

I became interested in the scholarly field of aging as an undergraduate when I decided to write a paper on personality and adaptation in the course I was taking on developmental psychology. However, the field of aging had personal relevance to me as well. My father was a physician who specialized in geriatrics (the medical practice of aging). His professional activities had a profound influence on me and made the choice of gerontology (the scientific study of aging) a natural one.

It is my hope and belief that you will find that the study of aging has many fascinating aspects. Not only is everyone around you aging, but the issues that are raised within this field extend from the philosophical to the practical. Why do living things age? Is there a way to slow down the aging process? How will society deal with the aging of the Baby Boomers? How will job markets be affected by our aging society? Will you age differently than your parents and grandparents? All of these, and more, are questions that you will find yourself asking as you explore the many complexities of the process that causes us to change and grow throughout our lives. At the same time, you will gain many advantages from learning the material in this course. You will learn the keys to healthy development in the years of adulthood. As a result, you will learn not only how we grow older but how to grow older in a way that is healthy and satisfying.

THEMES OF THE BOOK

The biopsychosocial model on which I have based the text is intended to encourage you to think about the multiple interactions among the domains of biology, psychology, and sociology. According to this model, changes in one area of life have effects on changes in other areas. The centerpiece of this model is identity, your self-definition. You interpret the experiences you have through the framework provided by your identity. In turn, your experiences often stimulate you to change your self-definition.

This is an exciting time to be studying adult development and aging. Not only is the topic gaining increasing media attention, but it is also gaining tremendous momentum as an academic discipline within life-span development. The biopsychosocial model fits within the framework of contemporary approaches that emphasize the impact of social context on individuals throughout all periods of life. Entirely new concepts, sets of data, and practical applications of these models are resulting in a realization of the dreams of many of the classic developmental psychologists whose work shaped the field in the early twentieth century.

ORGANIZATION

There is a logical organization to the progression of chapters in this book, essentially from the "bio" to the "psycho" to the "social." However, this is not a strict progression. Instructors may find that they would prefer to switch the order of certain chapters or sections within chapters, and that will be fairly easy to do. I have stuck to the integrative theme of the biopsychosocial model in that many of the topics, regardless of where they appear in the book, bring together this multifaceted approach.

I felt strongly about having the final chapter be not about death and dying, as is often the case in other books in the field, but about successful aging. In fact, as you looked at the cover, you may have wondered what is meant by the swirl of brightly colored squares. It is actually a collage by Henri Matisse, who you will read about in Chapter 14, where I discuss creativity and aging. It is his last work, a remarkably vivid expression of the vitality that characterizes successful aging.

Features

- Up to date research
  The topics and features in this text are intended to involve you in the field of aging from a scholarly and a personal perspective. You will find that the most current research is presented throughout the text, with careful and detailed explanations of the studies that highlight the most important scholarly advances.

- Thought questions
  Critical thinking questions are presented in highlighted boxes in a feature called "What Do You Think?"), as well as throughout the text. Some of these are intended to encourage you to apply the material to your personal life and others to examine critically the research.

- Assess Yourself Boxes
  Web-based surveys used in teaching the course are presented in these boxed features. Ranging from thinking about what you will be like "When I'm 64," to planning your own funeral, they give you a chance to think about how the material directly applies to your own life. I think you will enjoy taking them, and instructors will very likely be interested in seeing how their classes respond to the questions. None of them are copyrighted, so instructors are free to administer them in class or online.

- Introductory quotes
  Each chapter opens with observations about aging from well-known authors, poets, and

celebrities. The individuals quoted are people who have lived to ripe old ages themselves, and reflect the wisdom that has accompanied their own journeys through life.

Student Learning Aids

- Numbered summaries
  Each chapter contains a numbered summary that will assist students in reviewing the important material from the chapter.

- Glossary terms
  Bold items in each chapter indicate glossary terms. Because students may encounter a term more than once after it is introduced in a particular chapter, all the glossary items appear at the end of the book, as do the references.

- Ample illustrations
  Tables and figures pick up on major points in the text. There are also photographs intended to highlight particularly interesting or relevant issues.

CHANGES IN THE THIRD EDITION

The first edition of *Adult Development and Aging: Biopsychosocial Perspectives* was intended to provide a fresh and engaging approach to the field of the psychology of adult development and aging by focusing on three themes: a multidisciplinary approach, positive images of aging, and the newest and most relevant research. The second edition maintained these three themes, as they have proven to be well-received by adopters and students. Now, with the third edition, I sought to have the text replicate as closely as possible the experience for students of participating in a live classroom. To accomplish this goal, I incorporated more of a conversational style– essentially "talking to" the student reading the text. I hope that this approach will make the instructor's job a little easier, because students will be more motivated to complete their readings if they think the text is more interesting.

I did not change the organization of chapters, although I moved some sections around within chapters. For example, I moved the section on sexuality and aging to the chapter on physical changes (Chapter 4). Rather than present socioemotional selectivity theory in the chapter on relationships (Chapter 9), I presented it in the chapter on personality (Chapter 8). Within the chapter on theories (Chapter 2), I moved the biological theories to the end and brought the psychosocial theories to the front. Instructors who have developed their course based on earlier editions will not need to change the basic structure of their lectures and assignments. However, I did condense some sections, deleted others, and introduced new sections to reflect changes in the field. I also deleted the boxed features that, in my experience, students were not reading. Instead, I integrated the Biopsychosocial Perspectives boxes from the previous editions into the text itself.

Throughout the third edition, references have been substantially updated. Approximately half of the references are from 2005 or later and one-third are from 2006 and 2007. To maintain the same length of the text, outdated references were deleted and sections were updated to reflect the new research. In addition to reshaping the research base of the text, greater emphasis was given in the text itself on walking students through the major studies, including explaining in depth the results presented in relevant figures and tables.

New U.S. Census data have been completely integrated into demographic material presented throughout the text, as have special reports on older adults published by the Administration on

Aging, the U.S. Department of Health and Human Services, and the Centers for Disease Control and Prevention. In addition to presenting updated information on the U.S., substantial information was added from international statistics particularly in the area of health. Since there are many Canadian users of the text, I also included a number of studies based on Canadian samples. Based on the feedback from my students, I gave particular attention to data that would catch the attention of the student reader, and also consolidated or deleted a number of the statistical tables from previous editions.

Another major change involved condensing the biological and physiological material. Feedback from instructors and my own students was instrumental in prompting this change of focus. As a result, the material is still amply documented and presented, but with much more attention to behavioral aspects of changes in physical functioning and health. For example, in the chapter on biological theories of aging (Chapter 2), I included data (and illustrations) from studies showing the effects of red wine and chocolate on longevity. Similarly, in the chapter on research methods (Chapter 5), I condensed the information on sequential methods, again, only focusing on the most central themes. In general, I aimed to provide studies that were as interesting as possible to illustrate major points.

Some of the other specific changes found in each chapter should also increase the relevance of the text. For example, in response to reviewer suggestions, I expanded the section on aging and driving in the chapter on information processing (Chapter 6). Within that chapter, I also added new theoretical perspectives that are taking hold within the field, such as context processing deficiency theory. I updated and expanded the section in that chapter on memory control beliefs and memory training studies. Throughout these chapters,

I also expanded the treatment of brain imaging studies, an area that has grown tremendously in the past three to four years. Along these lines, new theories and treatments of Alzheimer's disease have also been included (Chapter 5). If an instructor would like a detailed list of changes, just email me and I will provide it (swhitbo@psych.umass.edu); obviously I would also be happy to answer any other questions that you may have.

One of the changes that I am most excited about is the addition of a table on "Age Busters" in the chapter on successful aging (Chapter 14). Those instructors who have used my powerpoint slides in the past know that I have built a special bonus lecture into the course that includes a multimedia show of highly successful aging people from the past and present who have broken out of traditional age barriers within their respective fields (such as the actress Katharine Hepburn who won three Academy Awards after the age of 60). For the present edition, I included the names, ages, and accomplishments of contemporary figures who fit this definition. Some of the inspiration for the names included in this table came from my own students, who I regularly poll online to find out who are their nominees. Feel free to add your own nominees to this list!

Supplements

Wiley is pleased to offer an online resource containing a wealth of teaching and learning material at http://www.wiley.com/college/whitbourne

Website Links

Active website links are available on our book companion website. These links are specific to this text and are constantly updated to reflect the latest advances in the field.

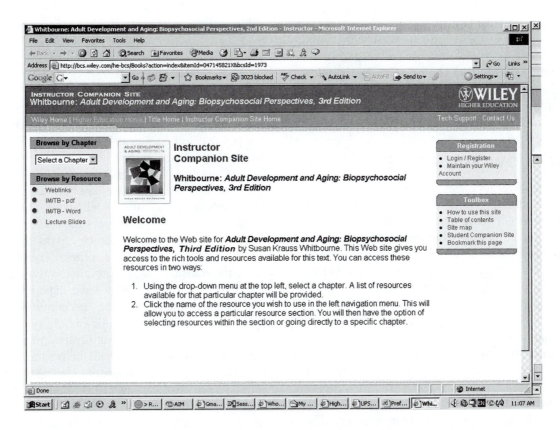

Instructor Resources (written solely by the Author)

• Instructor's Manual

The content in the Instructor's Manual reflects over 30 years of experience in teaching this course. Provides chapter outlines, key terms, learning objectives, and lecture suggestions. Video suggestions are also provided as well as resources for finding documentaries, movies, and even pop music.

• PowerPoint slides
Prepared for use in lectures, a complete set of PowerPoint slides tailored to the book are available for download. Contained on the slides are highlights of chapters and extensive visual illustrations of chapter concepts and key terms.

• Test Bank
A complete downloadable test bank includes 50 to 70 questions in each chapter that follow along with the order that the concepts are presented in the text. Each multiple-choice question is labeled according to which concept it tests, along with its difficulty level. There are also short answer and essay questions corresponding to each section of the chapter.

- Supplemental Lecture Notes
  Prepared to accompany the PowerPoint slides, lecture notes include outlines, diagrams, and tables taken from the text that students can bring to class. Instructors can download these and reprint them for distribution to students.

ACKNOWLEDGMENTS

My first set of acknowledgements go to my long-suffering family, who have put up with the hours I have spent holed away in my upstairs study preparing this third edition: My husband Richard O'Brien, as always, provided both important substantive help (his field is biology), but also continued to encourage me at every step along the way. My two daughters keep me up to date with what is on the minds of students, and as both of them decided to pursue careers in psychology, they are excellent test audiences for some of my material. Not only were both of my daughters students in my Psychology of Aging course (an interesting experience!), my older daughter, Stacey Whitbourne, received her Ph.D. from Brandeis in social psychology with a focus on aging, carrying on the family tradition to one more generation. Jennifer O'Brien, my younger daughter, will be entering the field of clinical psychology, carrying on that tradition as well. Finally, my mother, Lisa Rock, deserves a special merit award for not only providing regular companionship around the dinner table, but also continuing to demonstrate so many of the qualities of creativity that make up successful aging as she pursues her career as an artist.

Throughout the writing of this book, the students in my Psychology of Aging class provided valuable insights and observations. As I was literally revising the book while I was preparing the lectures, their input allowed me to work back and forth between teaching and writing. Their good humor, patience, and willingness to experiment with some new ideas made it possible for me to help add the all-important student viewpoint to the finished product.

My editor at John Wiley & Sons, Chris Johnson, has provided tremendous inspiration and support in the planning of this revision. His positive and enthusiastic approach has been greatly appreciated as has been the support of Jay O'Callaghan, Vice President and Publisher. I would also like to give special thanks to Maureen Clendenny, who is about as quick to reply to an email as anyone I have ever met. Her assistant, Eileen McKeever, serves in her role with efficiency and effectiveness. They have made the transition to the production team also about as smooth as any I have experienced. Elle Wagner, Photo Manager, has continued to show resourcefulness and efficiency in fulfilling my desires for outstanding illustrative material, and I have also received terrific help from Janet Foxman, the production editor. The marketing team, Jeffrey Rucker, Marketing Manager, and Rachel Cirone, Marketing Assistant, have helped to ensure that you and your colleagues know all about the book. Finally, the work of Hope Miller, the Designer, has ensured that the book is attractively presented. These individuals provide behind the scenes help that every author knows is invaluable to the creation of an excellent text.

My final thanks go to the reviewers who provided helpful comments and suggestions throughout the revision process. Their insightful observations and thoughtful proposals for changes helped me tighten and focus the manuscript and enhance the discussion of several key areas of interest in the field. Thank you to Gary Creasey (Illinois State University), Carrie Andreoletti, (Central Connecticut State University), Richard Tucker (University of Central Florida), Renee Babcock (Central Michigan University), Susan Bell (Georgetown College) and

Victoria Hilkevitch Bedford (University of Indianapolis). I have also benefited from informal reviews provided by my colleagues who use the book in their teaching and greatly appreciate their helpful suggestions. I have tried my best to honor your input.

In conclusion, I hope that I have given you something to look forward to as you venture into the fascinating field of adult development and aging, and that the subsequent pages of this book will fulfill these expectations. I have tried to present a comprehensive but clear picture of the area and hope that you will be able to apply this knowledge to improving your own life and the lives of the older adults with whom you may be preparing to work. I hope you will come away from the course with a positive feeling about what they can do to "age better" and with a positive feeling about the potentialities of later life. And maybe, just maybe, as has happened on many past occasions with people who have read this book, you will decide to pursue this field and I can welcome you as colleagues in the coming years.

Susan Krauss Whitbourne, Ph.D.
June 2007

ABOUT THE AUTHOR

Susan Krauss Whitbourne, Ph.D., Professor of Psychology at the University of Massachusetts Amherst, received her Ph.D. in Developmental Psychology from Columbia University in 1974 and completed a post-doctoral training program in Clinical Psychology at the University of Massachusetts Amherst, having joined the faculty there in 1984. Her previous positions were as an Associate Professor of Education and Psychology at the University of Rochester (1975–84) and an Assistant Professor of Psychology at SUNY College at Geneseo. Currently Psychology

Departmental Honors Coordinator at the University of Massachusetts Amherst and Director of the Office of National Scholarship Advisement, she is also Faculty Advisor to the University of Massachusetts Chapter of Psi Chi, a position for which she was recognized as the Eastern Regional Outstanding Advisor for the year 2001 and as the Florence Denmark National Faculty Advisor in 2002. She served as Eastern Region Vice President of Psi Chi in 2006–07. Her teaching has been recognized with the College Outstanding Teacher Award in 1995 and the University Distinguished Teaching Award in 2001. Her work as an advisor was recognized with the Outstanding Academic Advisor Award in 2006. In 2003, she received the American Psychological Association (APA) Division 20 (Adult Development and Aging) Master Mentor Award and the Gerontological Society of America (GSA) Behavioral and Social Sciences Distinguished Mentorship award.

Over the past 20 years, Dr. Whitbourne has held a variety of elected and appointed positions in APA Division 20 including President (1995–96), Treasurer (1986–89), Secretary (1981–84), Program Chair (1997–98), Education Committee Chair (1979–80), Student Awards Committee Chair (1993–94), Continuing Education Committee Chair (1981–82), and Elections Committee Chair (1992–93). She currently chairs the Fellowship Committee and served for six years as the Division 20 Representative to the APA Council (2000–2005). She is a Fellow of Divisions 1 (General Psychology), 2 (Teaching of Psychology), 12 (Clinical Psychology), and 20. She has served on the APA Committee on Structure and Function of Council and chaired the Policy and Planning Board in 2007.

Dr. Whitbourne is also a Fellow of the Gerontological Society of America, and has served as Chair of the Student Awards Committee and Distinguished Mentorship Committee. A founding member of the Society for the Study of Human Development, she was its President from 2005 to 2007. She has also served on the Board of Directors of the National Association of Fellowship Advisors. In her home of Amherst, Massachusetts, she has served on the Council on Aging (2004–07) and is currently the President of the Friends of the Amherst Senior Center.

Her publications include twenty four published books and over 125 journal articles and chapters, including articles in *Psychology and Aging, Psychotherapy, Developmental Psychology, Journal of Gerontology, Journal of Personality, and Social Psychology*, and *Teaching of Psychology*, and chapters in the *Handbook of the Psychology of Aging,*

Clinical Geropsychology, Comprehensive Clinical Psychology (Geropsychology), the *Encyclopedia of Psychology* and the *International Encyclopedia of the Social and Behavioral Sciences*. She has been a Consulting Editor for *Psychology and Aging* and serves on the Editorial Board of the *Journal of Gerontology* and is a Consulting Editor for *Developmental Psychology*. Her presentations at professional conferences number over 175, and include several invited addresses, among them the APA G. Stanley Hall Lecture in 1995, the EPA Psi Chi Distinguished Lecture in 2001, and the SEPA Invited Lecture in 2002.

CONTENTS

CHAPTER 6

Basic Cognitive Functions: Information Processing, Attention, and Memory   139

CHAPTER 7

Language, Problem Solving, and Intelligence   163

CHAPTER 8

Personality and Patterns of Coping   190

Themes and Issues in Adult Development and Aging

> **"***I had to wait 110 years to become famous. I wanted to enjoy it as long as possible.***"**
>
> — Jeanne Louise Calment
> (1875–1997)

f you are reading this book, you are an "adult." Even if you are, by all accounts, an average-aged college student, you nevertheless fit many of the criteria for this age category of human beings. The term "adult," which may conjure up the image of someone who is a "grown-up," refers to all individuals who have reached a certain level of physical, psychological, and social maturity. You and your fellow students may have difficulty entering certain commercial establishments without valid proof of age. Nevertheless, you are considered in many ways able to enjoy the privileges and carry out the responsibilities of those whom you tend to think of as from the "older generation." For those of you reading this book who have no difficulty thinking of yourselves as adults, you may be struggling with the issue of whether you are a "young" or "middle-aged" version of this category of humans. And for

those students who clearly identify themselves as members of the older generation of adults, the issues you face with regard to self-definition may involve contemplating your status as a "senior citizen."

Questions involving self-definition based on age are very relevant to the scope and coverage of this book. We will be examining definitions of adulthood, the meaning and definition of "age," and the approaches researchers have taken to understanding the biological, psychological, and social changes that take place from the years of adolescence through old age. Readers will find that this information is of personal as well as theoretical and professional interest. We will explore the many ways individuals can affect their own aging processes through incorporating into their daily lives behaviors and activities that can maintain maximum levels of functioning well into the later decades of life. For college students of traditional age (18–22) taking the course, we will see that it is never too early to begin to make these adaptations. For those college students of nontraditional age, we will see that it is never too late to initiate these important interventions.

THE BIOPSYCHOSOCIAL PERSPECTIVE

The theme of this book is the **biopsychosocial perspective**, a view of development as a complex interaction of biological, psychosocial, and social processes. Biological processes incorporate the changes within the body associated with the passage of time that alter the body's functions and structures. Psychological processes are those that involve cognition, personality, and emotions. The social processes in development are those that reflect the environment or context, and they include indicators that reflect the individual's position within the social structure. Theories and models of life-span development, discussed in Chapter 2, attempt to sort out the relative influence of these sets of factors on the individual's progression through life.

The biopsychosocial model implies that biology, medicine, nursing, sociology, history, and even the arts and literature provide crucial perspectives to the psychology of adulthood and aging. Knowledge, theories, and perspectives from a variety of areas each contribute importantly to the study of the individual over time. Within this model, the concept of **identity** will have a central role. An individual's identity is defined as a composite of self-representations in biological, psychological, and social domains. The interaction of these domains as interpreted in terms of the individual's view of the self forms a central organizing concept within the biopsychosocial perspective.

PRINCIPLES OF ADULT DEVELOPMENT AND AGING

The field of adult development and aging is built on a set of principles that form the foundation of this book. Although theoretical differences exist within the discipline, there is general agreement on these underlying premises.

Changes are Continuous over the Life Span

The first principle of the study of adult development and aging is that changes over the life span occur in a continuous fashion. In other words, the changes that occur in later adulthood build on those that have occurred over the previous years of life. This principle has theoretical as well as practical implications.

Theories of adulthood and aging, from the biological to the sociological, take it as a given that the changes in old age occur against the backdrop of the individual's prior developmental history. For example, in the biological realm, changes that occur in later life in a particular organ system, such as the cardiovascular system, depend in many ways on the prior functioning of that system throughout life.

The continuity principle has practical implications for the ways that individuals feel about themselves and the ways that others feel about them. We do not feel that we become different

Although people change in outward appearance over their lifetimes, they still feel they are the "same" inside.

people because we reach a certain birthday. In fact, you might have heard older adults say that they do not feel they have changed very much on the "inside" and that they still feel the same way they always have. Unfortunately, outward appearance plays a large role in the ways we are perceived by others. Consequently, when others look at a middle-aged or older adult, they are likely to focus on that person's age rather than on some other characteristic of personality or ability. It is important to keep in mind that as people develop through adulthood they think of themselves as the "same," but older, and that many of them will resent being treated in a particular way because of their age. Think of the way you feel when you are lumped together with all other college students (for better or for worse) on the basis of your age and position in life rather than on "who" you are as an individual.

"What do you think?"   *1-1*

Have you ever heard anyone say that they don't feel any older but when they look in the mirror they see that they appear this way?

It is the Survivors Who Grow Old

The second principle of adult development and aging is one that is perhaps obvious but worth pointing out nevertheless. Simply put, in order for people to become old, they have to not die. When I say this to my class, I usually preface it by pointing out that although this may not not seem like the most remarkable piece of information they will learn in the class, it is in some ways the most profound. The people who have become old (and not died) are the ones who survived

TABLE 1.1
Five Ways to Shorten Your Life

The Centers for Disease Prevention and Control regards these five behaviors as the major obstacles that prevent people from living a longer and healthier life

1	Being overweight
2	Drinking and driving
3	Eating inadequate amounts of fruits and vegetables
4	Being physically inactive
5	Smoking

Source: Kamimoto et al., 1999.

the many threats to life that cause other people to fall by the wayside. They are the people who did not get involved in fatal vehicular accidents, war, natural disasters, human-made disasters, or risky behavior such as excessive drug or alcohol use. The fact that people manage to avoid death from these conditions suggests that they have inherited a good set of genes, made wise choices in lifestyles, and managed to avoid misfortune.

When you consider what it takes to become old then, you realize that the people who survive to later adulthood have some special characteristics indeed. This fact has implications for the way that we make sense out of scientific data on human aging. All older people are survivors of the conditions that took away the lives of others. With increasing age into later life, they become even more select in important characteristics such as physical functioning, health, intelligence, and probably even personality. Consequently, if you are looking at the differences between younger and older people on any given characteristic, you should realize that the older people are a more restricted (and perhaps superior) group than the younger ones. The younger ones have not been subjected yet to the same conditions that could threaten their lives.

A concrete example might help illustrate this principle. Consider the data on the psychological characteristic of cautiousness. One of the tried and true findings in psychology and aging for many years was that older people are less likely to take risks than are younger people. Along similar lines, older adults are also less likely to engage in criminal behavior. Why is this? One possibility is that people do in fact learn to moderate their behavior as they get older. They choose not to engage in behaviors that will bring them harm or get them arrested. The other possibility is that

the high risk-takers are no longer in the population because their risky behavior led to an early accidental death. The criminals are no longer in the population for study because they were either killed in their professional exploits or were imprisoned and could no longer commit illegal acts. Another example of the selectivity of increasingly older populations can be seen in Table 1.2, which summarizes the characteristics of "super" centenarians (people 110 years and older). Their superior health status shows that they clearly are not representative of the population and probably never were.

Individual Differences Must Be Recognized

A long-held myth regarding development in adulthood and old age is that as people age, their individuality fades as the aging process takes its toll on the body and the mind. This view is refuted by this third principle of adult development and aging: that as people grow older, they become more different from each other, not more alike. Increasingly older age groups of adults are a highly diverse segment of the population in terms of their physical functioning, psychological performance, and conditions of living. Supporting this point, in one often-cited study, researchers examined a large number of studies of aging and compared the amount of variability in measures of older compared to younger adults. The researchers found that the variability was far greater in measures taken from older adults, suggesting increasing diversity over the adult years (Nelson & Dannefer, 1992).

This finding of increasing diversity with age in adulthood points to the importance of experiences in adulthood as shaping development. As

TABLE 1.2
Characteristics of Supercentenarians

Illustrating the point that people who live to older ages are increasingly select, consider the following characteristics of 32 individuals studied at the ages of 110 or older. All rates of medical conditions are significantly lower than those rates found in the typical older adult population.

Medical history	N (%)
Myocardial infarction	2 (6)
Cardiac arrhythmia	1 (3)
Pacemaker inserted	0 (0)
Angina pectoris	0 (0)
Stroke	4 (13)
Treated hypertension	7 (22)
Adult-onset diabees mellitus	1 (3)
Chronic obstructive pulmonary disease	0 (0)
Hypothyroidism	5 (16)
Other thyroid condition	2 (6)
Osteoporosis	14 (44)
Cataract	28 (88)
Parkinson's disease	1 (3)
Cancer	8 (25)
Bladder	1 (3)
Breast	2 (6)
Colon	2 (6)
Skin	2 (6)
Unknown	1 (3)
Functional status (Barthel Index score), n(%)	
Totally dependent (<20)	3 (9)
Very dependent (20–39)	10 (31)
Partially dependent (40–59)	6 (19)
Requires minimal assistance (60–79)	8 (25)
Independent (80–100)	5 (16)

Source: Schoenhofen et al., 2006.

people get older, their lives diverge increasingly from each other because of the many choice points that are offered to them and the many different choices they make. They may have gone to college or not gone to college, they may have joined the army or not joined the army, they may have moved to New York City or landed in Wichita, Kansas. They may have gotten married or not, had children or not, and as a result, they might have had grandchildren or not. Even little decisions can affect later outcomes in life although at the time they might not seem so. For example, perhaps you decide to go out to a movie on a stormy night, leading you to end up with a broken leg after your car skids through an intersection. Now, instead of being able to take a vacation in the Bahamas, you spend several weeks recuperating at home and, as a result, have a chance to study more thoroughly for your midterms which ultimately allows you to be accepted into the graduate school of your choice. The many possibilities we can spin out of this simple example show that the permutations of events in our lives are virtually endless. In a similar way, each individual's personal history moves in increasingly idiosyncratic directions with each passing day, year, and decade of life.

The principle that people become more different from each other with age relates to the notion of **interindividual differences**. Moreover, as shown in Figure 1.1, people of the same age may differ so much from each other that they more closely resemble people from different age groups entirely, even on measures typically thought to decline with age.

Another aspect of the principle of individual differences relates to differences within the individual, or **intra-individual differences**. This principle is also referred to as the **multidirectionality of development** (Baltes & Graf, 1996). According to this principle, not all systems develop at the same rate within the person—some functions may show positive changes and others negative changes over time. Even within the same function, such as intelligence, the same individual may show gains in one area, losses in another, and stability in yet a third domain.

<u>FIGURE 1.1</u>
Scatterplots of Brain Volumes by Age

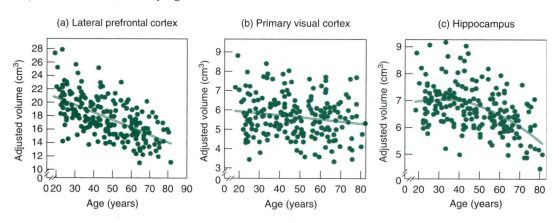

This scatter plot of the age-adjusted volume of three regions of the brain shows that it is possible for individuals in their 70s and 80s to be similar to or higher than people in their 20s on a measure typically thought to decline in later life, the volume of parts of the brain. This extreme variation illustrates the principle of individual differences in development.

Source: Hedden & Gabrieli, 2004.

One important and very intriguing consequence of the principle of individual differences is that it is possible to find older adults whose performance on a given measure is superior to that of younger people. Average-age college students may think that they can run faster, lift heavier weights, or solve crossword puzzles faster than a person two or three times their age. However, a middle-aged or older adult who exercises and remains active may very well be quicker, stronger, and mentally more adept than a sedentary or inactive younger person. There is no reason for all functions to "go downhill" as people get older.

"Normal" Aging Is Different from Disease

The fourth principle of adult development is the need to differentiate between **normal**, **impaired**, and **optimal** aging. A set of normal aging changes built into the hard wiring of the organism occurs more or less in all individuals, although at different rates, and is different from those changes associated with disease. **Impaired aging** implies the existence of changes that result from diseases and do not occur in all individuals. Optimal aging is also called "successful aging." This concept implies that the individual has avoided changes that would otherwise occur with age through preventative and compensatory strategies.

Another term for normal aging is **primary aging**, referring to age-related changes that are universal, intrinsic, and progressive. This constrasts with the term **secondary aging**, which is used to refer to changes that are due to disease (Aldwin & Gilmer, 1999). The basis for this distinction is the importance of differentiating between normal age-related changes that occur throughout life and the disease that eventually causes death by leading a vital life function to shut down. Many people remain healthy well into their later adult years, acquiring the disease that ends their life only close to the time of their death.

It is important for practical as well as scientific reasons to distinguish between normal aging and disease. Health care specialists who work with middle-aged and older adults should recognize and treat a disease when it occurs rather than attribute it to the normal aging process or dismiss it as simply "getting older." For example, a 60-year-old adult who suffers from symptoms of depression can be successfully treated but only if the psychologist is aware that the symptoms of depression are not inherently a feature of normal aging. Personality development in adulthood does not inevitably lead to the depressive symptoms of lowered self-esteem, excessive guilt, changes in appetite, or lack of interest in activities. If the psychologist mistakenly thinks that these symptoms are part of the normal aging process, that individual will fail to provide the necessary therapy that could ultimately alleviate the depressed person's suffering.

THE MEANING OF AGE

The study of aging implies that age is a variable of major interest. However, what does chronological age represent? Technically, it is defined as the difference between your date of birth and the present date, usually measured in years. Our society uses this number to describe us because it is convenient to calculate, but as a scientific index, it is flawed. After all, chronological age is a number based on events in the universe that occur independently of events inside our body. If you think even further about the meaning of age, you come to the realization that age, like time, is a purely human invention. Scientists on our planet have decided to use seconds, minutes, days, weeks, and years as the way to segment units of the dimension called time, but these numbers are in some ways arbitrary. Our bodies do not "keep time" in these units, and although some of our biological functions do seem to operate according to an internal clock, we do not yet know if these functions have anything to do with the aging process or with changes that take place over many years. To say that chronological age (or time) "means" anything with regard to the status of our body's functioning is, based on current evidence, questionable.

Using Age to Define "Adult"

One of the most difficult words to define is the very basic term "adult." As indicated at the very opening of this chapter, people tend to think of this term as synonymous with the word "mature." We assume that a person who has become an adult has achieved some degree of full-fledged growth. When we think of the term "mature," we might think of an apple that is ready to be eaten or a cat that is no longer a kitten. Fortunately or unfortunately, humans are not like apples or cats, and the point of reaching maturity is much harder to quantify.

We cannot use physical maturity alone as a criterion for maturity because then we might consider a 15-year-old or even a 13-year-old who has reached full physical growth to be an adult. Can we use some other criterion based on ability? This might lead us to use the age of 16 years old, which is when people can legally drive. Alternatively, maturity in the eyes of the U.S. government is 18 because that is when a person is eligible to vote. However, various states may use other criteria for adulthood, such as the "age of consent," which is when a person can marry without the consent of a parent. In South Carolina, this is 14, but in most other states it is 16 or 18. Alternatively, the age of 21 years may be the final mark of maturity because that is when it is legal to drink in most states. However, it may seem inappropriate or unjustifiable to consider the age when you will not be arrested for ingesting alcohol as an overall criterion of adulthood.

Because of all these contradictory definitions, it might be wise to recommend that the age given as the crossing-over point into adulthood depends on the individual's having reached the chronological age that has associated with it the expectations and privileges of a given society or subculture. For example, in a particular county and state of the United States, individuals may be considered to have reached adulthood at the age when they are eligible to vote, drink, drive, and get married. In that state, the age of 21 would be considered the threshold to adulthood. In another country, these criteria may be reached at the age of 18. In any case, the first three or four years of adulthood represent a transition prior to assuming the responsibilities associated with adulthood, a period given the label "emerging adulthood" (Arnett, 2000). These responsibilities may either occur during the years that follow college graduation or, for those individuals who are not in college, whenever they face the need to find full employment or make family commitments.

Divisions by Age of the Over-65 Population

Traditionally, 65 years of age has been seen as the entry point for "old age." However, those individuals who are close to the age of 65 face very different issues and challenges than those who are close to the age of 85 or older. These issues and challenges relate mainly to the quality of physical functioning and health, but they also involve different economic constraints and social opportunities. Therefore, the period of 65 and older is divided into three age ranges: **young-old**, which incorporates ages 65 to 74, **old-old**, which includes ages 75 to 84, and **oldest-old**, or ages 85 and older. Although people do not magically shift from one period to the other on their 65th, 75th, and 85th birthdays, there is an understanding in this system that some changes will become

ASSESS YOURSELF: "When I'm 64"

How will you change over the next 40 or so years? In this exercise, you will put yourself into the future and imagine what will happen to you when you get older.

1. Compared to myself today I will be:
   A. taller
   B. the same height
   C. shorter

2. Compared to myself today my weight will be:
   A. heavier
   B. lighter
   C. the same

3. Regarding my hair:
   A. I will let it go gray naturally
   B. I will dye it to cover the gray

4. If I become very wrinkled, I will:
   A. seek plastic surgery
   B. find other treatments than plastic surgery
   C. not try to change it

5. With regard to my work:
   A. I will seek to retire as early as possible
   B. I will seek to continue working as long as possible

6. With regard to my relationships:
   A. I will be married
   B. I will be single
   C. I will be divorced
   D. I will be widowed

7. With regard to my friendships:
   A. I will have the same friends I have now
   B. I will not be friends with the people who are my friends now

8. With regard to my family:
   A. I will have grandchildren
   B. I will not have grandchildren

9. My physical abilities will be:
   A. the same or better than they are now
   B. somewhat worse than they are now
   C. much worse than they are now

(contd.)

ASSESS YOURSELF

11. I will be sick:
    A. none of the time
    B. some of the time
    C. most of the time
12. People will respect me:
    A. less than they do now
    B. more than they do now
    C. the same as they do now

apparent within a year or two of that birthday that may lead to significant changes in functioning.

As more and more people are living to advanced ages, even the three ages used to demarcate the 65 and older period are being recognized as having limitations. **Centenarians**, people over the age of 100, and **supercentenarians**, those over the age of 110 (as described in Table 1.2), are the two newest age categories to be added to the divisions of the 65 and older population.

Alternative Indices of Age

As an alternative to chronological age, researchers have suggested indices of age based on specific aspects of functioning. Using this system, an individual may have more than one "age" based on the level of performance reached on a set of measures or tests. The advantage of using these alternative indices of aging is that, were they to be adopted, the individual would be more accurately characterized than through the simple chronological system used now. Many people use these indices informally when talking about other people, as when you say that someone is "young for her age."

The quality of functioning of the individual's organ systems is the basis of **biological age**. Standards of performance on various biological measures for an individual can be compared with the age norms for those measures. For example, a 50-year-old may have the blood pressure values of those in the 25–30 segment of the population and therefore would have a youthful biological age on that measure.

"What do you think?"   1-2

How could the alternative indices of age be implemented in a practical sense so that they would replace chronological age?

A similar logic forms the basis for calculating **psychological age**, which represents the quality of an individual's functioning on psychological measures such as intelligence, memory, and learning ability. People would be classified according to their abilities to perform cognitive tasks, which are important aspects of functioning in everyday life. Since such performance is known to be affected by the aging process, an index of psychological age would accurately characterize a person's ability to meet the cognitive demands of the environment.

The third component of the equation for calculating age according to alternative indices is **social age**, that is, the characterization of a person's age based on occupying certain social roles. Social age takes into account the person's family, work, and possibly community roles. For example, a grandparent would have an older social age than would a parent, although the grandparent might easily be chronologically younger than would the parent. Similarly, a retiree would have an older social age than would a person still working although again, their chronological age might be in reverse order.

As stated earlier, the advantage of using these alternative indices of aging is that the individual is more accurately characterized than happens with the chronological system currently used. However, a major disadvantage is the fact that they require frequent upgrading to make sure that they are still accurate. For example, a biological index based in part on blood pressure may have to be adjusted as health practitioners change the definition of what is considered "old" on a particular scale. In the area of social age, the fact that there are diverse subcultures within a single society means that social age has to be defined according to the particular group of which the individual is a part. Furthermore, given the fact that people make major life decisions based on their own expectations of what is appropriate rather than by what society believes, social age may be becoming increasingly irrelevant. With all its faults, chronological age may be the more expedient index for most uses.

Personal vs. Social Aging

Researchers in developmental psychology face the challenge of attempting to separate processes intrinsic to the individual as the cause of changes in behavior over time from changes due to exposure to events in the world. Changes within the individual are referred to as **personal aging**, or more formally, ontogenetic change (with "onto" referring to "being," and "genesis" to development). Theoretically, it should be possible to isolate the changes within the cells of the individual's body that are tied to alterations with time in structure and function. This process would then lead to an understanding of the inherent nature of aging.

However, people exist within the context of their societies, and therefore changes that occur in societies over time can have an impact on the individuals within those societies. Changes in societies over time are responsible for the process of **social aging**, in which people change along with or perhaps as the result of historical change. Factors extrinsic to the individual can cause direct changes in the individual or can interact with personal aging. For example, as people are exposed to improvements in health care and education over their lifetimes, their rate of personal aging may slow down because they are able to take advantage of preventative strategies, such as avoiding the poor health habits listed in Table 1.1.

The term "normative," as used in this categorization system, implies that the influence is one that occurs as the "norm"—in other words, it is expected to happen in the lives of the majority of individuals within a given culture or society. Normative changes, then, are those that happen to most people within that social group. Nonnormative changes are those that are idiosyncratic to the life of the individual. Combining the concepts of normative and nonnormative influences specific to the individual and more general to historical time provides a set of three interacting systems of influence that regulate the nature of life-span development. These influences, developed by psychologist Paul Baltes (2005), are normative age-graded influences, normative history-graded influences, and nonnormative influences.

The first set of normative influences to consider is in some ways the easiest to understand in relation to age. They are the **normative age-graded influences** on life that lead people to choose certain experiences that their culture and historical period attach to certain ages or points in the life span. In Western society, individuals are affected by normative age-graded influences that lead them to graduate from college as expected when they are in the early 20s, get married at some later point, begin a family in the 20s or 30s, retire in their 60s, and become grandparents in their middle to later years. We expect that people will have these experiences at these ages because most people do, and we do not think it is unusual when they happen.

Events that occur in response to normative age-graded influences occur in part because a given society has developed expectations about what is desirable for people of certain ages. The decision to retire at the age of 65 years can be seen as a response to the norm regarding when it is appropriate and desirable to leave the labor market. Graduation from high school occurs at about the age of 18 years for most people because in our society, children start school at the age of 5 or 6 and the educational system is based on 12 or 13 grades. Biological factors also play a role in the optimal timing of certain events, however, such as parenthood, which has traditionally been limited to the years between 20 and 40 at the peak of a woman's years of fertility. Some normative age-graded events set the pattern for later events to occur in response, so that if an adult becomes a parent at the age of 30, a lower limit is set on the age at which the adult can become a grandparent. If the child also follows a normative age-graded influence, the parent will become a grandparent

The victims of Hurricane Katrina faced devastating losses, tragic examples of normative history-graded influences. Such events affect the lives of many thousands of people living at one time and place in history.

for the first time somewhere between the ages of 55 and 65 years.

Normative age-graded influences are associated, then, with the life span of the individual, even though they may reflect environmental or social factors. By contrast, influences that transcend the individual's life and are associated with changes in society as a whole are referred to as **normative history-graded influences.** These are events that occur to everyone within a certain culture or geopolitical unit and include large-scale occurrences such as world wars, economic trends, or sociocultural changes in attitudes and values. The impact of these events on people's lives may be felt immediately, but they can have continuing impact for many years on subsequent patterns of work, family, and quality of life. For example, World War II veterans who entered the military after their families were already established were more likely upon their return to get divorced or separated, to suffer career setbacks, and even experience poorer physical health after they turned 50 (Elder, Shanahan, & Clipp, 1994). The historical events may not even directly affect the individual, but they may have an indirect influence by virtue of the changes they stimulate in social awareness, anxiety, or sensitivity, as was true for the current generation of people in their mid 50s and early 60s who were in high school and college during the Vietnam War years. Many people in the United States and around the world now are currently being affected by such historical events as the war in Iraq, global warming, and the aftermath of disasters such as Hurricane Katrina.

If the course of life were influenced only by the two types of normative changes just examined, it would be relatively easy to predict the route of development taken by people of the same age living in the same culture. However, each individual's life is also affected by random, chance factors that occur due to a combination of coincidence, the impact of earlier

Kansas resident Nola Ochs broke a Guinness World Record when she graduated from college at the age of 95.

decisions made on later events, and relationships with other people. Little is written about these **nonnormative influences** in the developmental literature because there is virtually no way of predicting their occurrence. Developmentalists can only observe these phenomena when they occur and then attempt to draw generalizations about the impact of certain unpredictable life events on individuals more or less after the fact.

There are almost an infinite number of examples of nonnormative influences. Some are due to good luck, such as winning the lottery or making a smart investment. Nonnormative influences can also be negative, such as a car accident, a fire, or the accidental death of a relative. One moment a person's life is normal, and the next moment everything is ruined. Other nonnormative influences may unfold over a gradual period, such as being fired from a job (due to personal reasons), developing a chronic illness not related to aging, or getting divorced.

As you were reading about these three types of influences on life, surely you were also thinking about ways that they may interact with each other. Consider the example of getting divorced. Although society's norms have changed considerably regarding this life event, many would still consider this a nonnormative occurrence because the norm (and certainly the hope) of married couples is to remain married. And although it is a very personal occurrence, a divorce may be seen in part as a response to larger social forces. Social-historical changes that have sensitized one of the marital partners to problematic areas within the marriage may give the individual the impetus to seek an end to the relationship. The wife may realize that her husband's resistance to her seeking outside employment has restricted her independence, or, conversely, the husband may wish that his wife would become more independent like the women he knows at work. In either case, the sensitivity of a partner in the relationship to such social issues may lead to a decision that permanently alters the course of the lives of all people involved including, of course, the children.

It is also interesting to consider what happens when individuals have experiences that would normatively occur at one age but instead occur at a different age. In a sense these are "nonnormative" because, although they are normative events, they have happened at an age when most people do not experience them. Such is the case when an individual marries for the first time in late adulthood, becomes a grandparent at the age of 30 years, enters the job market at age 60, or retires from a sport at the age of 18 years.

SOCIAL FACTORS IN ADULT DEVELOPMENT AND AGING

The study of adult development and aging involves an understanding of concepts that describe the characteristics of individuals according to certain social factors or indicators. Along with age, these social factors help to shape the structures of opportunities available to people throughout their lives.

Sex and Gender

The term **gender** refers to the individual's identification as being male or female. It is generally considered distinct from a person's biological sex, which refers to an individual's anatomy. Both sex and gender are important in the study of adult development and aging.

Physiological factors relevant to sex influence the timing and nature of physical aging processes, primarily through the operation of sex hormones. For example, the sex hormone estrogen is thought to play at least some role in affecting a woman's risks of heart disease, bone loss, and possibly even cognitive changes.

Social and cultural factors relevant to gender are important to the extent that the individual assumes a certain role in society based on being viewed as a male or female. Opportunities in education and employment are two main areas in which gender influences the course of adult development and becomes a limiting factor for women. Although progress has certainly occurred in both of these domains over the past several decades, women nevertheless face a restricted range of choices and the prospects of lower earnings than do men. Furthermore these differences are particularly likely to have affected older cohorts who were raised in an era with more traditional gender expectations than currently exist.

Race

A person's **race** is defined in biological terms as the classification within the species based on physical and structural characteristics. However, the concept of race in common usage is broader than these biological features. Race has come to be applied in a broad fashion to refer to the cultural background associated with being born within a particular biologically defined segment of the population. The "race" that people use to identify themselves is more likely to be socially than biologically determined. In addition, because few people are purely of one race in a biological sense, social and cultural background factors assume even greater prominence.

The U.S. Census 2000 defined race on the basis of a person's self-identification. In addition to using race, the census also included categories based on national origin (see Table 1.3). The 2000 census also made it possible for individuals to identify themselves as belonging to more than one racial category.

To the extent that race is biologically determined, however, racial differences in functioning in adulthood and aging may reflect differences in genetic inheritance. People who have inherited a risk factor that has been found to be higher within a certain race are more likely to be at risk for developing that illness during their adult years. Racial differences in risk factors may also interact with different cultural backgrounds associated with a particular race. For example, people at risk for a disease with a metabolic basis (such as inability to metabolize fats) will be more likely to develop that disease depending on whether high-fat foods are a part of their culture.

Social and cultural aspects of race may also alter an individual's development in adulthood through the structure of a society and based

TABLE 1.3
Race Categories Used in the U.S. Census 2000

How are the race categories used in Census 2000 defined?

"White" refers to people having origins in any of the original peoples of Europe, the Middle East, or North Africa. It includes people who indicated their race or races as "white" or wrote in entries such as Irish, German, Italian, Lebanese, Near Easterner, Arab, or Polish.

"Black or African American" refers to people having origins in any of the black racial groups of Africa. It includes people who indicated their race or races as "black, African Am., or Negro," or wrote in entries such as African American, Afro American, Nigerian, or Haitlian.

"American Indian and Alaska Native" refers to people having origins in any of the original peoples of North and South America (including Central America), and who maintain tribal affiliation or community attachment. It includes people who indicated their race or races by marking this category or writing in their principal or enrolled tribe, such as Rosebud Sloux, Chippewa, or Navajo.

"Asian" refers to people having origins in any of the original peoples of the Far East, Southeast Asia, or the Indian subcontinent. It includes people who indicated their race or races as "Asian Indian," "Chinese," "Filipino," "Korean," "Japanese," "Vietnamese," or "Other Asian," or wrote in entries such as Burmese, Hmong, Pakistani, or Thai.

"Native Hawallan and Other Pacific Islander" refers to people having origins in any of the original peoples of Hawaii, Guam, Samoa, or other Pacific Islands. It includes people who indicated their race or races as "Native Hawaiian," "Guamanian or Chamorro," "Samoan," or "Other Pacific Islander," or wrote in entries such as Tahitian, Mariana Islander, or Chuukese.

"Some other race" was included in Census 2000 for respondents who were unable to identify with the five Office of Management and Budget race categories. Respondents who provided write-in entries such as Moroccan, South African, Belizean, or a Hispanic origin (for example, Mexican, Puerto Rican, or Cuban) are included in the some other race category.

The 2000 U.S. Census was the first census conducted in which racial categories were expanded to include national origin. In addition, it was the first census in which individuals were given the option of self-identifying as a member of more than one racial category.

on whether there are systematic biases against people who identify with that race. As is shown repeatedly throughout this book, health problems are higher for African Americans than for whites. Part of the differences in health may be attributed to lack of opportunities for education and well-paying jobs, but it is thought that systematic discrimination also takes its toll on health by increasing the levels of stress experienced by African Americans (Clark, Anderson, Clark, & Williams, 1999).

Ethnicity

The concept of **ethnicity** captures the cultural background of an individual, reflecting the predominant values, attitudes, and expectations in which the individual has been raised. Along with race, ethnicity is often studied in adult development and aging as an influence on a person's family attitudes and experiences. For example, people of certain ethnic backgrounds are thought to show greater respect for older adults and feel a stronger sense of obligation to care for their aging parents. Ethnicity also may play a role in influencing the aging of various physiological functions, in part through genetic inheritance and in part through exposure to cultural habits and traditions. Finally, discrimination against people of certain ethnic backgrounds may serve the same function as race in limiting the opportunities for educational and occupational achievements.

"What do you think?"   **1-3**

Do you feel that your ethnicity is an important influence on your development?

Socioeconomic Status

An individual's **socioeconomic status**, or "social class," is a function of level of education and level of occupation. Various researchers have developed scales of socioeconomic status. Although the exact calculations may vary, these scales weight some combination of education and occupational level in ranking people from low to high. Higher education and a higher level of occupation, in terms of prestige and status, contribute to a higher socioeconomic status. Income levels are not necessarily associated with socioeconomic status because high-prestige jobs (such as teacher) often are associated with mid- or even low-level salaries. However, as a proxy for or in addition to socioeconomic status, some researchers use income as the basis for analyzing social class differences in health and opportunities.

Religion

Although relatively uninvestigated, **religion**, which is an individual's identification with an organized belief system, is being given increasing attention as a factor influencing development in adulthood. Organized religions form an alternative set of social structures that is at least partly connected with race and ethnicity. More important, religion provides many people with a source of coping strategies, social support in times of crisis, and a systematic basis for interpreting one's life experiences (Klemmack et al., 2007).

THE BABY BOOMERS GROW UP: CHANGES IN THE MIDDLE-AGED AND OLDER POPULATIONS IN THE UNITED STATES AND THE WORLD

You can see a quick snapshot of the U.S. population according to age and sex by looking at Figure 1.2 (He, Sangupta, Velkoff, & DeBarros, 2005). The age-sex structure provides a useful way of looking at a population. A "young" population is shaped like a pyramid, and an

FIGURE 1.2
Age-sex Structure of the U.S. Population Showing the Number of Men and Women in Each 5-year Age Group

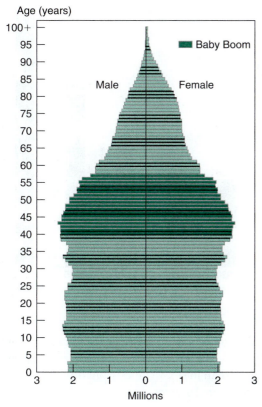

Source: He et al., 2005.

"old" population by an upside-down pyramid. A stable population is shaped like a rectangle. You can clearly see that in this figure there is a "bulge" in the middle of this structure, reflecting the **Baby Boom** generation of people who were born between 1945 and 1964. As this bulge continues to move upward throughout the 21st century, this generation will have a continued impact on the nature of society, as indeed it already has (Whitbourne & Willis, 2006).

In 1900, the number of Americans over the age of 65 years was 3.1 million (about

4% of the population). By 2004, this number increased more than twelve times to 36.3 million. People 65 and older now represent 12.4% of the total U.S. population. As you can see from Figure 1.3, this number is estimated to rise to nearly 87 million by the year 2050, or 21% of the total U.S. population (U.S. Bureau of the Census, 2007h). As is also shown in this figure, there will be a disproportionate rise in the population 85 years and older. Most impressive of all the statistics is the growth in the number of **centenarians**, people 100 and older. In 1990, an estimated 37,306 centenarians lived in the United States. By 2004 this number increased 73% to 64,658, and by 2050 there will be over 1.1 million of these very hardy individuals (see Figure 1.4).

The major reason for these large increases in the 65 and older population is the movement of the Baby Boomers through the years of middle and later adulthood. However, it is not just that those people were born but that they are expected to continue to live into their 80s, 90s, and 100s, and hence will increase the

FIGURE 1.3
Growth of U.S. Population 65 and Older, 2000–2050

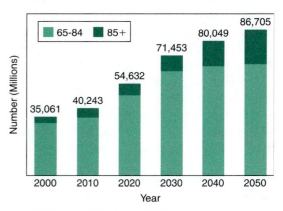

Source: U.S. Bureau of the Census, 2007b.

FIGURE 1.4

Growth in Centenarians, U.S. 1990–2050

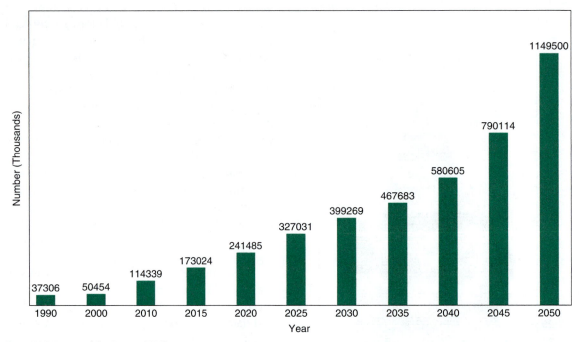

Source: U.S. Bureau of the Census, 2007h.

numbers of very-old individuals throughout the century.

Increases in the aging population, then, reflect the huge gains that have taken place in the average length of life. This value, known as **life expectancy**, is the average number of years of life remaining to the people born within a similar period of time. To calculate life expectancy, statisticians take into account the death rates for a particular group within the population and project how long it will take for that entire group to die out completely.

Life expectancy from birth rose overall from 62.9 years in 1940 to 77.5 years in 2003 (Hoyert, Heron, Murphy, & Kung, 2006). Many factors have contributed to increases in life expectancy, including reduced death rates for children and young adults. In addition, however, people are

living longer once they make it to age 65, with the life expectancy at age 65 (which is always higher than life expectancy from birth) estimated to be about 18 years.

"What do you think?"   **1-4**

What do you think the world will be like when you are 65?

Geographic Variations within the United States

Not only are older people living longer, but people are living to different ages depending on where they live in the United States. As of 2005 slightly over one-half of persons 65 and over lived in nine states. With 3.9 million people 65 and older, California has the largest number of older adults, but because the state's population is so large, this age group constitutes a relatively small proportion (11%) of the population. It is Florida that has the highest percent of people 65 and older (16.8%), and the county with the highest proportion of people over 65 is Charlotte, where 35.5% of the population is 65 or older. Interestingly, Florida, a state associated with large numbers of retirees, has a percentage of over-65 similar to that of some midwestern states. This is because young people are moving out of the farm belt states, leaving behind a higher proportion of

people in the 65 and older age group (Greenberg, 2006).

Gender and Racial Variations in the Over-65 Population

Women over the age of 65 currently outnumber men, amounting to about 58% of the total over-65 population. The "gender gap" gets wider for each successively older age group, until by the age of 100, there are 4 times as many men as women in the population (U.S. Bureau of the Census, 2007e). This disparity between the genders is expected to diminish by the year 2030, when the Baby Boomers reach advanced old age. At that time, 56% of the 65 and older

FIGURE 1.5

Percent 65 and Older in the United States by State, 2005

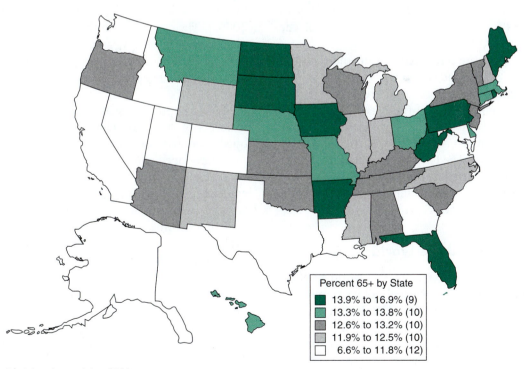

Source: Administration on Aging, 2006.

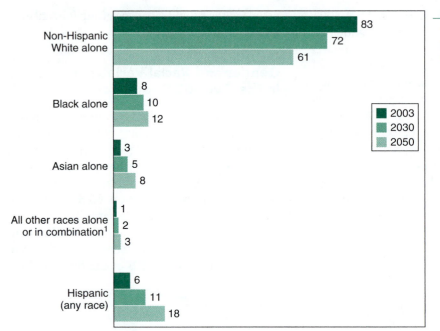

FIGURE 1.6

Changes in the Racial and Ethnic Composition of U.S. Population, 2003–2050

Source: He et al., 2005.

population in the United States will be females and 44% will be males (U.S. Bureau of the Census, 2007h).

Changes are also occurring in the distribution of white and minority segments of the population. As can be seen from Figure 1.6, in 2003, about 17% of the over-65 population was made up of members of racial and ethnic minorities, but this number will rise to 39% by the year 2050. The Hispanic population of older adults is expected to grow at the fastest rate, increasing from about 6 million in 2003 to over 18 million by 2050 (He et al., 2005).

Aging Around the World

The statistics from around the world confirm the picture of an increasingly older population as we move through the 21st century. As of the year 2006, there were 483 million people worldwide over the age of 65 and predictions are that this number will nearly double to 974 million

by the year 2030 (U.S. Bureau of the Census, 2006c). The country with the largest number of older adults both now and as projected by the year 2030 is China, but Italy has the highest percentage of people 65 and older (He et al., 2005).

World population statistics are often reported in terms of "more developed" and "less developed" countries or "developing" countries. The more developed countries represent the industrialized nations, and the less developed countries are those that have an agrarian-based economy, typically with low levels of health care, education, and income. As can be seen in Figure 1.7, projections of world population trends estimate that the proportion of the population of adults 65 years and over living in the less developed countries will rise disproportionately between now and the year 2050. The largest increase is projected to occur in Singapore, which will experience a 372% rise in people 65 and older (Kinsella & Veloff, 2001).

FIGURE 1.7
Population Aged 65 and Over for Developed and Developing Countries by Age: 2000 to 2050 (in millions)

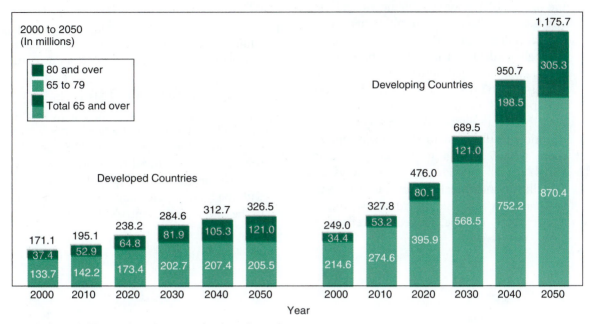

Growth of 65 and older population by groups of 65–79 and 80 and over.
Source: He et al., 2005.

What are the implications of these figures for your future as you move into your adult years? First, you will be more likely to have friends and associates to socialize with than is true of the current older population. And if you are a man, the news is encouraging: you will be more likely to live into old age than was true for current cohorts of older adults. For those of you who are younger than the "Baby Boomers," the statistics are encouraging if you are considering a career related to the field of aging: Older clientele is definitely going to be on the increase. Changes in various aspects of lifestyle can also be expected in the next decades, as adjustments are made to an aging population in the entertainment world and the media. Just as we are getting used to the idea of an aging Mick Jagger, many others will follow in his footsteps to change the way we regard prominent celebrities in Western society and, indeed, around the world.

SUMMARY

1. This book is based on the biopsychosocial model that regards development as a complex interaction of biological, psychological, and social processes.

2. The four principles of adult development and aging are that changes are continuous over the life span, the survivors grow old, individual differences must be recognized, and "normal" aging is different from disease. Distinctions must be drawn between primary and secondary aging.

3. It is difficult to define the term "adult" as there are many possible criteria. In this book, the age of 18 for individuals not in college and the postcollege years for individuals who attend college from 18 to 22 will serve as a rough guideline. The over-65 population is generally divided into subcategories of young-old (65–74), old-old (75–84), and oldest-old (85 and over). These divisions have policy implications, as well as draw attention to the need to distinguish among those over 65. Biological, psychological, and social age all provide alternative ways to describe an individual. Personal aging refers to changes within the individual over time. Social aging can be viewed as reflecting normative age-graded influences, normative history-graded influences, and nonnormative influences.

4. Social factors that are important in the study of adult development and aging include gender, race, ethnicity, socioeconomic status, and religion.

5. The world and the United States are "graying." There are now 36.3 million people in the United States over the age of 65, which constitute 12.4% of the total U.S. population. Countries around the world will show increases in the over-65 population as well, with the highest percentage growth occurring in the developing countries.

CHAPTER 2

Models of Development: Nature and Nurture in Adulthood

> *"Too many people, when they get old, think that they have to live by the calendar."*
> —John Glenn at age 77

The study of adult development and aging has evolved as an expansion of the field of developmental psychology to incorporate the years past childhood and adolescence into a unified view of the life span. For many years, the field of developmental psychology was synonymous with the field of child development, but starting in the 1960s, the emphasis began to shift to models that would explain changes within the individual from "cradle to grave." It did not make sense to designate a point in life when people stopped developing. To a certain extent, traditional developmental psychology retains a focus on youth, but as knowledge about and interest in the adult years expands, the emphasis is slowly shifting toward a more all-encompassing view of change. This shift toward understanding development as continuous from childhood through old age is reflected in the **life span perspective**.

Along with a shift from the early years of life to the middle and later portions of the life span, developmental psychology now incorporates social or **contextual influences on development**. This shift arose out of the now outdated "nature versus nurture" debate concerning whether development reflected genetic inheritance ("nature") or the effects of parenting and society ("nurture"). With movement away from the "versus" in this debate, developmental psychology began to treat life span change as a function of both sets of factors. Reflecting this change, we now use the term **developmental science** rather than developmental psychology (Magnusson, 1996).

"What do you think?"   **2-1**

Why is a life span perspective necessary to understanding development in adulthood and later life?

Replacing psychology with science implies that rather than looking within the individual alone to understand change, we need to look at multiple factors as influences on development. This means expanding the study of processes within the individual from psychological domains such as cognition and personality to areas of functioning that fall more traditionally into other fields such as biology or health. At the same time, the broadening of the term to developmental science means that it is no longer considered sufficient to look in the individual's immediate environment in order to understand change over time. It is also important to study the role of social context in development and to see the individual as part of the larger community and society (Ford & Lerner, 1992). Developmental scientists look at a wide variety of processes, then try to understand dynamic interactions among and within each level of analysis of change, from the biological to the contextual (Lerner, 2003).

With the refocus toward developmental science, researchers in the field are more explicitly attempting to explain the mechanisms or underlying processes of development rather than simply to describe developmental changes. In a descriptive approach to development, researchers attempt to establish the ages at which different events occur within the individual. This approach characterized the work of the early child psychologists, such as Arnold Gesell, who wrote books on "the child at two," "the child at three," and so on. Developmental scientists are clearly attempting to discover orderly principles underlying growth through life: the "whys" and not just the "whats."

MODELS OF INDIVIDUAL-ENVIRONMENT INTERACTIONS

Classic developmental psychology evolved around the notion that growth in childhood occurred primarily as a result of "nature." This was the assumption of some of the earliest writers in the early 20th century who, like Gesell, believed that their task was to chronicle accurately and thoroughly the changes that occurred from birth onward. These changes, it was thought, would reflect the influence of ontogenesis, or maturational processes, as they unfolded within the child. The role of the environment (specifically the parents) was to understand this sequence of changes and then provide the right growing conditions, much as one provides water and light to a plant seedling. However, it was not long until the "nurture" position began to emerge among child psychologists. The founder of American behaviorism, John B. Watson, writing some 20 years after Gesell, claimed that a child's future could be molded entirely by the environment provided by the parents.

The nature-nurture debate stimulated many of the classic studies in child development, and many findings were presented on either side to provide support for one position or the other. Gradually it became increasingly evident to scholars in the field that both sets of factors interact to influence the course of development in early life. Moreover, it became clear that the interaction was not just a matter of X% of genetics and X% of the environment (although such data certainly were presented). With the introduction of the concept of **niche-picking** (Scarr & McCartney, 1983), the notion began to take hold that the interaction of nature and nurture is an active and dynamic one.

According to the idea of niche-picking, genetic and environmental factors together work to influence the direction that children's lives take. The process works this way. A child has the genetic potential to be talented in a particular area, such as dancing. She has a great deal of flexibility, poise, and a good sense of rhythm. Let's say she has strong "dance" genes. Now, at the age of 4, she is taken to a ballet performance by her parents. The child sits glued to her seat,

fascinated by the pirouettes and leaps of the performers. This event triggers her to beg her parents to let her start ballet lessons, and soon they do. The child has chosen her "niche" of dancing, having been exposed to the sight of ballet dancers, and now that she has found her niche, she has continued to thrive. Thus, her "dance genes" lead her to develop an interest in exactly the activity that will allow her talents to flourish.

At the same time as the notion of a gene-environment interaction was being suggested by researchers and theorists in the area of child development, others were beginning to look at expanding the focus of child development to incorporate the years of adulthood. The middle years of adulthood, which were being studied primarily by educators in the field of adult learning, became swept along in the general movement to integrate the previously disparate studies of development. People in the field of **gerontology**, the study of the aging process, became interested in general issues pertaining to development prior to old age. Out of these converging interests, a unified view of the life span began to evolve.

These young children are expressing an interest in dance, which will become their "niche" as they continue to develop further their interests and abilities.

TABLE 2.1
Models of Individual-Environmental Interactions

	Organismic	*Mechanistic*	*Interactionist*
Nature of Change	Qualitative	Quantitative	Multidirectional Multidimensional
Contribution of Organism	Active	Passive	Active
Main force in Development	Biological-intrinsic maturational changes	External stimuli from environment	Reciprocal relations with environment

Source: Adopted from Lerner, 1995.

The general philosophical and theoretical discussions revolving around the expansion of child psychology to life span development produced very clear but divergent statements of the models underlying the nature-nurture debate. Table 2.1 presents the essential elements of these models. The **organismic model** (taken from the term "organism") is based on the notion that "nature" is the prime mover of development. Growth in childhood and beyond is seen as the manifestation of genetic predisposition as it is expressed in the physical and mental development of the individual. Changes are proposed to occur through qualitative or structural alterations in the individual's psychological qualities such as intelligence and personality. This model is the basis for stage theories of development, which postulate that change over the life span occurs in "leaps" or steps rather than in a continuous fashion.

The **mechanistic model** of development (taken from the word "machine") is based on the premise that "nurture" is the primary force in development. Growth throughout life is postulated to occur through the individual's exposure to experiences that present new learning opportunities. Because this exposure is gradual, the model proposes that there are no clear-cut or identifiable stages. Instead, development is a smooth, continuous set of gradations as the individual acquires experience.

On the column in the extreme right of Table 2.1 is the **interactionist model**, the perspective that is represented by the evolving field of developmental science. According to this model, not only do genetics and environments interact in complex ways (as suggested by the niche-picking concept), but the individual actively participates in his or her development through reciprocal relations with the environment. Another important aspect of this model is the proposition of multidirectionality, a term introduced in Chapter 1. According to the principle of multidirectionality, there are multiple paths in development, so that it is not possible to describe development according to a series of linear stages. **Multidimensionality** is another principle of the interactionist model. This term means that there are multiple processes in development. Finally, the model is based on the assumption that there is **plasticity** in development, meaning that the course of development may be altered (is "plastic"), depending on the nature of the individual's specific interactions in the environment.

Each theory of development falls within one of these three models. Theories that propose that development is the result of ontogenetic changes within the individual fall within the organismic model. Learning theory, which proposes that development proceeds according to environmental influences, falls within the mechanistic model.

Theories that regard development as the product of joint influence fit within the interactionist model. A less formal term than theory is **perspective**, which presents a position or set of ideas. The biopsychosocial perspective falls within the interactionist model of development.

As we explore the processes of development in adulthood and old age, the usefulness of the concepts of multidimensionality, multidirectionality, and plasticity will become apparent. We have already discussed the need to examine the aging process from a multidimensional point of view, and along with this notion goes the idea that development can proceed in multiple dimensions across life. The concept of plasticity fits very well with the notion of compensation and modifiability of the aging process through actions taken by the individual, another point that will be explored throughout this book. The interactionist model, then, provides an excellent backdrop for the biopsychosocial perspective and a basis for viewing the processes of development in later life on a continuum with developmental processes in the early years.

Reciprocity in Development

As emphasized by the interactionist model, adults are, at least in part, products of their experiences. However, adults also shape their own experiences, both through active interpretation of the events that happen to them and through the actions they take. These observations emphasize the **reciprocal nature of development**, the explicit recognition that people both influence and are influenced by the events in their lives (Bronfenbrenner & Ceci, 1994).

Consider the reciprocal process as it has affected your own life. You were influenced by earlier events to choose a particular course of action that has brought you to your current point in life. Perhaps your best friend from high school chose to go to the college you are attending now, and that influenced you to attend this school. Perhaps you chose this college because you knew you wanted to major in psychology and you were impressed by the reputation of the faculty in your department. Or just perhaps your choice was made randomly, and you're not sure what led to your being in this place at this time. In any case you are now at this place having been influenced one way or another by your prior life events. That is one piece of the reciprocal process.

The second piece of the reciprocal process has to do with the effect you will have on the environment of which you are a part, and this in turn will affect subsequent events in your life. For example, by virtue of your very own existence, you are having an effect on the people who know you. It is not an exaggeration to suppose that their lives may be forever altered by their relationships with you. Furthermore you may be having an impact on your college that will alter the events that happen to you as a function of your being a student here. We all know of great student athletes, scholars, or musicians who bring renown to their institutions. Even if you are not fortunate enough to have such vast and recognized talents, your contributions to the school may alter it nevertheless. You may ask a question in class that stimulates your professor to investigate a new research question, and the investigation may ultimately produce new knowledge in the field, drawing attention to your school's contributions to the area. For example, a student at the University of Massachusetts brought his history professor a World War II political cartoon drawn by Dr. Seuss (who hailed from nearby Springfield). Intrigued by this item, the professor went on to conduct research on the early political cartoon career of this well-known children's writer.

Thus, we are not passive recipients of environmental effects. Instead, our choices and behaviors leave a mark on the environment of which we are a part. Subsequently the changes in that environment may further alter us in significant ways, causing us to affect our surroundings, and so on. Reciprocal views of development regard these spiraling processes as both ongoing and unpredictable.

SOCIOCULTURAL MODELS OF DEVELOPMENT

The models of development we have just examined set the stage for looking in more depth at particular theoretical approaches to adult development and aging. We begin by focusing on those approaches that give relatively more emphasis to the environment as an influence on development.

Ecological Perspective

The **ecological perspective** (Bronfenbrenner, 1979, 2001) identifies multiple levels of the environment that interact with individual processes of change (see Figure 2.1). The inner biological level refers to physiological changes that take place over time to affect the individual's functioning. Next at the level of individual functioning includes cognition, personality, and

FIGURE 2.1
Bronfenbrenner's Ecological Perspective

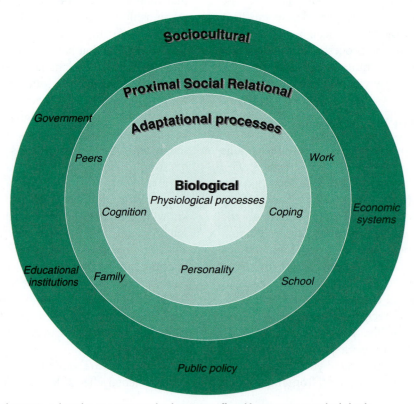

According to Bronfenbrenner's ecological perspective, our development is affected by processes at multiple levels.

other processes of adaptation. The third level is the **proximal social relational level**, involving the individual's relationships with significant others, peers, and members of the nuclear family. At the **sociocultural level** are relations with the larger social institutions of educational, public policy, governmental, and economic systems. Although interactions at both social levels occur throughout development, those occurring at the proximal level in the immediate environment, as these occur over time, are regarded as having the greatest impact on the individual's life (Bronfenbrenner, 1995; Lerner, 1995).

> *"What do you think?"*   **2-2**
>
> What are influences on your development from each of the three levels described within the ecological perspective?

Figure 2.2 summarizes findings from a study that provides a perfect example of Bronfenbrenner's model in action. In the Longitudinal Study of Aging in Amsterdam, the Netherlands, a sample of nearly 2,600 older adults were followed over a nine-year period to determine who was at higher risk for developing depression (Koster et al., 2006). Although we normally think of depression as a condition that develops at the inner psychological level, this study showed that the symptoms of this disorder are systematically related to social context.

The Life Course Perspective

The **life course perspective** emphasizes the importance of age-based norms, roles, and attitudes as influences that shape events throughout development. Through the life course perspective, sociologists and social gerontologists are attempting to forge links between these broad social factors and individual adjustment.

FIGURE 2.2
The Role of Context in Depression in Older Adults

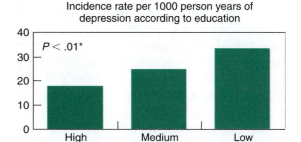

Incidence rate per 1000 person years of depression according to education

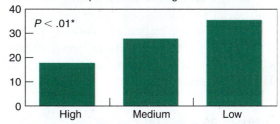

Incidence rate per 1000 person years of depression according to income

Incidence rate of depression according to education and income in a sample of 2,600 Dutch elders studied over a 9-year period. Both education (top) and income (bottom) were related to the probability of an individual's development of depression.
Source: Koster et al., 2006.

One of the first theories to emerge regarding the role of society as an influence on individual adjustment was **disengagement theory** (Cumming & Henry, 1961). According to disengagement theory, there is an optimal relationship between the older individual and society—one in which the older person retreats from active involvement in social roles. According to this view, society withdraws support and interest in the individual during the later years of life through phenomena such as retirement. At the same time, though, starting in late middle age, the individual chooses to disengage from social involvements. Successful aging, according to this view, involves a process of mutual withdrawal of the individual from society.

Disengagement theory was considered a direct assault on the underlying tenets of the prevailing views in social gerontology holding in the mid-20th century that it is harmful to the well-being of older adults to force them out of productive social roles (most people in the field still feel this way at some level). This prevailing view was known as **activity theory** (Cavan, Burgess, Havighurst, & Goldhamer, 1949). Following considerable debate and further research, **continuity theory** (Atchley, 1989) provided a resolution of the issue. According to continuity theory, older adults will suffer a loss of well-being and negative effects of being excluded from social roles if this exclusion goes against their will. The implication of continuity theory is that either forced retirement or forced activity will lead to lower adjustment and self-esteem in middle-aged and older adults.

Ageism as a Social Factor in the Aging Process

This discussion of disengagement theory brings up the related issue of **ageism** which, as with the "isms" of racism and sexism, is a set of beliefs, attitudes, social institutions, and acts that denigrate individuals or groups based on their chronological age. The components of ageism represent stereotyped views of different age groups. Theoretically the term could apply to teenagers as well as to older persons, such as when teenagers are stereotyped as lazy, impulsive, rebellious, or self-centered. However, for all practical purposes, ageism is used as a term referring to stereotyped views of the over-65 or perhaps the over-50. Disengagement theory was thought of by its critics as a justification for ageism, as a way to put older people on the shelf. Moreover, by stating that all older people prefer to remove themselves from society, the theory stereotypes the aged as having the same personalities.

Thus the negative feature of ageism is that, like other stereotypes, it involves making overgeneralizations about individuals based on an outward characteristic that they possess. However, ageism may take the form of overly positive attitudes as well as attitudes that are more negatively valenced (Kite & Wagner, 2002). For example, older adults may be seen as "cute" or "kindly," labels that, though perhaps favorable (if not patronizing), cannot possibly apply to each and every older person. For the most part, however, ageist views portray older adults in a negative light—as cranky, "senile," ridiculous, and incompetent. Closeness to an older person is seen as disgusting or frightening, and, consequently, young people attempt to avoid direct or prolonged contact. Ageism may also take the form of making older adults "invisible"; that is, as not included in representations of people in general. In the workplace, although prohibited by law (see Chapter 10), ageism takes many forms, such as penalizing older workers for making mistakes that would be forgiven if made by younger workers (Rupp, Vodanovich, & Crede, 2006).

There are many possible causes of ageism, but one plausible notion is that negative attitudes toward aging represent fear of death and dying. By their presence, the old remind younger people of the inevitability of their own mortality (Martens, Greenberg, Schimel, & Landau, 2004). Unlike the case for the other "isms," people who hold these stereotypes will eventually become the targets of their own negative beliefs as they themselves grow old. Those young people most likely to experience ageist attitudes are actually the ones who identify most strongly with their own age group. Young adults who have less of an identification with their own age group have more favorable attitudes toward older adults (Packer & Chasteen, 2006).

Although there is ample evidence for ageism, there is little consensus on its cause. One prominent theory of ageism proposes that the status of older adults is negatively related to the degree of industrial development in a given society. According to the **modernization hypothesis**, the increasing urbanization and industrialization of Western society have led to lower social value for older persons (Cowgill & Holmes, 1972). However, critics argue that this hypothesis is overly simplistic (Luborsky & McMullen, 1999). For example, in the United States, even when life expectancy was much lower and the prevalence of older persons in the population was less common than in modern times, attitudes toward aged were not consistently positive (Achenbaum, 1978). Furthermore, evidence for negative attitudes toward elders is found in current preindustrialized societies. Conversely, in some highly developed countries, older adults are more likely to be treated with reverence and respect and are well provided for through health care and economic security programs. The status of older adults in a given society is determined by many complex factors.

Related to the concept of ageism is the **multiple jeopardy hypothesis** (Ferraro & Farmer, 1996). According to this view, older individuals who are of minority status, particularly women, are affected by additional biases beyond those caused by ageism. Systematic biases against women, minorities, and working-class people are thought to interact with age to produce greater risk for discrimination in attitudes and the provision of services to specific subgroups of older adults. Alternatives also exist to the multiple jeopardy hypothesis, however. One alternative is the age-as-leveler view, which proposes that as people become older, age overrides the other "isms." All older adults, including the supposedly favored white males, become victim of the same stereotypes. Therefore, minorities and women are no more disadvantaged than are other persons of their age. A second alternative is the inoculation hypothesis. According to this view, older

minorities and women have become immune to the effects of ageism through years of exposure to discrimination and stereotyping. Sadly, due to their history of discrimination, they are actually in a better position than white males to withstand the negative attitudes they experience as older adults.

At least some of the preoccupation that people have about age is based on a process known as the **social clock**, the normative expectations for the ages at which major life events should occur (Hagestad & Neugarten, 1985). Events such as parenthood have a biological component; other life events are based on calendars that are set by society, such as the need to make progress up the career ladder by the early 30s. Such events in one's own life and the lives of others are evaluated according to whether they are "on-time" or "off-time" with regard to the social clock. When a person's life is off-time, the individual may feel a great deal of personal distress and perhaps criticism from others who expect that people will follow the normative prescriptions for their age group. Nonevents, which are the failure to experience an expected life change, may have as much of an influence on an individual's life as actual events.

Increasingly, however, individuals are setting their own unique social clocks, as exemplified by people like John Glenn, quoted at the beginning of the chapter. At the age of 77, Glenn joined the Space Shuttle Discovery crew on a 9-day orbital mission. His ability to meet the arduous physical requirements of the voyage supports the notion that people do not, as he asserted in his quote, have to be limited by "the calendar."

These views of ageism become important in examining the health and well-being of older adults. Interestingly enough, neither ageism nor multiple jeopardy appears to have deleterious effects on feelings of happiness and well-being, as will be seen in Chapter 14. However, the effects of less access to health care and exposure to negative views of aging on those who are subjected to the "isms" may take their toll on physical health and therefore are a matter of vital concern.

PSYCHOLOGICAL MODELS OF DEVELOPMENT IN ADULTHOOD

In the broadest sense, psychological models attempt to explain the development of the "person" in the person-environment equation from the standpoint of how adaptive abilities unfold over the course of life. It is taken as a given that the body undergoes significant changes, but of interest within the psychological approaches are the changes that occur in the individual's self-understanding, ability to adjust to life's challenges, and perspective on the world.

Erikson's Psychosocial Theory

Perhaps the best known life span psychological theory is Erik Erikson's (1963), which focuses on the development of the self or **ego** through a series of eight stages. In this theory, each stage of development is defined as a crisis in which particular stage-specific issues present themselves as challenges to the individual's ego. The theory is called **psychosocial**, but it could easily be characterized by the term biopsychosocial.

Erikson proposed that individuals pass through a series of transitions in which they are particularly sensitive or vulnerable to a complex interaction of biological, psychological, and social forces characteristic of their period of life. For example, during the intimacy versus isolation stage, the young adult is biologically capable of engaging in sexual relationships, psychologically capable of serious emotional involvement with another adult, and socially expected to "settle down" and find a partner. The "crisis" is not

truly a crisis in the sense of being a catastrophe or disaster. Instead, each psychosocial stage is a time during which the individual may move closer either to a positive or negative resolution of a particular psychosocial issue. This is why each stage is described in terms of a favorable attribute versus an unfavorable attribute. These attributes are qualities of the ego that will develop based on how the crisis is resolved. Depending on the outcome of the stage, you will be more or less able to adapt to the changing demands that life presents to you.

Another crucial aspect of Erikson's theory is the **epigenetic principle**, which means that each stage unfolds from the previous stage according to a predestined order. These stages are set in much the same manner as is the program for the biological development of the individual throughout life. They are built, according to Erikson, into the hard-wiring of the human being.

Erikson's theory has fascinated researchers and developmental theorists, in part because his writing is so compelling and in part because it presents an organized, cohesive view of development from birth to death. The matrix of ages by stages, which forms the heart of the theory, is shown in Figure 2.3. This chart is elegant but deceptively simple. At first glance, it might appear that development proceeds in a series of steps moving steadily from childhood to old age. A more careful inspection of the figure shows that the diagonal line is not the only possibility for development of the ego, although it may be the most evident. The matrix format of this chart implies that there may be developments occurring in boxes that lie outside the diagonal line. Thus, the issues characterizing each stage (such as "trust versus mistrust" for infancy) may coexist as relevant concerns throughout adulthood. Any stage may reach ascendancy in response to events that stimulate its reappearance.

FIGURE 2.3

Stages in Erikson's Psychosocial Theory

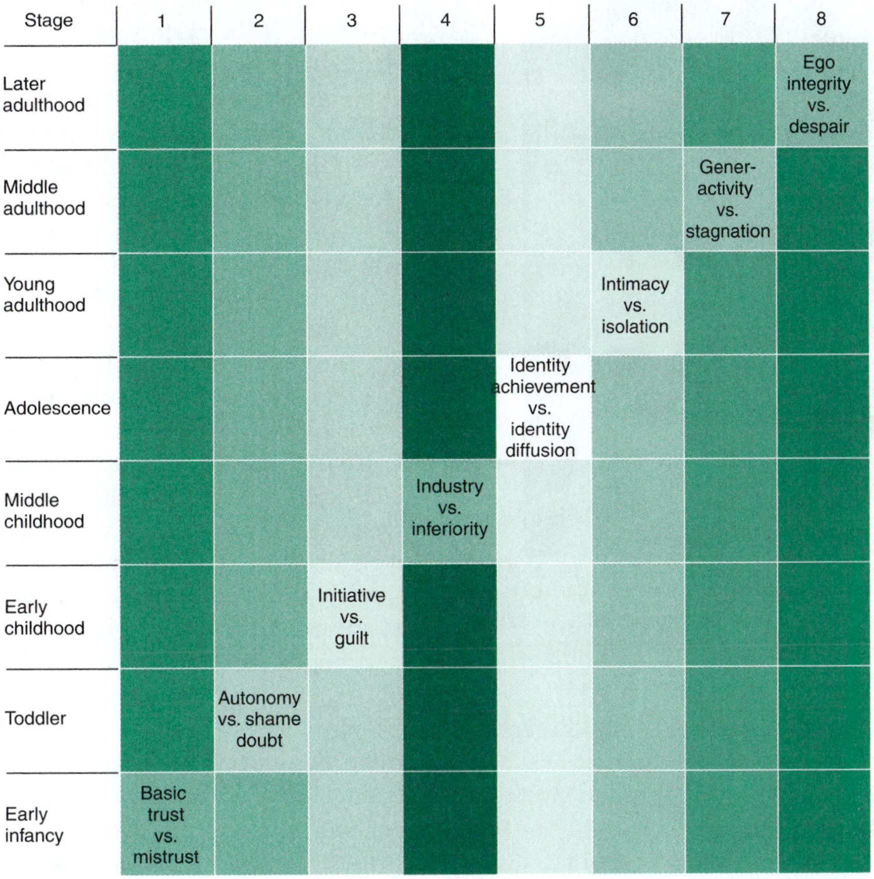

Stage	1	2	3	4	5	6	7	8
Later adulthood								Ego integrity vs. despair
Middle adulthood							Gener-activity vs. stagnation	
Young adulthood						Intimacy vs. isolation		
Adolescence					Identity achievement vs. identity diffusion			
Middle childhood				Industry vs. inferiority				
Early childhood			Initiative vs. guilt					
Toddler		Autonomy vs. shame doubt						
Early infancy	Basic trust vs. mistrust							

Source: Adapted from Erikson, 1963.

Consider the example of an 80-year-old woman who is mugged while walking on a city sidewalk, robbed of her purse and beaten around the head and neck. This incident will leave her traumatized for weeks, and in the process she becomes suspicious and fearful to the point where she will not leave her home. She is essentially, in Erikson's terms, reliving issues of "trust" in which she must regain the feeling that she is safe in her environment. Autonomy may be revisited as an issue in later adulthood when the individual begins to experience limitations

in mobility associated with the physical aging process (Erikson, Erikson, & Kivnick, 1986).

Another implication of the matrix concept is that a crisis may be experienced before its "time." A 35-year-old woman diagnosed with breast cancer may become faced with issues relevant to Ego Integrity versus Despair, the psychosocial crisis normally reserved for a much older person. The crisis stages are best thought of as "critical periods" during which certain issues are likely to become prominent, but they are not meant to be discrete, age-related segments of the life span.

Adults who serve as mentors for younger persons are thought by Erikson to be expressing a sense of generativity.

Given these qualifications regarding the correspondence of the stages with chronological age, let us move on to look at the stages that most typically are associated with the adult years. The first of the eight stages that is directly relevant to adulthood is **Identity Achievement versus Identity Diffusion**. This stage first emerges in adolescence, but it persists in importance throughout adulthood and forms a cornerstone of subsequent adult psychosocial crises (Erikson, 1959; Whitbourne & Connolly, 1999). An individual who achieves a clear identity has a coherent sense of purpose regarding the future and a sense of continuity with the past. By contrast, identity diffusion, the opposite of identity achievement, involves a lack of direction, vagueness about life's purposes, and an unclear sense of self.

The next stage emerging in early adulthood is **Intimacy versus Isolation**. The attainment of intimacy involves establishing a mutually satisfying close relationship with another person to whom a lifelong commitment is made. We can think of the perfect intimate relationship as the intersection of two identities but not a total overlap because each partner preserves a sense of separateness. The polar opposite is the state of isolation in which the person never achieves true mutuality with a life partner. Theoretically isolation is more likely to occur in an individual who lacks a strong identity because in order to establish a close relationship with others, the individual must be secure from within.

The motive for caring for the next generation emerges from the successful resolution of the intimacy psychosocial crisis. The stage of **Generativity versus Stagnation** focuses on the psychosocial issues of procreation, productivity, and creativity. The most common route to generativity is becoming a parent and in this way becoming directly involved in care of the next generation. However, those who do not have children can nevertheless develop generativity in the activities of teaching, mentoring, or supervising younger people. A career that involves producing something of value that future generations can enjoy is another form of generativity. The main feature of generativity is a feeling of concern over what happens to the young and a desire to make the world a better place for them. Stagnation, by contrast, occurs when the individual turns concern and energy inward or solely to others of one's own age group rather than to the young. A person who is high on the quality of stagnation lacks interest or may even go so far as to reject the younger generation. Of course, being a parent is no guarantee of achieving generativity; the crucial component of generativity is concern and care for the people who will follow one's own generation.

Toward the end of adulthood, the individual faces psychosocial issues related to aging and growing closer to death, and begins to enter the stage of **Ego Integrity versus Despair**. The older individual who establishes a strong sense of ego integrity can look back over the years lived thus far with acceptance. Ego integrity also involves an ability to look at and accept the positive and negative attributes of one's life and self, even if it may be painful to acknowledge past mistakes or personal flaws. This sense of acceptance of the past and present self allows the individual who has attained ego integrity to look at mortality similarly with acceptance that life inevitably must end. It may be difficult for a young person to imagine how a person who is happy with life could also be happy or at least not devastated by the thought of death. However, according to Erikson, acceptance of the past and present helps us attain acceptance of the end of life. In contrast, despair is the outcome of the individual's realization that death is unavoidable and that it will come too soon to make possible a righting of previous wrongs. The individual in a state of despair feels discontent with life and is unhappy to the point of despondency at the thought of death. Even though this person's daily existence is filled with complaints and misery, the thought of ending that life before past mistakes can be corrected is even more frightening.

Erikson's views about development were a radical departure from the theories about personality prevalent at the time of his writing. He proposed his theory as a reaction to those of other psychologists who felt that we were completely formed by, if not childhood, then certainly no later than adolescence. Identity, intimacy, generativity, and ego integrity are now regarded as central themes of adult development and indeed inform much of what is covered in this book.

Piaget's Cognitive-Developmental Theory

Jean Piaget was a Swiss psychologist who became fascinated with the development of

intelligence after watc gain mastery of thei infancy and early cl was to come to envis reciprocal relationship physical-social environ theory was cognitive d but the terms and concepts central to this theory can be applied more generally to a life span model of psychological functioning in general.

A major feature of Piaget's theory was his description of a series of stages in childhood cognition. More generally, however, Piaget identified two basic ways in which people interact with their experiences. The process of **assimilation** is engaged when individuals interpret new experiences in terms of their existing mental structures, what he called **schemas**. The term assimilation, in this context, does not have its common meaning, as when we say that a person has become assimilated to a new culture. In Piaget's model, assimilation has actually almost the opposite meaning, referring to the situation in which individuals are trying to fit their experiences into their schemas or current ways of viewing the world.

As an example of assimilation, let's say that you have a very meager understanding of different varieties of birds, and you call all little birds "sparrows" and all large birds "crows." You are forcing into two categories what actually may be eight or ten different varieties of birds in your neighborhood. According to Piaget, people engage in this assimilative process until they are able to gain experiences that allow them to refine their concepts or schemas. If you go for a walk with an avid bird watcher who points out the differences among sparrows, finches, and chickadees (all small birds), you will emerge with a refinement to your previous categorization system. In Piaget's terms, you have changed your existing schema, a process he referred to as **accommodation**.

et's theory, children become better able
dapt to the world through alternating
tween assimilation and accommodation. The
ideal state is one in which we are able to
interpret our experiences through a consistent
framework (assimilation) but are able to change
this framework when it no longer is helpful in
organizing experiences (accommodation). Such
an ideal state is referred to as an **equilibrium**,
and the process of achieving this balance is called
equilibration.

Identity Process Theory

Integrating Erikson's and Piaget's theories provides an excellent vantage point for making
predictions about psychosocial development in
adulthood and, in particular, the way that people
adapt to the aging process. According to **identity
process theory** (Whitbourne, 2002), the processes of assimilation and accommodation can
account for interactions between the individual
and experiences through the framework provided
by identity.

In identity process theory, we assume that
people approach their experiences from the vantage point provided by their personal identities,
namely, their ideas or concepts about the self.
There is a certain bias that we all have to view
ourselves in a favorable light. Most of us like
to think of ourselves as physically and mentally competent, liked by others, and as adhering
to ethical principles such as being honest and
concerned for the welfare of others.

Using Piaget's terminology, **identity assimilation** refers to the tendency that we have to
interpret new experiences relevant in terms of
these ideas as being competent, well liked, and
ethical. Identity assimilation has its good features
in that it allows us to feel happy and effective. We
can continue to feel good about ourselves despite

being less than perfect. But identity assimilation
can also lead us to twist the way we interpret
experiences that might challenge this sunny view
of who we are. For example, failure such as
receiving a low grade on a test is an experience
that could potentially cause you to conclude that
you are intellectually flawed in some way. Using
identity assimilation, you might blame the test
or the professor rather than question your own
abilities and you therefore will not suffer a loss
of self-esteem.

Although identity assimilation preserves a
positive view of the self, continued failure
experiences that we refuse to incorporate into
our self-appraisals can ultimately have negative
consequences. As with the example of the bird
classification, a discrepancy between a certain
way of viewing the self or the world and the
reality of an experience that is incongruent or
inconsistent with that view at some point may
need to be resolved. You cannot go on blaming
the professor or the test forever if you keep
getting low grades. At some point you have to
confront your own limitations, whether it means
you are in the wrong set of courses, you do not
study enough, or you are not as smart as you
thought you were. This realization stimulates the
process of **identity accommodation**, through
which people change their identity.

Identity accommodation is not always a
negative process, however. For example, people
who are able to cope successfully with a tragedy
may find that they have inner strength that
they did not know had existed. As with identity
assimilation, however, it is possible to rely too
heavily on identity accommodation. Individuals
who define themselves entirely on the basis
of their experiences, such as how others treat
them, have the potential to be devastated by
a negative event such as being rejected by a
romantic partner.

According to the Multiple Threshold Model, age-related changes in appearance can lead some adults to undergo changes in their identity.

"What do you think?"   **2-3**

Can you give an example of identity assimilation and identity accommodation from your own life or from examples in literature or film?

Ideally, as in Piaget's theory, there is a balance or dynamic equilibrium between identity assimilation and identity accommodation in adulthood. Piaget proposed that it is a natural tendency to use assimilation when confronted with a new situation. We use what has worked in the past to help us understand what is happening to us now. However, to be as well adjusted as possible, we need to be able to make accommodations when the situation warrants changes.

Throughout adulthood, identity processes are constantly being called into play with regard to the changes in our physical and cognitive

functioning. We can think of these changes as occurring through a sequence of phases over time, a set of "multiple thresholds" (Whitbourne & Collins, 1998). The **multiple threshold model** of change in adulthood proposes that people pass through a series of steps of feeling "old" at different times for different systems of the body. Each new age-related change brings with it the potential for another threshold to be crossed. The area or areas that are of greatest significance to our identities are likely to be observed with great care or vigilance. Some thresholds are crossed without much notice because they are in areas that are not of particular importance to that individual. You may find that gray hair provides a threshold for you but that you don't care much about the fact that your muscles have gotten somewhat weaker than they used to be. Someone else may disregard gray hair entirely but become obsessed with the first signs of loss of muscle strength. At the point of crossing a threshold, we are stimulated to recognize the reality of the aging process in that particular area of functioning. At that point we move from identity assimilation to identity accommodation as we attempt to adjust to the crossing of the threshold and, in so doing, reach a new state of balance.

Figure 2.4 illustrates how a person's identity can influence the way that we react to age-related changes. We tend to interpret our experiences in terms of our existing identities, which for most people is favorable. Then we have a "threshold" experience such as noticing an age-related change, experiencing a health problem, or feeling that our cognitive abilities have worsened. At that point, we use one of the three identity processes.

In identity accommodation, we take that experience very seriously, to the point that we let it redefine our identities. If it is a case of, for example, feeling out of breath or in a little bit of pain after an arduous workout, we might decide that we are "over the hill" and have lost our youthful prowess. Another possible outcome of using identity accommodation is that we form a new identity around the illness and go overboard in terms of the extent to which we worry about the consequences of the illness and try to fight it off.

In this regard, a term that has unfortunately (in my opinion) gained popularity among Baby Boomers is the "senior moment," generally used humorously when a person forgets a well-known piece of information such as someone's name or telephone number. Looking at this term from the vantage point of the multiple threshold model, it essentially is describing the point at which an individual crosses over the memory threshold. It is interesting that this term is almost always used in a joking manner, but it can have more ominous overtones in people who are seriously concerned that their memory is taking an irreversible turn for the worse. In fact, as will become clear later in the book, it can almost take on the quality of a self-fulfilling prophecy.

Overuse of identity accommodation is a maladaptive way to react to an age-related change, because it leads us either to feel that there is nothing we can do to change our fate or to let our illness overtake the rest of our lives. Similarly overuse of identity assimilation presents problems. In unhealthy denial people fail to take advantage of preventative measures that could help them maintain their optimal functioning. They may not cut back on harmful foods, refuse to exercise, or continue to engage in various

FIGURE 2.4
Identity Process Theory

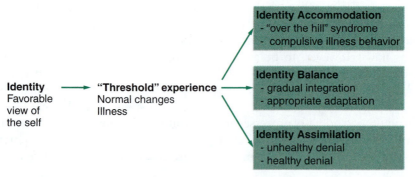

We interpret "threshold" experiences that have the potential to change the way we think about ourselves in one of three ways: identity accommodation (changing our view of the self), identity balance (maintaining a stable sense of self but making some adaptations), or identity assimilation (not allowing the change to affect our sense of self).

ASSESS YOURSELF: What Is Your Identity Process?

According to Identity Process Theory, we react to new experiences in adulthood according to one of three processes: Identity Assimilation, Identity Accommodation, and Identity Balance. In this survey, you will be asked questions involving each of these three processes and how closely they apply to you. You can keep a tally of your score because feedback for each question shows how it would be rated. In addition to learning about your identity processes, the ratings for each question show you more specifically how the identity processes are defined.

Identity Assimilation = IAS
Identity Accommodation = IAC
Identity Balance = IBL

1. When it comes to thinking about myself and my experiences:
   A. I prefer not to think too much about "who" I am. (IAS)
   B. I am constantly learning from my experiences. (IBL)
   C. I am constantly trying to figure out "who" I am. (IAC)

2. Regarding my goals:
   A. I have always been very sure of my goals (IAS)
   B. I do not have a clear sense of my goals. (IAC)
   C. I have a pretty good idea of my goals, but I am open to change if necessary. (IBL)

3. When it comes to thinking about my mistakes:
   A. I realize that I have made some but I don't become preoccupied with them. (IBL)
   B. I figure that what's done is done and it is not worth thinking about them. (IAS)
   C. I find myself thinking constantly about how I could do things differently. (IAC)

4. When I think about my life so far, I find that I
   A. often wonder about how my life could be different than it is. (IAC)
   B. like to see myself as stable, consistent, and unlikely to change. (IAS)
   C. am challenged but not overwhelmed by change. (IBL)

5. With regard to my behavior on a daily basis:
   A. I spend little time wondering why I act the way I do. (IAS)
   B. I am constantly trying to understand why I act the way I do. (IAC)
   C. I think about why I act the way I do, but am not preoccupied with it. (IBL)

6. With regard to other people I
   A. behave according to what I think others want from me. (IAC)
   B. am not very interested in advice from others. (IAS)
   C. like to listen to other viewpoints and then make up my own mind. (IBL)

7. When I think about myself getting older, I
   A. prefer not to focus on how I will change. (IAS)
   B. am very concerned about what will happen to me. (IAC)
   C. feel confident that I will be able to adapt to changes. (IBL)

deleterious behaviors such as smoking. However, denial may not always be bad. In healthy denial, people avoid thinking about the deeper implications of the fact that they are experiencing age-related changes. Yet they manage to engage in healthy, preventive behavior anyway. They take advantage of health-preserving activities without giving them a great deal of thought.

Identity balance is the most positive way to react to age-related changes or alterations in health. People who use identity balance accept the fact that they are aging but do not become fatalistic. They take steps to ensure that they will remain healthy but they are not preoccupied with any conditions or limitations that they may already have developed. At the same time, they are not living with the illusion that they will be young forever.

The advantages of identity balance and even healthy denial are that the aging person adopts an active "use it or lose it" approach to the aging process. By remaining active, we can ward off negative changes ranging from loss of muscle strength to memory. On the other hand, there are many "bad habits" or ways in which our behavior can accelerate the aging process. Some of the most well known of these negative behaviors were described in Chapter 1 (see Table 1.1). Ideally, people adapt to the aging process by taking advantage of the use-it-or-lose-it approach and avoiding the bad habits. We will place less of a strain on both identity assimilation and identity accommodation if we can maintain our functioning as long and as well as possible by maintaining our good health.

BIOLOGICAL APPROACHES TO AGING IN ADULTHOOD

Biological changes throughout later life, as is true of those in the years of infancy, childhood, and adolescence, are based on certain genetically

determined events or at least changes in physiological functioning brought about by intrinsic changes within the organism. As described at the beginning of this chapter, the interactionist model of development predicts that environmental factors influence the expression of biological or genetic predispositions. According to the principle of reciprocity, the individual's activities, both in direct relation to these changes and through more general behaviors we call "lifestyle," interact with our preset biological programs. The result is that large individual differences occur in the nature and timing of age-related changes in physical and cognitive functioning. Ultimately, however, it is the aging of the body that sets the limit to the life span. We can compensate through behavioral measures for many of the changes associated with the aging process. Yet an inevitability is associated with the passage of time. The body's biological clock continues to record the years.

Having acknowledged this "fact of life" regarding the biological aging process, next we can turn to the question of why it happens. Why must living things grow old and die? Science fiction fans enjoy stories of worlds in which biological aging does not occur, or at least not at the rate it does on our planet, and people live forever or for hundreds of years. If you contemplate such a world or think about how they are portrayed in fiction, you can think of some obvious problems associated with prolonged or eternal life. Overpopulation, lack of resources, and intergenerational strife (lasting hundreds, not tens of years) are just some of the possible outcomes. Alternatively the birthrate may be reduced to a virtual standstill in one of these planets to avoid some of those problems.

Another futuristic possibility is that perhaps people can constantly be "reborn" and the same individual can live on in multiple bodies despite apparent physical death. In any case the problems of a static society may be just as unpleasant as the alternatives. Perhaps it is far more "efficient" to have a world such as ours, in which the older generations are constantly being swept aside to make room for the new ones whose entry into the population assures its vitality. But can we assume that there is some advantage to aging and death that has led to its association with life? Although some of the biological theories are based on this assumption, maybe those fictional worlds in which death did not occur had some other advantages that we will not be able to enjoy until we unlock the secret of eternal life. Perhaps it is preferable to have a society in which people's wisdom and experience continue to accumulate and the lessons of history do not need to be painfully relearned with every generation. Perhaps being old and full of years is the ideal state, and being young and naive is an unpleasant hurdle that must be suffered through by each new flock of young people. Maybe we were not meant to die after all, and aging is some terrible accident that can ultimately be corrected.

The idea that aging is the result of a correctable defect in living things is a premise that underlies some of the major biological theories that we will turn to shortly. Or, as a third possibility reflected in these theories, perhaps organisms are programmed to survive until reaching sexual maturity. Having guaranteed the survival of their species, either organisms are programmed to deteriorate or they simply fade away because there are no genes programmed to keep them alive past that point. We have to be around long enough to reproduce, and after that there is no particular set of guidelines for what happens to us next.

Genes and DNA

Inherited characteristics are found in genome, the complete set of instructions for "building" all the cells that make up an organism (see Figure 2.5). The human genome is found in each nucleus of

FIGURE 2.5
Genes and DNA

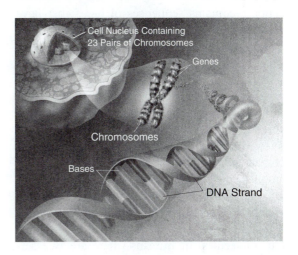

a person's many trillions of cells. The genome for each living creature consists of tightly coiled threads of the molecule **deoxyribonucleic acid (DNA)**. The DNA resides in the nucleus of the body's cells as two long, paired strands spiraled into a double helix, a shape that resembles a twisted ladder. The components of DNA encode the information needed to manufacture proteins, which are large, complex molecules made up of long chains of subunits called amino acids. Protein is the primary component of all living things. There are many kinds of proteins, each with different functions. Some proteins provide structure to the cells of the body, whereas others called enzymes assist biochemical reactions that take place within the cells. Antibodies are proteins that function in the immune system to identify foreign invaders that need to be removed from the body. The entire process of protein manufacture is orchestrated by the genetic code contained in the DNA.

A **gene** is a functional unit of a DNA molecule carrying a particular set of instructions for producing a specific protein. Human genes vary widely in length, but only about 10%

of the genome actually contains sequences of genes used to code proteins. The rest of the genome contains sequences of bases that have no apparent coding or any other function. Some of the proteins that the genes encode provide very basic housekeeping functions in the cell. These genes stay active all the time in many types of cells. More typically, however, a cell activates just the genes it needs at the moment and suppresses the rest. Through this process of selective activation of genes, the cell obtains its character as a skin cell, for example, rather than a bone cell.

The genome is organized into **chromosomes**, which are distinct, physically separate units of coiled threads of DNA and associated protein molecules. In humans, there are two sets of 23 chromosomes, one set contributed by each parent. Each set has 23 single chromosomes: 22 are called "autosomes" and contain nonsex-linked information, and the twenty-third is the X or Y sex chromosome. A normal female has a pair of X chromosomes, and a male has an X and Y pair. The presence of the Y chromosome determines maleness. Although each chromosome always has the same genes on it, there is no rhyme or reason to the distribution of genes on chromosomes. A gene that produces a protein that influences eye color may be next to a gene that is involved in cellular energy production.

Genes may undergo alterations, called **mutations**, when DNA reproduces itself. When a gene contains a mutation, the protein encoded by that gene is likely to be abnormal. Sometimes the protein will be able to function even though it is damaged, but in other cases, it will be totally disabled. If a protein that is vital to survival becomes severely damaged, the results of the mutation are obviously going to be very serious. Genetic mutations can be either inherited from a parent or acquired over the course of one's life. Inherited mutations originate from the DNA of the cells involved in reproduction (sperm and egg). When reproductive cells containing mutations are combined in one's offspring, the mutation will be in all the bodily cells of that offspring. Inherited mutations are responsible for diseases such as cystic fibrosis and sickle cell anemia or may predispose an individual to cancer, major psychiatric illnesses, and other complex diseases. Acquired mutations are changes in DNA that develop throughout a person's lifetime. Remarkably, cells possess the ability to repair many of these mutations. If these repair mechanisms fail, however, the mutation can be passed along to future copies of the altered cell. Mutations can also occur in the mitochondrial DNA, which is the DNA found in the tiny structures within the cell called mitochondria. These structures are crucial to the functioning of the cell because they are involved in producing cellular energy.

Biologists have provided many fascinating perspectives on the aging process. Their theories share the common thread of being attempts to solve one of, if not the greatest, mysteries of life.

Programmed Aging Theories

The biological theories of aging are divided into two categories (Hayflick, 1994): programmed aging and random error. Programmed aging theories are based on the assumption that aging and death are built into the hard-wiring of all organisms. Following from this assumption is the notion that there are "aging genes" that count off the years past maturity as surely as "development genes" lead to the point of maturity in youth. One argument long used in support of this assumption is based on the fact that the life span varies according to species, suggesting that life span is part of an organism's genetic makeup. For example, butterflies have life spans of 12 weeks, and giant tortoises have life spans of 180 years. Humans, the mammals with the longest life spans, are in between these points with life spans of 120 years.

This deermouse, shown in the wild, is one of the species examined in the Gompertz function shown in Figure 2.6.

The relationship between the age span of a species and the age of its death (or life span), is expressed in the **Gompertz equation**, a mathematical function showing the relationship between age and probability of death. The originator of the Gompertz equation was Benjamin Gompertz, an 18th century British mathematician who worked as an actuary. In 1825 he applied calculus to mortality data and showed that the mortality rate increases in a geometric progression with age. When plotted as a logarithmic function, it takes the form of a straight line. Figure 2.6 compares the Gompertz functions of several species of field and deer mice (Sacher, 1977). The horizontal axis of this graph shows the age of the organism in days with the longest-living species reaching about 9 years and the shortest-living about a year and a half. The

vertical axis shows the death rate per day and the plot points show the number that die per day with increasing age of the species. There is a different Gompertz function for each species, supporting the idea that longevity is an inherited, species-specific trait.

Findings in support of genetic theories are particularly intriguing in view of the considerable progress being made in the field of genetics. The ability to identify and then control the "aging" gene or genes would go a long way toward changing the very nature of aging. However, despite the appeal of a genetic theory based on the concept that one or multiple genes control the aging process from birth to death, a simple genetic theory does have its problems. We cannot say for sure that evolution has selected for the aging process along the lines of the argument that old generations must die to make room for new ones. The fact is that, historically, few species survived until they were old enough to grow old and be exposed to the evolutionary selection process. A more defensible variant of the genetic theory is that evolution has selected for species that are vigorous up to the point that sexual maturity has passed. In the postreproductive years, "good genes gone bad" (Hayflick, 1994) take over and lead to the ultimate destruction of the organism. Researchers continue to investigate the notion that the very genes that have a positive effect on development during early life create susceptibility to a variety of diseases in later life (Caruso et al., 2000), particularly those that affect our ability to fight off infection through the immune system (Franceschi et al., 2007).

The most compelling attempts to explain aging through genetics are based on the principle of **replicative senescence**, the loss of the ability of cells to reproduce. Scientists have known for a long time that there are a finite number of times (about 50) that normal human cells can proliferate in culture before they become terminally incapable of further division (Hayflick &

FIGURE 2.6
Gompertz Curve

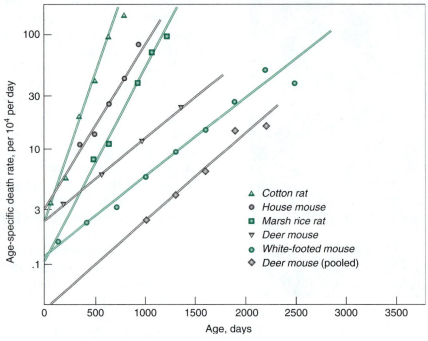

This figure shows the relationship between the age in days of six species of mice and rats and the rate of dying per day. The fact that different species have different functions supports the notion of genetic contributions to longevity.

Source: Sacher, 1977.

Moorhead, 1961). Until relatively recently, though, scientists did not know why this happened. It was only when the technology developed sufficiently to allow them to look closely at the chromosomes that at least some of the mystery behind this process was revealed.

As we saw in Figure 2.2, the chromosome is made up largely of DNA. However, not entirely, because at the ends of the chromosomes are **telomeres**, repeating sequences of proteins that contain no genetic information. At each cell division, the telomeres become shorter, and as they do, changes occur in patterns of gene expression that affect both the functioning of the cell and the organ system in which it operates. Adjacent chromosomes fuse, the cell cycle is halted, and ultimately the cell dies

(Shin, Hong, Solomon, & Lee, 2006). Evidence linking telomere length to mortality in humans suggests that the telomeres may ultimately hold the key to understanding why we age (Graakjaer, Londono-Vallejo, Christensen, & Kolvraa, 2006).

> *"What do you think?"*   **2-4**
>
> Do you think that aging can or should be controlled through genetics?

However, biology does not tell the whole story, even with telomeres. Supporting the idea of biopsychosocial interactions in development, researchers have linked telomere length to social factors. Analyzing blood samples from over 1,500

FIGURE 2.7
Telomeres

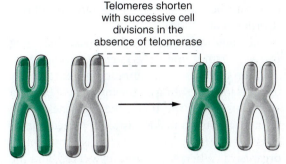

Telomeres shorten
with successive cell
divisions in the
absence of telomerase

Telomeres are the nongenetic material at the ends of chromosomes that protect against gene loss. During each cell division, the telomeres become shorter and shorter. Eventually they are no longer present, and genetic material is lost when cells divide.

female twins, researchers in the United Kingdom found that telomere length was shorter in women from lower socioeconomic classes (Cherkas et al., 2006). There was a difference of seven "biological years" (measured in terms of telomeres) between twins with manual jobs and their co-twins in higher-ranking occupations. The researchers attributed this difference to the stress of being in a lower-level occupation in which people have less control over their day-to-day activities. Body mass index, smoking, and lack of exercise were additional factors influencing telomere length.

Although many cells in the body are thought to be affected by the shortening of the telomeres, not all of them experience this effect of the aging process. For example, when tumor cells are added to normal cells, they replicate indefinitely. Because of the danger posed by indefinitely replicating tumor cells, senescence may be thought of as a form of protection against cancer. The trick in extending the life span based on the telomere theory would be for scientists to find a way to keep cells replicating longer without increasing the risk of cancer cell proliferation (Geserick & Blasco, 2006).

Random Error Theories

Random error theories are based on the assumption that aging reflects unplanned changes in an organism over time. The wear and tear theory of aging is a theory that many people implicitly refer to when they speak of "falling apart" as they get older. According to this view, the body, like a used Ford truck, acquires more and more damage as it is exposed to the use and abuse it takes on a daily basis. Eventually, as more and more of its parts give out, it stops running altogether. Programmed aging theories, in contrast, would suggest that the truck was not "built to last," but to deteriorate over time in a systematic rather than idiosyncratic fashion.

Cross-linking theory proposes that aging causes deleterious changes in **collagen**, the protein that makes up about one-quarter of all bodily proteins. Collagen provides structure to the body, supporting the skin, strengthening the tendons, and connecting the softer tissues of the body to the skeleton. The collagen molecule is composed of three chains of amino acids wound together in a tight helix. Strands of collagen molecules are attached through horizontal strands of cross-linking proteins, like the rungs of a ladder. Increasingly with age, the rungs of one ladder start to connect to the rungs of another ladder, causing the molecules to become increasingly rigid and to shrink in size. Researchers agree that the process of cross-linking affects the efficiency of functioning of many structures in the body (Avery & Bailey, 2005), but it is unlikely that the process is a primary cause of aging.

The **free radical** theory, also known as the oxidative stress theory (Sohal, 2002), focuses on a set of unstable compounds known as free radicals, produced when certain molecules in cells react with oxygen. The free radicals then seek to bind to other molecules. When this binding takes place, the molecule to which the free radical has become attached loses its functioning.

There is experimental support for the free radical theory (Krause, 2006). Some of this support comes from research involving antioxidants, which are chemicals that prevent the formation of free radicals. Antioxidants include vitamin E and vitamin C. Free radicals can be destroyed by superoxide dismutase (SOD). Although antioxidants receive a good deal of attention in the antiaging drug and cosmetic markets, many in the scientific community remain skeptical about whether these supplements will ultimately deliver what they promise (Howes, 2006).

One implication of the free radical theory relates to caloric restriction. Biologist Roy Walford, devoted his career to proving the **caloric restriction hypothesis**, the view that restriction of caloric intake is the key to prolonging life (Walford, Mock, Verdery, & MacCallum, 2002). Caloric restriction is thought to have its beneficial impact in part because it reduces the formation of free radicals. Although impressive results have been shown in studies involving caloric restriction in rats (Hyun, Emerson, Jo, Mattson, & de Cabo, 2006), there is still insufficient evidence to support the caloric restriction hypothesis, in part because of the lack of controlled studies on humans (Dirks & Leeuwenburgh, 2006a).

Some promising findings regarding free radical theory have been obtained involving resveratrol, a component of red wine. Laboratory mice fed on a high calorie diet plus resveratrol have a survival rate approximating that of mice on a normal diet, both of whom had higher survival rates than animals on a high calorie diet (Baur et al., 2006). Although it has now become fairly well established that red wine is related to longer life, researchers debate the cause of these positive effects. Rather than having its effects through mechanisms involving free radicals, other researchers propose that red wine's benefits are the result of procyanidins, tannens

present in red wine, which have beneficial effects on the arteries. The wines of Southwest France are thought to have the most protective effect on longevity because of their high tannen content (Corder et al., 2006).

The autoimmune theory proposes that aging is due to faulty immune system functioning. In addition to a loss of the immune system's ability to do its job in fighting off the invasion of bacteria and viruses into the body, the immune system actually begins to make mistakes in recognizing cells of the body versus the cells of invading organisms. When autoimmunity occurs, and the body attacks its own cells, damage results to bodily tissues. Autoimunity is at the heart of certain diseases that become more prevalent in older adults (but are not restricted to them), such as some forms of arthritis (Giunta, 2006).

Error theories are based on the proposal that mutations acquired over the organism's lifetime lead to malfunctioning of the body's cells. According to one variant of this theory, the error catastrophe theory, it is not just random errors that lead to the changes associated with aging, but errors in the manufacturing of proteins, a process that play a key role in the maintenance of the body's cells. Like a bridge that has suddenly collapsed after gradually accumulating damage over the years, the impairment in the cell would lead to widespread tissue and organ malfunction. Although researchers have not established error catastrophe as a generalized process leading to aging, there is evidence that it may have applicability to certain age-related diseases as well as more widespread changes throughout the bodily tissues (Conley, Amara, Jubrias, & Marcinek, 2006). The source of the errors is thought to be in the mitochondrial DNA (Trifunovic, 2006).

As we can see, biologists have spanned a large spectrum in trying to solve the puzzle of why we, and our counterparts across the animal kingdom, experience the changes associated with

FIGURE 2.8
Map of France

Researchers believe that wine from the southwestern region of France provides the greatest protection against the aging process.

the aging process that eventually lead to death. At the present time, genetic theories are definitely considered more likely to hold the ultimate answer, but none of the other approaches can be ruled out just yet.

In looking at perspectives on the aging process that derive from the social sciences, it is important to keep in mind the central role of biological factors. These factors form the "nature" component to the complex "nature-nurture" interactions assumed to characterize development in the adult years. Clearly all three models must be brought to bear in attempting to understand the complexities of nature and nurture.

SUMMARY

1. The life span perspective is increasingly replacing the view of development as ending in adolescence. Current life span models emphasize contextual influences on development, and the term "developmental science" is emerging to reflect the need to take a broad, interdisciplinary approach to the study of change over time.

2. Interactionist models of development emphasize processes such as niche-picking in which there is a reciprocal interaction between the individual and the environment. Organismic models regard development as an unfolding

of genetic processes, and mechanistic models emphasize the role of the environment in shaping development. Interactionist models include the concepts of multidimensionality and multidirectionality, and they regard plasticity as an important element of development. Reciprocal processes in which individuals affect and are affected by their environment are a focus of interactionist models. The biopsychosocial perspective fits within the interactionist model.

3. Sociocultural models of development emphasize the effects of the environment on individuals, focusing on variables such as age and sex structures within the population, income, and social class. The life course perspective highlights age-related norms, roles, and attitudes as influences on individuals. Ecological perspectives examine multiple levels of organization within the environment, such as the proximal social relational level and the sociocultural level.

4. Ageism is a set of stereotyped views about older adults, reflected in negative as well as positive images. Some historians believe that older adults were more highly regarded in preindustrial societies, a view known as the modernization hypothesis. However, it appears that mixed views of aging have existed throughout history and across cultures. Theories that relate the well-being of the older individual to the level of social involvement include disengagement theory, activity theory, and continuity theory. These propose different relationships between individuals and society. According to the multiple jeopardy hypothesis of aging, older adults who are of minority status and are female face more discrimination than white male individuals.

5. Erikson's psychosocial development theory is an important psychological model of development in adulthood. It proposes a series of eight psychosocial crisis stages that correspond roughly to age periods in life in the growth of psychological functions. The eight stages follow the epigenetic principle, which means that each stage builds on the ones that come before it. However, later stages can appear at earlier ages, and early stages can reappear later in life. According to Piaget's theory of development, individuals gain in the ability to adapt to the environment through the processes of assimilation and accommodation. The ideal state of development is one of equilibration or balance. According to the identity process theory, identity assimilation and identity accommodation operate throughout development in adulthood as the individual interacts with experiences. The multiple threshold model was proposed as an explanation of how identity processes influence the interpretation of age-related events such as changes in physical or cognitive functioning.

6. There are two major categories of biological theories, all of which regard aging as the result of changes in the biological makeup of the organism. Programmed aging theories are based on the observation that species differ in life spans (represented by the Gompertz equation) and propose that aging is genetically determined. The telomere theory, which emerged in part from observations of replicative senescence, proposes that cells are limited in the number of times they can reproduce by the fact that each replication involves a loss of the protective ends of chromosomes known as telomeres. Random error theories view aging as an accident resulting from cellular processes that have gone awry. Studies on caloric restriction provide support for the free radical theory, which also proposes that antioxidants can slow down the aging process.

CHAPTER 3

The Study of Adult Development and Aging: Research Methods

> *"Nature gives you the face you have at twenty; it is up to you to merit the face you have at fifty."*
>
> Coco Chanel
> (1883–1971)

Aging is intimately tied up with the passage of time. It is this intrinsic relationship between age and time that researchers in adult development and aging must struggle with in designing their studies. As difficult as questions are regarding the nature of change over time, it is crucial that such research be conducted. Without empirical data, we would have no solid ground for establishing a basis for gathering a clear view of how aging affects people. In this chapter, we examine the strategies that researchers have devised to provide the information needed to gain an accurate view of the processes of development in adulthood and later life.

VARIABLES IN DEVELOPMENTAL RESEARCH

A variable is a characteristic that "varies" from individual to individual. Behavioral scientists attempt to understand why some people are high on a particular variable and some people are low. This is the **dependent variable**, the variable on which people differ. The **independent variable** is the variable that explains or "causes" the range of scores in the dependent variable. Although developmental psychologists treat age as an independent variable, it is not technically correct to do so because the experimenter cannot control its value. However, there are other ways around this challenge.

An **experimental design** involves the manipulation of an independent variable followed by the measurement of scores on the dependent variable. Respondents are randomly assigned to treatment and control groups. It is assumed that people vary on the dependent measure because they were exposed to different levels of the independent variable. Since age is not an independent variable, we cannot state that aging "caused" people to receive the scores they did on a dependent variable of interest, but we can determine whether different age groups varied in their responses to different levels of the independent variable. Such situations are referred to as interactions among variables. If a manipulation produces a different effect in a younger age group than it does in an older age group, we may infer that the treatment has some relationship to age. For example, consider an experiment in which special instructions are given for a memory test to two different age groups of adults. If older adults are helped more in their performance than are younger adults, we can infer that there is something about age that makes people particularly sensitive to the type of manipulation involved in these instructions.

In cases where the characteristics of a group cannot be manipulated experimentally, the design is said to be quasi-experimental. In a **quasi-experimental design**, groups are compared on predetermined characteristics. We cannot conclude that the predetermined characteristic caused the variations in the dependent variable, but we can describe the differences between groups. If we feel that other explanations have been ruled out, and if we can repeatedly demonstrate differences based on age, we can make the cautious inference that aging had something to do with the variations in people's scores.

Solid theories and careful ruling out of alternative explanations are the key to drawing conclusions about the "effect" of age on variables of interest. We will return to this point on numerous occasions throughout the text.

DESCRIPTIVE RESEARCH DESIGNS

The major challenge facing researchers is to separate the effect of aging from the effects of time. The three variables used in this process are age, cohort, and time of measurement.

These three factors are thought to influence jointly the individual's performance on any given psychological measure at any point in life. As we will see, these variables are highly related to each other. It takes both creativity and scientific rigor to try to disentangle these factors.

TABLE 3.1
Age, Cohort and Time of Measurement

Term	Definition	Index of
Age	Chronological age, measured in years	Change within individual
Cohort	Year of period of birth	Influences relative to history
Time of measurement	Time of testing	Current influences on individuals being tested

These are the three major variables investigated in research carried out within the field of development science.

Age, Cohort, and Time of Measurement

Age is measured as chronological age, usually in years. As you know from Chapter 1, age is an objectively determined measure based on the passage of time, not a direct measure of an individual's internal characteristics. The older a person is, the more calendar years that person has experienced. There may or may not be a direct connection between the movement of the calendar and changes going on within the person. Developmental psychologists use age as a convenient shorthand but understand that age is an imperfect index of the phenomena they investigate.

"What do you think?" 3-1

Why is it that cohort, time of measurement, and age cannot truly be separated from each other?

Social aging is represented by the two factors of cohort and time of measurement. **Cohort** is determined by the year of the individual's birth. This term is used in studies on adult development and aging to signify the general era in which a person was born. Conceptually, the term cohort may represent the more familiar term generation in that it is intended to refer to people who were born (and hence lived through) some of the same social influences. For example, members of the 1950 cohort were in college during the Vietnam War era and shared certain experiences specific to this period of history. By contrast, the college experiences of people in the 1960 cohort were far more quiescent.

Time of measurement is the year or period in which testing has occurred. It is a convenient way of representing the social and historical influences on the individual at the point when data are collected. Time of measurement is linked to cohort in that people of a certain age being tested at a particular time must, by necessity, be from the same cohort.

Conceptually, time of measurement is intended to be an index of current environmental conditions. For instance adults tested now are more proficient at using computers than were adults tested in the 1980s, when personal computers were far less available or accessible. A measure of development that depends on being able to use the computer, then, would be highly influenced by the year in which the study is conducted. The inherent connection between time of measurement and cohort creates logical difficulties when investigators attempt to disentangle these indices of social and historical context.

Many studies in the psychology of adult development and aging involve simple designs in which people of different ages are compared on the variable of age. No efforts are made in these studies to investigate contextual effects relating to historical or social contextual factors.

The two variants of these descriptive research designs are **longitudinal**, which involves comparing the same people at different ages, and **cross-sectional**, which involves comparisons between people of different ages at the same point of measurement. A summary of these designs is shown in Table 3.2.

Longitudinal Designs

The goal of a longitudinal study is to examine what happens to people over time. By observing and studying people as they get older, researchers feel confident that their participants have changed as the result of intrinsic aging changes that have occurred with the passage of time. The longitudinal study is analogous to attending a high school reunion. You and everyone else are wearing badges with your copies of your senior yearbook photos displayed over your names. As you compare the faces of the people

TABLE 3.2
Characteristics of Descriptive Research Designs

	Advantages	Disadvantages	Corrective Step
LONGITUDINAL	Measures age changes and therefore "development"	Effects of aging cannot be separated from historical change. Takes many years to complete. Expensive. Researcher will not have publishable results. Selective attrition of respondents. Practice effects on tests may lead to improved performance. Original test may become outdated.	Devote administrative resources to maintaining the respondents in the study. Use alternate forms of the test to avoid practice effects. Rescore outdated measures using newer theoretical frameworks. Examine data from multiple studies conducted at different time periods.
CROSS-SECTIONAL	Quick and inexpensive. Latest theories can be tested	Measures differences between age groups and not changes over time. Results may reflect cohort differences and not differences due to aging. Tasks may not be equivalent for different cohorts. Survivor problems exist because the older adults are a select group. Appropriate age ranges are difficult to determine.	Control for cohort differences by careful attention to selection of samples. Validate test procedures on different age groups before comparing them. Regard results as tentative rather than conclusive. Replicate studies, preferably with more sophisticated methods.

There are advantages and disadvantages to each of the descriptive research designs. Investigators must weigh the pros and cons of each method before embarking on a particular study.

on the badges with the faces of the people as they appear in person now, you are struck by the way some people look the same and others look like completely different individuals. This, in effect, is your own longitudinal study. You are comparing people with the way they were at one point in time with the way they are now on the rather obvious (and subjective) variable of physical appearance. You may wonder why Jane, the former prom queen, now looks somewhat faded and frumpy, or how Harold, the former math freak, has evolved into a charming and desirable stockbroker. As you speak to these people, you learn more about how they have changed over the years. That prom queen has gotten a great deal more serious than she was in high school, and the math freak has now become a great deal worldlier. The hypotheses you spin out regarding these people are the kinds of inferences that researchers interested in adult development and aging attempt to make based on similar observations of people over time.

As intuitively appealing as is the longitudinal design, it has serious drawbacks. From a theoretical point of view, researchers cannot know with certainty that the changes observed over time are the results of the person's own aging or the result of the person having been subjected to a changing environment. The individual cannot be removed from the environment to see what would happen in a different set of circumstances. In longitudinal studies, there is an inevitable coincidence of personal and historical time.

Practical problems also plague longitudinal research. The most obvious problem is that longitudinal research takes many years to conduct. To be of value as a study of adult development and aging, a longitudinal study should span at least a decade or more. Both patience and a solid research budget are required because the study will be costly. Furthermore the results of the study will not be available for many years, which may create problems for researchers whose careers depend on their publication records. The

study may even outlive at least its original investigator.

The participants in a longitudinal study are also likely to be lost over time, a problem referred to as **subject attrition**. The loss of participants from the original sample creates a host of practical and theoretical problems. From a practical point of view, as the number of subjects dwindles, it becomes increasingly difficult to complete statistical analyses on the data. Even if there is a respectable number in the total sample, there may be too few to permit more refined analysis of, for example, differences according to sex, social class, or race.

The loss of participants also creates difficulties when the investigator wants to draw inferences from the sample to the population as a whole. The people who disappear from the sample do so for a variety of reasons such as poor health or death, lack of motivation, or an inability to continue in the study because they have moved from the area or are otherwise unreachable. The survivors, those who remain in the study, may be higher on all or some of these factors. Conclusions made

Participants in a high school reunion have a chance to witness their own longitudinal study as they watch the aging of their fellow classmates.

about the survivors, then, may not apply to the general population.

The result of this attrition problem is that data from a longitudinal study will be skewed by the fact that different types of people are present in the samples at Time 1 and Time 2 (or later testings). If both the dropouts and the survivors are included in the data set for Time 1 but only the survivors are present for Time 2, the scores are likely to be more favorable at Time 2 than they were at Time 1 by virtue of the fact that only the healthier, smarter, or more motivated people are left. The researcher may erroneously conclude that people in the sample "improved" from Time 1 to Time 2, when all that happened was that the sicker and less motivated ones died off or dropped between testings. The survivors may not have changed at all.

An example of this problem of selective attrition is shown in Figure 3.1. If the person whose scores are shown here had been tested at age 86 with other people who were not on a downward trajectory, this person's scores would have brought down the mean for the entire group.

How do researchers tackle these problems of attrition? First, let's look at the practical side. Large-scale longitudinal studies are often housed in established institutions or agencies that have clerical help for the investigator. It is then possible to set aside administrative resources to provide for the "care and feeding" of the sample in between test occasions. The research staff may send out greeting cards every year (birthday and holiday), as well as newsletters and e-mails keeping them up to date on progress in the study, or may make telephone calls to establish a more personal touch. Many longitudinal studies now have a Web site that participants can visit.

These special efforts not only keep the respondents more motivated, but also they make it more likely that the research team will find out when a person has moved or is no longer available due to illness or death. Another way

FIGURE 3.1
Example of Problem of Attrition

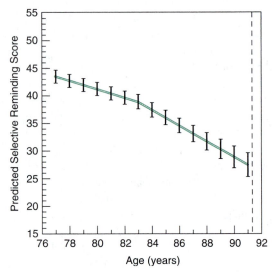

This figure shows predicted mean memory scores and 95% confidence intervals (bars) for an individual tested annually from age 77 to 91, who died 6 months after the last assessment.
Source: Sliwinski et al., 2006.

to tackle this problem is to conduct a simulated longitudinal design in which several cohorts are followed up over a five- or ten-year period. For example, a study would include people in their 30s, 40s, and 50s, who would be followed up over a ten-year period. A second study would include people in their 50s, 60s, and 70s. Then the results would be combined to produce a simulated longitudinal design from ages 30 to 70. Sophisticated statistical methods are now making analyses from studies spliced together in this way more feasible.

Practice effects are another complication in longitudinal studies. The survivors have had at least one, if not several, opportunities to practice taking the tests they are being given. If the test is one of intelligence, they may learn the answers in between testings. The same problem may plague personality studies, should a participant suspect or find out later that a certain response means admitting to a personality flaw. On the next test occasion, the respondent will be less likely to admit to having that particular problem. Researchers may use alternate forms of their tests on different test occasions to avoid these problems.

Another issue relating to the test itself is that the original test may become outdated. One option to get around this problem is to find a way to reanalyze or rescale the test scores to correspond to contemporary ways of thinking about the variable under scrutiny. This was the strategy used in studies of personality development by researchers at the Institute for Human Development in Berkeley, who have followed the same samples from infancy to old age. Previous measures were rescored using newer theoretical and empirical frameworks to allow analysis over time to be conducted without sacrificing data. Some of these studies are described in Chapter 8.

Despite these limitations, longitudinal studies have the potential to add invaluable data on psychological changes in adulthood and old age. Furthermore, as data accumulate from multiple investigations concerning related variables, it is possible to overcome the limitations of any one particular study.

Cross-Sectional Designs

In a cross-sectional design, the researcher compares the performance of people selected on the basis of their ages at one point in time. The goal of cross-sectional research is to describe age differences, but it is assumed that performance differences between age groups are the result of changes associated with the aging process. To ensure that such an assumption is valid, the researcher attempts to control for cohort differences that would obscure or exaggerate the effects of age. This control is achieved by selecting

samples comparable in important factors such as amount of education and social class. Like the longitudinal design, the cross-sectional design has the problem of providing results applicable to only one historical period. The age differences obtained in this study are specific to the cohorts of people compared. People born in the 1950s and tested in the 1990s at the age of 40 may be higher on an attribute than people born in the 1970s and tested in the 1990s at the age of 20 due to environmental factors. A similar difference between 20- and 40-year-olds may not be encountered among people compared in a study conducted in the 1980s, when the samples were born 10 years earlier. For example, although commonsense wisdom regards young adults as less conservative than middle-aged adults, it is possible that middle-agers who lived through the 1960s are less conservative than young people growing up in the 1980s. The same difference between age groups may not show up if the study is conducted in a different historical era.

Figure 3.2 illustrates this problem of cohort differences in cross-sectional studies. The graph is from an investigation of the relative amounts of white matter in the brains of young, middle-aged, and older adult samples (Brickman et al, 2006). The higher the amount of white matter, the better the individual's brain functions, so it is clear that the older adults are functioning less well than the younger age groups. Yet, in addition to differing in age, the three samples differed in education, with the older adults having the least amount of education. Because of this cohort difference, it is not possible to know with certainty whether it is age or education that is affecting the white matter of these three age groups.

Practical problems also beset the cross-sectional study. One is the matter of the survivors. Although participants might not die in the middle of the study, as is true in a longitudinal study, the fact that they are around for testing in their 60s, 70s, 80s, or beyond means that they are,

FIGURE 3.2

Cross-sectional Differences in White Matter

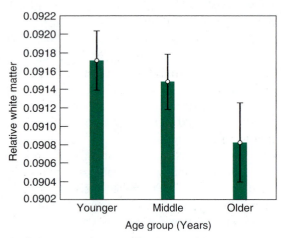

This figure shows a comparison by age group of the relative amount of white matter in the brains of younger, middle, and older adults. The participants differed not only in age, but also in years of education, with the older groups having significantly less education (about 12 years) than the younger (nearly 15 years) and middle-aged (14 years).

Source: Brickman et al., 2006.

by definition, survivors compared with their age peers who already have died. Thus, they may represent a healthier or luckier group of people. They may also be the people who are more cautious, perhaps smarter, and born with sturdier genes that have enabled them to avoid the many diseases that could have killed them off prior to old age. As a result, the older adults in a cross-sectional study may look different from the younger ones because the two groups are drawn from two different populations—those who die young (but are still represented in the young adult group) and those who will live to be old. If young adults are drawn exclusively from a college population, they may not be representative of their cohort either.

The next practical problem has to do with the ages selected for the samples. How do researchers decide on the age spans for the different samples? If they are working with a young adult college student sample, then the age range will be 18 to 22 or perhaps 25 at most. This is a span of four to seven years. The older adult sample is rarely defined so narrowly. Older adult volunteers are difficult to entice into the laboratory, and most researchers have to settle for an age range that is larger than they would prefer. That age range may be as high, in some studies, as 20 to 30 years. In some studies, the "older" sample is defined as including all respondents over the age of 50 or 60.

Related somewhat to this problem of acceptable age ranges is the question of how to divide the adult age range when selecting samples. Is it better to divide samples of people in cross-sectional studies into decades and then examine age differences continuously across the adult years? Or is it better to compare people at the two extremes of the adult span? Some researchers use three groups: young adult, middle-aged, and older adult. With three groups there is a greater sense of confidence in the appropriateness of "connecting the dots" between their scores on measures of psychological functioning.

With regard to test procedures, researchers conducting cross-sectional studies must also be sensitive to how different age groups will react to the test materials. In studies of memory, for example, there is a risk that the older adults will find some of the measures too challenging and perhaps intimidating. Young adults are far more comfortable with test situations because they are in school or were recently in school where they were frequently tested. To an older adult, particularly one who is sensitive to memory loss, anxiety alone about the situation can result in lowered performance than would otherwise be obtained (see the section in this chapter titled Laboratory Studies).

Task equivalence also applies to the way different cohorts react to measures of personality and social attitudes. The same item may have very different meanings to people of different generations or people of different educational or cultural backgrounds. One common problem that occurs in research on personality and mental health is that a measure of, for example, depression, may have been tested for use on a young adult sample but not on an older sample. Items on such a scale that concern physical changes, such as alterations in sleep patterns presumably related to depression, may in fact reflect normal age-related differences. Therefore older adults will receive a higher score on the depression scale by virtue of changes in their sleep patterns alone, not because they are more depressed.

Researchers must attempt to validate their measures on samples of different ages before they make conclusions about differences between age groups on that measure. More about this issue follows in the section on Measurement Issues in research on adult development and aging.

These problems aside, cross-sectional studies are relatively quick and inexpensive compared with longitudinal studies. Another advantage of cross-sectional studies is that they can be used with the latest technology, whether in the biomedical area or in the psychological and social domains. If a new tool comes out one year, it can be tested cross-sectionally the next. Researchers are not tied to obsolete methods that were in vogue some 30 or 40 years ago.

Perhaps the best that can be said about cross-sectional studies is that they provide descriptions of differences between groups of varying ages. The more effort the investigators put into controlling for differences other than age, the greater the likelihood that the age differences they observe are not the result of differences in the backgrounds or life experiences of the participants. Furthermore, most researchers regard their cross-sectional findings as tentative descriptions of the effects of aging on the function of

interest. There is great sensitivity in the field to the need for their findings to be replicated and, ultimately, verified through studies employing a longitudinal element.

SEQUENTIAL RESEARCH DESIGNS

It should be clear by now that the perfect study on aging is virtually impossible to conduct. Age can never be a true independent variable because it cannot be manipulated. Furthermore, age is inherently linked with time, and so personal aging can never be separated from social aging. However, considerable progress in some areas of research has been made through the application of **sequential designs**. These designs consist of different combinations of the variables age, cohort, and time of measurement. A sequential design involves a "sequence" of studies, such as a cross-sectional study carried out twice (two sequences) over a span of 10 years. The sequential nature of these designs is what makes them superior to the truly descriptive designs conducted on one sample, followed over time (longitudinal design) or on different-aged samples, tested on one occasion (cross-sectional design).

The Most Efficient Design

One of the most influential articles to be published in the field of adult development and aging was the landmark work by psychologist K. Warner Schaie (1965) in which he outlined the **Most Efficient Design**, a set of three designs manipulating the variables of age, cohort, and time of measurement.

The general layout for the Most Efficient Design is shown in Table 3.3. Researchers organize their data by constructing this table that combines year of birth (cohort) with

TABLE 3.3
Layout for Sequential Studies

Year of Birth (Cohort)	Year of Testing (Time of Measurement)			
	1980	1990	2000	2010
1940	40 years old	50 years old	60 years old	70 years old
1930	50 years old	60 years old	70 years old	80 years old
1920	60 years old	70 years old	80 years old	90 years old

This table shows the way that an investigator would lay out the data for a sequential study. The rows represent longitudinal follow-ups of three samples born 10 years apart. The columns represent their years of testing. The sequential designs typically involve two or more longitudinal studies or two or more cross-sectional studies, or both.

year of testing (time of measurement). The three designs that make up the Most Efficient Design and the respective factors they include are the time-sequential design (age by time of measurement), the cohort-sequential design (cohort by age), and the cross-sequential design (cohort by time of measurement). When all three designs are analyzed, they theoretically make it possible for the researcher to obtain separate estimates of the effects of each of the three factors.

Depending on the pattern of significant effects, the researcher may be able to make some conclusions about the relative influence of personal and historical aging. For example, if age effects are significant in the time-sequential and cohort-sequential designs, and there are no significant effects of time of measurement or cohort in the cross-sequential design, then a strong argument can be made for the possibility of "true" aging effects. Another scenario involves significant effects of time of measurement in both the time-sequential and cross-sequential designs. If there are no age effects, then the researcher may be able to make the case that the variable being studied was sensitive to current historical influences. Similarly, if the cohort factor is significant in the two designs in which it is used, and there are no significant age or time

of measurement effects, then the researcher may look toward environmental factors specific to the early years of childhood in these samples.

Figure 3.3 shows the advantages of conducting a sequential design. The data are from my study of psychosocial development (Whitbourne, Zuschlag, Elliot, & Waterman, 1992), begun by a previous investigator by testing college students

FIGURE 3.3
Results from a Sequential Study of Psychosocial Development

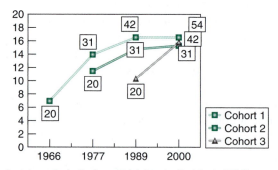

Participants in the Rochester Adult Longitudinal Study (Whitbourne, et al., in preparation) were followed up over four testing occasions. This figure shows their scores on the Eriksonian measure of Industry versus Inferiority (Stage 4), representing identification with the work ethic. By comparing the curves of the three cohorts, it is possible to see that the increases between the ages of 20 to 31 were steeper for the cohort first tested in 1966 than for later cohorts.

in the mid-1960s. Starting in the late 1970s, I followed up the college student sample (who were now in their early 30s) and added a new group of college students, who themselves were followed up again approximately 11 years later. There are now three cohorts, with the oldest one having been tested from 20 to 54 years.

As can be seen, there were different patterns of age changes over time for the three cohorts on the particular measure illustrated in Figure 3.3. Had only Cohort 1 been tested over this age span, the results would have looked very different because they showed the steepest pattern of increases between the ages of 20 to 31 years. The data are superior to what would have been obtained through traditional longitudinal methods because it was based on the study of more than one cohort over more than one test occasion.

"What do you think?" | **3-2**

Why are sequential designs referred to as "sequential"?

CORRELATIONAL DESIGNS

An alternative approach to describing group differences using the quasi-experimental design is the **correlational design**, in which relationships are observed among variables as they exist in the world. The researcher makes no attempt to divide participants into groups or to manipulate variables.

Simple Correlational Designs

Comparisons of age groups or groups based on divisions such as year of birth or time of measurement are useful for many research questions in the field of gerontology. However, in some situations this approach is neither the most efficient nor the most informative. Recall that at the beginning of the discussion about variables, it was mentioned that researchers attempt to "explain" or account for the reasons that people differ in their performance.

For example, let's say we want to know why someone is higher on the variable of response speed than someone else. If we suspect that age differences can "explain" this difference in response speed, then we might set up a cross-sectional study in which we compare groups of people who differ in age and see if they also differ in response speed. This approach, based on the model of the experimental method (although it is not an experimental design, for reasons discussed earlier) is clear and intuitively sensible. However, apart from all of the problems involved in cross-sectional studies, another problem is directly tied in with the notion of grouping people according to age. The variable of age is a continuous variable, meaning that it does not have natural cutoff points as does a categorical variable such as gender. When we put people into groups based on their age, we are losing information. There may be a difference between people of 42 and people of 45 years of age, but when they are all grouped in the "40-year-olds" this distinction is obscured.

In the correlational design, the relationship is observed between two or more variables, producing the statistic known as the correlation (represented as the letter r) whose value can range from $+ 1.0$ to $- 1.0$. A correlation greater than zero indicates that the two variables are positively related so that when the value of one variable increases, the other one does as well. A correlation less than zero indicates that the two variables are negatively related so that when one increases in value the other one decreases. A correlation of zero indicates no relationship between the variables.

One advantage of the correlational design for the study of aging is that age can be treated as a continuous variable, and so there is no loss of information owing to the necessity of collapsing people into age groups. In the example of the study on the relationship between aging and response speed, the values of age can be directly inserted into the equation, as can the values of response speed.

Studies based on the correlational design differ not only in the statistics that are used to analyze the data but also in the underlying assumptions about the nature of the variables under scrutiny. In experimental designs, researchers explain the variance in the dependent variable by assuming that differences among people in their scores are caused by their differences on the independent variable. By manipulating the values of the independent variable, the researcher has caused people to differ on the dependent variable. In a correlational study, the researcher makes no assumptions about what caused what—there are no "independent" or "dependent" variables. A correlation between two variables means simply that the two variables are related, but like the proverbial chicken and egg, the researcher cannot say which came first.

> ## "What do you think?"   3-3
>
> Can you think of an example in which two variables that have a correlation are related to each other due to the influence of a third variable?

Let's return to the example of the relationship between age and response speed. The correlation between these variables would quite likely be found to be positive; when age increases, response speed increases as well. (A higher response speed indicates slower performance.) When interpreting this relationship, the researcher may be tempted to conclude that age "caused" the increase in response speed. However, this conclusion is not justified because age was not experimentally manipulated. In a correlational study, since there are no independent or dependent variables, the possibility that variable A accounts for variable B is equal to the possibility that B accounts for A. Now, you are probably saying to yourself, "Response speed can't cause age, it must be the other way around!" However, the truth is that because an experiment was not conducted, even the apparently silly possibility that increased response speed caused aging cannot be ruled out. Think of another example that might help firm up this point. There is a correlation between certain personality characteristics known as Type A behavior and cardiovascular disease. People with the Type A personality, who are hard-driving, competitive, somewhat hostile, and impatient, are more likely to have heart disease. Does the personality type cause heart disease (which might seem logical to you), or does heart disease cause people to have personality problems? Because the design is correlational, neither possibility can be excluded.

You may have learned these facts about correlational studies already; it is probably fair to say that most psychology students have ingrained into their nervous systems the phrase "correlation does not equal causation." The possibility that either of the two variables could have "caused" the other is part of the basis for this statement. There is yet another alternative, namely, that a third but unmeasured variable accounts for the apparent relationship between the two observed variables. In the case of the relationship between age and response speed, this third variable might be "number of functioning brain cells." Age may be related to number of brain cells, and number of brain cells may be related to response speed. The apparent correlation between age and response speed might disappear entirely when number of brain cells is measured and factored into the relationship. Similarly the correlation between Type A behavior and heart disease might be accounted for entirely by an unmeasured third variable such as cigarette smoking. Perhaps people with certain personality types are more likely to smoke cigarettes, and cigarette smoking is related to heart disease. This unmeasured variable could be responsible for the apparent relationship between the other two.

When examining the data from a typical correlational study, then, it is essential to repeat to yourself like a mantra "correlation does not equal causation" and be on the lookout for competing hypotheses related to unmeasured variables. This is no less true of gerontology than it is for all the other sciences, but in gerontology it is particularly easy to fall into the trap because arguments related to age seem so compelling. Interestingly, however, the need to look for possible third variables is not all that different from the problems we reviewed in quasi-experimental studies when groups of different ages are compared. In these cases, generational differences in important background variables (education, health status, environmental stimulation) could account for age differences rather than age per se. In those studies, particularly cross-sectional studies, we must also be aware of potential confounds with age that could account for older and younger groups showing different levels of performance.

Correlational studies can contain a wealth of information, despite their limitations in terms of determining cause and effect. The value of the correlation itself provides a useful basis for calculating the strength of the relationship. Furthermore, it is possible to manipulate a larger number of variables at one time than is generally true in studies involving group comparisons. Finally, within the last 20 years, advanced correlational methods have become increasingly available that allow researchers to get around the problems involved in causality with traditional correlational methods.

Multivariate Correlational Designs

In contrast to simple correlational designs, which involve determining the statistical relationship between two variables (also called a bivariate relationship), a multivariate correlational design involves the analysis of relationships among multiple variables. A multivariate design makes it possible for the researcher to analyze a set of complex interconnections among variables. Instead of being restricted to the study of two variables, which can result in the researcher overlooking an important third (or fourth) variable, the researcher using a multivariate design can evaluate simultaneously the effects of many potentially important factors.

Multivariate correlational methods also enable researchers to test models in which a set of variables is used to "predict" scores on another variable. In **multiple regression analysis**, the predictor variables are regarded as equivalent to the independent variables used in experiments, and the variable that is predicted is regarded as equivalent to a dependent variable. Although the design is still correlational in that the experimenter does not manipulate an independent variable, the statistics involved enable investigators to suggest and test inferences about cause-effect relationships.

A variant of multiple regression is **logistic regression**, in which researchers test the likelihood of an individual receiving a score on a discrete yes-no variable. For example, a group of investigators may want to test the probability that a person will receive a diagnosis of cardiovascular disease or not, depending on whether the person has one of several risk factors.

Multivariate correlational designs have the potential to test complex models in which there are relationships predicted among age and scores on measures predicted to have a relationship to age. In structural equation modeling (SEM), researchers develop hypotheses regarding the relations among observed (measures) and latent (underlying) variables or factors (Hoyle, 1995).

SEM serves purposes similar to multiple regression, but in a more powerful way, taking into account the possibilities that there are complex relationships among the variables and factors of interest. This method, illustrated in Figure 3.4,

FIGURE 3.4
Study of Religious Participation and Mortality

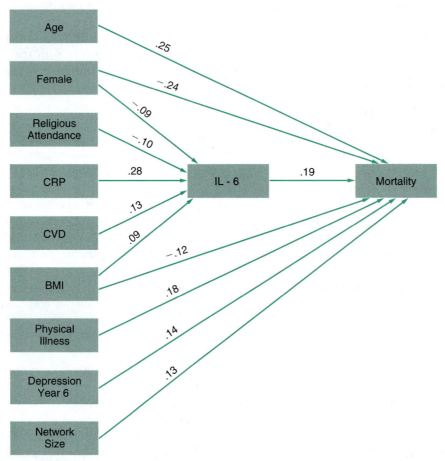

This figure shows the relationship between a set of predictor variables and mortality over a 12-year period among a sample of 557 older adults. The coefficients on each pathway represent the direction and strength of the relationship between the variable and mortality. CVD stands for cardiovascular disease, BMI stands for body mass index, CRP stands for C-reactive protein (a harmful factor in the body), and IL-6 stands for interleukin-6 (a harmful immune system factor). Each of the physiological and categorical variables were related to mortality, but what is most impressive is the fact that religious attendance predicted mortality through the route of immune functioning. This finding could not have been discovered using any other method. All of the paths shown were significant.

Source: Lutgendorf et al., 2004.

helped to identify religious participation as a predictor of mortality above and beyond the effects of physical functioning.

The newest multivariate method to be introduced into developmental research is **hierarchical linear modeling** (HLM), a method used for longitudinal studies (Raudenbush & Bryk, 2002). In this method, individual patterns of change are investigated rather than simply comparing mean scores. This is important because in a longitudinal study, not every participant shows the same changes over time. Some individuals may increase, others may decrease, and some may not change at all. Looking at the overall mean scores fails to capture this individual variation. In HLM, these individual patterns can be investigated statistically as well as examining whether particular variables affect some individuals more than others. For example, in my study shown in Figure 3.3, some people decreased, others increased sharply, and some remained stable. HLM provides a way to understand the individual differences in patterns of change overtime.

TYPES OF RESEARCH METHODS

Data on adult development and aging can be gained using a variety of data collection strategies, or research methods. Each has advantages and disadvantages which must be weighed according to the particular field of study, the nature of the sample, available resources, and desired applications.

Laboratory Studies

The majority of information about physical and cognitive changes associated with the aging process through adulthood comes from **laboratory studies**, in which participants are tested in a systematic fashion using standardized procedures. This method is considered the most objective way of collecting data because each participant is exposed to the same treatment, using the same equipment and the same data recording procedures. For example, in a study of memory, participants would be given a set of items to be recalled, probably shown on a computer. Then they would be asked at some later point to recall as many of those items as possible, again, using some type of automated response system.

There are obvious advantages to the laboratory study. The objective and systematic way in which data are recorded provides the investigator with assurance that the results are due to the variables being studied rather than to extraneous factors. In the memory study, for instance, all participants would be presented with the items to be remembered in a way that does not depend on the voice inflections of the researcher, the quality of the visual stimuli, or the amount of time used to present the items.

On the negative side, the laboratory study is removed from the real-life experiences of most adults. It is possible that the older person feels uncomfortable when tested in an impersonal and possibly intimidating manner using equipment that is unfamiliar. Consequently the findings may underestimate the individual's abilities in everyday life.

Qualitative Studies

There are often instances in which researchers wish to explore a phenomenon of interest in an open-ended fashion. The investigation of social influences on adult development such as, for example, personal relationships, may demand the researcher use a method that captures potentially relevant factors within a broad spectrum of possible influences (Allen & Walker, 2000). Qualitative methods allow for the exploration of such complex relationships outside the narrow restrictions and assumptions of quantitative methods. In other cases, researchers may be working in an area in which conventional methods are neither practical nor appropriate for the problem under investigation. Qualitative methods are also used in the analysis of life history information, which is likely to be highly varied from person to person and not easily translated into numbers. The main point in using qualitative methods is that they provide researchers with alternative ways to test their ideas and that the method can be adapted in a flexible manner to the nature of the problem at hand.

Archival Research

In **archival research**, investigators use existing resources that contain data relevant to a question about aging. The archives might consist of a governmental data bank, or the records kept by an institution, school, or employer. Another source of archival data is newspaper or magazine reports.

An advantage of archival research is that the information is readily accessible, especially given the growth of web-based data sets including those of the U.S Census. Data files can be downloaded directly from the Internet, or publications can be accessed using portable document files (PDFs) that are easily read and searched. Disadvantages are that the researcher does not necessarily have control over the form of the data. For instance, a governmental agency may keep records of employment by age that do not include information on specific occupations of interest to the researcher. Another disadvantage is that the material may not be systematically collected or recorded. Newspaper or school records, for example, may have information that is biased or incomplete.

Surveys

Researchers rely on the **survey** method to gain information from a sample that can then be generalized to a larger population. Surveys typically are short and easily administered with simple rating scales to use for answers, for example, the surveys given to poll voters on who they will be casting their ballots for in upcoming elections. Occasionally, more intensive surveys may be given to gain in-depth knowledge about aging and its relationship to health behaviors, health risks, and symptoms. The U.S. Census, mentioned earlier as an archival data source, was collected through survey methodology. However, it is considered archival in that it has extensive historical records going back to the year 1750 when the first U.S. Census was conducted.

Surveys have the advantage of providing data that allows the researcher to gain insight into the behavior of more people than it would be possible to study in the laboratory or other testing site. They can be administered over the telephone or, increasingly, in a web browser. Interview-based surveys given by trained administrators provide knowledge that is easily coded and analyzed while still providing comprehensive information about the behavior in question. Typically, however, surveys tend to be short with questions that are subject to bias by respondents, who may attempt to provide a favorable impression on the researcher. Consequently, although the data may be generalizable to a large population, the quality of the data itself may be limited.

Case Reports

When researchers want to provide an in-depth analysis of particular individuals, they use the **case report**, which summarizes the findings from multiple sources for those individuals. Data may be integrated from interviews, psychological tests, observations, archival records, or even journal and diary entries. The focus of the case report is on the characteristics of the individual and what has influenced his or her development and life experiences. Personal narratives may also be obtained with this method, in which individuals describe their lives as they have experienced them along with their ideas about why their lives have evolved in a given manner.

Although the case report has the benefit of providing insights into the lives of individuals as they change over time, it relies heavily on clinical judgments by the researcher. Therefore, for a case report to provide valuable information, a high level of expertise is required so that the findings are presented in a manner that balances the objective facts with the subjective analysis of the researcher.

Focus Groups

A less formal research method is a **focus group**, which is a meeting of a group of respondents oriented around a particular topic of interest. In a focus group, an investigator tries to identify important themes in the discussion and keep the conversation oriented to these themes. By the time the focus group ends, concrete research

questions to pursue in subsequent studies will be identified. For example, attitudes toward mental health providers by older adults may be assessed by a focus group in which participants 65 and older share their concerns and experiences with counselors and therapists.

An advantage of the focus group is that issues can be identified through a focus group prior to conducting a more systematic investigation. This approach is particularly useful when there is little preexisting research on the topic. An obvious disadvantage is that the method is not particularly systematic, and the data cannot readily be analyzed or systematically interpreted.

Observational Methods

In the **observational method**, researchers draw conclusions about behavior through careful and systematic examination in particular settings. Recordings may be made using either videotapes or behavioral records. In one type of observational method known as participant-observation, the researcher participates in the activities of the

In the scene shown here, the researcher records the behaviors of people at a delicatessen counter, illustrating the observational method.

ASSESS YOURSELF: Aging Behavior Checklist

The observational method is an important means of collecting data on the aging process. For this quiz, you are to copy the following chart onto a sheet of paper and take it with you for the next 24 hours. Record every instance in which you see an older adult (a person 65 or older) and write down both the behavior and when it occurred. After you have done so, try to generate hypotheses about what might have affected the older person's behavior in this situation. What empirical studies might you conduct to follow up on these hypotheses? Think about these as you progress through the rest of the course and see if any of your hypotheses and possible studies have in fact been proposed.

AGING BEHAVIOR CHECK LIST

Date	Time	Brief description of person (approximate age, sex, other)*	Behavior	Situation in which behavior occurred

*Please note that you should not identify the person by name.

respondents. For example a researcher may wish to find out about the behavior of staff in a nursing home. In participant observation, the researcher would spend several days living with people in the nursing home. The researcher's subjective experiences would become part of the "data."

There are elaborate procedures available for making behavioral records in which the researcher defines precisely the behavior to be observed (the number of particular acts) and specifies the times during which records will be made. This procedure may be used to find out if an intervention is having its intended effects. If an investigator is testing a method to reduce aggressive behavior in people with Alzheimer's disease, behavioral records could be made before and after the intervention is introduced. After observing the effects of the intervention, a final check on the method's effectiveness would involve a return to baseline condition to determine whether the aggressive behavior increases without the intervention.

MEASUREMENT ISSUES IN ADULT DEVELOPMENT AND AGING

Research designs, no matter how cleverly engineered, cannot yield worthwhile results if the methods used to collect the data are flawed. Researchers in adult development and aging, like all other scientists, must concern themselves with the quality of the data-gathering instruments. The task is made more difficult because the instruments must be usable with people who are likely to vary in ability, educational background, and sophistication with research instruments. Earlier we pointed out the problems involved in comparing older and younger adults on measures used in cross-sectional studies. Here we will look specifically at some of the ways developmental researchers can ensure that their measures are equivalent across age groups.

The first measurement issue to consider is that of **reliability**. A measure is reliable if it yields consistent results every time it is used. The importance of reliability can be seen if you consider the analogy of a measure that you would use in cooking. If your tablespoon were unreliable (if it was made of floppy plastic), you would be adding different amounts of ingredients every time you used it. Your brownies might come out flat and soggy one day but sky high the next. A psychological test must also provide the same scores every time it is given, or at least, it should result in a similar placement of individuals along the scale of measurement on each occasion. Thus the first quality that psychologists look for in a measure is its ability to provide consistent scores. Reliability can be assessed by test-retest reliability, which is based on giving the test on two occasions and determining whether respondents receive similar scores on both occasions. The internal consistency of the measure is another form of reliability, indicating whether respondents are giving similar answers to similar items.

"What do you think?"   **3-4**

How might psychological measures vary in their psychometric qualities when applied to adults of different ages?

The second criterion used to evaluate a test is **validity**, meaning that the test measures what it is supposed to measure. A test of intelligence should measure intelligence, not how good your vision is. Returning to the example in the kitchen, if a tablespoon were marked "teaspoon," it would not be measuring what it is supposed to measure, and your baking products would definitely be ruined.

Tablespoons are fairly easy to assess for validity, but unfortunately psychological tests present a far greater challenge. In fact, validity is a much more elusive quality than is reliability.

There are different kinds of validity, depending on the potential use of the measure. Content

Standardized tests, such as the one being taken by this student, must be reliable and valid.

validity provides an indication of whether a test that assesses factual material is correctly measuring that material, as would be the case in a test of a student's knowledge of psychology that includes questions about experimental methods. Criterion validity indicates whether a test score accurately predicts performance on a criterion measure, as would be used in a test of vocational ability that claims to predict success on the job. Finally, construct validity is used to assess the extent to which a measure that is intended to assess a psychological construct appears to be able to do so. Construct validity is difficult to establish and requires two types of evidence. Convergent validity is needed to show that the measure relates to other measures that are theoretically similar to it. A test of intelligence should have a positive relationship to another test of intelligence that has already been validated. Divergent validity is needed to show that the measure does not relate to other measures that have no theoretical relationship to it. A test of intelligence should not be correlated with a test of personality unless the personality test assesses some aspect of intelligence.

Although psychologists are generally aware of the need to establish the reliability and validity of their measures as used in both research and practical settings, less attention tends to be paid to psychometrics when used in gerontological research. Measures whose reliability and validity were established on young adult samples are often used inappropriately without testing their applicability to samples of adults of varying ages. The process can become very complicated, as you can imagine. If Form A of a measure is found to be psychometrically sound with college students but only Form B has adequate reliability and validity for older adults, the researcher is faced with the prospect of having to use different forms of a test for different samples within the same study. Nevertheless, sensitivity to measurement issues is crucial if the conclusions drawn from the research are to have value.

ETHICAL ISSUES IN RESEARCH

All scientists who engage in research with humans or other animals must take precautions to protect the rights of their participants. In extreme cases, such as medical research, the life of an individual may be at stake if that individual is subjected to certain procedures. Equally important for other reasons, research in which respondents are being tested or put through an experimental manipulation also requires that the researcher follow a certain protocol. Recognizing the importance of these considerations, the American Psychological Association developed a comprehensive set of guidelines for psychologists that includes the appropriate treatment of human participants in research (American Psychological Association, 2003).

Researchers must present a potential respondent as full a disclosure as possible of the risks and benefits of becoming involved in any research project. When the individual is a minor child or an adult who is not able to make independent decisions, the researcher is obligated to inform the legal guardian of that individual about the nature of the study. Having provided information about the study, the researcher must then obtain a legal signature indicating that the participant understands the risks and benefits involved in the study. At this point the researcher is able to obtain the full **informed consent** of the respondent or the respondent's legal representative. When the individual is an animal, the researcher is similarly bound to ensure that the animal is not mishandled or subjected to unnecessary harm, although different protective procedures are followed.

Research participants are also entitled to know what the study was about after it has been completed, a process called **debriefing**. If you have ever been a participant yourself, then you were probably curious during the course of the study to know what was being tested. In some cases you might have been surprised to find out about the "real" purpose of the study. Perhaps you were told that you were going to be asked to fill out a series of questionnaires in a quiet laboratory room. In the middle of the questionnaire, you hear a loud noise out in the hallway, and then you hear a man scream. The researcher is really interested in finding out if you will get up from your chair and see what is wrong with the man. The questionnaires were just a ruse. After the experiment is over, the researcher is obligated to give you the correct information about the purpose of the study. You may not feel very good about yourself if you in fact did not get up to help, but at least you have a right to know that you were being tested on this attribute. In fact the debriefing would probably make you feel better because you would realize that your response of not helping reflected the experimental manipulation rather than a malevolent personality attribute you possess.

As this example illustrates, research participants may learn information about themselves that is potentially upsetting or damaging. In fact, ethical guidelines for research in psychology dictate that the researcher not only provides feedback but also must be ready to suggest support or counseling for people who become distressed while involved in the experiment. Respondents are also entitled to withdraw from a study without risk of penalty should they choose to do so. The experimenter should not coerce them into completing the study, and even if they decide to discontinue participation, they should still receive whatever reimbursement they were initially promised. If they are students in a class or clients receiving services (such as hospital patients), they should not fear having their grades lowered or services withheld from them.

Finally, research participants are entitled to know what will happen to their data. In all cases, the data must be kept confidential, meaning that only the research team will have access to the information provided by the participants. The other condition usually attached to the data is that of anonymity. Participants are guaranteed that their names will not be associated with their responses. The condition of anonymity obviously cannot be kept if the study is a longitudinal one because the researchers must maintain access to names for follow-up purposes. In this case, the condition of confidentiality applies, and the researchers are obligated to ensure that all records are kept private and secure.

These ethical standards are enforced in all institutions receiving federal funding for research through Institutional Review Boards (IRBs), which review all proposed studies to be carried out at that institution or by anyone employed by that institution. These reviews ensure that the rights of research participants are adequately protected according to the criteria discussed here. In addition, the American Psychological Association's ethical guidelines ensure that studies specifically in the field of psychology meet predetermined criteria for protection of human and animal subjects. An important development in the area of protection of human participants was the implementation in April 2003 of national standards within the United States to protect the privacy of personal health information. The Health Insurance Portability and Accountability Act, referred to as HIPAA, is the first-ever federal privacy standards to protect patients' medical records and other health information provided to health plans, doctors, hospitals and other health care providers. HIPAA protects research participants by ensuring that a researcher must meet standards to maintain the privacy of health-related information. With these guidelines in place, there is assurance that respondents in research will be appropriately treated.

SUMMARY

1. The study of aging is intimately tied up with the passage of time, and researchers on aging have attempted to develop innovative methods to increase the reliability of their findings. The variables in developmental research are age, cohort, and time of measurement. Age represents processes going on within the individual, and cohort and time of measurement are regarded as measures of social aging. These three variables are interdependent because as soon as two are known, the third is determined.

2. Descriptive research designs include longitudinal and cross-sectional. Both of these designs are quasi-experimental because they do not involve the manipulation of age as an independent variable. Each has advantages and disadvantages, but the main problem is that they do not allow for generalizations to be made beyond a single cohort or period of history. Sequential designs are necessary to attempt to control for the effects of social aging because they allow researchers to make estimates of the influence of factors other than age on performance. The Most Efficient Design was developed by Schaie to provide a framework for three types of sequential studies.

3. Correlational designs involve studying the relationship between age (or another variable) and other measures of interest. A simple correlational design involves two variables, and a multivariate correlational design involves analyzing relationships among multiple variables. Structural equation modeling is a form of multivariate correlational analysis in which complex models involving age can be statistically evaluated. In hierarchical linear modeling, patterns of change over time are analyzed, taking into account individual differences in change.

4. There are several methods of research available to investigators who study aging. In the laboratory study, conditions are controlled, and data are collected in an objective manner. Archival research uses existing records, such as census data or newspaper records. Surveys involve asking people to provide answers to structured questions, with the intention of generalizing to larger populations. Case reports are used to provide in-depth analyses of an individual or small group of individuals. Focus groups gather information about people's views on particular topics. Observational methods provide objective data on people in specific settings and under specific conditions.

5. Researchers in adult development and aging must concern themselves with finding the most appropriate measurement tools available. The science of studying measurement instruments is known as psychometrics. Of particular concern is the need to establish the appropriateness of the same measurement instrument for adults of different ages. Reliability refers to the consistency of a measurement instrument, and validity assesses whether the instrument measures what it is intended to measure.

6. Ethical issues in research address the proper treatment of participants by researchers. Informed consent is the requirement that respondents be given adequate knowledge about a study's procedures before they participate. Debriefing refers to notification of participants about the study's real purpose. Respondents also have the right to withdraw at any time without penalty. Finally, respondents must be told what will happen to their data, but at all times the data must be kept confidential. All research institutions in the United States are required by federal law to guarantee the rights of human and animal participants.

CHAPTER 4

Physical and Sensory Changes in Adulthood and Old Age

According to the biopsychosocial perspective, changes in physical functioning interact with psychological processes and social context. Biologically based changes have an effect on our behavior, which in turn can modify the expression of these changes. Furthermore, the changes that occur in our bodies reflect social factors such as class, race, and gender. These social factors also affect how we interpret the physical changes. Identity plays an important role in this process, for the way that we feel about ourselves is affected in part by our physical appearance and competence. In this chapter, changes in the body, brain, and sensory systems throughout middle and later adulthood are examined, with an emphasis on their interactions with identity processes. Special attention is paid to preventive measures that you can begin right now, that will help you age more successfully regardless of how old you are now.

APPEARANCE

Outward appearance is the first cue we use when we are trying to guess someone's age. The face provides the most information about how old people are, but there are other hints that we have about age based on body build and the condition of a person's hands, hair, teeth, and other parts of the body that we can readily see. We make these guesses about age on the basis of our experience in which we learn what most people look like at particular ages. However, often we are surprised to learn the age of someone who looks prematurely old, on the one hand, or seems to possess the secret of eternal youth, on the other. Unfortunately, people in Western society have very negative attitudes toward looking "old." Consequently, people can become highly sensitive to these outward signs of aging, even though in reality these changes do not interfere significantly with their everyday activities.

When you ask someone about the most obvious physical changes associated with the aging process, chances are that the person will mention wrinkles and gray hair. Though readily observable, these outward signs are not necessarily good indices of what is happening inside the body. However, starting in middle age, many adults regard these as some of the most important aspects of the changes that occur as they get older.

Skin

The wrinkling and sagging of the skin are processes that can take on significance starting as early as the 20s and 30s, although they are hardly evident in most people until much later in life. Gradually, however, the number and depth of skin wrinkles increase. At the same time, parts of the skin lose their resilience, and it becomes more and more translucent so that the veins and bones can be seen underneath.

To understand what happens to the skin, it is necessary to be aware of its structure. The skin is composed of three layers: the outermost layer or epidermis, the middle layer or dermis, and the innermost layer of subcutaneous fat. With increasing age in adulthood, the cells in the epidermis lose their regularity and become more random in their arrangement. However, the most significant effects of aging are in the cells of the dermis layer. These cells are composed of collagen, the ubiquitous protein molecule that supports the matrix of skin cells, and elastin which, as the name implies, helps to maintain the elasticity of the skin. As years of constant movement take their toll, the skin literally cannot return to its original state of tension after it has been stretched out through so many repeated movements. At the same time, the sebaceous glands, which normally provide oils that lubricate the skin, become less active. Consequently, the skin surface becomes drier and more vulnerable to damage from being rubbed or chafed.

Changes also occur in the subcutaneous fat layer of the skin. In young adults, it is the subcutaneous fat layer that gives the skin its opacity and smoothes the curves of the arms, legs, and face. The fat layer begins to thin in middle adulthood, providing less support underneath to hold up the two layers above it. This might seem like good news, but, unfortunately, the fat does not disappear. Instead it collects as fatty deposits around the torso.

Other changes in the skin involve the development of discolored areas, colloquially referred to as "age spots" (officially called *lentigo senilus*). These areas of brown pigmentation (on fair-skinned people) are more likely to develop in the sun-exposed areas of skin on the face, hands, and arms. Other changes in the coloring of the skin occur through the development of pigmented outgrowths (moles) and elevations of small blood vessels on the skin surface (angiomas). Capillaries and arteries in the skin may become dilated and in general are more visible due to the loss of subcutaneous fat.

Large irregularities in the blood vessels known as varicose veins may develop and appear on the skin of the legs.

We might not think of the nails as part of the skin, but technically they are. As people get older nail growth rate slows down. The nails also become yellowed in color. The toenails especially are likely to develop ridges and thickened areas, and they may even become curved to the point of looking like hooks.

Now, we return to the aging of the face. Our face's appearance is affected by these changes in the skin. In addition, though, the face changes shape due to bone loss in the skull, particularly loss of bone in the jaw. Changes in the cartilage of the nose and ears cause them to lengthen, further altering the face's shape. The teeth become somewhat discolored due to loss of their enamel surface and staining from coffee, tea, food, and tobacco. Tooth loss also occurs; in the United States about 20% of all adults 65 and older have lost all their natural teeth (Pleis & Lethbridge-Cejku, 2006). Current generations of middle-aged adults may suffer less from problems related to tooth loss than their previous counterparts because of improvements in dental hygiene in the past several decades, particularly flossing. In addition, tooth loss is related to lower levels of education, given that there are increasingly higher education levels in younger and younger cohorts, tooth loss should be less of a problem for future older adults (http://apps.nccd. cdc.gov/nohss/DisplayGraphV.asp?DataSet=2& nkey=7931&grp=4).

The eyes also change with age, further affecting the face's appearance. In addition to eyeglasses, which many middle-aged adults must wear for reading, if not distance, the areas around the eyes become baggy in their appearance through the accumulation of fat, fluid, and dark pigmentation. On the positive side, as people age, they are less likely to blush or show other signs of skin sensitivity (Guinot et al., 2006).

Genetic background affects the rate at which the skin ages, with fair-skinned people showing more rapid effects of aging than those who have darker skins, but there are also important contributions made by the individual's lifestyle. Primary among these lifestyle factors is **photoaging**, age changes caused by exposure to the sun's harmful radiation (Rabe, Mamelak, McElgunn, Morison, & Sauder, 2006). Parts of the body that are more exposed to the sun are more likely to show the microscopic changes described here than are parts of the body that are not exposed. Sunscreen that effectively blocks the rays of the sun (at least level 15 SPF) is the most effective prevention. Staying away from toxins such as cigarette smoke can also help to protect the skin from damage (Rexbye et al., 2006).

In recent years, perhaps reflecting advances in understanding of age-related changes in the skin, a host of cosmetic products has been introduced into the market intended to help people look younger. Some of these products have a scientific basis and others reflect nothing more than advertising hype. The prices can range from a few dollars at a discount chain store to several hundreds of dollars at specialty department or online stores. However, it is not necessary to splurge in order to buy a basic treatment to help ease the changes associated with the aging process. Moisturizer used on a daily basis can help to counteract the fragility, sensitivity, and dryness of the exposed areas of skin. The addition of alpha-hydroxy acid agents to a basic moisturizer can help stimulate cell growth and renewal to offset sun damage (Yamamoto et al., 2006). Retinol (vitamin A) is an antiwrinkle agent that helps to preserve the collagen matrix of the skin, but it has the drawbacks of being chemically unstable and also causing unpleasant side effects such as skin redness. Researchers are attempting to find synthetic alternatives that will still have the same benefits (Lee et al., 2006). Other over-the-counter products that claim to replace

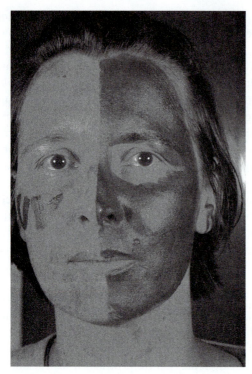

Sun damage not visible to the naked eye (left) can be seen under a uv-light (right).

collagen are also available (and can become very expensive indeed); controlled studies to demonstrate their effectiveness are generally not available to the public. *Caveat emptor* (or buyer, beware!) applies if you are seeking to purchase one of these products.

Other antiaging treatments for the face can only be provided by a plastic surgeon or dermatologist. The most popular by far is the injection of botulinum toxin (Botox®). In a Botox® treatment, a syringe containing a small amount of this substance, a nerve poison, is injected into the area of concern such as around the eyes or in the middle of the forehead muscle. This procedure paralyzes the muscle, hence relaxing the skin around it and causing a temporary reduction in the appearance of the wrinkle. Although cosmetics companies have

invested heavily in finding over-the-counter alternatives, at present there are no substitutes for this procedure (Beer, 2006).

Finally, apart from facelifts, in which a plastic surgeon removes the excess skin from the area of concern, there are a number of other dermatologic procedures intended to offset the effects of aging on the face. These include injections of artificial fillers, laser resurfacing treatments, and microdermabrasion. Advances in these procedures are certain to occur, given the enormous population of aging Baby Boomers who will wish to avail themselves of ways to stay young looking for as long as possible.

Hair

As people get older their hair becomes gray and eventually turns white. Equally likely, but especially of course for men, the hair also gets thinner. Despite what you might think, changes in the color of the hair are actually not due to the accumulation of gray but to the increasing loss of pigmentation in the hairs that remain on the head as the production of melanin ceases. The actual shade of gray in one's hair color is the result of the mixture of the white (unpigmented) hairs with the remaining pigmented hairs. Eventually, for most people, all the hairs are unpigmented, and the overall hair color is white. People vary tremendously in the rate at which their hair changes color.

The thinning of the hair, though more obvious in men, actually occurs in both sexes. Hair loss in general results from the destruction of the germination centers that produce the hair in the hair follicles. The most common form of hair loss to occur as people get older is male pattern hair loss and female pattern hair loss, technically known as **androgenetic alopecia**. This is a condition that affects, to some degree, 95% of adult men and 20% of adult women. In this form of hair loss, the hair follicles stop producing the long, thick pigmented hairs known as terminal

ASSESS YOURSELF: Your Aging Body

How are you treating your aging body? Answer these questions as honestly as you can to assess your chances of maximizing your body's functions for as long as possible.

1. With regard to eating patterns:
   A. I avoid eating high fat foods such as bacon, sausage, or donuts.
   B. I enjoy eating junk food, even though I know it's no good for me.
   C. I don't pay much attention to what I eat.

2. Being perfectly honest, I have to admit that I:
   A. smoke a lot of cigarettes a day.
   B. smoke a few cigarettes a day.
   C. smoke, but only under certain conditions (such as going out with friends).
   D. used to smoke but I've stopped.
   E. never have smoked, do not smoke, and don't plan to start.

3. I hang out with friends who:
   A. smoke very frequently.
   B. occasionally smoke.
   C. never smoke.

4. When I'm listening to music, such as in the car, on my stereo, or using my personal music device (mp3 player or walkman), I:
   A. turn up the volume so loud it almost hurts my ears.
   B. keep the volume turned up but just moderately loud.
   C. listen at a very low volume; just enough to be in the background.

5. When I'm outside during the day, I:
   A. always wear sunglasses, even if it is not very bright outside.
   B. only wear sunglasses if it is very sunny.
   C. never wear sunglasses.

6. With regard to brushing my teeth:
   A. I brush twice a day and floss at least once a day.
   B. I brush once a day and floss if I can remember.
   C. I brush once a day but don't bother flossing.
   D. I brush less than once a day.

7. The shoes I wear:
   A. are not very comfortable but they are very fashionable.
   B. are comfortable and I don't care if they are fashionable or not.
   C. are sometimes comfortable and sometimes fashionable, but fashion matters more than comfort.
   D. are sometimes comfortable and sometimes fashionable, but comfort matters more than fashion.

(contd.)

ASSESS YOURSELF

8. With regard to stress,
   A. I know that I get very stressed out, but there's nothing I can do about it.
   B. I try to do yoga, meditation, or other relaxation exercises.
   C. I don't get very stressed out, and therefore I don't really do much to control stress.

9. Again, being very honest, this is how often I drink:
   A. every night, sometimes as much as a six pack a night.
   B. two or three times a week, and usually drink up to one six pack (or equivalent) each time.
   C. two or three times a week, but no more than one or possibly two drinks, max.
   D. once a week, usually drink up to a six pack (or equivalent) each time.
   E. once a week, but no more than one or possibly two drinks, max.
   F. less than once a week.

hair and instead produce short, fine unpigmented and largely invisible hair known as vellus hair. Eventually, even that hair is not visible, because it no longer protrudes from the follicle which itself has shrunk. Although hair stops growing on the top of the head where it is desired, it may appear in larger amounts in places where it is not welcome, such as the chin on women, the ears, and in thicker clumps around the eyebrows.

Pharmaceutical companies are actively working on the solution to the problem of baldness. Improvements in hair stimulation products are probably not far off in the future.

BODY BUILD

Throughout adulthood, the body is a dynamic entity, changing size and shape continuously. We are used to considering ourselves fully grown by the early 20s, but in reality our height and weight change significantly over the course of the adult years. For better or for worse, by the time people are in their 50s and 60s, their bodies may have only a passing resemblance to what they looked like when they first reached physical maturity.

The first set of changes in our body build involves height. Cross-sectional and longitudinal studies convincingly show that we become shorter as we get older, a process that is more pronounced for women. The loss of height is caused by loss of bone material in the vertebrae that leads the spine to collapse and shorten in length (Pfirrmann et al., 2006).

Our weight also changes in adulthood, a process quantified by two measures. One is fat-free mass (FFM), an index of the amount of lean tissue in the body. The second is **Body Mass Index (BMI)**, an index of body fat that equals weight in kilograms divided by (height in meters) squared. An ideal BMI is one that is about 23 in men and 21 in women. Total body weight increases from the 20s until the mid-50s, but declines after that. Most of the weight gain that

FIGURE 4.1
BMI Changes in Adulthood

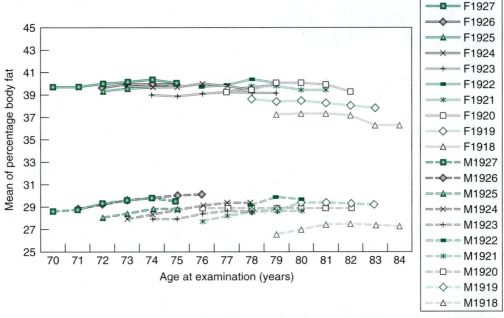

Among successive older cohorts of older adults, the percent of body fat has continued to increase, as shown in this figure. Also illustrated is the fact that the percent of body fat increases over time. For example, the bottom half of the figure shows that among men born in 1927, body fat increased from the age of 70 to 76 years (bottom half of figure, first set of data points).

Source: Ding et al., 2007.

occurs through the years of middle adulthood is due to an increase in BMI (see Figure 4.1) (Ding et al., 2007) which is manifested mainly as the accumulation of body fat around the waist and hips (called "middle-aged spread"). The loss of body weight in the later years of adulthood is not due to loss of this accumulated fat. Older adults lose pounds because they suffer a reduction of FFM. The loss of FFM is due to inadequate food intake, a condition called **anorexia of aging**. The reduction of food intake occurs because of hormonal changes in regulation of hunger (Di Francesco et al., 2007).

Even people well into middle age can take preventative and compensatory measures to offset these changes. Regular involvement

in aerobic exercise can help maintain muscle tone and reduce the fat deposits of middle-aged spread. Involvement in active leisure time activities, ranging from 15 to 90 minutes a day, can reduce age-related accumulation of body fat (Raguso et al., 2006). Exercise has its beneficial effect in large part due to the prevention of the increase in BMI that occurs when people are sedentary (Kyle et al., 2001). Resistance training (weight lifting or Nautilus) in particular can help to offset age losses in bone content that contribute to the loss of height. By engaging in vigorous walking, jogging, or cycling for 30 to 60 minutes a day, three to four days a week, the sedentary adult can see positive results within two to three months.

"What do you think?"   *4-1*

What will future generations of older adults (who exercised when young) look like compared with current older adults?

It is also important to consider interactions with identity when discussing the individual's decision to take advantage of exercise as a preventive measure against negative changes in body build. In one intriguing study, older adults were tested on a measure of "social physique anxiety," the extent to which one is afraid of what other people think of one's body. Over the course of a six-month exercise training study, social physique anxiety significantly decreased along with improvements in feelings of fitness and a measure of self-efficacy, or the feelings of confidence in being able to complete physically demanding tasks (McAuley, Marquez, Jerome, Blissmer, & Katula, 2002). These findings may be interpreted in terms of the identity process theory as indicating the advantages of helping older adults to achieve a balanced and self-accepting image instead of accommodative approach to the changes associated with the aging process in physical appearance and fitness.

MOBILITY

We are able to move due to the actions of the structures that support movement, including the bones, joints, tendons, and ligaments that connect the muscles to the bones, and the muscles that control flexion and extension. In the average person, all these structures undergo age-related changes that compromise their ability to function effectively. Beginning in the 40s, or earlier in the case of injury, each component of mobility undergoes significant age-related losses. Consequently, there is a gradual reduction of the speed of walking (Shumway-Cook et al., 2007). You may be aware of some of these changes from your own experience or your experience with older relatives or friends, who probably take longer than you do to reach the same destination.

Muscles

The adult years are characterized by a progressive loss of muscle mass, a process known as **sarcopenia**. There is a reduction in the number and size of muscle fibers, especially the fast-twitch fibers involved in speed and strength (Karakelides & Sreekumaran Nair, 2005). As muscle mass decreases, it is replaced at first by connective tissue and then ultimately by fat. The rate of yearly decrease is 1 to 2% (Marcell, 2003), so that between the ages of 50 and 80 years, people lose 30% of their skeletal muscle fibers (Kosek, Kim, Petrella, Cross, & Bamman, 2006). Variations in the rate of sarcopenia exist by gender and race. Among average men and women, the process is more pronounced in men (see Figure 4.1) (Castillo et al., 2003). Racial differences among women have been identified. Compared to white women, black women lose muscle at a lower rate (Aloia, Vaswani, Feuerman, Mikhail, & Ma, 2000). However, for women at least, sarcopenia rates can be reduced by exercise of three or more times per week (Castillo et al., 2003).

As indicated in cross-sectional studies, muscle strength as measured by maximum force reaches a peak in the 20's and 30's, remains at a plateau until the 40's to 50's, and then declines at a faster rate of 12 to 15% per decade (Kostka, 2005). By contrast, muscular endurance as measured by isometric strength is generally maintained throughout adulthood (Lavender & Nosaka, 2007). There are also relatively minor effects of age on eccentric strength, involved in lowering arm weights, slowing down while walking, and going down the stairs. Eccentric strength is preserved through the 70s and 80s in men

FIGURE 4.2
Prevalence of Sarcopenia by Age and Sex

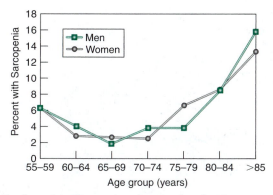

This figure shows the prevalence by age and gender of sarcopenia, or loss of muscle mass, among a large sample of men and women. Sarcopenia was defined as a fat-free mass of 2 standard deviations or more below the fat-free mass of a young comparison group.

Source: Castillo et al., 2004.

and women (Horstmann et al., 1999). These findings are consistent with the known patterns of atrophy of the fast-twitch and slow-twitch fibers.

Although decreases in muscle force can account in part for losses of muscle strength (Morse, Thom, Reeves, Birch, & Narici, 2005), muscle mass changes do not completely predict age-related reductions in strength in adulthood (Hughes et al., 2001). There seem to be disruptions in the signals the nervous system sends to the muscles telling them to contract (Klass, Baudry, & Duchateau, 2006). Also increased tendon stiffness can contribute to reduced muscle strength (Narici & Maganaris, 2006).

Strength training is the number one preventative measure that can counteract the process of sarcopenia in adulthood (Hunter, McCarthy, & Bamman, 2004). Although older adults do not achieve as high a degree of improvement as do younger adults, only 16 weeks of resistance training can improve fast-twitch muscle fiber numbers to the size of those found in the young (Kosek et al., 2006). People as old as 100 years of age

can benefit from this form of exercise. Effective training typically involves eight to twelve weeks, three to four times per week, at 70 to 90% of the one-repetition maximum. Caloric restriction is also being investigated as a possible mechanism to slow down sarcopenia (Dirks & Leeuwenburgh, 2006b). At the same time, nutrition plays an important role in preserving muscle strength (Dreyer & Volpi, 2005), particularly maintaining adequate protein intake (Morais, Chevalier, & Gougeon, 2006).

Bones

Bone is living tissue that constantly reconstructs itself through a process of bone remodeling in which old cells are destroyed and replaced by new cells. The general pattern of bone development in adulthood involves an increase in the rate of bone destruction compared to renewal and greater porosity of the calcium matrix, leading to loss of bone mineral content. The remodeling process that leads to these changes is controlled in part by a set of protein-like substances that act on the bone cells (Cao et al., 2005). These substances are, in turn, under the influence of the sex hormones estrogen (Bord, Ireland, Beavan, & Compston, 2003; Carnevale et al., 2005; Keles et al., 2006) and testosterone (Mellstrom et al., 2006), particularly in older adults (Khosla, Melton, Achenbach, Oberg, & Riggs, 2006). Therefore, as people experience decreases in sex hormones, they also lose bone mineral content (Sigurdsson et al., 2006).

Estimates of the decrease in bone mineral content over adulthood are about .5% per year for men and 1% per year for women (Emaus, Berntsen, Joakimsen, & Fonnebo, 2006). Further weakening occurs due to microcracks that develop in response to stress placed on the bones (Diab, Condon, Burr, & Vashishth, 2006). Part of the older bone's increased susceptibility to fracture can be accounted for by a loss of

FIGURE 4.3
Changes within the Bones with Age

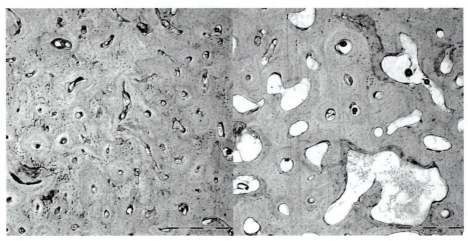

This photo shows two areas of bone from the same 78-year-old woman. On the left is an area of dense bone, and on the right is an area showing significant bone loss.

Source: Augat & Schorlemmer, 2006.

collagen, which reduces the bone's flexibility when pressure is put upon it (Seeman & Delmas, 2006). The problem is particularly severe for the upper part of the thigh bone right below the hip, which does not receive much mechanical pressure during walking and therefore tends to thin disproportionately (Mayhew et al., 2005).

We lose bone loss at varying rates as the result of a number of other causes. Genetic factors are estimated to account for as much as 70% of bone mineral content in adulthood (Ferrari & Rizzoli, 2005). Heavier people in general have higher bone mineral content, and so they lose less in adulthood, particularly in the weight-bearing limbs that are involved in mobility. However, it is not the weight but the amount of muscle mass that is important because greater fat mass is related to higher loss of bone mineral content (Hsu et al., 2006). Perhaps reflecting their greater mobility, people living in rural areas have higher bone density than people living in urban environments (Pongchaiyakul et al., 2005). Bone loss is greater in women,

especially whites, who lose bone at a higher rate than do African American women (Cauley et al., 2005).

The process of bone loss is not a significant problem until at least the 50s or 60s. However, well before then there are ways that we can slow down the rate of bone loss, even if these biological factors will ultimately work against us. Smoking (Baheiraei, Pocock, Eisman, Nguyen, & Nguyen, 2005), heavy alcohol use (Samelson et al., 2006), and poor diet exacerbate the process. Physical activity can slow it down (Chen et al., 2006; Engelke et al., 2006). Resistance training with weights (Suominen, 2006), high protein intake (Devine, Dick, Islam, Dhaliwal, & Prince, 2005) increased calcium intake prior to menopause, and use of vitamin D (Dawson-Hughes et al., 2005; Montero-Odasso & Duque, 2005) can also lower the rate of bone loss. Adequate intake of magnesium also seems to reduce the risk of bone loss (Ryder et al., 2005; Strotmeyer, Cauley, Schwartz et al., 2005). Environmental factors play a role as well. People who live in climates with sharp demarcations between the seasons appear to be more likely to suffer from earlier onset of bone loss; for example, people living in Norway have among the highest rates of bone fracture of anyone in the world (Forsmo, Langhammer, Forsen, & Schei, 2005).

Joints

Although most adults do not feel that they are getting "creaky" until their 40s, deleterious processes are at work even before we reach the age of skeletal maturity. These changes continue steadily throughout the adult years (Ding, Cicuttini, Scott, Cooley, & Jones, 2005). By the 20s and 30s, the arterial cartilage that protects the joints has already begun to degenerate, and as it does so, the bone underneath wears away. Over the course of adulthood, joint problems are exacerbated by outgrowths of cartilage that begin to develop, further interfering with the smooth movement of the bones against each other. The fibers in the joint capsule become less pliable, reducing flexibility even more.

Unlike muscles, joints do not benefit from constant use. On the contrary, our joints lose flexibility and become more painful the more we stress them. In fact, over half of the adults in the United States report that they experience chronic joint pain or movement restriction (Leveille, 2004).

Exercise cannot compensate for or prevent these changes in the joints. However, there are variations in the rate of change of joint functioning over time, reflecting differences in the types of preventive measures that we can take to minimize joint pain, stiffness, and limitation of movement as we get older. Strength training that focuses on the muscles that support the joints can be beneficial in helping the individual to use those joints while placing less stress upon impaired tendons, ligaments figments, and arterial surfaces (Boling, Bolgla, Mattacola, Uhl, & Hosey, 2006). In addition to increasing muscle strength (see below), resistance training in which people use weight machines can also increase the flexibility of the tendons, allowing the muscle to operate more effectively (Reeves, Narici, & Maganaris, 2006).

Because the increased weight associated with obesity contributes to joint pain and stiffness, an exercise program should also focus on lowering body fat. Particularly important is flexibility training that increases the range of motion of the joint (Oken et al., 2006).

Precautions taken when you are young can reduce the chance of losses in middle age and

Wearing running shoes with adequate support can help preserve our joints as we age.

beyond. Most important is proper footwear, particularly during exercise. Although it might not always be practical, people who engage in occupational activities that involve repetitive motions of the wrist should try as much as possible to minimize damage by the use of ergonomically designed accessories. Middle-aged individuals already experiencing joint damage can benefit from flexibility exercises that expand a stiff joint's range of motion. Exercise that strengthens the muscles supporting the joint also helps to improve its functioning. Both kinds of exercise have the additional benefit of stimulating circulation to the joints, thereby enhancing the blood supply that promotes repair processes in the tendons, ligaments, and surfaces of the exercising areas.

VITAL BODILY FUNCTIONS

Our survival is ultimately determined by the quality of the bodily systems that support life such as the heart, lungs, and kidneys. Overall estimates place the rate of age-related changes across all bodily systems in the neighborhood of .5% per year (Bortz, 2005). Despite the impressive nature of this figure, there is much that people can do to reduce or offset the impact on aging on the majority of these functions.

Cardiovascular System

Aging of the cardiovascular system involves changes that begin in middle age in both the heart itself and the arteries that circulate blood throughout the body. The component of the heart that has the most relevance to aging is the left ventricle, the chamber that pumps oxygenated blood out to the arteries. Unfortunately, this important structure becomes less efficient over time. Its wall becomes thicker and less compliant, so that less blood is ejected into the aorta with

each contraction (Nikitin et al., 2006). The arteries become less able to accommodate the flow of blood that spews from the left ventricle (Otsuki et al., 2006). Complicating matters further is the continuing deposit of plaque along the arterial walls consisting of cholesterol, cellular waste products, calcium, and fibrin (a clotting material in the blood).

Our cardiovascular efficiency is indexed by **aerobic capacity**, the maximum amount of oxygen that can be delivered through the blood, and **cardiac output**, the amount of blood that the heart pumps per minute. Both indices decline consistently at a rate of about 10% per decade from age 25 and up so that the average 65-year-old has 40% lower cardiovascular efficiency than the young adult (Maron et al., 2001). The decline is more pronounced in males than females (Hollenberg, Yang, Haight, & Tager, 2006). Maximum heart rate, the heart rate achieved at the point of maximum oxygen consumption, also shows a linear decrease across the years of adulthood.

Declines in aerobic capacity occur even in highly trained athletes, but those who continue to exercise at a high level of intensity maintain their aerobic capacity longer than non-athletes (Tanaka & Seals, 2003). The major factor determining whether an athlete remains fit appears to be the difficulty of maintaining an active training program in the late 70s. Complications other than those involving the cardiovascular system, such as joint pain, interfere with the ability of even the most motivated person to participate in high-intensity exercise (Katzel, Sorkin, & Fleg, 2001).

Continued involvement in exercise throughout adulthood therefore does not appear to result in stopping the biological clock. However, exercise can slow down that clock by benefiting functional capacity, lifestyle, and control over body mass. Add to this the benefits of avoiding cigarette smoking, and the impact

FIGURE 4.4

Aerobic Capacity in Sedentary and Trained Men

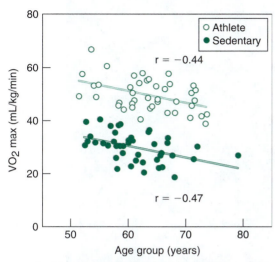

Longitudinal decreases in VO_2 max (aerobic capacity) in men who are athletes and men who are sedentary. The decline in athletes was related to the amount of exercise they continued to engage in, with those who stopped training showing a greater decrease than those who remained active.

Source: Katzel, Sorkin, & Fleg, 2001.

on cardiovascular functioning and hence the quality of daily life of these positive health habits can be significant (Christensen, Stovring, Schultz-Larsen, Schroll, & Avlund, 2006).

Short-term training studies provide more consistent findings about the value of exercise for middle-aged and older adults (Woo, Derleth, Stratton, & Levy, 2006). To be maximally effective, exercise must stimulate the heart rate to rise to 60 to 75% of maximum capacity, and this training must take place three to four times a week. Some recommended aerobic activities are walking, hiking, jogging, bicycling, swimming, jumping rope, and roller skating. However, even moderate or low-intensity exercise can have positive effects on previously sedentary older people.

In part, improvements in blood pressure associated with short-term training may reflect the favorable effect that exercise has on enhancing lipid metabolism. Exercise increases the fraction of **high-density lipoproteins (HDLs)**, the plasma lipid transport mechanism responsible for carrying lipids from the peripheral tissues to the liver where they are excreted or synthesized into bile acids. It is beneficial to have a high level of HDLs and a low level of low-density lipoproteins (LDLs). As is true for the effects of exercise on aerobic power and muscle strength, even moderate levels of exercise can have a beneficial impact on cholesterol metabolism (Knight, Bermingham, & Mahajan, 1999). Conversely, smoking has deleterious effects on cholesterol, leading to decreased HDLs and increased LDLs, as well as the accumulation of other harmful forms of fat in the blood (Kuzuya, Ando, Iguchi, & Shimokata, 2006).

"What do you think?" | **4-2**

Do you know people who exercise extensively? How much do you think a desire to avoid negative cardiovascular changes fits into their exercise goals?

In summary, even though there are a number of deleterious changes associated with aging, they are by no means uniformly negative (Ferrari, Radaelli, & Centola, 2003). More important, there are many ways that we can both prevent and compensate for these changes. In what will become a much-repeated message throughout this chapter (and the book as a whole), exercise is one of the best ways you can slow down the rate of your body's aging process.

Respiratory System

The function of the respiratory system is to bring oxygen into the body and move carbon dioxide

This couple is engaging in exercise, an activity that can slow the effects of aging on many bodily functions.

out of it. Our respiratory system accomplishes these goals through the mechanical process of breathing, the exchange of gases in the inner-most reaches of tiny airways in the lungs, and the transport of gases to and from the body's cells that occur in these airways. Aging affects all of these components of the respiratory sys-tem. The respiratory muscles lose the ability to expand and contract the chest wall, and the lung tissue itself is less able to expand and con-tract during inspiration and expiration (Sprung, Gajic, & Warner, 2006). Consequently, all mea-sures of lung functioning in adulthood show age-related losses from about age 40 and on, par-ticularly under conditions of exertion (DeLorey & Babb, 1999; Ishida, Sato, Katayama, & Miyamura, 2000). These changes are thought to affect women more than men, particularly when stress is placed on the respiratory system during exercise (Harms, 2006).

However, exercise has positive effects on the respiratory system, strengthening the chest wall and thereby compensating for some loss of pumping capacity of the respiratory muscles. People who do not exercise show significantly worse respiratory functioning than those who do (Jakes et al., 2002). However, we cannot overcome the changes in the lung tissue itself, even through aerobic exercise (Womack et al., 2000). The best that we can hope for is to minimize the effects of aging on the lungs. We can do so in one of two ways. The first is pretty obvious—stay away from cigarette smoking. People who smoke show a greater loss

FIGURE 4.5
Expiratory Volume and Aging

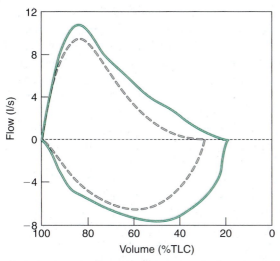

This figure shows the effects of aging on respiratory flow. The solid line shows the data for a young adult, and the dashed line for an older adult. The upper curves show the amount of air blown out during expiration, and the lower curves show the amount of air taken in during inspiration.

Source: Babb & Rodarte, 2000.

of forced expiratory volume in later adulthood than those who do not (Morgan & Reger, 2000). Although it is better to quit smoking than continue smoking, there are unfortunately deleterious change in the body's cells that remain for at least several decades after a person has quit smoking (Masayesva et al., 2006).

Maintaining a low BMI is the second way to preserve the functioning of the respiratory system. Researchers are finding that at least among men, body fat and fat-free body mass are associated with improved respiratory function (Wannamethee, Shaper, & Whincup, 2005).

Urinary System

Our bodies must rid themselves of the by-products of cellular metabolism, and we do so through the functioning of the urinary system. Making up the urinary system are the kidneys, bladder, ureters, and urethra. The kidneys are composed of nephron cells that serve as millions of tiny filters as the blood passes through them to be cleansed of metabolic waste. These waste products combine in the bladder with excess water from the blood to be eliminated as urine through the urethra.

At one time it was thought that the fate of the kidneys in older adults was to decline steadily due to loss of nephrons over time. However, it then became evident that the normal aging process actually does not impair these important cells. Many factors other than age can compromise the nephrons, one of which is cigarette smoking which, in fact, can cause serious kidney disease in older adults with other risk factors (Stengel, Couchoud, Cenee, & Hemon, 2000). Studies conducted on samples in the past may have yielded exaggerated estimates of the effects of normal aging, reflecting instead the unhealthy effects of the once widespread habit of smoking. However, it is also true that when the kidneys of the older person are placed under stress, such as illness, extreme exertion, or extreme heat they are less able to function normally (Fuiano et al., 2001).

Regardless of the cause, there are important implications of the aging of the kidney. Older adults are likely to have slower excretion rates of chemicals from the body. Levels of medications must be carefully monitored in middle-aged and older adults to avoid inadvertent overdoses (Wyatt, Kim, & Winston, 2006).

Changes with aging may also occur in the elastic tissue of the bladder such that it can no longer efficiently retain or expel urine. Older adults also experience some changes in the perception that they need to urinate although the bladder itself does not shrink in size in normal aging (Pfisterer, Griffiths, Schaefer, & Resnick, 2006). Adding to intrinsic changes in the bladder which lower the rate of urinary flow in men is the fact that many men experience hypertrophy (overgrowth) of the prostate, a gland that sits on top of the bladder. This puts pressure on the bladder and can lead men to feel frequent urges to urinate.

Approximately 30% of all adults 65 and older suffer from the form of urinary incontinence known as urge incontinence, in which the need to urinate occurs suddenly and the individual is therefore unable to resist the need to void. Among individuals living in nursing homes, however, the percentage is far higher, rising to 50% (see Figure 4.6) (Erdem & Chu, 2006). A related condition is overactive bladder, whose symptoms may include urge incontinence but whose chief symptom is urinary frequency. Overactive bladder affects 25% of the population 65 and older (Wagg, Wyndaele, & Sieber, 2006). These are distressing conditions, but fortunately, as you can see from these percentages, the large majority of older adults are symptom-free when it comes to the functioning of their bladders.

For those older adults who do experience overactive bladder and incontinence, there can be associated psychological problems, including

FIGURE 4.6
Age-related Increases in Overactive Bladder Symptoms

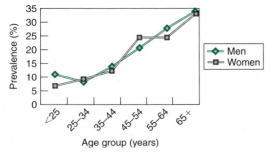

As shown in this figure, older men and women are more likely to experience symptoms of an overactive bladder.

Source: Erdem & Chu, 2006.

symptoms of depression, difficulty sleeping, and sexual dysfunction. Embarrassment and concern over having an accident further add to the difficulties experienced by older men and women with bladder problems. Also related to these conditions is a greater prevalence of falls and fractures because people with bladder problems may be more likely to try to make a quick exit from a social situation in order to reach the bathroom. Unfortunately, because there is a strong tendency for our society to regard bladder problems as a normal part of the aging process, people who could benefit from treatment do not even raise the issue with their physicians and therefore miss out on the opportunity for treatment (Tyagi, Thomas, Hayashi, & Chancellor, 2006).

Medications are becoming increasingly available to help people with bladder problems, but there are also a number of behavioral controls that can be effective in controlling the symptoms of overactive bladder and incontinence (Subak, Quesenberry, Posner, Cattolica, & Soghikian, 2002). Pelvic muscle training is particularly effective for this purpose (Norton & Brubaker, 2006). In this exercise, you contract and relax the urinary sphincters for about one minute at a time (both men and women can engage in this exercise). Apart from these strategies, the older individual can avoid some of the behaviors that can exacerbate renal dysfunction such as not becoming dehydrated, particularly during hot weather or while exercising.

Digestive System

We hear a great deal in the media about middle-aged and older people requiring aids to their digestive system, such as treatments for heartburn (acid reflux), gas, bloating, and bowel irregularity. Surprisingly, the reality is that most older people do not actually experience significant losses in their ability to digest food.

For example, physiological changes in the esophagus are relatively minor (Achem & Devault, 2005), and (for people in good health) as are changes in the remaining organs consisting of the stomach and lower digestive tract (Bharucha & Camilleri, 2001). It is true that less saliva is produced (Eliasson, Birkhed, Osterberg, & Carlen, 2006), there is less gastric juice secreted, and the stomach empties more slowly in older adults (O'Donovan et al., 2005). There is also a decrease in liver volume and blood flow through the liver (Serste & Bourgeois, 2006). However, these changes vary tremendously from person to person, as well as considerably according to overall health status (Drozdowski & Thomson, 2006).

Despite the image propagated by the media, problems such as fecal incontinence affect only a small fraction of even the over-65 population (7%). As is true with urinary incontinence, training people in coping methods and behavioral controls can help to manage the condition (Norton, 2004).

It is not only the physiology that determines how well our digestive systems function in later life. Many lifestyle factors that can change in middle and later adulthood contribute to overall digestive health. For example, families typically become smaller, financial resources may decrease, and age-related mobility and cognitive problems can make it harder for the older adult to cook. All these factors can detract from the motivation to eat. However, the constant hawking by advertisers of the need for dietary supplements, digestive aids, and laxatives after the age of 40 or 50 can make people expect to and then ultimately see changes in their digestion.

BODILY CONTROL SYSTEMS

Each of the organ systems we have looked at so far plays a crucial role in our daily functioning, but overseeing much of the way these operate is the job of the endocrine and immune systems. Researchers are increasingly learning about their important roles in a variety of control processes that can range from the way our bodies utilize energy to our sleep habits to our sexuality.

Endocrine System

The endocrine system is a large and diverse set of glands that regulates the actions of the body's other organ systems (called "target" organs). **Hormones** are the chemical messengers produced by the endocrine systems.

Changes in the endocrine system can occur at many levels. The endocrine glands themselves may release more or less of a particular hormone. The target organs may also respond differently to stimulation from the hormones. Making matters more complicated is the fact that the endocrine system is highly sensitive to levels of stress and physical illness. Alterations that appear to be due to normal aging in adulthood may instead reflect other factors such as the effects of disease.

The hypothalamus and anterior (front) section of the pituitary gland, located deep within the base of the brain, are the main control centers of the endocrine system. Hypothalamus-releasing factors (HRFs), hormones produced by the hypothalamus, regulate the secretion of hormones in turn produced by the anterior pituitary gland. However, the HRFs are not the only source of stimulation for pituitary hormones. Signals from target organs carried through the blood, indicating that more pituitary hormones are needed, can also lead to greater hormone production. HRFs may also be stimulated by information sent from other parts of the nervous system.

Six hormones are produced by the anterior pituitary: thyroid-stimulating hormone (TSH), adrenocorticotropic hormone (ACTH), follicle-stimulating hormone (FSH), luteinizing hormone

(LH), growth hormone (GH, also called soma-totropin), and prolactin. Each of these hormones acts on specific target cells within the body and some (such as TSH) stimulate the production of other hormones.

Growth hormone.   One of these hormones receiving extensive attention by researchers is GH. In youth, GH stimulates the growth of bones and muscles, but throughout life, it affects the metabolism of proteins, lipids, and carbohydrates. A related hormone produced by the liver, IGF-I (insulin-like growth factor-1), stimulates muscle cells to increase in size and number.

Together, GH and IGF-1 are called the somatotrophic axis (GH and IGF-1). Their decline is called **somatopause of aging** (Burgess et al., 1999). The somatopause is thought to account for a number of age-related changes in body composition across adulthood, including loss of bone mineral content, increases in fat, and decrease in muscle mass as well as losses in strength, exercise tolerance, and quality of life in general (Lombardi et al., 2005). In young people, GH production shows regularly timed peaks during nighttime sleep; in older adults, this peak is smaller (Russell-Aulet, Dimaraki, Jaffe, DeMott-Friberg, & Barkan, 2001). GH also rises during exercise, but in adults age 60 and older this response is attenuated (Weltman et al., 2006).

"What do you think?"   **4-3**

Why might hormones be thought of as the key to aging?

Given the importance of GH to so many basic processes affected by aging, GH replacement therapy has been increasingly seen by some as the magic potion that can stop the aging process (Hermann & Berger, 2001). Low doses,

administered with testosterone to men, have been shown to have positive effects in increasing lean body mass and reducing fat mass, and improving overall aerobic capacity (Giannoulis et al., 2006). However, there are still many questions about both the practicality of this approach as well as its safety. In addition to being extremely expensive ($10,000 to 25,0000 USD per year), researchers maintain that the side effects of this treatment include substantial negative effects that outweigh any of its possible advantages (Perls, Reisman, & Olshansky, 2005). GH is linked to joint pain, enlargement of the heart, enlargement of the bones, diabetes, high blood pressure, and heart failure.

Cortisol.   We turn next to cortisol, the hormone produced by the adrenal gland. The fact that cortisol provides energy to the muscles during times of stress has led researchers to regard it as the "stress hormone." When it increases, not only does cortisol energize the body, but it unfortunately also has negative effects on memory and other forms of cognitive functioning in older adults (Li et al., 2006). Sleep impairments, which are more common in older adults, are also related to higher cortisol levels (Prinz, Bailey, & Woods, 2000). The idea that aging causes dangerous increases in cortisol levels is known as the **glucocorticoid cascade hypothesis**. The reason that cortisol increases, according to this view, is that the endocrine system is attempting to energize the body to make up for losses of muscle tissue.

Not all studies support the glucorcorticoid cascade hypothesis. Some researchers find that there are no age changes under normal conditions (Feldman et al., 2002). Others have questioned whether there are age differences in the reaction to stress (Kudielka, Schmidt-Reinwald, Hellhammer, Schurmeyer, & Kirschbaum, 2000). Most significant is the fact that when the data are collected longitudinally rather than cross-sectionally (which is true for all of the above studies), individual variations exist in the pattern of changes over time. Yearly testing of healthy older adults over a three- to six-year period revealed that some older individuals increase, some decrease, and some remain stable in cortisol levels (Lupien et al., 1996). Interestingly, positive associations were found in this longitudinal study between anxiety and cortisol, suggesting that variations in time in cortisol level may relate to individual differences in personality. Another factor that may play a role in cross-sectional studies is obesity, which is positively related to cortisol levels, at least in middle-aged men (Field, Colditz, Willett, Longcope, & McKinlay, 1994). Of course it is impossible to determine whether increases in obesity reflect cause or effect in relation to cortisol levels. Nevertheless these findings create doubt regarding the validity of the glucocorticoid cascade hypothesis.

Thyroid hormones. Controlling the rate of metabolism, also known as the basal metabolic rate (BMR), are hormones produced by the thyroid gland, located in the neck. The BMR begins to slow in middle age and is responsible for the weight gain that occurs even when a person's caloric intake remains stable. We hear these complaints very often from middle-aged people, who state that their metabolism is slower than it used to be and that is why they are unable to lose weight. Changes in BMR are related to age-related decreases in thyroid hormones over adulthood (Weissel, 2006). By the 60s, subclinical hypothyroidism can reach as high as 15 to 18% (Diez & Iglesias, 2004).

Melatonin. Our sleep-wake cycles are controlled in part by the hormone melatonin, which is manufactured by the pineal gland, located deep within the brainstem. Our **circadian rhythm**, the daily variations we experience in various bodily functions, is therefore affected by this hormone.

As we will see later, there are significant changes in circadian rhythm throughout middle and later adulthood, possibly corresponding to the fact that melatonin production declines across adulthood (Mahlberg, Tilmann, Salewski, & Kunz, 2006).

Some researchers believe that melatonin supplements can reduce the effects of aging and age-associated diseases, especially in the brain and immune system. Melatonin supplements for women have been shown to lead to improved pituitary and thyroid functions (Bellipanni, Bianchi, Pierpaoli, Bulian, & Ilyia, 2001) and to reduce the incidence of sleep problems (Gubin, Gubin, Waterhouse, & Weinert, 2006). Although melatonin supplements would therefore seem to provide a logical solution to the problem, the side effects have still not been completely identified, and the purity of the available supplements on the market has not been assured. Melatonin supplements can also interfere with sleep cycles if taken at the wrong time. There are also significant side effects, including confusion, drowsiness, headaches, and constriction of blood vessels, which would be dangerous in people with high blood pressure. Finally, the dosages usually sold in over-the-counter medications may be as high as 40 times the amount normally found in the body, and the effect of such large doses taken over a long term has not been determined.

DHEA. The most abundant steroid in the human body, dehydroepiandrosterone (DHEA) is a weak male steroid (androgen) produced by the adrenal glands located adjacent to the kidneys. It is a precursor to the sex hormones testosterone and estrogen and is believed to have a variety of functions such as increasing production of other sex steroids and availability of IGF-1 and positively influencing some central nervous system functions.

DHEA, which is higher in males than females, shows a pronounced decrease over the adult years, reducing by 60% between the ages of 20 and 80 (Feldman et al., 2002). This phenomenon, termed **adrenopause**, is greater in men, although men continue to have higher levels than women throughout later life because they start at a higher baseline. Extremely low levels of DHEA have been linked to cardiovascular disease, some forms of cancer, immune system dysfunction, and obesity (von Muhlen, Laughlin, Kritz-Silverstein, & Barrett-Connor, 2007).

Although there are no definitive answers about DHEA's role in aging other than the fact that the decline in DHEA is probably a reliable one, DHEA replacement therapy is rivaling GH and melatonin in the antiaging industry. However, like GH therapy, there are health risks, notably liver problems and an increase in risk of prostate and breast cancer (Acacio et al., 2004; Arnold, Le, McFann, & Blackman, 2005). A natural substitute for some of the positive effects of DHEA replacement therapy is exercise, which can help to compensate for its loss in the later adult years (Ravaglia et al., 2001).

Female sexual changes.   Technically speaking, **menopause** is the point in a woman's life when menstruation stops permanently. As used in common speech, however, menopause has come to mean a phase in middle adulthood covering the years in which reproductive capacity diminishes. The more precise term for this gradual winding down of reproductive ability is **climacteric**, a term that applies to men as well. For women, the climacteric occurs over a three- to five-year span called the **perimenopause**, ending in the menopause when the woman has not had her menstrual period for one year. The average age of menopause is 50 years, but the timing varies among individuals. Menopause occurs earlier in women who are thin, malnourished, or who smoke.

Throughout the perimenopause, there is a diminution in the production by the ovarian follicles of estrogen, the primary female sex hormone. Since the other female hormone, progesterone, is produced in response to ovulation, progesterone levels also decline during this time. The process of estrogen decline begins about 10 to 15 years before menopause, at some point in the mid-30s. By the mid-40s, the ovaries have begun to function less effectively and produce fewer hormones. Eventually, menstrual cycles by the early to middle 50s have ended altogether. There is still some production of estrogen, however, as the ovaries continue to produce small amounts and the adrenal glands stimulate the production of estrogen in fat tissue. FSH and LH levels rise dramatically during the perimenopausal period as the anterior pituitary sends out signals to produce more ovarian hormones. In turn, the hypothalamus produces less gonadotropin-releasing factor (GnRH).

Although women vary considerably in their progression through the menopause (as they do during puberty), there are certain characteristic symptoms, many of which you have probably heard discussed by middle-aged and older women (there was even an off-Broadway musical called *Menopause*). One of the most prominent is the occurrence of "hot flashes," which are sudden sensations of intense heat and sweating that can last from a few moments to half an hour. These are the result of decreases in estrogen levels, which cause the endocrine system to release higher amounts of other hormones that affect the temperature control centers in the brain. Fatigue, headaches, night sweats, and insomnia are other physiological symptoms thought to be the result of fluctuating estrogen levels. Menopausal women also report that they experience psychological symptoms such as irritability, mood swings, depression, memory loss, and difficulty concentrating, but the evidence regarding the connection between these symptoms and the physiological changes involved in menopause is far from conclusive.

Along with hormonal changes, menopause is associated with alterations in the reproductive tract. Because of lower estrogen levels, there is a reduction in the supply of blood to the vagina and surrounding nerves and glands. The tissues become thinner, drier, and less able to produce secretions to lubricate before and during intercourse. The result is the possibility of discomfort during intercourse. In addition, women may become more susceptible to urinary problems such as infections and stress incontinence in which urine leaks out of the urethra upon exertion.

More widespread throughout the body are other effects of menopause associated with the impact of decreasing estrogen levels on other bodily systems. Weaker bones, high blood pressure, and cardiovascular disease become more prevalent among postmenopausal women. It appears that estrogen provides protection against these diseases which is lost at menopause. There are also changes in cholesterol levels in the blood associated with menopause, causing postmenopausal women to be at higher risk of atherosclerosis and associated conditions.

Estrogen-replacement therapy (ERT) was introduced in the 1940s to counteract the negative effects of estrogen loss on postmenopausal women. Later, estrogen was combined with the hormone, progestin, to reduce cancer risk. Administration of both hormones is referred to as **hormone replacement therapy** (**HRT**).

Initial studies on HRT's effects on the body provided enthusiastic support, citing positive effects on skin tone and appearance, bone mineral density, immune functioning, thickness of the hair, sleep, accidental falls, memory, and mood. Through the summer of mid-2002, health professionals working with menopausal women felt confident that they were making the right decision by prescribing HRT. Then,

in the summer of 2002, everything changed with the publication of a major international study on the relative risks and benefits of HRT. This study, the Women's Health Initiative (WHI) funded by the U.S. National Institutes of Health and an Italian medical foundation, involved 161,809 postmenopausal women ranging from 50 to 79 years. After five years, researchers discontinued the study when they observed an increase in the number of invasive breast cancer cases and heart attacks in women taking HRT. In addition there was a higher risk of heart attacks among women taking HRT. The study's authors suggested that rather than prescribing HRT, physicians should provide postmenopausal women with medications designed to target specific conditions associated with estrogen loss such as bone loss or sleep problems (Rossouw et al., 2002).

The second major finding to call into question the benefits of HRT was in the area of well-being. A randomized clinical trial on over 16,000 women in the United States, 10% of whom were studied over a three-year period, showed that there were no significant effects of HRT on general health, vitality, mental health, depressive symptoms, or sexual satisfaction. Although small improvements were observed after one year in some quality of life symptoms, these were not clinically meaningful nor did they persist in the group studied over the entire three years of the study (Hays et al., 2003).

Since the publication of the 2002 findings, researchers have continued to investigate the risks versus benefits of HRT. Now, as it turns out, not all studies show an increased risk of breast or ovarian cancer (Stefanick et al., 2006; Zhang et al., 2006). Other researchers believe that the timing is critical and that estrogen can be beneficial if taken at the time of the menopause rather than waiting until several years later (Grodstein, Manson, & Stampfer, 2006; Sherwin, 2006). One of the problems with the WHI study was that early postmenopausal women were ineligible, thus preventing researchers from investigating the impact of HRT at the start of the menopause (Henderson, 2006). It is also important to recognize the fact that there are various forms of estrogen and progestin as well as variations in dosages, all of which can impact the findings of studies on the value of HRT (Turgeon, Carr, Maki, Mendelsohn, & Wise, 2006). Some researchers are concerned that as a consequence of the WHI and the publicity it has received, many symptomatic women remain untreated (Ness, Aronow, & Beck, 2006).

For women who do not want to experiment with HRT given all these conflicting data, there are alternatives. Other recommended approaches to use instead of HRT to counteract the effect of hormonal changes include exercise, giving up smoking, lowering the cholesterol in the diet, and perhaps, more enjoyably, having one alcoholic drink a day.

Male sexual changes.   Although men do not experience a loss of sexual function comparable to the menopause (despite what you might hear about the "male menopause"), there is an **andropause**, which refers to age-related declines in the male sex hormone testosterone. The decline in testosterone is equal to 1% per year after the age of 40 years, a decrease observed in longitudinal as well as cross-sectional studies (Feldman et al., 2002). The term "late onset hypogonadism" or "age-associated hypogonadism" is beginning to replace the term andropause, but all three are currently in use.

When men undergo the andropause, they also experience a number of changes in body composition and physiology, including reduced lean body mass, increased body fat, decreased bone mineral density, and reduced numbers of red blood cells (Heaton & Morales, 2001; Longcope, Feldman, McKinlay, & Araujo, 2000). However,

there are large individual variations in testosterone levels across adulthood—about 25% of men over 75 years old have testosterone levels within the upper 25% of values for young men (Vermeulen, Goemaere, & Kaufman, 1999). These variations may reflect differences within older populations in cholesterol levels, percent of body fat, cigarette smoking, and behavioral tendencies that predispose an individual to developing cardiovascular disease (Zmuda et al., 1997).

Although common wisdom for a number of years was that testosterone supplements for aging men are an unnecessary and potentially dangerous proposition, they are now gaining greater empirical support and acceptance in the medical community with the condition that the treatment is accompanied by regular medical screening (Schulman & Lunenfeld, 2002; Tenover, 2000). Benefits associated with testosterone supplements include maintained or improved bone density, greater muscle strength, lowered ratio of fat to lean muscle mass, and increased strength, libido, and sexual function. There is emerging evidence that mood also seems to be positively affected although more controlled studies are needed (Seidman, 2006). Most significantly, in contrast to the findings of early studies, there is no evidence that prostate mass is increased as long as the treatment maintains a man's testosterone within a normal range. Also, in contrast to early findings, a higher rather than a lower testosterone level is associated with lowered cardiovascular risk, including more favorable cholesterol levels (i.e., higher HDLs), lower blood pressure, and lower levels of substances in the blood that contribute to atherosclerosis (van den Beld et al., 2003; Vermeulen, 2000).

Erectile dysfunction (ED), a condition in which a man is unable to achieve an erection sustainable for intercourse, is estimated to affect slightly over one-half of the noninstitutionalized population of men over 40. The prevalence of

ED increases with age in adulthood, from a rate for complete ED of 5% at the age of 40 to 15% at the age of 70. Moderate ED doubles over that period, from 17 to 34%. ED is also related to health problems, including diabetes, hypertension, and arthritis. Smoking also plays a role in ED as current smokers under treatment for heart disease have a much higher risk than nonsmokers receiving treatment for the same disease (Goldstein, 2004).

ED has an impact on the female partners of men who have the disorder. They suffer a number of significant effects, including lower frequency of orgasm, lower sexual satisfaction, and lower frequency of intercourse (Fisher, Rosen, Eardley, Sand, & Goldstein, 2005).

You are probably aware of the so-called "cure" for ED, the little blue pill known as Viagra. Phosphodiesterase type 5 inhibitors, including this medication (the technical term is sildanefil), can be effective in treating ED, alleviating the difficulties experienced by men and their sexual partners. Vardenafil (Levitra) is a similar medication that serves as an effective alternative for men with health conditions that make Viagra an unsafe medication for them to take (Goldstein et al., 2003). Though not effective for everyone, these medications have certainly helped to alleviate symptoms among millions of men, and, by extension, the problems experienced by their partners.

Immune System

Regulating our body's ability to fight off stress, infection, and other threats to our well-being is the immune system. In addition to its role in protecting the body against these challenges, the immune system is intimately connected to the nervous system and, consequently, behaviors, thoughts, and emotions (Glaser, 2005). Stress and negative emotions are thought to have deleterious effects on immune functioning

which, in turn, can result in tissue damage and vulnerability to disease.

Researchers believe that there are widespread age-related declines in immune system functioning, a process captured by the term **immune senescence** (Allman & Miller, 2005). The two primary types of immune cells are "T cells" and "B cells," both of which are involved in destroying bodily invaders known as antigens. In immune senescence, these cells fail to develop properly and lose their ability to perform the job effectively (Min, Montecino-Rodriguez, & Dorshkind, 2005).

This being said, there are many interactions between the immune system and other physical and psychological processes. Moderate exercise can play a role in enhancing immune functioning as can be seen in Figure 4.7 (Stasser, Skalicky, & Viidik, 2006). In terms of diet, additives such as zinc and vitamin E improve immune responsiveness (Chandra, 2004). Conversely, older people

FIGURE 4.7

Exercise and the Immune System

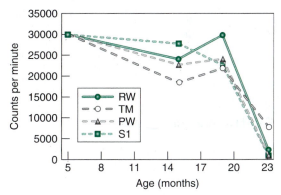

This figure compares the lymphocyte counts of rats under four conditions of exercise and dietary control. The RW rats voluntarily ran on treadmills, the PW rats were restricted in their food intake, TM rats were forced to run on treadmills, and the S1 rats were sedentary. After nearly two years, the treadmill-running (TM) rats showed improved immune functioning, as compared to the other groups.

Source: Strasser, Skalicky, & Viidik, 2006.

who eat low-protein diets have deficient immune functioning (Ahluwalia, 2004). It is possible that lack of control for diet and exercise in previous studies has contributed to an overly pessimistic view of the effect of aging on the immune system. For example, one study of a small sample of healthy volunteers found no age differences in a variety of immune system measures (Carson, Nichol, O'Brien, Hilo, & Janoff, 2000). Control for lifestyle factors would seem to be important as researchers attempt to determine the extent to which aging affects the immune system.

For the present time, it is best to be aware of the potentially negative effect aging may have in people who do not maintain ideal levels of diet and exercise. A malfunctioning immune system, as in the case of cancer, is a major contributor to mortality in middle and later adulthood.

NERVOUS SYSTEM

Our behavior is controlled by the nervous system. The central nervous system makes it possible for us to monitor and then prepare responses to events in the environment, conceive and enact our thoughts, and maintain connections with other bodily systems. The autonomic nervous system controls involuntary behaviors, our body's response to stress, and the actions of other organ systems that sustain life.

Central Nervous System

Early research on nervous system functioning in adulthood was based on the hypothesis that, because neurons do not reproduce, there is a progressive loss of brain tissue across the adult years that is noticeable by the age of 30. The model of aging based on this hypothesis was called the **neuronal fallout model**. However, in the years intervening since that early research, it has become clear that, in the absence of disease,

the aging brain maintains much of its structure and function. The first evidence in this direction was provided in the late 1970s by an innovative team of neuroanatomists who found that mental stimulation can compensate for loss of neurons.

According to the **plasticity model**, although some neurons die, the remaining ones continue to develop, and, in fact, some areas of the brain involved in complex language and word processing skills do not completely mature until middle age (Bartzokis et al., 2001). Research continues to accumulate supporting the notion of plasticity (Burke & Barnes, 2006), including studies on the value of diet and physical exercise as a way to maintain brain function (Pinilla, 2006) and, consequently, cognitive functioning (Dishman et al., 2006). Aerobic exercise in particular appears to be most beneficial in preserving and maximizing brain functioning (Colcombe et al., 2006).

Over the past 20 years, the increasing availability and sophistication of brain imaging methods, most importantly, magnetic resonance imaging (MRI) brain scans (the method used in Figure 4.8) has produced a wealth of new data about the impact of aging on the central nervous system. Normal aging seems to have its major effects on the prefrontal cortex, the area of the brain most involved in planning and the encoding of information into long-term memory (Hedden & Gabrieli, 2004). The hippocampus, the structure in the brain involved in consolidating memories, becomes smaller with increasing age in adulthood (Schiltz et al., 2006), although this decline is more pronounced in abnormal aging. These patterns of findings are interpreted as providing a neurological basis for the behavioral observations of changes in memory and attention in adulthood (Townsend, Adamo, & Haist, 2006).

Aging is also associated with changes in the frontal lobe in the form of abnormalities known as

FIGURE 4.8
Impact of Aerobic Exercise on Brain Functioning

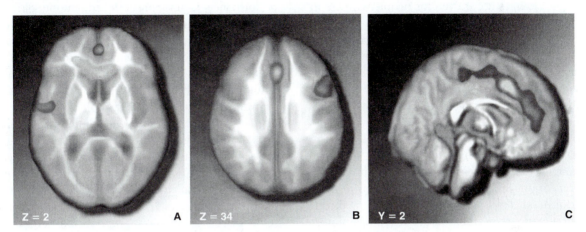

MRIs of the brains of older adults who engaged in an aerobic fitness training program compared with older adults who participated in a stretching and toning program. A and B show horizontal slices of the brain, and C shows a vertical slice. The dark areas indicate increased gray matter volume, and the lighter highlighted regions show increased white matter, all areas that help promote memory.

Source: Colcombe et al., 2006.

white matter hyperintensities (WMH). These abnormalities are thought to be made up of parts of deteriorating neurons. However, there is great variability among the older adult population, reflecting the probable inclusion of participants in studies of so-called normal aging who suffer from various abnormalities affecting their brain functioning (Raz & Rodrigue, 2006).

Sleep

The literature on sleep in adulthood clearly refutes a common myth about aging, namely, that as people grow older they need less sleep. Regardless of age, everyone requires seven to nine hours of sleep a night (Ancoli-Israel & Cooke, 2005). In fact, sleeping eight hours or more a night is associated with higher mortality risks, as is use of prescription sleeping pills (Kripke, Garfinkel, Wingard, Klauber, & Marler, 2002). However, changes in various aspects of sleep-related behavior and sleep problems can affect the mental and physical well-being of

the middle-aged and older adult (Moore, Adler, Williams, & Jackson, 2002). These changes relate in part to lifestyle as well as physiology. We all know how much more difficult it is to sleep when we are under stress. Middle-aged people living with high degrees of job-related stress, not surprisingly, also suffer sleep disturbances. Furthermore, hormonal changes, such as those associated with the menopause and somatopause affect the individual's sleep patterns throughout the adult years. Alcohol intake is another potentially negative factor affecting sleep patterns of older adults (Brower & Hall, 2001).

Changes in sleeping patterns emerge gradually in later adulthood. Older adults spend more time in bed relative to time spent asleep. They take longer to fall asleep, awaken more often during the night, lie in bed longer before rising, and have sleep that is shallower and more fragmented, meaning that it is less efficient. EEG sleep patterns show some corresponding age alterations, including a rise in Stage 1 sleep and a large decrease in both Stage 4 and REM (rapid eye movement) sleep (Kamel & Gammack, 2006). These changes occur even for people who are in excellent health.

Perhaps related to the changes in sleep is the fact that at some point in middle to later adulthood, people shift from a preference to working in the later hours of the day and night to a preference for the morning. As can be seen in Figure 4.9, older (over 65-year-old) adults tend to be "morning" people and the large majority of younger adults are "evening" people. The biological basis for this shift in preferences presumably occurs gradually throughout adulthood, along with changes in hormonal contributors to sleep and arousal patterns (Benloucif et al., 2006).

One intriguing implication of changes in circadian rhythm with age is that when studies of cognitive functioning take place at nonoptimal times of day, older adults perform relatively more poorly than do young adults tested at their off-peak times (Rowe, Valderrama, Hasher, & Lenartowicz, 2006). To the extent that cognitive researchers fail to take this into account, there is a systematic bias against the older participants. Interestingly, the effect of time of day on memory performance is less pronounced among older adults who engage in regular patterns of physical activity compared with their sedentary peers (Bugg, DeLosh, & Clegg, 2006).

Changes in sleep patterns in middle and later adulthood may be prevented or corrected by one or more alterations in sleep habits. A sedentary lifestyle is a major contributor to sleep problems at night; therefore, exercise (during the day) can improve sleep at night. A variety of psychological disorders and medical conditions can also interfere with the sleep of middle-aged and older adults (Riedel & Lichstein, 2000). Depression, anxiety, and bereavement are psychological causes of sleep disturbance. Medical conditions that disturb sleep include arthritis, osteoporosis, cancer, chronic lung disease, congestive heart failure, and digestive disturbances. People with Parkinson's disease or Alzheimer's disease also suffer serious sleep problems. Finally, the normal age-related changes that occur in the bladder lead to a more frequent urge to urinate during the night and thereby cause sleep interruptions. During menopause, hot flashes at night due to hormonal changes can cause breathing difficulties and lead to frequent awakenings. Periodic leg movements during sleep (also called nocturnal myoclonus) can awaken the individual. All of these conditions, when they interrupt sleep, can lead to daytime sleepiness and fatigue. A vicious cycle begins when the individual starts to establish a pattern of daytime napping, which increases the chances of sleep interruptions occurring at night (Foley et al., 2007).

One physical condition in particular that interferes with sleep at any age but is more prevalent in middle-aged and older adults is **sleep apnea**, also called sleep-related breathing disturbance. People with this condition experience a particular form of snoring in which

FIGURE 4.9
Age Differences in Circadian Rhythm

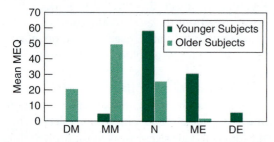

Scores on the morning-eveningness questionnaire show clear differences in circadian rhythm with greater percentages in older people who are "definitely morning" (DM) and "mostly morning" (MM) compared with younger persons, who tend more to be "mostly evening" (ME) and "definitely evening" (DE).

Source: Hasher, Goldstein, & May, 2005.

a partial obstruction in the back of the throat restricts airflow during inhalation. A loud snore is followed by a choking silence when breathing actually stops. When the airway closes, the lack of oxygen is registered by the respiratory control centers in the brain, and the sleeper awakens. There may be 100 such episodes a night, and to make up for the lack of oxygen that occurs during each one, the heart is forced to pump harder to circulate more blood. As a result, there are large spikes in blood pressure during the night as well as elevated blood pressure during the day. Over time, the person's risk of heart attack and stroke is increased. In addition, the individual experiences numerous periods of daytime sleepiness that interfere with everyday activities.

Although changes in sleep patterns occur as a normal feature of the aging process, severe sleep disturbances do not. Exercise can be helpful in resetting disturbed circadian rhythms (Van Someren, Lijzenga, Mirmiran, & Swaab, 1997). Sleep specialists can offer innovative approaches such as light therapy, which "resets" an out-of-phase circadian rhythm, and encouragement of improvements in sleep habits (Klerman, Duffy, Dijk, & Czeisler, 2001).

Temperature Control

It is standard news fare as parts of the country suffer extreme weather that older adults are at risk of dying from hyper- or hypothermia, conditions known together as **dysthermia**. In the 20-year period from 1979–1999, over 8,000 deaths occurred in the United States due to heat exposure (http://www.cdc.gov/nceh/hsb/extreme heat/). Over a similar period (1979–1998), a total of 13,970 deaths were attributed to hypothermia. The majority of deaths due to dysthermia occur in people over the age of 65, and the percentages rise sharply with each age decade. Most people

who die from hyperthermia have heart disease (Luber & Sanchez, 2006). (See Figure 4.10).

As shown in Figure 4.11, there are also increasing numbers of deaths due to hypothermia in older adults (Fallico, Siciliano, & Yip, 2005). The cause of the higher death rates under conditions of hypothermia may be an impaired ability of older adults to maintain their core body temperature during extremely cold outside temperatures (DeGroot & Kenney, 2007).

SENSATION AND PERCEPTION

A variety of changes occur in adulthood throughout the parts of the nervous system that affect sensation and perception. These changes reduce the quality of input that reaches the brain to be integrated in subsequent stages of information processing.

Vision

One of the major set of changes that people notice as they get older involves vision. Changes in vision take several forms. One is a loss of visual acuity, the ability to see details at a distance. The level of acuity in an 85-year-old individual is about 80% less than that of a person in their 40s. By raising the level of illumination, it is possible to compensate somewhat for this loss, but in dimly lit surroundings, older people have a great deal more trouble when they must observe details at a distance. On the other hand, after we reach the age of 40 years, we become increasingly sensitive to glare. As a result, making lights brighter may actually impair rather than improve our visual acuity.

The change that most affects people in midlife and beyond is **presbyopia**, which is the loss of the ability to focus vision on near objects. The cause of presbyopia is a thickening and hardening of the lens, the focusing mechanism of the eye,

FIGURE 4.10
Heat-related Deaths, United States

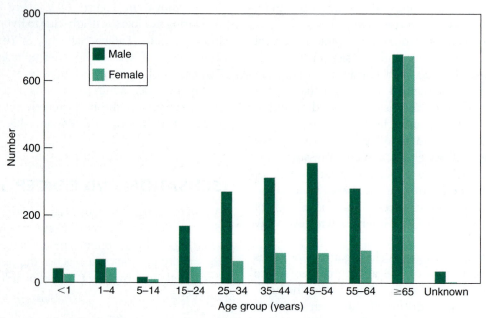

Number of heat-related deaths by sex and age group, United States, 1999–2003. The total number of deaths due to heat exposure during this period was 3,442.

Source: Luber & Sanchez, 2006.

(Strenk, Strenk, & Koretz, 2005). As a result, the lens cannot adapt its shape when needed. By the age of 50, presbyopia affects literally 100% of the population. There is no treatment for it other than to wear corrective lenses in the form of bifocals (Kasthurirangan & Glasser, 2006). However, we may be able to slow down the process. For example, smoking accelerates the aging of the lens (Kessel, Jorgensen, Glumer, & Larsen, 2006).

In addition to experiencing normal age-related changes in vision, we become increasingly susceptible to certain diseases as we age. About one-half of adults over the age of 65 years report that they have experienced some form of visual impairment. The most common impairment is a **cataract**, a clouding that develops in the lens. This results in blurred or distorted vision because

images cannot be focused clearly onto the retina. Actually, the term "cataract" reflects the previous view of this condition as a waterfall behind the eye that obscured vision.

Cataracts usually start as a slight cloudiness that progressively grows more opaque. They are usually white, but they may take on color such as yellow or brown. Cataracts seem to develop as a normal part of the aging process, but other than the fact that they are due to changes in the lens fibers, their cause is not known. Heredity, prior injury, and diabetes may play roles in causing cataract formation. Indicating perhaps its effects on the lens as mentioned earlier, cigarette smoking is another risk factor for the development of cataracts (Mukesh et al., 2006). Some evidence suggests that a high intake of carbohydrates may increase the probability of developing cataracts (Chiu, Milton, Gensler, & Taylor, 2006). Conversely, taking multivitamins may slow their formation (Milton, Sperduto, Clemons, & Ferris, 2006).

Cataracts are the main visual impairment experienced by older adults in surveys of self-reported health status, affecting about 25% of the over-65 population (Desai, Reidy, & Minassian, 1999). The development of cataracts occurs gradually over a period of years during which the individual's vision becomes increasingly blurred and distorted. If the cataracts have a yellow or brown tone, colors will take on a yellow tinge similar to the effect of wearing colored sunglasses. Vision becomes increasingly difficult both under conditions of low light, as acuity is reduced, and under conditions of bright light, due to increased susceptibility to glare. Bright lights may seem to have a halo around them. These are significant

limitations and can alter many aspects of the person's everyday life. It is more difficult to read, walk, watch television, recognize faces, and perform one's work, hobbies, and leisure activities. Consequently, people with cataracts may suffer a reduction in independence, as they find it more difficult to drive or even go out at night with others.

Despite the common nature of cataracts and their pervasive effect on vision, they need not significantly alter an older adult's life. Enormous strides have been made in the treatment of cataracts due to advances in surgical procedures. Currently, cataract surgery is completed in about an hour or less, under local anesthesia, and with no hospital stay. Visual recovery is achieved usually within one to seven days, and for many people vision is so improved that they rely only minimally on corrective lenses.

FIGURE 4.11
Cold-related Deaths, United States

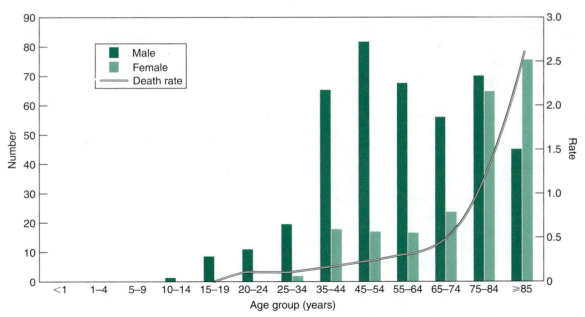

Number and rate, per 100,000 population of hypothermia-related deaths by age group and sex in the United States, 2002.
Source: Fallico, Siciliano, & Yip, 2005.

A second significant form of blindness that becomes more prevalent in later adulthood is **age-related macular degeneration**, one of the leading causes of blindness in those over the age of 65. An estimated 15% of people 80 and older have this disease (ONeill, Jamison, McCulloch, & Smith, 2001).

Age-related macular degeneration involves destruction of the photoreceptors located in the central region of the retina known as the macula, leaving dark or empty areas in the center of the afflicted individual's vision. This area of the retina is normally used in reading, driving, and other visually demanding activities so that the selective damage to the receptors in the macula that occurs with this disease is particularly incapacitating. There is no known treatment for this disorder. However, diet may play a role in prevention. People who eat diets high in omega-3 fatty acids (found in fish, for example), have a lower risk of developing age-related macular degeneration (Johnson & Schaefer, 2006). Conversely, cigarette smoking (once again) serves as a risk factor (Chakravarthy et al., 2007). Exposure to light is another risk factor, so wearing protective lenses may serve as prevention (de Jong, 2006).

Glaucoma is a group of conditions causing blindness. The most common type of glaucoma develops gradually and painlessly, without symptoms, meaning that it may not be detected until the disease reaches advanced stages. Eventually glaucoma causes a loss of peripheral vision and, over time, may cause the remaining vision to diminish altogether. More rarely the symptoms appear suddenly, including blurred vision, loss of side vision, perception of colored rings around lights, and experience of pain or redness in the eyes.

Glaucoma is the third most common cause of blindness in the United States, and the most common form of glaucoma is estimated to affect about 3 million Americans. It is diagnosed in 95,000 new patients each year. Blacks are at higher risk than whites, as are people who are nearsighted, have diabetes, or have a family history of glaucoma. Arthritis (Perruccio, Badley, & Trope, 2007) and obesity are additional risk factors (Cheung & Wong, 2007). Some forms of glaucoma can be controlled but not cured, and others can be treated successfully through surgery.

Hearing

Hearing loss is a common occurrence in later adulthood, as is shown in Table 4.1. The most common form of age-related hearing loss is **presbycusis** in which degenerative changes occur in the cochlea or auditory nerve leading from the cochlea to the brain. Presbycusis is most often associated with loss of high-pitched sounds. Fortunately, although hereditary factors play a role in presbycusis, we can take steps to protect ourselves because there are a number of environmental contributors. In one large study of older adults, smokers had a 68% greater chance of developing presbycusis (Helzner et al., 2005). Various health problems such as diabetes, heart disease, high blood pressure and the use of some medications such as aspirin and antibiotics can also put a person at higher risk. However,

TABLE 4.1
Hearing and Vision Problems by Age

Age Group (Years)	Hearing Trouble	Vision Trouble
18–44	8.2	5.5
45–64	19.2	11.2
65–74	30.4	13.2
75 years and older	48.1	22.0

Age-adjusted percentages of adults with hearing and vision trouble from the National Health Interview Survey, 2005.
Source: Pleis & Lethbridge-Cejku, 2006.

exposure to loud noise is the most frequent cause of presbycusis. The next time you turn up your iPod or go to a live rock concert, think about the long-term effects on your hearing. Although exposure to occupational noise used to place workers (mainly men) at risk for hearing loss, exposure to loud music now serves as the main risk factor.

Another hearing disturbance that is relatively common in older people is **tinnitus**, in which the individual perceives sounds in the head or ear (such as a ringing noise) when there is no external source for it. The condition can be temporarily associated with use of aspirin, antibiotics, and anti-inflammatory agents. Changes in the bones of the skull due to trauma and the buildup of wax in the ears may also contribute to tinnitus.

With the many improvements in hearing aids, much of the age-associated hearing loss can be corrected without needing to rely on an outwardly detectable device. These miniature devices, which are effectively invisible to the outside observer, considerably reduce the social stigma associated in many people's minds with the need to wear a hearing aid. In addition, certain communication strategies can be used by others to ensure that they are heard, such as avoiding interference, speaking in low tones, and facing the person while speaking.

Hearing loss clearly has an effect on the older adult's ability to engage in conversation (Murphy, Daneman, & Schneider, 2006). However, there are a variety of communication strategies we can use to be sure we are heard by a person with presbycusis. One is to face the person directly in a well-lit situation so that he or she can see your face. It is also important to avoid background noise such as a television or a radio in the room so there will be minimal interference from competing sources of sound. In restaurants and social gatherings, it is better to find a place to talk that is as far as possible from crowded or noisy areas. You should not be chewing food or gum. Rather than shouting, which increases interference with the speech signal, you should use a low, clear voice and be sure to enunciate carefully. It is especially important not to talk to the person as if he or she was a child. Similarly, you should not talk about the individual in the third person or leave the person out of the conversation altogether. Providing context is also useful. Most important, do not become frustrated or upset with the listener and try to maintain a positive and patient attitude.

FIGURE 4.12
Hearing Loss in Older Adults

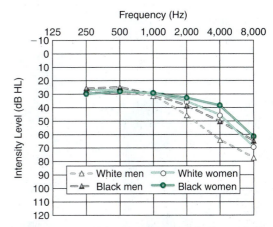

Mean hearing threshold levels by sex and race for the ear that has poorer hearing. The points in this figure represent the intensity level needed for sounds of various frequencies to be heard. The decrease is illustrated by the fact that louder levels of intensity are needed to be heard for sounds of increasingly higher pitch.

Source: Helzner et al., 2005.

Balance

As important as our senses are to our ability to enjoy the sights and sounds of our world, it is the sense of balance that can mean the difference between life and death, particularly for an older adult. Loss of balance is one of the main factors responsible for falls (Dickin, Brown,

FIGURE 4.13

Age-adjusted Rates of Nonfatal Falls in Men and Women, United States

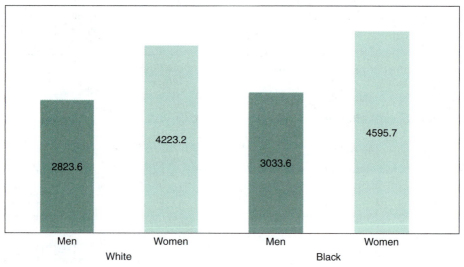

Age-adjusted rates, per 100,000 in the population by sex and race from nonfatal falls, United States.

Source: Stevens, Ryan, & Kresnow, 2006.

& Doan, 2006). In 2003 alone, more than 13,700 people 65 and older died from injuries related to falls; 1.8 million were treated in emergency departments for fall-related nonfatal injuries, and about 460,000 of these people were hospitalized (Stevens, Ryan, & Kresnow, 2006).

It is natural that people who have the painful and perhaps frightening experience of a fall become anxious the next time they are in a situation where they feel insecure; subsequently they become even more unsteady in their gait (Brown, Gage, Polych, Sleik, & Winder, 2002). The "fear of falling" or what is also called "low self-efficacy" about avoiding a fall can create a vicious cycle in which the older individual increasingly restricts her movements, further increasing the risk of losing strength.

Age-related alterations in the vestibular system that controls balance contribute to increased risk of falling in older adults (Jang, Hwang, Shin, Bae, & Kim, 2006; Moffat, Elkins, & Resnick, 2006). Older individuals have more difficulty detecting body position, leading them to be more likely to lose their balance or fail to see a step or an obstacle in their path on a level surface.

The two symptoms most frequently associated with age-related vestibular dysfunction are dizziness and vertigo. Dizziness is a feeling of lightheadedness and the sense that one is floating. **Vertigo** is a sense of movement when the body is actually at rest, usually the sense that one is spinning. Because the vestibular system is so intimately connected to other parts of the nervous system, symptoms of vestibular disturbance may also be experienced as problems such as headache, muscular aches in the neck and back, and increased sensitivity to noise and bright lights. Other problems can include fatigue, inability to concentrate, unsteadiness while walking, and difficulty with speech. Increased sensitivity to motion sickness is another common symptom. Some of these changes may come about with diseases that are not part of normal aging, and others may occur as the result of normative alterations in the vestibular receptors.

"What do you think?" | **4-4**

Can you balance for a minute on one foot holding onto the other foot behind you? If not, this is something you should work on to improve your own balance.

Older adults can be helped to compensate for factors that increase their chance of falling, such as receiving assisted practice in stepping (Hanke & Tiberio, 2006), strengthening the leg muscles (Takahashi, Takahashi, Nakadaira, & Yamamoto, 2006), and reducing medications taken for other conditions that can cause confusion or disorientation (Kannus, Uusi-Rasi, Palvanen, & Parkkari, 2005). Compensation for deficits or abnormalities of the vestibular system involves ensuring proper eyeglass prescriptions, use of a prosthetic aid in walking, outfitting the home with balance aids such as handrails, and developing greater sensitivity to the need to take care while walking. Balance training, including Tai Chi, can also be an effective preventative method to lessen the likelihood of falling (Taylor-Piliae, Haskell, Stotts, & Froelicher, 2006).

It is also important to correct for sensory losses in other areas that could contribute to faulty balance. The proper eyeglass prescription is obviously very crucial because vision provides important cues to navigating the environment. Older adults with uncorrected visual problems are more vulnerable to falls (Vitale, Cotch, & Sperduto, 2006). Second, an older individual with vestibular problems can obtain an aid to balance such as a walking stick and learn how to use it. In the home, it is important to find ways to substitute sitting for standing in situations that might pose a risk. For example, a shower chair or bath bench can be used in the tub, and a handheld

shower head can be installed. The individual can also get used to sitting while performing ordinary grooming tasks around the bathroom. This further reduces the need to maintain balance while engaging in delicate operations such as shaving. Similar adaptations can be made in the kitchen, such as sitting down rather than standing at the counter to cut vegetables. Having multiple telephones in the home is another useful strategy so that it is not necessary to run (and possibly fall) when trying to answer a phone in another room.

In addition to such practical remedies, older individuals can learn to develop greater sensitivity to the need to be careful when moving from one floor surface to another, such as stepping onto a tile floor from a carpet. This type of adjustment is particularly important when the individual is in an unfamiliar environment. Similarly, the individual should develop the habit of waiting a minute or two when getting up from a horizontal position. Reminding oneself of the need to use railings on stairways is another useful adjustment, or if there is no railing, using the wall for balance when moving up or down the stairs.

Smell and Taste

We are able to enjoy our food due to the operation of the taste buds, which are responsible for the sense of gustation, with the assistance of the smell receptors, which are responsible for the sense of olfaction. Smell and taste belong to the chemical sensing system referred to as chemosensation. The sensory receptors in these systems are triggered when molecules released by the substances around us stimulate special cells in the nose, mouth, or throat. Despite the fact that the olfactory receptors constantly replace themselves, the area of the olfactory epithelium shrinks with age, and ultimately the total number of receptors becomes reduced throughout the adult years. At birth, the olfactory epithelium covers a wide area of the upper nasal cavities, but by the 20s and 30s, its area has started to shrink noticeably.

Approximately one-quarter of all older adults suffer some form of olfactory impairment (Murphy et al., 2002). The loss of olfactory receptors reflects intrinsic changes associated with the aging process, as well as damage caused by disease, injury, and exposure to toxins. In fact, these environmental toxins may play a larger role than changes due to the aging process. Chronic diseases, medications, and sinus problems may be a more significant source of impairment over the life span (Rawson, 2006).

We come next to a major source of interference with taste and smell, and that is tobacco smoke. Although people who quit smoking eventually experience an improvement in their sense of smell, this can take many years (equal to the number of years spent smoking).

Dentures are another cause of loss of taste sensitivity because these may block the receptor cells of the taste buds.

Cognitive changes also appear to be associated with loss of smell sensitivity (Wang et al., 2002). In fact, older adults who have experienced the greatest impairment in cognitive functioning may be the most vulnerable to loss of odor identification abilities. In one longitudinal study following older adults over a 3-year period, people with the most rapid decline in cognitive processes had the greatest rate of decline on the ability to label various odors (Wilson, Arnold, Tang, & Bennett, 2006).

Although there is nothing you can do to reverse age-related losses of smell and taste, once they occur, people who suffer from severe losses may benefit from medical evaluations and treatments for underlying conditions (Forde, Cantau, Delahunty, & Elsner, 2002). Apart from such interventions, older people can also take advantage of strategies to enhance the enjoyment of food, such as expanding their food choices, planning meals in pleasant environments, and finding good dining companions!

Somatosensory System

We are able to move around in our environment through the operation of our somatosensory system, which translates information about touch, temperature, and position to our nervous system. Bodily position is made possible by proprioception, which provides information about where the limbs are placed when we are standing still. Kinesthesis applies to the knowledge that receptors in the limbs provide when the body is moving. Through proprioception, you would know that you are poised at the top of a staircase, ready to take your first step downward, and through kinesthesis you would know that you are actually moving down those stairs.

Touch.   There is a well-established body of evidence linking loss of the ability to discriminate touch with the aging process throughout adulthood. Age differences have been documented in such areas as the ability to discriminate the separation of two points of pressure on the skin and the detection of the location of a stimulus applied to the skin. One estimate places the loss at 1% per year over the years from 20 to 80. However, the rate of loss varies by body part. The hands and feet are particularly subject to the effects of aging compared with areas located more centrally, such as the lip and tongue. These losses can compromise the adult's ability to grasp, maintain balance, perform delicate handwork, and can even interfere with speech (Wickremaratchi & Llewelyn, 2006).

Pain.   The question of whether older adults are more or less sensitive to pain is a topic of considerable concern for health practitioners. Changes in pain perception with age could make life either much harder or much easier

FIGURE 4.14

Prevalence of Chronic Back Pain by Age

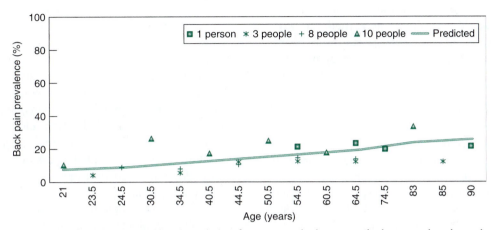

Prevalence of chronic back pain by age. The solid line shows the best-fitting curve to the data points. The data points show the number of people.

Source: Dionne, Dunn, & Croft, 2006.

for individuals with illnesses (such as arthritis) that cause chronic pain. There is no evidence that older adults become somehow immune or at least protected from pain by virtue of age changes in this sensory system. Lower back pain, the most common form of chronic pain, is experienced as a chronic symptom in approximately 10.5 million or 30% of all older adults. An additional 5 million older adults suffer from chronic neck pain (Lethbridge-Cejku, Rose, & Vickerie, 2006). Although benign back pain shows a decrease across adulthood, back pain that is more severe and disabling increases in the later years (Dionne, Dunn, & Croft, 2006). Most older adults are able to maintain their daily functioning despite the presence of chronic pain, but as we would expect, the pain makes it more difficult for them to carry out their everyday activities (Hartvigsen, Frederiksen, & Christensen, 2006).

In addition to being a limitation in an individual's everyday life, the experience of pain can also interfere with cognitive performance. In one sample of over 300 older adults, poorer performance on tests of memory and spatial abilities was observed among individuals who suffered from chronic lower back pain (Weiner, Rudy, Morrow, Slaboda, & Lieber, 2006). This finding is of interest in its own right, but should be kept in mind when evaluating studies of cognitive performance in older adults when researchers do not control for chronic pain.

Psychological factors may also interact with the experience of pain in older adults. One reason that symptoms of benign pain may be diminished in older, compared to middle-aged, adults is that the older adults have become habituated to the daily aches and pains associated with changes in their bones, joints, and muscles. It is also possible that cohort factors interact with intrinsic age changes to alter the likelihood that complaints about pain will be expressed. The experience of pain is associated with the personality trait of stoicism (the tendency to suffer in silence) (Yong, 2006). Older adults may simply not wish to admit to others, or even themselves, that they are feeling some of those aches and pains.

In summary, changes in physical functioning have important interactions with psychological and sociocultural factors, and can influence the individual's identity in the middle and later years of adulthood. Fortunately, there are many preventative and compensating steps that people can take to slow the rate of physical aging.

SUMMARY

1. Appearance is an important part of our identities, and throughout adulthood, changes in the components of appearance all undergo change. Many age changes in the skin are the result of photoaging. The hair thins and becomes gray, and in men in particular, baldness can develop. There are significant changes in body build, including loss of height, increase of body weight to the 50s followed by a decrease, and changes in fat distribution. However, adults of all ages can benefit from exercise, which can maintain muscle and lower body fat.

2. Mobility reflects the quality of the muscles, bones, and joints. The process of sarcopenia involves loss of muscle mass, and there is a corresponding decrease in muscle strength. Strength training is the key to maintaining maximum muscle functioning in adulthood. Bones lose mineral content throughout adulthood, particularly in women. Diet and exercise are important areas of prevention. The joints encounter many deleterious changes, and exercise cannot prevent these, but middle-aged and older adults can benefit from flexibility training, which maintains range of motion even in joints that are damaged.

3. The cardiovascular system undergoes changes due to alterations in the heart muscle and arteries that lower aerobic capacity, cardiac output, and maximum heart rate. It is crucial for adults to avoid harmful fats in the diet and to engage in a regular pattern of aerobic exercise to minimize changes in the cardiovascular system. The respiratory system loses functioning due to stiffening of lung tissue. The most important preventive action is to avoid (or quit) cigarette smoking. Changes in the urinary system make the kidney more vulnerable to stress and less able to metabolize toxins, including medications. The bladder of older adults becomes less able to retain and expel urine, but the majority of people do not become incontinent. Behavioral methods can correct normal age-related changes in urinary control. The digestive system becomes somewhat less efficient in older adults, but there is not a significant loss of functioning. Many older people are misinformed by the media and take unnecessary corrective medications to control their gastrointestinal functioning.

4. The endocrine system is the site of many changes in the amount and functioning of the body's hormones. The climacteric is the period of gradual loss of reproductive abilities. After menopause, women experience a reduction in estrogen. Decreases in testosterone level in older men are not consistently observed. Changes in the immune system, referred to as immune senescence, are observed primarily in a decline in T-cell functioning. Diet and exercise can counteract loss of immune responsiveness in older adults.

5. Normal age-related changes in the nervous system were once thought of as neuronal fallout, but it is now recognized that there is much plasticity in the aging brain. Brain scans reveal considerable variation in age-related alterations in brain structure. There is a rise in Stage 1 and a decrease in Stage 4 and REM (dream-related) sleep. Changes in circadian rhythms lead older adults to awake earlier and

prefer the morning for working. Poor sleep habits and the coexistence of psychological or physical disorders (such as sleep apnea) can interfere further with the sleep patterns of middle-aged and older adults. In many cases, dysthermia is related to the presence of disease.

6. Visual acuity decreases across adulthood, and presbyopia leads to a loss of the ability to focus the eye on near objects. Cataracts, age-related macular degeneration, and glaucoma are medical conditions that can lead to reduced vision or blindness. Presbycusis can interfere with the ability to communicate. Older adults are more vulnerable to loss of balance, particularly when they suffer from dizziness and vertigo. Balance training can compensate for these changes. Smell and taste show some losses with age, but both senses are extremely vulnerable to negative effects from disease and environmental damage. Findings on pain are inconclusive. There is loss of the perception of the position of the feet and legs, adding to other age-related changes in balance.

CHAPTER 5

Health and Prevention

> **"**Do not try to live forever, you will not succeed.**"**
>
> George Bernard Shaw
> (1856–1950)

Chronic illnesses can significantly interfere with the quality of our daily life. In addition, they can present complicating factors in the diagnosis and treatment of psychological disorders among older adults. These illnesses are cases of secondary aging and, as pointed out in Chapter 1, need to be distinguished from primary aging because they are not an inherent part of the aging process.

In this chapter, we will look at the major physical diseases that affect older adults. We also examine the set of conditions known as dementia in which individuals suffer cognitive changes due to neurological damage and diseases that may become prevalent in later life. Although all of these conditions have the potential to be highly disabling, individuals can take advantage of many preventative strategies starting early in the adult years.

DISEASES OF THE CARDIOVASCULAR SYSTEM

Cardiovascular diseases affect the heart and arteries. Because the distribution of blood throughout the body is essential for the normal functioning of all other organ systems, diseases in this system can have widespread effects on health and everyday life.

Cardiac and Cerebrovascular Conditions

In the normal aging process, as described in Chapter 4, fat and other substances accumulate

TABLE 5.1
Prevalence of Chronic Health Conditions by Age and Sex

Condition		25–44	45–64	65–74	75–84	85+
Heart disease	Males	3.7	13.4	33.1	42.4	42.9
	Females	5.3	11.6	22.4	31.8	36.9
Hypertension	Males	9.4	30.8	47.1	51.2	41.9
	Females	8.5	29.6	51.1	59.5	54.6
Stroke	Males	0.4	2.6	8.3	11.8	15.4
	Females	0.6	2.2	6.1	9.9	14.6
Chronic bronchitis	Males	2.1	2.9	4.5	5.1	n.a.
	Females	4.2	6.7	7.7	7.1	4.7
Arthritis	Males	7.5	25.3	39.9	47.2	45.9
	Females	11.3	33.5	51.8	57.6	60.4
Diabetes	Males	2.1	10.3	21.3	17.9	13.5
	Females	2.5	8.8	15.4	16	11.6

This table shows the prevalence of the major chronic health conditions faced by older adults in the United States broken down by age group and sex.
Source: Centers for Disease Control and Prevention, 2007a.

in the walls of the arteries throughout the body. In the disease known as **atherosclerosis** (from the Greek words *athero* meaning paste and *sclerosis* meaning hardness), these deposits collect at an abnormally high rate, to the point that they substantially reduce the width of the arteries. **Arteriosclerosis** is a general term for the thickening and hardening of arteries, a condition that also occurs to some degree in normal aging. **Atherogenesis** is the term that refers to stimulation and acceleration of atherosclerosis. Many people live with atherosclerosis and do not encounter significant health problems. However, the progressive buildup of plaque that occurs with this disease may eventually lead to partial or total blockage of the blood's flow through an artery. The organs or tissues that are fed by that

artery will then suffer serious damage due to the lack of blood supply. When this occurs in the arteries that feed the heart muscle, the condition becomes known as **coronary artery disease** (or **coronary heart disease**). A **myocardial infarction** occurs when the blood supply to part of the heart muscle (the myocardium) is severely reduced or blocked.

Hypertension is the term given to the disease in which the individual chronically suffers from blood pressure that is greater than or equal to the value of 140 mm Hg systolic pressure and 90 mm Hg diastolic pressure (systolic and diastolic refer to blood pressure at the stages of the heart during contraction and at rest, respectively). Changes in the arteries associated with atherosclerosis are thought to be due to the damaging effects of

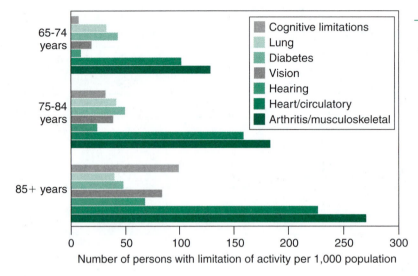

Although chronic diseases are prevalent among older adults, the majority of older adults do not experience major limitations in their activities.

Source: Centers for Disease Control and Prevention, 2006.

FIGURE 5.1

Activity Limitations due to Chronic Health Conditions in Older Adults, 2003–2004, United States

hypertension. The fact that a person's blood pressure is virtually always elevated means that the blood is constantly putting strain on the walls of the arteries. Eventually, the arterial walls develop areas of weakness and inflammation, particularly in the large arteries where the pressure is greatest. Damage to the walls of the arteries makes them vulnerable to the accumulation of substances that form plaques. Furthermore, hypertension increases the workload on the heart, which is forced to pump harder than it otherwise would. Consequently, people with hypertension are more likely to develop hypertrophy (overgrowth) of the left ventricle of the heart. It is estimated that as a result of this damage to the circulatory system, adults with even mild levels of hypertension have a greater likelihood of dying from cardiovascular disease (Bowman, Sesso, & Gaziano, 2006).

Congestive heart failure (or heart failure) is a condition in which the heart is unable to pump enough blood to meet the needs of the body's other organs. Blood flows out of the heart at a slower and slower rate, causing the blood returning to the heart through the veins to back up. Eventually the tissues become congested with fluid. This condition can result from coronary artery disease, scar tissue from a past myocardial infarction, hypertension, disease of the heart valves, disease of the heart muscle, infection of the heart, or heart defects present at birth. People experiencing this condition are unable to exert themselves without becoming short of breath and exhausted. They develop a condition known as edema, in which fluid builds up in their bodies, causing their legs to swell. They may also experience fluid buildup in their lungs along with kidney problems.

The term "cerebrovascular disease" refers to the disorders of the circulation to the brain. This condition may lead to the onset of a **cerebrovascular accident**, also known as a "stroke" or "brain attack," an acute condition in which an artery leading to the brain bursts or is clogged by a blood clot or other particle. The larger the area in the brain that is deprived of blood, the more severe the deterioration of the physical and mental functions controlled by that area. Another condition caused by the

FIGURE 5.2

Buildup of a Plaque Inside an Artery

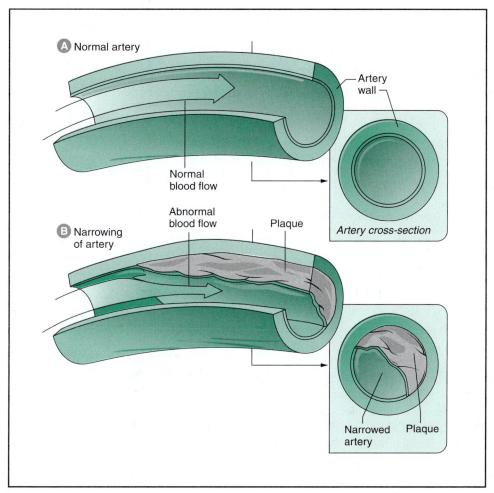

Plaque is made up of fat, cholesterol, calcium, and other substances found in the blood. As it grows, the buildup of plaque narrows the inside of the artery and, in time, may restrict blood flow. The illustration shows a normal artery with normal blood flow (Figure A) and an artery containing plaque buildup (Figure B).

development of clots in the cerebral arteries is a **transient ischemic attack (TIA)**, also called a ministroke. The cause of a TIA is the same as that of a stroke, but in a TIA, the blockage of the artery is temporary. The tissues that were deprived of blood soon recover, but the chances are that another TIA will follow. People who have had a TIA are also at higher risk of subsequently suffering from a stroke.

Incidence Rates

Heart disease is the number one killer in the United States, resulting in 28% of all deaths in the year 2003 (Heron & Smith, 2007). However,

TABLE 5.2

Causes of Death by Age and Sex, 2003 United States

Sex	Age Group (Years)	Heart Disease	Stroke	Cancer	Lung Disease
Male	25–44	13.6	1.9	10.1	0.0
	45–64	26.9	3.3	29.0	3.0
	65–74	28.3	4.6	33.6	6.6
	75+	32.6	7.0	21.4	6.4
Female	25–44	11.5	3.2	23.2	1.1
	45–64	18.0	4.2	39.5	4.4
	65–74	22.9	5.5	34.9	8.0
	75+	32.9	9.4	15.3	5.2

The risk of death varies by age group and sex.
Source: Heron & Smith, 2007.

because deaths occur disproportionately in the population, with over half of all deaths occurring in people 75 years and older, it is technically more correct to say that heart disease is the number one killer among this segment of the population.

Together, heart and cerebrovascular disease accounted for 39% of all deaths in the United States (among people over the age of 65 in the year 2003) and about 36% of the 65 plus population in Canada (Canadian Institutes of Health Research, 2006; Heron & Smith, 2007). As can be seen in Figure 5.3, however, there are substantial variations by sex and race in the risk of dying from cerebrovascular disease.

Worldwide, coronary heart disease was the leading cause of death in 2002, amounting to 7.2 million deaths or nearly one-third of all deaths around the globe. Another 5.5 million per year die from cerebrovascular disease. The countries with the highest numbers of death from heart disease in 2002 were China, Russia, and India (Mackay & Mensah, 2006; Rosamond et al., 2007).

FIGURE 5.3

Death Rates (adjusted for age) for Stroke Among Persons Aged Less Than 75 Years by Race and Age Group—United States, 2002

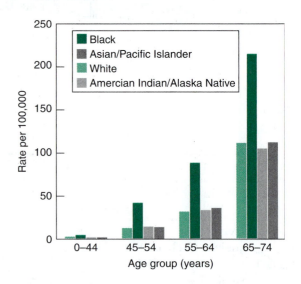

This figure shows age-adjusted death rates for stroke. Blacks have an elevated risk for stroke at all ages (http://www.cdc.gov/mmwr/preview/mmwrhtml/mm5419a2.htm).

Behavioral Risk Factors

Understanding the contribution of lifestyle factors to heart disease is one of the most heavily researched topics in the biomedical sciences. The positive side of this research is the fact that although the genetics behind these conditions cannot be controlled, behavioral risk factors are potentially within the individual's control.

What lifestyle choices can people make to reduce their risk of developing heart disease? There are essentially four areas of lifestyle choices, many of which we have seen in the context of the normal age-related changes discussed in Chapter 4. Here we will see how these factors play out in terms of raising or lowering the individual's risk in this particular area of functioning.

"What do you think?"	*5-1*

Do you know people who have one or more of these diseases? How are their lives affected?

A sedentary lifestyle is the first major risk factor for heart disease. Unfortunately, the majority of adults at highest risk for heart disease (i.e., those 75 and older) are the least likely to exercise. As can be seen from Figure 5.4, 78% of those 65 to 74 and 88% of those 75 and older do not engage in any vigorous leisure activity (Pleis & Lethbridge-Cejku, 2006). The relationship between leisure activity and heart disease is well established, with estimates ranging from a 24% reduction in the risk of myocardial infarction among nonstrenuous exercisers to a 47% reduced risk among individuals engaging in a regular pattern of strenuous exercise (Lovasi et al., 2007).

The second risk factor for heart disease is smoking. Although it is not known exactly why smoking increases the risk of heart disease, most researchers believe that smoking damages the arteries, making them more vulnerable to plaque formation. Approximately one-fifth of all adults in the United States are current smokers. The rates of current smokers decrease across age groups of adults from rates of 26% of those under 65 to 9.2% of those 65 to 74 and 4.7% of those 75 and older (Pleis & Lethbridge-Cejku, 2006). It is very possible that the smoking rates decrease not only because older adults are less likely to smoke but also because the nonsmokers are more likely to survive.

Body weight is the third risk factor for cardiovascular disease. In one study of over 8,300 adults in the United States, among those with the highest risk of developing cardiovascular disease over a 10-year period, 61% were overweight (Ajani, Ford, & McGuire, 2006). According to the CDC, dramatic increases in overweight and obesity have occurred among United States adults over the past 20 years. Currently 30.3% of the United States population is considered obese by government standards. According to the International Organization for Economic Development, this is the highest percent in the world (Organisation for Economic Co-operation and Development, 2007).

The importance of BMI as a factor predicting health status extends beyond cardiovascular disease, as will be seen throughout this chapter. In addition to its relationship to a variety of chronic diseases, a high BMI is associated with declines in perceived health over time. A longitudinal study of nearly 8,000 adults in their 50s revealed that people with high BMIs (30–35) were more likely to experience decreases in a measure of health-related quality of life. In addition to the impact on actual and subjective health, a high BMI was also associated with declines in mobility (Damush, Stump, & Clark, 2002). The increased weight carried around by a person with a high BMI places more burden on the lower extremities.

FIGURE 5.4

Percent of U.S. Population Engaging in Vigorous Leisure Activity, 2005

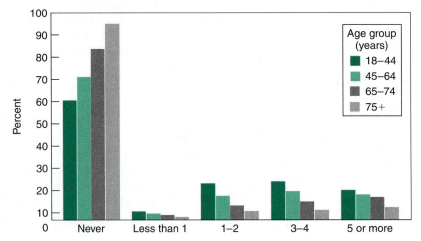

Percent of adults in the U.S. population by age according to number of times per week engaging in vigorous leisure activity.

Source: Pleis & Lethbridge-Cejku, 2006.

Although a high BMI is associated with increased risk of heart disease in middle and later adulthood, people with high BMIs in childhood and young adulthood are not necessarily at higher risk of developing cardiovascular disease. A study of nearly 15,000 young people in Great Britain revealed no association between early BMI and the later development of either cardiovascular disease or stroke (Lawlor et al., 2006). These findings are encouraging because they mean that even if you were overweight or obese as a child or teen, you can still engage in preventive behaviors now to lower your risk of developing these diseases.

Variations in stroke rates by race/ethnicity, social class, and poverty have emerged as causes of national concern in the United States (Casper et al., 2003). The southeast of the United States constitutes a "stroke belt" due, most likely, to the high consumption of sodium, monounsaturated fatty acids, polyunsaturated fatty acids and cholesterol, and the low consumption of dietary fiber (see Figure 5.5).

Combining these risk factors for cardiovascular disease is the concept of **metabolic syndrome**, which involves high levels of abdominal obesity, abnormal levels of blood cholesterol (low "good" cholesterol or HDL and high "bad" cholesterol or LDL), hypertension, insulin resistance, high blood fats (known as triglycerides), high levels of C-reactive proteins in the blood (an indication of inflammation), and the presence of coronary plaques. The metabolic syndrome is increasing with alarming speed in the United States, where it is estimated that almost half of the population possesses three or more of its unhealthy traits (Smith, 2007). Ironically, then, as the population becomes healthier in terms of decreasing the amount of cigarette smoking, we have become unhealthier in terms of this potentially deadly syndrome.

The fourth risk factor for cardiovascular disease is alcohol intake. This has been a controversial matter, with evidence accumulating pro and con about how much alcohol is "good" and how much is "bad." It is difficult to separate

FIGURE 5.5

Stroke Rates by State, United States 2005

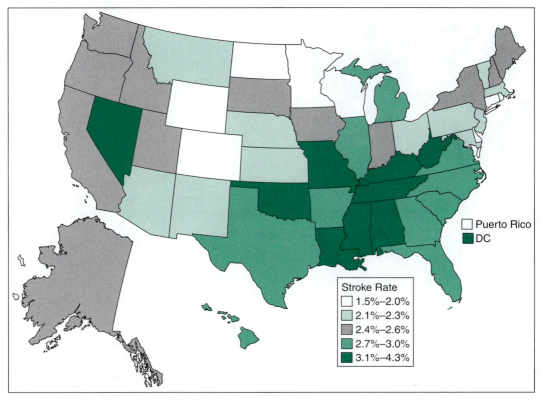

Stroke Rate
☐ 1.5%–2.0%
☐ 2.1%–2.3%
☐ 2.4%–2.6%
☐ 2.7%–3.0%
■ 3.1%–4.3%

☐ Puerto Rico
■ DC

*Age adjusted to the 2000 U.S. standard population of adults.

The "stroke belt" can be seen in this map as the Southeastern portion of the United States where stroke rates are highest.

Source: Centers for Disease Control and Prevention, 2007b.

the effect of alcohol intake from the effect of diet (Barbaste et al., 2002). However, it seems that moderate alcohol consumption has a protective effect on the risk of cardiovascular disease (Byles, Young, Furuya, & Parkinson, 2006; Vasdev, Gill, & Singal, 2006). Beyond that point, heavy alcohol intake (more than 60 grams of alcohol or 2 beers or 2 glasses of wine a day) may be associated with increased stroke risk (Reynolds et al., 2003).

Negative emotions also play a role in mediating the relationship between social class and health. People with low socioeconomic status

(SES) are more likely to experience negative emotions and perceptions of the world. Their lower SES means that they are exposed to more stressful situations which in turn create more negative views of the world. These views, in turn, make them more vulnerable to negative health outcomes (Gallo & Matthews, 2003). Ethnicity may also interact with emotions in affecting illness. For example, in a study comparing Eastern Europeans with Americans of European descent, negative affect was found to increase the risk of arthritis in Eastern Europeans only. When comparing African Americans with Caribbeans,

Southern fried chicken may look and taste good, but it is one of the factors contributing to high stroke rates.

negative emotion had a greater impact among African Americans (Consedine, Magai, Cohen, & Gillespie, 2002).

National differences in risk of heart disease, as well as other major illness, are also apparent when comparing the United States with other countries. Eastern European countries, such as Russia, Bulgaria, Romania, and Poland have the highest death rates from cardiovascular disease (Rosamond et al., 2007). However, the United States ranks high on the list of heart disease rates around the world. An international team of researchers comparing large national studies in the United States and England found that although social class is related to incidence of chronic disease in both countries, the United States has higher rates of the six major chronic diseases associated with mortality (Banks, Marmot, Oldfield, & Smith, 2006).

Prevention of Heart Disease and Stroke

Ultimately, the success of the vast research enterprise on the causes of heart disease will rest on its ability to provide the public with safe and effective medical or dietary supplements to lower cardiovascular death rates. Drugs called statins, which lower the levels of harmful cholesterol in the blood, help people maintain low levels of cholesterol which, combined with control of diet, can significantly reduce their risk of heart disease (Davignon & Leiter, 2005). However, the simplest and cheapest measures that people can take to protect against heart disease involve diet and exercise. As noted in Chapter 1, eating fruits and vegetables significantly lowers mortality; this benefit on mortality is mainly due to the reduction of cardiovascular disease (Bazzano, 2006). Researchers also advocate the

FIGURE 5.6

Chronic Disease in the United States and England

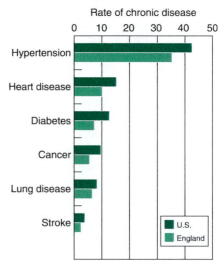

Controlling for a variety of risk factors, including socioeconomic status, researchers have found that rates of chronic disease are higher in the United States than in England.

Source: Banks, Marmot, Oldfield, & Smith, 2006.

ASSESS YOURSELF: Why Exercise?

Everybody exercises for different reasons and in different ways. Please answer these questions about your exercise and health prevention patterns. What do your answers say about your chances of maintaining your health as you get older?

1. I go out of my way to exercise at least:
   A. 4 times a week or more.
   B. 1–3 times a week.
   C. 1 time a week.
   D. Less than 1 time a week.

2. What is the main reason you exercise (or if you don't exercise, what would be the main reason you would exercise if you did):
   A. To look attractive to others.
   B. To look attractive for my own self-esteem.
   C. To keep myself healthy.
   D. To hang out with my friends.

3. When you exercise (or if you were to exercise), what part of your body would be of most concern for you to work on?
   A. Arms
   B. Chest
   C. Abdomen
   D. Thighs
   E. Buttocks

4. My exercise workout includes weights:
   A. all of the time.
   B. most of the time.
   C. sometimes.
   D. hardly ever.

5. You have just joined a local gym and are about to go to work out when a friend calls and asks if you would rather see a movie. What are you likely to do?
   A. Go to the gym anyway.
   B. Go to the movie with your friend.

6. When you know you will be outside during the day for more than a few minutes, do you:
   A. Put on sunblock.
   B. Not do anything special.

7. With regard to your eating patterns
   A. I avoid eating high fat foods such as bacon, sausage, or donuts.
   B. I enjoy eating junk food, even though I know it's no good for me.
   C. I don't pay much attention to what I eat.

Exercise can significantly reduce a person's chance of developing heart disease and other illnesses in adulthood.

benefits of the "Mediterranean diet," which is high in minimally processed fruits, vegetables, nuts, seeds, grains, olive oil, and fruits, low amounts of red meat and dairy foods, and low to moderate amounts of wine (Serra-Majem, Roman, & Estruch, 2006). Finally, exercise is a vital component of all preventive programs aimed at reducing the prevalence of heart disease (Marcus et al., 2006).

Of course, it is not only the availability of preventive treatments that counts. People have to be motivated to engage in these preventive measures and to maintain their motivation throughout any program of dietary improvements or exercise. The field of behavioral medicine is increasingly addressing these concerns, particularly as they apply to preventive and treatment measures for older adults (Siegler, Bastian, Steffens, Bosworth, & Costa, 2002).

CANCER

Cancer is a generic term for a group of more than 100 different diseases. Each type of cancer has its own symptoms, characteristics, treatment options, and overall effect on a person's life and health. In 2006, it was estimated that about 1.3 million Americans received a diagnosis of cancer (not including skin cancer or noninvasive cancers) and that about 10.5 million are living with the disease (United States Cancer Statistics Working Group, 2006). The lifetime risk of developing cancer is about 1 in 2 for men and 1 in 3 for women (American Cancer Society, 2006). Skin cancer is the most prevalent type of cancer in the United States, with about one million new cases occurring each year. However, lung cancer is the most frequent cause of death; in 2002 it accounted for more deaths than breast cancer, prostate cancer, and colon cancer combined (United States Cancer Statistics Working Group, 2005).

Risk Factors and Prevention

All cancer is genetically caused in the sense that it reflects damage to the genes that control cell replication. Some damage is associated with genetic mutations linked to an inherited tendency for developing cancer, most often involving breast and colon cancer. About 5% of women with breast cancer have a hereditary form of this disease. Similarly, close relatives of a person with colorectal cancer are themselves at greater risk, particularly if it has affected many people within the extended family. However, most cancer is not of the inherited variety. Instead, cancer develops when random mutations occur that cause the body's cells to malfunction. The mutations develop either as a mistake in cell division or in response to injuries from environmental agents such as radiation or chemicals.

Most cancers become more prevalent with increasing age in adulthood because age is associated with greater cumulative exposure to harmful toxins (carcinogens) in the environment. Lifestyle also plays a vital part. The three greatest lifestyle risk factors for the development of cancer during adulthood are exposure to the sun, cigarette smoking, and lack of control over diet.

Skin cancer, the most common form of cancer in adults, is directly linked to exposure to ultraviolet (UV) radiation from the sun. In the United States, for example, melanoma is more common in Texas than it is in Minnesota, because the levels of UV radiation from the sun are stronger in the south. Around the world, the highest rates of skin cancer are found in South Africa and Australia, areas that receive high amounts of UV radiation. Even artificial sources of UV radiation, such as sunlamps and tanning booths, can cause skin cancer despite the claims that the manufacturers make about their safety.

"What do you think?"	5-2
How might public health efforts be better directed at reducing the risk for cancer in this country?	

Cigarette smoking is the next greatest health risk, and in many ways it is more dangerous than UV exposure because the forms of cancer that are related to cigarettes are more likely to be lethal than skin cancer typically is. It is known that most lung cancer is caused by cigarette smoking, and exposure to cigarette smoke is a risk factor for developing cancers of the mouth, throat, esophagus, larynx, bladder, kidney, cervix, pancreas, and stomach. The risk of lung cancer begins to diminish as soon as a person quits smoking. People who have had lung cancer and stop smoking are less likely to

get a second lung cancer than are patients who continue to smoke. Exposure to cigarette smoke ("secondhand smoke") can be just as great a risk, if not greater, for lung cancer.

Diet is the third risk factor for cancer. A nationwide study of over 900,000 adults in the United States who were studied prospectively (before they had cancer) from 1982 to 1998 played in important role in identifying the role of diet. During this period of time, there were over 57,000 deaths within the sample from cancer. The people with the highest BMIs had death rates from cancer that were 52% higher for men and 62% higher for women compared with men and women of normal BMI. The types of cancer associated with higher BMIs included cancer of the esophagus, colon and rectum, liver, gallbladder, pancreas, and kidney. Significant trends of increasing risk with higher BMI's were observed for death from cancers of the stomach and prostate in men and for death from cancers of the breast, uterus, cervix, and ovary in women (Calle, Rodriguez, Walker-Thurmond, & Thun, 2003). We can conclude from this study that maintaining a low BMI is a critical preventive step in lowering your risk of cancer.

Not only BMI but eating specific foods seems to play a role in helping to prevent cancer. Stomach cancer is more common in parts of the world—such as Japan, Korea, parts of Eastern Europe, and Latin America—in which people eat foods that are preserved by drying, smoking, salting, or pickling. By contrast, fresh foods, especially fresh fruits and vegetables, may help protect against stomach cancer. Similarly, the risk of developing colon cancer is thought to be higher in people whose diet is high in fat, low in fruits and vegetables, and low in high-fiber foods such as whole-grain breads and cereals. For instance New Zealand and the United States have the higher rates of colon cancer and also consume the largest amount of meat

FIGURE 5.7
Age-adjusted Cancer Death Rates, Males by Site, United States, 1930–2003

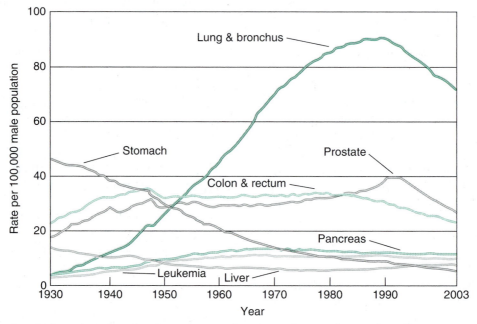

As can be seen from this figure, deaths due to lung disease among men have decreased since reaching a peak in 1990.

Source: American Cancer Society, 2006.

(http://press2.nci.nih.gov/sciencebehind/cancer/cancer57.htm).

In addition to these three general risk factors, there are other specific types of experiences that seem to make certain people more vulnerable to cancer. Environmental toxins such as pesticides, electromagnetic fields, engine exhausts, and contaminants in water and food are being investigated for a possible role in the development of breast cancer. Carcinogens in the workplace, such as asbestos and radon (a radioactive gas), also increase the risk of lung cancer. The risk of prostate cancer may be increased by exposure to cadmium, a metal involved in welding, electroplating, and making batteries. Fumes and dust from an urban or workplace environment may also increase the risk of stomach and colorectal cancer.

A host of other lifestyle habits and choices that people make can further contribute to the risk of developing cancer. In the intensive efforts being made to find the causes of breast cancer, various personal history factors have been suggested, such as amount of alcohol consumed and having an abortion or a miscarriage. The evidence is somewhat stronger for the effect of personal history in the case of cervical cancer, which has a higher risk among women who began having sexual intercourse before age 18 and/or have had many sexual partners. For men, efforts are underway to determine whether having had a vasectomy increases their risk for prostate cancer.

In addition to a person's lifestyle and history of disease, variations due to race and ethnicity are observed among certain types of cancers. It is known that skin cancer is more likely to develop

FIGURE 5.8

Age-adjusted Cancer Death Rates, Females by Site, United States, 1930–2003

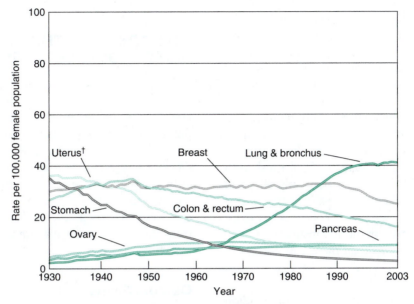

In contrast to males, females have shown a steadily increasing lung cancer rate since 1990.

Source: American Cancer Society, 2006.

in people with fair skin that freckles easily. Black people are less likely to get any form of skin cancer. Other cancers that vary according to race are uterine cancer, which is more prevalent among whites, and prostate cancer, which is more prevalent among blacks. Stomach cancer is twice as prevalent in men and is more common in black people, as is colon cancer. However, rectal cancer is more prevalent among whites.

Finally, hormonal factors are thought to play an important role in the risk of certain forms of cancer. Although the cause of prostate cancer is not known, it is known that the growth of cancer cells in the prostate, like that of normal cells, is stimulated by male hormones, especially testosterone. Along similar lines, estrogen is thought to increase the likelihood of a woman's developing uterine cancer. It is possible that the link between weight and uterine cancer in women

may be due to the fact that women with a higher amount of body fat produce more estrogen and that it is the estrogen, not fat, that increases the risk of uterine cancer. Similarly, the finding that diabetes and high blood pressure increase the risk of uterine cancer may be related to the fact that these conditions are more likely to occur in overweight women who have higher levels of estrogen.

Treatments

The best way to treat cancer is to prevent it. Cancer detection with frequent screenings is the primary step in treatment. Organizations in the United States such as the American Cancer Society and the Canadian Cancer Society in Canada publicize the need for tests such as breast self-examination and mammograms for women, prostate examinations for men, and colon cancer screenings for both men and women. There is mixed evidence for the effectiveness of this publicity. In the case of mammograms, for example, it does appear that women have responded. The percentage of women in the United States population who have had this screening procedure in the past two years rose from 29 to 70% in the years between 1987 and 2003. However, the distribution of women who take this preventative step varies by education and poverty status, as do so many other aspects of health care. In the year 2003, of those with less than a high school education, only 58% had gotten a mammogram compared with 75% of those with at least one year of college. Over twice as many women with health insurance (76%) receive mammograms than those without health insurance (37%) (Centers for Disease Control and Prevention, 2006).

Depending on the stage of cancer progression at diagnosis, various treatment options are available. Surgery is the most common treatment for most types of cancer when it is likely that all of the tumor can be removed. Radiation therapy is the use of high-energy X-rays to damage cancer cells and stop their growth. Chemotherapy is the use of drugs to kill cancer cells. Patients are most likely to receive chemotherapy when the cancer has metastasized to other parts of the body. Biological therapy is treatment involving substances called biological response modifiers that improve the way the body's immune system fights disease and may be used in combination with chemotherapy to treat cancer that has metastasized. As more information is gathered through the rapidly evolving program of research on cancer and its causes, new methods of treatment and prevention can be expected to emerge over the next few decades. Furthermore, as efforts grow to target populations at risk for the development of preventable cancers (such as lung cancer), it may be expected that cancer

deaths will be reduced even further in the decades ahead.

DISORDERS OF THE MUSCULOSKELETAL SYSTEM

Although not usually fatal, musculoskeletal diseases can be crippling and may even lead to injury or bodily damage that does prove to take the afflicted individual's life. Two primary disorders of the musculoskeletal system affect middle-aged and older adults: arthritis and osteoporosis. These disorders, which unfortunately are relatively common, can range in their effects on the individual from minor but annoying limitations to severe disability.

Osteoarthritis

Arthritis is a general term for conditions that affect the joints and surrounding tissues. It refers to any one of several diseases that can cause pain, stiffness, and swelling in joints and other connective tissues. The most common form of arthritis is known as **osteoarthritis**, a painful, degenerative joint disease that often involves the hips, knees, neck, lower back, or the small joints of the hands. Osteoarthritis typically develops in joints that are injured by repeated overuse in the performance of a particular job or a favorite sport. Obesity, associated with the carrying of excess body weight, is another risk factor.

Eventually, injury or repeated impact thins or wears away the cartilage that cushions the ends of the bones in the joint so that the bones rub together. The articular cartilage that protects the surfaces of the bones where they intersect at the joints wears down, and the synovial fluid that fills the joint loses its shock-absorbing properties. Joint flexibility is reduced, bony

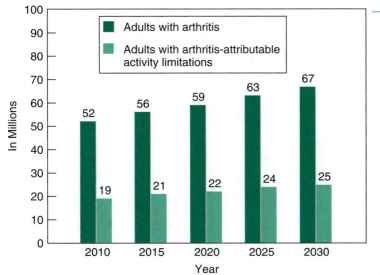

FIGURE 5.9

Projected Number of Adults with Arthritis and Arthritis-attributable Activity Limitations, 2005–2030

Over the coming two decades, there will be a steady increase in adults with arthritis and limitations due to arthritis.

Source: Hootman & Helmick, 2006.

spurs develop, and the joint swells. These changes in the joint structures and tissues cause the individual to experience pain and loss of movement.

Pain management is an important feature of the treatment for osteoarthritis and typically involves medication. The medications most likely to be used for pain control include aspirin, acetaminophen, ibuprofen, and aspirin-like drugs called nonsteroidal anti-inflammatory drugs (NSAIDs). Unfortunately, the NSAIDs can cause the person to develop gastrointestinal problems, including ulcers. Corticosteroids can also be injected directly into joints to reduce swelling and inflammation. These drugs are used sparingly, however, because chronic use can have destructive effects on bones and cartilage. Pain medications only alleviate symptoms; they do not provide any kind of cure for the disease. More active forms of treatment are becoming available to people who have osteoarthritis, including injection of a synthetic material into an arthritic joint to replace the loss of synovial fluid. A second option is injection of sodium hyaluronate

into the joint, an injectable version of a chemical normally present in high amounts in joints and fluids. Increasingly common is the total replacement of an affected joint, such as a hip or a knee. Although this sounds like a drastic measure, it is one that typically proves highly satisfactory.

"What do you think?"   **5-3**

Do you know anyone with arthritis? How is that person's life affected by the disease?

Osteoporosis

As we saw in Chapter 4, normal aging is associated with loss of bone mineral content due to an imbalance between bone resorption and bone growth. This loss of bone mineral content is technically called **osteoporosis** (literally, "porous bone") when it reaches the point at which bone mineral density is more than 2.5

standard deviations below the mean of young white, non-Hispanic women.

It is estimated that 10 million individuals in the United States over the age of 50 have osteoporosis, the large majority of whom are women (United States Department of Health and Human Services, 2004). Women are at higher risk than men because they have lower bone mass in general. Menopause, with its accompanying decrease in estrogen production, accelerates the process. Women vary by race and ethnicity in their risk of developing osteoporosis; white and Asian women have the highest risk, and blacks and Hispanics the lowest. In addition women who have small bone structures and are underweight have a higher risk for osteoporosis than heavier women.

Alcohol and cigarette smoking increase the risk of developing osteoporosis. Conversely, risk is reduced by an adequate intake of calcium through dairy products, dark green leafy vegetables, tofu, salmon, and foods fortified with calcium such as orange juice, bread, and cereal (a regimen similar to that recommended to prevent heart disease). Vitamin D, obtained through exposure to sunlight (while wearing sunblock of course) or as a dietary supplement, is another important preventative agent because it plays an important role in calcium absorption and bone health. Exercise and physical activity are also significant factors in reducing the risk of osteoporosis.

Prevention and treatment of osteoporosis involve attempting to restore bone strength through nutritional supplements and a regular program of weight-bearing exercise. Medication may also be prescribed to slow or stop bone loss, increase bone density, and reduce fracture risk. Alendronate is a bisphosphonate used to increase bone density, and calcitonin is a naturally occurring hormone involved in the regulation of calcium and bone metabolism. Each of these has advantages but also can have serious side effects that make them more or less useful for particular individuals. For example they may increase bone loss in the jaw among patients with dental problems.

DIABETES

A large fraction of the over-65 population suffers from Type 2 diabetes, a disease that begins in adulthood. This form of diabetes is associated with long-term complications that affect almost every organ system, contributing to blindness, heart disease, strokes, kidney failure, the necessity for limb amputations, and damage to the nervous system.

Characteristics of Diabetes

Diabetes is caused by a defect in the process of metabolizing glucose, a simple sugar that is a major source of energy for the body's cells. Normally, the digestive process breaks food down into components that can be transported through the blood to the cells of the body. The presence of glucose in the bood stimulates the beta cells of the pancreas to release insulin, a hormone that acts as a key at the cell receptors within the body to "open the cell doors" and let in the glucose. Excess glucose is stored in the liver or throughout the body in muscle and fat. After it is disposed of, its level in the blood returns to normal. In Type 2 diabetes, the pancreas produces some insulin, but the body's tissues fail to respond to the insulin signal, a condition known as insulin resistance. Because the insulin cannot bind to the cell's insulin receptor, glucose cannot be transported into the body's cells to be used. Eventually the excess glucose overflows into the urine and is excreted. The body therefore loses a main source of energy, although large amounts of glucose are potentially available in the blood.

Projected Prevalence of Osteoporosis and/or Low Bone Mass of the Hip in Women, Men, and Both Sexes, 50 Years of Age or Older

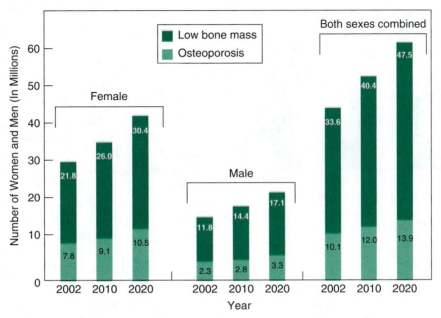

Over the coming decade, osteoporosis will increase in both women and men.

Source: http://www.surgeongeneral.gov/library/bonehealth/chapter_4.html.

The symptoms of diabetes include fatigue, frequent urination (especially at night), unusual thirst, weight loss, blurred vision, frequent infections, and slow healing of sores. These symptoms develop more gradually and are less noticeable in Type 2, compared with Type 1 (child-onset), diabetes. If blood sugar levels become too low (hypoglycemia), the individual can become nervous, jittery, faint, and confused. When hypoglycemia develops, the individual must eat or drink something with sugar in it as quickly as possible. Alternatively, the person can also become seriously ill if blood sugar levels rise too high (hyperglycemia). Women who develop diabetes while pregnant are more likely to experience complications, and their infants are more likely to develop birth defects.

Incidence and Risk Factors

It is estimated that 10 million Americans have been diagnosed with diabetes, and there may be as many as 5 million people who have the disease but have not received a diagnosis. The disease is estimated to afflict 10.3 million people 60 years of age and older, which is about 21% of adults in this age category. The CDC estimates that having diabetes doubles the risk of death compared with other people in one's own age group (http://www.cdc.gov/diabetes/pubs/estimates05 .htm#prev).

According to the World Health Organization, the number of people suffering from diabetes worldwide is projected to grow by more than twofold from the 150 million reported in 2000 to 300 million by the year 2025. The rise in cases

FIGURE 5.11
Percent of Adults 50 and Older with Diabetes, United States and Canada, 2002–2003

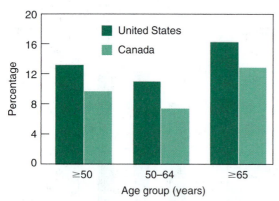

There are differences between the United States and Canada in the prevalence of diabetes, suggesting the role of lifestyle and health care as risk factors for this disease.

Source: Powell-Griner, Blackwell, & Martinez, 2005.

will approach 200% in developing countries and 45% in developed countries. Nearly 900,000 deaths worldwide in 2000 were due to this disease (World Health Organization, 2002).

The main risk factors for diabetes are obesity and a sedentary lifestyle. Epidemiologists attribute the rise in diabetes to the increase in BMI, noted earlier in the chapter as a risk factor for heart disease (Centers for Disease Control and Prevention, 2003a). Researchers in this area warn that older adults are becoming increasingly likely to experience metabolic syndrome, noted earlier in the chapter as a dangerous combination of obesity, insulin resistance, high lipid levels, and hypertension, leading to greater risk of cardiovascular and kidney disease (Bechtold, Palmer, Valtos, Iasiello, & Sowers, 2006).

Other risk factors contributing to diabetes risk are race and ethnicity. The incidence of diabetes is about 60% higher in African Americans and 110 to 120 percent higher in Mexican Americans and Puerto Ricans compared with whites. The highest rates of diabetes in the world are found among Native Americans. Half of all Pima Indians living in the United States, for example, have adult-onset diabetes.

Prevention and Treatment

Given the clear relationship between obesity and diabetes, the most important means of preventing Type 2 diabetes are control of glucose intake, control of blood pressure, and control of blood lipids. Moderate alcohol consumption also seems to offer a protective effect (Nakanishi, Suzuki, & Tatara, 2003).

Once an individual has Type 2 diabetes, diet and exercise continue to be important. Frequent blood testing is also necessary to monitor glucose levels. Much of this treatment involves trying to keep blood sugar at acceptable levels. Some people with Type 2 diabetes must take oral drugs or insulin to lower their blood glucose levels. In addition to medication and monitoring of diet, people with diabetes are advised to develop an exercise plan to manage their weight and to lower blood pressure and blood fats, important steps which can lead to reductions in blood sugar levels.

RESPIRATORY DISEASES

The main form of respiratory disease affecting adults in middle and late life is **chronic obstructive pulmonary disease (COPD)**, a group of diseases that involve obstruction of the airflow into the respiratory system. Two related diseases—chronic bronchitis and chronic emphysema—often occur together in this disease. People with COPD experience coughing, excess sputum, and difficulty breathing even when performing relatively easy tasks, such as putting on their clothes or walking on level ground. Over 10 million individuals in the United States were diagnosed with COPD in 2000, and estimates are that 80 million people worldwide suffer from this disorder (http://www.who.int/respiratory/copd/burden/en/index.html). Women are more likely to have this disease than men, and the rates increase linearly from about 39 per 1,000 to 96 in the 65 to 74 year-old age group and 106 in those 75 and older (Mannino, Homa, Akinbami, Ford, & Redd, 2002).

Chronic bronchitis is a long-standing inflammation of the bronchi, the airways that lead into the lungs. The inflammation of the bronchi leads to increased production of mucus and other changes, which in turn lead to coughing and expectoration of sputum. People with this disorder are more likely to develop frequent and severe respiratory infections, narrowing and plugging of the bronchi, difficulty breathing, and disability. Chronic emphysema is a lung disease that causes permanent destruction of the alveoli. Elastin within the terminal bronchioles is destroyed, leading to collapse of the airway walls and an inability to exhale. The airways lose their ability to become enlarged during inspiration and to empty completely during expiration, leading to a lowering of the quality of gas exchange. For people with COPD, the symptom they are most aware of is shortness of breath. They also suffer from restrictions in their ability to enjoy daily life, including limitations in mobility, as shown in Figure 5.12 (Reardon, Lareau, & ZuWallack, 2006).

Although the cause of COPD is not known, it is generally agreed that cigarette smoking is a prime suspect. Exposure to environmental toxins such as air pollution and harmful substances in the occupational setting also may play a role, particularly for people who smoke. The specific mechanism involved in the link between smoking and emphysema is thought to involve

FIGURE 5.12

Functional Status and Quality of Life in Chronic Obstructive Pulmonary Disease

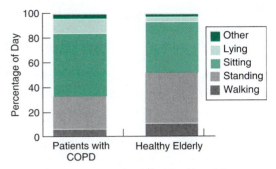

People with COPD, compared with healthy older adults, are more likely to spend time sitting and lying.

Source: Reardon, Lareau, & Zu Wallack, 2006.

the release of an enzyme known as **elastase**, which breaks down the elastin found in lung tissue. Cigarette smoke stimulates the release of this enzyme and results in other changes that make the cells of the lung less resistant to elastase. Normally there is an inhibitant of elastase found in the lung, known as alpha-1 antitrypsin (AAT). However, cigarette smoke inactivates AAT and allows the elastase to destroy more lung tissue. Of course, not all smokers develop COPD, and not all people with COPD are or have been smokers. Heredity may also play a role. There is a rare genetic defect in the production of AAT in about 2 to 3% of the population that is responsible for about 5% of all cases of COPD.

Apart from quitting smoking, which is obviously the necessary first step in prevention and treatment, individuals with COPD can benefit from medications and treatments. These include inhalers that open the airways to bring more oxygen into the lungs or reduce inflammation, machines that provide oxygen, or, in extreme cases, lung surgery to remove damaged tissue.

DEMENTIA AND RELATED NEUROLOGICAL DISORDERS

Dementia is a clinical condition in which the individual experiences a loss of cognitive function severe enough to interfere with normal daily activities and social relationships. Dementia can be caused by a number of diseases that affect the nervous system, including cardiovascular disorders, a variety of neurologically based disorders, and abnormalities in other bodily systems. The disorder that has received the most attention by far is Alzheimer's disease, which is also the most common cause of dementia.

Alzheimer's Disease

The disorder now known as **Alzheimer's disease** has been given many names over the years, including senile dementia, presenile dementia, senile dementia of the Alzheimer's type, and organic brain disorder. The current terminology reflects the identification of the condition as a disease by Alois Alzheimer (1864–1915), a German neurologist who was the first to link changes in brain tissue with observable symptoms. Alzheimer treated a patient, Auguste D., a woman in her 50s who suffered from progressive mental deterioration marked by increasing confusion and memory loss. Taking advantage of what was then a new staining technique, he noticed an odd disorganization of the nerve cells in her cerebral cortex. In a medical journal article published in 1907, Alzheimer speculated that these microscopic changes were responsible for the woman's dementia. The discovery of brain slides from this patient confirmed that these changes were similar to those seen in the disease (Enserink, 1998). In 1910, as more autopsies of severely demented individuals showed the same abnormalities, one of the foremost psychiatrists of that era, Emil Kraepelin (1856–1926), gave the name described by his friend Alzheimer to the disease.

Prevalence

The World Health Organization estimates the prevalence of Alzheimer's disease worldwide of people over 60 as 5% of men and 6% of women (World Health Organization, 2001). The incidence rates of new cases is less than 1% a year for those aged 60 to 65 or possibly as high as 6.5% in those 85 and older (Kawas, Gray, Brookmeyer, Fozard, & Zonderman, 2000). A commonly quoted figure regarding the number of people in the United States with Alzheimer's disease is 5 or 5.5 million people, representing a rate of over 12% of the over-65 age groups but 50% or higher of those over 85 years of age. The media and other sources have projected this number to soar into the mid-twenty-first century, reaching a staggering 14 million individuals who will suffer from the disease by 2050 unless a cure is found. However, a more careful look at the statistics reveals an estimated prevalence of about half the media number at 2.3 million (Brookmeyer & Kawas, 1998; Hy & Keller, 2000). Furthermore, norms for diagnostic tests for the disorder vary by education and age, so estimates of its prevalence in the oldest-old and the less well educated might result in inflated figures (Beeri et al., 2006). The numbers presented in the media, though drawing attention to an important problem, present an unfortunate reinforcement of the notion that "senility" is an inevitable feature of aging.

Psychological Symptoms

The psychological symptoms of Alzheimer's disease evolve gradually over time. The earliest signs are occasional loss of memory for recent events or familiar tasks. Although changes in cognitive functioning are at the core of this disease's symptoms, changes in personality and behavior eventually become evident as well. By the time the disease has entered the final stage, the individual has lost the ability to perform even the simplest and most basic of everyday functions. The rate of progression in Alzheimer's disease varies from person to person, but there is a fairly regular pattern of loss over the stages of the disease. The survival time following the diagnosis is 7 to 10 years for people diagnosed in their 60s and 70s, and drops to 3 years for people diagnosed in their 90s (Brookmeyer, Corrada, Curriero, & Kawas, 2002).

Biological Changes

One set of changes that Alzheimer discovered in the brain of Auguste D. consisted of what looked like the accumulated waste products of collections of dead neurons. Now known as **amyloid plaques**, they develop as long as 10 to 20 years before symptoms become noticeable and are thought to be one of the first events in the pathology of the disease, and possibly at the root of the illness (Hardy & Selkoe, 2002). Consequently the term **amyloid cascade hypothesis**, proposing that the formation of amyloid plaques causes the death of neurons in Alzheimer's disease, has emerged as a primary explanation of the cause of the disorder (Hardy, 2006). **Amyloid** is a generic name for protein fragments that collect together in a specific way to form insoluble deposits (meaning that they do not dissolve). The form of amyloid most closely linked with Alzheimer's disease consists of a string of 42 amino acids and is referred to as beta-amyloid-42.

The abnormal processes that occur in the formation of beta amyloid are shown in Figure 5.13 in the top portion. Beta amyloid is formed from a larger protein found in the normal brain, referred to as **amyloid precursor protein (APP)**. As it is being manufactured, APP embeds itself in the neuron's membrane (Figure 5.13a). A small piece of APP sticks inside the neuron and a larger part remains outside. At this point, the APP is trimmed at both ends by enzymes known as proteases (Figure 5.13b). In healthy aging,

the part of APP lying outside the neuron is trimmed by enzymes called **secretases** so that it is flush with the neuron's outer membrane. In Alzheimer's disease, this process is faulty. If the APP is snipped at the wrong place by one type of secretase, beta-amyloid (−42) is formed (Vassar et al., 1999). The fragments eventually clump together into abnormal deposits that the body cannot dispose of or recycle (Figure 5.13c).

Apart from its tendency to form insoluble plaques, beta amyloid seems to have the potential to kill neurons. **Caspase** theory proposes that beta amyloid stimulates substances called caspases, which become enzymes that destroy neurons. The destruction of neurons, called **apoptosis**, is what then ultimately leads to the loss of cognitive functioning that occurs in Alzheimer's disease (Galvan et al., 2006).

The second mysterious change observed in Auguste D.'s brain was a profusion of abnormally twisted fibers within the neurons themselves, known as **neurofibrillary tangles** (literally, tangled nerve fibers). It is now known that the neurofibrillary tangles are made up of a protein called **tau**, which seems to play a role in maintaining the stability of the microtubules that form the internal support structure of the axons. The microtubules are like train tracks that guide nutrients from the cell body down to the ends of the axon. The tau proteins are like the railroad ties or crosspieces of the microtubule train tracks. In Alzheimer's disease, the tau is changed chemically and loses its ability to separate and support the microtubules. At that point, it twists into paired helical filaments, which resemble two threads wound around each other. This collapse of the transport system within the neuron may first result in malfunctions in communication between neurons and eventually may lead to the death of the neuron.

Like the formation of plaques, the development of neurofibrillary tangles seems to occur early in the disease process and may progress

FIGURE 5.13
Stages in the Formation of a Beta Amyloid Plaque

(a)

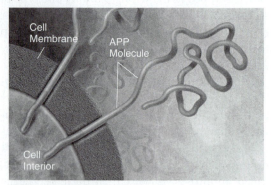

(b)

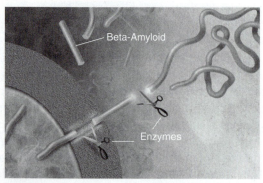

(c)

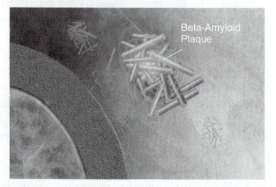

The three stages of formation of a beta-amyloid plaque. See text for details.

quite substantially before the individual shows any behavioral symptoms. The earliest changes in the disease appear to occur in the hippocampus and the entorhinal region of the cortex, which is the area near the hippocampus; these are the areas that play a critical role in memory and retention of learned information (Scheff & Price, 2006). Throughout the course of the disease, tangles continue to accumulate in the hippocampus along with the destruction of neurons in this critically important area of the brain (Kril, Patel, Harding, & Halliday, 2002).

Causes of Alzheimer's Disease

One certainty about Alzheimer's disease is that it is associated with the formation of plaques and tangles, pa ticularly in areas of the brain controlling memory and other vital cognitive functions. The great uncertainty is what causes these changes. It is also not clear whether the development of plaques and tangles is the cause of neuron death or whether these changes are the result of another, even more elusive, underlying process that causes neurons to die and produces these abnormalities in neural tissue as a side product. Moreover, the existence of these changes in the brain is not a sure sign that an individual will have cognitive symptoms, highlighting the fact that this is a disorder that can be affected by environmental as well as biological factors (Knopman et al., 2003). Although the progression of the disorder tends to lead to an inevitable loss of functioning, there is variability in its physical and cognitive symptoms (Burton, Strauss, Hultsch, Moll, & Hunter, 2006).

The theory guiding most researchers is that genetic abnormalities are somehow responsible for the neuron death that is the hallmark of Alzheimer's disease (Schellenberg, 2006). This theory began to emerge after the discovery that certain families seemed more prone to a form of

FIGURE 5.14
Formation of a Neurofibrillary Tangle in Alzheimer's Disease

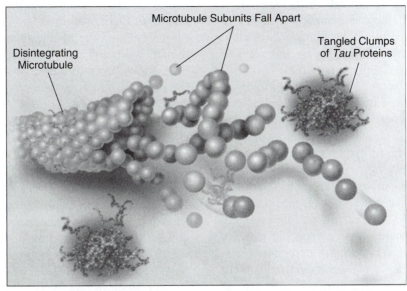

The formation of a neurofibrillary tangle, showing the stages of disintegration as the microtubule within the neuron starts to break apart.

the disease that struck at the relatively young age of 40 to 50 years. These cases are now referred to as **early-onset familial Alzheimer's disease**, and though tragic, scientists have been able to learn a tremendous amount from studying the DNA of afflicted individuals. Since the discovery of the early-onset form of the disease, genetic analyses have also provided evidence of another gene involved in familial Alzheimer's disease that starts at a more conventional age of 60 or 65 years. This form of the disease is called **late-onset familial Alzheimer's disease**. The four genes that have been discovered so far, which are thought to account for about half of all early-onset familial Alzheimer's disease, are postulated to lead by different routes to the same end-product, namely, excess amounts of beta-amyloid protein. Furthermore, the changes in the brain produced by these genes are thought to be the same as those involved in nonfamilial, or **sporadic Alzheimer's disease**. Only 5% of all cases of Alzheimer's

disease are familial, leaving the large majority as sporadic (Harman, 2006).

Aided by the discovery of familial patterns of early-onset Alzheimer's disease along with the burgeoning technology of genetic engineering, genetic research has led within a surprisingly short time to some very plausible suspects for genes that cause the brain changes associated with the disease. One of the prime candidates is involved in the late-onset familial pattern of the disorder. This is the **apolipoprotein E (ApoE) gene**, located on chromosome 19. ApoE is a protein that carries blood cholesterol throughout the body, but it also binds to beta-amyloid, and hence may play a role in plaque formation. Although the ApoE gene has received more attention, the first genetic defects found to be associated with familial Alzheimer's disease were on the **APP gene** on chromosome 21. The APP gene appears to control the production of the protein that generates beta-amyloid. Most early-onset familial Alzheimer's disease cases are associated with defects in the so-called **presenilin genes (PS1 and PS2)**. Researchers speculate that these genes somehow lead APP to increase its production of beta-amyloid which in turn causes neurofibrillary tangles and amyloid plaques (Goedert & Spillantini, 2006).

There may also be nongenetic biological causes of the increase in beta-amyloid associated with Alzheimer's disease. One possibility is that electrical activity in the hippocampus contributes to the formation of this substance. According to this view, the background activity of the brain produces an excess of electrical activity that leads to overproduction of the harmful form of beta-amyloid. By engaging in purposeful mental activity, people actually lower their risk of developing Alzheimer's disease because they are exercising the parts of the brain that do not contribute to a rise in this harmful form of electrical activity (Selkoe, 2006).

Higher education and continued mental activity throughout life are known to be protective environmental factors. In addition to the statistical association between higher education and lower risk of Alzheimer's disease, as pointed out earlier, a high level of cognitive activity predicts lower risk of Alzheimer's disease in an individual's later years (Wilson et al., 2002). An extensive social network can also be a protective factor, reducing the risk even among people who have high levels of brain pathology (Bennett, Schneider, Tang, Arnold, & Wilson, 2006).

The extent to which the individual participates in exercise may be another lifestyle contributor to the development of or progression of Alzheimer's disease. Both physical exercise and exercise in the form of stimulation along multiple sensory channels are of value in slowing down cognitive decline in general and therefore could potentially be successfully applied to individuals with dementia (Briones, 2006). Finally, one of the most intriguing prospects in the search for causes of Alzheimer's disease relates to diet. As shown in Figure 5.15, people who follow the Mediterranean diet, high in tomatoes, olive oil, and even some red wine, have been shown to have a lower risk of developing the disease, even controlling for factors such as ApoE4 genotype, BMI, age, sex, smoking and ethnicity (Scarmeas, Stern, Mayeux, & Luchsinger, 2006).

Diagnosis

The diagnosis of dementia is made by psychiatrists and clinical psychologists when the person meets the criteria for clinical signs of dementia. These signs include progressively worsening memory loss, aphasia (loss of language ability), apraxia (loss of ability to carry out coordinated movement), agnosia (loss of ability to recognize familiar objects), and disturbance in exeutive functioning (loss of the ability to plan and organize) (American Psychiatric Association, 2000).

FIGURE 5.15

The Mediterranean Diet and Alzheimer's Disease

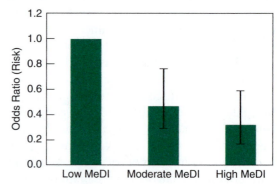

People who eat a diet low in Mediterranean content ("LoMeDi") have a greater risk of Alzheimer's disease than people with moderate or high Mediterranean diets.

Source: Scarmeas, Stern, Mayeux, & Luchsinger, 2006.

The diagnosis of Alzheimer's disease through clinical methods is traditionally done by exclusion because there is no one specific test or clinical indicator that is unique to the disorder. As has been the case for decades, a definite diagnosis is possible only through autopsy, which identifies the characteristic neurofibrillary tangles and beta-amyloid plaques known to occur in the disease. In the mid-1980s, spurred by the desire to arrive at as comprehensive a set of diagnostic guidelines as possible, a joint commission of the National Institute of Neurological and Communicative Disorders and Stroke and the Alzheimer's Disease and Related Diseases Association addressed the problem (McKhann et al., 1984). They developed a set of medical and neuropsychological screening tests, behavioral ratings, and mental status measures that at the time significantly improved the chances of a correct diagnosis to 85 to 90% accuracy in the disease's later stages. However, with the continued improvement of MRI, which has resulted in a virtual explosion of studies on diagnosis of Alzheimer's disease through brain imaging, it is likely that the ability to provide a reliable diagnosis in the early to moderate stages of the disorder is forthcoming (Jagust et al., 2006). Ultimately, as treatments improve, it would be optimal to be able to provide this diagnosis when there is an opportunity to intervene and either slow or stop the degeneration of the brain.

Of particular interest and importance is the need to differentiate the type of moderate memory loss that may reflect the early form of the disease from what is known as **mild cognitive impairment (MCI)**, a subtle loss of memory and learning abilities (Levey, Lah, Goldstein, Steenland, & Bliwise, 2006). This is a controversial diagnosis (Petersen, 2004), in part because it is not clear whether this is a separate entity from Alzheimer's disease. However, even as researchers attempt to identify whether there are changes in the brain that indicate an intermediate stage between normal aging and Alzheimer's disease, there remains the issue of whether there is a direct correspondence between pathological changes in the brain and symptoms of memory loss (Petersen et al., 2006).

Medical Treatments

Even as the search for the cause of Alzheimer's disease proceeds, researchers are attempting to find medications that will alleviate its symptoms. Although the drugs currently being tested have yet to produce significant improvements in Alzheimer's patients, they are seen as having the potential to lead to treatments that will.

"What do you think?" | 5-4

If a test is developed that can predict whether a person has a high chance of developing Alzheimer's disease, would you want to take that test and find out the results?

Two drugs approved by the Food and Drug Administration (FDA) for the treatment of Alzheimer's disease target the neurotransmitter acetylcholine. These drugs are the **anticholinesterase treatments** given the names THA or tetrahydroaminoacridine (also called tacrine and given the brand name Cognex) and donepezil hydrochloride (Aricept). They are called anticholinesterase because they work by inhibiting the action of acetylcholinesterase (also called cholinesterase), the enzyme that normally destroys acetylcholine after its release into the synaptic cleft. Declines in the levels of acetylcholine, particularly in the hippocampus, are thought to be a factor in the memory loss shown by people with Alzheimer's disease. By inhibiting the action of acetylcholinesterase, these drugs slow the breakdown of acetylcholine, and therefore its levels are not as drastically reduced.

Initial excitement accompanying the approval of tacrine in 1993 was followed by disappointing reports that it could produce toxic effects in the liver if taken in required doses. Aricept was approved three years later, although it also has gastrointestinal side effects related to the effects of acetylcholinesterase inhibitors (diarrhea and nausea). However, its required dose is lower, and it does not interfere with liver function. Both drugs give the patient a few months to a year of relief from the troubling cognitive symptoms that occur in the early stages of the disease. Other drugs that inhibit acetylcholinesterase activity are citicoline, arecoline, and ENA 713 (Exelon). Rivastigmine (Exelon) is another medication in this category that operates in a similar manner but causes fewer gastrointestinal side effects.

The effects of the medications that operate on acetylcholine have been less than impressive (CME Institute of Physicians Postgraduate Press, 2006), leading investigators to seek new approaches. The latest medication is **memantine**, which operates on the glumatate system. Glutamate is an excitatory neurotransmitter found widely throughout the brain. The theory is that glutamate essentially overexcites the neurons and leads to deleterious chemical changes that cause neuron death. By targeting glutamate, memantine is thought to exert a protective effect against this damage (Lipton, 2006).

Antioxidants are also being experimented with, based on the theory that when beta-amyloid breaks into fragments, free radicals are formed that damage the surrounding neurons. Researchers are also testing an Alzheimer's vaccine that would increase the body's immune response against beta amyloid to prevent or reduce plaque formation (Dasilva, Aubert, & McLaurin, 2006). Most recently, agents that inhibit the activity of the secretases that are instrumental in

producing beta-amyloid are being tested (Tomita & Iwatsubo, 2006).

Researchers believe that a medical cure for Alzheimer's disease will eventually be found. However, it is unlikely that one "magic bullet" will serve this function. Instead, treatments will need to be targeted for specific at-risk individuals based on their genetic vulnerability, medical history, and exposure to environmental toxins (Roberson & Mucke, 2006).

Psychosocial Treatments

As intensively as research is progressing on treatments for Alzheimer's disease, the sad truth is that there is currently no cure. Meanwhile, people with this disease and their families must find ways to deal, on a daily basis, with the incapacitating cognitive and sometimes physical symptoms that accompany the relentless deterioration of brain tissue. Clearly, until a cure can be found, mental health workers will be needed to provide assistance in this difficult process, so that the individual's functioning can be preserved for as long as possible.

A critical step in providing this kind of management of symptoms is for health care professionals to recognize the fact that Alzheimer's disease involves families as much as it does the patients. Family members are most likely to be the ones providing care for the patient, especially wives and daughters. These individuals, called **caregivers**, have been the focus of considerable research efforts over the past two decades. It is now known that people in the role of caregivers are very likely to suffer adverse effects from the constant demands placed on them. The term **caregiver burden** is used to describe the stress that these people experience in the daily management of their afflicted relative. As the disease progresses, caregivers must provide physical assistance in basic life functions, such as eating, dressing, and toileting. As time goes by, the caregiver may experience health problems that make it harder and harder to provide the kind of care needed to keep the Alzheimer's patient at home.

Given the strain placed on caregivers, it should come as no surprise that health problems and rates of depression, stress, and isolation are higher among these individuals than among the population at large. Fortunately, support for caregivers of people with Alzheimer's disease has become widely available. Local chapters of national organizations in the United States such as the Alzheimer's Association provide a variety of community support services for families in general and caregivers in particular. Caregivers can be taught ways to promote independence and reduce distressing behaviors in the patient, as well as to learn ways to handle the emotional stress associated with their role.

An important goal in managing the symptoms of Alzheimer's disease is to teach caregivers behavioral methods to maintain functional independence in the patient. The idea behind this approach is that, by maintaining the patient's functioning for as long as possible, the caregiver's burden is at least somewhat reduced. For example, the patient can be given prompts, cues, and guidance in the steps involved in getting dressed and then be positively rewarded with praise and attention for having completed those steps. Modeling is another behavioral strategy, in which the caregiver performs the desired action (such as pouring a glass of water) so that the patient can see this action and imitate it. Again, positive reinforcement helps to maintain this behavior once it is learned (or more properly, relearned). The caregiver then has less work to do, and the patients are given the cognitive stimulation involved in actively performing these tasks rather than having others take over their care completely.

Another strategy that caregivers can use to maintain independence is to operate according to a strict daily schedule that the patient can learn to follow. The structure provided by a regular routine of everyday activities can give the patient additional cues to use as guides. In addition to increasing the extent to which people with Alzheimer's disease engage in independent activities, caregivers can also use behavioral strategies to eliminate, or at least reduce the frequency, of undesirable acts such as wandering or being aggressive. In some cases this strategy may require ignoring problematic behaviors, with the idea that by eliminating the reinforcement for those behaviors in the form of attention, the patient will be less likely to engage in them. However, it is more likely that a more active approach will be needed, especially for a behavior such as wandering. In this case the patient can be provided with positive reinforcement for not wandering. Even this may not be enough, however, and the caregiver may need to take such precautions as installing a protective device in doors and hallways.

It may also be possible for the caregiver to identify certain situations in which the patient becomes particularly disruptive, such as during bathing or riding in the car. In these cases the caregiver can be given help in targeting those aspects of the situation that cause the patient to become upset and then modify it accordingly. For example, if the problem occurs while bathing, it may be that a simple alteration such as providing a terry cloth robe rather than a towel helps reduce the patient's feeling of alarm at being undressed in front of others.

Creative approaches to managing the recurrent stresses involved in the caregiver's role may help to reduce the feelings of burden and frustration that are so much a part of daily life. Along with the provision of community and institutional support services, such interventions can go a long way toward helping the caregiver and ultimately the patient (Callahan et al., 2006).

Other Neurological Diseases That Can Cause Dementia

The condition known as dementia is frequently caused by Alzheimer's disease in later life, but many other conditions can affect the status of the brain and cause loss of memory, language, and motor functions.

Vascular dementia. In **vascular dementia**, progressive loss of cognitive functioning occurs as the result of damage to the arteries supplying the brain. Dementia can follow a stroke, in which case it is called acute onset vascular dementia, but the most common form of vascular dementia is **multi-infarct dementia** or **MID**, caused by transient ischemic attacks. In this case, a number of minor strokes ("infarcts") occur in which blood flow to the brain is interrupted by a clogged or burst artery. Each infarct is too small to be noticed, but over time, the progressive damage caused by the infarcts leads the individual to lose cognitive abilities. There are important differences between MID and Alzheimer's disease. The development of MID tends to be more rapid than Alzheimer's disease, and personality changes are less pronounced. However, the two conditions may often coexist (Charlton, Morris, Nitkunan, & Markus, 2006).

Fronterotemporal dementia. Dementia that attacks specifically the frontal lobes of the brain is known as **frontotemporal dementia (FTD)** and is reflected in personality changes such as apathy, lack of inhibition, obsessiveness, and loss of judgment. Eventually the individual becomes neglectful of personal habits and loses the ability to communicate. This type of dementia can be divided into two types—one with primarily behavioral changes and the second with primarily disturbances of language (Sjogren & Andersen, 2006).

Parkinson's disease. People who develop **Parkinson's disease** show a variety of motor disturbances, including tremors (shaking at rest), speech impediments, slowing of movement, muscular rigidity, shuffling gait, and postural instability or the inability to maintain balance. Dementia can develop during the later stages of the disease, and some people with Alzheimer's disease develop symptoms of Parkinson's disease. Patients typically survive 10 to 15 years after symptoms appear.

There is no cure for Parkinson's disease, but medications have been developed that have proved relatively successful in treating its symptoms. The primary drug being used is Levadopa (L-dopa), but over the years this medication loses its effect and may even be toxic. Major advances have also been made in neurological treatments, with the most recent being high-frequency deep brain stimulation of subcortical movement areas of the brain that in the past were excised surgically (Espay, Mandybur, & Revilla, 2006).

Lewy Body dementia. **Lewy bodies** are tiny spherical structures consisting of deposits of protein found in dying nerve cells in damaged regions deep within the brains of people with Parkinson's disease. Lewy body dementia, first identified in 1961, is very similar to Alzheimer's disease with progressive loss of memory, language, calculation, and reasoning, as well as other higher mental functions. Estimates are that this form of dementia accounts for 10 to 15% of all cases of dementia (McKeith, 2006).

The dementia associated with the accumulation of Lewy bodies fluctuates in severity, at least early in the disease. The disease also includes episodes of confusion and hallucinations, which are not typically found in Alzheimer's disease. Individuals with pure Lewy body dementia also show impairments in motor skills and in specific skills, including tasks demanding concentrated attention, problem solving, and spatial abilities.

Pick's disease.   A relatively rare cause of dementia is **Pick's disease**, which involves severe atrophy of the frontal and temporal lobes. This disease is distinct from fronterotemporal dementia because, in addition to deterioration of these areas, there is an accumulation of unusual protein deposits (called Pick bodies). The symptoms of Pick's disease include disorientation and memory loss in the early stages, but the disorder eventually progresses to include pronounced personality changes and loss of social constraints, similar to fronterotemporal dementia. Eventually the individual becomes mute, immobile, and incontinent.

Reversible dementias.   **Reversible dementias** are due to the presence of a medical condition that affects but does not destroy brain tissue. If the medical condition is allowed to go untreated, permanent damage may be done to the central nervous system, and the opportunity for intervention will be lost. Furthermore, if the condition is misdiagnosed as Alzheimer's disease, the patient will be regarded as untreatable and not be given the appropriate care at the appropriate time.

A neurological disorder known as **normal-pressure hydrocephalus**, though rare, can cause cognitive impairment, dementia, urinary incontinence, and difficulty in walking. The disorder involves an obstruction in the flow of cerebrospinal fluid, which causes the fluid to accumulate in the brain. Early treatment can divert the fluid away from the brain before significant damage has occurred. Head injury can cause a **subdural haematoma**, which is a blood clot that creates pressure on brain tissue. Again, surgical intervention can relieve the symptoms and prevent further brain damage. The presence of a brain tumor can also cause cognitive deficits, which can be prevented from developing into a more severe condition through appropriate diagnosis and intervention.

Delirium is another cognitive disorder that is characterized by temporary but acute confusion that can be caused by diseases of the heart and lung, infection, or malnutrition. Unlike dementia, however, delirium has a sudden onset. Because this condition reflects a serious disturbance elsewhere in the body, such as infection, it requires immediate medical attention.

Prescribed medications given in too strong a dose or in harmful combinations are included as other potentially toxic substances that can cause dementia-like symptoms. The condition called **polypharmacy** in which the individual takes multiple drugs, sometimes without the knowledge of the physician, can be particularly lethal. Recall that the excretion of medications is slower in older adults because of changes in the kidneys, so that older adults are more vulnerable to such toxic effects of medications.

Wernicke's disease is an acute condition caused by chronic alcohol abuse involving delirium, eye movement disturbances, difficulties maintaining balance and movement, and deterioration of the nerves to the hands and feet. Providing the individual with vitamin B1 (thiamine) can reverse this condition. Unfortunately, if it is not treated, Wernicke's disease progresses to the chronic condition known as **Korsakoff syndrome**.

Depression is another condition that can mimic the cognitive changes involved in Alzheimer's disease. In older adults, the symptoms may also include confusion, distraction, and irritable outbursts, and these symptoms may be mistaken for Alzheimer's disease. When these symptoms appear, causing impairment like that of dementia, the disorder is referred to as **pseudodementia**. Depression may also occur in conjunction with dementia, particularly in the early stages. In either case, the depression is treatable, and when appropriate interventions are made, the individual's cognitive functioning can show considerable improvement.

Clearly Alzheimer's disease and the variety of dementias described here are major potential limitations on the lives of older adults. Fortunately they afflict a minority of people. Nevertheless breakthroughs in their treatment, along with contributions to understanding other major diseases, will be among the most significant achievements of science in the 21st century.

SUMMARY

1. Diseases in middle and later adulthood can be highly disabling. However, many are preventable, starting with actions taken in early adulthood. Cardiovascular diseases in which there are pathological changes in the arteries are arteriosclerosis and atherosclerosis. Heart disease includes coronary artery disease, myocardial infarction, and congestive heart failure. Cerebrovascular accidents involve a cutting off of blood to the brain and may be acute or transient. Cardiovascular diseases are the leading cause of death in the over-75 population, with men having a higher risk, particularly black men. Behavioral risk factors include sedentary lifestyle, smoking, high BMI, and excessive alcohol intake. Heart disease can be largely prevented by careful monitoring of diet and exercise.

2. Cancer is a group of diseases in which there is abnormal cell growth. Skin cancer is the most prevalent form in the United States in the adult population overall. Breast cancer is the most frequent cancer in women, but lung cancer is the deadliest for men and women. There are many behavioral risk factors for cancer, including smoking, sun exposure, and lack of control over diet. Environmental toxins can increase cancer risk. Cancer treatment includes surgery, radiation therapy, chemotherapy, and biological therapy.

3. Several musculoskeletal disorders are more common in older adults than in the younger population. Osteoarthritis is a degenerative joint disease in which the cartilage deteriorates. Osteoporosis is an extreme loss of bone mineral content that primarily affects women. Preventative steps include calcium intake, vitamin D, exercise, dietary control, and estrogen-replacement therapy.

4. Type 2 diabetes is an increasingly common chronic disease in older adults caused by a defect in metabolizing glucose. Prevention and treatment involves weight control and exercise.

5. Chronic respiratory diseases, including chronic emphysema and chronic bronchitis, are thought to be caused primarily by cigarette smoking. They have no cure at present. Dementia is a clinical condition involving loss of memory and other cognitive functions.

6. Alzheimer's disease is the most common form of dementia, affecting an estimated 7% of the over-65 population. Biological changes include development of amyloid plaques and neurofibrillary tangles. Alzheimer's disease is thought to have genetic causes, possibly involving abnormalities on the ApoE, APP, and presenilin genes that lead to formation of plaques and tangles. The caspase theory focuses on the neurotoxic role of amyloid. Diagnosis of Alzheimer's disease can be made only from autopsy, but there are improved methods such as those involving brain scans. Medical treatments being tested include anticholinesterases and memantines. Psychosocial treatments attempt to control behaviors and to provide support to caregivers. Other forms of dementia are vascular dementia, fronterotemporal dementia, Parkinson's disease, Lewy body dementia, and Pick's disease. There are also reversible dementias, including pseudodementia, which, if treated, can lead to a return to normal cognitive functioning.

CHAPTER 6

Basic Cognitive Functions: Information Processing, Attention, and Memory

> **"**By the time you're eighty years old you've learned everything. You only have to remember it.**"**
>
> George Burns

Our abilities to learn, remember, solve problems, and become knowledgeable about the world are basic to our sense of self and ability to adapt. As these change during adulthood, they also have the potential to change our fundamental understandings of ourselves and our world.

The field of **cognition** is a central one in the field of adult development and aging. In addition to being of theoretical and scientific interest, there are practical ramifications of changes in the ability to apply cognitive skills to situations in everyday life, ranging from job performance to driving to the enjoyment of leisure activities.

The popular concept of the "senior moment" is intended to be humorous, but it may relate to a more deep-seated anxiety that middle-aged individuals have about losing their memories. In

FIGURE 6.1
Ballot from the 2004 Sarasota County Election

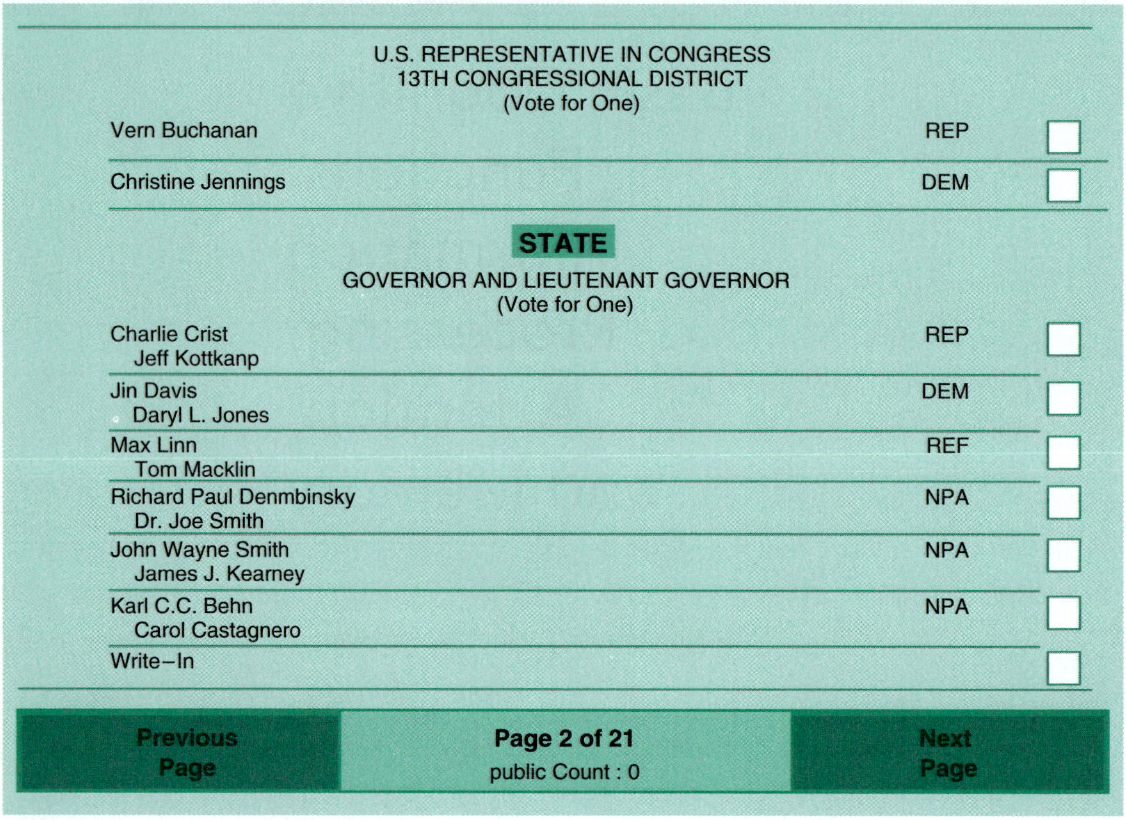

U.S. REPRESENTATIVE IN CONGRESS
13TH CONGRESSIONAL DISTRICT
(Vote for One)

Vern Buchanan	REP	☐
Christine Jennings	DEM	☐

STATE
GOVERNOR AND LIEUTENANT GOVERNOR
(Vote for One)

Charlie Crist / Jeff Kottkanp	REP	☐
Jin Davis / Daryl L. Jones	DEM	☐
Max Linn / Tom Macklin	REF	☐
Richard Paul Denmbinsky / Dr. Joe Smith	NPA	☐
John Wayne Smith / James J. Kearney	NPA	☐
Karl C.C. Behn / Carol Castagnero	NPA	☐
Write—In		☐

Previous Page	Page 2 of 21 public Count : 0	Next Page

This ballot was used in the 2004 election in Sarasota County, Florida. About 18,000 ballots were recorded as not having picked a candidate for Congress, even though most of these same voters cast a vote in every other race. Looking at the ballot's layout, we can see why it would be confusing, particularly for older adults, because the vote for Congress was not highlighted. Approximately 29% of Sarasota county residents are 65 and older.

this chapter, we will see whether such anxiety is warranted. As a preview, it is safe to say that although there are some losses in speed and memory as we get older, normal age-related changes are not entirely negative. Furthermore, in terms of identity processes, there are many ways that people can compensate for memory changes as long as they manage to adopt a balanced approach to this important aspect of self-definition.

INFORMATION PROCESSING

Researchers working within the **information processing** perspective regard the cognitive functioning of humans as comparable to the functioning of a computer. The "data" from experience are entered into the brain through the various sensory routes, where they progress through a series of stages of analysis. Like a computer the brain either stores the information

Although this older female executive may be experiencing changes in her information processing abilities, she is nevertheless able to make use of high-tech equipment to meet the demands of her job.

or prepares it to be used instantaneously. Studies of information processing in adulthood attempt to determine whether and how the aging process alters the efficiency and effectiveness of these analytical phases. Even though these studies can be highly technical, findings from laboratory studies on information processing can have significant effects on daily life.

Psychomotor Speed

Theories about changes in the overall quality of information processing in adulthood are based on the results of studies on **psychomotor speed**, which is the amount of time it takes us to process a signal, prepare a response, and then execute that response. Researchers believe that psychomotor speed reflects the integrity of the central nervous system (Madden, 2001).

The basic framework of a study on psychomotor speed is fairly straightforward. You enter a laboratory that is equipped with a computer set up to record your responses. The screen flashes a stimulus array that you are asked to examine. Your instructions will typically tell you how to respond when a particular stimulus, known as a target, appears in that array. Then your time to respond (called **reaction time)** is recorded. Although the reaction time study procedure sounds simple enough, what adds to the complexity and elegance of the research design is the experimenter's creation of various conditions intended to measure different facets of cognitive functioning. What happens if you are given a prompt that provides a clue regarding where the target will appear? Conversely what happens when the task of finding the target is made more difficult by the presentation of a misleading or irrelevant cue? It is the observation of the effects of these variations on individuals of different ages that forms the basis for research on adult age differences in psychomotor speed.

Researchers know with certainty that your reaction time as a young adult will be lower (i.e., you will be quicker) than it will be as you get older. The question is how much and under what circumstances. Increases in reaction time with age in adulthood are typically a matter of several hundreds of milliseconds, not enough to be particularly noticeable in everyday life, but enough to be significant under the scrutiny of the laboratory researcher. Thus, although with increasing age in adulthood there is increasing variability in reaction times, the net effect is in a negative direction toward greater slowing (Deary & Der, 2005).

Why do we get slower as we age? According to the **general slowing hypothesis** (Salthouse, 1996), the increase in reaction time reflects a general decline of information processing speed within the nervous system of the aging individual. Related to this idea is the **age-complexity**

FIGURE 6.2

Brinley Plot

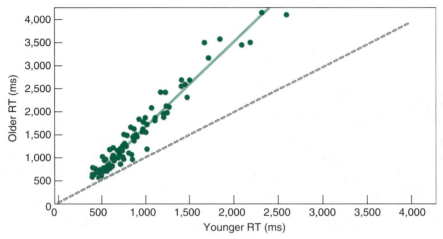

The Brinley plot is a graph that is used to compare the reaction times of young adults with those of older adults. If there were no age differences in reaction time, the increase in reaction time of young adults would match those of older adults. Instead, as the task becomes harder and the required reaction time gets longer, older adults are disproportionately slower, producing the line in this graph.

Source: Sliwinski & Hall, 1998.

hypothesis, which proposes that through slowing of central processes in the nervous system, age differences increase as tasks become more complex and our processing resources are stretched more and more to their limit.

The general slowing hypothesis was arrived at through observations in cross-sectional studies showing the reaction times of an older group of adults plotted against the times of younger adults on a graph called a **Brinley plot**. As you can see from Figure 6.2, older adults perform at similar speeds on tasks that can be completed relatively quickly by a young adult (500 ms). On tasks that take longer for young adults (1,000 ms), older adults take proportionately longer (1,500–2,000 ms) than they do on the relatively easy, 500 ms, tasks.

Although not particularly elegant in terms of a theoretical model, the general slowing hypothesis is consistent with a large body of data on reaction time performance in adulthood. Salthouse's model does not identify any particular stage or component of information processing as the culprit causing age differences in reaction time. All that he is saying is that older adults are slower. The general slowing hypothesis is also used to explain age differences in memory, as we will see later. Loss of speed leads to memory impairments because there is a backlog in cognitive processes when multiple operations must be completed simultaneously or within a limited time.

Attention

The slowing of reaction time with age may be attributed to many factors, but one that has intrigued researchers is the possibility that older adults are particularly disadvantaged in the attentional stage of information processing. **Attention** involves the ability to focus or concentrate on a portion of experience while ignoring other features of experience, to be able to shift that focus as demanded by the situation, and to be able to coordinate information from multiple sources. Once you have paid attention to a piece of information, you can then perform further cognitive operations on it, such as those involving memory or problem solving.

If you are one of the many people who has difficulty concentrating or focusing your attention for long periods of time, you are certainly aware of the price that you pay. It is annoying to others and frustrating to oneself to have an important piece of information fly by without having had the chance to absorb it. Attentional problems can have serious consequences, as is true for people who have attention deficit disorder. A lapse in attention at a crucial moment of decision making, as in when to apply the brakes or turn the wheel of the car, can have serious consequences.

Researchers have examined adult age differences in attention by comparing people of different ages performing under various conditions, including when they must shift attention, divide attention among multiple inputs, and sustain their attention over an extended period of time. Studies of attention are considered important for understanding the cognitive functions of adults of varying ages and their abilities to function in various real-life situations in which cognitive resources must be focused on some target or goal. For the most part, these studies suggest that people become less efficient as they get older in the use of attentional processes.

One theory to explain age differences in attention regards attention as a process reflecting the allocation of cognitive resources. When you must focus on a particular object, you must dedicate a certain proportion of your mental operations to that object. The theory of **attentional resources** and aging proposes that older adults have less energy available for cognitive operations than do their younger counterparts across a wide domain of tasks (Blanchet, Belleville, & Peretz, 2006). In contrast,

the **inhibitory deficit hypothesis**, suggests that aging reduces the individual's ability to inhibit or tune out irrelevant information (Hasher, Zacks, & May, 1999). As was just discussed, one important feature of attention is the ability to focus on one element of a stimulus array and ignore others. If older adults cannot tune out that irrelevant information, their attentional performance will suffer.

The inhibitory deficit hypothesis has accrued considerable data to support it, including studies that combine psychological and electrophysiological methods. For example, studies of event-related potentials, which measure the brain's electrical activity in response to stimuli, show that older adults are less able to block out distracting stimuli when they are trying to complete a task. The pattern of responding they show suggests that there are deficits in the prefrontal cortex, which is involved in the control of inhibiting irrelevant information (West & Schwarb, 2006).

The inhibitory deficit hypothesis would imply that middle-aged and older adults are able to focus more effectively when distractions are kept to a minimum. Some of these distractions might, ironically enough, involve concern over the quality of one's performance. Imagine that you are a computer programmer anxious about the possibility of being laid off or reassigned because of problems in performance. Your concern over your job security may actually increase your odds of losing your job. Attention, by definition, is a fleeting cognitive state, a necessary step prior to subsequent and more detailed analysis of incoming information. Factors that can serve to limit its effectiveness, such as concern over the quality of your functioning, will make it even more difficult for you to put it to use in further cognitive operations. In a similar way, people who are worried about the aging of their cognitive abilities may be more likely to engage in identity accommodation, the "over-the-hill" mentality, and suffer even more declines than they otherwise would.

Although, for the most part, older adults are slower when they must process information from visual displays, there is one area in which their performance seems to be maintained intact. Remembering where an item was in a visual display seems to be an ability that is not affected by the aging process—in fact, in one study, older adults were more efficient in remembering where an item had appeared on a display. Their visual search was more rapid than that observed in young adults (Kramer et al., 2006).

Another important area of attentional performance involves dividing the focus of attention between multiple inputs. Commonly known as "multitasking," you most likely engage in dividing your attention on a pretty regular basis throughout your day. You may be attempting to listen to a telephone conversation while watching television or playing a video game, or trying to eat and drive at the same time. Experiments that attempt to replicate this real-life situation use a **dual task** (also called **divided attention** task), in which the individual is given information from two input sources. Although everyone is disadvantaged to a certain degree when monitoring more than one input, the disadvantage becomes progressively greater in increasingly older groups of adults (Verhaeghen, Steitz, Sliwinski, & Cerella, 2003). However, older adults appear to make up for the disadvantage somewhat by reducing the activity of frontal regions of the brain that younger adults activate during this task and increasing the activity in other brain regions that store visual and spatial information (Fernandes, Pacurar, Moscovitch, & Grady, 2006).

Most psychology students are familiar with the Stroop test in which you are given the task of naming the ink used to print a word such as "green" that is actually printed in yellow. Evidence from the Stroop task supports the view that older adults have more difficulty on this task than do younger adults, adding further weight to the idea that older adults suffer disproportionately on tasks that involve the inhibition of one response ("green") in order to provide the correct response ("yellow") (Brink & McDowd, 1999; Hartley, 1992).

As important as divided attention is to our everyday life, we also need to be able to maintain our attention over a prolonged period of time, the ability known as **sustained attention**. In a laboratory task of sustained attention, you would be asked to watch the computer screen as a series of stimuli are presented and to respond only when you see the target stimuli (such as the letter "X"). The experimenter manipulates the stimuli to make you either more or less likely to respond when you see the target.

The **context processing deficiency** hypothesis of aging and information processing proposes that aging affects our ability to take the context of information into account when making judgments in situations such as the sustained attention task. We have to keep the context in mind during this task, because we have to remain conscious of the fact that our responses are supposed to come only to certain targets. The theory proposes that older adults are particularly affected under these circumstances because they have fewer resources to devote to the task when they must constantly remind themselves of the instructions (Braver & Barch, 2002).

To measure context processing, researchers use the AX-CPT paradigm, a sustained attention task. The "CPT" in AX-CPT stands for "continuous performance task." Participants must perform one response to a target, such as pushing the "d" key on the computer, and another to the nontarget, such as pushing the "k" (see Figure 6.3). They are shown a series of continuously presented letters and instructed to make the target response only when they see an "X" that has been preceded by an "A." In this case,

FIGURE 6.3
AX-CPT Paradigm

Percent of trials	Cue	Probe	Target response (yes or no)
70	A (valid cue)	X (probe)	Yes
10	B (invalid cue)	Y (invalid probe)	No
10	A (valid cue)	Y (invalid probe)	No
10	B (invalid cue)	X (probe)	Yes

In the AX-CPT paradigm, the participant is instructed to give the target response when presented with the probe. The majority of trials involve the presentation of the valid cue with the probe (AX), but in the other conditions, they are either presented with an invalid cue prior to an invalid probe (BY), the valid cue and the invalid probe (AY), or an invalid cue and the probe (BX).

the A is a valid cue for the probe. The majority of trials consist of AX pairings between the valid cue and the probe (the "AX" in "CPT-AX"). The participants come to expect that when they see the valid cue, it will be followed by the probe, not another letter. Figure 6.3 shows the entire AX-CPT paradigm.

A typical set of findings from the AX-CPT task comparing older and younger adults is shown in Figure 6.4 (Rush, Barch, & Braver, 2006). Looking at the top set of results (Figure

FIGURE 6.4
Age Differences on the AX-CPT

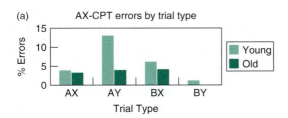

(a) AX-CPT errors by trial type (b) AX-CPT reaction time by trial type.

Source: Rush, Barch, & Braver, 2006.

6.4a), you might wonder why it is that older adults make fewer errors in the AY condition than do young adults. However, looking at the results in another way, it becomes clear that older adults perform at about the same level on the AX, AY, and BX tasks. If they were paying attention to context (i.e., preparing to make the target response when they see the valid cue), then they would make far more errors in the AY condition than the AX condition because the "A" is priming them for the valid probe. The fact that they do not make more errors in this condition suggests that they are not really paying attention to the cue, but only paying attention to the probe. They do not take advantage of the information provided by the cue to prepare their response. Young adults, in contrast, are using the "A" as a guide or prime to prepare them for making the target response so they make more errors.

Now look at the bottom half of Figure 6.4, which shows reaction times of older and younger adults in these four conditions. Young adults take disproportionately longer to respond on the AY trials, so not only do they make more errors in this condition, but they are slower as well. Older adults also take longer on the AY trial, so both age groups are slower when incorrectly primed by the context ("A"). However, older adults are particularly disadvantaged in their reaction time in the BX trials. It is as if when they see the valid probe (X), they have to go back to try to

FIGURE 6.5
Deaths in Passenger Vehicles, 2005

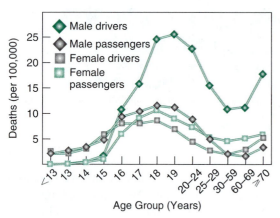

Deaths per 100,000 people by seating position, age, and gender.
Source: Insurance Institute for Highway Safety, 2005.

FIGURE 6.6
Crash Involvement Rate Per Million Miles, 2005

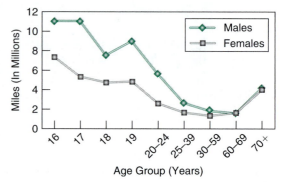

Passenger-related vehicular crashes, including those that are fatal and nonfatal, per million miles by age.
Source: Insurance Institute for Highway Safety, 2005.

remember whether the X was preceded by an A or not because they were not attending to the context. As it turns out, even if the cue remains in front of them during the trial, older adults are less able to use the context provided by the cue information to their advantage (Paxton, Barch, Storandt, & Braver, 2006). Age differences in performance on the AX-CPT are not readily explained by the inhibitory deficit or general slowing hypothesis, but instead suggest a unique contribution of context processing difficulties to the slower reaction time of older adults as demonstrated in laboratory tasks (Rush et al., 2006).

"What do you think?"   **6-1**

How might attentional problems in older adults influence their ability to perform everyday tasks?

DRIVING AND AGING

Age-related changes in information processing have effects on many aspects of daily life, but perhaps having the greatest practical importance is in the area of driving. There are a number of changes in the visual system that can impair performance in older drivers, including loss of visual acuity, increased sensitivity to glare, and difficulty seeing in the dark. In addition, many driving situations involve rapid cognitive judgments that may present a challenge for older adults. As we have just seen, reaction time is greater for older adults, and they may be particularly disadvantaged when they need to evaluate a quickly changing context before they make a response.

Do these changes in cognition translate into higher accident rates for older adults? According to the Insurance Institute for Highway Safety, teenagers present a greater threat on the road than do drivers in their 60s and older, particularly teenage male drivers. Female drivers retain a low rate of dying in motor vehicle accidents

FIGURE 6.7
Alcohol and Fatal Crash Involvement, United States 2003

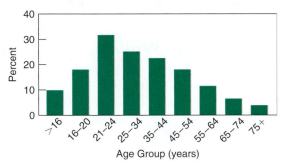

Percent by age group of drivers with blood alcohol levels 0.08 g/dl or higher involved in fatal crashes by age group.

Source: National Highway Traffic Safety Administration, 2005.

Younger people are also involved in many more crashes than older drivers per number of licensed drivers. However, even on a per-mile basis (rather than per driver), the oldest drivers still are not as dangerous as the youngest drivers. On a statistical basis, then, older drivers are safer than younger ones.

The highest number of crashes for people in all age groups occurs when the vehicle is traveling in a straight direction just prior to the accident. For young drivers that vehicle is likely to be traveling over the speed limit. Among teenage male drivers involved in fatal crashes in 2003, 39% were speeding at the time of the crash. Poor judgment, lack of seat belt use, and especially driving while intoxicated are more prevalent among young drivers (http://www.cdc.gov/ncipc/factsheets/teenmvh.htm). By contrast older adults are more likely to be involved in a crash at an intersection when making a left-hand turn, at least in the United States.

up through the 70s and beyond; older male drivers, although showing an upturn in fatalities, never reach the high point of young male drivers.

The lights and the signs at this intersection present a complex visual array and may create confusion in older drivers.

ASSESS YOURSELF: Aging Driver Survey

These questions concern the topic of aging drivers. Please answer each question as honestly as you can.

1. What would cause you to be most concerned about the driving of an older relative?
   A. Vision impairment
   B. Inability to remember names
   C. Recent illness
   D. Seeing unexplained dents in the car

2. Should older adults be forced to take road tests based only on their age?
   A. Yes
   B. No

3. If yes, at what age do you think older people should be required to take a road test?
   A. 65
   B. 70
   C. 75
   D. 80
   E. Not applicable

4. What do you think is of most concern in general when it comes to aging drivers?
   A. Drinking and driving
   B. Driving too fast
   C. Slowed reaction times
   D. Restrictions in movement

5. How comfortable would you feel talking to an older relative about not being able to drive any more?
   A. Completely comfortable
   B. Mostly comfortable
   C. Mostly uncomfortable
   D. Completely uncomfortable

6. What would make it most difficult for you to talk to an older relative about driving less or not at all?
   A. Hurting the person's feelings
   B. Concern over lack of alternatives to driving
   C. Falsely accusing the person of losing his or her driving skills
   D. Feeling that it is not any of your business

7. Who do you think would be most likely to be able to talk to your older relative in a sensitive and helpful manner?
   A. Me or another relative
   B. Physician
   C. Police officer
   D. Social worker

(contd.)

ASSESS YOURSELF

8. What aspect of taking away your relative's ability to drive do you think would be most difficult for your relative?
   A. Losing his or her independence
   B. Not being able to take a vacation
   C. Being unable to afford public transportation
   D. Not being able to find public transportation

9. What conditions do you think are hardest for older drivers?
   A. Driving in the bright sun
   B. Being a passenger when an unsafe driver is at the wheel
   C. Driving at night
   D. Being able to control drinking and driving

10. Which driver do you think is safest?
   A. 18-year-old who has just had two drinks
   B. 75-year-old who is driving in bad weather

The opposite is true in Australia, where people drive on the left, making a right-hand turn more complex and dangerous there (Braitman, Kirley, Chaudhary, & Ferguson, 2006).

Sociocultural factors add to biological and psychological processes to influence further the driving behavior of older adults. The link between driving and independence is highly reinforced in U.S. society, and loss of the ability to drive is seen as a major blow to a person's sense of autonomy. There are also practical implications of not being able to drive. Older adults who live in suburban or rural areas with limited or no public transportation lose an important connection to the outside world, and they risk becoming housebound and socially isolated. Prejudice against them by younger people can exacerbate whatever fears and concerns older drivers already have about their changing abilities.

Despite these problems, many older drivers seem to be able to adjust their behavior and attitudes so that they compensate for changes in cognitive and perceptual abilities (Vance et al., 2006). Younger people may not always like being on the road with an older driver who is a bit more slow and cautious, but the fact that older people have fewer accidents per person indicates that they are doing something right. Interestingly, the data on aging and driving correspond closely to what we know about aging and crash prevalence among older airline pilots, who seem to have fewer fatal and nonfatal accidents than younger pilots (Broach, Joseph, & Schroeder, 2003). Older, experienced pilots also seem to be better able to take advantage of training sessions to improve their performance in flight simulators, where decision time and judgment both play an important role (Taylor, Kennedy, Noda, & Yesavage, 2007).

As the number of older drivers continues to increase with the increased longevity of the Baby Boomer generation, appropriate safeguards are being investigated, such as driving tests and safety classes for older drivers. Unfortunately, safety classes are not effective if they give the older driver a false sense of security (Owsley, McGwin, Phillips, McNeal, & Stalvey, 2004). Instead, highway safety experts are exploring alternatives to the traditional intersection, such as substituting well-designed roundabouts for the type of complex junction that can cause so many accidents while turning. Along with these safeguards, we can hope for changes in the attitudes of current middle-aged people as they themselves become the "older driver."

MEMORY

One of the most feared changes to occur with aging is loss of memory. The data on the effects of aging on memory suggest that the aging process indeed has negative effects on many aspects of memory but not all aspects of memory are affected in the same way by aging nor is everyone affected the same way by the aging process.

Working Memory

Working memory, the part of memory that keeps information temporarily available and active, seems to be particularly vulnerable to the effects of aging. In a laboratory test of working memory, you are asked to perform a cognitive task while simultaneously trying to remember some of the information for a later memory task. One of the most common working memory tests is the "n back" task. You are asked to repeat the "nth" item back in a list of items. For instance, 1-back would be one item back, 2-back would be two items back, and so on. The further back in the list, the harder the task because the more demands are placed on working memory.

There are four components theorized to be part of working memory (Baddeley, 2003). The phonological loop consists of a memory store for speech-based information called the phonological store. This information can be rehearsed by repeating the material over and over again "in your head" such as trying to keep a street address in mind while you search for it. The visuospatial scratch pad is, like the name implies, the part of working memory that records and maintains visual and spatial images. For instance, the visuospatial scratch pad may be used when you are figuring out a shorter route between your home and the closest convenience store. The third component brings information from long-term memory into working memory, and is known as the episodic buffer. The central executive, the fourth component of working memory, puts this all together. The central executive is responsible for deciding how to allocate cognitive resources such as whether to rehearse the address or to form a mental street map. Through the central executive, we allocate our attentional resources to specific operations.

"What do you think?"	6-2

Why is working memory an important aspect of cognition?

Decreases in working memory are presumably tied in with deficits in the hippocampus, the part of the brain responsible for processing working memory. Yet, older adults are also able to compensate in part through increasing their activation of the frontal lobes of the brain (Persson et al., 2006).

The inhibitory deficit hypothesis (Hasher, et al., 1999) proposes that we experience an increasing difficulty with age in our ability to inhibit information that is not relevant to the task (Hedden & Park, 2001; Malmstrom & LaVoie, 2002). Presumably this occurs because the prefrontal cortex is less efficient at inhibiting irrelevant information (Hedden & Yoon, 2006).

In support of this proposal, white matter hyper-intensities that accumulate in this part of the brain are in fact associated with working memory declines in older adults (Nordahl et al., 2006). However, other researchers suggest that another region in the front part of the brain, the anterior cingulate cortex, also plays a role in decreases in working memory in later adulthood (Otsuka, Osaka, Morishita, Kondo, & Osaka, 2006).

Information is eventually either forgotten or consolidated in **long-term memory**, the repository of information that is held for a period of time ranging from several minutes to a lifetime. Long-term memory contains information ranging from the recent past, such as remembering where you put your cell phone half an hour ago, to information from many years ago, such as what happened at your fourth birthday party. The model of working memory shown in Figure 6.8 shows the relationships among the components of working memory and long-term memory.

The episodic buffer integrates information from the phonological and visuospatial components of working memory with information pulled out of long-term memory. Essentially, it is the information brought into your conscious awareness, either from experiences being processed anew or from memories retrieved from your long-term memory. For example, when you are trying to get directions to a friend's house in a familiar part of town, you would listen to and perhaps visualize where the new instructions would take you, as well as integrate that information with knowledge about the town from your previous visits to nearby locations.

Episodic memory is memory for events, or "episodes" in your life. Most of the testing that occurs in a memory experiment assesses your episodic memory. **Semantic memory** is the equivalent to "knowledge," and it includes the words and definitions of words found in your vocabulary or storehouse of historical facts.

Nonverbal memories are stored in **procedural memory**, which is the knowledge of how to perform certain activities such as using a complicated computer program, sewing on a button, or cooking up a batch of chocolate chip cookies.

Contemporary researchers believe procedural memory is a variant of what is known as **implicit memory**, the recall of information that was acquired unintentionally. To test implicit memory, you might be shown a list of words (but not asked to recall them) containing, for example, the word "apple." When you are then asked to name three fruits, you will be more likely to include "apple" as one of those fruits.

FIGURE 6.8
Multicomponent Model of Working Memory

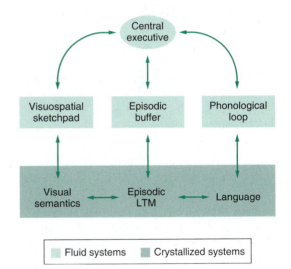

In this model of memory, working memory is shown in the top portion as including the central executive, visuospatial sketchpad, episodic buffer, and phonological loop. Long-term memory is shown in the bottom as consisting of visual semantics, episodic long-term memory, and language. The dark purple areas represent "crystallized" knowledge, which is gained through experience. The episodic buffer serves as an interface between working memory and long-term memory.

Source: Baddeley, 2003.

Another way to test implicit memory is through repetition priming. Here you would be shown the list of words containing the word "apple." Then a word fragment such as "a – p – –" would be presented, and you would be asked to fill in the remaining three blanks. Implicit memory is shown when you say "apple" rather than "ample." Cognitive researchers regard procedural memory as a variant or form of implicit memory because it involves the recall of information that is not available to conscious awareness. To illustrate this point, consider what you would say to someone if you were trying to describe the processes involved in tying a shoelace. Although you are very familiar with these actions, it is hard to put these actions into words because they are not thought of in verbal terms.

The majority of verbal memory tasks involve **explicit memory**, in which you consciously attempt to recall a list of words or other stimuli. You know before you are presented with a list of items that you will be asked to remember as many as possible.

In **source memory**, also called **source monitoring**, you are asked to state where you saw or heard a piece of information. In everyday life, source memory may be required when you are trying to recall who told you where you could buy concert tickets or where you saw a drug store coupon for one dollar off on disposable shavers.

Two other long-term memory phenomena relate to recall of information from the past. **Remote memory** involves, as the term implies, recall of information from the distant past, and **autobiographical memory** is recall of information from your own past. Finally there is another form of memory, which is the recall of events to be performed in the future, or **prospective memory**. In this type of memory, you must remember your intention to perform an action.

Effects of Aging on Long-Term Memory in Adulthood

If you think of working memory as your capacity for "mental work," then it would make sense that a reduction in this capacity would have widespread effects on how well you can acquire and store new information. Indeed, cognitive aging researchers assume that the effects of aging on working memory can be viewed as deficits in processing resources that account for other age differences in episodic memory for information acquired during the course of experiments. Because older adults are deficient in processing newly presented information, they do not engage in effective encoding and retrieval of this material, and so their long-term recall suffers as a result.

The theorized reduction across adulthood in processing resources and in being able to engage in self-initiated processing is reflected primarily in age differences in episodic memory (Wingfield & Kahana, 2002). It is a well-established finding that older adults are both slower and less accurate in performing episodic memory tasks (Verhaeghen, Vandenbroucke, & Dierckx, 1998). Although the vast majority of memory studies on aging are cross-sectional and hence subject to cohort effects, longitudinal data are available to confirm the general pattern of negative age effects in recall memory after the age of 55 years (Davis, Trussell, & Klebe, 2001; Zelinski & Burnight, 1997).

The memory deficits of older adults do not generalize to all areas, however. Consider the case of "flashbulb" memories, which are important and distinctive events personally experienced by the individual. When they form such memories, older adults are as likely as younger adults to recall them correctly, as was discovered in a study assessing recall of source memory for the news of the September 11 terrorist attacks (Davidson, Cook, & Glisky, 2006).

Semantic memory is also spared from the negative effects of the aging process (Wiggs, Weisberg, & Martin, 2006). Older adults are able to remember word meanings and a broad array of factual informaion.

In the area of procedural memory, it appears that as we get older, we are able to retain well-learned and practiced motor skills such as playing an instrument, typing on a computer keyboard, or riding a bicycle, at least while it is physically possible for us to perform these actions. Even when it comes to learning new motor skills, older adults appear to maintain procedural memory. In one particularly impressive study, a sample of approximately 500 adults ranging from 18 to 95 years of age were tested on their learning of a task in which they had to slide a small nut off a rod as quickly as possible. Not only did older adults show significant improvement in performance over a series of five learning trials, but they retained their memory for the task for as long as two years later with no dropoff at all in performance (Smith et al., 2005).

Even though they may be slower (Jastrzembski, Charness, & Vasyukova, 2006), the greater experience of older adults can serve to compensate for changes in speed and working memory in areas involving procedural expertise such as bridge playing, chess, reading, cooking, gardening, and typing (Mireles & Charness, 2002). The experienced bridge player is able to examine a round of cards without giving each individual card a great deal of thought or study. Through years of playing, many of the choices about which card to play follow established conventions and rules, so that the older bridge player does not have to remember as much about each hand of cards.

The findings on procedural memory are important in pointing to an area that appears to be spared from the effects of aging. As we saw earlier, procedural memory is one form of implicit memory. The results of research on age differences in implicit memory parallel the findings on procedural memory in adulthood. Tasks such as repetition priming that involve no conscious effort at recall show no age differences (Caggiano, Jiang, & Parasuraman, 2006).

An area that is not spared from aging's effects, though, is source memory. Older adults seem to have greater difficulty on memory tasks that require judging where they previously encountered an item (Thomas & Bulevich, 2006). Not only are older persons less able to remember where or how an item of information was presented, but they also are more likely to have illusory memories in which they recall something that never happened (Dodson, Bawa, & Slotnick, 2007). They may think that one person said something when in reality it was said by someone else.

Along these lines, older adults are also more susceptible to the planting of false memories. In a manipulation of false memory known as the Deese-Roediger-McDermott (DRM) paradigm, individuals are presented with a list of words from a category (such as "cake," "honey," "candy," etc.) but not the category label. The critical test of false memory is to ask participants if the category label ("sweet") was on the list. Very few people are immune from this effect, but when warned, younger participants are better able to avoid the false memory implantation. One interpretation for the greater vulnerability of older adults to false memories is that it is a variant of the difficulty they experience in inhibiting irrelevant information (Jacoby & Rhodes, 2006). In fact, older adults whose frontal lobes function normally do not show this effect (Butler, McDaniel, Dornburg, Price, & Roediger, 2004).

Problems in retrieval from long-term memory appear in research on the tip-of-the-tongue phenomenon in adulthood. You are most likely to have a tip-of-the-tongue experience when you are trying to remember a name such as the name of a person, place, or movie, such as what was the name of the 1990 movie starring Julia Roberts and Richard Gere? (answer: *Pretty Woman*). The tip-of-the-tongue effect is observed more in older adults in both laboratory and everyday life situations (Burke & Mackay, 1997). Young adults occasionally experience this effect when they are trying to retrieve an abstract word, but for older persons, it is more likely to occur when trying to remember a person's name (Evrard, 2002), particularly when the person has a name that sounds similar to someone else's (O'Hanlon, Kemper, & Wilcox, 2005). Although the information eventually can be recalled, the experience can lead to inconvenience and embarrassment, such as when you see someone you know out of context and cannot come up with that person's name.

Information that is stored and not accessed from remote memory appears to become increasingly difficult to retrieve with the passing years. It is often assumed that older people can remember information from many years in the past better than they can remember information to which they have more recently been exposed. However, this apparent truism is not supported by data on remote memory (Piolino, Desgranges, Benali, & Eustache, 2002). This finding was established a number of years ago in a study asking older adults to recall events from television shows. Their memory for recent programs was actually superior to that of programs in the more distant past (Squire, 1989). It seems that over time, our memory for past events becomes less vivid and loses detail no matter how old we were when we experienced the events (Cohen, 1996).

The exception to this finding on remote memory is in the area of autobiographical memory, or recall of one's own past. The events in your life that have a great deal of personal relevance and are rehearsed many times, such as achieving an important goal, do retain their clarity (Cohen, 1998a). Particularly salient to many adults is a "reminiscence bump" of memories from the ages of 10 to 30 (Rubin, Rahhal, & Poon, 1998), especially happy memories (Berntsen & Rubin, 2002). These memories are preserved because people often think and talk about them and they are central to their sense of identity (Piolino et al., 2006). For those remote memories that do not have the same personal relevance, the effect of aging and time is for those memories to fade away with the passing years.

The ability to remember to "do" something, or prospective memory, is another area of interest with regard to changes in adulthood. A common complaint of older adults is that they become absent-minded, such as forgetting what they were intending to get when they go from one room to another. In event-based prospective memory, you attempt to remember to engage in a particular activity, such as following through on your promise to go to a friend's house after dinner. In time-based prospective memory, you attempt to remember to do something at a particular time, such as meeting that friend at 7:00 P.M.

Prospective memory is important in everyday life because everyone hates to forget to do something important. It is a nuisance, both to yourself and to others, when you forget to be at a certain place at a certain time. For instance, if you forget your dental appointment, you are inconveniencing the dentist, who now has an unfilled time slot, and yourself, because it will probably take you months to reschedule your appointment, not to mention paying a no-show fee. There are also potential health risks associated with a decrease in prospective memory, as when an individual forgets to take medication at the right time or, as in many cases, with a meal.

Older people appear to have greater difficulties with prospective memory than do younger adults. For example, in a simulated shopping task requiring participants to remember the items on their list, older adults showed poorer memory performance than did young people (Farrimond, Knight, & Titov, 2006).

Identity, Self-Efficacy, Control Beliefs, and Stereotype Threat

The empirical evidence we have just seen supports the commonly held belief that our memory will suffer as we get older—the only question is perhaps how much and when. However, there is a countervailing set of data suggesting that how we think about our memory may play just as important a role as our actual age. In this section, we look at four of these factors to investigate possible connections between the way we feel about our memory and how our memory holds up with age.

The "over-the-hill" form of identity accommodation predicts that people who allow their views of their cognitive abilities to be invaded by society's negative stereotypes about aging actually suffer more severe age effects than people who are able to shore up their identities through identity assimilation. The over-the-hillers start on a downward spiral that causes them to be painfully aware of each instance of forgetting and to become even more pessimistic about their memory performance in the future. We know that middle-aged adults are highly sensitive to age-related changes in memory (Whitbourne & Collins, 1998). How does this sensitivity affect their actual performance?

Researchers investigating the related concepts of memory self-efficacy, control, and anxiety about memory performance are providing evidence to suggest that the way we feel about our memories can in fact influence how well we do, particularly as we get older. For example, people who interpret memory failures as due to an uncontrollable loss of capacity and feel that the forces that determine their memory functioning are outside their control are more likely in fact to have lower memory test scores (Riggs, Lachman, & Wingfield, 1997).

Memory self-efficacy is one component of the way we feel about our memory—it refers specifically to the degree to which you feel that you can successfully complete a memory task (Cavanaugh, 1989; Ryan & See, 1993). The higher your self-efficacy, the greater the chance that you will be able to perform to your maximum ability. Although your self-efficacy may be too high, leading you to be overly confident about your memory, most people as they get older feel less and less confident about their memory. They are affected by the so-called "implicit theory" about aging and memory: namely, that memory functioning suffers an inevitable decline in later life (McDonald-Miszczak, Hertzog, & Hultsch, 1995).

An impressive display of the power of memory self-efficacy comes from a six-year longitudinal study conducted in the Netherlands of a healthy community sample of over 1,800 individuals 55 and older (Valentijn et al., 2006). Individuals with a lower sense of memory self-efficacy, particularly with regard to the belief that their memory has changed, showed poorer memory performance over the course of the study. Whether their lower self-efficacy caused their poorer performance or reflected negative changes that were actually occurring was impossible to determine. However, other investigations suggest that having lower memory self-efficacy may in fact be somewhat of a self-fulfilling prophecy.

The notion of **stereotype threat** supports the idea that believing that memory declines with age might be enough to throw off the performance of an older adult on a memory task. Initially developed in research on the standardized test performance of African-Americans, the concept of stereotype threat refers to our tendency to perform in ways consistent with negative stereotypes of the group to which we belong

The way that instructions are worded may influence the performance of an older adult on a memory test.

(Steele, Spencer, & Aronson, 2002). Since older adults are stereotyped as having poorer memories, stereotype threat would mean that they will receive lower scores on a memory test because, at some level, they have come to accept society's views of their cognitive abilities. Although through identity assimilation older adults can overcome stereotype threat (Whitbourne & Sneed, 2002), it still remains difficult to be entirely impervious to society's negative views about aging and memory (Cuddy, Norton, & Fiske, 2005).

In the aging stereotype threat paradigm, participants are asked to complete several questionnaires prior to the memory test to assess their memory-related beliefs, including self-efficacy. They are then assigned to a positive or negative memory stereotyping condition. In the positive condition, they read a news article that contradicts memory stereotypes and in the negative condition, a news article that supports memory stereotypes. They are then given a memory recall task. In addition to measuring self-efficacy, researchers using the stereotype threat paradigm also assess **memory controllability** (Lachman, Weaver, Bandura, Elliott, & Lewkowicz, 1992), a scale tapping into a variety of beliefs about the effects of the aging process on memory,

such as the extent to which the individual believes that memory decline is inevitable with age.

In investigating stereotype threat, researchers have proposed that identification with negative images of aging interferes with memory performance in older adults by lowering their feelings of memory controllability and, ultimately, their use of mnemonic strategies to improve memory performance (Hess, Auman, Colcombe, & Rahhal, 2003). However, there are variations in the ways that people respond to stereotype threat. In a further study with a range of adults from the 20s to the 80s, researchers found that rather than being more negatively affected by stereotype threat, the oldest participants were relatively immune to its impact (Hess & Hinson, 2006). Although identity processes were not investigated in this particular study, the investigators proposed that individual differences in response to threat may mediate the way that older individuals react to negative information about aging and memory. We might hypothesize that identity assimilation was protecting these elders from the harmful effects of believing that aging is associated with inevitable memory loss.

It is very difficult to estimate the impact of memory beliefs on performance in the sense that even the hint that the situation is a memory test can activate stereotype threat and hence worsen the performance of older adults. In a study comparing traditional and nontraditional instructional conditions in relation to memory for trivia (Rahhal, Colcombe, & Hasher, 2001), age differences were observed in the traditional, but not the nontraditional, instructional condition. We do not even know exactly when stereotype threat starts to come into play as a factor affecting memory performance because there is evidence that concern over poor memory performance on the basis of age may be higher for middle-aged than older adults (O'Brien & Hummert, 2006).

The notion of memory controllability stems from a model of memory control and aging that focuses on the actions we can take to regulate our own memory performance, regardless of age (Lachman, 2006). According to Lachman's model, self-efficacy contributes to our beliefs that we can control our memory, which ultimately influences actual memory performance along with a host of other psychological variables, including our use of mnemonic strategies. If we

believe that we can control our memories, as was shown in the stereotype threat studies, then we are more likely to take advantage of the strategies that can ensure that we actually can perform better (Lachman, 2006; Lachman & Andreoletti, 2006).

Memory and Health-Related Behaviors

Given the relationship of various health-related behaviors to the functioning of the central nervous system, it should not come as a surprise to learn that memory in later adulthood is related to similar health-related behaviors. For example, cigarette smoking is known to cause deleterious changes in the brain. One unique longitudinal study conducted in Scotland provided impressive data showing that people who had been tested as children and were then followed up at ages 64 and 66 years had significantly lower memory and information processing scores (Starr, Deary, Fox, & Whalley, 2007). Particularly impressive about this study was the fact that the longitudinal design made it possible not only to observe changes over time but also to control for early life intelligence scores.

A second health-related behavior relevant to memory is fish consumption. Certain types of fish are high in omega-3 fatty acids and other substances that have been shown to be related to enhanced cognitive functioning. Participants in the Chicago Health and Aging Study were followed over a six-year period during which they were asked to report their food consumption. Of the over 3,700 people followed over the course of the study, about 20% ate two or more fish meals per week. Controlling for a host of relevant factors, the rate of cognitive decline in individuals who had one or more fish meals a week was reduced by 10 to 13% per year (Morris, Evans, Tangney, Bienias, & Wilson, 2005).

FIGURE 6.9
Control Beliefs and Memory

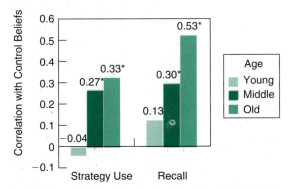

In this figure, with data from Lachman and Andreoletti (2006), age differences in correlations between control beliefs, strategy use, and recall are illustrated. For older adults, having strong beliefs in memory controllability was predictive of both strategy use and recall.
Source: Lachman & Andreoletti, 2006.

FIGURE 6.10
Cognitive Decline and Flavonoid Intake

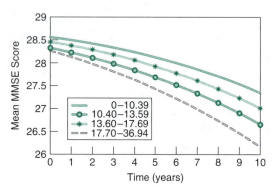

Changes in Mini-Mental State Examination (MMSE) scores by amount of daily flavonoid intake in men in the PAQUID (Personnes Age'es Quid) Study aged sixty-five to seventy years at baseline, who had a high educational level, were nonsmokers, and had a normal body mass index and average fruit (286.15 g/day) and vegetable (242.44 g/day) consumption.

Source: Letenneur, Proust-Lima, Le George, Dartigues, & Barberger-Gateau, 2007.

Investigators have also established a link between enhanced memory performance in older adults and other dietary components, including vitamin B_{12}, vitamin B_6, and folate (Calvaresi & Bryan, 2001). Conversely, among a sample of over 450 Chinese adults age 55 and older, cognitive functioning was negatively related to intake of homocysteine, an amino acid found in the blood and acquired mainly from eating meat. Vitamin D is another dietary component thought to be linked to cognitive functioning (Wilkins, Sheline, Roe, Birge, & Morris, 2006). Flavonoids, found in certain foods ranging from fruits and vegetables to red wine and dark chocolate, can also have a beneficial influence on cognition. In a longitudinal study conducted in France over a 10-year period, high levels of flavonoid intake were associated with significantly lower memory declines (Letenneur, Proust-Lima, Le George, Dartigues, & Barberger-Gateau, 2007).

In contrast to the positive effects of these substances, one supposed natural memory cure shows no beneficial effects. Ginko biloba extracts, sold as a nutritional supplement to improve memory, was associated with improved memory performance on only one measure among a host of cognitive tests administered to older and younger adults in a placebo-controlled study (Burns, Bryan, & Nettelbeck, 2006).

In Chapter 4, we saw that aerobic exercise can contribute to increases in brain areas involved in cognition. A number of other researchers have also shown that older people who are aerobically fit are also mentally more fit (Newson & Kemps, 2006). Mirroring those findings is research showing that strength training through weight lifting can improve the performance of older adults (Lachman, Neupert, Bertrand, & Jette, 2006). It is not even necessary to belong to a gym to be able to benefit from resistance exercise, as the participants in this study exercised in their own homes.

Health may also play a role in cognition through the route of metabolic factors. As we saw in Chapter 5, people with metabolic syndrome are at increased risk for Alzheimer's disease. Impaired glucose tolerance, a component of metabolic syndrome, shows a clear relationship to cognitive functioning in normal aging individuals (Di Bonito et al., 2007). Older adults with diabetes are more likely to experience slowing of psychomotor speed as well as declines in memory (Ryan, 2005). Even impaired glucose tolerance, a condition known as pre-diabetes, can be a risk factor for greater declines in cognition. High-fat diets appear to play an important role in this process (Greenwood & Winocur, 2005).

One possible route through which metabolic factors can affect psychomotor slowing and memory involves insulin growth factor-1 (IGF-1), one of three growth hormones involved in insulin regulation, which also has a protective effect on neurons. As part of the Nurses' Health Study, a nationwide investigation involving over 120,000 women studied from midlife on, researchers obtained blood samples and then several years later conducted telephone interviews of cognitive functioning from a sample of 590 women who were 70 years of age and older. After adjusting for a large possible number of confounding factors (such as education, smoking history, alcohol use, and BMI), the researchers found that the women with low levels of IGF-1 showed slower decreases with age in cognitive functioning than women with high levels of this substance (Okereke et al., 2007).

As we saw in Chapter 5, health-related behaviors include those that are involved in the management of stress. It would make sense that to the extent that stress takes its toll on our health and emotions, it would also affect our cognitive functioning. You undoubtedly have had the experience of forgetting something important when you were being preoccupied with other concerns such as worries about finances, too much work, or relationship problems. Researchers investigating this issue in older adults have provided support for the notion that stress can interfere with their memory performance. In one intriguing investigation of this notion, a sample of over 300 older adults in the Veterans Administration Normative Aging Study were asked to keep a daily diary of their interpersonal stressors and their memory failures. By tracking the relationship of stressful experiences on a daily basis, researchers were able to establish the lagged effect showing that stressors on one day predicted memory failures on the next (Neupert, Almeida, Mroczek, & Spiro, 2006).

That emotions can interfere with memory is also an experience to which you can most likely attest. When you are sad, you may feel that you are not at the peak of your cognitive abilities. A prospective longitudinal study of widows, i.e., begun before the widows lost their husbands, confirmed this idea among older women. Independently of the effect of losing a spouse on depressive symptoms, women in

the Longitudinal Aging Study Amsterdam were found to have lower memory performance when studied over a six-year period. Although the women who eventually lost their husbands had started out with lower memory scores, even when controlling for their initial status, the widows showed greater memory loss over the course of the study (Aartsen, Van Tilburg, Smits, Comijs, & Knipscheer, 2005).

Looking directly at memory performance and its relationship to stress, another group of investigators has also provided impressive evidence supporting the idea that at least some of the deficit shown by older adults on working memory tasks can be accounted for by the experience of daily stressors (Sliwinski et al., 2006). In this study, a group of over 100 older adults living in the community with intact mental status were compared with young adults on the n-back working memory task. The amount of daily stress was determined through an interview in which participants were asked questions such as "Did you have an argument or disagreement with anyone?" and "Did anything happen to a close friend or relative that turned out to be stressful for you?" Testing occurred over six occasions, allowing the investigators to examine within-person variations in the relationship between stress and memory as well as between-person age group differences.

Interestingly, the young adults in the sample were more likely to say "yes" to these and the other four questions assessing interpersonal stress. For instance, young adults said they had an argument on 26% of the days on which a given stressor occurred compared to 5% for older adults. However, on days in which people experienced stress, their performance was significantly worse for both age groups, as can be seen in Figure 6.11, which shows reaction times for the 2-back working memory task.

Why does stress interfere with memory performance? Sliwinski and his colleagues (2006)

FIGURE 6.11
Relationship Between Stress and Working Memory in Young and Older Adults

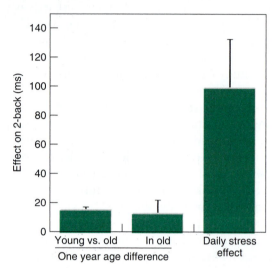

Older and younger adults were compared in the impact of daily stress on working memory in the 2-back test. The left bar shows the effect of a 1-year age difference (based on a young-older comparison) on response time, the middle bar shows a 1-year age difference based on just the older sample, and the right bar shows the effect of one daily stressor on reaction time. Error bars indicate the standard error of the effect.

Source: Sliwinski, Smyth, Hofer, & Stawski, 2006.

maintain that preoccupation with stress occupies attentional resources that could otherwise be devoted to the memory task. The lack of age differences in the stress-memory relationship suggests that all of us, regardless of our age, perform more efficiently when we are free from the competing attentional demands of stress. However, there is evidence that older adults are more anxious about their memories, and that their anxiety interferes with their memory performance (Andreoletti, Veratti, & Lachman, 2006).

Memory Training Studies

It seems safe to say that one mission of researchers who study aging and memory is to find ways to help older adults offset deleterious changes in their working memory, episodic memory, and other functions of long-term memory. Many of the researchers in this field are true "gerontological optimists" who believe that their work can help improve cognitive functioning in older adults. They have established, for example, the fact that even simple practice can produce significant improvements in memory task performance, offsetting the negative effects of mental inactivity (Belleville et al., 2006). Interventions aimed at improving episodic memory can be beneficial even with individuals who suffer from mild cognitive impairment (Belleville et al., 2006).

Even though simple practice alone can suffice to result in enhanced memory performance, there are advantages to encouraging strategy use among older adults. Giving them training in ways to improve their memories also has the benefit of increasing feelings of self-efficacy (Lachman, Andreoletti, & Pearman, 2006).

One of the most ambitious cognitive training interventions in the field is a multisite study known as Advanced Cognitive Training for Independent and Vital Elderly ("ACTIVE") carried out over a two-year period on over 2,800 adults 65 to 94 years of age (Ball et al., 2002). Training sessions consisted of 10 sessions lasting about an hour over a 5- to 6-week period. The participants were trained in one of three types of cognitive skills—memory, reasoning, or speed of processing. The control group received no training. These types of training were selected because in small laboratory studies they showed the most promise. Also, these were cognitive functions related to everyday living tasks (e.g., telephone use, shopping, food preparation, housekeeping, laundry, transportation, medication use, and management of personal finances). For instance, those who received memory training were taught ways to remember word lists and sequences of items, text, and the main ideas and details of stories. Training in the area of reasoning involved learning how to solve problems that follow patterns, such as reading a bus schedule or filling out an order sheet. Training in speed of processing involved learning how to identify and locate visual information quickly for use in tasks such as looking up a phone number, finding information on medicine bottles, and responding to traffic signs.

In testing at the end of the training period, the majority of participants in the speed (87%) and reasoning (74%) groups showed improvement; about one-quarter (26%) in the memory group showed improvement. Two years later, the gains were still maintained, although these were larger for participants who participated in booster sessions.

"What do you think?" | *6-3*

If you were going to open a memory clinic for older adults, what types of strategies would you teach? Why?

In conclusion, attentional and memory processes in adulthood are important in everyday life. Older adults appear to suffer some deleterious changes, but these changes are by no means universally or irreversibly negative. Identity seems to play an important role in determining whether individuals are able to take advantage of compensatory strategies. Future research will help uncover more of these personality-memory linkages as well as identify which strategies can be most effective in maximizing cognitive performance throughout middle and later adulthood.

SUMMARY

1. Cognitive functions are an important component of an individual's identity, and in middle and later adulthood, individuals become concerned about the loss of these abilities. However, many cognitive abilities are maintained well into later life, and there are preventative strategies individuals can use. Psychomotor speed, measured by reaction time, is an important variable in research on cognitive aging. There is a consistent increase of reaction time throughout adulthood. The general slowing hypothesis explains this increase as a decline of information processing speed, and the related age-complexity hypothesis proposes that the loss is greater for more difficult tasks. Studies of attention and aging involve the tasks of priming, search, divided attention, and sustained attention. Patterns of age differences on these tasks are interpreted in terms of the theory of attentional resources and aging, which proposes that older adults have limited resources, and by the inhibitory deficit hypothesis, according to which older adults are less able to inhibit irrelevant information in attentional tasks. The context processing deficiency proposes that older adults are less able to take advantage of cues from the environment.

2. Memory is studied in terms of its components. The study of aging and memory involves attempts to determine how each component is affected by age-related changes in the processes of storing, encoding, and retrieving information. Working memory is significantly poorer in older adults.

3. In long-term memory, tasks of episodic memory are most sensitive to age effects, and older adults have more difficulty in everyday memory tasks as well as in standard laboratory experiments. Semantic memory, however, is not affected by the normal aging process. Procedural memory is also retained in older adults, as is implicit memory. However, older adults have more difficulty with tasks involving source memory, tip-of-the-tongue, and

remote memory. Certain personal memories are well retained into later life, particularly those from adolescence and early adulthood. Prospective memory is retained when an individual can be prompted by the time rather than by an event. Researchers are attempting to establish connections between changes in the nervous system and age-related deficits in working memory.

4. Researchers are investigating the interaction of memory changes with changes in control beliefs, identity, and self-efficacy. The concept of stereotype threat implies that older adults may perform more poorly on memory tasks that activate negative stereotypes about aging and memory.

5. Memory in later adulthood is related to a variety of health-related behaviors, including cigarette smoking, consumption of fish high in omega-3 fatty acids, vitamin B_{12}, vitamin B_6, folate, and flavonoids. Aerobic exercise can contribute to increases in brain areas involved in cognition. Health may also play a role through the route of metabolic factors. Impaired glucose tolerance, a component of metabolic syndrome, shows a clear relationship to cognitive functioning in normal aging individuals. Stress can also interfere with memory performance.

6. Interventions aimed at improving episodic memory can be beneficial, particularly those that teach strategy use among older adults. One of the most ambitious cognitive training interventions was a multisite study known as Advanced Cognitive Training for Independent and Vital Elderly (ACTIVE) which found that training in memory and reasoning improved the performance of older adults on daily living tasks.

CHAPTER 7

Language, Problem Solving, and Intelligence

> **"**_The wiser mind mourns less for what age takes away than what it leaves behind._**"**
>
> William Wordsworth
> (1770–1850)

As critical as information processing and memory are to the ability to adapt to everyday life, the ability to analyze, reason, and communicate with others guides your use of judgment, knowledge, and decision making. Without these abilities, your potential to learn new information and integrate it with your existing body of knowledge would be very limited.

Researchers have a great interest in finding out about the higher level cognitive functions in adulthood and later life. Such findings help address the practical need to determine how well older workers can perform (as is discussed in Chapter 10). Furthermore, information on thinking and learning in later adulthood can provide a greater understanding of the potential for, as it is termed, "lifelong learning."

LANGUAGE

The use of language involves a wide range of cognitive functions, including comprehension, memory, and decision making. As shown in Chapter 6, many of these functions are negatively affected by the aging process. Somewhat surprisingly, then, most researchers believe that, overall, the average healthy older adult does not suffer significant losses in the ability to use language effectively under normal speaking

These older adults, participating in an Elder Hostel educational program in Washington, D.C., are clearly enjoying their ability to communicate about shared experiences through language.

conditions (Titone et al., 2006). The basic abilities to carry on a conversation, read, and write are maintained throughout later life.

Cognitive Aspects of Language

Given an overall picture of stability in language, there are nevertheless changes with age in cognitive processes that may affect an older adult's ability to use language effectively. At the most basic level, reading rate slows down in later adulthood, even in people with good visual acuity (Lott et al., 2001). The changes in hearing and speech perception described in Chapter 4 may influence language use in later adulthood. When conversing, older adults may find it more difficult to hear particular words, so that they have to work harder to interpret what other people say.

The slowing of cognitive processing also affects the quality of interpretations that older adults derive from spoken language. Retrieval deficits can cause older adults to make mistakes in spelling, leading them to be unable to recall how

to spell a word they once knew (Burke & Mackay, 1997). Compared with young adults, they may speak in simpler sentences (Kemper, Marquis, & Thompson, 2001). Their writing also becomes simpler, both in terms of expression of ideas and in terms of grammatical complexity (Kemper, Greiner, Marquis, Prenovost, & Mitzner, 2001).

A second major factor influencing spoken and written language is the existence of working memory deficits (Kemper & Sumner, 2001). As discussed in Chapter 6, working memory is the ability to hold one piece of information in mind while processing other information. Declines in this capacity can cause older adults to lose track of what they wish to say as they speak or the content of what they read.

On the other hand, there are compensating factors that can counteract the negative effects of aging on the processes involved in speech production and comprehension. A major benefit for older adults is the fact that they do not lose the ability to understand individual words (James & MacKay, 2007). They can grasp and remember the descriptions provided in language describing the thoughts and actions of a character in a story (Stine-Morrow & Miller, 1999). Older adults are also able to use strategies effectively to maximize their comprehension of written text (Stine-Morrow, Milinder, Pullara, & Herman, 2001). When listening to someone speaking, they show no impairment in the ability to put together the structure of the sentence along with the emphasis the speaker uses while talking (Titone et al., 2006).

Neuroimaging evidence supports the view that older adults use compensatory strategies by activating parts of the frontal cortex while reading to augment their working memory deficiencies (Grossman et al., 2002). There is even some evidence that older adults activate the right hemisphere of the brain when processing speech, a reversal of the left hemispheric dominance seen in most younger adults. It is possible that this changing brain activation is an attempt to compensate for age-related losses (Geal-Dor, Goldstein, Kamenir, & Babkoff, 2006).

Another important compensating factor for changes in memory and speed is the effect of experience on understanding context in language, particularly for those older adults who have developed an extensive vocabulary over their lifetimes (Federmeier, McLennan, De Ochoa, & Kutas, 2002). Older adults have a rich backlog of experiences from which to draw when they listen or read. Even if they cannot hear each word, they can use the context of a situation to draw the correct meaning. While reading, they can skim for information rather than stop and examine every word or phrase.

As will be seen later in the topic of expertise, older adults have well-developed structures of information that allow them to anticipate and organize information that may overwhelm a novice. Even in situations that do not involve expert knowledge of a skill, previous experience can make up for slower processing of new linguistic information. For example, the avid soap opera fan who watches the same program every day can anticipate what the characters will say rather than needing to hear every single word that is spoken. When reading magazines or newspapers, a knowledgeable older reader is able to make up for changes in working memory by building more effective structures for retrieving related information from written text (Stine-Morrow & Miller, 1999).

Social Aspects of Language

Along with changes in language use and comprehension throughout adulthood are changes in the social aspects of communication. One of these is the tendency of older adults to share with others their reminiscences about the past. Such a change can have very positive outcomes. Our ability to tell a good story may improve as we get older as we develop greater richness and elaboration of linguistic and metaphorical abilities. Reminiscences about the past may also serve a function in solidifying relationships with and building shared identities with others from our own generation. Through such processes, older adults are able to use language to enhance their relationships with others.

With the increased tendency to reminisce, there is also the unfortunate possibility that an older adult will be perceived negatively by a younger person who finds the older person's speech overly repetitive or too focused on the past (Bieman-Copland & Ryan, 2001). The greater verbosity among older people further complicates intergenerational relationships to the extent that the aging individual focuses on current disabilities or health limitations. Talking extensively about a topic in which the listener has no interest or which makes the listener uncomfortable can have an effect opposite to that intended and possibly isolate the older individual.

The third and possibly the most serious change in communication patterns between young and older adults comes not from the

ASSESS YOURSELF: How We Treat Older Adults

Elderspeak and the associated patterns of treating older adults like children can have detrimental effects. Even though people mean well, they often inadvertently engage in this behavior. See whether you are one of the people who does so:

1. When I talk to an older adult, I find that I talk:
   A. in my normal voice.
   B. much louder than normal.

2. The average older adult prefers it when strangers call him or her by:
   A. first name.
   B. terms such as "dear" or "honey."
   C. "Mr." or "Mrs./Ms."

3. If an older adult has physical infirmities, it means that he or she:
   A. may or may not suffer from cognitive deficits.
   B. certainly suffers from cognitive deficits as well.

4. If I had the opportunity to plan the events in a nursing home, I would think the most enjoyable activities for residents would include:
   A. coloring books and cutouts.
   B. holiday decorations such as Easter bunnies.
   C. current events discussion groups.

5. I think that it is better for older adults to:
   A. be discouraged from talking about the past.
   B. talk about whatever comes to their minds.
   C. be encouraged to talk about the past.

older adult, but from younger people. Based on outward physical appearance, the young person can make the incorrect assumption that the elder is frail, cognitively impaired, and handicapped in the ability to speak. This assumption can lead the younger person to adopt the linguistic pattern known as **elderspeak**, which is a simplified speech pattern directed at older adults who presumably are unable to understand adult language.

According to the **communication predicament model** of aging, the use of elderspeak constrains the older person from being able to participate fully in conversations with others.

(See Figure 7.1.) Lack of cognitive stimulation due to the adoption of simple speech patterns directed toward the older person can accelerate whatever cognitive declines might otherwise have occurred. Furthermore, the kind of patronizing speech that is involved in elderspeak (e.g., "Can I help you, honey?" or referring to someone by first name) forms part of a pattern of overparenting and failure to encourage independent behaviors in the older person (Ryan, Hummert, & Boich, 1995). Such patterns of speech are most likely to be used by young adults when speaking to a target whom they believe to be infirmed (Hummert, Shaner, Garstka, & Henry,

FIGURE 7.1
Communication Predicament Model

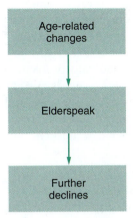

According to the communication predicament model, older adults who are treated in an infantilizing manner suffer greater declines in cognitive functions.

Source: Ryan, Hummert, & Boich, 1995.

1998). Through this process of infantilization, the older person loses the incentive to attempt to regain self-sufficiency in the basic activities of daily life (Whitbourne, Culgin, & Cassidy, 1995; Whitbourne & Wills, 1993). Moreover, when older adults in a residential facility are treated by younger staff in an infantilizing manner, they are also less likely to want to socialize with each other, potentially leading to social isolation (Salari & Rich, 2001).

"What do you think?"   **7-1**

When have you seen older people spoken to with elderspeak? How do you think this makes them feel?

EVERYDAY PROBLEM SOLVING

Closely related to the issue of language development in later adulthood is the question of how we change over the course of adulthood in our ability to apply our cognitive processes to the problems we encounter in our daily lives. Over the past several decades, researchers have increasingly moved away from investigations of abstract reasoning abilities as applied to academic problems (such as anagrams or puzzles). Instead, current investigations focus on how people tackle the everyday challenges of managing such tasks as personal finances, maintaining medications, and monitoring diet (Allaire & Marsiske, 2002).

Characteristics of Problem Solving

Psychologists approach the "problem" of problem solving by identifying types of problems and the stages involved in successfully approaching and resolving them. Essentially, problem solving involves assessing the current state of a situation, deciding on what is the desired end-state, and finding ways of transforming the current into the desired state. For example, when you are planning your budget for the month, you begin by assessing how much money is in your checkbook (current state). You then decide on how much money to allocate to food, entertainment, and transportation based on your desired end-state (having some money left at the end of the month).

Problems vary tremendously, however, in their structure and complexity. This example of a monthly budget is one that is fairly well structured in that the constraints are clear (there is only so much money in one's checkbook), and a set of steps must be followed. With problems that lack clear goals or when the steps that must be followed are difficult to discern, an increased cognitive burden is placed on the individual.

Some of these problems we face in our lives involve high-tech objects that are becoming increasingly commonplace and are relatively easy for computer savvy people to use but challenging for many older adults (and even a fair number of middle-aged adults). For example, programming

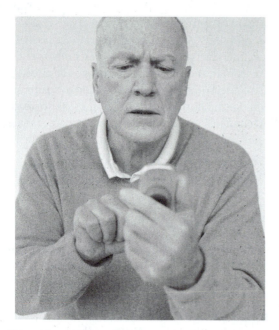

This older adult is showing some of the frustration many of us feel when trying to figure out how to use a new gadget.

cell phones, cameras, and digital video recorders, not to mention word processing software and printers, often involves interpreting instructions that require multiple steps. Instruction manuals, notorious for containing uncertain or ambiguous specifications, now are increasingly less likely to be packaged with the product and must be downloaded on the Internet, itself often a major challenge. However, complex instructions are present in many "low-tech" areas as well, such as cooking, handcrafts, and work with mechanical objects (such as the infamous vague instructions provided for the assembly of a desk chair or bicycle). Therefore, we must apply our problem-solving skills to a wide range of situations, many of which are less than ideal.

Problem Solving in Adulthood

Given the pervasiveness of complex problems in daily life, researchers are naturally interested in

determining the factors that influence successful solutions. In everyday problem solving, unlike problem solving in the laboratory, the problems are multidimensional, and the steps in solving them vary from person to person. Taking these factors into account, everyday problem solving is defined as involving problems that typically occur in people's everyday lives, that can be solved in more than one way, and that require the problem solver to decide which strategy will lead to the desired result (Thornton & Dumke, 2005).

"What do you think?"	7-2

Can you give examples of the most important problems in your life?

Throughout the adult years, there is a tradeoff in the factors affecting everyday problem-solving between alterations in speed of processing and working memory, and gains in experience as individuals encounter a wider variety of problems as well as more depth in their own fields of expertise. Experience can enhance both problem solving performance (Crawford & Channon, 2002) and feelings of self-efficacy (Artistico, Cervone, & Pezzuti, 2003).

The acquisition of expertise through years of exposure to certain kinds of problems is a major influence on the way middle-aged and older adults approach familiar everyday situations. They develop an ability to search for the relevant factors in a problem, and this increased selectivity to information allows them to avoid becoming burdened with excess information. Think of the experienced automobile mechanic who, with a single glance at an engine, is able to arrive at an instant diagnosis of the cause of the strange sounds it has been making for the past week. A novice (such as perhaps yourself) might spend hours searching through the car manual, various instruction books, and the seemingly hundreds of valves and gauges under the hood. By the time you have finished, you may not even remember what you have already checked out.

Expert problem solvers are able to avoid information overload by zeroing in on specific areas that experience has taught them are important to consider. They may also make better choices. In one fascinating study of decision making, older adults were found to avoid what is known as the "attraction effect," a trap that younger people fall into when choosing between alternatives. In this study, decisions were compared when people were given 2 versus 3 choices. For example, if you say you prefer vanilla ice cream when given the choice of vanilla or chocolate, then logically speaking, you should also say you prefer vanilla when presented with the choice of vanilla, chocolate, or strawberry. The attraction effect refers to the tendency to find a less than optimal choice between two alternatives to be more attractive when a third

alternative is presented. With these three choices, you would actually be more likely to choose chocolate.

When comparing older adults with young adults, researchers found that young adults are more likely to fall prey to the attraction effect than are older adults, whose decisions are consistent regardless of the alternatives (Tentori, Osherson, Hasher, & May, 2001).

Supporting the notion that older adults are better problem solvers than younger adults are data from a study comparing younger and older adult pilots. Older pilots (60 to 84 years of age) did show memory deficits on a task requiring them to read back messages that were read to them. However, there were no age differences when younger and older pilots were compared in tasks that required expertise in interpreting information about air routes from charts and messages (Morrow, Menard, Stine-Morrow, Teller, & Bryant, 2001). Adding to

Researchers have found that older adults are likely to make better choices at the grocery store than are younger adults.

the data about aging pilots discussed in Chapter 6, this finding further reinforces the notion that when you are flying on a commercial airplane, you are safer with an experienced pilot in the cockpit!

Although positive from the standpoint of efficiency, the ability that older problem solvers have to discount potentially irrelevant factors may have negative consequences. Because experienced problem solvers tend to seek answers to familiar problems by seeking familiar solutions, they may miss something important that is unique to a particular problem. For example, an automobile mechanic who goes directly to the distributor as the source of the problem may not notice a more serious wiring flaw elsewhere. Older problem solvers may think that they are doing a better job at solving the problem but, by objective criteria, may not be considering alternative solutions as effectively as do younger adults (Thornton & Dumke, 2005).

In addition to focusing on one solution rather than considering others, older adults may also tend to stick with one pattern of responding when the situation calls for being able to call on a range of ideas. Tests of verbal fluency ask respondents to produce as many items as possible, such as producing all possible words that begin with the letter "K." Older adults are more likely to perseverate on such a task, meaning that they continue to produce the same words, such as saying "King," "Knock," "Knee," "King," "Kite," where "King" counts as a perseveration. Although perseveration is often taken in clinical settings as indicative of frontal lobe deficits, a certain deficiency seems to be associated with normal aging on this type of cognitive task (Henry & Phillips, 2006). This deficiency may make it harder for older adults to generate novel solutions to problems, because they continue to repeat the ones they have already produced.

Further evidence of difficulties in problem solving comes from a study of the planning ability of a species other than humans, Japanese monkeys. In this study, the monkeys were given the task of finding food contained behind small openings in a panel (see the photograph). There were nine openings. In the experimental condition (shown in the photograph), the food was hidden behind white plastic circles. In the

Apparatus used to test planning abilities in monkeys. Food was either visible or not visible behind the openings in the panel.
Source: Kubo, Kato, & Nakamura, 2006.

control condition, the food was visible through clear plastic plates. As there were nine holes that could contain food, the best performance the monkey could achieve would be to retrieve all food items in nine consecutive attempts. Errors were counted if the monkey went back to a hole from which food had already been retrieved.

In this unique study, comparison between older and younger monkeys showed that the older monkeys made considerably more errors on the experimental trials, the ones in which the food was hidden behind the white plates (Kubo, Kato, & Nakamura, 2006). Not only did the older monkeys make more errors, but they also were inconsistent in their selection strategies, suggesting that they had experienced a decreased ability to plan.

Making up for losses in the ability to plan their strategies, older problem solvers have the advantage of more experience and improved

FIGURE 7.2

Errors in Problem Solving in Young and Older Monkeys

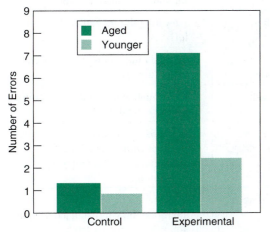

Older monkeys in the experimental condition in which they could not see the food behind a covered window made significantly more errors than younger monkeys reflecting poorer planning ability.

Source: Kubo, Kato, & Nakamura, 2006).

access to relevant information. People with experience have well-organized storehouses of knowledge that they can easily access and put to use. The expert on international travel, for example, can quickly tell you the pros and cons of a trip you are planning to a foreign country. Knowledge about the country's hotels, places of interest, and weather patterns is systematically stored in what is essentially a mental file cabinet of major travel destinations. Sports trivia buffs have a similar mastery of large amounts of content matter because it has been organized into systematic units.

Research on the speed of decision making in adults of varying ages confirms that older persons are able to reach an answer more quickly than are younger persons who do not have their knowledge bases as well sorted or categorized. However, it also appears that older persons make quicker decisions even in areas in which they are not particularly expert. Furthermore, they are less likely to seek additional information once their decision has been made than are young adults. It is possible that the more rapid problem solving shown by older adults reflects the fact that in many areas of decision making, their greater experience has given them an edge. Therefore they do not feel as dependent on incoming information as do younger adults. It is also possible that older adults are less able to use multiple sources of information and that this is why they make decisions on the basis of their experience rather than on the basis of the incoming data about the problem (Marsiske & Margrett, 2006).

The notion that older adults are faster at solving problems conflicts with much of the other data on cognition in adulthood. However, the types of measures used in studies of problem solving do not quantify responses in terms of milliseconds, as is true for studies of psychomotor speed. Instead, studies of problem solving involve measures based on the amount of information

TABLE 7.1
Examples from the Everyday Problems Test

Area	Problem	Sample Question
Recipe instructions	Items in a recipe are listed along with instructions for mixing	Which ingredients are mixed together?
Choosing furniture polishing products	Effects of various furniture polishing products are described	What type of polish would you use to provide the greatest shine?
Telephone bill	Charges for one month's phone calls	To which city were the most calls made?
Drivers' right of way	Laws for giving right of way while driving	Who can go first when there is a four-way stop sign?
Membership application	Fees for family membership	How much would you pay for yourself and your two children?
Medical symptoms	Indicate whether you have experienced a symptom or not	What box should you check if you have frequent back pain?
Dosages for medication	Directions provided for proper adult dosage	How many times can you take the medication in a 24-hour period?
Rebate coupon	Amount of money that can be claimed in a rebate	What information must you provide to receive the rebate?
Cab rates	Cab rates according to distance traveled	How much would the cab fare be if you traveled 3/4 of a mile during heavy traffic?
Tax return	Tax form with instructions	How much can you claim in deductions for your apartment rental?
Instructions for preparing a food product	Instructions are provided for how to prepare a prepackaged food	How long should you cook the mixture for?
Fixing a broken appliance	Troubleshooting list of instructions for the appliance failing to work	What should you do if your oven light won't turn on?
Payments schedule for health insurance	Benefits are described for a health insurance plan	How much will insurance cover of a 3-day hospital stay?
Nutritional information for loaf of bread	Calories, carbohydrates, and fats are listed in terms of recommended daily allowances on a loaf of bread	If you have two slices of bread, how much of your recommended daily allowance of cholesterol will you be consuming?
Time periods for receiving discounts on service	Schedule of discounts by day of week and time of day are provided	If you take a bus on a Sunday afternoon, how much of a discount can you receive on your fare?

In evaluating the problem-solving abilities of older adults, items such as these are used on the Everyday Problems Test.
Source: Willis & Marsiske, 1997.

that is gathered prior to making a decision, and these are not as sensitive to what are effectively fairly tiny changes in reaction time. Supporting the findings from studies of aging and cognition are results from neuropsychological testing. For midlife adults, performance on the familiar problem-solving tasks used in this context such as sorting cards appears to be maintained even while the ability to solve new problems may suffer impairments (Garden, Phillips, & MacPherson, 2001).

There are variations within the older population in factors that affect everyday problem solving. Education, as might be expected, is related to scores on the Everyday Problems Test (Burton, Strauss, Hultsch, & Hunter, 2006). Among African Americans, in particular, health status plays a role in influencing the quality of decisions they make on this task (Whitfield, Allaire, & Wiggins, 2004).

In everyday situations involving practical decision making, then, middle-aged and older adults appear to have an advantage when confronted with familiar choices. Their greater experience and expertise in terms of content and process allow them to appraise the problem, come up with a strategy, and then proceed to enact that strategy. However, when a familiar dilemma appears with a new twist, or when a premature decision leads to avoiding important information, older adults are relatively disadvantaged. Young problem solvers may suffer from their lack of familiarity with many situations, but because they can process larger amounts of information in a shorter time, they may avoid some of the traps that befall their elders.

Adult Learners

The literature on problem solving obviously emphasizes the ability to come to a resolution when dealing with a dilemma. However, the ability to "find" problems seems to be an equally compelling aspect of adult cognition. Research and theory on this aspect of adult cognition was stimulated, in part, by Swiss psychologist Jean Piaget's concept of **formal operations**, the ability of adolescents and adults to use logic and abstract symbols in arriving at solutions to complex problems. Adult developmental researchers have proposed that there is a stage of **postformal operations**, referring to the way that adults structure their thinking over and beyond that of adolescents (Commons, Richards, & Armon, 1984; Sinnott, 1998). Postformal thinking incorporates the tendency of the mature thinker to use logical processes that are specifically geared to the complex nature of adult life. The postformal thinker is also able to judge when to use formal logic and when, alternatively, to rely on other and simpler modes of representing problems. For example, it is not necessary to use the rules of formal logic to unplug a stopped drain. Hands-on methods are generally suitable for dealing with practical situations like this one involving actions in the physical world.

Related to the postformal stage of cognitive development is that of **dialectical thinking**, which is an interest in and appreciation for debate, arguments, and counterarguments (Basseches, 1984). Adult thinking involves the recognition that often the truth is not "necessarily a given," but that common understandings among people are a negotiated process of give and take. We may not be able to find the ideal solution to many of life's problems, but through the process of people sharing their alternative views with each other, we can at least come to some satisfactory compromises.

The proposition of a postformal stage of thinking has a great deal of intuitive appeal. Many questions that adults face have no right or wrong answer—just think of some of the cases that are brought to the Supreme Court every year. There are at least as many ambiguities

Adult learners often are more challenging and interested in debate in the classroom.

and uncertainties even in the dilemmas that the average person faces in resolving interpersonal conflicts with friends, family, or colleagues. Furthermore some people seem to seek out and relish the opportunity to engage others in dialogue and intellectual engagement. It would be boring for such individuals to face a world in which all the gray areas were removed from life's "real" problems.

The possibility that adults operate according to postformal operations leads to a variety of interesting implications about adults as thinkers, problem solvers, and, particularly, learners. Adult learners are increasingly becoming part of the concerns of those who teach at the college level; as of 2005 over half of the adult population age 16 to 40, and large percentages of adults over 40 (48% of those 41 to 50 and 41% of those 51 to 65) were involved in adult education (U.S. Bureau of the Census, 2007g). The distribution of adults by age involved in specific adult educational programs are shown in Figure 7.3.

In the classroom, adult learners may rely more on attaining mastery of the material through using strategies such as taking more copious notes and relying on them more heavily as they are trying to acquire new information (Delgoulet & Marquie, 2002). The adult learner is also more likely to challenge the instructor to go beyond the information and explore alternative dimensions. Such tendencies, though fascinating in the classroom, can lead to problems when it comes to evaluation. For a person who can see all the alternate angles to a standard multiple-choice exam question, it can be very difficult to arrive at the correct answer because more than one has virtues that merit attention. The adult thinker and learner may find it equally fascinating to ponder ambiguities rather than settle on one choice even though only one choice is graded as correct.

Not all adult learners have these character- istics, of course, and variation from person to person may be related to personality factors, such as willingness to be open to new experiences (dis- cussed in Chapter 8). However, the emergence of alternative modes of thought, and their con- tinued evolution throughout adulthood, provide an important counterpoint to the findings on

FIGURE 7.3

Adult Learners in the United States

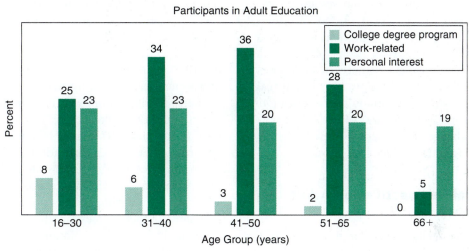

Source: U.S. Bureau of the Census, 2007g.

the adult's tendency to become more potentially more closed minded with age and experience.

INTELLIGENCE

When you think of "intelligence," you probably have some notion that it represents the quality of a person's ability to think. Formal definitions of intelligence in psychology come very close to this simple idea of intelligence as an individual's mental ability. Psychologists have struggled for decades with defining the specific meaning of the term intelligence beyond the notion that it represents the overall quality of the individual's mental abilities. For nearly as long, psychologists have grappled with the issue of determining the course of development in adulthood for this elusive quality of the human mind.

The potential existence of age effects on intelligence in adulthood has many practical as well as theoretical ramifications. For practical reasons, it is important to find out the relative strengths and weaknesses of younger versus older workers. As indicated in the earlier discussion of problem solving, there appear to be fairly distinct differences in the styles that adults of different ages use when making decisions. Employers in the public and private sectors can make practical use of the analyses generated by psychologists on the more quantified data that emerge from studies using standard intelligence test scores. From a theoretical standpoint, research on intelligence in adulthood has provided new perspectives on the components of thought. This research has also provided insight into the perennial question of how mental processes are affected by "nature versus nurture" as researchers have continued to exploit and explore the application of complex research designs to data on intelligence test scores in adulthood.

Just as our physical abilities partially define our identities, intelligence serves as an attribute of the person that forms part of the sense of self. People have a good idea of whether they are "smart" or "dumb," a self-attribution that they can carry for years (Leonardelli, Hermann, Lynch, & Arkin, 2003). For some people, their intelligence forms a significant part of identity. Those who value the products of the mind, such as their ability to solve tough crossword puzzles and the scores they obtain on board games, will be more vigilant for changes in intelligence associated with aging than people whose pride comes from physical competence. In some cases, these changes may be more imagined than real, as people respond to common characterizations of older people as having lost some of their wits. When the changes are present, however, this may prove to be a tough threshold to cross.

Historical Perspectives on Adult Intelligence

Research on intelligence in adulthood emphasizes the description and analysis of individual differences in the years from the 20s and older. The individual differences approach is reflected in the use of standardized intelligence tests as basic data for these studies. In fact, historically, it was the desire to develop age norms across adulthood for tests of intelligence that were originally developed on children that formed the impetus for the first studies on aging. The first intelligence test, the Stanford-Binet, was designed to evaluate the mental abilities of children. When it became evident that this was not a suitable tool for measuring adult intelligence, the search for appropriate tests and normative standards prompted investigations of the performance of adults of different ages.

"What do you think?"	**7-3**
Why is it so difficult to define intelligence?	

The initial forays into the field of adult intelligence involved cross-sectional and longitudinal comparisons. For example, David Wechsler, who developed the widely used **Wechsler Adult**

Intelligence Scale in the 1930s, administered the tests that comprise this instrument to representative samples of adults drawn from each succeeding decade ranging from early adulthood to old age. Standardization data were developed from these scores, but they were also used to describe age-related differences in performance on various facets of intelligence.

Early findings proposed that age differences across adulthood followed the "classic aging pattern" (Botwinick, 1977) of an inverted U-shaped pattern, with a peak in early adulthood followed by steady decline. Wechsler scales are divided into Verbal and Performance (i.e., nonverbal) scales, and older samples are consistently found to maintain their scores on the Verbal scales, particularly vocabulary (Kaufman, 2001). This differential age pattern for verbal and nonverbal abilities is the foundation for one of the major theoretical approaches to adult intelligence that is still in use today, the "fluid-crystallized" ability distinction, which is discussed shortly.

Results from the Wechsler scales, which supported the view that intelligence generally erodes over succeeding decades in adulthood, were in conflict with a smaller but consistent body of evidence from longitudinal studies. When samples of adults were followed through repeated testings using the Wechsler scales or another standardized test, the finding was either no decline or a decline that did not become apparent until very late in life.

In the 1950s, K. Warner Schaie began what is now the primary source of data on adult intelligence. Schaie's doctoral dissertation involved a comparison of 500 persons, 50 from each of 10 five-year age intervals, who were part of a prepaid medical plan consisting of 18,000 members in the Seattle, Washington, area. The first set of studies produced the typical cross-sectional age differences, showing negative age effects beginning in the 50s. However, seven years later, Schaie published a follow-up in which people's scores were compared within age groups between 1956 and 1963. Here were some surprising findings. For most abilities, there was an increase or no change between the first and second testings, even among the oldest age group. The stage was set for what has now become a 40-year plus search for the factors accounting for the aging, or the nonaging, of intelligence. Schaie's foresight in planning a study that would make possible the sophisticated developmental research designs described in Chapter 3 has provided a wealth of information on intelligence in adulthood and the factors that affect its fluctuations.

Theoretical Perspectives on Adult Intelligence

Theories of ingelligence differ in the number and nature of abilities that are postulated to exist. Fortunately, for our purposes, researchers working in the field of adult development and aging have come to a resolution, in theory if not practice, when characterizing the nature of adult intelligence. Most operate from the assumption that there are two main categories of mental abilities corresponding roughly to verbal and nonverbal intelligence.

The Concept of "g".   As background to the current state of theory in adult intelligence, it is necessary to take one more venture back into the history of the field. At the turn of the twentieth century, British psychologist Charles Spearman set about on the ambitious task of formulating a comprehensive theory of intelligence (1904; 1927). He proposed the existence of a "general factor" of intelligence, referred to as "g," which encompasses the ability to infer and apply relationships on the basis of experience. According to Spearman, individuals with high levels of "g" should be able to receive high scores on various tests that tap into specific

mental abilities (each of which is called "s" for specific). Such tests included the intelligence test devised by Binet, now known as the Stanford-Binet. The concept of a unitary factor in intelligence has emerged again in a large statistical analysis of age-performance relationships among adults 18 to 84 years. Salthouse identified a broad "g-type" factor associated with age that was also related to age-related deficits in speed and memory (Salthouse, 2001; Salthouse & Ferrer-Caja, 2003).

Primary Mental Abilities.   Despite the popularity of intelligence tests based on "g," the idea that intelligence is a unitary construct can be criticized for being overly simplistic. Contrasting theories involve proposals of multiple abilities or dimensions of abilities that together comprise intelligence. The multidimensional approach that has proven to be the most productive for understanding adult intelligence was the **primary mental abilities** framework proposed by Thurstone (1938). According to Thurstone, there are seven primary mental abilities: verbal meaning, word fluency (the ability to generate words following a certain lexical rule), number (arithmetic), spatial relations, memory, perceptual speed, and general reasoning. These seven abilities are considered separate and distinct from one another, and together they are thought to cover all possible abilities that characterize intelligence.

Fluid-Crystallized Theory.   Out of the primary mental ability theory emerged the proposal by theorist Raymond Cattell (1963) that the seven abilities actually group into two broad sets: one based on educational training and one set based on untutored thought processes. Cattell regarded these abilities as **secondary mental abilities**, a concept based on a statistical method of analysis that attempts to capture the broad constructs that underlie specific abilities.

In writing about the characteristics of these abilities, Cattell, in conjunction with psychologist John Horn (1966), defined them as "so pervasive relative to other ability structures and so obviously of an intellectual nature that each deserves the name intelligence" (p. 254). The first ability, **fluid intelligence** (also called **Gf**), is defined as the individual's innate abilities to carry out higher-level cognitive operations involving the integration, analysis, and synthesis of new information, "the sheer perception of complex relations" (Cattell, 1971). Fluid intelligence reflects the quality of biopsychological factors such as the functioning of the nervous system and sensory structures and cannot be trained or taught.

The second broad set of abilities within the Cattell model is **crystallized intelligence** (also called **Gc**), which represents the acquisition of specific skills and information acquired through familiarity with the language, knowledge, and conventions of one's culture. It involves the learned ability to infer relationships, make judgments, analyze problems, and use problem-solving strategies. Together, fluid and crystallized intelligence form a biopsychosocial definition of intelligence. They incorporate the biological factors related to the integrity of the nervous system, the psychological factors involved in cognitive processing, and the social factors derived from education and experience in one's culture.

Tests of fluid intelligence measure the ability to develop and infer abstract relationships independently of culture-specific information. The items on these tests either are novel combinations of figures and shapes or are well within the inventory of any individual such as letters and common words. For instance, in a fluid intelligence test, you may be asked to predict the next letter in a series based on the pattern that is set in the question (e.g., what letter would follow "A-C-E-G"?). You probably recall items such as

these from the SATs in which you had to imagine what an abstract shape or figure would look like when it was rotated 180 degrees.

By contrast, tests of crystallized intelligence include items involving language, logic, and factual information. In keeping with the definition by Cattell and his colleagues of crystallized intelligence as culturally based ability, some of the other tests used in their studies assessed such functions as the use of tools and the ability to solve everyday problems, such as computing gasoline mileage or balancing a checkbook.

Definitions and measurement of secondary mental abilities are based on the notion that they are statistically and conceptually independent from each other, but in reality, the two have an intrinsic connection. Many years after the theory was proposed, this connection was put to the test. A longitudinal investigation of 111 participants originally tested through the ages of 4 to 64 showed that over time fluid abilities helped to shape crystallized (McArdle & Hamagami, 2006). To acquire the skills and knowledge specific to your culture and system of education, it is necessary to have the fluid abilities to support the learning of new information.

The hypothesized life-span course of crystallized and fluid intelligence reflects the combination of factors thought to affect each of the two secondary abilities. Figure 7.4 depicts the adult course of fluid and crystallized intelligence as observed in an early study (Horn, 1970). The peak of fluid intelligence is hypothesized to be achieved in the years of adolescence, when the integrity of the nervous system and sensory structures are, at least theoretically, at optimum levels. From this point on, the changes associated with aging that reduce the efficiency of these systems lead to a downward trajectory in fluid intelligence. A contrasting age-related trend is proposed for crystallized intelligence, which continues to grow throughout

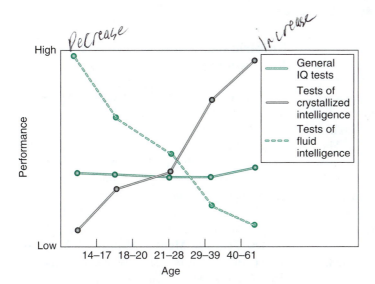

FIGURE 7.4
Pattern of Adult Age Differences in Fluid and Crystallized Abilities

Source: Horn, 1970.

adulthood as the individual acquires experience and culture-specific knowledge

It makes sense that vocabulary, information about the world, and understanding of why and how things work are all abilities that continue to evolve in the adult years as people gain more day-to-day exposure to people, places, and things (Beier & Ackerman, 2001). Consider, for example, what happens every time you solve a daily crossword puzzle. The chances are very high that you will learn at least one new word or fact each time. For example, did you know that the word topa means "any one of a variety of fish found in aquaria"? Yet this was a correct answer to a clue in a recent popular weekly newspaper's puzzle. Assuming you remember this seemingly useless information in the future, you would have increased your crystallized intelligence by coming across this word in the puzzle. As these experiences accumulate over a lifetime, this component of your intelligence will continue to grow.

Alternative Views of Intelligence

If you feel that the traditional views of intelligence are overly restrictive in the way they define this ineffable human quality, you are not alone.

Critics of traditional intelligence theories have proposed alternative views based on their belief that intelligence should be defined in terms of knowledge of the world and our ability to adapt to it.

The **theory of multiple intelligences** by Howard Gardner (1983; 1993) proposes that there are eight independent categories of intelligence, each of which can contribute to an individual's ability to adapt to the world. In addition to the usual areas included in other theories of intelligence, such as knowledge of math and vocabulary, Gardner's theory goes beyond what we learn in school to include a number of other qualities that help us to succeed in the world, ranging from musical to naturalistic intelligence. You may be high in one area, such as the ability to use your body effectively in sports or dance, but low in another area, such as understanding other people. According to Gardner, each of us has a range of strengths and weaknesses, not just one or two overall abilities.

Challenges to traditional views of intelligence were also raised by Robert Sternberg (1985), who based his **triarchic theory of intelligence** on analyses of the strategies used by expert problem solvers. The three aspects of intelligence proposed by Sternberg are componential (the ability to think and analyze), experiential (creativity), and contextual (practical). The contextual aspect of intelligence is perhaps the most interesting in the sense that it corresponds to the kind of "street smarts" we need to handle many of life's dilemmas, but it is not an ability usually tested in a standard intelligence test. The experiential component is relevant as well, corresponding to conceptions of creativity, which are discussed with regard to aging in Chapter 14. Like Gardner's approach, Sternberg's emphasizes a variety of non-academic skills needed in daily life.

Sternberg expanded his theory to make more explicit the notion that doing well on an intelligence test does not necessarily give us the ability to do well in life. He defined **successful intelligence** as the ability to achieve success in life according to your personal standards and in the framework of your sociocultural context (Sternberg, 1999). Included in successful intelligence are the processing skills identified in the triarchic theory (renamed analytical, creative, and practical). People high in successful intelligence are able to apply these skills to adapt, shape, and select environments, and they are able to capitalize on their strengths and correct and compensate for their weaknesses.

Although not yet applied directly to the study of adult intelligence, Sternberg's theory seems to have potential to enhance and enrich current formulations. For example, Sternberg's **balance theory of wisdom** (Sternberg, 1998) views wisdom as the ability to integrate the various components of intelligence outlined in the theory and to apply them to problems involving the common good or welfare of others. This approach complements the frameworks developed within the tradition of life-span developmental psychology by Baltes and his colleagues (see below). Together, these formulations greatly expand the notion of intelligence as a quality that goes beyond the ability to receive good test scores.

Empirical Evidence on Adult Intelligence

Schaie's study of intelligence on the Seattle sample (referred to briefly in Chapter 3) has produced a compelling literature on the complex nature of adult intelligence and the factors that affect its development. The archives of the Seattle Longitudinal Study (SLS) are now considered to be the major repository of data on intelligence in adulthood; the study is therefore the focus of this next section of the chapter.

The **Primary Mental Abilities (PMA) test** developed by Thurstone is the basis for the SLS data. According to Schaie (1996), combinations of PMA scales can be used to understand all the abilities involved in a person's everyday life. PMA scores can also be interpreted in terms of the fluid-crystallized distinction. Inductive Reasoning is the closest measure of G_f and verbal meaning measures G_c.

Longitudinal estimates of changes in the PMA scales are shown in Figure 7.5. The overall picture appears to be one of stability until the 50s or 60s, followed by decline through the oldest age tested. However, there are some cautions that may be helpful to consider (Schaie, 1996). First, although some individuals may show declines in intelligence by the mid-50s, there are not significant losses until the decade of the 70s. A second point is that none of the participants showed general deterioration of functioning, even at the oldest age tested of 88 years. Thus the age changes in cognitive functioning, though in a negative direction, did not occur significantly across the board. Fortunately, most people are able to retain competent performance of familiar skills, particularly those that are of importance to the individual.

Although based on a cross-sectional analysis, data from another large investigation provided an intensive look at age differences between 20 and 50 years, a period of time typically

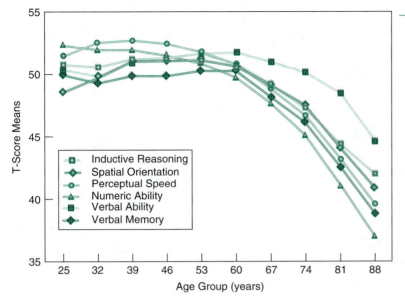

FIGURE 7.5
Seattle Longitudinal Study
Findings

Longitudinal estimates of age changes on
the primary mental abilities in the Seattle
Longitudinal Study are shown here.
Source: Schaie, Willis, & Caskie, 2004.

underrepresented in studies of intelligence in
adulthood (Schroeder & Salthouse, 2004). A
sample of nearly 5,400 individuals seeking
vocational aptitude testing provided data on a
variety of key intellectual variables. The pattern of
scores revealed in this study provides impressive
data in support of the notion of increases
in crystallized intelligence (vocabulary) through
middle adulthood, as can be seen in Figure 7.6.

Cross-sectional studies are, however, subject
to cohort effects, even in the most rigorous of
investigations. In Figure 7.7, you can see the
different patterns of performance on the PMA
scales of successive cohorts ranging from those
born in 1889 to those born in 1973. There
have been overall increases across cohorts in
verbal meaning, word fluency, spatial orientation, and inductive reasoning. By contrast,
numerical ability has shown a downward trend.
Exposure to different socialization and educational experiences across the decades seems to
have resulted in different strengths and weaknesses across historical cohorts (Schaie, Willis,
& Caskie, 2004).

With these analyses, it is possible to draw
some inferences about the effects of aging across
adulthood on the primary mental abilities. Verbal
meaning scores appear to reach a peak by the 50s
to 60s on cross-sectional studies and somewhat
later on longitudinal. Approximately 10 years
later, these scores start to drop, and by age 88
they are about half the level of their highest point.
Numerical ability also peaks in middle age, and
its drop becomes detectable by the 60s as well.
As measured longitudinally, spatial orientation,
inductive reasoning, and word fluency remain
stable until the late 60s and drop steadily
thereafter. Both spatial orientation and inductive
reasoning, however, descended downward from
a peak in young adulthood. Cohort differences
on these abilities consistently favored younger
cohorts from the 1989 cohort and on.

Given that verbal meaning is regarded as
a crystallized ability, the pattern of findings
discussed here may seem to be in conflict
with the propositions of crystallized-fluid theory. However, more recent longitudinal data on
the fluid-crystallized theory do show declines in

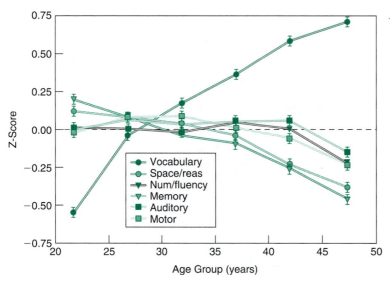

FIGURE 7.6
Intelligence from Age 20 to 50

Means (and standard errors) by five-year age intervals of intelligence scores among job seekers ranging from 20 to 50 years of age.
Source: Schroeder & Salthouse, 2004.

crystallized as well as fluid intelligence, although the decline in crystallized is less than in fluid (McArdle, Ferrer-Caja, Hamagami, & Woodcock, 2002). At the same time, fluid intelligence may reflect an individual's knowledge in crystallized domains. An intriguing study of players with varying levels of expertise in the game *Go* revealed that among those with high levels of expertise, the expected decline in memory-based measures of fluid intelligence was not observed (Masunaga & Horn, 2000).

One obvious factor that would seem to affect intelligence test scores is the individual's health status. As we saw in Chapter 3, retrospective studies show that people who are fated to die within a period of several years show diminished intellectual functioning. It would make sense that health status would be related to intelligence test performance, and indeed, this has been found in the SLS. Arthritis, cancer, and osteoporosis are health conditions shown to be associated with intelligence test scores (Schaie, 1996). Sensory functioning is also associated with intelligence test scores (Ghisella & Lindenberger, 2005).

Given the theoretical basis of fluid intelligence as reflective of neurological functioning,

a relationship between test scores and measures of brain functioning would be expected. Over a 4-year time period, a sample of over 400 older adults showed a considerable degree of overlap between speed and fluid intelligence (Zimprich & Martin, 2002). Variations in neurological abilities may also account for the fact that older individuals with lower fluid intelligence also show greater fluctuations in scores over time. Perhaps these older individuals are more vulnerable to the physiological changes that can exacerbate the aging of the abilities that underlie fluid intelligence (Ram, Rabbitt, Stollery, & Nesselroade, 2005).

Another important source of individual differences is that of gender, and differences between men and women are indeed observed in intelligence test performance in adulthood. Men outperform women on numerical skill, the crystallized ability of knowledge of general information, and spatial orientation. However, women receive higher scores on a fluid intelligence measure called Digit Symbol, involving the substitution of symbols for digits in a speeded coding task (Kaufman, Kaufman, McLean, & Reynolds, 1991; Portin, Saarijaervi, Joukamaa,

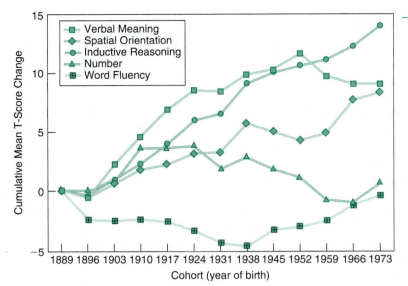

FIGURE 7.7
Cross-sectional Differences in the Seattle Longitudinal Study

In this figure, cross-sectional differences for cohorts born from 1889 to 1973 are compared on the five abilities of the PMA.
Source: Schaie, Willis, & Caskie, 2004.

& Salokangas, 1995). In terms of changes over adulthood, women tend to decline earlier on fluid abilities and men show earlier losses on crystallized abilities (Dixon & Hultsch, 1999). Another gender difference emerges in the risk factors for cognitive decline in both crystallized and fluid intelligence with obesity being more strongly related to deficits in men than in women (Elias, Elias, Sullivan, Wolf, & D'Agostino, 2005).

Individual differences in intelligence test scores are related to social and cultural factors as assessed in the SLS (Schaie & Zanjani, 2006). Higher socioeconomic status seems to provide protection from the negative effects of aging on intelligence (Aartsen, Smits, van Tilburg, Knipscheer, & Deeg, 2002). People with higher levels of education receive higher scores even on fluid intelligence measures and, in fact, when controlling for education, even cross-sectional differences in middle adulthood disappear (Ronnlund & Nilsson, 2006). In general, the more stimulating a person's environment after retirement, the greater the chances of maintaining his or her intellectual abilities (Schaie, Nguyen, Willis,

Dutta, & Yue, 2001). As is true for cognitive functioning in general, participation in exercise training can also benefit intelligence by promoting brain plasticity (Kramer, Colcombe, McAuley, Scalf, & Erickson, 2005).

Personality may also play a role in the maintenance or decline of cognitive abilities. Feeling confident in your abilities, being liberal and autonomous in attitudes, and having an open-minded approach to new experiences, thoughts, and feelings are also related to higher PMA scores over time (Schaie et al., 2004). Adding perhaps to the complexity of understanding the relationship between lifestyle factors and intellectual changes in adulthood are findings on personality and its relationship to intellectual functioning. Anxiety has a negative relationship to intelligence test performance in that higher anxiety during testing is related to poorer performance on a variety of fluid and crystallized tasks (Wetherell, Reynolds, & Gatz, 2002).

The problem of cause and effect is clearly present in some of this research on lifestyle and intelligence. Do the intellectually more able seek out more stimulating environments, or does involvement in a rich environment lead to greater preservation of mental abilities? Perhaps older people with high levels of intelligence purposefully search for ways to maximize their abilities. They may also seek out certain complex problems and situations because these fit with their abilities. Another possibility is that people with higher intellectual abilities who have better problem-solving abilities are better able to take advantage of health maintenance and treatment strategies.

Crystallized intelligence can also facilitate learning among older individuals. In one study, researchers assessed the extent to which scores on fluid and crystallized intelligence predicted learning about health-related topics. Although prior knowledge about the topic was related to the amount of new learning that took place, people higher in crystallized intelligence were able to learn more independent of the amount of previous knowledge they had about the topic. Thus, focusing only on deficits in fluid intelligence can therefore provide an unduly negative portrayal of the learning abilities of older adults (Beier & Ackerman, 2005).

Turning to twin studies, which provide a classic method of contrasting genetic with environmental effects, a study of Swedish twin pairs from 41 to 91 years of age provided insight into the relative influence of these effects on levels of ability and changes in ability over time. Although heredity seemed to influence individual variations in ability levels, environmental factors had effects on the rate of change over time (Reynolds, Finkel, Gatz, & Pedersen, 2002). Similar findings were obtained in a study of Danish twins, studied using a cohort-sequential design and retested every two years for up to four testings. As with the Swedish study, overall intellectual ability appeared to be a function of genetics, but the rate of change over time was a function of environmental influences (McGue & Christensen, 2002).

Training Studies

The documentation of changes in intelligence over the years of adulthood may seem to have somewhat of a downside in that many of the changes are in a negative direction. Furthermore, as you have just seen, the people who are aware of just how much their mental abilities are aging may have somewhat of an advantage in terms of gains and losses. However, at the same time that Schaie and his coworkers attempt to provide an accurate picture of intelligence in adulthood, they just as actively seek methods of intervention. There is a long tradition within the developmental perspective advocated by Schaie, Baltes, and Willis of seeking ways to help preserve people's functioning as strongly as possible for as long as possible (Schaie, 2005).

To put into perspective the findings on training studies, it is necessary to take a few steps backward and present the evolution of the underlying theoretical and philosophical perspective. A quote from the mid-1970s from an influential article by Baltes and Schaie (1976) states this perspective with eloquence: "Our central argument is one for plasticity of intelligence in adulthood and old age as evidenced by large interindividual differences, multidirectionality, multidimensionality, the joint significance of ontogenetic and historical change components, and emerging evidence on modifiability via intervention research" (p. 724). To put it more simply, Baltes and Schaie argued for the need to see intelligence as "plastic" or modifiable. This proposal is based on research we have already seen regarding the existence of individual differences, multiple dimensions of intelligence, and the interaction of aging and cohort effects. Although the research of the 1990s obviously was not available in the 1970s, the basic assumption that adult intelligence is responsive to interventions permeates the later research program of the SLS. According to Baltes and Schaie, if older adults could be taught ways to improve their intelligence test scores, this would serve as a major victory for the plasticity model.

In a handful of early studies conducted in the early 1970s at Penn State University, Baltes, Willis, and their colleagues demonstrated that, given practice and training in test-taking strategies, older adults could improve their scores on tests of fluid intelligence (Hofland, Willis, & Baltes, 1980; Plemons, Willis, & Baltes, 1978; Willis, Blieszner, & Baltes, 1981). Current studies continue to confirm and expand these findings. For example, training older adults in the strategies used to solve inductive reasoning problems can lead to gains in scores, particularly for older adults with higher education (Saczynski, Willis, & Schaie, 2002).

Remember that fluid intelligence is theoretically intended to be a "pure" measure of ability, uninfluenced by educational experiences. The Penn State studies, part of the Adult Development and Enrichment Project (ADEPT), involved pretest posttest designs, with the intervention consisting of five hours of group training in the requisite skills demanded by the fluid ability tests. Similar training methods, but with individual rather than group instruction, were used with members of the SLS sample. The longitudinal nature of the study made it possible to examine additional factors relevant to the effects of training over time. Even after a seven-year period in between training and testing, older adults who were part of the intervention study were able to maintain their advantage over their non-trained age peers (Schaie, 1994). Furthermore, these positive training effects were evident with people who had shown a previous decline in their intellectual functioning in the period prior to training. Booster sessions also proved helpful in maintaining gains in between training and testing. Impressively, the gains shown in training studies generalize from one test of a particular ability to another test of that same ability involving different sets of items.

Most recently, the ADEPT findings were expanded in ACTIVE, the large multisite intervention study described in Chapter 6, which showed a positive impact of training on the cognitive functions of memory, reasoning, and speed of processing. In an innovative variant on the overall training paradigm, the ACTIVE researchers investigated the impact of training in these areas on actual abilities to maintain functional independence in everyday life. Training in the area of reasoning had a significantly positive impact

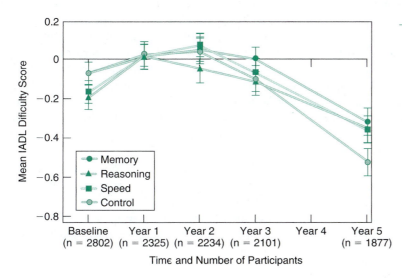

FIGURE 7.8
ACTIVE Study Results on Functional Abilities

Mean scores on Instrumental Activities of Daily Living (IADLs) for groups in the ACTIVE study trained in four specific abilities.

Source: Willis et al., 2006.

on the ability of the older adults in the study to manage in daily activities an effect that was maintained over a 5-year period (Willis et al., 2006).

THE PSYCHOLOGY OF WISDOM

In moving from training studies to broader conceptualizations of intelligence in adulthood, Baltes suggested several principles that highlight and extend the notions of variability and modifiability. The principle of **reserve capacity** is that older adults possess abilities that are normally untapped and therefore unproven (Staudinger, Marsiske, & Baltes, 1995). Training studies allow adults the opportunity to express this reserve capacity by making it possible for them to reach their maximum potential. You can think of reserve capacity as your ability to perform to your highest level when you are highly motivated by a teacher, coach, competitor, or friend. You may not have even thought such a strong performance was possible until you completed it successfully.

Following on the principle of reserve capacity is that of **testing the limits**. This is the method developed by Baltes and Kliegl (1992) to determine just how much the performance of older adults can be increased through training. By using this method, the amount of reserve capacity that is available can be quantified and compared to that of younger people.

The method of testing the limits was used in a innovative study on reaction time to show that even on this type of task, which clearly declines in later adulthood, there can be a developmental reserve capacity that is normally untapped (Bherer et al., 2006). In this study, there was an auditory task and a visual task. For the auditory task, participants listened to tones presented through headphones and decided whether they were high or low in pitch, pressing a key on the keyboard in front

of them corresponding to what they heard. For the visual task, they identified the letter on the screen as "B" or "C." The auditory and visual tasks were presented separately and then in a mixed fashion, so the participant did not know which type of task would be coming next, making the task considerably harder.

The main feature of this study that distinguishes it from other reaction time studies and made it one of "testing the limits" is that participants were given feedback and guided instructions on their performance. This made it possible for them to improve their performance across successive practice trials. Both younger and older adults improved their speed and accuracy through practice, but the older adults showed a larger improvement in accuracy than did the young; in fact, they were able to reach the accuracy levels of young adults at the end of their practice sessions (see Figure 7.9).

The concept of reserve capacity also leads to another principle developed by Baltes, that of **selective optimization with compensation** (Baltes & Baltes, 1990). According to this principle, explored earlier with regard to Sternberg's balance theory, adults attempt to preserve and maximize the abilities that are of central importance and put less effort into maintaining those that are not. Given that resources become increasingly limited as we move into later adulthood, people make conscious decisions regarding how to spend their time and effort. Through training, they may be given the incentive and necessary skills to bring an atrophied ability back up to a higher level, but if left to themselves, adults become increasingly likely to pick and choose their battles.

The principle of selective optimization with compensation implies that at some point in adulthood, we deliberately begin to reduce our efforts in one area in order to focus more on achieving success in another. It is likely that the areas we choose to focus on are those that

FIGURE 7.9
Testing the Limits in Reaction Time and Aging

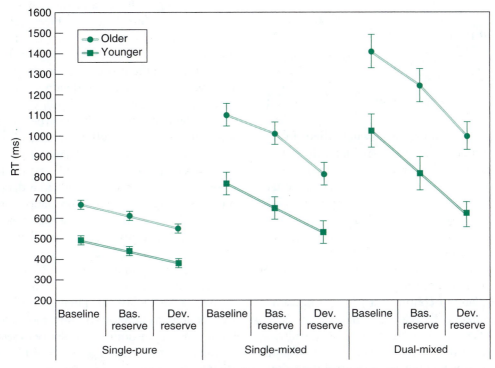

Mean reaction times for older and younger adults as a function of conditions of testing by type of trial. Baseline refers to the beginning of testing, Bas. Reserve (Baseline Reserve) refers to the first session of training, and Dev. Reserve (Developmental Reserve) refers to the end of training, when "testing the limits" has occurred. Single-Pure, Single-Mixed, and Dual-Mixed refers to whether the auditory and visual trials were presented alone or in mixed format.

Source: Bherer et al., 2006.

are of greater importance and in which the chances of success are higher. Time and health limitations may also be a factor. If someone who has enjoyed high-impact aerobics finds the activity too exerting or too hard on the knees, this person may decrease this involvement but compensate by spending more time doing yoga. Similar processes may operate in the area of intellectual functioning. The older individual may exert more effort toward solving word games and puzzles and spend less time on pastimes that involve spatial and speed skills, such as fast moving computer games. If reading becomes too much of a chore due to fading eyesight,

the individual may compensate by switching to audio books.

We may add some ideas from the identity model into this analysis, specifically, concepts from the multiple threshold model. People may make these choices of what to emphasize based on what aspects of functioning are central to their identities. Those who value the mind will compensate for changes in mental abilities by finding other intellectually demanding activities that they can still perform rather than switching their focus entirely. Those who are able to make accommodations to age-related changes without becoming overwhelmed or preoccupied will be able to reestablish a sense of well-being after what may be an initially difficult period.

"What do you think?" | 7-4

Do you agree with the definition of wisdom provided by Baltes? How would you define wisdom?

Ultimately, adults may switch their focus almost entirely away from intellectually challenging activities to activities that involve the successful completion of life tasks. Those of us still in school may find it both enjoyable and relevant to devote our energies to games and activities of the mind, but for many people, cognitive activities hold no compelling interest or attraction. You probably know many people who look forward to college graduation and have no plans to continue anything approaching an academic lifestyle once they are on their own. Baltes referred to this switch from cognitive efforts to involvement in personal enjoyment and relationships as the movement toward the **pragmatics of intelligence**, in which people apply their abilities to the solution of real-life problems. Such problems may involve how to help a troubled granddaughter whose parents have divorced, how to rescue an unsuccessful business venture, or whether to move to a warmer climate after retirement. These abilities become more important to adults than the **mechanics of intelligence**, which involve the cognitive operations of speed, working memory, and fluid intelligence.

Baltes believed that adults become increasingly capable of dealing with higher level conceptual issues that are not tested by conventional intelligence tests. Through his research on the pragmatics of intelligence, he showed that cognitive development in adulthood involves growth in the ability to provide insight into life's many dilemmas, particularly those that are psychosocial or interpersonal. This is where the quality of wisdom emerges.

According to Baltes and those who worked with him, **wisdom** is a form of expert knowledge in the pragmatics of life (Baltes & Staudinger, 2000). With increasing age in adulthood, through the process of selective optimization with compensation, individuals develop an increasing interest in and capacity to exercise their judgment. The insights that people gain as wisdom develops include awareness of the finitude of life and the role of culture in shaping our lives and personalities ("life-span contextualism"). They become less likely to judge others, and they have a greater appreciation for individual differences in values, life experiences, and beliefs ("value relativism"). People who are wise also possess a rich base of factual or declarative knowledge and an extensive background of procedural knowledge (Baltes, Staudinger, Maercker, & Smith, 1995). Finally, another quality, not always emphasized in the more cognitive approaches to wisdom, is the ability to recognize and manage uncertainty as a fact of life (Ardelt, 2004).

These conclusions about wisdom were arrived at through studies identifying the characteristics of people nominated by others to be wise and by observing the types of decisions made by these people in real-life dilemmas. Through such research, Baltes and his coworkers observed that people who are "wise" are more likely to be found among the older adult population (Staudinger, Smith, & Baltes, 1993). However, age alone does not foster wisdom. The development of this mature form of intelligence is brought about through a set of favorable life influences, including a willingness to learn from experience, interest in the welfare of others, training, and mentoring by others. Simply clocking more hours on the planet is not sufficient; you must be able to take advantage of what life's lessons (and teachers) have to offer.

SUMMARY

1. The higher cognitive functions include language, problem-solving ability, and intelligence. Changes in memory contribute in part to age-related losses in language such as the ability to derive meaning from spoken or written passages, spell, and find words. As a result older adults use simpler and less specific language. However, many language abilities are maintained, and older adults are able to use nonlanguage cues to help them derive meanings from language. The way that younger persons speak to older adults can also be problematic if this involves elderspeak, which is patronizing and infantilizing speech directed at an older person. The communication predicament describes the negative effects on cognition and language when older persons are communicated to in this manner.

2. Throughout the adult years, there is a trade-off in the factors affecting everyday problem solving between alterations in speed of processing and working memory, and gains in experience as individuals encounter a wider variety of problems as well as more depth in their own fields of expertise. However, because experienced problem solvers tend to seek answers to familiar problems by seeking familiar solutions, they may miss something important that is unique to a particular problem. In addition to focusing on one solution rather than considering others, older adults may also tend to stick with one pattern of responding when the situation calls for being able to call on a range of ideas.

3. There are a number of theories of intelligence, but the majority of research on adult intelligence is based on the fluid-crystallized theory. Studies on the primary mental abilities support the theory's proposal that fluid (unlearned, nonverbal) abilities decrease gradually throughout adulthood. By contrast the crystallized abilities that are acquired through education and training steadily increase through the 60s and show a decrease only after that point. Other conceptions of intelligence, including the theory of multiple intelligences and triarchic theory, have not been tested yet on adults of varying ages but hold potential to offer a broader view of intelligence. The most extensive study of adult intelligence is the Seattle Longitudinal Study in which sequential methods have been applied to the Primary Mental Abilities test. In addition to providing data on age patterns in intelligence test scores, this study has highlighted relationships with intelligence among health, personality, lifestyle, and sociocultural factors.

4. Intervention studies in which older adults are given training in the abilities tapped by intelligence test scores have yielded support for the notion of plasticity. Even five hours of training can result in improved scores across tests for as long as a seven-year period. Following from these training studies, researchers have proposed establishing the reserve capacity of older adults not demonstrated in ordinary life by using a method known as testing the limits. According to the principle of selective optimization with compensation, older adults attempt to maximize the abilities that are important to them and do not seek opportunities to expand the abilities that are not of interest or relevance. Many older adults turn to the pragmatics of intelligence, or the practical use of knowledge, and away from the mechanics of intelligence, or the skills typically measured on tests of ability. The quality of wisdom in later life develops as individuals become more interested in developing their abilities in the pragmatics of life.

CHAPTER | 8

Personality and Patterns of Coping

> "*He who is of a calm and happy nature will hardly feel the pressure of age, but to him who is of an opposite disposition, youth and age are equally a burden.*"
>
> Plato
> (427–346 B.C.)

W e use the term personality in many ways in everyday language, but the most common meaning is as an unobservable quality thought to be responsible for our observable behavior. Someone pays you a compliment because that person is "nice," or "generous," or "friendly." Although within psychology the term has a number of technical definitions, in general, it refers to an unobservable influence on our outward behavior.

Discussions of personality in adulthood and later life typically are based on one or more theories of personality. Although these theories may be traced back to the time of the Greek physician Hippocrates, who developed the notion that there were four basic temperaments or dispositions, contemporary approaches generally begin with a discussion of Sigmund Freud's psychodynamic theory.

PSYCHODYNAMIC PERSPECTIVES

Freud is credited with having "discovered" the unconscious mind. As it turns out, this claim may be somewhat of an exaggeration, but it is true that Freud was the first to develop a comprehensive theory that incorporated multiple components of personality into an integrated whole. Many current theories of adult development and personality are based on the psychodynamic perspective even if they do not explicitly consider the role of unconscious forces in behavior. At the same time, cognitive processes are increasingly being incorporated into the more traditional focus of psychodynamic approaches.

Having left a rich body of work that later theorists would subsequently revise and reshape, unfortunately Freud paid relatively little attention to the years of adulthood and old age. According to Freud, the major work of personality development is completed in each of us by the age of 5 years old, with some additional touches added when we go through adolescence. At the same time, Freud believed that therapy could not be of much value to individuals over the age of 50, who he believed had personalities so rigidly set that they could not be radically altered.

Much of personality, Freud theorized, was hidden in the unconscious, with the conscious mind being simply the small tip of a much larger iceberg. The structure in personality most accessible to conscious awareness is the **ego**, which performs the rational, executive functions of the mind and organizes the individual's activities so that important goals can be attained. **Defense mechanisms** are intended to protect our conscious mind from knowing the improper urges of our unconscious mind, which include a wide range of socially unacceptable behaviors such as rape, incest, and murder. Freud believed that unconscious urges could drive us not only toward the expression of love and sexuality, but also to the potential destruction of the self and others.

The ultimate goal of development, according to Freud, is the ability to "love and work"; in other words, to be able to live our everyday lives without experiencing undue conflict. Freud maintained that although we can never be entirely free from improper desires, we can develop defense mechanisms that will allow us to function with a minimum of anxiety. Maturity and healthy use of defense mechanisms, according to Freud's view of the world, are less likely to be found in people who fail to resolve their childhood conflicts. They may spend a large proportion of their adult years involved in unsuccessful efforts to rid themselves of inappropriate sexual attachments to parents or parent figures. Similarly people who are not able to regulate their aggressive urges may find themselves plagued with guilt or anxiety about the harm that they have caused or might cause to others.

Ego Psychology

For many current psychologists who operate from a psychodynamic position, the most interesting and important component of personality is the ego. Freud regarded the ego as not having an independent role in personality but merely as serving the desires of the id. However, to other theorists, the ego is equivalent to the conscious mind, performing the functions of integration, analysis, and synthesis of thought. The term **ego psychology** is used to describe the view that the ego plays a central role in actively directing our behavior.

Theories of ego psychology give primary attention to the ego as the organizer of experience. The main concern in studying development, from this perspective, is to learn how aging influences the ego's ability to adapt to the conditions and constraints of the outside world and yet manage to achieve expression of the individual's personal needs and interests. Often, but not necessarily, the ego is equated with the self, as in Erikson's use of the term "ego identity" to indicate the individual's self-attribution of personal characteristics.

In Chapter 2, we reviewed the major principles of Erikson's theory of psychosocial development. To recapitulate briefly, the theory proposes that there are eight crisis stages in the maturation of the ego. Each stage represents a point of maximum vulnerability to biological, psychological, and social forces operating on the individual at that particular point in the life span. The outcome of each crisis stage may either be favorable (as in the attainment of identity) or unfavorable (as in the failure to achieve a coherent identity). The resolution of earlier stages forms the basis for resolution of later stages, according to Erikson, and the epigenetic principle lays out the ground plan for the unfolding of psychosocial crises throughout life. Although certain ages are associated with certain stages, earlier issues may arise at a later point in life, and the later stages may move to the forefront in earlier periods if conditions develop that stimulate the individual to confront those issues.

"What do you think?"	*8-1*

What factors other than age could account for increases in identity and intimacy from college to early adulthood?

University of Rochester campus as it was in the 1960s at the start of the RALS.

The most extensive study based specifically on Erikson's theory is the one conducted by this author and my colleagues in the Rochester Adult Longitudinal Study (RALS), a sample of undergraduates and alumni from the University of Rochester. This study began in 1966 when Constantinople (1969) administered a questionnaire measure of psychosocial development to a sample of over 300 students in the classes of 1965–1968. The original sample was followed up 11 years later in 1977 when a new sample of 300 undergraduates was added to allow for sequential analyses (Whitbourne & Waterman, 1979). In the second follow-up in 1988–1989, yet another undergraduate sample was added. Sequential comparisons could then be made among three cohorts of college students and two cohorts of adults in their early 30s. Longitudinal follow-up analyses were also made of adults from college up to age 43. Additional data were also collected on other measures of identity and life events at each of the follow-up testings (Whitbourne & van Manen, 1996; Whitbourne, Zuschlag, Elliot, & Waterman, 1992).

The heart of the findings from the RALS regarding psychosocial development was the consistency of age changes across two cohorts in the two stages theorized to change the most in college and early adulthood: identity versus identity diffusion and intimacy versus isolation. Analysis of data from another measure given in 1988 to respondents from all three cohorts specifically intended to assess identity development showed convergent support for the notion of continued growth on this dimension during adulthood (Whitbourne & van Manen, 1996).

The RALS has also shown psychosocial development scores to be related to life events in a predictive manner. In one of the investigations, psychosocial development scores from college were used to predict marital, family (number of children), and career status at the ages of 31 and 42 among the men and women in Cohort 1. The identity scores that these women attained at age 31 predicted their socioeconomic attainments by their early 40s, as well as their identity scores at that same age. However, this relationship was in a direction opposite to that of prediction.

Women with higher identity scores at age 31 were in *lower*, not higher, status occupations at the age of 42. This was because women who were full-time homemakers received the lowest socioeconomic status scores. We concluded that women who had strong identities in their early 30s were more likely to remain in the home rather than invest their energies into their careers (Van Manen & Whitbourne, 1997). In current work on the RALS, some of which appears in Chapter 3, the alternative paths from college to midlife are being explored (Whitbourne, in press).

A somewhat comparable investigation of women was begun in the 1950s to 1960s by Ravenna Helson and colleagues at Mills College, a private school in California. Although not originally intended as a study of Eriksonian development, a number of the findings were interpreted in terms of his theory. The original intention of the study was to investigate the personality characteristics and plans for the future of college women (Helson, 1967). At each follow-up, the women were asked to complete standardized personality measures and to provide information about their life events up to that time (Helson & Moane, 1987; Helson & Wink, 1992).

Although Helson's early findings presented evidence for considerable personality stability, there were several notable exceptions. The women increased in the qualities of assurance, independence, and self-control, and decreased on a scale measuring how feminine the women felt they were. Overall, these findings were taken to suggest increased personality integration and movement in middle adulthood to becoming a positive contributor to society. There were also individual differences in personality change patterns which the investigators linked to variations in level of ego development and identity. For example, women higher in identity at age 43 were more likely to have achieved higher levels of generativity at age 48 (Vandewater, Ostrove, & Stewart, 1997). Similar findings were obtained

in a later analysis in which the identity of a woman at age 43 was seen to influence the effects of personality scores at age 21 in predicting her well-being at the age of 60 (Helson & Srivastava, 2001). Social roles have also been found to influence the development through late midlife of such qualities as dominance, masculinity/femininity, flexibility and achievement (Helson & Soto, 2005).

Closely related to Erikson's notion of psychosocial development is that of Jane Loevinger (1976), whose view of the ego incorporates how we think as well as the structure of our personalities. Loevinger defines the ego as the structure within personality that attempts to synthesize, master, and interpret experiences. She regards the ego as involved in our ability to regulate impulses, relate to others, achieve self-understanding, and think about what is going on around us. The development of the ego proceeds in a series of stages that move from lower to higher levels in these characteristics (see Table 8.1).

Individuals in the Conformist stage have only a very basic understanding of self, others, and the reasons for following society's rules. They have simple views of what is right and what is wrong, and it is hard for them to understand why others think and feel the way they do. Most adults are in the second stage, known as the Conscientious-Conformist stage. Developmentally this is the stage when people first have an internalized sense of right and wrong and are able to be aware of their own motives as well as those of other people. Next to follow is the Conscientious stage, when people develop a true conscience, one that is an internalized understanding of society's rules and the reasons for those rules. People in the Conscientious stage are also able to have insight into their own emotions as well as the emotional needs of others.

The final three stages involve an increasing sense of individuality and self-determination. In the Individualistic stage, as the name implies,

TABLE 8.1
Stages of Ego Development in Loevinger's Theory

Stage	*Description*
Conformist Stage	Obeys rules to be accepted by the group and to avoid disapproval. Simple view of emotions. Prone to stereotyping others. Concerned about appearances and reputation.
Conscientious-Conformist Level	The most frequently observed level among adults. Transition between conformist and conscientious stages. Increase in self-awareness of an inner life. Able to see alternatives and exceptions to rules.
Conscientious Stage	Major elements of adult conscience, including long-term personal goals and ideals, sense of responsibility, and internalization of rules. May choose to break the law if it violates personal standards. Complex inner life and ability to understand emotions of self and others.
Individualistic Level	Greater sense of individuality and ability to be emotionally dependent on others. Ability to tolerate uncertainty and contradiction.
Autonomous Stage	Ability to think about and cope with inner conflict, such as conflict between personal needs and duties to others. Sees reality as complex and multidimensional. Recognizes the needs of others for autonomy but cherishes personal ties. Holds to broad, abstract, social ideas.
Integrated Stage	Rarely found in adults. Similar to autonomous stage but in addition has a strong sense of identity and ability to achieve complete expression of the true, inner self.

Source: Loevinger, 1976.

an appreciation and respect for individuality emerges. Next, in the Autonomous stage, inner standards have become even more clearly articulated. Various personality attributes begin to emerge as the individual's cognitive abilities allow for the recognition of complex causes of the behavior of self and others. The ability to live with uncertainty also becomes more fully developed in people who are in the Autonomous stage. Finally, the Integrated stage, which Loevinger proposed would be reached by relatively few people, is one in which the individual has a clear sense of self, is able to recognize inner conflicts, and highly values individuality. In this stage, the individual is able to achieve the expression of the true "inner self."

Loevinger's theory combines ego psychology with moral development, and in that sense is not a "typical" psychodynamically based theory. In fact, scores on Loevinger's measure of ego development have a strong cognitive component. A large scale analysis of studies on over 5,600 participants in which ego development and intelligence were assessed in the same individuals showed strong correlations between ego level and intellectual abilities. At the same time, however, ego level is not completely synonymous with intelligence. Higher levels of ego development according to Loevinger's stage are associated with personality variables such as assertiveness, conformity, and fearfulness, even after controlling for intelligence test scores (Cohn & Westenberg, 2004).

The ego development theory proposed by George Vaillant (2000), places heavy emphasis on the development of our use of defense mechanisms. As mentioned earlier, intended to help protect our conscious mind from knowing about our unconscious desires, defense mechanisms are strategies that we use almost automatically to protect us from knowing about our innermost urges and desires.

Unlike Freud, who proposed that personality is invariant after childhood, Vaillant regards the ego defense mechanisms as becoming increasingly adaptive, helping us to cope with life's challenges as we move through our adult years. When we are younger, we tend to use less mature, and more maladaptive defenses such as acting out or denial. These defense mechanisms can create their own problems. An example of the immature defense mechanism of acting out is to react to a parking ticket by kicking in your car's bumper. This action may temporarily relieve your anger, but it causes unnecessary physical damage and you appear to others to be out of control (besides costing more money than the ticket). Using a mature defense mechanism such as humor would help you feel better and avoid the social and practical cost of a rash action. Vaillant believed that as we get older, we are more likely to react with mature defense mechanisms in situations that stir up angry or painful feelings. Vaillant's (1993) Study of Adult Development, which investigated the use of defense

mechanisms through middle adulthood, incorporated three very diverse samples. The first was the Harvard Grant Study sample, which began in 1938 on a sample of college men in excellent physical and psychological health. Men in the second group, called the Core City sample, were chosen based on their residence in the inner city. The third sample was composed of 40 women who were first tested as part of a study on gifted children when young and then interviewed again when they were in their late 70s.

The initial set of findings provided evidence within each of the three samples for a positive relationship between maturity of defenses and various outcome measures. Further analyses supported these findings. For instance, Core City men who used immature defenses (such as acting out) were more likely to experience alcohol problems, unstable marriages, and antisocial behavior (Soldz & Vaillant, 1998). Another investigation showing positive relationships between ego defenses and adaptation was a 24-year longitudinal study conducted by Cramer (2003) in which over 150 men and women were followed from early to middle adulthood. Individuals using

TABLE 8.2
Categories of Defenses Identified by Vaillant

Category	Examples
Psychotic	*Delusional projection*—attributing one's own bizarre ideas and feelings to others *Denial*—disclaiming the existence of a feeling, action, or event *Distortion*—significantly exaggerating and altering the reality of feelings and events
Immature	*Projection*—attributing unacceptable ideas and feelings to others *Hypochondriasis*—expressing psychological conflict as exaggerated physical complaints *Acting out*—engaging in destructive behavior that expresses inner conflicts
Neurotic	*Displacement*—transferring unacceptable feelings from the true to a safer object *Repression*—forgetting about a troubling feeling or event *Reaction formation*—expressing the opposite of one's true feelings
Mature	*Altruism*—turning unacceptable feelings into behavior that is helpful to others *Sublimation*—expressing unacceptable feelings in productive activity *Humor*—being able to laugh at an unpleasant or disturbing feeling or situation

Source: Vaillant, 1993.

immature defense mechanisms had less favorable scores on personality dimensions representing several facets of adjustment (NEO scores, discussed below).

In addition to investigating the correlates of immature and mature defense mechanisms, other researchers have examined the relationship between age and defense mechanisms (Diehl, Coyle, & Labouvie-Vief, 1996; Labouvie-Vief & Medler, 2002). Consistently, these studies show that older adults are able to manage their emotions through the use of mature defense mechanisms that involve controlling negative emotions or trying to put the situation into perspective. In terms of coping, older adults similarly show less of a tendency to react in self-destructive or emotional ways. They are more likely to attempt to understand the situation and figure out a way around it. If they are stressed, they suppress their negative feelings or channel those feelings into productive activities. Younger people, including adolescents and young adults, are more likely to react to psychologically demanding situations by acting out against others, projecting their anger onto others, or regressing to more primitive forms of behavior.

Consistent gender differences have also emerged in studies of defense mechanisms and coping (Diehl et al., 1996; Labouvie-Vief & Medler, 2002). Regardless of age, women are more likely to avoid unpleasant or stressful situations, to blame themselves when things go wrong, and to seek the support of others. Men are more likely to externalize their feelings and to use reaction formation, a defense mechanism in which people express in behavior the opposite of their unconscious feelings.

Adult Attachment Theory

Attachment theory emphasizes the earliest of relationships in life—those with our parents (or caregivers)—as the root of personality (Shaver & Mikulincer, 2005). The work of British psychoanalyst John Bowlby (1969) provided the basis for this theory. According to Bowlby, our relationship with our mother sets the parameters for the development of our sense of self. A caregiver who attends to the child's needs enables the child to feel that he or she has favorable attributes. Caregivers who are unresponsive or hurtful to the child plant the seeds for the growth of negative self-conceptions (Bowlby, 1973).

Attachment style is the term used to describe the way we relate to our primary attachment figure who, in adulthood, shifts from the mother (or other caregiver) to our romantic partner. Psychologist Mary Ainsworth tested Bowlby's ideas by developing a clever, if somewhat stressful, experimental procedure to see how toddlers would react when their mothers first left and then reentered the laboratory playroom (Ainsworth, Blehar, Waters, & Wall, 1978). The child with a secure attachment style is not made angry or anxious by the mother's temporary departure and, upon her return, seeks contact with her. The child with avoidant attachment style resists contact with the mother, and the child with the anxious attachment style appears to want to make contact with the mother but resists her. Because of the mixed behavior of this last group of children, the anxious attachment style is also referred to as the anxious-ambivalent attachment style. The majority of children fall into the secure attachment style, and the remaining two types, together considered "insecure," are in the minority.

"*What do you think?*"	8-2

Do you think people's personalities become more "mature" as they get older?

Later researchers working in attachment theory decided to subdivide the avoidant attachment style (Bartholomew & Horowitz, 1991).

People who are afraid of closeness are said to have a fearful attachment style, and those who do not want to be close to others are called, appropriately, dismissive.

Just as the majority of infants are securely attached, so are the majority of adults. In fact, there are fewer anxiously attached adults in older than younger age groups (Mickelson, Kessler, & Shaver, 1997). However, there is a tendency for older individuals to lower their emotional attachments to other people, perhaps as a way of protecting themselves from interpersonal losses (Diehl et al., 1996). It is also possible that older adults interpret the questionnaires differently than do young adults, the population for whom they were originally developed (Shaver & Mikulincer, 2004).

Attachment style is most likely not a stable trait despite the fact that it emerges early in life. If attachment style is thought of as a reflection of the individual's social relationships, to the extent that these relationships change over time so too may attachment style. Following a sample of adults over a period of six years, Zhang and Labouvie-Vief (2004) observed that in fact, attachment style showed considerable variation over the course of the six-year period. Changes in attachment style also seemed related to changes in depressive symptoms and feelings of well-being. When individuals were feeling depressed or low in well-being, they also appeared to be less securely attached. Interestingly, over the course of the study, among the oldest groups there were increases both in secure and in dismissing attachment styles.

Theoretically, early socialization plays a role in the development of attachment style. This aspect of the theory was tested in an investigation of a large cross-sectional sample of older and younger adults who were asked to recall how they were raised by their parents (Magai, Consedine, Gillespie, O'Neal, & Vilker, 2004). For both age groups, recollections of a punitive childhood were associated with an ambivalent attachment style in adulthood, as well as to negative emotional outcomes. Interestingly, however, older adults seemed less negatively affected by the punitive experiences they recalled from childhood. This finding may reflect cohort differences in that the childhood experiences of older adults were more likely to include punishment. In contrast, more recent cohorts are less likely to have been exposed to punitive parental practices. It is also possible that this finding reflects what we will observe later in the context of emotions and aging, namely, that older adults seem to be better able to maintain positive emotional states even in the face of adversity.

TRAIT APPROACHES

When you think about how to describe the personality of a friend, relative, or coworker, you most likely begin by coming up with a list of a characteristics or qualities that seem to fit the person's observable behavior. These characteristics are typically adjectives such as "generous," or "outgoing," or perhaps, "quiet" and "unfriendly." Trait theories of personality propose that adjectives such as these capture the essence of the individual's psychological makeup. The fact that people use these adjectives in everyday life to describe themselves and others agrees with the basic principle of trait theory, namely, that personality is equivalent to a set of stable characteristic attributes.

A **trait**, then, is defined as a stable, enduring attribute that characterizes one element of an individual's personality. Trait theories of personality are based on the assumption that the organization of these specific personal dispositions guides behavior. Trait theory is also increasingly coming to be viewed in terms of genetic or constitutional theories of personality. According to these views, there is a constitutional basis for personality that endures throughout life and that is at least partially inherited (Bouchard, 2004).

The Five Factor Model

The predominant trait theory in the field of adult development is based on Costa and McCrae's proposal that there are five major dimensions to personality in adulthood. The **Five Factor Model** (also called the "Big Five") is a theory intended to capture all the essential characteristics of personality in a set of five broad dispositions, each of which has six facets, making a total of 30 personality components.

The five personality traits in the Five Factor Model are neuroticism, extraversion, openness to experience, agreeableness, and conscientiousness (you can remember these as spelling "OCEAN,"

TABLE 8.3
Five Factor Model

Trait Name	Description	Facets
Neuroticism	Tendency to experience psychological distress, overreactiveness, and instability	Anxiety Hostility Depression Self-consciousness Impulsiveness Vulnerability
Extraversion	Preference for social interaction and lively activity	Warmth Gregariousness Assertiveness Activity Excitement seeking Positive emotions
Openness to experience	Receptiveness to new ideas, approaches, and experiences	Fantasy Aesthetics Feelings Actions Ideas Values
Agreeableness	Selfless concern for others, trust, and generosity	Trust Straightforwardness Altruism Compliance Modesty Tender-mindedness
Conscientiousness	Organization, ambitiousness, and self-discipline	Competence Order Dutifulness Achievement striving Self-discipline Deliberation

Source: Costa & McCrae, 1992.

or "CANOE"). A complete characterization of an individual on the five factors involves providing scores or ratings on each of the facets.

The chief measure used to assess an individual's personality according to the Five Factor Model is the **NEO Personality Inventory-Revised (NEO-PI-R)** (Costa & McCrae, 1992). The "NEO" stands for the original three factors in the model, which are neuroticism, extraversion, and openness. "PI" stands for Personality Inventory, and the "R" for Revised. Data from the NEO-PI-R can be reported in terms of both self-ratings and the ratings that others make of the individual. The scores can then be compared to determine whether respondents agree in their self-ratings with the assessments of others. Comparisons can also be made of scores over time in both sets of ratings.

Trait theories regard personality as an entity that reflects constitutional or innate predispositions (McCrae, 2002). According to the Five Factor Model, we are programmed by these five particular dispositions to be, for example, sociable, warm, intellectually curious, and concerned about others.

The notion that personality affects the course of an individual's life is an important component of the Five Factor Model (McCrae & Costa, 2003). Intuitively, many people believe that personality development in adulthood is affected by the course of life events. People become cynical after having been betrayed or are less likely to seek out exciting adventures after being injured in pursuit of a pastime full of thrills and chills. However, according to trait theory, experiences only rarely cause personality changes (Costa, Herbst, McCrae, & Siegler, 2000). Instead, the shape of people's lives is strongly influenced by the nature of their personalities. Cynical people may be more likely to become betrayed because they themselves are less trusting in the first place. Adventurous people are more likely to place themselves in situations where they are likely to be injured because they are more open to engaging in risk-taking behavior. People choose situations as a function of their personalities. Once in those situations, people are subject to the force of the events as they unfold.

Research Based on the Five Factor Model

> *"What do you think?"* | **8-3**
>
> Is it depressing to think that personality might be fixed so early in adulthood? What would you like to change about yourself and do you think you'll be able to do so?

Studies based on the Five Factor Model show a high degree of consistency over time in the scores of individuals on these scales, with estimates as high as .70–.75 over the course of adulthood (Roberts & DelVecchio, 2000). Although analyses of intra-individual change over time reveal a pattern of modest changes, still it is claimed that as much as 85% of the variation in personality scores over adulthood is due to stable individual differences (Terracciano, McCrae, Brant, & Costa, 2005).

Despite the enthusiasm with which such claims of stability are pronounced, there are reasons to regard this estimate as overly high. In addition to the measure itself being biased toward showing stability, the samples on which the data are based are selective because the individuals in these studies have initially agreed to be willing to participate over a period of many years (Ardelt, 2000). The fact that there are high test-retest correlations in traits such as neuroticism after the age of 30 (Terracciano, Costa, & McCrae, 2006) may not justify the conclusion that the traits are "stable" (Fraley & Roberts, 2005).

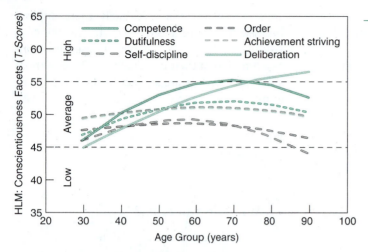

FIGURE 8.1
Longitudinal Changes in
Conscientiousness

Longitudinal curves for the six facets of conscientiousness.

Source: Terracciano, McCrae, Brant, & Costa, 2005.

Apart from these concerns, researchers have also raised the overarching question of whether it is both empirically and theoretically valid to use just five, and these particular five, traits to describe personality (Block, 1995). Although the Five Factor Model can have a great deal of utility as a way to characterize personality profiles, it may not be as sensitive as other models to developmental processes (Mroczek, Spiro, & Griffin, 2006).

Health and Personality

Apart from these questions regarding stability, the Five Factor Model has had utility in helping to investigate relationships between personality and health in adulthood, a topic of great interest in the fields of health psychology and behavioral medicine. Since the first intriguing data supporting such a relationship were first reported, investigators have sought to determine whether people with certain personality types are more susceptible to chronic or even fatal illnesses such as cardiovascular disease and cancer.

Much of the interest in the topic of health and personality has centered on the **Type A behavior pattern**, a collection of traits thought to increase a person's risk of developing cardiovascular disease (Friedman & Rosenman, 1974). People with Type A personalities are competitive, impatient, feel a strong sense of time urgency, and are highly achievement oriented. They also show unusually high degrees of hostility or anger directed toward others. The Type A-cardiovascular disease connection was for many years considered a case of correlation not equaling causation. However, researchers have been able to use longitudinal data to help overcome the limitations of correlational approaches to the problem. Investigators at Duke University followed male participants over a 10-year period, measuring their levels of hostility, depression, and anger, as well as their levels of proteins (C3 and C4) considered to be strong indicators of heart disease or the risk of heart disease (Boyle, Jackson, & Suarez, 2007). Men who had high levels of personality risk also showed greater increases over the course of the study in both C3 and C4 (see Figure 8.2).

High levels of anxiety may also serve as risk factors for cardiovascular disease. In comparing the personality factors of anxiety, general levels of distress, and anger, researchers investigating predictors of cardiovascular heart disease over a 14-year period found that anxiety in particular was related to the subsequent development

FIGURE 8.2

Type A Risk Factors and Heart Disease

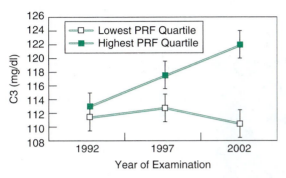

Adjusted C3 levels for the lowest and highest psychological risk factor quartiles at each examination. High levels of C3 are indicative of heart disease and heart disease risk.

Source: Boyle, Jackson, & Suarez, 2007.

of illness, even when controlling for other risk factors such as smoking, cholesterol, BMI, and blood pressure (Kubzansky, Cole, Kawachi, Vokonas, & Sparrow, 2006).

The relationship between personality and health may go back as far as childhood. Researchers have observed relationships between low scores in childhood on the trait of conscientiousness and higher death rates in adulthood (Friedman et al., 1995). Being low in conscientiousness might lead people to be more careless about many aspects of life and to the extent that factors such as BMI can be controlled, may be associated with higher rates of weight gain during adolescence and early adulthood (Pulkki-Raback, Elovainio, Kivimaki, Raitakari, & Keltikangas-Jarvinen, 2005). By middle age, it is more difficult to lose the weight that was gained during previous decades. In one investigation of personality predictors of BMI in midlife, lower scores on conscientiousness were related to greater weight gains during adulthood, particularly for women. In the same study, shown in Figure 8.3, high scores on neuroticism were linked to greater weight gains; again

the relationship was stronger for women than men (Brummett, et al., 2006). Low scores on conscientiousness and high scores on neuroticism also relate to the likelihood of cigarette smoking (Terracciano & Costa, 2004). Oddly enough, the trait of cheerfulness is negatively related to health outcomes, perhaps because people who are high on this trait also tend to be careless about their health (Martin, et al., 2002).

Conscientiousness continues to play a role in mortality in later adulthood as well. Among a sample of over 1,000 Medicare recipients ranging from 65 to 100 years of age followed over a three- to five-year period, conscientiousness, and particularly self-discipline, one facet of conscientiousness, predicted lower mortality risk over a three-year period. It is possible that high levels of self-discipline relate to a greater tendency to be proactive in engaging in behaviors that are protective of health and to avoid those behaviors that are damaging to health (Weiss & Costa, 2005).

High levels of hostility in early adulthood may also pose a risk factor for the development of depression during the ensuing years. Alumni of the University of North Carolina who had been tested in college were followed up at the age of 47 years through mail surveys assessing their personality scores and the experience of depression. Those individuals who had received high scores on hostility in college and then went on to experience an increase in levels of hostility were at a significantly higher risk for developing depression in midlife. High levels of hostility in college were also associated with higher rates of health risk behaviors, including smoking, drinking, and negative changes in family life. Changes in hostility over the study period predicted obesity, failure to exercise, high-fat diets, social isolation, poor health, and, for women, lower income (Siegler et al., 2003).

Clearly personality factors must be considered in a biopsychosocial model of development

FIGURE 8.3
BMI and Conscientiousness

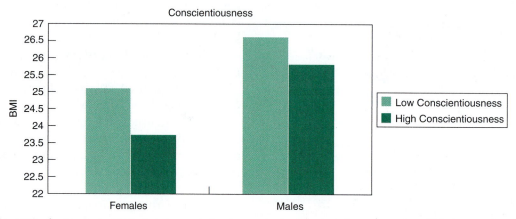

Over the course of a 14-year longitudinal study, people low in conscientiousness showed a greater gain in BMI than people with high conscientiousness scores.
Source: Brummett et al., 2006.

in adulthood and old age. Traits and behavior patterns that have their origins in inherited predispositions or through early life experiences influence the health of the individual through a variety of direct and indirect pathways. However, even though personality traits may be an inherent part of "who" we are, they can modulate and change over adulthood (Staudinger & Kunzmann, 2005) even as they influence some of the most basic components of our ability to remain healthy.

SOCIAL COGNITIVE APPROACHES

Our feelings and moods result from the interplay of emotions within our personalities. Although most personality psychologists tend to look at the way our personalities are structured, there is a growing interest within the field in the factors that cause us to be happy or sad. Some of this interest focuses on subjective well-being, which is the focus of the last chapter of the book, and some of the interest is more

specifically on our emotions. Researchers are also becoming increasingly interested in the "why's" of behavior—that is, motivation. Traditionally two very old topics in psychology—emotions and motivation—are still the source of a great deal of speculation and theorizing.

Some of the growing interest in emotions stems from a desire to help people feel better about themselves and their experiences, and some is based on a resurgence of a topic that has always been within the domain of psychology. In looking at aging and emotions in particular, researchers are also gaining an increased appreciation for the ways that older adults are able to focus their attention on the positive, rather than negative, aspects of their daily lives. Research on motivation and aging helps provide insight into our goals, desires, and needs as we grow older.

According to one developing viewpoint in adult development and aging, emotions and motivation are intimately linked. **Socioemotional selectivity theory** proposes that throughout adulthood, we structure the nature and range of our relationships to maximize gains

According to socioemotional selectivity theory, couples who have been together throughout their adult lives have found ways to maximize the emotional benefits they experience in the relationship.

and minimize risks (Carstensen, 1987). According to this theory, we change gradually over the years of adulthood and into old age with regard to the functions that interactions with others serve for our sense of well-being. Ultimately, it is these functions that both motivate us and cause us to experience particular emotions.

To understand how this theory works, it is necessary to take a step back and look at the roles that our relations with others play in our daily lives. One is an informational or knowledge function. We learn many practical things from other people that help us operate more effectively in the world. For instance, when you moved into your college dormitory, you probably sought out the people who seemed to know the most about where to buy necessary items such as textbooks, school supplies, and the cheapest and best cup of coffee. The second role of relations with others is emotional. Whether we are feeling good or bad on a given day often depends on whether the people who are close to us are pleased or displeased with us. It is not at all enjoyable to have your best friend, lover, or parent angry at you, regardless of the reason.

Socioemotional selectivity theory proposes that as we grow older, we become more focused on maximizing the emotional rewards of our relationships and less interested in seeking information or knowledge through their interactions with others (see Figure 8.4). This shift, according to the theory, occurs as people become increasingly sensitive to the inevitable ending of their lives and recognize that they are "running out of time."

It is not aging so much as this recognition of less time left to live that triggers the shift in what we want out of our interactions. Young adults, when placed either under artificial time constraints through experimental manipulations or under real time constraints, as for those who are HIV positive, show similar preferences toward the emotional functions of social interactions as do older adults (Carstensen, Isaacowitz, & Charles, 1999). Endings of any kind bring out strong emotions and cause us to want to spend time with the people who have been closest to us. Think of what happens to you at the end of each school year. No longer are you particularly interested in learning something new, although you may be trying to find out where people are getting summer jobs. The chances are that you are trying to spend as much "quality" time with your friends as possible to take advantage of the emotional benefits of being near them.

The desire to maximize emotional rewards leads adults increasingly to prefer spending time in their relationships with people who are familiar to them rather than seeking out new friends and acquaintances. Family and long-time friends are the people who will serve the positive emotional functions of self-validation and affect regulation. Older adults are less interested in meeting new people and broadening their social horizons because such individuals do not serve the same emotional functions (Lang & Carstensen, 2002).

In one particularly intriguing research paradigm, Isaacowitz and colleagues (2006) used socioemotional selectivity theory as the basis for

FIGURE 8.4
Socioemotional Selectivity Theory

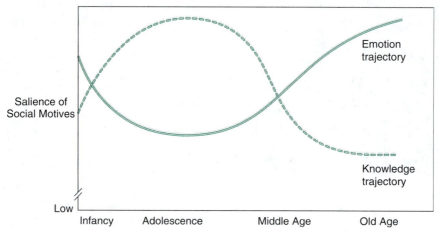

According to socioemotional selectivity, the importance of motives for social interactions changes over life, with knowledge being more important in the early years and emotion taking on increased importance in the later years.

Source: Carstensen, Gross, & Fung, 1997.

examining age differences in reactions to faces conveying happy, sad, and neutral emotional expressions. Older and younger adults were compared in their eye movement fixations to the parts of faces showing these emotions. Older adults were less likely than younger adults to look at parts of the face conveying anger and sadness, and more likely to look at the parts conveying happiness. This study's findings imply that older adults would prefer, literally, to "accentuate the positive" when it comes to reading other people's facial expressions.

Note that the theory does not imply that older people are less capable of showing or feeling emotions or that they are not interested in forming new relationships. The intensity of emotion experienced by an individual does not change over adulthood (Carstensen & Turk-Charles, 1994), although older adults may take longer to respond to emotionally provoking situations (Wieser, Muhlberger, Kenntner-Mabiala, & Pauli, 2006).

In keeping with the findings of personality research and aging, emotional understanding and

control appears to improve in the adult years (Magai, Consedine, Krivoshekova, Kudadjie-Gyamfi, & McPherson, 2006). There is also evidence that older adults actually have fewer negative emotions, perhaps because they are better able to regulate their affective experiences. A longitudinal study of over 2,800 adults studied from 1971 to 1994 revealed that as people get older, they are less likely to experience negative affect (Charles, Reynolds, & Gatz, 2001).

Nevertheless, older adults can experience strong emotions when prompted with relevant stimuli. In one investigation of age differences in emotional reactivity, older adults were compared with younger adults in their reactions to movies with specific, age-relevant themes intended to provoke sadness (Kunzmann & Grühn, 2005). Older adults felt appropriate levels of sadness as acutely as did young adults to the depiction of situations appropriate for their age group, such as loss associated with bereavement and chronic illness.

As is true for identity assimilation, which also causes people to minimize negative information, the desire to focus on the positive implied in socioemotional selectivity theory can have undesirable consequences. There are times when it is necessary to focus on the possibility of negative outcomes, particularly in the area of health. In fact, older adults do appear to be able to switch their motivational focus when given an incentive to do so, as when learning about negative consequences of failing to make the right health-related decision could have unfavorable consequences (Luckenhoff & Carstensen, 2007).

COGNITIVE PERSPECTIVE

Returning to the issue of motivation, the cognitive perspective sees us as driven by the desire to predict and control our experiences. Emerging from the cognitive perspective are the cognitive self theories proposing that individuals view the events in their lives from the standpoint of the relevance of these events to the self. These theories also place emphasis on coping, the mechanisms that people use to manage stress.

Because certain tendencies are inherent in the makeup of the self, events may not always be

FIGURE 8.5
Visual Fixation Patterns on Faces Varying in Emotional Expression

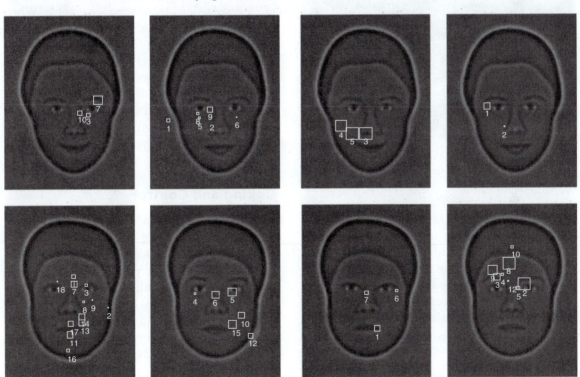

These figures show the fixation patterns of a younger adult (two left panels) and an older adult (two right panels) to the same face images for a happy-neutral (top row) and angry-neutral (bottom row) pair. The numbers signify the order of fixation, with 1 being the first fixation. The size of the boxes indicates fixation strength. Older adults preferred to look at the smiles of the happy-neutral faces and away from the frowns of the angry-neutral faces, in comparison to younger adults, who studied the eyes and the mouths of the angry-neutral faces.

Source: Isaacowitz, Wadlinger, Goren, & Wilson, 2006.

When writing about personal experiences in a diary, people may create a "life story" consistent with their current identities.

theorized to serve as psychological resources that can both motivate us toward future behavior and defend us against current threats to our well-being. They continue to shift throughout adulthood, and individuals can continue to be future oriented and hopeful of change until well into later life (Smith & Freund, 2002). One variant of the possible selves model states that older adults are particularly oriented toward possible selves that revolve around health (Frazier, Johnson, Gonzalez, & Kafka, 2002; Hooker & Kaus, 1994).

We are motivated to strive to achieve a hoped-for possible self and will attempt to avoid a dreaded or feared possible self. To the extent that we are successful in this process, positive feelings of life satisfaction are theorized to emerge. When the individual is unable to realize a hoped-for possible self or to avoid the dreaded possible self, negative self-evaluations and affect will follow. However, protective mechanisms can come into play at this point and lead to a revision in the possible self to avoid future disappointment and frustration. The revised possible self is more consistent with our current experiences.

viewed from a realistic perspective. One of these tendencies of the self is to attempt to maintain consistency (Baumeister, 1996; 1997); people prefer to see themselves as stable and predictable. Another basic tendency is for people to view their abilities and personal qualities in a positive light (Baumeister, Bratslavsky, Finkenauer, & Vohs, 2001).

Possible Selves Theory

The **possible selves** model (Markus & Nurius, 1986) proposes that the individual's view of the self, or self-schema, guides the choice and pursuit of future endeavors. Possible selves are

Coping and Control

Researchers have been interested in the relationship between aging and feelings of control because of the presumably inevitable fact that as we get older, we may have less control over what happens to us, both in terms of the aging of our bodies and in terms of changes in the social environment. **Coping**, a related process, is how we attempt to manage stress by changing the environments or ourselves in order to enhance adaptation to our environments.

The MacArthur Study of Adult Development, a large national survey of almost 3,500 adults, showed that despite awareness of increasing constraints in their lives, older adults (over 60) feel that they do have high levels of control in their lives. They are able to view their resources and potential in a positive way rather than focusing on losses (Plaut, Markus, & Lachman, 2003).

One of the outcomes of coping successfully with stressful situations is an improved mood. By definition, we feel better when we are able to rid ourselves of a nagging problem or work our way out of a situation that threatens our well-being. One longitudinal investigation of coping in midlife adults followed over a 10-year period found that, in turn, people who are more likely to resolve problematic situations are those who are less depressed to begin with. Successful coping was also facilitated by being in good health and having extensive social networks (Brennan, Schutte, & Moos, 2006).

Being resilient, or having a personality that allows you to "bounce back" readily from stressful life experiences, can be another positive attribute that can facilitate the coping process. A sample of older adult widows and widowers followed intensively over a six-week period rated their daily experiences of stressful events and emotional reactions (Ong, Bergeman, Bisconti, & Wallace, 2006). The measure of resilience tapped such qualities as the respondent's ability to overcome negative emotions and adapt to new situations. The more resilient individuals were able to maintain a positive mood even on days when they experienced high degrees of stress, suggesting that personality plays an important role in influencing our ability to cope with difficult situations in life.

Although some discussions of coping in later life regard older adults as passive rather than active copers, it is not necessarily a given that as we get older we adopt a fatalistic approach to managing our fortunes. Older adults can show initiative in managing their situations and making efforts to alter the course of events in their lives. At the heart of their coping efforts is a desire to maintain a feeling of independence, even if they have been forced to relinquish some of their actual independence due to functional changes in their abilities (Duner & Nordstrom, 2005). Improved health may also be an outcome of this type of active coping. The ability to take charge of potentially stressful situations, before they become problems, was found in one study of community dwelling, active, older adults to be related to fewer health-related stressful situations (Fiksenbaum, Greenglass, & Eaton, 2006).

That aging may bring with it more effective ways of coping with stress was illustrated in one intriguing study comparing learning under stress between older and younger rats. The stress in this experiment consisted of being kept in restraint for a period of 21 days. The younger rats showed impairments in spatial and nonspatial memory and learning tasks that were not present in the older animals (Bowman, 2005). Interestingly, research comparing the cardiovascular reactivity of older and younger humans found that older adults actually increased their blood pressure more in response to stress than did their younger

FIGURE 8.6

Stress and Negative Affect in Older and Younger Adults

When asked to rate their negative affect during episodes of daily stress, younger adults had higher scores, as shown here, even though their blood pressure did not rise as much as did the blood pressure of stressed older adults. This figure shows negative affect as a function of age and daily stress (no, yes). Neg. = negative.

Source: Uchino, Berg, Smith, Pearce, & Skinner, 2006.

counterparts. However, as you can see from Figure 8.6, the older adults managed to keep their negative emotions in check, even when it was apparent that their bodies were registering heightened levels of stress (Uchino, Berg, Smith, Pearce, & Skinner, 2006).

"What do you think?"	8-4

Do you agree that as people get older they are better able to handle the stress in their lives?

Researchers in this area regard it as a given that social support is an important resource for people of any age to have when faced with stressful experiences. We all know how important it is to be able to talk to someone who can, if not help, at least hear us out when we have had something bad happen to us. Loss of functional abilities is certainly one important stressful area for older adults. In investigating responses of anxiety, depression, and self-esteem to loss of abilities in married older adults, researchers found that high levels of marital closeness were a protective factor for psychological problems. Older adults with functional losses were able to maintain positive mood and self-regard if they were in marital relationships characterized by such factors as feeling loved, understood, and able to communicate (Mancini & Bonanno, 2006).

Identity Process Theory

In identity process theory, the goal of development is optimal adaptation to the environment through establishing a balance between maintaining consistency of the self (identity assimilation) and changing in response to experiences (identity accommodation). The actions we take upon the environment reflect our attempts to express who we are by engaging in the activities we regard as important and worthwhile. Through identity assimilation, we interpret events in a way that is consistent with our present identity. If an event occurs that is so discrepant we cannot interpret it in terms of our identity at the moment, identity accommodation comes into play.

Most of us have fairly positive views of ourselves, but as we get older, more and more of the experiences we have can potentially erode our self-esteem. However, research on identity processes shows that adults increasingly rely on identity assimilation, and this is how older people are able to maintain a positive self-esteem. The edge that assimilation has over accommodation is theorized to be just enough to maintain this positive view without leading individuals into self-views that are so off base as to be completely out of sync with experiences.

The multiple threshold model, described in Chapter 2, predicts that individuals react to specific age-related changes in their physical and psychological functioning in terms of the identity processes. This model was tested out in a study of nearly 250 adults ranging in age from 40 to 95 years (Whitbourne & Collins, 1998). Individuals who used identity assimilation with regard to these specific changes (i.e., they did not think about these changes or integrate them into their identities) had higher self-esteem than people who used identity accommodation (i.e., became preoccupied with these changes). A certain amount of denial, or at least minimization, seems to be important with regard to changes in the body and identity.

Later studies have examined the relationship between identity and self-esteem more generally and found self-esteem to be higher in people who use both identity balance and identity assimilation (Sneed & Whitbourne, 2003). Identity accommodation, by contrast, is related to lower levels of self-esteem throughout adulthood. However, men and women differ in their use of identity processes in that women use identity accommodation more than do men (Skultety

& Whitbourne, 2004). In addition, some women who use identity assimilation may claim that they use identity balance to appear as though they are flexible and open to negative feedback when in reality, they are not with looking inward and perhaps confronting their flaws (Whitbourne, Sneed, & Skultety, 2002).

That there may be an advantage to identity assimilation in terms of health and mortality was suggested by a fascinating analysis of self-perceptions of aging and longevity (Levy, Slade, Kunkel, & Kasl, 2002). Older adults who managed to avoid adopting negative views of aging (which may be seen as a form of identity assimilation) lived 7.5 years longer than those individuals who did not develop a similar resistance to accommodating society's negative views about aging into their identities.

The tendency to use identity assimilation when thinking back on your life and how you have changed is a general bias that pervades the way many of us recall our previous experiences, a phenomenon known as the life story (Whitbourne, 1985). This tendency was demonstrated in a recent study investigating retrospective reports of personality change in a sample of nearly 260 men and women in their early 60s. Men, in particular, were likely to see themselves as having gained in such attributes as "confident power" between the 20s and the 60s (Miner-Rubino, Winter, & Stewart, 2004).

Identity assimilation may also serve a protective function in other contexts in which older adults are faced with potentially negative information about their abilities. One group of researchers used a novel opportunity to study this process among older drivers referred to driver education classes due to a history of auto accidents. Those older drivers who overestimated their driving abilities became less depressed after receiving feedback about their actual driving abilities than older drivers who took a more pessimistic view of whether their driving

abilities had changed (De Raedt & Ponjaert-Kristoffersen, 2006).

Midlife Crisis Theories and Findings

Lying outside the domain of any particular theory is the notion of the **midlife crisis**, which is derived from an age-stage approach to personality in adulthood. Erikson's theory and, to a certain extent, Vaillant's also attempt to divide the years of adulthood into segments based on broad psychosocial issues. The midlife crisis approach emerged from this framework but took it much further by attempting to pinpoint specific psychological events occurring at specific ages. The most well known of these events is the midlife crisis.

Theory of the Midlife Crisis

It is safe to say that every well-educated person in contemporary American society is familiar with the term "midlife crisis." The topic of the midlife crisis has become a permanent fixture in popular psychology. A recent search of a popular commercial Web site revealed over 100 books on the topic, and there is no sign of diminishing interest in the foreseeable future. It may therefore surprise you to learn that the concept is largely discounted in academic psychology. Despite the lack of supporting evidence, the midlife crisis is commonly referred to in common speech and in the media, with books, magazine articles, and movies portraying the phenomenon along with ways to get through it. Given its impact on the popular psyche, it is worth exploring the thinking and research that went into its original conceptualization.

The term midlife crisis originated in the early 1970s as a description of the radical changes in personality that supposedly accompanied entry into the midpoint of life (age 40 to 45). At this age, it was theorized, the individual is involved in extensive and intensive questioning of goals, priorities, and accomplishments. The prompt for this self-scrutiny, according to theory, was the individual's heightened awareness of the inevitability of death (Jaques, 1965).

The concept of the midlife crisis was first aired in the media when journalist Gail Sheehy (1974) published a best-selling paperback book called *Passages: Predictable Crises of Adult Life*. This book, which was based on a study being conducted at the time by Yale psychologist Daniel Levinson, described the supposed changes that occurred at each decade marker of adulthood. The years of the early 40s, according to this view, were marked by inner turmoil and outer acts of rebellion against the placid, middle-aged lifestyle into which the individual was fated to slip by the 50s. Shortly after the publication of *Passages*, Levinson published his own best-seller called *The Seasons of a Man's Life*, which was a collaborative effort of a team of Yale psychologists, psychiatrists, and sociologists (Levinson, Darrow, Klein, Levinson, & McKee, 1978). This book focused exclusively on the experience of men in midlife through analysis of the interviews of 40 men ranging in age from the mid-30s to mid-40s. The men in the sample were intended to represent men from diverse backgrounds, with 10 from each of the following occupations: business executive, academic biologist, blue-collar worker, and novelist. In addition to these interviews, the authors included informal analyses of the biographies of famous men and the stories of men portrayed in literature.

The core of Levinson's theory of adult development is the **life structure**, defined as "the basic pattern or design of a person's life at a given time" (Levinson et al., 1978, p. 41). To analyze the individual's life structure, it is necessary to look at the sociocultural world, conscious and unconscious self, and participation in the world. Both central and peripheral themes can

be identified in the life structure. These include family, work, friendship, religion, ethnicity, and leisure. According to Levinson and his colleagues, the life structure evolves through an orderly series of universal stages in adulthood. These stages alternate between periods of tranquility and periods of transition, and each stage has a specific focus. The stages and their associated ages are shown in Figure 8.7. During periods of stability, the man builds his life structure around the decisions he made in the previous stage. If he chose to pursue a certain career path, he continues in that path throughout the period of stability. However, as the period reaches its close, the man becomes driven by both internal and external factors to question his previous set of commitments. For the next four or five years, during the transitional period that ensues, he explores different alternatives and seeks a new life structure or a modification of the existing one. Levinson believed that these transitional periods are inevitable. Choices are always imperfect, and as the outcome of one set of choices plays itself out, the individual begins to experience regrets and a desire for change. As stated by Levinson (p. 200), "no life structure can permit the living out of all aspects of the self."

The period called the midlife transition has a special quality compared to other transitional periods because it involves the most significant shift, from early to middle adulthood. As shown in Figure 8.7, the period of the midlife transition ("crisis") is targeted as 40 to 45. As described in the text of the study, however, its beginning can occur anywhere between 38 and 43, and its ending can occur anywhere between the years of 44 to 47. This extends the period of the midlife crisis potentially to nine years. This large time span allotted for the midlife crisis is but one of many problems with the theory, as it encompasses nearly the whole of the 40s. Nevertheless, returning to the substance of the midlife crisis, according to Levinson and

FIGURE 8.7
Stages of Adult Development According to Levinson

Levinson proposed that there are three important transitions in adulthood, with the midlife transition serving as the basis for the "midlife crisis."
Source: Levinson, Darrow, Klein, Levinson, & McKee, 1978.

colleagues, it is oriented around several themes. The first is overcoming disillusionment due to failure to achieve the dreams of youth that inevitably cannot be fully realized. A new set of aspirations, more realistic ones, must be established. The second theme of the midlife crisis involves making decisions about how to pursue the life structure during middle adulthood. During this time, the man questions his marriage, comes to grips with the maturing of adolescent children, handles promotions or demotions at work, and reflects on the state of the nation and the world. He may begin to establish mentoring relationships with younger persons so that he may pass along the torch of what

was handed to him during his early adulthood. Finally, the man must resolve the polarities of his personality involving masculinity and femininity, feelings about life and death, and the needs for both autonomy and dependence on others.

Although Levinson's theory predicts that the stage sequences are universal, it does allow for variations in progress through the late thirties that would affect the specific nature of the midlife crisis. In the most frequently observed pattern reported in the sample, the man advanced steadily through a stable life structure but then encountered some form of failure. Usually, this was not a catastrophic loss, such as being fired or thrown out of the house, but it may have been failure to achieve some particular desired goal by a certain age. For instance, he may not have won an award or distinction for which he was striving such as the biologist who knows he will never win a Nobel Prize. Most people would not be distraught over such a "failure," particularly if they were generally well regarded in their profession or community. However, if this goal was part of an individual's "dream," it can lead to serious disappointment and self-questioning. Some men in the sample did in fact realize their dreams, others failed completely, and still others decided to change their life structures entirely out of boredom.

The characteristics of the midlife crisis are by now well known through their representation in contemporary literature, theater, movies, and song. For many people, they seem almost synonymous with the particular characteristics of the Baby Boomers whom current society regards as being obsessed with aging, determined to stay young, and selfishly concerned with their own pleasure. However, as mentioned before, Levinson regarded the midlife crisis to be a virtually universal process that has characterized human existence for at least 10,000 years. In his subsequent publication on women, which was greeted with far less fanfare, Levinson claimed that similar alternations between change and stability characterize adult women (Levinson & Levinson, 1996). Other theories also emerged at about the same time as Levinson's, such as Gould's theory of transformations (Gould, 1978). Vaillant (1977) also temporarily espoused the midlife crisis concept but then renounced this view: "I believe transitions are merely by-products of development . . . development creates transitions; transitions do not create development" (p. 163). Although Vaillant's view of adult development does depict the growth of the ego as occurring in stages, the midlife crisis is not one of them.

In this pivotal scene from *American Beauty*, Kevin Spacey plays with his "midlife crisis" toy, a red car.

Critiques and Research on the Midlife Crisis

Apart from the original investigation by Levinson and colleagues, little empirical support has been presented for the existence of the midlife crisis as a universal phenomenon (Lachman, 2004). Even before the data were available, however, psychologists in the adult development field expressed considerable skepticism about the concept of the midlife crisis based on what at the time appeared to be extrapolation far beyond the available evidence (Brim, 1976; Whitbourne, 1986a).

One of the most significant criticisms of the midlife crisis was the heavy reliance of the Levinson framework on age as a marker of development. On the one hand, Levinson and the other midlife crisis theorists were somewhat vague about exactly when the midlife crisis was supposed to occur. Was it 40 to 45, 38 to 47, or, as some had argued, at exactly age 43? The vagueness and fluidity of the age range is one type of weakness. People with any problems in their late 30s to almost 50 can claim that they are having a midlife crisis when things are not going their way in life. On the other hand, specificity of age 43 as the time of the event is another type of weakness because adults simply do not have such regularly timed events coinciding with a particular birthday. In some ways, the Levinson (and Sheehy) approaches are like horoscopes, telling us that the calendar determines our personality. People like reading their horoscopes because it gives them some ways to be able to predict what will happen to them, but, of course, the basis for these predictions is highly flawed. If horoscopes were valid, everyone with the same birth date (day, month, or year) would be the same, and clearly, this is not the case.

The Levinson study had other logical and theoretical problems. One was the nature of the original sample. Of the 40 men whose interviews formed the basis for the sample, one-half represented the highly educated and intellectually oriented strata of society. Another one-quarter of the sample consisted of successful business executives. The biased nature of this sample would not have been a problem if Levinson had not tried to generalize to the entire population (now and for all time). However, Levinson did make such extreme claims based on this highly educated, introspective, and financially privileged group of men. Their concerns, such as running companies, publishing novels, and competing for Nobel Prizes, are hardly those of the average man or woman. A second theoretical problem has to do with the inspiration for the study and its source in the personal life of the investigator. Levinson was very clear in stating his own motivations for beginning the study: "The choice of topic also reflected a personal concern: at 46, I wanted to study the transition into middle age in order to understand what I had been through myself" (p. x). He speculated that perhaps the study's results reflected the "unconscious fantasies and anxieties" (p. 26) of himself and his middle-aged male colleagues. A third problem with the basis for the study was perhaps more technical. The process of rating the life stages was never clearly explicated. The usual standard procedures of establishing agreement among judges for rating interview material were not described. Furthermore, the interview questions were not published, so that the interviews themselves as well as the ratings were likely biased in the direction of proving the researchers' hypotheses. Given the many weaknesses in the study, it is understandable that other researchers subsequently were unable to replicate Levinson's findings.

One of the first empirical challenges to the midlife crisis concept came from the laboratories of McCrae and Costa, who used their extensive database on personality in adulthood to test predictions based on Levinson's theory (McCrae & Costa, 2003). As we have already seen, their studies have shown remarkable stability on all personality dimensions across the middle years of adulthood. However, they thought it seemed worthwhile to test specifically the possibility that a midlife crisis would be revealed with more careful analysis. When they plotted scores on the NEO scales by year across the supposed midlife crisis peak years, the scores were essentially flat; in fact neuroticism was lower by a very small amount in the 43-year-olds.

Having explored this indirect approach McCrae and Costa created a Midlife Crisis Scale and administered it to 350 men ages 30 to 60 years. Items on this scale concerned emotions thought to be related to the midlife crisis such as feelings of meaninglessness, turmoil, and confusion, job and family dissatisfaction, and fear of aging and death. If any questions had detected a midlife crisis, these surely would have. Yet they did not, either on the initial sample or in a different group of 300 men tested with a slightly shorter version (Costa & McCrae, 1978). The most telling data of all, however, emerged in this second study on the Midlife Crisis Scale. The data had been obtained from men participating in the Boston Normative Aging Study, one of the longitudinal personality investigations that eventually became part of the basis for the Five Factor Model. Men who had received higher scores on the neuroticism factor 10 years earlier were the ones who received higher scores on the Midlife Crisis Scale. This finding suggests that those with chronic psychological problems are more likely to experience a phenomenon such as the midlife crisis, not the average person.

So far, all the data contradicting the existence of the midlife crisis were derived from the laboratories of McCrae and Costa. There is ample documentation, however, from many other sources. One was a study I conducted on nearly 100 adult men and women between the ages of 24 and 61 (Whitbourne, 1986b). Extensive interview data were collected on identity and life histories. None of the participants, even those in their 40s, fit the criteria for a midlife crisis even when they were asked specifically about the impact of aging on their identities. A second study at around that time was conducted by another investigator on a sample of over 300 men ranging from ages 38 to 48, who completed survey questionnaires and semistructured interviews in the years 1971–1974 (Farrell & Rosenberg, 1981). A smaller group of 20 men participated in a more intensive study involving further questionnaires, interviews, and even family interviews. Once again, however, the midlife crisis failed to appear either in the surveys or the interviews.

Looking broadly at data spanning early to late adulthood on trait-based personality measures, including those administered in the Mills and Radcliffe studies, continuity rather than change tends to be the dominant theme in midlife (Caspi & Roberts, 2001). Interestingly, in one of the Mills studies on women in midlife, the usual sort of factors that might be expected to trigger a midlife crisis among women did not have any effects on personality. Such potential triggers included menopause, having to care for parents, and being concerned about the children leaving the home. Having experienced these events did not lead to negative changes in personality as would be predicted from the midlife crisis theory (Helson & Wink, 1992).

More recently, a nationwide survey of midlife adults known as MIDUS added another nail in the coffin to the midlife crisis concept. The overall percentage of those who stated they had experienced a midlife crisis was 26%, more than the 10% previously reported in studies carried out in the 1980s (Wethington, 2000). However, the reason for this large percentage was the broad scope that respondents used to characterize the phenomenon. Their criteria for saying they had

ASSESS YOURSELF: Assess Yourself: Midlife Crisis Quiz

Take this quiz to evaluate whether your answers are consistent with what researchers have found about the midlife crisis.

1. Do you know anyone who has experienced a midlife crisis?
   A. Yes
   B. No

2. If you answered ''yes'' to Question 1, how old was this person? (If you answered no to Question 1, please check option E.)
   A. 20–30
   B. 31–40
   C. 41–50
   D. 51–60
   E. Not applicable

3. If you answered ''yes'' to Question 1, what is the main reason leading you to think that the person had a midlife crisis?
   A. Ended a long-term relationship for no apparent reason
   B. Suddenly changed careers
   C. Became depressed
   D. Told you he or she was having a midlife crisis
   E. Bought a new ''youthful'' car
   F. Picked up roots and moved somewhere new
   G. Not applicable

4. How prevalent do you think the midlife crisis is?
   A. Happens to almost everyone
   B. Happens to about half the midlife population
   C. Happens to almost no one

5. Do you think you will have a midlife crisis?
   A. Yes
   B. No

6. If people have a midlife crisis, what do you think is the main reason?
   A. Loss of physical abilities
   B. Changes in memory
   C. Lack of job fulfillment
   D. Unhappiness in relationships
   E. Problems with children
   F. Fear of dying
   G. Changes in personality

7. What advice would you give to someone who you think is having a midlife crisis?
   A. Everyone has one, so don't get too upset over yours.
   B. Use this opportunity to learn more about yourself.
   C. Everyone gets older, so just learn to deal with it!

FIGURE 8.8
Percent of Adults Reporting Midlife Crisis

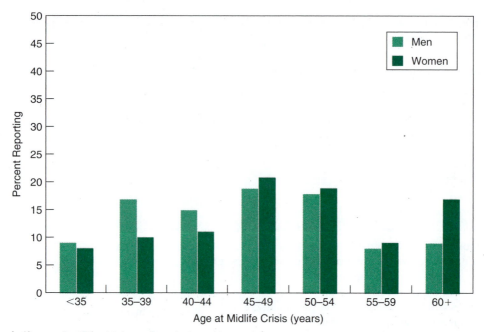

Distribution of self-reported midlife crisis by gender and age at crisis.
Source: Wethington, 2000.

undergone a crisis included awareness of the passing of time. Even so, when categorized by age, there was no particular peak in the mid-40s, as would be expected. Some of the women in the sample even declared that the age of their midlife crisis was over 60, hardly considered "midlife" in the sense of being at the middle of life.

As a scientific concept, the midlife crisis simply fails to withstand multiple tests. By now you must surely be wondering why a concept so thoroughly debunked by the data continues to remain alive. Some argue that, the idea of a midlife crisis makes a "good story" (Rosenberg, Rosenberg, & Farrell, 1999). People in their middle years, settled into stable patterns of both personality and social roles, find it exciting to think about getting that proverbial red sports car or leaving their jobs behind them and moving to

some exotic new place. Sensational events such as hurricanes, tornadoes, and other disasters capture the attention of millions of television viewers. Similarly the idea that personality is subject to major upheavals in the middle years may lead to the persistence of this phenomenon in the public mind far longer than warranted by the data.

In summary, personality is characterized in multiple ways in psychology. Studying how this entity develops over adulthood leads us to the realization that we need not become hardened into a rigid pattern of set dispositions. Change is possible throughout our lives, if not in predictable stages, at least in ways that allow us to feel better about ourselves as we grow older. As researchers explore relationships between health and personality, we will gain greater understanging of how we can maximize our chances of maintaining our physical functioning as well.

SUMMARY

1. Studies of personality in adulthood are based on theories that attempt to define the nature and structure of personality. Within psychodynamic theory, ego psychology focuses on the role of the ego, the structure in personality that is theorized to perform the executive functions of personality. Ego psychologists include Erikson, Loevinger, and Vaillant. Several major longitudinal studies have provided tests of ego psychology theories. Psychosocial development from college to midlife was the focus of the Rochester Adult Longitudinal study, which also examined the relationship of life experiences to personality among men and women. In the Mills and Radcliffe studies, college women were followed using measures testing Erikson's and Loevinger's theories, as well as the interaction of personality and social context. The Vaillant study examined the use of ego defense mechanisms in three samples of adults. Coping and defense mechanisms have also been examined in several large national samples. Together the findings from this research suggest that through middle age and beyond, individuals become more accepting of themselves and better able to regulate their negative feelings. Social context also affects the course of development, and personality in turn affects the way individuals select and react to their experiences.

2. Attachment theory proposes that the earliest interactions with caregivers relate to adult personality and relationships. Studies on adult age differences in attachment style show that older adults are less likely to be anxiously attached and more likely to be dismissive compared with younger adults. However, the majority of adults are securely attached.

3. Socioemotional selectivity theory proposes that, over the course of adulthood, individuals select social interactions that will maximize the emotional rewards of relationships. Older adults appear better able than their younger counter parts to regulate negative affect.

4. Within the trait perspective, the Five Factor Model has stimulated a large body of longitudinal and cross-sectional studies on personality in men and women throughout the adult age range. There are also important individual differences in changes in personality over time, many of them related to health and behavioral risk patterns, such as the Type A behavior pattern.

5. Cognitive self theories propose that individuals view the events in their lives from the standpoint of the relevance of these events to the self. Identity process theory and the possible selves model fit into this category of theories.

6. According to the midlife crisis theory, there is a period in middle adulthood during which the individual experiences a radical alteration in personality, well-being, and goals. Midlife crisis theory was developed by Levinson and colleagues through an interview study of 40 adult males and has gained strong support in the popular culture. However, subsequent researchers using a variety of empirical methods have failed to provide support for this theory, and it is generally disregarded within the field of adult development.

CHAPTER | 9

Relationships

"I was married by a judge. I should have asked for a jury."

Groucho Marx
(1890–1977)

R elationships with others are essential to our existence. Developmental processes interact at every level throughout life with the ties that we have with our intimate partners, family, friends, and the wider social circles in which we carry out our everyday activities. It is difficult to capture the essential qualities of these many relationships, and it is perhaps even more challenging to study the way these relationships interact with individual developmental processes. As important as we know these relationships are at an intuitive level, it is just as crucial to be able to quantify the nature and impact of social processes in adulthood.

Anyone who reads the newspaper or listens to the television news is aware that patterns of marriage and family life are changing with each passing year. Fewer people are getting married, and those who do are waiting longer than was true in previous generations. Families are changing in composition as people leave and reenter new long-term relationships, often involving children and extended families as well. In this chapter, these changing family patterns are examined along with attempts by theorists to understand the qualities of close relationships

and how they interact with the development of the individual.

MARRIAGE AND INTIMATE RELATIONSHIPS

The marital relationship has come under intense scrutiny in contemporary society. The union between two adults is thought to serve as the foundation of the entire family hierarchy that is passed along from generation to generation. We hear about the death of marriage as an institution, yet interest in marriage itself never seems to wane in the popular imagination, the media, and the professional literature. The decision to marry involves a legal, social, and, some might say, moral commitment in which two people promise to spend the rest of their lives together. Given the current divorce statistics, we know that many people are not able to maintain the hopeful promises they make to each other in their wedding vows. What factors contribute to a successful marital relationship, and what might lead to its downfall? Social scientists are nowhere near answers to these questions, but there are many, many theories.

Marriage

In the year 2005, 122.3 million adults were married, a number that represents 56% of the population age 18 and older. The percentage of adults who have ever been married is far higher, however. Among the entire population 18 and older, 75% have been married, but among those 55 and older, 96% were married at some point in their lives (U.S. Bureau of the Census, 2006a).

The median age of marriage is 27 for men and 25.5 for women, a number that has been steadily rising from where it was at the early 20s in 1970 (U.S. Bureau of the Census, 2007c).

As a social institution, **marriage** is defined as a legally sanctioned union between a man and a woman. People who are married are expected to pay joint income tax returns and are given virtually automatic privileges to share the rest of their finances, as well as other necessities such as health care and housing. They often share a last name, usually that of the husband's, although some couples create a new, hyphenated last name. Generally, marital partners are entitled to retirement, death, and other insurance benefits, as well as the entire portion of the estate when one partner dies. Although marriages need not legally fit in with the statutes of a religion, they are often performed in a religious context.

Having explained the legal definition of marriage, we can clearly see what is excluded.

As the confetti rains down on this newly-wedded couple, we can hope for their sake that they will be able to beat the odds and remain happily married.

People who are not legally married are not automatically entitled to the benefits available to those who are. Individuals living within a committed and long-term relationship not sanctioned by the law must seek exceptions to virtually all of the conditions that are set forth for married people. If these individuals are of the same sex and living within a committed homosexual relationship, they face additional barriers to the benefits granted to married persons.

Obviously, the legal definition of marriage includes no mention of the partners' emotional relationship with each other. People can be legally married and live apart, both literally and figuratively. Most social scientists distinguish between an intimate and a marital relationship because the two need not exist within the same couple. The legal commitment of marriage adds a dimension to an intimate relationship that is not present in a nonmarital close relationship in that it is technically more difficult to end a marital than a nonmarital relationship. Furthermore, many people view their marriages as moral and spiritual commitments that they cannot or will not violate.

Definitional concerns aside, there is a body of evidence on marriage in adulthood suggesting that adults who are married have many advantages compared with those who are unmarried. An analysis of the findings of over 50 studies, including more than 250,000 older adults from a variety of countries, showed a 9 to 15% reduction in mortality risk for married adults, both men and women (Manzoli, Villari, Pirone, & Boccia, 2007). This protective effect of marriage was greater in countries from Europe and North America compared to studies from Asia and the country of Israel. Marriage also confers with it greater happiness, a fact that came into question (particularly for women) in the 1980s, but now is accepted as well established (Lee & Bulanda, 2005).

Among all adults 18 and older, over half of whites (56%) are married. Asians (61.7%) have the highest marriage rates, and blacks (34%) the lowest. Of all who identify themselves as biracial, 39.3% are currently married (U.S. Bureau of the Census, 2007b).

Corresponding to sex differences in marital status among the older adult population are differences in family living situations. As can be seen in Figure 9.1, men are almost twice as likely to be living with a spouse; by contrast women are more likely to be living alone or in other situations, but there are also substantial variations by age, race, and ethnicity.

Cohabitation

Living in a stable relationship prior to or instead of marrying is referred to as cohabitation. Since the 1960s, there has been a steady increase in the number of couples who choose this lifestyle. In 1960 a total of 439,000 individuals in the United States reported that they were cohabitating with a person of the opposite sex. By 2005 this number had risen to 4.9 million, or a total of 5% of the population age 18 and older (Johnson & Dye, 2005; U.S. Bureau of the Census, 2006a). From 50 to 60% of all marriages are now preceded by cohabitation (Stanley, Whitton, & Markman, 2004), but there is no evidence that the experience of living together contributes positively to the success of a marriage. In fact the opposite seems to be true. In contrast to commonsense notions about the advantages of cohabitation before marriage, data on divorce patterns show that there is a greater risk of marital breakup among people who cohabitated.

The greater likelihood of divorce among couples who cohabitate before marriage is referred to as the **cohabitation effect** (Cohan & Kleinbaum, 2002). One explanation for the cohabitation effect is that couples who would not have gotten

<u>FIGURE 9.1</u>

Percent Married with Spouse Present by Sex, Age, Race, and Hispanic Origin: 2003

MEN

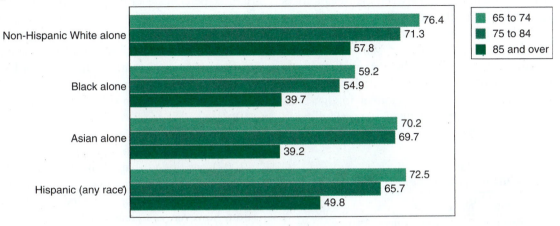

WOMEN

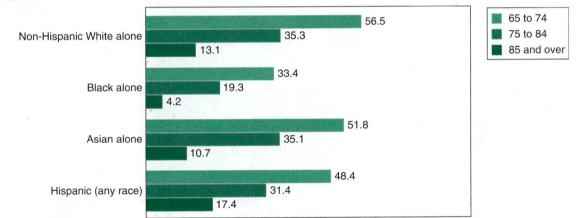

As can be seen from this figure, the percent married decreases within each population group from ages 65 to 85 and older, with the lowest percent married with a spouse present among black women 85 and older.

Source: He, Sangupta, Velkoff, & DeBarros, 2005.

married "slide" into marriage through inertia; in other words, the fact that they were already living together becomes the basis for entering into marriage even if the fit between the two partners is not all that good. Eventually they divorce due to the fact that they were not well matched at the outset (Stanley, Rhoades, & Markman, 2006). Whatever the cause the cohabitation effect seems to hold across a variety of ethnic and racial categories, with the exception of foreign-born Mexicans living in the United States (Phillips & Sweeney, 2005).

"What do you think?" | **9-1**

Do you know of anyone who has experienced the cohabitation effect? Why do you think it happens?

Along with a rise in the overall numbers of couples who cohabitate is a parallel increase in the number of cohabitating adults with children under the age of 15. In 1960 this number amounted to 197,000, but by 2000 it was estimated to have increased by a factor of almost 10 to 1.95 million (U.S. Bureau of the Census, 2006a).

Same-Sex Couples

Gay marriage was first legalized in the United States by the Commonwealth of Massachusetts in 2004, having already been legalized in the Netherlands in 2001, Belgium in 2003, and Spain and Canada in 2005. Other U.S. states are considering similar legislation. Clearly, based on the extent of debate about this issue in the United States and other countries, it is a topic that will remain on political agendas for the coming years.

As of the 2000 U.S. Census, 594,000 people (1 in 9 of all unmarried couple households)

identified themselves as living with a member of the same sex; nearly equal numbers involved male-male and female-female partnerships. The largest percentage (1.6%) of same-sex partners involved people of two or more races. San Francisco, Seattle, and Portland, Oregon, were the cities with the highest numbers of same-sex partnerships. It is estimated that 34% of lesbian couples and 22% of gay male couples who live together have children (Simmons & O'Connell, 2003).

In a comprehensive review of the characteristics of same-sex couples, Peplau and Fingerhut (2007) concluded that, compared with heterosexual couples, there are many similarities in the dynamics of the relationship. One notable exception, however, is a greater sharing of household tasks among lesbian and gay couples. Although there is little research on the factors contributing to the longevity of these relationships and partner satisfaction, the available evidence suggests that because most of the individuals living in these relationships are not legally bound to each other, they are more likely to dissolve when the partnership is not working out. However, the majority of same-sex couples would prefer to legalize their relationship.

Divorce and Remarriage

Approximately 10% of the adult population in the United States is divorced (United States Bureau of the Census, 2007e). The divorce rate is highest among men in their 50s (Kreider, 2005b). Taking into account all marriages that end in divorce, the average length of first marriage prior to divorce is about 8 years (Kreider, 2005b). Divorce statistics also show important variations by race. Blacks and Hispanics have higher divorce rates than white or Asian women (Bramlett & Mosher, 2002).

Divorce rates have been declining since reaching a peak in 1980. Many factors can

<u>FIGURE 9.2</u>
The Cohabitation Effect

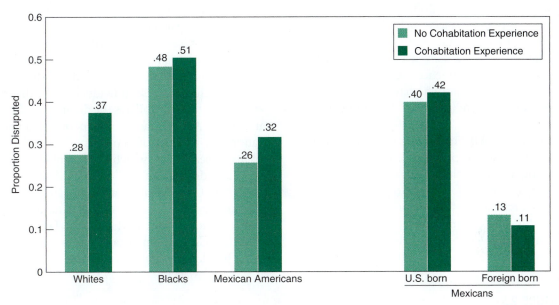

Estimated proportion of women's first marriages disrupted within 10 years, by race and ethnicity, nativity, and cohabitation experience. Disruption refers to separation or divorce.

Source: Phillips & Sweeney, 2005.

account for the decreasing divorce rate. One is that people are marrying at later ages; the older a woman at marriage, the lower the probability that she will become divorced (Bramlett & Mosher, 2002). The skyrocketing divorce rates have also increased consciousness in society about the need for prevention. Suggesting that such efforts can pay off, a study of over 2,200 households in the Midwest of the United States showed that couples who participated in premarital education had higher levels of marital satisfaction, lower levels of conflict, and reduced odds of divorce (Stanley, Amato, Johnson, & Markman, 2006).

The dissolution of a marriage is ordinarily perceived by those involved as a disappointment and a sad event. One or both of the partners may be relieved to see the end of an unsuccessful relationship, but they are nevertheless affected in many ways by the inevitable consequences of the divorce on their daily lives, the lives of children, and the lives of extended family members. A range of practical issues must be resolved, such as changes in housing and financial affairs, but the greatest toll is the emotional one. For many couples, child custody arrangements present the most significant challenge caused by their altered status as a family.

Earlier the advantages of marriage were discussed in terms of benefits to health, financial security, well-being, and lifestyle. Studies on divorced (compared with married) individuals show that they have lower levels of psychological well-being, poorer health, higher mortality rates, more problems with substance abuse and depression, less satisfying sex lives, and more negative life events (Amato, 2000). These effects may persist for many years, particularly for individuals who remain psychologically attached to their ex-partner, experience conflict in coparenting, or who have unusual difficulty in being alone (Sweeper & Halford, 2006). Divorce in older adults has negative effects on health in that newly divorced older adults experience more physical limitations in their daily lives (Bennett, 2006). The negative consequences of divorce are more severe for individuals who have young children, especially women (Williams & Dunne-Bryant, 2006).

Increases in the rate of divorce in the last 30 to 40 years are widely publicized, and the disturbing statistic is often cited that one out of every two marriages will end in divorce. However, the divorce statistics are much more complicated than this simple formula would imply. Those who divorce in a given year are generally not the same people as those who have gotten married, so the number of divorces cannot simply be compared with the number of marriages to determine the odds of divorcing. Furthermore, the divorce rate in any given year includes those people who are divorcing for a second or third time, people who tend to have a higher divorce rate than those who are getting a first divorce, as will be discussed below. Including these individuals in the divorce statistics artificially inflates the divorce rate for all marriages. Another factor influencing the divorce rate is the number of people in the population of marriageable age, which itself is influenced by birth and death rates.

In the United States., approximately 18% of all marriages are second marriages, and 4% are third marriages (Kreider, 2005b). The average duration of a second marriage that ends in divorce is slightly longer than that of a first marriage—8

FIGURE 9.3
Percent Ever Divorced by Age, 2001

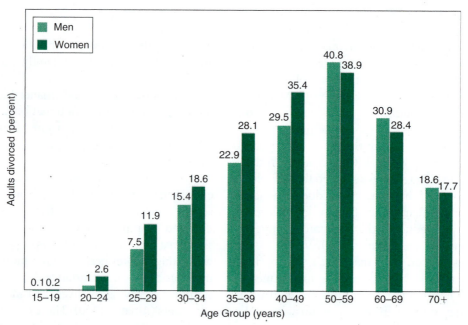

As can be seen here, men in their 50s are the most likely group of adults to ever have been divorced.
Source: Kreider, 2005.

years for men and 9 years for women (Kreider, 2005b). The probability of a second marriage ending in divorce after 10 years is .39, slightly higher than that of the ending of a first marriage, which is .33 (Bramlett & Mosher, 2002).

Approximately one million new children each year are affected by divorce, a figure that has remained constant since 1980 (U.S. Bureau of the Census, 1998). About half (46%) of marriages ending in divorce involve custody arrangements for children. In the majority (72%) of cases, the wife receives custody, compared with only 16% in which joint custody is given and 9% in which custody is given to the husband. There is a greater chance of joint custody being awarded if the couple is between the ages of 35 and 44. Men are also more likely to be awarded custody if they are white, in their late 40s, and are ending their first marriage (Clarke, 1995).

As difficult as it is for children to be caught in between parents who are divorced, it may be just as hard, if not harder, to be caught in between parents who are in a high conflict marriage. Children 19 years of age and older whose parents were interviewed as part of a large longitudinal study on marriage were asked to state whether they felt they had been caught in between parental arguments. The children of parents whose marriages were characterized by a high degree of conflict were least likely to say they had never been involved in conflict between their parents. Their feelings of being caught in the middle were related to lower feelings of subjective well-being and poorer relationships with their parents. Thus, in some ways, the children were better off when their parents divorced rather than remained together in an unhappy marriage (Amato & Afifi, 2006).

Widowhood

Each year it is estimated that about 800,000 individuals in the United States become widowed, the majority of whom are women 65 years and older (National Institute of Mental Health, 2005). When a marriage ends in the death of a partner, the survivor is faced with enormous readjustments in every aspect of life. Even when there is time to prepare, adjustment to widowhood is a difficult and painful process. Depressive symptoms may persist for at least several years after the loss (Wilcox et al., 2003).

Men seem particularly vulnerable to depression after the death of their wives (Bennett, Smith, & Hughes, 2005). Without remarriage, their levels of well-being may not return to preexisting levels even for as long as 8 years after the spouse has died (Lucas, Clark, Georgellis, & Diener, 2003). Adaptation to widowhood is influenced by prior levels of well-being; those who are more vulnerable to widowhood's effects are people whose well-being was lower prior to the death of the spouse (Bennett, 2005). Nevertheless, grief reactions may continue for as long as six decades following widowhood, with the surviving partner continuing to experience memories about and talking to the deceased. Anniversary reactions may continue for as long as 35 years following the spouse's death (Carnelley, Wortman, Bolger, & Burke, 2006).

The likelihood of being a widow is about three times as high for women 65 and older (44%) as for men (14%). By the age of 85 and older, the majority of women are widows (78.3%), over double the rate for men (34.6%). The highest rate of widowhood is among black women 85 and older, among whom the large majority (87.5%) have lost their spouses (He, Sangupta, Velkoff, & DeBarros, 2005). In what is called the **widowhood effect**, there is a greater probability of death in those who have become widowed (Manzoli et al., 2007). The effect is particularly pronounced for Mexican American men, who have an increased risk of death for almost three years after becoming widowers (Stimpson, Kuo, Ray, Raji, & Peek, 2007). Whites married to

FIGURE 9.4
Frequency of Conversations with the Deceased Spouse

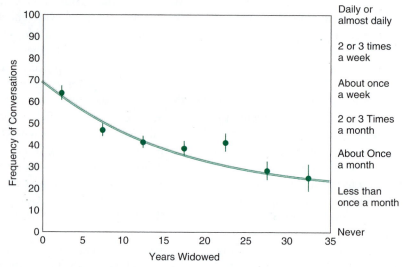

Even for as long as 35 years after becoming widowed, women still report having a "conversation" with their deceased spouse.
Source: Carnelley, Wortman, Bolger, & Burke, 2006.

whites and black men married to white women also show elevated rates of mortality (Elwert & Christakis, 2006).

Women who remarry after becoming widows, not surprisingly, are favored in a number of ways over women who remain widows. The remarried have fewer depressive symptoms, worry less about money, and have higher incomes than women who remain widowed (Moorman, Booth, & Fingerman, 2006). Widows also engage in behaviors that are potentially harmful to their health, particularly after recently becoming widowed. Some of these riskier behaviors include eating fewer fruits and vegetables, foods with higher fat content, and engaging in less physical activity. Longer-term widows are more likely to smoke. By contrast, women who remarry engage in generally healthier behaviors with the exception of alcohol consumption. Perhaps reflecting the use of alcohol in social situations, remarried women are more likely to drink (Wilcox et al., 2003).

Psychological Perspectives on Long-Term Relationships

Throughout the vicissitudes of marriage, divorce, remarriage, and widowhood, most adults actively strive to maintain gratifying interactions with others on a day-to-day basis. Furthermore, for many adults, the feeling of being part of a close relationship or network of relationships is the most salient aspect of identity (Whitbourne, 1986b). Whether this relationship is called "marriage," "family," "friendship," or "partnership" is not as important as the feeling that one is valued by others and has something to offer to improve the life of other people.

Poets, philosophers, playwrights, and novelists, among others, have attempted for centuries to identify the elusive qualities involved in close relationships. Although they have not been around for as long, psychologists and sociologists have also contributed their share of theories to account for why people develop these relationships and what factors account for their maintenance or dissolution over time. Early theories tended to focus on what now seem like simplistic notions such as whether "opposites attract" or whether, instead, "like attracts like." Explanations of relationship satisfaction across the years of marriage attempted to relate the quality of marital interactions to the presence of children in the home and their ages. As relationships in the real world have seemed to become more complicated, however, so have the theories, and there is now greater recognition of the multiple variations that are possible when adults form close relationships. The emotional factors involved in long-term relationships are also gaining greater attention, as it is realized that some characteristics of human interactions transcend specific age- or gender-based boundaries.

Socioeconomic selectivity theory, described in Chapter 8, implies that older adults would prefer to spend time with their marital partner (and other family members) rather than with new people. They should regard the long-term marital relationship as offering perhaps the most potential to serve emotional functions as their experience together over the years has allowed them to understand and respond to each other's needs. In addition, if older adults are better able to control their emotions, particularly the negative ones, they should get along better with their partner because each is less likely to irritate the other one. Finally, if older adults are

FIGURE 9.5
The Widowhood Effect

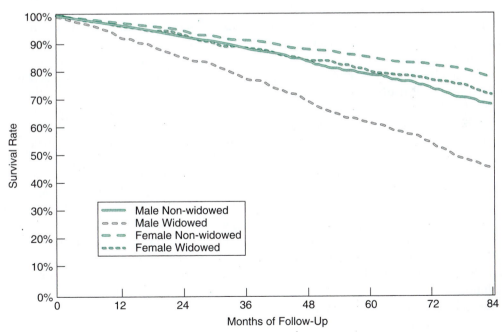

Age-adjusted survival rate for Mexican American men and women in widowed and non-widowed status; similar findings are obtained across racial and ethnic groups.

Source: Stimpson, Kuo, Ray, Raji, & Peek, 2007.

nevertheless able to experience strong feelings, their affection for one another should not fade.

"What do you think?" | **9-2**
Who would you rather spend time with if you knew that you would be moving away within 24 hours, a close friend or a person you have just met?

Attempts by sociologists and social psychologists to understand the dynamics of long-term relationships go back to the 1930s, when interest in marriage and the family had its formal beginnings as a field of inquiry. Some of the questions that researchers working in this tradition ask include the age-old puzzles involved in explaining why some relationships "work" and others do not. Within these traditions, researchers try to account for the factors that cause two people to be attracted to each other. For sociologists, these explanations often involve socioeconomic status or geographic residence. For social psychologists, these explanations involve people's perceptions of themselves and others, as well as their ability to read interpersonal signals in relationships.

One rather significant factor thought to be involved in predisposing a couple to divorce is involvement in an extramarital affair. If you have ever given this matter any thought, you have probably wondered about whether involvement in such a relationship is the cause or the result of an unhappy marriage. Taking advantage of a unique 17-year longitudinal study on marital dissolution, researchers were able to identify the pathways leading from marital happiness to divorce through the pathway of infidelity. Among the nearly 1,500 adults in a nationally representative sample, **divorce proneness** (the tendency to think that your marriage in trouble and to contemplate divorce) predicts involvement in an extramarital affair. However, once one or both partners have engaged in an affair, marital happiness is further eroded by the experience along with an increased risk of divorce (Previti & Amato, 2004).

Social exchange theory attempts to predict the stability and dissolution of social relationships in terms of rewards and costs of an interaction. Relationships continue when partners perceive that the rewards of remaining in the relationship outweigh the rewards associated with its alternatives (Previti & Amato, 2003). The rewards of marriage include love, friendship, and feelings of commitment. When considering a breakup, these rewards are weighed against the barriers presented by legal, financial, social, and religious constraints, as well as the presence of children. The theory predicts that relationships dissolve when the balance shifts so that rewards no longer outweigh the costs. Conversely, increasing levels of intimacy and commitment to a relationship occur over time as the intrinsic rewards of being in the relationship increase and as couples develop increasing levels of dependency. Over time, then, the attractiveness of alternatives tends to fade.

In support of the notion of social exchange as a factor in relationship formation, there is evidence that the earning potential of young women is becoming more important in determining their desirability as mates. As women have made strides in the labor market, their income is now being seen by husbands as an important asset in their own movement up the occupational career ladder (Sweeney & Cancian, 2004). However, there are still some very traditional determinants of what makes men happy, at least in the early years of marriage. In a three-year longitudinal study of characteristics important in a mate, men were found to place higher value on good looks, a pleasing disposition, and a dependable character over time rather than financial prospect of favorable social status (Shackelford, Schmitt, & Buss, 2005).

A variant of social exchange theory is **equity theory**, in which the cost-benefit analysis in the relationship is extended to a comparison of the benefits that each partner brings to the couple (Walster, Walster, & Berscheid, 1978). Dissatisfaction with a relationship is theorized to occur when partners perceive that they are over-benefited (the reward-cost ratio is more in favor of them than the partner) or under-benefited (the partner is receiving more than they are). Commitment to the relationship, and hence its stability, decreases as feelings of inequity grow (Sprecher, 1988). Decreased commitment to the relationship in turn decreases the likelihood that couples will remain together (Floyd & Wasner, 1994).

Having had some practice in close relationships in families may give couples a better basis for getting along with each other. Among a sample of participants asked to reflect on conflict in their relationships during their early 20s, both men and women without siblings recalled more difficulties in getting along with romantic partners than did their counterparts who had brothers or sisters. The sibling effect appears to disappear by the late 20s when, presumably, relationships with romantic partners help to make up for this lack of socialization to close relationships (Chen et al., 2006).

The **behavioral approach to marital interactions** emphasizes the actual behaviors that partners engage in with each other during marital interactions as an influence on marital stability and quality (Karney & Bradbury, 1997). People will be more satisfied in a long-term relationship when their partners engage in positive or rewarding behaviors (such as expressing affection). Punishing or negative behaviors (such as criticism or abuse) decrease satisfaction. These include the husband's rejection of a wife's influence, negative behavior by wives in solving marital problems, and failure of husbands in reducing the negative feelings of their wives (Gottman, Coan, Carrere, & Swanson, 1998). Partners who reject or invalidate the communications of their spouses also experience diminished marital satisfaction over time (Markman & Hahlweg, 1993). Not surprisingly, high levels of hostility expressed by partners are another contributor to unhappy relationships (Matthews, Wickrama, & Conger, 1996).

The use of behavioral observations of marital interactions proved to provide unique insights into predicting who would divorce over the course of a 14-year period in research by Gottman and colleagues. Couples whose marriages were described as "passionless" (showing neither positive nor negative affect) divorced later than couples who were more volatile emotionally during the early married years. Interestingly one of the most predictive interactions of later divorce was the one in which husbands and wives shared the details of their everyday experiences over the course of an 8-hour period during the day. If these lacked positive affect, the couple was at particular risk for subsequent ending of the relationship (Gottman & Levenson, 2000;2002).

Intimacy is also created in smaller and less obvious ways in what Gottman and colleagues call "bids" for the connection with the partner. Partners who use the conflict-escalating reactions of turning away from or turning against the partner who makes the bid for connection increase the extent to which the couple experiences conflict. This effect of bids for connection seems to be stronger for men, whose responses to their wives play a stronger role in escalating or deescalating conflict (Gottman & Driver, 2005).

Another perspective on long-term relationships is provided by theorists who examine the role of similarity and assumed similarity between partners over time. According to the

need complementary hypothesis, people seek and are more satisfied with marital partners who are the opposite of themselves (Winch, 1958). However, the evidence seems to favor the **similarity hypothesis**, which proposes that similarity of personality and values predicts interpersonal attraction and satisfaction within long-term relationships (Gaunt, 2006).

Wives and husbands who manage to remain together often start to interpret their interactions in ways that may have an inner logic not immediately perceptible to outsiders. One pattern of interaction observed in studies of younger adults to be associated with higher physiological levels of stress, measured in terms of cortisol levels, is the "wife demand husband withdraw" pattern of communication in resolving conflicts. For older, but not younger, couples, the perception by both partners of this pattern of communication is associated with higher levels of stress, as measured by cortisol levels (Heffner et al., 2006). We might expect that couples habituate to these high levels of stress. However, researchers investigating the impact of marital discord on various measures of well-being found that even in individuals in their later years, couples who were constantly in conflict with each other suffered in terms of well-being as measured by symptoms of depression and anxiety, lower self-esteem, and lower levels of life satisfaction independently of personality (Whisman, Uebelacker, Tolejko, Chatav, & McKelvie, 2006).

Love that is "in the eye of the beholder" may also prove beneficial in promoting marital happiness over time. In a 13-year longitudinal study of marital relationships, researchers found that couples who perceived each other as higher in agreeableness than they actually were in reality were more in love during the early stages of marriage and more likely to remain in love over time (Miller, Niehuis, & Huston, 2006).

If couples stay together through middle and later adulthood, they have the opportunity to enjoy more leisure-time activities together as a result of retirement and the **empty nest**, or the departure of children from the home (Gagnon, Hersen, Kabacoff, & Van Hasselt, 1999). Interestingly, despite the negative connotations that we ofen hear to the empty nest phenomenon, researchers find that women are not more likely to experience depressive symptoms when their last child moves out of the home (Schmidt, Murphy, Haq, Rubinow, & Danaceau, 2004). Perhaps on a related note, when children do return home for whatever reason, the quality of a couple's sexual relationship may decline at least in terms of frequency of sexual activities (Dennerstein, Dudley, & Guthrie, 2002). In fact a survey of over 15,000 midlife Canadian women showed that the predictors of sexual activity within the past 12 months included age, marital status, race, income, alcohol use, smoking and empty nest status (Fraser, Maticka-Tyndale, & Smylie, 2004). Women whose children were still living in the home were less likely to have intercourse than women who were empty nesters.

Apart from what might be a temporary glitch in an older couple's expression of sexuality, many older individuals are able to maintain enjoyable sexual relations well into their later years. Although physiological factors clearly play a role, as described in Chapter 4, the individual's interest in sexuality and availability of partners are more significant factors in keeping the sexual flames alive among older couples (DeLamater & Sill, 2005). An intensive study of a small sample of Canadian women married after the age of 50 found a shift away from an emphasis on sexual intercourse to greater valuing of other expressions of intimacy, such as cuddling, companionship, and affection. These women still felt that they had strong sexual chemistry with their husbands, even though the expression of that chemistry had changed from the passion of youth (Hurd Clarke, 2006).

FAMILIES

The transformation of a marriage into a "family" traditionally is thought to occur when a child enters the couple's life on a permanent basis. Most of the psychological literature on children and families focuses on the children and their adjustment to the various arrangements for living worked out by their parents (Hetherington & Kelly, 2002). However, there is considerable interest in the literature on the period in which a first child is born, the so-called **transition to parenthood**. From a biopsychosocial perspective, this event involves biological changes (when the mother bears the child) as her body adapts to rapid hormonal and other physiological alterations. Psychological changes include the emotional highs and lows associated with first-time parenthood. In addition, the individual's identity begins to incorporate the concept of being a parent. Social changes involve the new role that adults acquire when they become parents, altering their status with other family members and the community. Clearly, once the transition has been passed, parenthood continues to make a multifaceted impact on the individual. Although biological factors recede in importance, psychological effects and social changes continue, in effect, for the rest of the individual's life.

Approximately 4 million women in the United States give birth each year (U.S. Bureau of the Census, 2007d). In 2004, the majority of children were born to mothers between the ages of 20 and 34 years old with the median age at first birth at 25.2 (Martin et al., 2006). Over the past two decades there has been a steady increase in the percentage of women who remain childless, from 10.2% in 1976 to 19.3% in 2004 (Dye, 2005). In 2003 the percentage of children born to unmarried women was 2.3 (U.S. Bureau of the Census, 2007d). Within the United States, there are racial and ethnic disparities between whites and blacks in the proportion of children born to single mothers. In 2004, 62% of all births to black women were to unmarried mothers compared with 32% for Hispanics, 24% for Asians, and 25% for whites (Dye, 2005).

Family Living Situations

Despite population trends toward more single-parent and cohabiting families, the large majority of households in the United States (67%) consist of people living together as a family. The average household size is 2.61 people. American households are most likely to consist of three-person families, and over half of all families have one or more members under the age of 18. Households with married couples constitute 50.4% of all households (U.S. Bureau of the Census, 2007a).

Now at an all-time low, approximately one in five households (22.4%) in the United States consist of married couples with children, the lowest percentage since at least 1970, when 40% of all households were composed of married couples with children (U.S. Bureau of the Census, 2007a). However, looking at the numbers from the perspective of children, a majority (71%) live in households with both parents; this percentage is virtually unchanged from 1990 to the present (Kreider, 2005a).

Another trend in families is an increase in the number of adult sons and daughters living with their parents (ages 25 to 34 years old), a situation referred to by the slang term "Boomerang" children in the United States and "Kids in Parents' Pockets Eroding Retirement Savings" (KIPPERS) in the United Kingdom. In 2000 this number in the U.S. was 18.5 million, up from 11.9 million in 1970. The peak year was 1990, when 21.4 million individuals 25 to 34 lived at home with their parents (U.S. Bureau of the Census, 2001).

A Canadian survey reported that there are cultural differences in the tendency of parents and young adult children to live together, with

Asian and Latin American born parents to be most likely to be hosting children in the age group of 20 to 24 years old (Turcotte, 2006). Although parents with live-in children were more likely than parents whose children did not live at home to experience feelings of frustration over the time spent taking care of their adult children, the percentage of these negative feelings was very low (8% with live-in children vs. 4% whose children did not live at home). The parents of children living at home also report more conflict about money, the children themselves, and the distribution of labor in household responsibilities. The situation seems more negative with boomerang children compared with children who had never left the home, particularly as mothers are likely to resent the fact that they are losing some of the freedom they gained when their children initially left the home. These parents are less likely to say that their children made them happier (57%) than the parents of non–boomerang children (68%). On the other hand, a larger percentage of parents of children living at home (64%) say they are satisfied with the amount of time spent with their offspring than are parents whose children had moved out (49%).

Changes in the family living situation in recent decades are often discussed in terms of **blended families**, also known as reconstituted families. Within these family situations, at least one adult is living with a child who is not a biological child of that adult. Often these family situations develop after a divorce and remarriage (or cohabitation) in which two adults establish a household together.

For women between the ages of 30 and 34 years, approximately 11% live with a nonbiological child. This percentage rises to 17% for women in their 40s. The majority of children in these situations are the son or daughter of a relative, friend, or partner. The dynamics within these relationships, though the subject of many fictional accounts, are only beginning to receive empirical attention as the numbers of blended families rise.

The Transition to Parenthood

Much of the literature on parenthood and its effects on adults developed through studies on the transition to parenthood within traditional two-parent families. The logic behind such research is that the most significant changes occur with the entry of the new member to the family. The original impetus for studies on the transition to parenthood was provided by the consistent finding that marital satisfaction dips during the childrearing years, a decline particularly marked for women, although there are variations across couples in the negotiation of this transition (Bradbury, Fincham, & Beach, 2000). At the same time as marital satisfaction may decrease, the satisfaction associated with coparenting can increase, particularly when the prebirth marital relationship was high (Van Egeren, 2004).

When wives do become less satisfied with their marriage, it is largely because the birth of the child carries with it changes in the allocation of household tasks. Typically, the division of labor in the home becomes more traditional after children are born. Working women without children already perform more household duties than men do, but after becoming mothers, the situation is exacerbated (Coltrane, 2000). Mothers assume more of the stereotypically female roles of performing household duties such as laundry, cooking, and cleaning, in addition to providing the bulk of the child care. Men increase their involvement in paid employment outside the home after the child enters the family (Christiansen & Palkovitz, 2001). In part, these changes reflect policies in the workplace as well as the beliefs that couples have about the equitable distribution of family responsibilities (Singley & Hynes, 2005).

Not only do fathers increase their paid employment, but their other patterns of social interaction also change significantly when they become fathers. A seven-year longitudinal study of nearly 3,100 fathers of children under the age of 18 referred to the process of becoming a father as transformative in that the relationships of fathers with other generations in the family change as they become more involved with parents, grandparents, and other relatives. Their fathers also become more involved with service-oriented groups and church. These effects occur along with the birth of each child, but are particularly pronounced when men become first-time fathers. One of the major findings of the study was the observation that the transition to the role of father permanently changes the man's life, particularly when he lives in the same household as the child (Knoester & Eggebeen, 2006).

Marital satisfaction may also be affected by the process referred to as **doing gender**. When the woman earns more money than her husband, this sets up a dynamic that violates normative expectations (Bittman, England, Sayer, Folbre, & Matheson, 2003). Rather than doing 50% or less of the housework, the wife actually takes on the majority of household duties, in the process enacting traditional gender expectations for women.

"What do you think?"	**9-3**

Why do couples tend to move toward more traditional roles after the birth of the first child?

Thus, many investigators see the decrease in marital satisfaction associated with the entry into parenthood as resulting from a shift in household duties (Cooke, 2006). Women who enjoy performing family work, are oriented toward family in terms of their overall life goals, and feel that they are particularly good at it seem to be able to avoid perceiving the unequal division of labor as unfair (Grote, Naylor, & Clark, 2002; Salmela-Aro, Nurmi, Saisto, & Halmesmaeki, 2001). However, once things start to come unglued and they feel that they are doing an unfair share of the labor, both they and their husbands become more psychologically distressed (Grote, Clark, & Moore, 2004).

Attachment style may also play a role in influencing the adjustment that a woman makes to parenthood. Among a sample of 106 couples experiencing this transition, it was the women with ambivalent attachment styles who were found to decrease in marital satisfaction if they perceived their husbands no longer supported them emotionally. Their perceptions of support from husbands decreased further over time if they entered the transition already having felt that their husbands were not providing them with the support they needed (Simpson & Rholes, 2002).

Early experiences with their own parents, or at least the recall of these experiences, may also influence adjustment through the transition to parenthood. In one study, interviews with couples becoming first-time parents revealed that if they recalled the marriages of their own parents as unhappy, their evaluation of their own marital quality was also more negative (Perren, Von Wyl, Bürgin, Simoni, & Von Klitzing, 2005). In another related investigation, couples who recalled their parents as having gotten along well were better able to maintain positive patterns of communication over the transition period (Curran, Hazen, Jacobvitz, & Sasaki, 2006).

Studying married couples over the 24 months following the birth of a child, another group of researchers found that fathers with insecure attachment styles had more negative interactions when the couple had experienced a high number of negatively escalating arguments. Unhealthy family alliances, in which one parent joined forces with a child against another parent, were more likely to occur in negatively escalating arguments when one parent was insecurely attached (Paley et al., 2005).

What are some of the factors that can lead to positive outcomes? In one investigation of pregnant women who were followed through motherhood, women who had high self-efficacy and were optimistic about their parenting role tended to weather the transition more favorably (see Figure 9.6). After becoming mothers they experienced fewer depressive symptoms than women with lower expectations and feelings of competence about their role. In fact, for the majority of women in the study, the bonding with their infant and enjoyment of their new role allowed them to feel good about the experience of becoming a mother, effects that persisted for at least four months into the postpartum period (Harwood, McLean, & Durkin, 2007).

Fatherhood is increasingly being studied as an aspect of identity in adulthood reflecting, in part, the increasing role of fathers in the raising of their children (Marsiglio, Amato, Day, & Lamb, 2002). The number of single fathers (sole parents) tripled between the 1980s and 1990s. By 2000, single-father families constituted 5% of all families, and of these as many as 10% were raising three or more children (Fields & Casper, 2001). The extent to which a single father is able to adjust to the role of solo parent is affected by the characteristics of the children, including their age and gender, and his own characteristics, including his age and educational level. The father's adjustment to this role is also affected by his ability to juggle the roles of parent and worker and maintain a relationship with his ex-wife or partner, as well as by his original desire to have custody (Greif, 1995).

Countering the trend toward more single fathers is the increase in the number of fathers who have no contact with their children. In 1960, it was estimated that 17% of children lived apart from their biological fathers; by the 1990s, this percentage had doubled (Popenoe & Whitehead, 1999). Considerably less is known about stepfathers, another increasing segment of the American population. Changes in marriage, divorce, and remarriage patterns over the past several decades have resulted in a larger number of men who take on the role of father to the children of a wife or partner (Marsiglio, 1992). Men in this role are more highly involved if they have biological children of their own, become stepfathers early in the child's life, have a good relationship with their ex-wife or partner, and have a good relationship with the biological father (Hetherington & Henderson, 1997).

An interesting and important variant on the issue of division of labor and the transition to parenthood among heterosexual couples comes from studies of parenting in lesbian couples. In one short-term longitudinal study of lesbian women becoming first-time parents (Goldberg & Sayer, 2006), researchers found that feelings of

FIGURE 9.6
Depression Scores by Parenthood Expectations

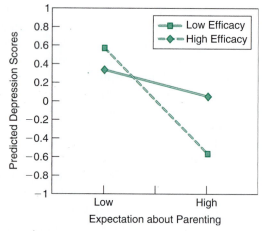

Women who had high efficacy scores regarding their ability to be good mothers had a more positive outcome after their children were born in terms of low depression scores.

Source: Harwood, McLean, & Durkin, 2007.

love tend to decrease and the amount of conflict tends to increase. As is also true with heterosexual couples, lesbian couples report that they have less time to spend with each other and are stressed by the new roles they have taken on as parents. Satisfaction with the allocation of duties seems to be an important factor in predicting the functioning of the children of that relationship. This is true for both lesbian and heterosexual couples (Agronick & Duncan, 1998).

Adult Parent-Child Relationships

Parent-child relationships maintain their importance throughout life (Allen, Blieszner, & Roberto, 2000). For older adults, these relationships can play a vital role in well-being, particularly with regard to the development of generativity, and particularly for women (An & Cooney, 2006). For example, the quality of parent-child relationships is related to mental health outcomes such as loneliness and depression among aging parents (Koropeckyj-Cox, 2002). Conversely, relationships with parents can play a particularly strong role for children who maintain strong attachment ties to their parents (Perrig-Chiello & Höpflinger, 2005). The majority of adult children (56%) state that they feel close to their parents, but another large group (38%) see their relationships as ambivalent. Fortunately only a small minority (6%) see them as problematic (Fingerman, Hay, & Birditt, 2004).

As children move through the years of adulthood, there are many facets of relationships with their own parents that can change. For example, as children have their own families, they begin to realize what it was like for their parents. On the one hand, the children may now appreciate what their parents did for them, but on the other hand, they may resent their parents for not having done more. Another changing feature of the relationship stems from the child's increasing concern that parents will require help

and support as they grow older. Adult children and their parents may also find that they do not agree on various aspects of life, from an overall philosophy and set of values (such as in the area of politics) to specific habits and behaviors (such as methods of food preparation). Whether parents and their adult children live in the same geographic vicinity and actually see each other must also be added into the equation.

In some unfortunate instances, the lines of communication break down considerably and a the result is an emotional gap known as a **developmental schism** (Fingerman, 2001). One manifestation of the developmental schism is the mother's tendency to regard her daughter as more important than the daughter does the mother and for the daughter to regard the mother as more intrusive than the mother does the daughter. Mothers are also more likely to regard their daughters as confidants than daughters do their mothers. Another possible source of tension is that the daughter still seeks the approval of the mother and feels guilty when she feels that she is not living up to her mother's expectations for her.

The term **role reversal** is occasionally encountered in the professional as well as the popular literature on the parents of adult children. According to this view, which is discredited among gerontologists, parents and their adult children switch responsibilities. The child becomes the parent because of physical, cognitive, and social changes in the parent's status. The concept is no longer considered valid in view of data showing reciprocal relationships of helping between adult children and their parents (Blieszner, 2006). Unfortunately, however, the idea that parents become their children's children is still prevalent in societal views of aging.

Children do undergo developmental changes that alter their relationships with parents, a concept referred to as **filial maturity** (Blenkner, 1963). During early adulthood, but particularly in the 30s, children begin to relate to their parents in a different way than they did before. By taking on the responsibilities and status of an adult (employment, parenthood, involvement in the community), the adult child begins to identify with the parent. Over time, the relationship may change as a consequence of this process, as parents and children relate to each other more like equals (Fingerman, 1996).

The idea that one might be forced to take on the role of parent to the parent, however, does create a certain amount of concern and worry in the adult child. This process is referred to as **filial anxiety** (Cicirelli, 1988). This phenomenon may be one that is particularly likely to occur in the United States and other Western industrialized nations where the prevailing values stress independence and the nuclear family. In other cultures, notably Hispanic, Asian, and African American, children have an attitude of **filial obligation** or **filial piety**, meaning that they feel committed to taking care of their parents should this become necessary. There are established traditions within African American (Wilson, 1986) and Hispanic (Keefe, Padilla, & Carlos, 1979) families of a broader definition of family to include the extended family rather than the nuclear family as the basic family unit. Similarly the norm in Asian cultures is for parents to live with their children. Even though there has been concern that westernization in these countries will erode that tradition, data from the mid-1990s would suggest that this tradition is still strong (Velkoff & Lawson, 1998).

The potential difficulties between adult children and their parents, particularly for women, are thought to rise to the point of crisis when there is the need to provide caregiving to the parent. Caregiving, first discussed in Chapter 5, consists of providing assistance in carrying out the tasks of everyday life to an infirm older adult. A large body of evidence has accumulated on this topic since the early 1980s (Zarit, Reever, &

Bach-Peterson, 1980), most of it cross-sectional. Based on this research, it was considered a foregone conclusion that the caregiving role was a traumatic one for the adult child. The daughters in this situation, referred to as "women in the middle" (Brody, 1981) or the **sandwich generation** (sandwiched between their mothers and their children), were thought to be victims of extreme stress due to their caregiver burden. However, longitudinal studies have since provided evidence of ameliorating factors in the caregiving situation and even the possibility that the daughters in these situations experience some benefits.

One factor that appears to play a role in reducing caregiving burden is that, consistent with exchange theory, monetary rewards in the form of an expected inheritance can balance out feelings of resentment toward aging parents (Caputo, 2002). The extent to which parents provided children with financial support when the children were younger also has an effect on the later social support provided as parents grow older (Silverstein, Conroy, Wang, Giarrusso, & Bengtson, 2002). In contrast to common myths about aging parents "taking" more than they "give," researchers find that the likelihood is far greater that parents provide financial support to their adult children than vice versa (Van Gaalen & Dykstra, 2006). Even when daughters are in the caregiving role for their parents, their feelings of obligation are tempered by gratitude for the help that the parents provided when the daughter's own children were young (Keefe & Fancey, 2002).

Among siblings there is a tendency to try to equalize the sense of shared responsibility, if not in reality then in the way that the situation is perceived (Ingersoll-Dayton, Neal, Ha, & Hammer, 2003). Caregiving stress can also be reduced by the provision of help by others in the family. Despite the belief that one child (the daughter) has sole responsibility for caregiving, close to two-thirds of caregivers have significant assistance from someone else, often the spouse (Martire, Stephens, & Townsend, 1998).

When parents do experience declines in health, it seems that the norms of filial responsibility lead to mutual adaptations between children and parents as they redefine their relationships (Silverstein, Gans, & Yang, 2006). Interestingly it seems that the Baby Boomers have become more oriented toward caring for their parents than was true of their own parents (Gans & Silverstein, 2006).

Rather than being a universally negative experience, then, caregiving may not present as traumatic a situation for middle-aged daughters as is often portrayed in the media. Although women in this age group face many demands on their time, they are also likely to be able to draw on other sources of help and emotional support.

A model incorporating the various dimensions present in the adult child-parent relations is the **intergenerational solidarity model** (Bengtson & Schrader, 1982; Silverstein & Bengtson, 1997). According to this model, six dimensions characterize the cohesiveness of these relationships: distance apart, frequency of interaction, feelings of emotional closeness, agreement in areas such as values and lifestyles, exchanges of help, and feelings of obligation. In research based on this model, the frequency of parent-child relationships was found to vary considerably according the gender of the parent. Five types of relationships were identified: sociable, tight-knit, obligatory, detached, and intimate but distant. The most common type of mother-child relationship was tight-knit, and the most common father-child relationship was detached. Altogether the results add up to a picture of greater intergenerational solidarity between mothers and adult children than between fathers and their children.

An extension of the intergenerational solidarity model to a German sample of adult

The nature of relationships in extended families show important variations by race and ethnicity.

daughters revealed further insights into adult parent-child relationships. Women who felt that they gave more than they received to their mothers felt less closely connected to them both in terms of intimacy and in terms of their admiration for them. In other words, daughters seemed to expect and desire more of a balanced relationship between their mothers and themselves. In general, the model had greater applicability to daughter-mother relationships than to daughter-father relationships (Schwarz, Trommsdorff, Albert, & Mayer,2005).

The intergenerational solidarity model was initially based on ratings by individuals within different generations of the quality of their relationships. Researchers in the Netherlands decided to approach their study of families on a set of behavioral criteria, identifying five basic types of parent-child relationships on the basis of how often parents and children saw each other, how much help was exchanged, and whether conflict was experienced over material and personal issues. Using these behavioral indicators, five types of parent-child relationships were identified: harmonious, ambivalent, obligatory, affective, and detached. The largest percentage (40%) consisted of harmonious relationships, but the second largest group consisted of ambivalent parent-child ties (29%). Relationships with mothers were more likely to be harmonious than relationships with fathers, and relationships with daughters more likely to be ambivalent than those with sons. Sons and fathers were more likely to have obligatory ties than were mothers and daughters (Van Gaalen & Dykstra, 2006). This study revealed the importance of examining ambivalence within parent-child relationships rather than looking only at solidarity versus conflict as two ends of a single continuum. Both solidarity and conflict can coexist in these complex intergenerational relationships.

SIBLINGS

The sibling relationship has many unique features within the constellation of family interactions (Van Volkom, 2006). Those who are siblings by birth share a genetic background, and those who have been raised together share many experiences dating to early childhood. By the time siblings reach later adulthood, it is quite possible that they are the only remaining members of their original family and that they have known each other longer than anyone else they have known in their entire lives. As is true for adult child-parent relationships, the sibling relationship is not one of choice, and, to be sure, many people allow their connections with brothers and sisters to fall by the wayside. However, even if they do not stay in frequent contact, they may still maintain the relationship and tend to value it in a positive manner (Bedford, Volling, & Avioli, 2000).

The potential exists for this relationship to be the deepest and closest of an adult's life, and to bring with that closeness both shared joy and shared pain. For the most part, it appears that although these relationships have different levels of intensity (Folwell, Chung, Nussbaum, Bethea, & Grant, 1997), they tend to be positive in

middle and later adulthood. The large majority (about 90%) report that they neither argue nor are competitive with their siblings (Cicirelli, 1982), and, conversely, only 10% fall into a sibling category with the self-evident label of "hostile" (Gold, 1989). Nevertheless siblings carry with them into midlife the perception that either they or their sibling was differentially favored by their parents. Some aspects of sibling rivalry, then, seem to persist throughout life (Boll, Ferring, & Filipp, 2003).

The sibling relationship is one that can, however, fluctuate throughout adulthood. Increased closeness between siblings is associated with a number of significant life events, such as marriage, the birth of children, divorce and widowhood, and the development of health problems or death of a family member (Connidis, 1992). Sibling ties seem to be particularly sensitive to these events. Such events can give siblings greater shared experiences, understanding of each other, and insight into the dynamics of their relationship.

GRANDPARENTS

For many older adults, the rewards of family life begin to grow much richer when they reach the status of grandparents. At this point, they are in a position to be able to enjoy the benefits of expressing their generativity through interacting with the youngest generation. However, they can avoid the more arduous tasks of parenthood. One of the most challenging aspects of life for the older person is loss of a spouse. The opportunity to be a grandparent can offset some of this loss. Unfortunately not all grandparents are able to enjoy the benefits of their status, nor do all grandparents want to assume this role. Furthermore, increasingly grandparents are being asked to substitute for a parent who is not present in the home, or whose job has extensive time commitments.

ASSESS YOURSELF: Your Grandparent

Please think of the grandparent to whom you are closest. If you have no grandparents, then think of one of your friends who is close to a grandparent and answer the questions on that basis. It's ok if one of the grandparents is a step-grandparent.

1. For birthdays and holidays, my grandparent:
   A. buys me great presents that I really like.
   B. gives me money.
   C. buys me presents that I really don't like.
   D. does not buy me presents or give me money.

2. When it comes to giving my grandparent a gift:
   A. I have trouble thinking of what he or she would like.
   B. It is easy for me to think of something to get him or her.
   C. I don't usually give my grandparent a gift.

3. If I could, I would:
   A. spend more time with my grandparent.
   B. spend about as much time as I do now with my grandparent.
   C. spend less time with my grandparent.

4. When I need advice from someone who is older than me, I:
   A. would not hesitate to ask my grandparent.
   B. would never ask my grandparent.
   C. might ask my grandparent but it would depend on what type of advice I need.

5. I see my grandparent:
   A. only on major family occasions (weddings, funerals, bar/bat mitzvahs, christenings).
   B. for major holidays such as Christmas, Chanukah, Thanksgiving.
   C. many times, usually whenever I visit my parents.

6. When I achieve something important, my grandparent
   A. is one of the first to congratulate me.
   B. might send me a note or might call me, but not always.
   C. does not usually acknowledge my achievement.
   D. probably does not know about my achievement.

7. The activity I most likely would engage in with my grandparent is:
   A. having fun together with my grandparent and no other family member.
   B. doing something around the house with no other family member present.
   C. sharing a meal or other family occasion, not usually alone.

8. If I can't see my grandparent in person, I:
   A. call him or her.
   B. e-mail him or her.
   C. don't really think about him or her.
   D. intend to call or e-mail but usually forget.

(contd.)

ASSESS YOURSELF

9. When I think about my parents and my grandparent, I:
   A. realize they really do not get along very well.
   B. think they love each other but don't always understand each other.
   C. hope that someday my own parents and I will get along that well.
10. If my family needs something, my grandparent:
    A. helps out by giving money or doing something specific that the family needs.
    B. seems interested in the situation but rarely offers assistance.
    C. is not even aware that my family needs something.
    D. refuses to provide money or specific help.

Many people still think of grandparents as the warm, generous, older adults who have ample time to spend with their families and want to do so. However, variations in patterns of grandparenting, along with a rapidly increasing growth in the number of grandparents in the population, may require that this image be changed.

Grandparents Raising Grandchildren

There are approximately 56 million grandparents in the United States (Fields, O'Connell, & Downs, 2006); about 11% (5.7 million) live with their under-18 years of age grandchildren (U.S. Bureau of the Census, 2007b).

In a number of families, the grandparent takes the primary responsibility as caregiver for the grandchild. As of 2001 there were 1.4 million children (1.9% of all children) living with grandparents and no parents present (Kreider, 2005a). This situation, referred to as a **skip generation family**, may occur for a variety of reasons, including substance abuse by parents, child abuse or neglect by parents, teenage pregnancy or failure of parents to handle children, and parental unemployment, divorce, AIDS, or incarceration (Pinson-Millburn, Fabian, Schlossberg, & Pyle, 1996).

Although only a small percentage (14%) of grandparents in these situations are over the age of 60 years, substantial percentages have a disability (40%) or live in poverty (21%). However, on the positive side, the role of surrogate parent can contribute positively to the grandparents' sense of identity, particularly for African American grandmothers (Pruchno & McKenney, 2002).

With life expectancy increasing, great-grandparents are becoming more and more prevalent. Relationships across more than two generations are taking on increasing importance and will continue to do so into the foreseeable future (Bengston, 2001).

Patterns of Grandparenting

The classic study of grandparenting conducted by Neugarten and Weinstein (1964) identified five types of grandparents. The first type, the formal grandparent, follows what are believed to

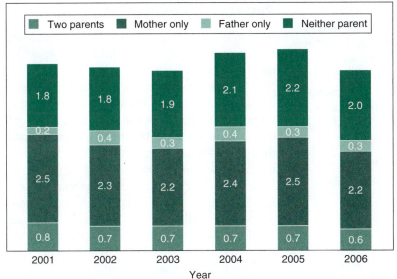

Two parents   Mother only   Father only   Neither parent

Year	2001	2002	2003	2004	2005	2006
Two parents	1.8	1.8	1.9	2.1	2.2	2.0
Father only	0.2	0.4	0.3	0.4	0.3	0.3
Mother only	2.5	2.3	2.2	2.4	2.5	2.2
Neither parent	0.8	0.7	0.7	0.7	0.7	0.6

Year

FIGURE 9.7

Children Living with Grandparents, 2001–2006

The percentage of children living with grandparents in the household and no parent has remained at about 2% of all children from 2001–2006.

Source: http://www.census.gov/population/ www/socdemo/hh-fam/cps2003.html

be the appropriate guidelines for the grandparenting role, which includes providing occasional services and maintaining an interest in the grandchild, but not becoming overly involved. By contrast, the fun seeker emphasizes the leisure aspects of the role and primarily provides entertainment for the grandchild. The surrogate parent, is the third type and as the name implies, takes over the caretaking role with the child. Fourth, the reservoir of family wisdom, which is usually a grandfather, is the head of the family who dispenses advice and resources but also controls the parent generation. Finally, the distant figure is the grandparent who has infrequent contact with the grandchildren, appearing only on holidays and special occasions.

Other attempts to characterize or delineate styles or categories of grandparenting have followed a similar pattern, with distinctions typically being made among the highly involved, friendly, and remote or formal types of grandparents (Mueller, Wilhelm, & Elder, 2002). The "remote-involved" dimension is one that seems to resonate in the attitudes that grandchildren have toward their grandparents as well (Roberto

& Stroes, 1992). The symbolic value of the grandparent in the family lineage, or the "family watchdog" (Troll, 1985), is another central component identified in several classifications.

Although these variations may exist in patterns of grandparenting, it is safe to say that the role of grandparent is an important one for the older adult (Harwood & Lin, 2000). Grandparents feel a strong sense of connection to the younger generation (Crosnoe & Elder, 2002)

There are a variety of patterns of grandparenting; clearly, the grandmother and grandchild shown here have a close and positive relationship.

and may play an important role in mediating relationships between parents and grandchildren during conflicts (Werner, Buchbinder, Lowenstein, & Livni, 2005). Grandparents who are unable to maintain contact with their grandchildren due to parental divorce or disagreements within the family are likely to suffer a variety of ill consequences, including poor mental and physical health, depression, feelings of grief, and poorer quality of life (Drew & Smith, 2002).

FRIENDSHIPS

Of the areas of relationships examined in this chapter, oddly enough, friendship has probably received the least attention regarding its function, meaning, and changes over the course of adulthood.

Theoretical Perspectives

Taking a life course perspective, Hartup and Stevens (1997) suggest that the major dimension that underlies close friendships is reciprocity, or a sense of mutuality. The fundamental characteristic of reciprocity is that there is give and take within the relationship at a deep, emotional level involving intimacy, support, sharing, and companionship. At the behavioral level, reciprocity is expressed in such actions as exchanging favors, gifts, and advice. Close friends in adulthood confide in each other, help each other in times of trouble, and attempt to enhance each other's sense of well-being. Although there may be developmental differences across the life span in the expression of reciprocity, the essence of all friendships remains this sense of deep mutuality. Another important function of friendships is socializing, or helping each other through life transitions in other spheres, such as changes in health, marital relationships, residence, and work.

Patterns of Friendships

As people enter long-term intimate relationships, they engage in "dyadic withdrawal," in which their individual friendships diminish and their joint friendships increasingly overlap (Kalmijn, 2003). Overall this means a decline will occur in a person's total number of friends. One exception occurs among women who have become divorced, whose number of close friendships increases (see Figure 9.8).

Friendship patterns at any age may be seen as following a developmental trajectory from formation to dissolution (Adams & Blieszner, 1994). You have probably experienced this trajectory with your own friends. The stage of friendship formation involves moving from being strangers to acquaintances to friends. The maintenance phase encompasses what is usually thought of as "friendship," during which friends sustain an active interest and involvement with each other. They may evaluate the quality of the friendship periodically during this phase, deciding to increase or decrease their level of involvement. In terms of Hartup's framework, it would be during the maintenance phase that reciprocity levels are highest. Friendships may remain in the maintenance phase for years, even decades, at varying levels of closeness. The end of a friendship, which occurs during the dissolution phase, may be hard to identify. A friendship may end gradually over a period of time as feelings of reciprocity diminish and the relationship essentially falls by the wayside. Friendships may also end through a conscious decision based on insurmountable disagreements and conflict.

"What do you think?"	9-4

What types of friends do you have? How many people would you count as close friends?

FIGURE 9.8
Friendships by Relationship Status and Sex

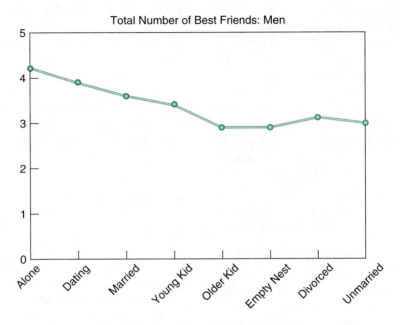

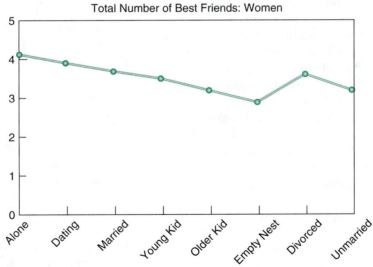

Number of close friends among men and women by relationship status.

Source: Kalmijn, 2003.

Friendships in adulthood may also be distinguished in terms of the closeness of the relationship, which may or may not change over time. People may maintain **peripheral ties**, which are not characterized by a high degree of closeness, for many years (Fingerman & Griffiths, 1999). Peripheral ties include people such as neighbors, coworkers, professional contacts, or the parents of one's children's friends. These relationships may be amicable and cordial but never progress beyond this level. Other peripheral ties may be those that are in the friendship formation stage and will later progress to close friendships. A third type of peripheral tie is one that was formerly a close friendship and has now moved to the dissolution/disinterest stage.

There may also be variations in friendship patterns in adulthood based on individual differences in approaches toward friends, called **friendship styles** (Matthews, 1986). Independent individuals may enjoy friendly, satisfying, and cordial relationships with people but never form close or intimate friendships. Discerning individuals are extremely selective in their choice of friends, retaining a small number of very close friends throughout their lives. Finally, acquisitive people are readily able to make and retain close friendships throughout their lives and therefore have a large social network.

People tend to choose as friends other people who are similar in gender, socioeconomic status, and ethnicity (Adams & Blieszner, 1995; Matthews et al., 1996). Throughout adulthood, close social ties serve as a buffer against stress and are related to higher levels of well-being and self-esteem. Relationships with friends may even be more predictive of high levels of self-esteem than income or marital status (Siebert, Mutran, & Reitzes, 2002). For people who have no family members, friendships serve as an important substitute for keeping an individual socially connected (Lang & Carstensen, 1994).

As you have learned in this chapter, our close social ties play an important role in our development. Even as relationships respond to a changing social context, they continue to influence our well-being and adaptation. There continue to be areas of research that need further work, however, particularly in the areas of grandparenting, siblings, and friendships. From a biopsychosocial perspective, this research will provide greater understanding of the interactions among health, personality, and social context.

SUMMARY

1. Close relationships form an important component of adult life, and although these patterns are changing in the United States, development in adulthood and later life interacts in important ways with the ties that people have with others. The large majority of adults get married, and although marriage rates are decreasing and people are waiting longer to get married than in previous decades, the majority of adults are living in a marital relationship.

2. Cohabitation rates have been increasing in recent decades. According to the cohabitation effect, people living together before marriage are more likely to divorce. Approximately 10% of the adult population in the United States is divorced. The divorce rate is highest among men in their 50s, and taking into account all marriages that end in divorce, the average length of first marriage prior to divorce is about 8 years. Divorce statistics also show important variations by race.

3. Birthrates have decreased over the past 20 years, and women are having children at later ages. Most women, however, have their first child before the age of 30. Women who have a child after they are 30 are more

highly educated and have higher incomes, but they also have a higher risk of encountering medical complications. Men with higher education and occupation are more involved in raising their children but spend less time in providing care. The number of single fathers is increasing, but there are also more fathers who have no contact with children.

4. Widowhood is a stressful event for men and women, but men are more likely to show the widowhood effect of increased mortality after becoming a widow. The effects of widowhood can persist for many years, and many people report various forms of attachment to their deceased spouse.

5. Studies of the transition to parenthood indicate that decreases in marital satisfaction are especially likely to occur when the division of labor assumes more traditional lines in the household. The study of adult child–parent relationships reveals a number of important phenomena related to changes in roles and their altered views of each other. Although caregiving is usually thought of in negative

terms, there is some evidence of positive outcomes. The intergenerational solidarity model proposes six dimensions to characterize the cohesiveness of these relationships.

6. Siblings are another important family tie in adulthood, and closeness between siblings varies over the adult years along with other family and life events.

7. The majority of older adults are grandparents, a relationship that tends to be positive, but there is a trend toward grandparents raising grandchildren in a "skip generation" (no parents present) household. Theoretical explanations of grandparenting focus on the remote-involved dimension, and various categorization schemes are based on this concept.

8. Friendships are another source of important close relationships in adulthood, and even if individuals are not involved in tight-knit friendships, they may have many important peripheral ties.

CHAPTER 10

Work, Retirement, and Leisure Patterns

> *"Old age hath yet his honour and his toil."*
>
> Alfred Lord Tennyson
> (1809–1892)

The majority of adults are involved in productive activities in some form of paid employment. For those of us who are lucky, the experience of work is positive, fulfilling, and expressive of our personal interests and abilities. Others are not so fortunate, and for those of us in this situation, work is a means to an end of supplying income that can be used toward fulfilling activities in the realms of leisure, recreation, or family. Regardless of the enjoyment that our work provides, however, it is the primary focus of life among people from the 20s and onward until we retire. Furthermore, the nature of our work, the amount of income it provides, and the conditions in which our work is conducted, carry over to virtually every other area of our lives. Finally, our identity is defined in important ways in terms of job title, prestige, security, and status.

Given the importance of work in adulthood, what is the impact of retirement? Researchers, theorists, and counselors have been intrigued with this question, and as you will learn, there are no easy answers. Although the thought of retirement may seem very far away to the average college-aged student, it must be planned for much sooner than you might think!

WORK PATTERNS IN ADULTHOOD

To understand work experiences and development in adulthood, it is best to begin by looking at the context in which employment occurs.

The **labor force** includes all civilians in the over-16 population who are living outside of institutions (prisons, nursing homes, residential treatment centers) and who have or are actively seeking employment. In 2007 the total civilian noninstitutionalized population over the age of 16 amounted to 230.8 million people, and of these, two-thirds were in the labor force. Almost all (96%) of these individuals were employed, meaning that 63% of all adults who could be employed in the United States are in fact employed (http://www.bls.gov/news.release/empsit .nr0.htm). Although whites, blacks, and Hispanics have similar labor force participation rates, the unemployment rates are higher for blacks (10%) and Hispanics (6%) than for whites (4.4%) and Asians (4%) (U.S. Bureau of the Census, 2007i).

Age Distribution

Labor force age dynamics have shifted over the past 40 years, reflecting the movement of the Baby Boom generation through the population. Beginning in the 1970s, when they entered the workforce, and projected through at least the year 2014, their impact has been felt in the labor market. Looking at Figure 10.1, you can see that although workers age 25 to 34 will actually have the largest representation in the labor force in 2014, workers 55 to 64 (the older Baby Boomers) will show the greatest and steadiest actual increase in percentages.

Not only are the Baby Boomers disproportionately represented in the labor force, but they are also among the wealthiest. As can be seen in Figure 10.2, adults aged 45 to 54 earned the

FIGURE 10.1

Labor Force Participation by Age

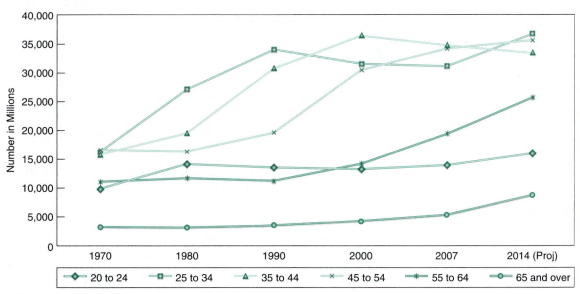

Total number of workers within each age group in the population as of 2007.

Source: U.S. Bureau of the Census, 2007f.

FIGURE 10.2
Median Income by Age, 2005

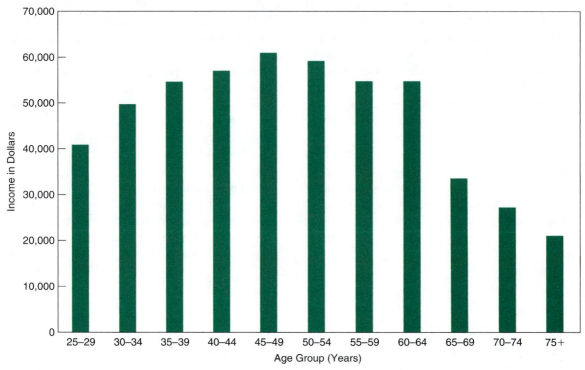

Median income in dollars, U.S. population.

Source: http://pubdb3.census.gov/macro/032006/hhinc/new02_001.htm

highest median incomes in the year 2005. These high incomes are due to the fact that the highest percentages of people in the managerial and professional levels, which are also the highest paying occupations, are within this age bracket (http://data.bls.gov/PDQ/servlet/SurveyOutputServlet)

Gender Patterns

Men are more likely than women to be represented in the labor force due to the tendency of women to remain at home with their children. However, the stay-at-home mother is becoming more and more a feature of the past. Since 1960 the percentage of married women in the workforce has steadily increased, particularly married women with young children. Among women with children under the age of 6, the labor participation rate increased by a factor of over threefold, from 19% in 1960 to 62% in 2004 (http://www.bls.gov/cps/wlf-databook2005.htm).

Despite their increasing involvement in the labor force, women still earn less than men, a fact referred to as the **gender gap** expressed as a proportion of women's to men's salaries. Estimates of the gender gap range from .60 to .80, depending on the data source used (the Census Bureau cites an overall figure for 2005 of .76) (Webster & Bishaw, 2006). The gender gap is particularly pronounced among women in the 55 to 64-year-old age group and lowest in the youngest group of workers.

FIGURE 10.3

Median Income by Age and Gender, United States, 2006

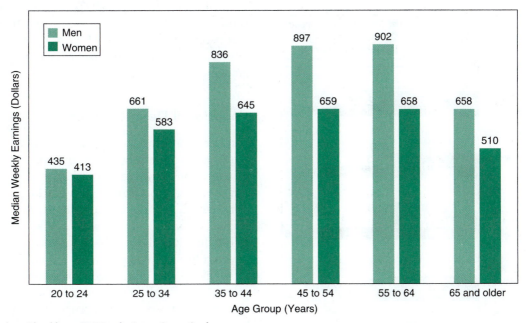

Source: http://data.bls.gov/PDQ/servlet/SurveyOutputServlet

In part, the discrepancy between men and women may be accounted for by the fact that women are more likely to have part-time jobs, which by definition provide a lower income. In addition women are more likely to be in the lower-paid service occupations. However, even among full-time sales workers, women earn only 64% of the salary of men. Moving up the occupational hierarchy, women do better, but female executives still earn only about 70% of the salaries of males (among full-time workers). Among female workers 25 years and older, those with professional degrees earn only 66% of the salaries of men (U.S. Bureau of the Census, 2007a).

Educational Level

Although students about to graduate from college often worry about whether they will get a job, the fact of the matter is that a college degree is definitely a benefit when it comes to occupational level and ultimately lifetime earning potential. Statistically speaking, your income is likely to rise with each increase in your educational level (U.S. Bureau of the Census, 2006b).

Unfortunately, education alone does not account for your earning potential. Even when controlling for education, black and Hispanic workers typically have lower earnings than do whites, a disparity particularly pronounced among men. For example, in 2005, among men with a bachelor's degree, whites earned a mean of $69,611, Hispanics $55,543, and blacks $50,992 (http://www.census.gov/population/www/socdemo/education/cps2006.html).

Educational levels within the United States vary considerably by age group. In general there has been an increasing trend over the past 40 years for older adults to have higher levels of education, with double the percentage in 2004

FIGURE 10.4
Income by Educational Level, United States, 2001

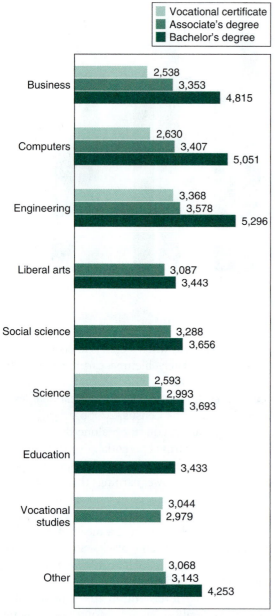

Average monthly earnings are shown by field of training; earnings are in dollars.

Source: U.S. Bureau of the Census, 2006b.

having received a college diploma (18.7%) than was true in 1985 (9.4%) (Centers for Disease Control and Prevention, 2007a). This trend is certain to continue, as is evident from the fact that people in the 25 to 34-year-old age bracket now includes the highest percentage of college graduates of all age groups of adults.

Vocational Development

Our development in the world of work is influenced in many ways by the social factors of education, race, gender, and age. However, our choice of an occupation, or **vocation**, reflects our personal preferences and interests as well; preferably we are doing what we want to do rather than what is available to us.

Your desire to enter a given field is what most likely has prompted your choice of a career path and hence your college major. You may be majoring in psychology, consumer studies, nursing, education, chemistry, or music. Assuming the process was not randomly made, and to be sure, this often happens, it is more likely that your choice reflects your personality, skills, and experience. These are the factors that vocational development theories take into account when they attempt to explain the career choices that people make and determine people's levels of happiness and productivity once they have acted on those choices.

Holland's Vocational Development Theory

According to **Holland's vocational development theory** (Holland, 1997), our vocational aspirations and interests are the expression of our personality. Holland proposed that there are six fundamental types (also called codes) that represent the universe of all possible vocational interests, competencies, and behaviors. Each of

FIGURE 10.5
Educational Attainment by Age Group, United States, 2006

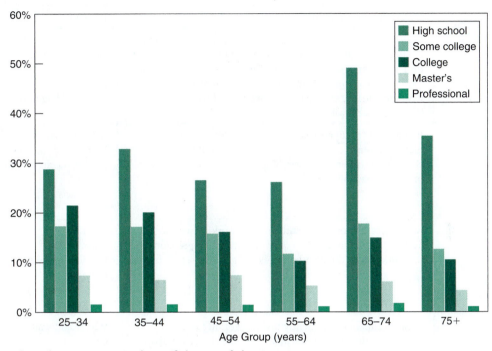

Percentage within each age group receiving the specified amount of education.

Source: http://www.census.gov/population/www/socdemo/education/cps2006.html

the six types is identified by its initial letter: Realistic (R), Investigative (I), Artistic (A), Social (S), Enterprising (E), and Conventional (C). Based on the letters that describe the six types, the theory is also referred to as the **RIASEC model**.

Occupations can be described in terms of the same six RIASEC types. According to Holland, occupations reflect particular patterns of job requirements and rewards that are characteristic of their environments. As such they serve as the settings that elicit, develop, and reward the specific interests, competencies, and behaviors associated with each of the types. There is a close correspondence between the interest types and the occupational types. For example, social occupations involve work with people, and realistic occupations involve work with one's hands.

In applying the RIASEC types, a combination of two or three of the initials are usually assigned rather than just one. The first letter reflects the primary type into which the interest or occupation falls ("S" for Social, for example). The second and third letters allow for a more accurate and differentiated picture of the individual or occupation. Both a construction worker and a corrections officer are R code occupations, and both have the RE code designation. They differ in their third code, which is C for the construction worker and S for the corrections officer.

In addition to the theorized vocational and occupational descriptions, personality descriptions

TABLE 10.1

RIASEC Types

Type	Description of Occupations	Examples
Realistic (R)	Realistic occupations frequently involve work activities that include practical, hands-on problems and solutions. They often deal with plants, animals, and real-world materials like wood, tools, and machinery. Many of the occupations require working outside, and do not involve a lot of paperwork or working closely with others.	Cook Dental technician Truck driver Electrician Chemical engineer Jeweler
Investigative (I)	Investigative occupations frequently involve working with ideas, and require an extensive amount of thinking. These occupations can involve searching for facts and figuring out problems mentally.	Insurance adjuster Respiratory therapist Market research analyst Biologist Pharmacist Surgeon
Artistic (A)	Artistic occupations frequently involve working with forms, designs, and patterns. They often require self-expression, and the work can be done without following a clear set of rules.	Actor Travel guide Fashion designer Editor Graphic designer Clergy
Social (S)	Social occupations frequently involve working with, communicating with, and teaching people. These occupations often involve helping or providing service to others.	Waiter and waitress Child-care worker Receptionist Registered nurse Personnel recruiter Counseling psychologist
Enterprising (E)	Enterprising occupations frequently involve starting up and carrying out projects. These occupations can involve leading people and making many decisions. Sometimes they require risk taking and often deal with business.	Bartender Real estate sales agent Retail salesperson Public relations specialist Economist Lawyer
Conventional (C)	Conventional occupations frequently involve following set procedures and routines. These occupations can include working with data and details more than with ideas. Usually there is a clear line of authority to follow.	Office clerk Computer operator Legal secretary Accountant Financial analyst Treasurer

Source: http://online.onetcenter.org/find/descriptor/browse/Interests/#cur.

RIASEC Model

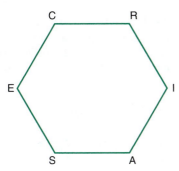

In Holland's RIASEC model, the six types are arranged around a hexagon with the distance between types reflecting the degree of difference among them.

are thought to characterize each of the six types, based on correspondence between the Holland codes and scores on the NEO-PI-R. The RIASEC codes can be translated in terms of the Five Factors Model of personality traits. Putting the two together, researchers have suggested that there are three underlying dimensions: interest in people versus things, preference for abstract versus concrete ideas, and striving for personal growth versus striving for accomplishment. However, personality traits do not completely map onto vocational interests (Mount, Barrick, Scullen, & Rounds, 2005).

The six RIASEC types are organized within the individual in a hexagonal structure. This structure implies that the types have a relationship to each other based on their distance from each other on the structure. Types that are most similar (such as R and C) are closest, and those that are the most dissimilar (such as C and A) are furthest away from each other.

The notion of the hexagon is an important one because it helps define the way that our interests correspond to our environments. We will be most satisfied in our jobs if we are in an environment that fits our personality type, a situation referred to as **congruence** or "fit." The hexagon can be thought of as two knobs, one on top of the other. Congruence is the situation where the two knobs are completely aligned.

Congruence also influences our ability to be effective on the job. If we are happy, we will also be most productive. Unfortunately, as you probably know, we cannot always find jobs congruent with our interests. In these situations, the RIASEC model predicts that we will experience low job satisfaction and a high degree of instability as we continue to seek more fulfilling work environments. If we are unable to do so, our satisfaction and work productivity may suffer. Researchers have found that individuals with Artistic interests working in Realistic environments, for example, have lower work quality than people whose interests match their environments (Kieffer, Schinka, & Curtiss, 2004).

The RIASEC theory is empirically derived from the responses of many thousands of individuals who have been tested over the years of its development. If you wanted to have your vocational interests assessed using this model, you would take one or both of the most common assessment instruments. The **Strong Vocational Interest Inventory (SVII)** (Harmon, Hansen, Borgen, & Hammer, 1994) consists of items in which respondents indicate their preferences for occupations, topics of study, activities, and types of people. The SVII is administered by a professional counselor and must be scored through a testing service. The second assessment method can be administered and scored on your own. The **Self-Directed Search (SDS)** (Holland, 1994) provides an assessment along the RIASEC dimensions, but also asks about your strengths, allowing you to determine the profile of your abilities as well as your interests (Gottfredson, 2002).

Just as people can be assessed along the RIASEC dimensions, work environments can also be assessed by rating the work activities

ASSESS YOURSELF: What's Your Vocational Profile?

For each of the questions below, indicate your preference. The feedback for each question will indicate into which of the 6 RIASEC categories your response belongs. When you are done, total up the number you have in each category. The top 3 scores indicate your vocational profile. The last question in the survey asks you which was your top rated category; please complete it based on your previous responses.

1. I like to:
   A. work outdoors (R).
   B. read scientific books or magazines (I).
   C. play in a band, group, or orchestra (A).
   D. help others with personal problems (S).

2. In my spare time, I enjoy:
   A. fixing electrical things (R).
   B. sketching, drawing, or painting (I).
   C. reading psychology articles and books (S).

3. My ideal job would involve:
   A. performing for others (A).
   B. operating my own service or business (E).
   C. checking paperwork or products for errors or flaws (C).
   D. applying mathematics to practical problems (I).

4. If I had my choice of occupation, it would involve:
   A. studying scientific theories (I).
   B. building things with wood (R).
   C. writing novels or plays (A).
   D. supervising the work of others (E).

5. I can often imagine myself in a job in which I:
   A. study scientific theories (I).
   B. work for a charitable organization (S).
   C. lead in a group accomplishing some goal (E).
   D. work in an office (C).

6. One of the things I can do well is to:
   A. operate power tools such as a drill press, grinder, or sewing machine (R).
   B. use a computer to study a scientific problem (I).
   C. take attractive photographs (A).
   D. talk with all kinds of people (S).

7. I feel most confident about my ability to:
   A. use algebra to solve mathematical problems (I).
   B. perform as a musical soloist (A).
   C. organize the work of others (E).
   D. file correspondence and other papers (C).

(contd.)

ASSESS YOURSELF

8. I can:
   A. make simple electrical repairs (R).
   B. Keep detailed records of expenses (C).
   C. working with people rather than with things or ideas (S).
   D. arrange or compose music (A).

9. At one time or another I have found that I can:
   A. do a good job painting the rooms of a house or apartment (R).
   B. do a painting, watercolor, or sculpture (A).
   C. get people to do things my way (E).
   D. keep accurate records of payment or sales (C).

10. Others tell me that I am a(n):
   A. careful and orderly person (C).
   B. easy person to tell your problems to (S).
   C. very persuasive person (E).

11. It is no problem for me to:
   A. use many different types of carpentry tools (R).
   B. help people who are upset or troubled (S).
   C. be a successful leader (E).
   D. write business letters (C).

12. Of the following, my ideal job would be a(n):
   A. electrician (R).
   B. medical laboratory technician (I).
   C. journalist (A).
   D. clinical psychologist (S).
   E. advertising executive (E).
   F. certified public accountant (C).

13. Now total up your scores and see in which category you have the most answers. Answer this question on the basis of this score:
   My top rated category in the RIASEC model is:
   A. Realistic.
   B. Investigative.
   C. Artistic.
   D. Social.
   E. Enterprising.
   F. Conventional.

College graduation is a time when young adults assess their talents and interests and try to find an ideal match in the world of work.

and institutional characteristics of occupations and work environments. The RIASEC codes now have become fully integrated into **O*NET**, the **Occupational Information Network** (http://www.onetcenter.org/), an online interactive national database of occupations used by vocational placement agencies and state labor departments in the United States. People who are trying to find a job that will fit their interests, training, and experience can be greatly aided by this system, even if they do not live in the United States. O*NET provides a comprehensive and searchable database of occupations, along with important data such as salary and expected growth (in the United States) in the next 10 years. Occupations that have a high priority are flagged.

Because of its widespread incorporation into occupational interest inventories and classification schemes, the RIASEC model is likely to be prominent for some time to come. Vocational counselors have adopted the RIASEC model as an easily interpretable and user-friendly system. Assessment tools for both people and jobs are readily available and inexpensive, and there is

adequate (if not perfect) empirical support for it from large-scale studies (McDaniel & Snell, 1999). Finally, from the standpoint of vocational counseling for young adults, the codes seem to be relatively stable during the crucial career development years of the late teens and early 20s (Low, Yoon, Roberts, & Rounds, 2005). However, there are individual differences in patterns of stability, possibly corresponding to variations in personality. For example, people who are more open to new experiences may be more likely to change their career interests over time (Rottinghaus, Coon, Gaffey, & Zytowski, 2007).

Within the field of industrial-organizational (I/O) psychology, congruence is now considered to be a major focus of matching people and jobs. At the same time, as anyone who has spent time in a workplace would attest to, it is also important to determine the fit or match among individuals working together as a team (Muchinsky, 1999). Does an RCE type get along better with another RCE, or would their similar styles lead to narrow thinking and lack of productivity among members of a work unit? Perhaps the RCE should be working alongside an SAI, who will complement the "thing"-oriented approach of the Realistic individual.

The notion of congruence between people and jobs has received considerable empirical support, not only in terms of job ratings but also in terms of career change behavior. All other things being equal, people will tend to move out of incongruent jobs and into ones that are more suited to their interests (Donohue, 2006). Unfortunately, for many people, factors outside their control, such as race and ethnicity, limit these choices. For individuals whose vocational situations are affected by such constraints, the role of identity and the possibility for realizing one's true vocational interests are far less significant than the reality of these sociocultural factors.

"What do you think?" | **10-1**

What are your vocational daydreams? Do you think you have the abilities to fulfill these daydreams? How would you find out if you did?

Super's Self-Concept Theory

The desire to achieve full realization of our potential is at the heart of **Super's self-concept theory** (Super, 1957; 1990). If you see yourself as an artist, then you will desire work in which you can express the view of yourself as an artist. In contrast to Holland's theory, which emphasizes vocational preferences (the fact that you prefer artistic work), Super's theory places the focus on the occupation that you see as most "true" to your inner self. Super's theory also takes into account the fact that the constraints of the marketplace mean that people are not always able to achieve full realization of their self-concepts. In a society with relatively little demand for artists, the person with the artistic self-concept will need to seek self-expression in a job that allows for a certain degree of creativity but will also bring in a paycheck. Such an individual may seek a career in computer graphic design, for example, because that is a more viable occupation than that of an oil painter.

According to Super, the expression of our self-concept through work occurs in a series of stages that span the years from adolescence to retirement in stages. In the exploration stage (teens to mid-20s), people explore career alternatives and select a vocation that they will find to be expressive of their self-concept. By the time they reach the establishment stage (mid-20s to mid-40s), people are focused on achieving stability and attempt to remain within the same occupation. At the same time, however, people seek to move up the career ladder to managerial

One of the most dramatic examples of a midlife career changer is that of actor Arnold Schwarzenegger, who became governor of California in 2003.

positions and higher. In the maintenance stage, (mid-40s to mid-50s), people attempt to hold onto their positions rather than to seek further advancement. Finally, in the disengagement stage (mid-50s to mid-60s), workers begin to prepare for retirement, perhaps spending more time in their leisure pursuits.

Variations in Vocational Development

When Super first wrote about career development, the job market was much more stable than it is at the present time. In the 1950s, the corporate world in particular tended to involve people being employed by one company for their entire careers. Climbing up the career ladder was also seen as a fairly typical goal, particularly for workers in white-collar occupations but also for blue-collar workers employed in such industries as steel or car manufacturing. This model began to change substantially as large corporations began programs of downsizing, particularly after the advent of computerized technology.

The modern workplace is likely to promote **recycling**, the process through which workers change their main field of career activity part way into occupational life. In recycling, middle-aged workers may find themselves once again in the establishment stage they thought they had left behind in their late 20s. Another variation on the traditional stages described by Super occurs when workers remain indefinitely in a maintenance-like period. **Plateauing** (Ettington, 1998), as this process is referred to, means that although your salary may increase, your job level remains static People may reach their plateau at a young age if they enter a so-called dead-end job, or if their moves within or between companies involve lateral changes rather than vertical advancement.

Recent approaches within the vocational developmental literature are increasingly speaking about the **boundaryless career**, meaning a career that does not follow a set pathway. Many workers who, in the past, were restricted by the opportunities presented to them by their organization are now progressing through their careers at their own pace. This increasing self-determination of one's own path is referred to as the **protean career**. Although the two concepts have some overlap, they are empirically distinct (Briscoe, Hall, & Frautschy DeMuth, 2006) and may in fact provide an alternative to the traditional notion prevalent for so many years in the vocational literature of one life and one career. As changes continue to occur in the workplace and society leading to greater and greater deviation from the standard organizational mentality of the mid-20th century, vocational counselors will increasingly be providing workers with ideas about ways to manage their own careers around internal rather than external goals and employer-developed criteria (Raabe, Frese, & Beehr, 2007).

Even as the corporate culture becomes less stable, there is still a desire among many employers to reduce turnover rates because training new workers can be costly and inefficient. In some ways this desire to keep turnover to a minimum is made more difficult by changes in the mind-set of employees, who look at such events in the world as corporate mergers and bankruptcies and worry about becoming too attached to their own companies. Vocational researchers have suggested, therefore, that the issue of job stability be examined in more depth. Using Super's theory can provide a framework for helping to maximize the sense of commitment among employees (Ng & Feldman, 2007). In the establishment stage, employees will feel more connected to their companies, and their professions in general, if they are given mentoring, adequate training, and favorable work hours. During the maintenance stage, being given opportunities to develop leadership and managerial skills will help them to feel more loyal to their organization. Finally, as they are looking toward retirement in the disengagement stage, they will feel more tied to companies that can guarantee them pension funds and adequate insurance benefits. At this stage in their career, they may also expand their focus to the profession as a whole if they are in a field that promotes broader occupational commitments such as through membership in a national organization.

VOCATIONAL SATISFACTION

Given that work takes up anywhere from one-third to one-quarter of our waking life during the week, we can assume that most people would prefer to maximize their level of satisfaction. Although not everyone can achieve full self-realization in their work, it is still possible for us to find sources of satisfaction either within our work itself or in the rewards it provides. On the other hand, a job may possess neither source of fulfillment but instead remain a daily grind that must be endured to maintain self and family. Theories and research on **vocational satisfaction** deal with these questions of how people find enjoyment in the work that they do or, conversely, of what factors limit their ability to achieve an optimal vocational situation.

Vocational satisfaction refers, very simply, to the extent to which a worker has positive views of the job or aspects of a job (Dawis, 1996). In turn, the more that workers view the job as providing a sense of "fit" with their needs, the more satisfied they will be and ultimately the stronger their commitment will be to the job and the organization (Verquer, Beehr, & Wagner, 2003).

Because of its presumed importance in determining both how productive and committed the worker is within the job, vocational satisfaction is one of the most heavily researched areas in vocational psychology. Although it may be relatively simple to define vocational satisfaction in general terms, it is surprisingly difficult to identify its components or, more importantly, determinants.

Intrinsic and Extrinsic Factors

A basic distinction that seems to cut across the various theories of vocational satisfaction is the difference between factors endogenous or inherent in the work itself and those that are exogenous or unrelated to the particular work involved in the job. The factors inherent in the work itself are referred to as **intrinsic factors** and include the physical and mental actions that the individual must perform in order to carry out the job. For example, sculpting involves the intrinsic physical activities of molding clay or stone, and accounting involves the intrinsic mental activities of manipulating numbers. Obviously, sculpting involves mental work, as the artist plans the piece before and during its completion. Conversely, intrinsic to accounting is the manipulation of keys on the keyboard or the writing of numbers on the page with a pencil. However, these are secondary activities compared with the nature of the work itself. The central defining feature of an intrinsic factor is that it cannot be found in precisely the same fashion in a different type of job. Molding materials is intrinsic to sculpting, and computing numbers is intrinsic to accounting.

Intrinsic factors can also be characterized as involving or engaging your sense of identity in that the work directly pertains to your feelings of competence, autonomy, and stimulation of personal growth. Work that is intrinsically rewarding allows the individual to feel truly "connected" to both the activities and purpose of the job and to experience a positive sense of competence and self-esteem (Mutran, Reitzes, Bratton, & Fernandez, 1997). Your ability to express autonomy and self-direction in the daily running of the job are also part of the intrinsic aspects of work because these factors are directly tied to the your sense of self. Furthermore, the engagement of intrinsic motivation in work that is cognitively challenging and self-directed maintains a constant stimulus for cognitive activity and may serve to enhance intellectual functioning over time (Schooler, Mulatu, & Oates, 1999).

The opposite of intrinsic factors in work are the **extrinsic factors**, which are the features that accompany the job but may also be found in other jobs with very different intrinsic characteristics. The easiest extrinsic factor to understand is salary. People may earn the same salary whether they harvest grain or provide care to preschool children. Paychecks are issued for work performed, and although some jobs earn more than others, the same salary can be earned in many alternative ways. A professional athlete may earn such a vast salary that it appears to be an inherent part of the job, but an oil magnate may earn the same amount of money for a very different set of job activities. Therefore, salary is not intrinsic to work. In the earlier example about accounting, using the pencil or keyboard is extrinsic because it is an activity that you can perform in a variety of jobs, from accounting to playwriting.

Other extrinsic factors are associated with the conditions of work such as the comfort of the environment, demands for travel, convenience of work hours, friendliness of coworkers, amount of status associated with the job, and adequacy of the company's supervision and employment policies. These aspects of work do not directly engage your sense of personal identity and competence. Although a high salary may certainly reinforce your sense of worth (particularly in Western society), as pointed out earlier, high salaries may be earned in many ways that are not necessarily tied to one's true vocational passions. The racial climate is another condition of the workplace that may be particularly important for workers from racial and ethnic minority backgrounds. Supervisors may not always be aware of the importance of maintaining an environment that is nonracist and promotes respect (Lyons & O'Brien, 2006).

You may or may not have had a job yet in which you felt involvement at an intrinsic level. However, you may be able to think of people you know whose work has intrinsic meaning to them. Perhaps you have encountered a sales or service person who seemed genuinely interested in helping you find a necessary item or solve a problem and was willing to work with you until you found the satisfactory solution. This may have been an employee who found the job to be intrinsically rewarding, feelings that were expressed in the apparent pride that he or she took in helping you with your situation.

Many vocational psychologists propose that intrinsic and extrinsic factors possess motivational properties. When workers are motivated for intrinsic reasons, they are thought to be doing so for the purpose of seeking personal expression, autonomy, and challenge. The control of their

behaviors comes from within themselves rather than from an outside sources such as a boss or the need to pay the rent. Conversely, extrinsic motivation is the desire to work to seek the benefits of pay, good job conditions, friendly coworkers, and an employer with fair and equitable policies. People motivated for extrinsic reasons are being controlled by forces outside of themselves because someone else is providing the rewards for their work. When considering these two forms of motivation, theorists have argued about which is more important or even whether the two are mutually exclusive.

One of the earliest theories about work motivation is the **two-factor theory** developed by Herzberg and colleagues in the late 1950s (Herzberg, Mausner, & Snyderman, 1959). According to this theory, intrinsic factors are motivators whose fulfillment allows the worker to achieve self-actualization. The extrinsic aspects of work are hygiene factors that either enhance or detract from an environment in which workers can realize their aspirations. The central hypothesis of the two-factor theory is that job motivators are more powerful than hygiene factors in leading to vocational satisfaction. Favorable hygiene factors could only prevent the development of job dissatisfaction, but they could not promote it. Growth, self-fulfillment, and feelings of achievement can only come from the fulfillment of job motivators.

A somewhat counterintuitive set of predictions regarding intrinsic and extrinsic work motivation is proposed by **cognitive evaluation theory** (Deci & Ryan, 1985) and its more recent update, **self-determination theory** (Gagne & Deci, 2005). According to this approach, the extrinsic rewards such as money actually reduce job satisfaction because they cause employees to feel less in control of their work-related activities, leading their performance to suffer. Not only is money not a motivator, as in the two-factor theory, but it is actually theorized to detract from the quality of performance when it is used as an incentive, a process called **motivational crowding out**—the idea that extrinsic rewards crowd out intrinsic satisfaction (James, 2005). You are probably thinking that this theory leaves a lot to be desired. Obviously, we all work for the extrinsic reward of money, and a theory that ignores this fact is bound to fall short of the mark (Bassett-Jones & Lloyd, 2005). The trick is for us to feel that even though we would not work without the pay, the work that we do is an expression of our identities. If we can feel that our paid work gives us the opportunity to develop our innermost goals and desires, we will perform at higher levels of persistence and discipline (Gagne & Deci, 2005). Herzberg's theory continues to receive empirical support, suggesting perhaps that workers are motivated, but only in part, by practical, economic concerns.

Positive and Negative Moods

Our job satisfaction can be affected not only by our motivation to work, but also our feelings about our jobs. We can have feelings on the job (such as being excited about the upcoming weekend) and feelings about the job (such as liking our job activities). According to **affective evaluation theory**, positive and negative emotions at work should be considered as influences on our satisfaction. If we experience positive events at work, such as having something good happen on the job (perhaps being complimented by a supervisor), we will have a positive emotional experience and if we experience negative events, such as conflict with a co-worker, we will have a negative reaction (Fisher, 2002).

Testing affective evaluation theory on one highly stressed group of employees, representatives who provide technical assistance at call service centers, researchers found that job satisfaction and positive emotions were correlated with such job characteristics as autonomy,

participation, supervisory support, and concern for employee welfare. Conversely, the stress of feeling overloaded was correlated with negative emotions but positively related to job satisfaction (Wegge, von Dick, Fisher, West, & Dawson, 2006). Thus, on a day-to-day basis, the impact of negative events at work (such as when the copy machine breaks down) can be more potent than the personality of the employee (Niklas & Dormann, 2005).

Contrary to affective evaluation theory, approaches emphasizing **dispositional affectivity**, the general dimension of a person's affective responding, regard a person's overall outlook on life as relatively stable over time (Bowling, Beehr, & Lepisto, 2006). A person may have the favorable trait of positive affectivity, meaning that he or she is upbeat and tends to look at the bright side of a situation. The converse, negative affectivity, refers to a state of being predisposed to experience negative mood states (Lease, 1998).

Research on this dimension of personality has found a relationship between affectivity and satisfaction, commitment, and intention to leave one's job (Cropanzano, Rupp, & Byrne, 2003). People with positive affectivity are more likely than those high on negative affectivity to be satisfied in their job, committed to it, and unlikely to leave when faced with problems or difficulties. Conversely, people with negative affect are more likely to feel unhappy and therefore be less satisfied. Looking at the intrinsic-extrinsic dimension, people with high neuroticism scores are less likely to feel that their jobs are intrinsically rewarding (Boudreau, Boswell, & Judge, 2001). Perhaps for this reason, neuroticism is negatively related to job satisfaction; by contrast, extraversion and job satisfaction are positively related (Judge, Heller, & Mount, 2002; Seibert & Kraimer, 2001).

In addition to personality affecting job satisfaction, however, it is possible that the direction can go the other way. In one longitudinal study of adults in Australia, although personality changes predicted changes in work satisfaction, the relationship went in both directions. Over time, workers who were more satisfied with their jobs became more extraverted (Scollon & Diener, 2006).

Occupational Reinforcement Patterns

Another influential theory of vocational satisfaction focuses on **occupational reinforcer patterns (ORPs)**, which are the work values and needs likely to be reinforced or satisfied by a particular occupation. According to the theory of work adjustment proposed by Dawis and Lofquist (1984), vocational satisfaction is directly related to the extent to which a worker feels that the environment fulfills his or her work-related needs. O*NET incorporated these work values into their job search system. Each occupation can be identified by the work values it satisfies. These values include achievement, independence, recognition, relationships, support, and working conditions.

Work Stress

We all know what it is like to have a "bad day" at work. However, what if every day is a bad day? Work stress can be a major threat to our feelings of well-being and eventually can come to take its toll on our health as well.

In Chapter 5, we learned about metabolic syndrome, a physical condition that places people at greater risk for heart disease. The Whitehall II Study, a longitudinal investigation of health in over 10,300 civil employees in Great Britain, has provided compelling data to show that the risk of developing this condition is linked to work-related stress (Chandola, Brunner, & Marmot, 2006). Carried out over five phases from 1985–1997, the study included measurements of

stress, social class, intake of fruits and vegetables, alcohol intake, smoking, exercise, and obesity status at the start of the study. Holding all other factors constant and excluding participants who were initially obese, men under high levels of work stress over the course of the study had twice the risk of metabolic syndrome. Although they were small in number, women with high levels of stress were over five times as likely to develop this condition. Maximizing workplace satisfaction, in addition to helping maintain worker productivity, also can make a key difference in promoting the health of the individual.

Conflict between Work and Family

When we become adults, we divide our time, energy, and role involvement in many areas of life, but the two that probably carry the most weight are the areas of occupation and family life. Both areas carry with them major obligations and responsibility, and both contribute heavily to our sense of identity.

There are three basic models of work-family interrelations. According to the **spillover model**, attitudes and behaviors associated with one domain have an effect on attitudes and behavior carried out in the other domain (Grzywacz & Marks, 2000). The negative spillover model proposes that unhappiness at work leads the individual to experience unhappiness at home, and vice versa. The positive variant of the spillover model proposes that there is role enhancement or enrichment between the domains of family and work (Greenhaus & Powell, 2006). The **role strain** model proposes that work and family involvement are inversely related, so that the higher the person's involvement in his or her work role, the lower the individual's involvement in the family. The workaholic, according to this view, has little energy or time for family relationships. Conversely, high involvement with

TABLE 10.2
Work Values

Value	Definition	Example
Achievement	Occupations that satisfy this work value are results oriented and allow employees to use their strongest abilities, giving them a feeling of accomplishment.	Commercial diver Home health aide Interior designer Chemist Civil engineer Landscape architect
Independence	Occupations that satisfy this work value allow employs to work on their own and make decisions.	Child-care worker Travel guide Chefs and head cooks Travel agents Upholsterers Clinical psychologists
Recognition	Occupations that satisfy this work value offer advancement, potential for leadership, and are often considered prestigious.	Model Air traffic controller Umpires and referees Choreographers Sales managers Educational administrators
Relationships	Occupations that satisfy this work value allow employees to provide service to others and work with coworkers in a friendly noncompetitive environment.	Taxi drivers and chauffeurs Bartenders Nurses aides Office clerks Dental hygienists Psychology teachers
Support	Occupations that satisfy this work value offer supportive management that stands behind employees.	Construction laborers Court clerks Retail salespersons Machinists Personnel recruiters Graduate teaching assistants
Working conditions	Occupations that satisfy this work value offer job security and good working conditions.	Bus drivers Pharmacy technicians Telemarketers Legal secretaries Auditors Veterinarians

Source: http://online.onetcenter.org/explore/workvalues/Working_Conditions/

family should preclude total commitment to the job.

When work-family conflict does occur, it takes its toll on the individual's physical and mental health, causing emotional strain, fatigue, perception of overload, and stress (Geurts, Kompier, Roxburgh, & Houtman, 2003). There are variations in the extent and impact of work-family conflict, however, and it is not experienced equally by all workers. Conflict is most likely to occur among mothers of young children, dual-career couples, and those who are highly involved with their jobs. Workers who devote a great deal of time to their jobs at the expense of their families ultimately pay the price in terms of experiencing a lower over-all quality of life (Greenhaus, Collins, & Shaw, 2003). However, there are individual differences in personality that affect the work-family balance. For example, people higher in negative affectivity, known to affect job satisfaction, also experience more work-family conflict (Bruck & Allen, 2003).

Jobs with flexible hours help reduce conflict by providing workers with the opportunity to meet more of their obligations at home within a broader time frame than the traditional work hours of 9 to 5 (Scandura & Lankau, 1997). Supportive supervisors, who recognize the inevitable commitments of family obligations and their possible impact on work performance, can also help ameliorate the experience of conflict (Schirmer & Lopez, 2001). In addition, if workers feel a strong sense of identification with their jobs, work can enrich family life. Conversely a strong family identity can promote feelings of satisfaction and commitment to the job (Wayne, Randel, & Stevens, 2006).

Age and Vocational Satisfaction

As people approach the end of their employment lives, do you think they are more or less satisfied

with their work? On the one hand, it might make sense that people would eagerly await the release from the daily grind that comes with retirement. On the other hand, older workers might have eased themselves into a position that is more satisfactory because they have taken advantage of seniority and promotions. In fact, the evidence indicates that there is a tendency for both older and younger workers to feel satisfied with their jobs. Many studies seem to produce U-shaped relationships between age and job satisfaction across adulthood (Clark, Ostwald, & Warr, 1996).

Making this relationship a hard one to investigate is the fact that age is usually related to job tenure, the length of time a person has spent in the job. Gender, level of employment, and salary also interact with age differences in job satisfaction (Riordan, Griffith, & Weatherly, 2003). People who reach a plateau in their career are likely to experience a drop in job satisfaction (Boudreau et al., 2001). Identity processes may then come into play as a way of coping with plateauing or failing to reach previously aspired-to career goals. People who have reached their own peak, but perhaps not the one they hoped to reach when younger, begin to focus through identity assimilation on the positive aspects of their work accomplishments rather than their inability to meet earlier career goals. This process may also increase the tendency to focus on family and nonwork commitments as a source of feelings of competence.

Identity assimilation with regard to work may also be part of a larger tendency to focus on positive aspects of life in general, a tendency reflected in higher life satisfaction scores among older adults (Warr, 1994). The reality of the situation is that most individuals will be retiring within the next 10 to 15 years, and they may be starting to make the mental shift toward the upcoming phase of life.

Another factor that may affect the older worker's commitment and involvement in the

This older woman seems to be satisfied with her apparently demanding job.

job is exposure to age discrimination in the workplace. Although older workers are protected by federal law prohibiting discrimination (see below), negative stereotypes about the abilities and suitabilities of older persons in the workplace persist (Rupp, Vodanovich, & Crede, 2006). Older workers may begin to disengage mentally when they feel that they are subject to these age stereotypes, pressures to retire in the form of downsizing, and the message that their skills are becoming obsolete (Lease, 1998). These pressures can lead older workers to be less likely to engage in the career development activities that would enhance their ability to remain on the job or find a new one when their job is eliminated due to downsizing.

This general picture by no means applies to all workers. Gender may also play a major role in this process, particularly as women's roles in the workplace have shifted radically since the time of some of the early studies. Furthermore, discrimination prohibits even the college-educated minority male from achieving his maximum employment potential, and therefore may keep him from reaching a point of perceived financial security in his late 40s and early 50s. Level of occupation is yet another factor, as a person in a managerial position who is earning a high salary has the resources to invest time and energy in nonwork options. Of course, with a higher level of employment may go higher daily job demands, leading to less time for leisure pursuits.

Individual differences in the extent to which an adult believes in the "work ethic" may also interact with the age-job satisfaction relationship. The work commitment of individuals with strong work ethic values may never taper off, even if it does not mean higher financial rewards.

Vocational satisfaction in later adulthood may also be affected by the extent to which the worker is experiencing age-related changes in physical and cognitive functioning that interfere with ability to perform the job satisfactorily. The aging process may alter the degree of person-environment fit between the individual and the job in important ways and indirectly have an impact on feelings of satisfaction and fulfillment.

AGE AND VOCATIONAL PERFORMANCE

Are older workers more or less competent on the job than younger workers? When you think about this question, perhaps you are balancing what you think are the benefits of experience against the limitations of some potentially job-relevant skills. We know that younger cohorts also are more highly educated as well as in better health than older workers. These and a host of other factors make the overall relationship between age and job performance a complex one.

Significant individual differences both in abilities and in attitudes toward work also affect job performance. Some older workers are focused on maintaining their current status and are planning how to finish out the end of their careers without jeopardizing this status. Others may have already experienced some disability and are in the process of attempting to compensate for their losses while still maintaining their position at work. Yet others have not and will not suffer apparent losses of functioning at work and can therefore maintain their high levels of performance until they retire.

Initial interest in the quality of job performance among older workers can be traced to the early 1940s, when it appeared that population shifts were leading to a rising proportion of older, and possibly less productive, workers. Following World War II and the subsequent Baby Boom, these concerns were temporarily allayed, as the shifts then moved in the reverse direction toward a younger workforce. However, with the aging of the Baby Boomers, employers and policy makers are once again becoming concerned about the characteristics and abilities of older workers and how their performance will affect the country's overall productivity. Obviously, society has moved in an increasingly technological direction since the 1940s, so concerns about older workers are less about physical functioning and more

about their cognitive abilities. Will the aging Baby Boomers be able to keep up their productivity in an increasingly technical marketplace?

Research on cognitive functioning in later life has provided insights on the potential trade-off experienced by older persons in speed and capacity versus accumulated skill and experience (Warr, 1994). For example, jobs that require crystallized intelligence (which does not decrease until well past retirement) and depend on experience theoretically should show improved performance in later adulthood. Older workers in jobs with high crystallized components should be highly motivated to put in the effort needed to perform well on the job because they realize that their efforts will most likely meet with success. By contrast, if the job is highly dependent on strength, speed, or working memory, older workers will be less able to perform well and at the same time will be less motivated to put in effort that they believe may not pay off (Kanfer & Ackerman, 2004). Because of the variations that exist in job performance based on the job's demands, tailored assessments that take into account the job's characteristics are needed rather than generic evaluations about the job capabilities of older workers (Sluiter, 2006b).

With this framework in mind, it is instructive to examine several areas of job performance that have been studied with regard to age. One area is that of shift work in which the individual's work hours change from the daytime hours to evenings or nights. Although these schedules present a challenge for workers of all ages, it is particularly hard on older workers (Bonnefond et al., 2006). This is a good example of a job in which age effects are decidedly negative (sleep patterns), and there is no benefit of experience because a person cannot improve over time in a shiftwork job on this aspect of performance.

Absentee rates are another important factor in examining worker productivity and aging. Voluntary absences, which are those in which an

FIGURE 10.7

Rate of Fatal Occupational Injuries—United States, 2005

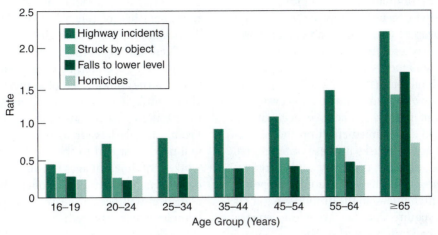

Rate of fatal injuries by category of injury per 100,000 workers aged 16 years and older.

Source: Pegula, Marsh, & Jackson, 2007.

employee decides not to report for work, are more frequent among younger workers by a factor of two to three. Thus, older workers are more reliable in this respect. It might be thought that older workers have higher rates of involuntary absenteeism, in which they are unable to work because of illness. However, this fact has not been established, and even so, when all rates of absenteeism are combined, older workers still have lower rates than younger workers (Warr, 1994).

Injuries are another area of investigation in analyzing the relationship between age and job performance. Overall, workers over the age of 55 are about half as likely to suffer a nonfatal injury as those who are 35 years and younger, but when older workers are injured, they typically require twice the length of time (12 days) to recover compared with workers in younger age groups (Bureau of Labor Statistics, 2006). In terms of fatal injuries, workers 65 and older are most likely to die in an accidental death. Driving-related accidents in the transportation industry have the highest fatality rate of all U.S.

industries, and it is in this job that older workers have the highest rate of dying as well (Pegula, Marsh, & Jackson, 2007).

With regard to overall physical fitness, decreases in strength and agility can certainly have a negative influence on job performance in some areas of employment, particularly when exertion is involved (Sluiter, 2006a). However, workers of any age can suffer from conditions that impair their performance, such as a cold or muscle ache. Furthermore, as pointed out by Warr (1994), every worker has restrictions in the kind of work that he or she can perform. The fact that older workers may have some limitations due to physical aging changes does not mean that they cannot achieve adequate performance on all types of jobs. People learn to cope with their limitations, and gravitate to jobs they are able to perform (Daly & Bound, 1996). If they become disabled enough, they will leave the job market altogether.

Passage of the **Age Discrimination in Employment Act (ADEA)** in 1967 made it illegal to fire or not hire workers on the basis of their age. This legislation was intended to provide protection for older workers (over 40) from discrimination by employers who would otherwise seek to replace them with younger, cheaper, and presumably more productive employees. In fact, the ADEA has resulted in settlements amounting to approximately $51.5 million in the year 2006 alone (http://www.eeoc.gov/stats/adea.html). However, the ADEA did not protect workers in occupations where age had a presumed effect on the performance of critical job tasks in these occupations. For example, this law does not cover workers in the protective service occupations of police officers and firefighters on the grounds that their occupations require that they be able to engage in highly demanding physical activity.

Airline pilots are another group not protected by the ADEA, as they face mandatory retirement at age 60. However, studies of airplane accident rates show that pilots make fewer errors through their mid-40s, followed by a leveling off of their error rates throughout the remaining years of their active work involvement (Kay et al., 1994). The performance of older (over 60) experienced pilots can even surpass that of younger (40 and under) pilots, as indicated in one study of performance in flight simulator training (Taylor, Kennedy, Noda, & Yesavage, 2007). As of 2007, the U.S. Congress was considering legislation to increase the mandatory retirement age of pilots but the Air Line Pilots Association opposes such changes.

These findings on age and job performance, like those in the area of vocational satisfaction, point to the importance of applying knowledge about adult development and aging in general to specific questions relating to older workers. From a human resources perspective, managers will need to attend to the varying capabilities of workers of different ages but also to take account of age dynamics as they play out in the workplace. Managers will need to learn how to balance the complementary strengths of workers of younger and older ages (Brooke & Taylor, 2005).

Unfortunately, older workers must battle against ageist stereotypes, held both by employers and by the workers themselves. Image norms, the view people have about how they "should" look in a particular occupation, may affect not only they way they are treated by their fellow workers but also the way they think of themselves (Giannantonio & Hurley-Hanson, 2006). As their self-image and abilities change, older workers can come to doubt their self-efficacy; in terms of the identity model, they over-accommodate

TABLE 10.3

Provisions of the Age Discrimination in Employment Act (1967)

What does the ADEA forbid?

Job ads or recruitment materials cannot mention age or say that a certain age is preferred.

Programs cannot set age limits for their trainees.

Age can not be a factor in making any decisions about workers.

This includes decisions about hiring, pay, promotions, or layoffs.

Employers cannot take action against workers who file a charge of age discrimination or who participate in any ADEA process.

With a few exceptions, employers cannot force employees to retire at a certain age.

Source: www.eeoc.gov

to the view that aging causes a loss of essential job skills. A self-fulfilling prophecy then develops and they then become, in fact, less able to keep up with new technologies. According to Maurer (2001), there are a set of factors that contribute to feelings of self-efficacy, including direct or vicarious (watching others) rewards, learning, persuasion, and changes in physiological functioning and health. Self-efficacy, in turn, influences attitudes toward training and development activities. Intervention at the point of raising self-efficacy can, then, give the older workers the confidence needed to engage in these important development activities so they can retain their job skills.

RETIREMENT

Retirement may be the furthest thing from your mind, if you are a college student in your late teens or early 20s. You are probably much more worried about getting a job than retiring from one. However, with increases in life expectancy, thinking about retirement, even before people have a job, is not all that far-fetched. Ideally, you will find a job that you will enjoy but one that will also give you a solid basis for being able to spend ten or twenty years (or more) enjoying your retirement years.

Traditionally, **retirement** is the end of an individual's work career. Many people think of retirement as an event that is marked by a ceremony such as the proverbial "gold watch" given to the retiree as thanks for years of loyal service. This traditional image of retirement is rapidly vanishing. In fact, even though it is a popular view, it may have ever applied in the past only to a minority of workers—men in the middle and upper middle social classes with organized or regular careers. Furthermore, compared with other celebratory rituals in adulthood, such as college graduation, marriage, and the birth of

children, retirement is more likely to carry with it ambivalent associations.

Just as labor force participation affects and is affected by the health of the economy, the opportunities for financial security available to retirees are heavily dependent on forces such as interest rates, tax policies, inflation, and the overall growth of the economy. The fate of the millions of retired persons in the United States will depend on how these forces play out in the coming decades. You might feel as though you are light years away from retirement and therefore are not affected by these debates, but if you take a close look at your paycheck at the section labeled Social Security taxes (called "FICA"), you will see that the topic is closer to you than you may think.

Definitions of Retirement

Retirement is defined simply as the withdrawal of an individual in later life from the labor force (Moen, 1996). This sounds simple but it is actually not all that easy a process to define. Most people do not just step off the job merry-go-round and into retirement. They usually go through a gradual set of phases.

There are least five phases in the retirement process (Sterns & Gray, 1999): an anticipatory period that may last for decades, the decision to retire, the act of retirement, continual adjustment following the actual event, and making further decisions regarding the structuring of the individual's life and activity patterns.

Even the notion that retirement proceeds in phases can be thought of as overly simplistic. Only about 10% of retirees show a "crisp" pattern of leaving the workplace in a single, unreversed, clear-cut exit. Another 15% experience a "blurred" exit in which they exit and reenter the workplace. They may have retired from a long-term job to accept bridge employment (Feldman, 1994), such as an insurance agent who retires from the insurance business but works as a crossing guard or server at a fast-food restaurant. Workers who have a long, continuous history of employment in private sector jobs tend not to seek bridge employment because they typically have sufficient financial resources (Davis, 2003), In general, involvement in bridge employment is strongly related to financial need. Ultimately, the criteria for retirement are met when the individual is collecting government benefits or a pension, considers himself or herself "retired," and does not spend time during the week at work (Talaga & Beehr, 1995).

Facts about Retirement

Even though they may arrive there in phases, by the time they reach the age of 65, the large majority of Americans are no longer in the labor force. Only 19% of men and 11% of women are either working or actively seeking employment. Virtually all of those 75 years and older have ended their full-time participation in the nation's workforce. However, many remain employed on a part-time basis; nearly half of all men and 61% of all women 70 years and older engage in some paid work (He, Sangupta, Velkoff, & DeBarros, 2005).

Approximately 10.5 million Americans receive pension benefits other than Social Security, and as of 2007, 33.4 million over the age of 65 were receiving Social Security benefits (http://www.ssa.gov/policy/docs/quickfacts/stat_snapshot/). The average Social Security benefit for a retired worker in 2007 was $1,046.50 (http://www.ssa.gov/policy/docs/quickfacts/stat_snapshot/).

In fact, the largest proportion of income for older adults comes from payments from Social Security (39%) and pensions not including Social Security (18%). The remaining shares of income come from work (24%) and assets such as interest income (16%) (He et al., 2005).

FIGURE 10.8

Sources of Income of People 65 and Older, United States

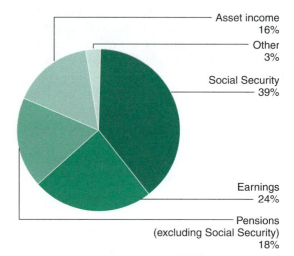

Sources of income for the population 65 and older, percent distribution.

Source: He, Sangupta, Velkoff, & DeBarros, 2005.

Retirement is in many ways a twentieth-century phenomenon (Sterns & Gray, 1999). Throughout the 1700s and mid-1800s very few people retired, and by 1900 about 70% of all men over 65 years were still in the labor force. The jobs held by older workers often held high status and prestige. Their wisdom and experience were valued, and it was considered a benefit to society to have their contributions to the workplace. However, pressures on the economy in combination with the growth of unions led, by the early 1930s, to the first instance in the United States of compulsory retirement (in the railroad industry). Because older workers were forced to retire but did not receive retirement benefits, they lived in poverty. The passage of the **Social Security Act** in 1935 provided much-needed financial relief for the older population. By 1940, the percentage of older workers in the labor force had dropped to slightly over 40%, and the numbers have continued to decrease.

Attitudes toward retirement were largely negative until the mid-1960s because lack of employment was associated with poverty. However, with increases in earnings and Social Security benefits, retirement began to gain more acceptance. Changes in federal policy toward older workers were also occurring. As mentioned earlier, the passage of the ADEA in 1967 meant that workers in the 40 to 65-year age range were protected from age discrimination. An amendment to the ADEA in 1978 eliminated mandatory retirement before the age of 70, and in 1986 mandatory retirement was eliminated from most occupations (Sterns & Gray, 1999). With these changes in retirement laws, it has also become easier for workers to continue in the jobs they have held throughout their lives or to find new employment even while they earn retirement benefits from their previous occupations. These changes in age discrimination and retirement laws have eased the potential stress of the transition, so that retired individuals no longer necessarily experience the poor health, low income, and loss of status that was associated with exit from the labor force earlier in the 1900s.

Furthermore, workers in the industrialized nations in Europe are increasingly looking favorably on retirement. The trend over the previous three decades is toward earlier retirement ages (Gendell & Siegel, 1996). Although this situation helps to give retirement a more positive image, it creates another problem by placing greater strain on pension plans, including Social Security in the United States (Binstock, 1999). In the year 2006, $460.5 billion were paid out in benefits to retired workers (http://www.ssa.gov/OACT/STATS/table4a4 .html). In the future, to reduce this pressure on retirement benefits it may be necessary to entice older workers to remain in the labor force rather than retire. Given that current Baby Boomers are less likely to save for retirement, however (Glass & Kilpatrick, 1998), there may be more financial incentives for them to remain in the labor market.

The Effects of Retirement on the Individual

Among sociological theories on the effect of aging on social roles, questions about the impact of retirement have consistently taken center stage. Does loss of the work role cause changes in mental and physical health? Do age-related losses in functioning precede retirement? Or is there no clear-cut relationship between changes in work patterns and health in later life? The answers to these questions have implications for both the health and well-being of millions of older Americans, as well as potential importance for employers and retirement counselors.

There are three major theoretical perspectives on the effect of retirement on the individual. The predominant view of retirement for many years was based on **role theory**. According to this perspective, the individual's roles, or normative expectations for behavior, provide a major source of fulfillment because they integrate the individual with society. The more roles the individual fills (worker, family member, friend, community member), the higher the individual's physical and psychological well-being. Among all the roles that adults may hold, the work role is one of the most important because it defines the individual's daily activities, status, and social group. As older workers lose their social roles, they lose their integration with society. Loss of the work role through retirement in particular leads a person to feel adrift, unimportant, depressed, anxious, and isolated. These negative effects can translate into poor health and ultimately a higher risk of mortality (House, Landis, & Umberson, 1988). Individuals who have had a strong psychological investment in their jobs are particularly likely to suffer after loss of their work role through retirement.

Retired individuals may become heavily involved in volunteer activity, as is true for these men working in a Habitat program in Coahoma, Mississippi.

Countering the role theory is the **continuity theory of retirement** (Atchley, 1989), which proposes that retirement does not lead to serious disruptions in the individual's sense of identity, social connections, or feelings of productivity. According to this perspective, the changes in work patterns associated with retirement do not lead to a significant loss of self-definition. Retirees maintain their previous goals, patterns of activities, and relationships, even though they are no longer reporting on a daily basis for work. Older adults view retirement as another stage of their careers, one that they have planned for and positively anticipated. The fact that many individuals maintain some form of employment after they have officially retired is further evidence in favor of continuity theory, suggesting that people can move into and out of the labor force with relative ease. What determines whether older adults are satisfied or not depends on whether the role is one that they desire, whether it is worker, retiree, or part-time worker (Warr, Butcher, Robertson, & Callinan, 2004).

The life course perspective views retirement as a normative stage of vocational development. Changes that are associated with this period of life are seen as logical outgrowths of earlier life events. The factors that shaped the individual's prior vocational development will have a persisting influence throughout retirement. For example, women's work lives are shaped by different factors than those of men, and these factors will continue to play out in the way that they experience retirement (Kim & Moen, 2001). The life course perspective also emphasizes the normative timing of events. According to this view, retirement will be stressful and create difficulties when its timing is unexpected. An individual who is forced to retire earlier than planned due to corporate layoffs will experience a higher degree of stress and disruption than an employee who is retiring "on time."

Retirement and Health

Implied in the role theory of retirement is the belief that loss of the work role leads to a general deterioration of the individual's well-being, both physical and mental. For many years, retirement researchers were convinced that lack of focus and sense of importance in life was the direct stimulus for a downturn in the retiree's health, with an associated increase in mortality. In other words, the retiree, without a purpose in life, soon became ill and died. In the extreme version of this scenario, the retiree commits suicide due to a general sense of uselessness and irrelevance. However, many researchers now believe that the relationship between retirement and poor health most likely exists due to the fact that poor health causes early retirement (Tsai, Wendt, Donnelly, de Jong, & Ahmed, 2005). This observation holds true not only for physical, but for mental health as well (Karpansalo et al., 2004).

> ### "What do you think?"   10-2
> Why might health decline after retirement? Why might it improve?

In terms of psychological health, there is evidence that retirement does not have deleterious effects on self-esteem or depression and may actually have a positive impact on feelings of well-being, a lowering of stress, and a reduction of anxiety and stress (Drentea, 2002). Having high levels of social support, being able to enjoy vacations, having a strong marriage, and participating in a set of enjoyable hobbies seems to be related to high retirement satisfaction (Vaillant, DiRago, & Mukamal, 2006).

In general, having a diverse set of physical, psychological, and social resources seems to ease the transition to retirement, even among individuals who initially experience poor adjustment. According to the **resource model** of retirement,

TABLE 10.4
Patterns of Retirement

Pattern	Characteristics	Percent
Maintaining	Hold a bridge job Actively engaged in retirement planning Married and had spouse present who is not working	70
Recovering	Retired from physically demanding jobs Retired from highly stressful jobs Had low job satisfaction	4
U-shaped	Experienced objective health declines during retirement transition Had an unhappy marriage Retired earlier than expected	26

In one large-scale study of health and retirement, three patterns of adjustment to retirement were identified, each associated with different patterns of activity and health.
Source: Wang, 2007.

adaptation even to difficult retirement transitions can be facilitated by being able to draw from a range of strengths and opportunities in a variety of life domains (Wang, 2007).

Factors That Influence Adjustment to Retirement

The timing of retirement is considered by researchers to be a major influence on the older individual's feelings of well-being. From a life course perspective, the exiting of the work role in an "off-time" or premature fashion is seen as more stressful or disruptive than going through the transition in an "on-time" or expectable fashion (Gill et al., 2006). Related to the timing of retirement is the reason for retiring. When early retirement suddenly becomes mandatory because of company downsizing, individuals lose control over the timing of their retirement and suffer negative consequences in terms of well-being (Armstrong-Stassen, 2001; Kalimo, Taris, & Schaufeli, 2003). If they lack sufficient financial resources at the time of being forced to retire, they are at higher risk of suffering from depressive symptoms than retirees with adequate wealth (Gallo et al., 2006). The amount of time allowed for retiring is another related factor. A minimum of two years planning prior to early retirement is related to a positive retirement experience compared with a decision made six months or less prior to retirement (Hardy & Quadagno, 1995). For men at least, the amount of planning for retirement may be one of the most important predictors of satisfaction (Dorfman, 1989).

Socioeconomic level has a complex relationship to retirement satisfaction. People at higher socioeconomic levels are less likely to retire, and they retire at later ages. Intrinsic satisfaction associated with work is more likely to be found in individuals in the higher occupational levels of professionals, executives, and managers, causing them to be less likely to engage in retirement planning (Kosloski, Ekerdt, & DeViney, 2001). However, higher socioeconomic status allows the individual to take advantage of the opportunities that retirement offers for productive and enjoyable leisure activities, such as involvement in retirement learning communities and the chance to travel. Individuals with higher levels of education and previous experience in managerial or professional positions may be better able to find part-time employment after retirement if they desire it. Past experience in community organizations and activities may also make it easier for such individuals to find rewarding opportunities for unpaid volunteer work and participation in clubs, organizations, and informal networks.

The continuity of an individual's work career is thought to be a further influence on the impact of retirement, at least for men. Those in **orderly careers** spend the majority of their employed years in related occupations. The higher the extent of orderliness in a people's careers, the higher their attachments to their communities, friends, and social activities. The social integration these individuals maintain during their careers eases their retirement transition and means that they are likely to be in better physical and psychological health. Individuals with more continuous work histories also have higher socioeconomic status and income than those in disorderly careers, and these are factors generally related to greater satisfaction with retirement. However, on the negative side, such workers may be more attached to their jobs and therefore less satisfied with retirement (Gee & Baillie, 1999).

There has been somewhat of a debate in the literature concerning the effect of retirement on a married couple's relationship. According to one school of thought, the "spouse underfoot syndrome," which traditionally applied to the husband, meant that partners were more likely to experience conflict now that they were in each other's presence for most of the daytime as well as nighttime hours. However, the contrasting view is of retirement as a second honeymoon, in which couples are now free to enjoy each other's company on a full-time basis without the constraints presented by the need to leave home for eight or more hours a day. It seems that the transition itself from work to retirement takes its toll on marital satisfaction when partners have high levels of conflict. The greatest conflict is observed when one partner is working while the other has retired. Eventually, however, these problems seem to subside, and after about two years of retirement for both partners, levels of marital satisfaction once again rise (Moen, Kim, & Hofmeister, 2001).

As we can see, work and retirement are broad and fascinating areas of study in the field of adult development and aging. Research from a developmental perspective has been somewhat slow to get off the ground. However, increasing information on the topics of vocational satisfaction and performance-retirement adjustment as these interact with personality and social structural factors are providing greater clarification regarding this significant component of adult life.

LEISURE PURSUITS IN LATER ADULTHOOD

Throughout adulthood, individuals express themselves not only in their work lives, but also in their hobbies and interests. Occupational psychologists and academics studying the relationship between job characteristics and satisfaction often neglect the fact that, for many adults, it is the off-duty hours rather than the on-duty hours that contribute the most to identity and personal satisfaction. In contrast, marketers recognize the value of developing promotional campaigns that appeal to older adults who potentially have resources to spend on leisure pursuits (Sterns & Gray, 1999).

This woman's involvement in the creative and leisure pursuit of pottery may help her maintain her cognitive skills, health, and psychological well-being.

> ### "What do you think?"   10-3
>
> Do you think people choose their leisure activities on the basis of the same or the opposite type that they express in the workplace?

As we move through adulthood and into retirement, it becomes more important for us to develop leisure interests so that we will have activities to provide our lives with a focus and meaning. In addition, leisure pursuits can serve important functions in helping us to maintain our health through physical activity and our cognitive

functioning through intellectual stimulation. The social functions of leisure are also of potential significance, particularly for people who have become widowed or have had to relocate due to finances, a desire for more comfortable climates, or health. Volunteer work can be an important part of the equation in leisure activities, serving as an important contributor to health outcomes (Luoh & Herzog, 2002a).

Researchers who study leisure time activities in later adulthood find strong evidence linking leisure participation to improvement in feelings of well-being, particularly among those who are trying to overcome deficits in physical functioning or social networks (Silverstein &

Parker, 2002). Furthermore, cognitively challenging leisure activities can have the same effect of helping individuals maintain their intellectual functioning over time as can cognitively challenging work (Schooler & Mulatu, 2001). The effects of leisure on physical health can also be striking. In one particularly impressive study, a sample of 799 men ages 39 to 86 were divided into groups on the basis of whether or not they were bereaved. Involvement in social activities was found to moderate the negative effects of stress on the physical functioning of the bereaved men. Being involved in volunteer work can also contribute to improved physical health. As was shown in a study of the oldest-old, involvement of over 100 hours a year in either paid or volunteer work was predictive of lower rates of illness and death (Luoh & Herzog, 2002b).

As was shown in Chapter 5, older adults are less likely than younger people to engage in physical activities as leisure time pursuits. There is evidence that, at least for men, public health efforts to increase the physical activity of older adults is having a moderately positive impact. In one large longitudinal study of health, over the two decades from the late 1970s to the late 1990s, there was a decline in the proportion of sedentary men. However, this decline was only slight. Given that the sample was recruited from a long-term study that tended to be heavily biased toward health-conscious individuals, however, this finding signifies that there are gaps between the efforts to educate the public to adopt more healthy lifestyle leisure choices and the actual behavior of older adults (Talbot, Fleg, & Metter, 2003).

It is one thing to be able to document the favorable effects of leisure activities on health and well-being and another to be able to help people select appropriate activities in which to become involved. Although it might be beneficial to become involved in highly social activities, for example, not everyone is going to seek out this type of experience. Similarly, not everyone will desire leisure activities that involve a high degree of cognitive stimulation. Based on this reasoning, researchers have found that the Holland RIASEC model can be applied to leisure activities in older adults (Kerby & Ragan, 2002). Just as people can be counseled to seek a person-environment fit for vocations, they might also be advised to find the leisure pursuit that will keep them motivated and, hence, active in a pursuit that will ultimately have value in maximizing their functional abilities.

In conclusion, changes in the labor force, the meaning of work, and the economic realities of an aging population will all affect the nature of work and the workplace. As you contemplate your future career, thinking about what you will find to be most fulfilling should be your number one concern. However, all workers will need to plan for these changes in the social context that will affect their adaptation to and satisfaction in the workplace.

SUMMARY

1. Work is a major focus of adult life from the 20s until retirement and beyond. Labor force age dynamics have shifted with movement of the Baby Boom generation and the aging of the labor force. There are disparities by race and gender in income levels, even controlling for educational attainment.

2. Contemporary vocational psychology is oriented primarily around Holland's RIASEC theory of vocational development, which is the basis for O*NET, a comprehensive catalog of occupations. The highest level of worker satisfaction and productivity is theorized to occur when there is congruence between persons and their environments. Super's self-concept theory proposes that individuals move through several stages of career development in which they attempt to

maximize the expression of their self-concept in their work. Rather than proceed straight through these stages, however, individuals may plateau at the maintenance stage or recycle through earlier stages after a career change. The boundaryless career captures the concept that individuals direct their own career progression.

3. Theories and research on vocational satisfaction attempt to determine the relative influence of intrinsic and extrinsic factors on worker's happiness and productivity in a job. Occupational reinforcement patterns are the work values and needs that are likely to be satisfied in a job, and if these are present, the individual will be more satisfied. Self-determination theory proposes that in the highest form of extrinsic motivation people's jobs become the basis for their identities. Conflict between work and family is a source of potential vocational dissatisfaction. Researchers have not established whether age is related to vocational satisfaction because the influence of job tenure must also be taken into account.

4. The question of whether older workers are as productive as younger workers is another focus of occupational research. Older workers are relatively advantaged in jobs that rely on experience and perform more poorly in jobs that demand speed. Older workers have higher fatalities but lower absentee rates. Passage of the ADEA in 1967 offered protection to workers over 40 from discrimination by employers, although several occupations are excluded from this legislation.

5. Retirement is defined as the individual's withdrawal from the labor force in later life. Rather than being a discrete event, however, for most people it spans a process that may last for years. Most retired people do not suffer a loss of health, either mental or physical, but some do experience the transition as stressful. The resource model of retirement proposes that people will be most satisfied in retirement if they can draw on physical, psychological, and social sources of support.

6. Leisure activities can serve a variety of important functions for adults throughout their working lives, but particularly in later adulthood after retirement. Researchers have identified positive effects of leisure involvement on physical functioning, well-being, and ultimately, mortality.

Mental Health Issues and Treatment

"Youth is an exhilirating, age a depressing theme."

G. Stanley Hall
(1844–1924)

U p until now, we have focused primarily on people who fit the definition "normal" as they traverse the adult years. Personality and social processes as applied to the individual's adaptation to life have focused on stability and change within the parameters of the average or expectable life. The people who have participated in studies discussed had no documented psychological disorders, and they lived in community settings, most likely their own homes. Although we can certainly make many generalities from within the framework of normal development, to do so means that we do not take into account the characteristics and developmental processes of individuals who fall outside that framework. In this chapter, we examine the factors that affect their lives.

PSYCHOLOGICAL DISORDERS IN ADULTHOOD

Psychological disorders significantly alter the individual's adaptation. The criteria used to judge behavior as "abnormal" include feeling personal or subjective distress, being impaired in everyday life, causing a risk to the self or other people, and engaging in behavior that is socially or culturally unacceptable (Halgin & Whitbourne, 2005). People who have a hobby of collecting coins would not be considered abnormal, for example, because they are engaging in a behavior that does not cause them harm and is culturally acceptable. By contrast, consider people who collect old newspapers, magazines, and cereal boxes until there is no room left in their house for anything else and they are living in squalor. These individuals might very well be considered to have a psychological disorder. These so-called "hoarders" are not only engaging in behavior that is outside the norm but may be putting themselves at risk for fire and other harm due to the filth and debris that have accumulated in their home.

Specific sets of behaviors that meet the conditions of abnormality are given a diagnosis according to the criteria set forth in the psychiatric manual known as the **Diagnostic and Statistical Manual**, the most recent version of which is the **Fourth Edition-Text Revision** known as the **DSM-IV-TR** (American Psychiatric Association, 2000). Unfortunately, the DSM-IV-TR was not developed with consideration of how the diagnostic categories for psychological disorders might change over the adult years. Given some of the distinctive characteristics of these disorders in later life, this creates problems in applying diagnoses to older adults. However, we have no alternative to this system, and therefore it forms the basis for how we look at and think about psychological disorders throughout adulthood.

The DSM-IV-TR has five axes along which the psychologist rates a client who is brought in for possible treatment. It is a little confusing to think of the term "axis" because we do not usually apply it outside the context of mathematics. In the DSM-IV-TR, an axis is really a dimension along which clients are evaluated.

Axis I includes clinical syndromes or disorders. These are collections of symptoms that together form a recognizable pattern of disturbance (comparable to an illness in medical terms). Included in Axis I are mood disorders, dementia, anxiety disorders, substance-related disorders, schizophrenia, sexual disorders, eating disorders, sleep disorders, and disorders first evident in infancy, childhood, and adolescence. On Axis II are personality disorders, which are disorders thought to reflect a disturbance within the basic personality structure of the individual. Mental retardation and disorders in the individual's ability to carry out the tasks of daily living are also included on Axis II. An individual may have both an Axis I disorder (such as major depression) and an Axis II disorder (such as paranoid personality disorder). The ratings on Axis III are of medical conditions that, although not a primary focus of treatment, have a bearing on the client's psychological condition. For example, an individual with diabetes may be faced with medical problems that alter or influence his or her symptoms of depression or anxiety. Ratings of psychosocial stressors and environmental problems are made on Axis IV, which allows the clinician to take into account any particular contextual conditions that pertain to the psychological disorder. Finally, on Axis V, the clinician provides an overall rating of the client's general level of functioning, which may range from suicidal (ratings of 1–20) to superior (91–100).

Major Axis I Disorders in Adulthood

The disorders on Axis I cause severe disturbances in the lives of afflicted adults. These conditions may persist for many years, and even if their symptoms dissipate over time, the individual may be on more or less constant alert for a renewed outbreak. Fortunately, a minority of adults experience these disorders, but those who do face struggles in their family relationships, work lives, and ability to live independently in the community. Table 11.1 lists the major Axis I disorders that are focused on in this chapter, with a description of how the symptoms are manifest

TABLE 11.1

Descriptions of Selected Axis I Disorders of the DSM-IV-TR as Observed in Older Adults

Category	Description	Examples of Specific Disorders	Variations in Older Adults
Mood disorders	Disturbance in mood	Major depressive disorder Bipolar disorder	Depression may appear as cognitive impairments, social isolation. Bipolar disorder may appear with hostility, irritability, and paranoia.
Anxiety disorders	Intense anxiety, worry, or apprehension	Generalized anxiety disorder Panic disorder Specific phobia Obsessive-compulsive disorder Post-traumatic stress disorder	Changes in health and physical symptoms interact with symptoms of anxiety.
Schizophrenia and other psychotic disorders	Psychotic symptoms such as distortion of reality and serious impairment in thinking, behavior, affect, and motivation	Schizophrenia Schizoaffective disorder Delusional disorder	Shift from positive to negative symptoms in older adults; depressive symptoms may coexist with symptoms of schizophrenia; poorer cognitive functioning than would be expected on the basis of age.
Substance-related disorders	Use or abuse of psychoactive substances	Substance dependence Substance abuse Substance intoxication	Older adults at higher risk than may be thought for these disorders.

in adults over the age of 65 (discussed within each disorder).

Mood disorders.   **Mood disorders** are psychological disorders involving abnormalities in the individual's experience of emotion. **Depressive disorders** are characterized by periods of dysphoria (sad mood), lasting varying amounts of time and involving varying degrees of severity. The experience of what is called a **manic episode** is one of the features of **bipolar disorder** (formerly known as manic depression). In a manic episode, an individual feels unusually "high," meaning elated, grandiose, expansive, and highly energetic.

"What do you think?"   **11-1**

For what reasons might older adults express symptoms of mood disorders differently than do younger adults?

Many older adults with treatable depression are reluctant to report symptoms or seek therapy.

Over the course of adulthood, the prevalence of major depressive disorder is estimated at 18.4% in the United States (Kessler et al., 2005). Therefore, a substantial percentage of individuals are affected by this disturbance of mood at some point in their lives. At any given time, about 1 to 5% of adults in the United States meet the diagnostic criteria for major depression or its milder form, known as dysthymia. At all ages the rates of major depressive disorder and dysthymia in women are about double the rates of men. However, persons over the age of 65 are less likely to experience these disorders than are people under the age of 65 (Kessler et al., 2003). There are, however, gender differences in the experience of depression in later life. Although women are more likely to suffer from depressive symptoms earlier in life, men seem to be more likely to develop depressive symptoms over the course of later adulthood than are women (Barefoot, Mortensen, Helms, Avlund, & Schroll, 2001).

The prevalence of a diagnosable mood disorder is lower in older than in younger adults, but many report symptoms of depressive disorders. From 8 to 20% of older adults living in the community experience depressive symptoms, with almost double that percentage (17 to 35%) in primary care settings (Gurland, Cross, & Katz, 1996). Even though older adults may not meet the diagnostic criteria for these disorders, they may nevertheless be troubled by significant depressive symptoms that do not improve over time (Beekman et al., 2002).

Older adults are less likely to report some of the traditionally recognized "psychological" symptoms of depression such as dysphoria, guilt, low self-esteem, and suicidal thoughts. They are more likely to seek treatment for somatic complaints such as pain and abdominal symptoms (Amore, Tagariello, Laterza, & Savoia, 2007). They may also seek treatment for other psychological symptoms that do not appear to be those of depression, such as anxiety, abnormalities in psychomotor functioning, cognitive dysfunction, suicidal behavior, and delusions that there is something wrong with their bodies or that they are being persecuted (King & Markus, 2000).

FIGURE 11.1
Major Depressive Disorders by Age Group

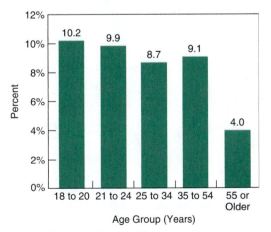

Percentage of adults aged 18 or older reporting a past year major depressive episode by age group: 2004 and 2005 National Survey on Drug Use and Health.

Source: Office of Applied Statistics, 2006.

Late-onset depression is mild or moderate depression that first appears after the age of 60. Risk factors for late-onset depression include becoming a widow, having had less than a high school education, experiencing impairments in physical functioning, and being a heavy alcohol drinker (United States Department of Health and Human Services, 1999). Late-onset depression is more likely to be accompanied by psychotic symptoms (Gournellis et al., 2001). These psychotic symptoms include hypochondriacal delusions and nihilistic delusions, or the belief that the self, others, or the world have ceased to exist. Depression may also occur in conjunction with dementia, particularly in the early stages as people begin to come to grips with the implications of the disease for their future (Harwood, Sultzer, & Wheatley, 2000).

Health care professionals are not well trained in recognizing the signs of depression in their older clients (Charney et al., 2003). In part this is because, as mentioned earlier, older adults do not necessarily report their symptoms in a manner that allows for accurate diagnosis. In addition, however, health care providers are not attuned to diagnosing psychological disorders in their older clients. Physicians spend less time per visit with an older patient than a younger patient. Furthermore, insurance companies reimburse for mental health diagnosis and intervention at a lower rate. Some health care providers may assume that depression is a natural consequence of aging and therefore pay less attention to its symptoms. Alternatively, a health care worker may wish to avoid stigmatizing older clients by diagnosing them with a psychological disorder (Duberstein & Conwell, 2000). Misdiagnosis may also occur because the symptoms of mood disorders may occur in conjunction with a medical condition, leading either to failure to detect the mood disorder or misattribution of the symptoms (Delano-Wood & Abeles, 2005).

There are a host of psychological factors that can increase the older individual's risk of developing depression. Older adults with hearing impairments, visual impairments, or both are more likely to experience depressive symptoms (Lupsakko, Mantyjarvi, Kautiainen, & Sulkava, 2002). Functional disability, the inability to provide basic self-care tasks, is also predictive of depressive symptoms, in part through its effect on lowering the individual's self-esteem (Yang, 2006). Problems with memory and cognition can also place the older person at risk of developing depressive symptoms (Gallo, Rebok, Tennsted, Wadley, & Horgas, 2003). Psychosocial issues such as bereavement, loneliness, and stressful life events can also serve as risk factors for depressive disorders in later adulthood (Bruce, 2002). An inability to employ successful coping strategies to deal with late-life stressors can also increase the individual's risk of developing depression. In one study covering a 10-year period, older adults who used ineffective coping methods, such as avoidance, were more likely to develop

FIGURE 11.2

Cumulative Lifetime Prevalence of Major Depressive Disorder

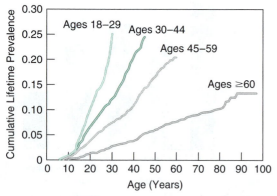

Major depressive disorder by age group as reported in the National Comorbidity Study.

Source: Kessler et al., 2003.

FIGURE 11.3
Relationship between Fitness and Depression

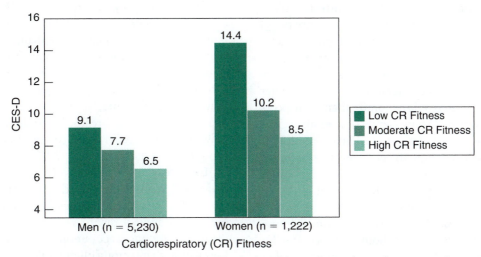

Mean scores for depressive symptoms by cardiorespiratory fitness level, adjusted for age, BMI, and year of participation. Superscripts indicate significant differences between fitness groups (all $P < 0.005$).

Source: Galper, Trivedi, Barlow, Dunn, & Kampert, 2006.

symptoms of depression compared with their age peers who attempted to handle their problems through direct, problem-focused coping methods (Holahan, Moos, Holahan, Brennan, & Schutte, 2005).

Medical disorders also present significant risk factors (Alexopoulos et al., 2002), even in people who have never experienced a depressive episode earlier in life (Sneed, Kasen, & Cohen, 2006). The prevalence of depressive symptoms and disorders is higher among older adults being treated in medical settings such as clinics, hospitals, and long-term care institutions. Prevalence rates in clinics and hospitals are estimated to range from 12 to 20% (Blazer, 1999). These figures rise to as high as 30% among older individuals living in long-term care settings (King & Markus, 2000). Unfortunately, older adults seen in medical settings are often not adequately diagnosed or treated (Charlson & Peterson, 2002).

Physical disability, such as that associated with arthritis, can also contribute to the development of depressive disorders in later adulthood (Oslin et al., 2002). Experiencing a hip fracture is associated with a 14.3% increased risk of developing major depressive disorder (Lenze et al., 2007). One physical concern that many psychologists might overlook is tooth loss. As pointed out in Chapter 4, tooth loss is a condition that affects a substantial number of older adults. Perhaps not surprisingly, researchers have found that depressed older adults are more likely to have experienced tooth loss (Persson et al., 2003). Another potentially overlooked risk factor is lack of sufficient vitamin D, which may also present a risk factor for cognitive impairment (Wilkins, Sheline, Roe, Birge, & Morris, 2006). Physical disorders present in the spouse may also contribute to depressive symptoms. An investigation of caregivers in the United States Health and Retirement Study identified a relationship between urinary incontinence in the wife and depressive symptoms in the husband (Fultz et al., 2005).

Over the long term, without receiving appropriate treatment in the form of medication or psychotherapy (see below), untreated older adults are at greater risk of a variety of impairments in physical and cognitive functioning. Over a 7-year period, older adults in their 70s who received high scores on a measure of depression-related distress showed a greater decline in cognitive functioning than their peers who did not have high depression scores (Chodosh, Kado, Seeman, & Karlamangla, 2007). Those older adults with more severe symptoms of depression and those whose depression is unremitting are more likely to suffer in terms of higher rates of mortality over time (Geerlings, Beekman, Deeg, Twisk, & Van Tilburg, 2002). One mechanism thought to account for the relationship between depression and higher morbidity is dysfunction in the immune system. Depression may activate cytokines that eventually increase the risk of cardiovascular disease, osteoporosis, arthritis, Type 2 diabetes, cancers, periodontal disease, frailty, and functional decline (Kiecolt-Glaser & Glaser, 2002).

The prevalence of bipolar affective disorder is far lower than major depressive disorder, with an estimated rate of 1.6% of the adult United States population (Kessler et al., 1994). Rates of bipolar disorder are lower in older adults (0.1%) than in the younger population (1.4%) (Robins & Regier, 1991). The likelihood of an individual experiencing a manic episode for the first time in old age is relatively low. The onset of a bipolar illness typically is in late adolescence or early adulthood. When bipolar disorder develops late in adulthood, it appears to be related a higher risk for cerebrovascular disease (Subramaniam, Dennis, & Byrne, 2006). The presence of white matter hyperintensities in individuals who develop bipolar disorder for the first time in later life reinforces the potential role of vascular contributions (Zanetti, Cordeiro, & Busatto, 2007).

Anxiety Disorders

The major symptom of an anxiety disorder is excessive anxiety, a state in which an individual is more tense, apprehensive, and uneasy about the future than is warranted by objective circumstances. The experience of anxiety also involves a focusing inward on the unpleasant feelings that accompany anxiety such as a pounding heart or shortness of breath. Often these feelings may become a major focus of the individual's symptoms.

Each year, approximately 12% of adults are diagnosed with an anxiety disorder (Kessler et al., 2005). Women at all ages have about twice the rate of anxiety disorders as men, and these disorders are more common in the under-65 population than among older adults (Beekman et al., 1998). Among a sample of Puerto Ricans 50 and older living in inner-cities in the Northeast, anxiety disorders were detected among 24%, with approximately equal distributions between men and women (Tolin, Robison, Gaztambide, & Blank, 2005). Anxiety disorders can have serious health implications. In one investigation of a sample of over 3,000 individuals in their 70s, symptoms of anxiety predicted mortality from heart disease, but only among African Americans, not whites (Brenes et al., 2007).

Psychologists who work with older adults are concerned that anxiety disorders fail to be recognized in clients within this age group. The major reason is the difficulty in arriving at an accurate diagnosis (Scogin, Floyd, & Forde, 2000). At any age, the symptoms of an anxiety disorder may be produced by or at least exist alongside a medical condition or the reporting of problems in mobility (Mehta et al., 2007). Health practitioners themselves may not be attuned to diagnosing psychological symptoms in an older individual with physical health problems. As a result, the presence of an anxiety disorder may be missed along with an opportunity for intervention. The implications of failing to diagnose anxiety disorders can be serious as the presence of anxiety symptoms has been linked to mortality risk, particularly in African American older adults (Brenes et al., 2007).

"What do you think?"	*11-2*

How can mental health professionals be better trained to diagnose anxiety disorders in older adults?

There are six categories of anxiety disorder. In **generalized anxiety disorder**, a person feels an overall sense of uneasiness and concern but cannot identify a specific focus. The primary symptom of this disorder is worry, especially over minor problems. Other symptoms are a general sense of restlessness, difficulty concentrating, fatigue, irritability, muscle tension, and sleep disturbance. In later adulthood, generalized anxiety disorder may be triggered by stress and concerns about health (Scogin et al., 2000). About 5% of adults have this disorder (Wittchen, Zhao, Kessler, & Eaton, 1994). Among older adults, the six-month prevalence (those who reported symptoms in the past six months) is 2%, and the lifetime prevalence is estimated to be 3.6% (Kessler et al., 2005). However, a higher percentage of older adults experience symptoms of generalized anxiety (Graham & Vidal-Zeballos, 1998), and some findings suggest that there is a more common "subsyndromal" version of generalized anxiety disorder among older adults whose symptoms are not severe enough to warrant a diagnosis of the disorder itself (Diefenbach et al., 2003).

The form of anxiety disorder known as **panic disorder** involves the experience of panic attacks, which are episodes in which the individual experiences physical symptoms involving extreme shortness of breath, a pounding heart, and the belief that death is imminent. People who suffer from panic disorder may have these episodes at unpredictable times, and eventually they may also develop agoraphobia, which is the fear of being trapped or stranded during a panic attack. To avoid this frightening and embarrassing situation, the individual then begins to stay at home and to avoid places such as elevators, shopping malls, or public transportation, where escape during an attack would be difficult. Estimates are that approximately 4.7% of adults have a diagnosis of panic disorder, with a higher percent in early and mid adulthood (Kessler et al., 2005).

The prevalence of agoraphobia is estimated to be much lower than panic disorder, affecting up to 1.4% of the adult United States population (Kessler et al., 2006). Agoraphobia is also less common among older adults than among adults in their 30s to 60s (Kessler et al., 2005). Unlike younger adults, who may develop agoraphobia following a panic attack, it is more likely that this condition in older adults is related to fear of harm or embarrassment (Scogin et al., 2000).

People with a **specific phobia** have an irrational fear of a particular object or situation. This disorder is the most commonly observed form of anxiety disorder in older adults, with a lifetime prevalence rate estimated at 12.5% and a prevalence rate in adults 60 and older at 7.5% (Kessler et al., 2005). There are many types of specific phobias ranging from fear of snakes to fear of enclosed places. A common form of specific phobia is blood-injury phobia, which is fear of seeing blood or seeing a surgical procedure.

People with **social phobia** have a form of anxiety disorder that applies to situations in which they must perform some action in front of others. In addition to the obvious scenarios that create distress for such individuals, including giving a public performance or speaking to a large group, ordinary situations such as eating in

FIGURE 11.4

Trajectories of PTSD Symptoms

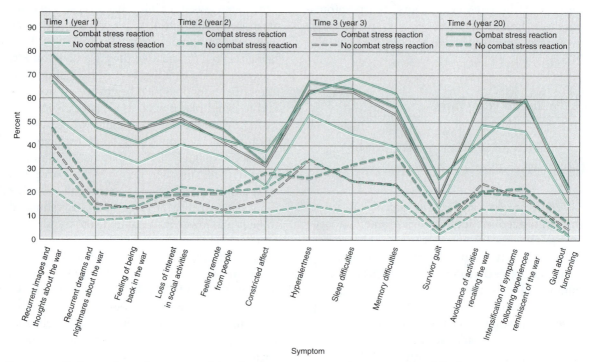

Symptom profile (percents) according to group and time of measurement among combat veterans of the 1982 Lebanon-Israeli War.
Source: Solomon & Mikulincer, 2006.

the presence of others can create high degrees of anxiety. Severe symptoms of social phobia are present in about 12% of adults, with a peak prevalence rate in adults in their 30s. Women are more likely to suffer from this disorder than are men (Kessler et al., 2005). A specific form of social phobia that applies only to public speaking also occurs, in which the individual can manage without distress as long as such situations can be avoided (Kessler, Stein, & Berglund, 1998).

Obsessive-compulsive disorder is a form of anxiety disorder in which people suffer from obsessions, or repetitive thoughts (such as the belief that one's child will be harmed) and compulsions, which are repetitive behaviors (such as handwashing). The obsessions and compulsions are unrelenting, irrational, and

distracting. This disorder is not the same as obsessive-compulsive personality disorder, in which an individual has the personality traits of being excessively rigid and perfectionistic. People with obsessive-compulsive anxiety disorder have unrelenting feelings of anxiety that are partially relieved only by performing compulsive rituals or thinking certain thoughts. The lifetime prevalence of obsessive-compulsive disorder is about 1.6% of the adult population (Kessler et al., 2005). The lifetime prevalence among older adults is estimated at 0.7%, making this a relatively rare disorder in this age group.

In the anxiety disorder known as **post-traumatic stress disorder (PTSD)**, an individual suffers prolonged effects of exposure to a traumatic experience, an event that is distressing, if not disastrous. Examples of traumatic experiences include earthquake, fire, physical assault, and war. Although many people who are exposed to these types of experiences suffer from an acute stress disorder for a period of time, some develop symptoms that persist for months or even years. People with PTSD may find themselves incapacitated by flashbacks or reminders of the event, intrusions of thoughts about the disaster, hypersensitivity to events similar to the trauma, and attempts to avoid these disturbing images and reminders. The individual may also become detached from other people and the ordinary events of daily life. In one study of Israeli veterans of the 1982 Lebanon War (see Figure 11.2), symptoms such as recurrent images, hypervigilance, and difficulties in sleep and memory persisted for as long as 20 years following combat. The likelihood of experiencing PTSD symptoms was particularly elevated in veterans who had experienced a stress reaction associated with involvement in combat (Solomon & Mikulincer, 2006).

Some clinicians expect that the incidence of PTSD among the older adult population will grow in future years due to the aging of Vietnam veterans. Estimates are that at the age of 19, the prevalence of PTSD among Vietnam soldiers was 15%. Since PTSD can arise many years after exposure to trauma, these numbers may well continue to increase (U.S. Department of Health and Human Services, 1999). Exposure to the terrorist attacks in the United States of September 11, 2001, may also increase the rate of PTSD among older adults, even those not directly exposed to the attacks themselves (van Zelst, de Beurs, & Smit, 2003).

In addition to suffering from PTSD after combat experiences, severe health problems can also increase the individual's risk of developing this disorder. For example, heart disease is linked to a higher risk of PTSD, especially in people with a history of depression (Spindler & Pedersen, 2005). PTSD, in turn, can also increase the individual's risk of developing heart disease. A longitudinal study of nearly 2,000 veterans in the Normative Aging Study revealed that, even after controlling for a number of risk factors, men who had experienced higher levels of PTSD were more likely to have heart attacks or develop coronary heart disease (Kubzansky, Koenen, Spiro, Vokonas, & Sparrow, 2007). Another risk factor associated with PTSD is impaired performance on laboratory tests of memory (Golier, Harvey, Legge, & Yehuda, 2006).

Anxiety may occur in conjunction with depression, a disorder being considered for inclusion in future DSMs that would have the name **mixed anxiety-depressive disorder**. In this disorder, the person experiences recurrent or persistent dysphoria for at least one month along with at least four symptoms of anxiety disorders such as worry, dread of the future, irritability, and sleep disturbance, along with other symptoms of depressive disorder such as low self-esteem and hopelessness. These symptoms, when present in older adults, can significantly lower their ability to carry out everyday activities. Unfortunately, people with mixed anxiety-depressive disorder

Researchers are concerned that troops currently in the Middle East will suffer long-term consequences of PTSD.

tend to be less responsive to treatment (Flint & Rifat, 1997).

Schizophrenia and other Psychotic Disorders.
The psychological disorder known as **schizophrenia** is perhaps the one that most mystifies students of psychopathology, because of its long association with the notion of "mental illness." A person with schizophrenia has a wide range of unusual symptoms, ranging from hallucinations (false perceptions) to delusions (false beliefs), which are known as positive symptoms. However, there may also be the so-called negative symptoms of apathy, withdrawal, and lack of emotional expression. Often, a person's speech may be disordered, and motor behavior may be extremely altered. There are variations by type of schizophrenia, but all share the common feature of involving a severe disturbance in the person's ability to remain in touch with reality.

It is estimated that schizophrenia has a lifetime prevalence of about 1%, with a peak prevalence at 1.5% for the 30 to 44 age group and 0.2% in people older than 65 years (Keith, Regier, & Rae, 1991). In part the apparent decrease in older age groups reflects the higher risk of mortality for people with this disorder. In the large majority of people who develop schizophrenia, the onset is before the age of 40, although the onset in women is about five years later than that of men. Reflecting the higher life expectancy of women, there is a crossover in the gender distribution of the disorder, with a higher prevalence of schizophrenia among older women than older adult men (Meeks, 2000).

The first systematic definition of schizophrenia as "premature dementia" (dementia praecox) was developed by the German psychiatrist Emil Kraepelin, and for many years it was thought of as a permanently disabling condition. However, it is now known that the long-term outcome of the disorder is highly variable. Approximately 20 to 25% of people who develop the disorder improve to the point of complete remission, and at the other end of the spectrum, 10% remain chronically impaired. Among the remaining 50 to 70%, the disorder shows a varying course with gradual improvements in social functioning and a reduction of psychotic symptoms (Meeks, 2000). Some individuals can achieve very significant recovery after many years of being chronically impaired, including being able to work, drive a car, and live independently in their own homes (Palmer et al., 2002).

Despite the favorable outcomes achieved by some who suffer from schizophrenia, there are serious ramifications of having had the disorder at some point in life. The nature of this disturbance and its association with other illnesses, suicide, or substance abuse mean that a person with this diagnosis faces serious threats to health and mortality throughout the adult years (Ruschena et al., 1998). Furthermore, although negative symptoms may become more prominent than positive symptoms, people who have this disorder in later adulthood continue to exhibit significant impairment. Depression, poorer cognitive functioning, and social isolation are complications that can be experienced by older adults with schizophrenia (Graham, Arthur, & Howard, 2002). Furthermore, the symptoms of schizophrenia themselves can lead to significant disruptions in everyday life as well as greater likelihood of negative life events (Patterson et al., 1997).

On the positive side, older adults who have suffered from schizophrenia for many years develop a wide range of coping skills (Solano & Whitbourne, 2001). Those naturally developing mechanisms can be augmented with clinical interventions that focus on skills for coping with everyday life problems. Emotional support is another important component of treatment for older individuals with a long history of this disorder (Semple et al., 1999).

Although not in the official diagnostic nomenclature, another apparent form of schizophrenia, known as **late-onset schizophrenia**, can occur among adults over the age of 45 years (Jeste et al., 1997), a condition also referred to as paraphrenia. In contrast to early-onset schizophrenia, the late-onset variety is more likely to involve paranoid symptoms, shows less severe cognitive impairment, and responds better to antipsychotic medications. Individuals with the late-onset form of schizophrenia appear to function at a higher level in their youth than do people who develop the more common form of early-onset schizophrenia. It is possible that individuals with the late-onset form of the disorder share the same genetic vulnerability thought to be involved in other forms of schizophrenia (Lohr, Alder, Flynn, Harris, & McAdams, 1997). For some reason, however, they were protected or had other advantages that prevented the emergence of symptoms (Meeks, 2000). The disorder may be triggered in later adulthood in connection with sensory losses such as changes in vision and hearing, which make it more difficult for the individual to perceive accurately the actions and speech of other people (Zarit & Zarit, 1998).

Delirium, Dementia, and Amnestic Disorders. Disorders involving significant loss of cognitive functioning as the result of neurological dysfunction or medical illness form the category in DSM-IV-TR known as **delirium, dementia, and amnestic disorders**. These disorders in previous versions of the DSM were called "organic" or "cognitive" disorders, indicating that they have different causes and characteristics than the other psychological disorders included in the diagnostic system. However, the terminology has moved toward the current descriptive one (which simply summarizes the disorders in this category) because it is becoming increasingly difficult to distinguish disorders that have a neurological or physiological basis from those that do not.

"What do you think?" | **11-3**

How can clinicians avoid making errors in diagnosing disorders that look like dementia?

The disorder known as Alzheimer's disease is technically regarded within DSM-IV-TR as a cause of dementia. The term dementia is used to apply to a change in cognitive functioning that occurs progressively over time. The symptoms include loss of memory and of the ability to use language (aphasia), to carry out coordinated bodily movements (apraxia), to recognize familiar objects, and to make rational judgments. As discussed in Chapter 5, Alzheimer's disease is one cause of dementia, but there can be others, such as long-term substance abuse, vascular disease, and Parkinson's disease, to name a few.

In contrast to the long-term changes that occur in dementia, the condition known as **delirium** is an acute state in which the individual experiences a disturbance in consciousness and attention. Cognitive changes may also occur including memory loss, disorientation, and inability to use language. The cause of delirium is a change in the brain's functioning due to substance use, improper medications, head injury, high fever, or vitamin deficiency. Most cases of delirium subside within days, but the condition may persist as long as a month. Although relatively frequent in acute care medical settings, it is uncommon within community-residing populations of older adults. When it does occur in nonacute settings, it should be a trigger for intervention because it clearly indicates the presence of an underlying condition requiring treatment (Andrew, Freter, & Rockwood, 2006). Unfortunately, the individual with delirium may be misdiagnosed with dementia, and an opportunity for intervention will have been lost or at least made more complicated.

ASSESS YOURSELF: Serious Psychological Distress

When the CDC measures serious psychological distress in the National Household Interview Survey, they use this single item "K6" scale. To date, the K6 has been used in general population surveys in 33 countries, including the United States. This was the measure used in Figure 11.8.

Use this rating scale when answering the following six questions:

ALL of the time

MOST of the time

SOME of the time

A LITTLE of the time

NONE of the time

During the PAST 30 DAYS, how often did you feel...

1. So sad that nothing could cheer you up
2. Nervous
3. Restless or fidgety
4. Hopeless
5. That everything was an effort; and
6. Worthless

You can compare your rating to others in your age group and if you feel it is overly high, you may wish to consult a mental health resource, such as www.samhsa.gov.

People who suffer from **amnesia** have as their main symptom profound memory loss. Their amnesia may involve an inability to learn or remember new information (anterograde) or the inability to recall information into the past (retrograde). An amnestic disorder may be due to chronic use of substances such as medications, psychoactive substances, or exposure to environmental toxins. However, amnesia may also be caused by head trauma, loss of oxygen supply to the brain, and the sexually transmitted disease of herpes simplex.

Substance-related Disorders. In 2005, illicit drugs were used by an estimated 19.7 million persons 12 years and older, representing 8% of the population (Substance Abuse and Mental Health Services Administration, 2006). The majority of adults who abuse or are dependent on alcohol or illicit drugs are in their late teens and early 20s. Very small percentages of adults 40 and older report abusing or being dependent on either illicit drugs or alcohol. Nevertheless researchers predict that the higher lifetime patterns of illicit drug use among Baby Boomers will lead to an increase in the prevalence of illicit drug use in adults 50 and older by the year 2020 (Colliver, Compton, Gfroerer, & Condon, 2006).

Older adults are particularly at risk for abuse of prescription drugs, as 36% of the medications used in the United States are taken by adults over the age of 65 years. One estimate places the potential of prescription drug abuse among older adults in outpatient treatment as ranging from a low of 5% to a high of 33%, with an estimated abuse rate (among women) at 11%. Further estimates are that the risk of abuse will rise dramatically between now and the year 2020 (Simoni-Wastila & Yang, 2006).

Attention has only recently been drawn to the problems of older drinkers. In part, this is because there is selective survival of people who do not use alcohol. The people who used alcohol to excess are no longer in the population by the time they reach their 60s and 70s. By the time they reach the age of 70, they have either become abstinent or died either from excessive alcohol use or from related high-risk behaviors

such as smoking (Vaillant, 2003). Estimates are that 2 to 5% of men and 1% of women over 65 abuse substances (Abeles et al., 1997) and that 1 to 2% of men and 0.3% of women over 65 are alcohol abusers (Grant et al., 1995). In contrast to the under-65 population, among those over 65 the prevalence rates of alcohol abuse are higher for African Americans. Hispanic females over 65 have the lowest rates of alcohol abuse. In the future, it is estimated that rates of alcohol abuse will increase significantly with the aging of the current cohort of Baby Boomers, who have higher rates of alcohol consumption than previous generations (U.S. Department of Health and Human Services, 1999).

Symptoms of alcohol dependence are thought to be present in as many as 14% of older adults

FIGURE 11.5

Past Month Illicit Drug Use among Persons Age 12 or Older: 2005

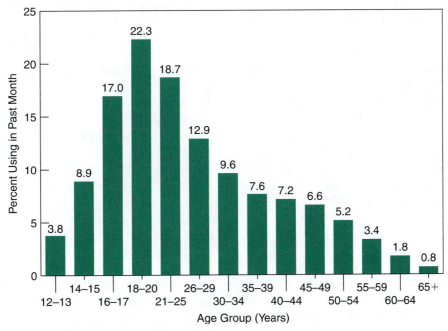

Percentage of adults in the United States using illicit drugs.

Source: Substance Abuse and Mental Health Services Administration, 2006.

who receive medical attention in hospitals and emergency rooms. It is also estimated that alcohol use is relatively prevalent in settings in which only older adults live, such as nursing homes and retirement communities. The risks of alcohol abuse among this population are considerable, ranging from cirrhosis of the liver (a terminal condition) to heightened rate of injury through hip fractures and motor vehicle accidents. Alcohol may also interact with the effects of prescription medications, potentially limiting their effectiveness. Even without a change in drinking patterns, an older person may experience difficulties associated with physiological changes that affect tolerance. Long-term alcohol use may also lead to changes in the frontal lobes and cerebellum, exacerbating the effects of normal aging on cognitive and motor functioning (National Institute on Alcohol Abuse and Alcoholism, 1998). In severe and prolonged alcohol abuse, dementia can develop, leading to permanent memory loss and early death (see Chapter 5).

There are treatment approaches that can be effective in reducing alcohol consumption among those older adults who continue to struggle with abuse and dependence. Alcoholics Anonymous, support from family and friends, and the use of adaptive coping mechanisms can be effective methods of reducing an older adult's reliance on alcohol. As is true for younger people, the context of drinking is important. One of the most effective treatments may be finding a new network of friends who do not engage in or approve of drinking (Moos, Schutte, Brennan, & Moos, 2004).

AXIS II DISORDERS

A **personality disorder** is a condition diagnosed on Axis II of the DSM-IV-TR to apply to long-standing and maladaptive dispositions. The prevalence of personality disorders in the general

population is estimated to be 9% (Samuels et al., 2002), a prevalence that is fairly steady across adulthood (Abrams & Horowitz, 1999).

The DSM-IV-TR diagnosis of antisocial personality disorder is characterized by **psychopathy**, a set of traits that are thought to lie at the core of the disorder. There are two dimensions or factors to psychopathy as measured by the Psychopathy Check List (PCL) (Hare, 1997). Factor 1 is a cluster of traits that represent disturbances in the capacity to experience emotions such as empathy, guilt, and remorse. This cluster also includes manipulativeness, egocentricity, and callousness. Factor 2 incorporates the unstable and impulsive behaviors that contribute to the socially deviant lifestyle of the individual with this disorder.

Studies of the relationship between age and antisocial personality disorder provide support for the notion that the maladaptive personality traits that constitute the essence of personality disorders are extremely stable over time (Harpur, Hart, & Hare, 2002). One large-scale study of psychopathy, conducted on nearly 900 male prisoners between the ages of 18 and 89, showed that there were no age differences on Factor 1, which represents the "personality" contribution to the disorder. By contrast, scores on the items that reflect socially deviant and impulsive behaviors show a dramatic decrease across age groups. This picture drawn from Factor 2 of the PCL scores corresponds closely to data on the numbers of prisoners by age reported by the U.S. Department of Justice (see Figure 11.6). The rate of imprisonment drastically decreases after the age of 45 (Harrison & Beck, 2005).

Changes over adulthood in the impulsive and antisocial element of psychopathy may reflect a number of factors other than changes in the personality disorder itself. The apparent decrease in antisocial behavior may reflect the fact that people who were high on Factor 2 of psychopathy

FIGURE 11.6

Number of Prisoners by Age, United States, 2004

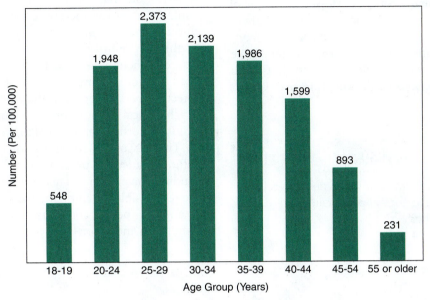

Number of sentenced prisoners by age group per 100,000 in the population, federal and state.

Source: http://www.ojp.usdoj.gov/bjs/pub/pdf/p04.pdf

are no longer alive. In addition to having been killed in violent crime or as the result of drug abuse, such individuals also have a higher than expected mortality rate due to higher rates of alcohol abuse and poor health habits (Laub & Vaillant, 2000). At the same time, the relative stability of Factor 1, which reflects the personality traits at the heart of psychopathy, attests to the insensitivity of this dimension to the effects of age or experience on people with this disorder. Older criminals learn to avoid incarceration, or else are motivated for other reasons to reduce their involvement in activities that will land them in prison.

Other personality disorders also change in prevalence over adulthood (Segal, Coolidge, & Rosowsky, 2000) There are lower rates for histrionic and borderline personality disorders in older adults. By contrast, the prevalence is higher for obsessive-compulsive and schizoid personality disorders as well as dependent personality disorder. These patterns fit the **maturation hypothesis**, which suggests that the "immature" personality types (borderline, histrionic, narcissistic, and antisocial) improve or at least become more treatable in older adults. By contrast, the "mature" types (obsessive-compulsive, schizoid, and paranoid) become more symptomatic over time (Engels, Duijsens, Haringsma, & van Putten, 2003). Possible explanations for such changes include brain injury, disease, and life stresses. Prior adaptation and the individual's social support network are additional factors that can influence the severity of personality disorders in later adulthood. For example, older adults with longstanding personality disorders become better at coping with their symptoms (Segal, Hook, & Coolidge, 2001).

To summarize, the major feature of personality disorders in later life is that they decrease in intensity and frequency. However, they may also take a modified form that makes them relatively more difficult for clinicians to manage. In addition, recovery from a depressive episode is more difficult for older adults who also have a personality disorder (Morse & Lynch, 2004).

> **"What do you think?"** | **11-4**
>
> How does the maturation hypothesis relate to changes in normal personality in middle and later life?

ELDER ABUSE

A condition that may become one of serious clinical concern is the abuse of an older adult through the actions taken by another person, or through self-neglect that leads to significant loss of functioning. The term **elder abuse** is used to refer to a large category of actions taken directly against older adults that inflict physical or psychological harm. To protect vulnerable adults, Adult Protective Services (APS) were mandated by Title XX of the Social Security Act in 1975. Although a federal program, there is little or no funding attached to it. This means that the states are responsible for enforcing the regulations and as a result, there is considerable variation in the definitions and reporting mechanisms for abuse.

TABLE 11.2
Forms of Elder Maltreatment

Type of Maltreatment	Definition
Abuse	Infliction of physical or psychological harm or the knowing deprivation of goods or services necessary to meet essential needs or to avoid physical or psychological harm
Neglect	Refusal or failure to fulfill any part of a person's obligations or duties to an elder. Neglect may also include failure of a person who has fiduciary responsibilities to provide care for an elder (e.g., pay for necessary home care services) or the failure on the part of an in-home service provider to provide necessary care. Neglect typically means the refusal or failure to provide an elderly person/vulnerable adult with such life necessities as food, water, clothing, shelter, personal hygiene, medicine, comfort, personal safety, and other essentials included in an implied or agreed-upon responsibility to an elder.
Financial or material abuse/exploitation	Illegal or improper use of an older person's or vulnerable adult's funds, property, or assets. Examples include, but are not limited to, cashing an older/vulnerable person's checks without authorization or permission; forging an older person's signature; misusing or stealing an older person's money or possessions; coercing or deceiving an older person into signing any document (e.g., contracts or will); and the improper use of conservatorship, guardianship, or power of attorney.
Self-neglect	An adult's inability, due to physical or mental impairment or diminished capacity, to perform essential self-care tasks including (a) obtaining essential food, clothing, shelter, and medical care; (b) obtaining goods and services necessary to maintain physical health, mental health, or general safety; and/or (c) managing one's own financial affairs. Choice of lifestyle of living arrangement is not, in itself, evidence of self-neglect

Source: Teaster et al., 2006.

Elder abuse is a notoriously difficult behavior to document, as it is surrounded by guilt, shame, fear, and the risk of criminal prosecution. Victims are afraid to report abuse due to concern over retribution, and the perpetrators obviously do not wish to reveal that they are engaging in this heinous activity. Estimates of the prevalence of elder abuse first became available in the 1980s when the issue received national attention after it was brought before the Select Committee on Aging in 1981. At that time, it was suggested that 4% of the 65 and older population are victims of moderate to severe abuse. By the year 2003, it was estimated that between 1 and 2 million adults 65 and older (5-6%) are the victims of abuse or mistreatment by someone on whom they depend for care (Committee on National Statistics, 2003). The prevalence rate based on reports to state adult protective services offices is estimated to be 2.7 per 1,000 older adults and vulnerable adults (who might be under 60), which represents an estimated increase of 19.6% from the reports received as of the year 2000 (Teaster et al., 2006).

The most likely perpetrator of elder abuse is a child or other relative under the age of 60 years old. States vary considerably in their rates of abuse, from a low of .4% in Oregon to a high of 24.5% in Connecticut. Caregiver and self-neglect are the most common forms of abuse (Teaster et al., 2006).

Clearly, the problem of elder abuse is a serious social and mental health issue. People who are victims of abuse, not surprisingly, have a higher mortality rate than their age peers, even controlling for medical conditions (Lachs, Williams, O'Brien, Pillemer, & Charlson, 1998). They are more vulnerable to psychological distress (Yan & So-kum, 2001). Although many individuals throughout life are potentially victims of abuse or neglect, it is the older adults who are in poor health who are at particularly high risk (Nadien, 2006). Targeting their caregivers, and

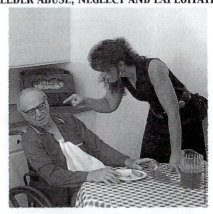

Posters such as this one attempt to bring to public attention the problem of elder abuse.

providing them with better coping skills as well as adequate reimbursement and social support, are seen as important preventative strategies to reduce the incidence of this very tragic situation (Nadien, 2006).

SUICIDE

Although not a diagnosis in the DSM-IV-TR, close to 90% of adults who complete suicide have a diagnosable psychiatric disorder. The most frequent diagnoses are major depressive disorder, alcohol abuse or dependence, and schizophrenia. Among suicide victims ages 65 years and above,

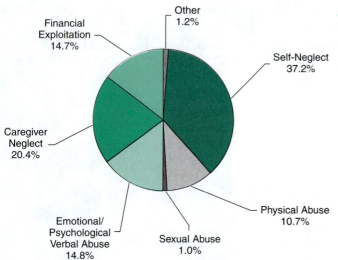

Other
1.2%

Financial
Exploitation
14.7%

Self-Neglect
37.2%

Caregiver
Neglect
20.4%

Emotional/
Psychological
Verbal Abuse
14.8%

Sexual Abuse
1.0%

Physical Abuse
10.7%

FIGURE 11.7
Prevalence of Major Forms of Elder Abuse

Substantiated reports by category for adults 60 and older in 19 U.S. states.
Source: Teaster et al., 2006.

rates of psychiatric disorders are nearly as high as in the general population, ranging from 71 to over 90%. The age-adjusted suicide rate in the United States of all age, race, and sex groups is highest for white males aged 85 and older (Centers for Disease Control and Prevention, 2006); however, this rate is so high because the total number of people in this age, sex, and race group in the population is relatively low. The actual number of deaths by suicide for this group is approximately 800 (Hoyert, Heron, Murphy, & Kung, 2006). Each year, approximately 31,000 people in the U.S. population as a whole die of suicide. The majority are ages 25 to 54 (Heron & Smith, 2007). Nevertheless, the issue of suicide in older adults is one of concern for those older white male individuals who have the risk factors of physical illness and widower status.

Depressive symptoms and major depressive disorder are strongly related to suicidal feelings in older adults (Barnow, Linden, & Freyberger, 2004). Among older adults with schizoaffective disorder, in which schizophrenia symptoms coexist with disordered mood, the rate of suicide attempts can rise to as high as 38% (Baran & Young, 2006). Symptoms of anxiety also are

present in older adults who commit suicide. Individuals who have a history of substance abuse, including alcohol abuse, are also at higher risk. The fact that mild to moderate symptoms of depression are observed in older adults before they commit suicide means that suicides are much more difficult to detect by health care workers (Duberstein & Conwell, 2000).

Certain personality disorders are more likely to be associated with completed suicide in older adults. These include avoidant personality disorder and schizoid personality disorder, which are characterized by withdrawal and social isolation (Duberstein & Conwell, 1997). Suicide risk is also heightened in individuals with lower levels of self-esteem (Szanto et al., 2007). Those who are anxious, rigid, and obsessional also are at heightened risk due, at least in part, to an inability to discuss their thoughts and feelings with others (Conwell, Duberstein, & Caine, 2002; Turvey et al., 2002).

The presence of a physical disease is another potential risk factor for suicide among older adults (Conwell et al., 2002). Impairments associated with cancer and cardiovascular disease in particular seem to be related to suicide risk.

Given the difficulty of diagnosing depression among older adults, as discussed earlier, it would seem particularly important for health care providers to be aware of these risk factors when working with older adults who have these diseases. Sadly, it is estimated that from 43 to 76% of all suicide victims had seen a health care provider within a month of their death (Duberstein & Conwell, 2000). Greater sensitivity to symptoms of mood disorders in conjunction with evaluation of the additional psychological and medical risk factors could potentially increase the chances that these health care providers would have been able to intervene (Heisel, 2006).

TREATMENT ISSUES IN MENTAL HEALTH CARE

The issue of health care, for both medical and psychiatric conditions, became a major problem in the United States at the turn of the 21st century. Changes in the composition of the population, occurring with the well-publicized increases in the Baby Boom generation, are of particular concern. As this population ages, it will undoubtedly put strains on an already overextended mental health care system, which is struggling to meet the needs of the current generation of older adults. Clearly, more training will be needed both for practitioners currently in the field and those who will be entering the ranks of therapists and other mental health care workers (Qualls, Segal, Norman, & Gallagher-Thompson, 2002).

Treatment for Psychological Disorders

The psychological disorders discussed in this chapter involve a variety of potential causes and, therefore, may be treatable by a variety of approaches. Psychological treatment involves the planning for and implementation of treatment by a clinician, a professionally trained individual

such as a clinical psychologist, psychiatrist, or social worker. Most clinicians who work with adult populations differentiate the approaches they take to young and middle-aged adults from the approaches they take to older adults (Zarit & Zarit, 1998). With the 2003 adoption of the APA Guidelines for Psychological Practice with Older Adults (American Psychological Association, 2004), it will now be clearer exactly how clinicians need to adapt their approaches to older clients.

In addition to potentially different etiologies for disorders at different points in adulthood, clinicians must take into account the potential effects of chronic medical conditions as well as normal age-related changes in physical, cognitive, and social functioning (Hinrichsen & Dick-Siskin, 2000). Finally, variations by ethnic and minority status must be recognized by clinicians. It is essential that clinicians become competent in assessing and treating individuals from a range of backgrounds (Ferraro, 2002; Lau & Gallagher-Thompson, 2002).

Within the professional realm of psychology, specialists are increasingly emerging who have received training in **geropsychology**, applications of the field of gerontology to the psychological treatment of older adults. Geropsychologists, for example, may specialize in assessment of cognitive disorders, such as dementia, that are found in the older population. Another term that may be used to describe professionals with this training is **clinical geropsychology**, which emphasizes the fact that this specialty is used primarily in applied settings such as hospitals, clinics, and long-term institutions.

Assessment

Clinicians begin their treatment of a client's psychological disorder by conducting a multifaceted clinical assessment. The **assessment** procedure involves evaluation of the psychological,

TABLE 11.3
APA Guidelines for Psychological Practice with Older Adults

In 2003, the American Psychological Association (APA) approved a set of guidelines containing recommendations for clinical work with older adults. These highlights from the guidelines describe specific ways in which psychologists are encouraged to

Work with older adults within their scope of competence and seek consultation or make appropriate referrals when indicated.

Recognize how their attitudes and beliefs about aging and about older individuals may be relevant to their assessment and treatment of older adults.

Gain knowledge about theory and research in aging.

Understand diversity in the aging process, particularly how sociocultural factors such as gender, ethnicity, socioeconomic status, sexual orientation, disability status, and urban versus rural residence may influence the experience and expression of health and of psychological problems in later life.

Be knowledgeable about psychopathology within the aging population and aware of the prevalence and nature of that psychopathology when providing services to older adults.

Be familiar with the theory, research, and practice of various methods of assessment with older adults, and knowledgeable of assessment instruments that are psychometrically suitable for use with them.

Develop skill in tailoring assessments to accommodate older adults' specific characteristics and contexts.

Develop skill at recognizing cognitive changes in older adults, and conduct and interpret cognitive screening and functional ability evaluations.

Be familiar with the theory, research, and practice of various methods of intervention with older adults.

Be familiar with and develop skill in applying specific psychotherapeutic interventions and environmental modifications with older adults and their families.

Understand the issues pertaining to the provision of services in the specific settings in which older adults are typically located or encountered.

Recognize issues related to the provision of prevention and health promotion services with older adults.

Understand the special ethical and/or legal issues entailed in providing services to older adults.

Increase their knowledge, understanding and skills with respect to working with older adults through continuing education, training, supervision and consultation.

Source: American Psychological Association, 2004.

physiological, and social factors that potentially affect the individual's current state of functioning. Most psychological assessments are intended to provide a diagnosis (according to the DSM-IV-TR) and lay the groundwork for a treatment plan. In some cases, assessments may be used for special purposes, as in making legal determinations of mental competence or in evaluating an individual's appropriateness for a particular occupation. When used in the context of treatment, however, psychological assessments focus on providing the most accurate reading possible of a client's specific disorder on which treatment can then be based.

All clinical assessment involves differential diagnosis, the process of ruling out alternative diagnoses. In the case of older adults, this process involves establishing whether the symptoms that appear to be due to psychological disorder could be better accounted for by a medical condition (Bartels & Mueser, 1999). Current and past substance abuse should be included in this evaluation. Another important determination that must be made in assessment is between dementia and other psychological disorders, such as depression, which can cause memory loss and difficulties in concentration. There are several significant differences in the symptom pattern of individuals with these disorders. In depression, the symptoms of **dysphoria** are more severe, and the individual is likely to exaggerate the extent to which he or she is experiencing memory loss. People who have dementia tend, in contrast, to be overconfident about their cognitive abilities. Recognition memory (stating whether an item was presented) tends to be satisfactory in people who are depressed, but they perform more poorly on tests of free recall, where they have to state verbally the items that were presented. People with dementia have memory problems on tests of both recall and recognition. Finally, people with depression report their memory loss as starting suddenly, and their mental status varies from test to test. People with dementia show a progressive loss of cognitive abilities. These differences are important for clinicians to note in their assessment of older adults because, as was pointed out in Chapter 5, if the depression is caught in time there is a good chance of successful treatment.

Assessment should also be tailored to the particular physical and cognitive needs of the individual, particularly for older adults. They should be made to feel comfortable and relaxed, and should be given sufficient time to ask questions about the procedure, which may be unfamiliar and even frightening to them. Some of the practical concerns of clients should be attended to, such as making sure they have the correct eyeglasses and a hearing aid if necessary. A person who has difficulty writing due to arthritis, for instance, will be unable to complete paper-and-pencil measures. Rest periods may be necessary during a lengthy testing session, or the session may have to be divided into shorter units. The clinician should also be aware of the changes in sensory abilities, motor functions, and cognitive processes that may hamper the client's understanding of problems or questions given during the assessment process. For example, materials should be presented in large print to visually impaired clients. Even something seemingly insignificant, such as the hum of office equipment in the background, may compromise an older adult's performance (Edelstein, Martin, & McKee, 2000) It is also important to be sensitive to cultural or language differences between clinician and client, regardless of the age of the client (Halgin & Whitbourne, 2005).

Clinical Interview.   In a **clinical interview**, the clinician asks questions of the client to establish insight into the client's psychological processes. The clinician can also use the opportunity to interact face-to-face with the client to observe the client's behavior. This interview may take the form of an unstructured interview, which involves a series of open-ended questions, or it may follow a structured format. An example of a structured clinical interview is the Composite International Diagnostic Interview (CIDI) developed by the World Health Organization to obtain international comparisons of psychological disorders (World Health Organization, 1997). The Structured Clinical Interview for DSM-IV-TR (SCID) was a similar tool used in the development and validation of the DSM-IV-TR (First, Spitzer, Gibbon, & Williams, 1997). These instruments are extremely important for establishing the prevalence of psychiatric disorders and are useful for individual diagnostic purposes. In some cases, however, it may be more appropriate or productive to use an interview that has less structure. Questions can be rephrased if they are unclear, and topic areas can be explored that may be of particular relevance to the client. An unstructured interview can also be beneficial in assessing older adults with cognitive difficulties who find it difficult to concentrate or need help in maintaining their focus (Edelstein et al., 2000).

Mini-Mental State Exam. An assessment instrument used extensively in the diagnostic process for older adults is the mental status examination, discussed in Chapter 5 as a tool in the psychological assessment of dementia. The most well known of these instruments is the Mini-Mental State Exam (MMSE) (Folstein, Folstein, & McHugh, 1975). Although it is quick and relatively easy to administer and is useful for charting changes in dementing symptoms over time, it is not particularly specific to dementia and does not allow for precise measurement of cognitive functioning (Edelstein et al., 2000). The MMSE is primarily a screening tool, and it should be followed with more thorough testing procedures. Another problem with the MMSE is that it is a less effective tool for African Americans (Mast, Fitzgerald, Steinberg, MacNeill, & Lichtenberg, 2001) and Mexican Americans (Espino, Lichtenstein, Palmer, & Hazuda, 2004). Given these and other problems with the MMSE, geropsychologists are increasingly turning to more sophisticated cognitive and neuropsychological testing methods that examine a broader range of abilities (Mast, MacNeill, & Lichtenberg, 2002).

Interview Measures for Specific Disorders. Several interview-based measures exist for the assessment of specific symptoms. The Geriatric Depression Scale (GDS) includes a true-false set of questions about depressive symptoms which excludes somatic disturbances likely to be endorsed by older adults regardless of their level

of depression (such as changes in energy level or sleep) (Yesavage et al., 1983). The Anxiety Disorders Interview Schedule (ADIS-R) (DiNardo & Barlow, 1988) is useful in assessing older adults, as it has been found to provide ratings in agreement with clinical diagnoses of social phobia, general anxiety disorder, simple phobia, and panic disorder (Scogin et al., 2000). The Hamilton Rating Scale of Depression (Hamilton, 1967) and the Hamilton Anxiety Rating Scale (Hamilton, 1959) have also been tested with older adults and are useful in evaluating both the severity and number of the individual's symptoms.

Self-Report Clinical Inventories. Easier to administer but at the cost of placing greater burden on the test-taker are self-report clinical inventories in which the client answers a set of questions concerning the experience of particular symptoms related to a diagnostic category. Many of these tests were developed for young or middle-aged adults, and therefore their applicability to older adults is either unknown or low. Unlike interviews, the clinician cannot adjust the administration of these measures to the needs or background of the client. Older adults and people from various cultural backgrounds may not interpret the questions as the authors of the test had intended, leading to results that do not provide a valid indication of the client's psychological status.

Treatment

By far, the most common method of medically-based treatments for psychological disorders involves **psychotherapeutic medications**, substances that by their chemical nature alter the individual's brain structure or function. These medications may be prescribed to adults of any age; however, when administered to older adults, clinicians must take precautions to avoid adverse drug reactions. As mentioned previously,

TABLE 11.4
Mini-Mental State Exam

MINIMENTAL LLC

NAME OF SUBJECT _____ Age _____

NAME OF EXAMINER _____ Years of School Completed _____

Approach the patient with respect and encouragement.
Ask: Do you have any trouble with your memory?   ☐ Yes   ☐ No   Date of Examination _____
May I ask you some questions about your memory?   ☐ Yes   ☐ No

SCORE	ITEM
5 ( )	**TIME ORIENTATION** Ask: What is the year _____ (1), season _____ (1), month of the year _____ (1), date _____ (1), day of the week _____ (1)?
5 ( )	**PLACE ORIENTATION** Ask: Where are we now? What's the state _____ (1), city _____ (1), part of the city _____ (1), building _____ (1), floor of the building _____ (1)?
3 ( )	**REGISTRATION OF THREE WORDS** Say: Listen carefully. I am going to say three words. You say them back after I stop. Ready? Here they are. PONY (wait 1 second), QUARTER (wait 1 second), ORANGE (wait 1 second). What were those words? _____ (1) _____ (1) _____ (1) Give 1 point for each correct answer, then repeat them until the patient learns all three.
5 ( )	**SERIAL 7s AS A TEST OF ATTENTION AND CALCULATION** Ask: Subtract 7 from 100 and continue to subtract 7 from each subsequent remainder until I tell you to stop. What is 100 take away 7? _____ (1) Say: Keep Going _____ (1) _____ (1) _____ (1) _____ (1)
3 ( )	**RECALL OF THREE WORDS** Ask: What were those three words I asked you to remember? Give one point for each correct answer. _____ (1) _____ (1) _____ (1)

(continued)

TABLE 11.4   (Continued)
Mini-Mental State Exam

2 ( )   NAMING
Ask:

What is this? (show pencil) _____ (1) What is this? (show watch)

_____ (1)

1 ( )   REPETITION
Say:

Now I am going to ask you to repeat what I say. Ready? No ifs, ands, or buts.

Now you say that _____ (1)

3 ( )   COMPREHENSION
Say:

Listen carefully because I am going to ask you to do something.

Take this paper in your left hand (1), fold it in half (1), and put it on the floor. (1)

1 ( )   READING
Say:

Please read the following and do what it says, but do not say it aloud. (1)

Close your eyes

1 ( )   WRITING
Say:

Please write a sentence. If patient does not respond, say: Write about the weather. (1)

_____

_____

1 ( )   DRAWING
Say: Please copy this design.

TOTAL SCORE _____ Assess level of consciousness along a continuum

	Alert	Drowsy	Stupor	Coma

	YES	NO		YES	NO	FUNCTION BY PROXY			
Cooperative:	☐	☐	Deterioration from			Please record date when patient was			
Depressed:	☐	☐	previous level of			last able to perform the following tasks.			
Anxious:	☐	☐	functioning:	☐	☐	Ask caregiver if patient independently			
Poor Vision:	☐	☐	Family History of			handles:			
Poor Hearing:	☐	☐	Dementia:	☐	☐		YES	NO	DATE
Native Language:			Head Trauma:	☐	☐	Money/Bills:	☐	☐	___
_____			Stroke:	☐	☐	Medication:	☐	☐	___
			Alcohol Abuse:	☐	☐	Transportation: ☐		☐	___
			Thyroid Disease:	☐	☐	Telephone:	☐	☐	___

Source: Folstein & McHugh, 1975.

medications take longer to clear the excretory system of the kidneys, so unless they are prescribed in lower doses for older adults, there is a risk of toxic accumulations in the blood. Another risk is that of **polypharmacy**, in which people receive multiple prescription medications. In addition to having potent effects of their own, psychotherapeutic medications can also interact with other prescription medications. Certain foods, such as cheese and chocolate, may also interact with certain medications, such as some antidepressants. Clinicians must take care to avoid these potentially lethal interactions.

Despite potential drawbacks and side effects, psychotherapeutic medications have proven highly effective (50 to 70%) for older adults in the treatment of depression. Antidepressants can be helpful in alleviating depression even in the oldest-old (Gildengers et al., 2002). These include selective serotonin reuptake inhibitors (SSRI's), the newest form of anti-depressant medications, SSRIs are particularly useful for older adults (Klysner et al., 2002; Mottram, Wilson, Ashworth, & Abou-Saleh, 2002). Unfortunately failure to diagnose depression correctly in older adults may lead to either undertreatment of depressive symptoms or treatment with the wrong medication, such as antianxiety medications rather than antidepressants (Sonnenberg, Beekman, Deeg, & Van Tilburg, 2003).

Lithium carbonate is an effective medication for the treatment of bipolar disorder. To prevent recurrence of manic episodes, the individual must take lithium on a continuous basis.

In cases of severe depression in which medications do not produce results, individuals may undergo **electroconvulsive therapy (ECT)**. In this treatment, an electric current is applied through electrodes attached across the head. The individual suffers seizure-likesymptoms (which can be controlled through muscle relaxants), but the main effect of the treatment is thought to result from the passage of electrical current through the brain. When this method was developed in the 1930s by an Italian neurologist for use in treating epilepsy, it was thought to be most useful for treating schizophrenia. The method fell into disfavor both because of its popular characterization in the media (Ken Kesey's *One Flew over the Cuckoo's Nest*) and its replacement by psychotherapeutic medications. Renewed interest in ECT began to develop in the 1980s when it was found to be an effective method of relief for very severe depression (Manning, 2003) and bipolar disorder (Malhi, Mitchell, & Salim, 2003). As a method of last resort, ECT appears to be an effective alternative for individuals over the age of 60 who have not responded to other forms of treatment (Stoppe, Louza, Rosa, Gil, & Rigonatti, 2006). However, relapse remains a significant concern (Dombrovski & Mulsant, 2007; Tharyan, 2007).

"What do you think?" | **11-5**

Why might the current generation of older adults be reluctant to become involved in therapy?

A number of psychotherapeutic medications are available for the treatment of anxiety disorders in adults. Benzodiazepines, which are the most frequently prescribed antianxiety medications, are highly addictive. They require higher and higher doses to obtain their intended effects, and they are likely to lead to significant withdrawal symptoms, so that the person's symptoms increase after treatment is discontinued. Older adults are particularly vulnerable to these effects and, furthermore, may experience a number of potentially dangerous side effects such as unsteadiness, daytime sleepiness, impaired cognitive functioning, and slowed reaction time (Paterniti, Dufouil, & Alperovitch, 2002). The

Although older adults may be reluctant to seek therapy, when they do, the odds are high that their treatment will be successful.

medication buspirone has fewer of these side effects and would therefore seem to be a safe alternative to benzodiazepines; unfortunately, however, little research has been done on the effectiveness of buspirone with older adults. Furthermore, it must be taken for six to eight weeks before it reduces anxiety, so that it is not helpful for treating the acute symptoms.

Other medications useful in treating anxiety in older adults are the beta-blockers, which reduce sympathetic nervous system activity (Sadavoy & LeClair, 1997). Older adults with certain chronic diseases cannot use this medication, however, because it affects other systems such as the cardiovascular system. SSRIs are another category of medications that are useful in treating people with anxiety disorders, particularly when they also have depressive symptoms. SSRIs are also effective in treating obsessive-compulsive disorder, panic disorder, and social phobias. Other antidepressants, such as tricyclics, tend to be useful in treating obsessive-compulsive and panic disorders.

Medications for the treatment of schizophrenia include the antipsychotic medications known as **neuroleptics**. These medications alter dopamine activity and are effective in reducing delusions and thought disorder and lowering the chance of an individual's experiencing a relapse.

People with early-onset schizophrenia are maintained on these medications for many years, allowing them to live independently in the community. Older adults who develop late-life schizophrenia also seem to respond to neuroleptics. However, they should be given smaller doses, and greater care must be taken with regard to side effects than is true for younger persons (Salzman, 1992). The side effects include confusion and agitation, dizziness, and motor disturbances. Some of these motor disturbances can resemble those of Parkinson's disease. The most serious side effect of neuroleptic medication is tardive dyskinesia, which involves involuntary, repetitive movements, particularly in the muscles of the face. These movements include chewing, moving the jaw from side to side, and rolling the tongue. Other abnormal movements of the body can also occur. Older adults are more likely than younger adults to experience tardive dyskinesia, even after treatment is discontinued (Jeste, Lohr, Eastham, Rockwell, & Caligiuri, 1998). Medications that alter serotonin functioning used for treatment of schizophrenia (clozapine and resperidone) do not produce these effects on motor functioning. However, clozapine can have fatal side effects and must be carefully monitored, particularly in older adults (Meeks, 2000).

Building on the finding that physical fitness is inversely related to mental health (Galper, Trivedi, Barlow, Dunn, & Kampert, 2006), researchers are beginning to explore the use of exercise as a therapeutic tool in the treatment of psychological disorders in later adulthood (Barbour & Blumenthal, 2005). As further data accumulate to support this less conventional intervention, it may increasingly become one of the recommended treatment options for a variety of symptoms experienced by older adults.

Psychotherapy. Although current treatment methods for older adults with psychological disorders tend to focus on the provision of medications, researchers are increasingly providing evidence for the efficacy of psychotherapy in addition to, or instead of, pharmacological interventions (Schulberg et al., 2007). There are challenges to providing psychotherapy for older adults, particularly those who also have physical illnesses and who also have experienced symptoms for a longer period of their lives (Mitchell & Subramaniam, 2005). Older adults, particularly those from diverse racial and ethnic backgrounds, may be either skeptical about or resistant to the idea of receiving psychotherapy. Yet, with appropriate modifications to treatments developed for younger individuals, older adults can benefit from psychotherapy (Zalaquett & Stens, 2006).

In **psychodynamic psychotherapy**, the clinician focuses on unconscious processes, such as conflicts, defense mechanisms, dreams, and issues based on early relationships with parents. The goal of therapy is to rework unconscious conflicts and through this process reduce so-called neurotic symptoms such as anxiety and self-defeating behavior. Therapy based on psychodynamic theory also attempts to strengthen or build the individual's sense of self, enabling the individual to develop clearer boundaries between the self and others. Although psychoanalysis in the classical or traditional sense was intended to be carried out intensively and over a period of many years, current applications within managed care systems (which limit the number of sessions a client may have) involve briefer and more focused therapy aimed at resolving specific issues.

Methods of **humanistic or client-centered therapy** form a second set of approaches to therapy. The emphasis in these methods is on helping the individual gain greater self-acceptance and ultimately achieving fuller expression of the true or underlying self. An important goal of humanistic psychotherapy is to free the individual from anxiety about being rejected or regarded as deficient by others who are important in that person's life. Clients are helped to communicate their needs and perspectives more clearly to others and, in the process, to improve in their relationships and their ability to express the true self.

Behavioral approaches to therapy take specific aim at particular problematic behaviors that the client seeks to change. Treatment of depression is based on the view that depressive symptoms result from lack of pleasant or positively reinforcing events in the individual's life. Clients are given "homework" assignments in which they are instructed to increase the number of pleasant events in their daily lives. Other behavioral methods involve procedures such as **systematic desensitization**, in which a client is taught to replace an unwanted response (such as fear) with a desirable response (such as relaxation). For an individual who is afraid of flying, for example, therapy might involve teaching the individual to relax rather than tense up in various situations that lead up to but do not include flying in an airplane. Another application of behavioral therapy is **contingency management**, in which a specific desirable outcome is made dependent (or "contingent") on the performance of a specific behavior. If you who were trying to stop smoking, for example, you would receive a reward for every period of time during which you did not smoke a cigarette. In behavioral therapies that take advantage of the social learning or social cognitive tradition, the client may be shown a successful "model" of the desired behavior. The **social-cognitive** approach to therapy attempts to raise a client's sense of self-efficacy by enabling the client to have steplike increments in success at completing a previously unattainable goal.

In **cognitive therapy**, the clinician attempts to change the client's maladaptive emotions and ways of coping with difficult situations by changing the client's thoughts (hence the term 'cognitive'). A client with depression, whose depression is related to feelings of low self-esteem, would be taught to avoid certain mental traps that lead to convictions of worthlessness and failure. For example, if you were convinced that any sort of failure is a negative reflection on your worth as a human being, you would obviously be very depressed following an experience in which you failed to attain a desired goal. Psychologists working from the framework of cognitive therapy use a method known as **cognitive restructuring**. The individual is encouraged to develop greater tolerance toward negative experiences and not make sweeping overgeneralizations such as equating one failure with total failure as a person (Ellis, 1998).

The cognitive variant of behavioral treatment, known as **cognitive-behavioral treatment**, involves encouraging the client to develop new behaviors and constructive ways of thinking about the self. For example, the depressed individual would be rewarded for spending more time in positive activities (behavioral) and would be trained to view failures from a more favorable perspective (cognitive).

Cognitive-behavioral therapy can be adapted to a variety of settings, including physician's offices and even the telephone (Arean & Ayalon, 2005). Increasingly, cognitive-behavior therapy is being seen as an effective alternative to antianxiety medications in treating anxiety disorders in older adults (Mohlman & Price, 2006). Relaxation training, a component of cognitive-behavioral therapy, can also be an effective intervention (Ayers, Sorrell, Thorp, & Wetherell, 2007). In this method, the client is taught systematic methods of reducing muscle tension, along with other methods such as deep breathing and education about anxiety.

A number of complicating factors can influence the provision of treatment to individuals seeking psychotherapy in the later adult years. These involve factors that alter both the nature of psychological difficulties experienced by older adults and the nature of the therapeutic process (Hinrichsen & Dick-Siskin, 2000). Older adults particularly those over the age of 75, have a greater probability of physical health impairments, problems that can compromise the effectiveness of therapy (Licht-Strunk, van der Windt, van Marwijk, de Haan, & Beekman, 2007). Changes in identity associated with these impairments can themselves stimulate the need for psychotherapy. However, by boosting the older adult's sense of mastery, even physical limitations can be overcome, and the older person's depressive symptoms can be alleviated (Steunenberg, Beekman, Deeg, Bremmer, & Kerkhof, 2007).

Psychosocial issues may also confront an older adult and should be taken into account in the provision of psychotherapy involving relationships with family. Death of family and friends, changes in relationships with children and spouses, and the need to provide care to a spouse or parent are additional problems faced by older adult clients. Finally, the social context can play an important role in influencing the outcome of treatment. Just as there are relationships between mental health and SES, there is a link between the effectiveness of antidepressant treatment and social class. Over the course of a 20-week period, older adults from lower social classes were found to be less likely to respond to a combination of psychotherapy and medication than individuals in middle and high income brackets (Cohen et al., 2006).

Clinicians have proposed treatments geared specifically to older adults. In a variant of traditional psychodynamic therapy, **life review therapy** (Butler, 1974) involves helping the older adult rework past experiences with the goal of gaining greater acceptance of previous life events. The purpose of this process is to facilitate the natural reminiscence process that accompanies the ego integrity versus despair psychosocial issue, as described by Erikson (see

Chapter 8). There is some evidence that life review therapy is beneficial to older adults with mild symptoms of depression, but for people with severe symptoms, the evoking of painful memories from the past can have negative effects (King & Markus, 2000).

Behavioral treatment that focuses on increasing the number of positive reinforcements in the individual's life is another beneficial treatment of depression in older adults (Teri, 1994). Such an approach is based on the notion that older adults may be experiencing depressive symptoms owing to decreases in pleasant events associated with physical changes, loss of friends, and loss of rewarding social roles. Cognitive-behavioral therapy appears to have considerable relevance to work with older depressed clients, particularly for those who have a tendency to focus excessively on age-related changes in physical functioning, memory, and health. The elements of cognitive-behavioral treatment for older adults

with depression include instructing clients to keep track of their pleasant and unpleasant events, helping them understand the relationship between their mood and these behaviors, looking for changes that can be made in daily life, increasing their social skills, and teaching them to be alert to and try to change their negative thoughts about the self (Satre, Knight, & David, 2006). Learning how to manage their health by taking an active role in their own treatment is another cognitive-behavioral intervention that can reduce the experience of depressive symptoms (Wrosch, Schulz, & Heckhausen, 2002). Social skills can also be taught through cognitive-behavioral methods to older adults suffering from schizophrenia, allowing them to have more satisfactory interactions with others in their environment (Patterson et al., 2003).

For these elements of therapy to succeed, older adult clients may need to be given help

FIGURE 11.8
Prevalence of Serious Distress by Age, United States

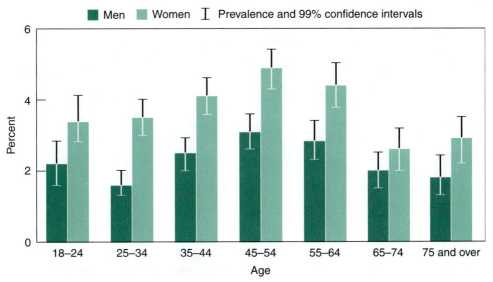

30-day prevalence of serious psychological distress by age and sex, National Health Interview Study 2001–2004.
Source: Pratt, Dey, & Cohen, 2007.

FIGURE 11.9

Psychological Distress by Age and Sex, Australians

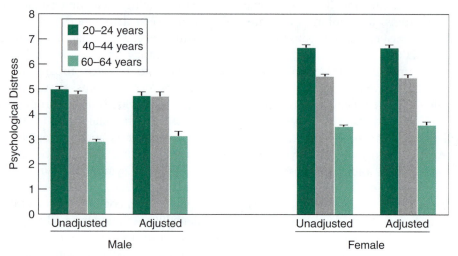

Psychological distress among males and females by age group, unadjusted and adjusted for risk factors.

Source: Jorm et al., 2005.

in learning to view therapy as a collaborative process in which they have an active role (King & Markus, 2000). This approach is more likely to have success with clients who have more education and are comfortable with the idea of receiving "homework." On the other hand, some clients who are seeking to gain greater insight into the nature of their symptoms may feel that cognitive-behavioral therapy does not delve deeply enough into underlying psychological processes (Zeiss & Steffan, 1996).

In contrast to treatment approaches focusing on one specific form of treatment, clinicians are also recommending that integration occur across models. In an integrative approach, the clinician working within one framework would select therapeutic methods based on other models that meet the client's specific needs and situations (Hillman & Stricker, 2002). For example a psychodynamically oriented clinician working with a depressed older adult woman may incorporate behavioral methods, psychotherapeutic medication, and the involvement of family and other health care providers.

Interpersonal therapy (IPT) integrates cognitive methods with a focus on social factors that contribute to psychological disturbance. Interpersonal therapy involves a combination of methods, but the main focus is on training in social skills, interpersonal relationships, and methods of conflict resolution. In one controlled study of the effects of monthly interpersonal therapy ("maintenance") combined with a tricyclic antidepressant, 80% remained free of symptoms for the three-year period during which they were followed. Even individuals in the over-70 group showed significant and lasting benefits from this combined treatment (Reynolds et al., 1999). Researchers investigating the long-term efficacy of IPT continue to demonstrate its effectiveness as an adjunct to or replacement of pharmacological interventions (Schulberg et al., 2007).

Generational differences between current cohorts of older adults and the middle-aged individuals more commonly seen in psychotherapy must be taken into account by clinicians working with this age group. Older adults may be skeptical about the therapy process, having been less socialized than younger cohorts to accept the need for psychological interventions. Part of therapy may involve educating older adult clients to feel less embarrassed or stigmatized by the process. An additional factor that can alter the nature of therapy for older adults is the existence of sensory and cognitive impairments, which affect the nature of communication between clinician and client. Finally, when the therapist is younger than the client, there is the possibility that the client sees the therapist as a "child" and therefore reacts differently than would be the case if the age differences were reversed. It is also possible that the therapist brings to the situation negative attitudes and stereotypes about aging that complicate the therapeutic relationship with the older adult client.

Although therapy can have many beneficial effects, equally important as treatment is prevention. Targeting specific older adults at risk, such as those who have become bereaved and have experienced illness or disability, can help to reduce not only the need for treatment but also maximize the psychological functioning of older adults who might otherwise develop disorders such as depression (Schoevers et al., 2006).

REPORTS OF SUBJECTIVE DISTRESS

Despite the presence of chronic physical health conditions in adulthood, the majority of older adults are able to retain a positive sense of subjective mental health. The National Health Interview Survey, which tracks the incidence of serious psychological distress, consistently reports lower rates of distress for adults 65 and older (2.3 in 65 and older vs. 2.8 in those 18 to 24), although these rates vary by gender, race, health and poverty status (Pratt, Dey, & Cohen, 2007).

These results are not limited to the United States. A large-scale investigation of nearly 7,500 adults in Australia ages 20 to 64 showed lower rates of anxiety and psychological distress among the older age groups (Jorm et al., 2005). Clearly, although older adults are at higher risk in an objective sense for experiencing psychological disorders, a combination of selective survival, enhanced use of coping mechanisms, and an ability to maintain an optimistic attitude toward adversity seem to offer significant protective factors against psychological problems in later adulthood. Increasingly, new methods of treatment are becoming available to provide services to those older adults who need assistance in these adaptive processes.

In summary, when we think of the aging process, we are likely to anticipate a number of ill effects. By contrast, the facts reveal that older adults are highly resilient to the physical, psychological, and social changes involved in the aging process. It is nevertheless true that there will be an increasing need for trained mental health workers in the coming decades, and there will also be an increased need for research on effective treatment methods for aging individuals in need of intervention.

SUMMARY

1. Psychological disorders are those behaviors that significantly alter the individual's adaptation. The DSM-IV-TR contains descriptions of the disorders that can affect children and adults; unfortunately it was not specifically written with the concerns of older adults in mind. In many cases, there are differences between the over-65 and under-65

populations of adults in the way that these disorders are manifested in behavior. Axis I disorders include clinical syndromes (organized patterns of disturbances), and Axis II includes personality disorders and mental retardation.

2. Epidemiological surveys place the prevalence of psychological disorders at between one-third to one-half of the adult population. There is a lower prevalence of all disorders among adults over the age of 65 years. Depressive symptoms are more likely to be found in the over-65 population than in the under-65 population. Older adults are more likely to experience physical symptoms of depression and are less likely to express emotional disturbances such as guilt or suicidality. Health care professionals may not be attuned to diagnosing depressive symptoms in older adults. Anxiety is also a relatively common disorder in the older adult population, and like mood disorders, estimates of anxiety symptoms are higher than estimates of the prevalence of anxiety disorders. It is thought that PTSD prevalence in the over-65 population will increase as Vietnam veterans become older. The majority of cases of schizophrenia emerge before the age of 40; cases that originate late in adulthood are referred to as late-onset schizophrenia. Delirium, dementia, and cognitive disorders form another category of Axis I disorders. Substance-related disorders are more likely to occur in younger adults. However, alcohol abuse and dependence are becoming an area of concern for the over-65 population, as are disorders related to the use of prescription medications.

3. The personality disorders are found in Axis II of the DSM-IV-TR. According to the maturation hypothesis, adults with personality disorders in the immature category experience fewer symptoms in later life. This hypothesis is consistent with data on a reduction in the traits and behaviors associated with psychopathy (antisocial personality disorder) among older adults.

4. Two additional topics of concern in the area of mental health and aging are elder abuse and suicide. According to nationwide surveys, the incidence of elder abuse is as high as 5% of older adults unfortunately, the large majority of cases normally escape detection. Adult children are most likely to be perpetrators of abuse. White men over the age of 85 have the highest risk of suicide in the population of the United States. The problem of suicide in older adults is exacerbated by the fact that older persons who are experiencing suicidal thoughts are unlikely to communicate these thoughts to health practitioners.

5. The field of clinical geropsychology involves the provision of psychological services to older adults. Treatment begins with thorough assessment. A number of tools are available that can be applied specifically to persons in later life. These tools range from clinical interviews to structured self-report inventories. Assessment of people within this age group requires that the clinician adapt the test materials and the testing situation to the specific needs and cognitive or sensory limitations of the older adult. Therapy methods range from somatic treatments such as ECT and medications to psychotherapy. Cognitive and interpersonal therapy methods appear to hold considerable promise for treatment of older adults.

6. Despite the many threats to positive mental health, the majority of older adults do not report elevated levels of subjective distress.

CHAPTER 12

Long-Term Care

> **"***A proud and resourceful nation can no longer ask its older people to live in constant fear of a serious illness for which adequate funds are not available. We owe them the right of dignity in sickness as well as in health.***"**
>
> John F. Kennedy
> (1917–1963)

Have you ever lived in an institutional facility? Your tendency may be to answer "no," unless you have been hospitalized for a physical or psychological disorder. However, think about the question in a slightly different way. An institutional facility is any residential setting in which nonfamily members are cared for under one roof. A dormitory is, according to this definition, an "institution." People living in dormitories, just as those who live in what we normally think of as an institution, must deal with problems inherent in communal living, such as noise, smell, the people in charge, poor food, rooms that are too hot or too cold, and rude or messy roommates. Imagine now what it would be like to adapt to these many problems in the environment if you were infirmed and in need of long-term care.

An institutional facility is one that provides individuals with medical or psychiatric care along with programs intended to restore lost functioning. Hospitals are short-term institutional facilities to which people are admitted with the understanding that they will be discharged when they no longer need round-the-clock treatment. At the other end of the spectrum are residential facilities into which an individual moves more or less permanently after no longer being able to live in an independent home setting.

Closely related to the issue of treatment is that of funding for health care, which is also covered in this chapter. Individuals in later life who must be hospitalized for physical and psychological problems increasingly are confronting the rising cost of health care as a barrier to effective resolution of their difficulties. In addition to the problems that result from failure to receive proper treatment, this situation creates considerable stress and anguish for the older individual.

Although you probably do not spend much time wondering about what coverage you will have for health care when you get older, if you have been following discussions of public funding for health insurance programs, you know that this is one of the most crucial issues facing the United States and many other countries as well. Changes are taking place in this area on almost a month-to-month basis in the current U.S. health care scene and are certain to become an even larger preoccupation in the years ahead.

INSTITUTIONAL FACILITIES FOR LONG-TERM CARE

People with chronic disabilities, cognitive disorders, or physical infirmities which keep them from living independently may receive treatment in one of a variety of institutional long-term care settings. These institutions range from hospital-like facilities to residential living situations with minimal food and services.

Nursing Homes

For individuals whose illness or disability requires daily nursing care as well as other support services, nursing homes provide comprehensive care in a single setting. A **nursing home** is a residence that provides a room, meals, skilled nursing and rehabilitative care, medical services, and protective supervision. The care provided in nursing homes includes treating problems that residents have in the areas of cognition, communication, hearing, vision, physical functioning, continence (regulation of the elimination of urine and feces), psychosocial functioning, mood and behavior, nutrition, oral and dental care, skin condition, and medications. Residents may receive urinary training programs, assistance with feeding and mobility, rehabilitative activities, and social services.

Typically, nursing homes are thought of as permanent residences for the older adults who

enter them, but about 30% of residents are discharged and able to move back into the community. About one-quarter of people admitted to nursing homes die there, and another 36% move to another facility (Sahyoun, Pratt, Lentzner, Dey, & Robinson, 2001).

| "*What do you think?*" | 12-1 |

Would you consider placing a chronically ill relative in a nursing home? Why or why not? What would you look for in a nursing home?

Nursing homes are certified by State and Federal governmental agencies to provide services at one or more levels of care. **Skilled nursing facilities** provide the most intensive nursing care available outside of a hospital. The nursing services provided at this level of care include applying dressings or bandages, providing bowel and bladder retraining, catheterization, enemas, full bed baths, injections, irrigation, nasal feeding, oxygen therapy, and measurement of temperature, pulse, respiration, or blood pressure. In an **intermediate care facility**, health-related services are provided to individuals who do not require hospital or skilled nursing facility care but do require institutional care above the level of room and board. There are also intermediate care facilities specifically designated for people who have mental retardation and are unable to live on their own in the community.

Nursing home services have become big business in the United States. In the year 2006, nursing home expenditures were estimated to be $126 billion, or about 6% of the total health care expenditures in the United States (Center for Medicare and Medicaid Services, 2007). As of 2004, there were approximately 16,000 nursing homes in the Unites States with a total of over 1.7 million beds, 86% of which were occupied (National Center for Health Statistics, 2006).

These residents of a nursing home are engaging in a lively conversation over a game of cards.

Residential Care Facilities

An alternative to a nursing home is a **residential care facility**, which provides 24-hour supportive care services and supervision to individuals who do not require skilled nursing care. The services they provide include meals, housekeeping, and assistance with personal care such as bathing and grooming. Some may provide other services such as management of medications and social and recreational activities.

Board and Group Homes.   Board and care homes are group living arrangements that are designed to meet the needs of people who cannot live on their own in the community but who also need some nursing services. Typically, these homes provide help with activities of daily living such as bathing, dressing, and toileting. Although it would seem from the name as though these homes provide a "homelike" setting, this is apparently not the case. A survey conducted by the Institute of Medicine determined that the

services provided in these facilities do not adjust the care they provide to the specific needs of the residents. They are typically understaffed and the staff who work in these settings are not required to receive training (Wunderlich, Kohler, & Committee on Improving Quality in Long-Term Care, 2001).

Group Homes.   Group homes provide independent, private living in a house shared by several older individuals. Residents split the cost of rent, housekeeping services, utilities, and meals.

Assisted Living Facilities.   **Assisted living** facilities are housing complexes in which older persons live independently in their own apartments. The residents pay a regular monthly rent that usually includes meal service in communal dining rooms, transportation for shopping and appointments, social activities, and housekeeping service. Some facilities have health services available on location. These facilities are

FIGURE 12.1

Percent Distribution of Nursing Homes by Bed size: United States Selected Years

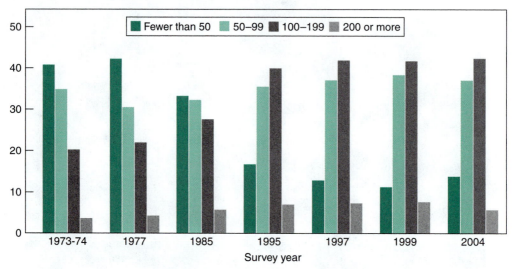

Percent of nursing homes by size from 1973 to 2004. As can be seen from the figure nursing homes are growing larger.

Source: http://www.cdc.gov/nchs/about/major/nnhsd/nnhschart.htm

professionally managed and licensed and may be one of several levels of care that are provided within the same housing community. The cost for living in an assisted living facility may range from hundreds to thousands of dollars a month. In some states, funds may be available for those who cannot afford to live in these facilities on their own through government support programs. However, most residents pay the rental and other fees out of their own funds.

The philosophy of assisted living is that private, residentially oriented buildings are combined with high levels of service that allow for "aging in place" so that residents can live within the same environment even if they undergo changes in their health or physical and cognitive functioning. However, many facilities do not achieve these goals. Moreover they are too expensive for the moderate- and low-income older adults and those that are affordable do not offer high levels of service or privacy (Wunderlich et al., 2001).

Adult Foster Care.   An older adult may receive adult foster care, in which a family provides care in their home. The services provided in these settings include meals, housekeeping and help with dressing, eating, bathing, and other personal care. These settings offer some advantages because of their home-like feeling, but because they are small and rely on a live-in caregiver for help with personal care, cooking, housekeeping, and activities, that caregiver's resources may be spread thin. If one resident becomes ill and must receive more nursing care, other residents may suffer from lack of attention. Another possible disadvantage is that residents may feel that they have less privacy than they do in a residential care setting (Wunderlich et al., 2001).

COMMUNITY-BASED FACILITIES

There are a variety of support services designed to allow older adults, even those with some form of disability, to live on their own in the community. Some of these services are offered by volunteer groups at no cost to the individual. Others are fee based and of these services, some may be paid for by Medicare.

Home Health Services

An increasing number of older adults who are ill or disabled are able to maintain an independent life in the community by utilizing **home health services**. A variety of services are available within this broad category of care. Such services include "Meals on Wheels," the provision of a hot meal once a day; so-called friendly visiting, in which someone comes to the home for a social visit; and assistance with shopping. Other home-based services can include laundry, cooking, and cleaning.

Researchers have found that home health care that simulates the types of restorative services provided in nursing homes such as physical therapy, speech therapy, occupational therapy, rehabilitation, and interventions targeted at particular areas of functional decline can help to maintain the older person in the home longer without needing to be institutionalized or needing emergency room care (Tinetti et al., 2002).

> *"What do you think?"* | **12-2**
>
> What would you think about living in an assisted living or continuing care retirement community when you become older? What might be the advantages and disadvantages of such an arrangement?

Meals on Wheels programs are often a part of home health services, which allow older adults to remain in their homes rather than requiring institutionalization. Volunteer Dr. Sheldon Ekland-Olson (left), Provost of the University of Texas, is shown here providing a packaged lunch to a participant in the Austin Meals on Wheels and More Program.

In 2000, nearly 1 million persons 65 years of age and over were home health care patients. The majority are women, and over half are 75 and older (Centers for Disease Prevention and Control, 2003b). Almost all live in private homes, and half live with family members (Munson, 1999). In the year 2006, $53.4 billion was spent by the U.S. government on home health care (Center for Medicare and Medicaid Services, 2007).

Geriatric Partial Hospital

In a **geriatric partial hospital**, daily outpatient therapy is provided with intensive, structured multidisciplinary services to older persons who have recently been discharged from a psychiatric hospital. The partial hospital may also serve as an alternative to hospitalization. Therapists in this setting focus on medication management and compliance, social functioning, discharge planning, and relapse prevention. A less intense program than the geriatric partial hospital program is **geriatric continuing day treatment** in which clients attend a day treatment program three days a week but are encouraged to live independently during the remaining days of the week. **Day care centers** are another form of community treatment in which individuals receive supervised meals and activities on a daily basis.

Accessory Dwelling Units

An older adult may be housed in a separate apartment in a relative's home. An accessory dwelling unit, also known as an "in-law apartment," is a second living space in the home that allows the older adult to have independent living quarters, cooking space, and a bathroom.

Subsidized Housing

Other alternatives in community care involve the provision of housing in addition to specialized services that can maintain the person in an independent living situation. **Subsidized senior housing** is provided for individuals with low to moderate incomes. People using subsidized housing live in low-rent apartment complexes and have access to help with routine tasks such as housekeeping, shopping and laundry.

Continuing Care Retirement Community (CCRC)

A more comprehensive community living setting is a **continuing care retirement community (CCRC)**, which is a housing community that provides different levels of care based on the residents' needs. The levels of care they provide range from independent living apartments to skilled nursing care in an affiliated nursing home. Within the same CCRC, there may be individual homes or apartments where residents can live independently, an assisted living facility, and a nursing home. Residents move from one setting to another based on their needs, but they continue to remain part of their CCRC community. Many CCRCs require a large payment prior to admission and also charge monthly fees. Some communities are beginning to allow residents to rent rather than buy into the facility.

Residents moving into CCRCs typically sign a contract that specifies the conditions under which they will receive long-term care. One option provides unlimited nursing care for a small increase in monthly payments. A second type of contract includes a predetermined amount of long-term nursing care; beyond this the resident is responsible for additional payments. In the third option, the resident pays fees for service, which means full daily rates for all long-term nursing care.

There are advantages to living in CCRCs. In addition to the relative ease of moving from one level of care to another, the CCRCs provide social activities, access to community facilities, transportation services, companionship, access to health care, housekeeping, and maintenance. Residents may travel, take vacations, and become involved in activities outside the community itself.

CCRCs are accredited by a commission sponsored by the American Association of Homes and Services for the Aging. To be accredited, a CCRC must pass a two and one-half day test that evaluates the facility's governance and administration, resident services, finance, and health care.

President Lyndon B. Johnson signing the Medicare bill into effect on July 30, 1965.

THE FINANCING OF LONG-TERM CARE

It is difficult to open the newspaper or turn on the television without hearing a discussion of the urgent need in the United States to address the economic issues involved in health care. These discussions often occur in the context of other issues affecting adults using a wide range of health care services, from outpatient medical care to private psychotherapy. Changes in health maintenance organizations (HMOs) have created havoc in many sectors of the health care industry, causing great anxiety among the public, politicians, and health care professionals. In many ways, the health care financing crisis is a function of the huge expenses associated with the long-term care of older adults. Insecurity over the financing of health care can constitute a crisis for adults of any age, but particularly so for older persons who have limited financial resources. The ability to receive proper treatment for chronic conditions is therefore both a social and an individual issue.

As you will see shortly, nursing homes and other facilities in which older adults receive treatment are subject to strict federal and state requirements to ensure that they comply with the standards set forth in the legislation that created the funding programs. The intimate connection between financing and regulation of these long-term care facilities has provided the incentive for nursing homes to raise their level of care so that they can qualify for this support.

Long-term health care financing has a history dating back to the early 1900s and the nation's first attempts to devise government health insurance programs. In the ensuing century, as these programs began to be established, their benefits structure and financing grew increasingly complex and diversified. Throughout this process, the developers of these plans, which involve state and federal agencies along with private insurance companies, have attempted to respond to the rapidly changing needs of the population and the even more rapidly changing nature of the United States economy.

Medicare

After considering and debating a variety of long-term health care plans for older adults, the U.S. Congress passed legislation as part of the Social Security Amendments of 1965 establishing the Medicare and the Medicaid programs. Title XVIII, known as **Medicare**, is entitled Health Insurance for the Aged and Disabled. The Medicare legislation established a health

insurance program for older adults to complement the insurance provided by Title II of the
Social Security Act to retirees, survivors, and
disabled persons. Since its enactment, Medicare has been subject to numerous legislative
and administrative changes designed to improve
health care services to older adults, the disabled, and the poor. In 1973 the program
was expanded to broaden eligibility to those
already receiving Social Security benefits, people
over 65 who qualify for Social Security benefits, and individuals with end-stage renal disease
requiring continuous dialysis or kidney trans-
plant. The Department of Health and Human
Services (DHHS) has the overall responsibility
for administration of the Medicare program, with
the assistance of the Social Security Administration (SSA). In 1977, the Health Care Financing
Administration (HCFA) was established under
the DHHS to administer Medicare and Medicaid;
it was replaced in July 2001 by the Centers for
Medicare & Medicaid Services (CMS) as part of
a large-scale reform of services to beneficiaries.
CMS has responsibility for formulation of policy and guidelines, oversight and operation of
contracts, maintenance and review of records,
and general financing. State agencies also play a
role in the regulation and administration of the
Medicare program in consultation with CMS.

"What do you think?"	12-3

Do you think that Medicare should provide
coverage for prescription drugs? Why or
why not?

Medicare Part A (Hospital Insurance or HI)
coverage includes the cost of a semiprivate
hospital room, meals, regular nursing services, operating and recovery room, intensive
care, inpatient prescription drugs, laboratory
tests, X-rays, psychiatric hospital, and inpatient

rehabilitation. All other medically necessary services and supplies provided in the hospital are
also completely covered. Luxury items, cosmetic
surgery, vision care, private nursing, private
rooms (unless necessary for medical reasons),
and rentals of television and telephone are not
included in coverage.

Coverage in a skilled nursing facility includes
rehabilitation services and appliances (walkers,
wheelchairs) in addition to those services normally covered for inpatient hospitalization. Home
health services are also included in Part A of
Medicare. Although there is no charge for these
services, patients must pay 20% of the costs of all
durable medical equipment. Finally, hospice care
is covered by Medicare Part A. Respite periods
are also covered for hospice care to allow a break
for the patient's caregiver.

Medicare Part B provides benefits available
to individuals age 65 and over with payment
of a monthly premium that, as of 2007, varies
according to the individual's income. Included in
Part B services are preventive treatments, including glaucoma and diabetes screenings as well as
bone scans, mammograms, and colonoscopies.
Other covered services include laboratory tests,
chiropractor visits, eye exams, dialysis, and mental health care, occupational therapy, outpatient
treatment, flu shots, and home health services. A
one-time physical is also included in Part B.

Part C of Medicare involves coverage
through private health plans. Established by
the Balanced Budget Act of 1997 (Public Law
105-33), it was put into effect in 1998. The
Medicare Moderanization Act of 2003 subsequently modified Medicare Part B. Beginning in
2006, Preferred Provider Organizations (PPOs)
began to serve beneficiaries on a regional basis.
The Department of Health and Human Services
identified 26 regions across the Nation in which
PPO plans compete to provide services. HHS
established these regions to ensure all Medicare
beneficiaries, including those in small states and

FIGURE 12.2
Health Care Expenditures Among Medicare Enrollees, 1992 and 2003

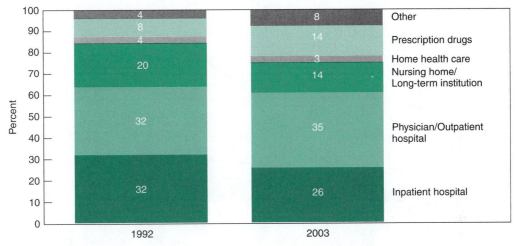

Out-of-pocket costs and costs covered by insurance for Medicare enrollees.

Source: Federal Interagency Forum on Aging-Related Statistics, 2006.

rural areas, would have the opportunity to enroll in a PPO and to encourage plans to participate. In 2006, 16 percent of beneficiaries were enrolled in Medicare Advantage plans, and by 2009, this number is projected to increase to 24 percent. Medicare beneficiaries who have both Part A and Part B can choose to get their benefits through a variety of risk-based plans including HMOs, PPOs, private fee-for service plans, and a health insurance policy administered by the federal government.

Beginning in 2006, **Part D of Medicare** went into effect, providing almost full prescription drug benefits. Medicare pays 75% of drug costs between a deductible of $250 and $2,250. Between $2,250 and $5,100 per year, beneficiaries pay all drug costs. However, when drug costs exceed $5,100 per year, Medicare pays 95%. Critics of the new legislation argue that these prescription privileges do not go far enough. In addition to the large deductible when costs are between $2,250 and $5,100, older adults who sign up for this plan are no longer eligible to receive prescription benefits through private insurance companies. Skyrocketing prescription drug costs exacerbate the problem. Of the 50 drugs most commonly used by older adults, the average annual cost per prescription is $1,000 or more. Hence the new prescription privileges leave many older adults with significant out-of-pocket expenses for medications required to maintain them in good health.

Medicare has grown enormously since its inception. In 1966 Medicare covered 19.1 million people at a cost of $1.8 billion. By 2007 over 36.7 million Americans 65 and older were covered (Center for Medicare and Medicaid, 2007). The total benefits paid out by Medicare totaled over $342 billion in 2005 or 17% of all expenditures by the United States on health care (http://www.cms.hhs.gov/NationalHealthExpend Data/02_NationalHealthAccountsHistorical.asp# TopOfPage) and 13% of the total United States budget (Roy & Cairns, 2007). The percent of the gross domestic product spent on Medicare is projected roughly to triple over the next 70 years.

FIGURE 12.3

Medicare Spending from 1971–2081

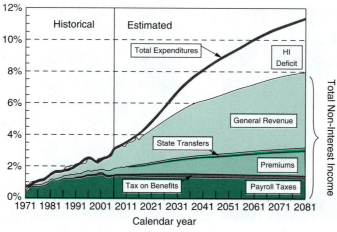

Medicare expenditures and noninterest income by source as a percent of the gross domestic product (GDP).

Source: Social Security Trust Fund Report, 2007.

Medicare's funding comes from payroll taxes, premiums, general revenue from income taxes, and some payments from the states. By the year 2015, there will be a deficit in the total Medicare budget because expenditures will be greater than its income. The gap between expenditures and income will continue to increase steadily through at least the year 2081. The situation was considered grave enough so that in its annual report of 2007, the Social Security Trustees issued a warning that the program is on its way to becoming unsustainable (Social Security Trust Fund Report, 2007).

Medicaid

Title XIX of the Social Security Act of 1965, known as **Medicaid**, is a federal and state matching entitlement program that pays for medical assistance for certain individuals and families with low incomes and resources.Initially, Medicaid was formulated as a medical care extension of federally funded programs providing income assistance for the poor, with an emphasis on dependent children and their mothers, the disabled, and the over-65. Eligibility for Medicaid has expanded, however, and now is available to a larger number of low-income pregnant women, poor children, and some Medicare beneficiaries who are not eligible for any cash assistance program. Changes in legislation have also focused on increased access, better quality of care, specific benefits, enhanced outreach programs, and fewer limits on services. Another change is the addition of managed care as an alternative means of providing health services.

Medicaid provides assistance for a wide range of medical services for those who fall in the category for their state of residence of being in need. For older adults these services include inpatient and outpatient hospital services, physician services, nursing facility services, home health care for persons eligible for skilled nursing services, laboratory and X-ray services, prescribed drugs and prosthetic devices, optometrist services and eyeglasses, rehabilitation and physical therapy services, and home and community-based care to cover certain chronic impairments.

Individuals covered by Medicare who are not otherwise "poor" may nevertheless require Medicaid when their benefits have run out and they cannot afford to pay their medical expenses. Many states have a "medically needy" program for such individuals, who have too much income to qualify as categorically needy. This program allows them to "spend down" to the point at which they are eligible for Medicaid by paying medical expenses to offset their excess income. Medicaid then pays the remaining portion of their medical bills by providing services and supplies that are available under their state's Medicaid program. Services that are covered by both programs will be paid first by Medicare and the difference by Medicaid, up to the state's payment limit. Medicaid also covers additional services (e.g., nursing facility care beyond the 100-day limit covered by Medicare, prescription drugs, eyeglasses, and hearing aids).

Medicaid is the largest source of funding for medical and health-related services for those in need of assistance. In 2005 it provided health care assistance amounting to $177 billion. Nursing homes received $53.5 billion from Medicaid in 2005. Together Medicare and Medicaid financed $519 billion in health care services in 2005, which was 26% of the nation's total health care bill (private and public funding combined) and 81% of all federal spending on health (http://www.cms.hhs.gov/NationalHealthExpend Data/02_NationalHealthAccountsHistorical.asp# TopOfPage).

LEGISLATIVE ISSUES IN CARE OF OLDER ADULTS

The regulation of nursing homes and community-based services for older adults and the disabled is a major focus of health policy and legislation in the United States. This is in large part because

funding of these services is provided by federal and state agencies.

1987 Omnibus Budget Reconciliation Act of 1987 (OBRA 1987)

The current laws governing the operation of institutional facilities have their origins in a report to Congress in 1986 by the Institute of Medicine called "Improving the Quality of Care in Nursing Homes." This report recommended major changes in the quality and nature of services provided to nursing home residents. The result of the report was the Omnibus Budget Reconciliation Act of 1987 that included the **Nursing Home Reform Act** ("reconciliation" in this context means an expedited process in the U.S. Congress that applies to government spending programs as a way of expediting the budgetary process in these cases). OBRA 1987 mandated that facilities must meet physical standards, provide adequate professional staffing and services, and maintain policies governing the administrative and medical procedures of the nursing facility. A significant component of this legislation was the provision of safeguards to assure quality of care and protection of residents' rights. The bottom line is that each resident must be provided with services and activities to attain or maintain the highest practicable physical, mental, and psychosocial well-being. Facilities are required to care for residents in a manner and an environment that promotes, maintains, or enhances quality of life.

The conditions of the Nursing Home Reform Act specify that nursing homes must be licensed in accordance with state and local laws, including all applicable laws pertaining to staff, licensing, and registration, fire, safety, and communicable diseases. They must have a governing body legally responsible for policies and the appointment of a qualified administrator. One or more physicians must be on call at all times to cover an emergency, and there must be 24-hour nursing care services, including at least one full-time registered nurse. The facility must admit eligible patients regardless of race, color, or national origin.

The specific services that are required in addition to availability of physicians and nurses are specialized rehabilitation, social services, pharmaceutical services, dietary services, dental services, and an ongoing activities program. The goal of the activities program should be to encourage self-care and the individual's return to normal life in the community through social, religious, and recreational activities, and by visits with relatives and friends. Nursing homes are required to maintain confidential records, employ appropriate methods for obtaining and dispensing medications, and have arrangements for obtaining required clinical, laboratory, X-ray, and other diagnostic services.

The series of resident rights developed as part of the Nursing Home Reform Act include choice of physician and treatment, freedom from physical and mental abuse, the right to privacy and treatment with respect and dignity, the right to confidential records, and the right to have needs and preferences met. In addition, residents have the right to refuse medications and treatments, voice their grievances, and transfer or leave the facility when appropriate. They are also required to be informed in writing about services and fees before entering the nursing home, to have the right to manage their own money (or choose someone to do so), and be able to keep personal belongings and property to the extent that these do not interfere with the rights, health, or safety of others.

The legislation also established procedures to ensure that all conditions are met for maintaining compliance with the law. These procedures include monitoring of the performance of facilities by outside survey agencies to determine whether they comply with the federal conditions of participation.

1997 Balanced Budget Act

Changes to the nursing home rates for posthospital care were incorporated into the Balanced Budget Act of 1997 and implemented in March 2000. These changes involved moving to a prospective payment system in which rates paid to **skilled nursing facilities** cover the costs of furnishing most covered nursing home services, excluding payment for physicians and certain other practitioner services. Under the prospective payment system, each facility receives a fixed amount for treating patients diagnosed with a given illness, regardless of the length of stay or type of care received. Prior to this system, nursing homes filed bills to Medicare based on fee-for-service. The intention of the change in payments was to curb the rapidly rising costs of Medicare as well as to adjust the payments to the specific needs of the patient. By paying more for the patients whose medical expenses are legitimately higher than those who have less expensive medical needs, nursing homes can provide better health care, adjusted for the needs of the individual resident.

1998 Nursing Home Initiative

Ten years after the Nursing Home Reform Act was put into place, a series of investigations and Senate hearings called attention to weaknesses in federal and state survey and enforcement activities that constituted serious threats to the well-being of residents (http://research.aarp.org/health/fs83_reform.html). In 1997, the U.S. Senate Committee on Aging received reports that documented inadequate care in California nursing homes that led to widespread death and suffering of residents. These reports triggered a hearing in 1998 by the Committee on California nursing homes. At this hearing, a General Accountability Office (GAO) report revealed that there was weak enforcement of the NHRA, putting many residents at risk of inadequate care. Fully 98% of nursing homes were found to have more than minimal (35%), substandard (33%), or serious (30%) deficiencies. Particularly troubling was the fact that even when serious problems were identified, there was no enforcement of actions that would ensure that the deficiencies were corrected and did not recur.

These shocking reports about nursing home abuse made it clear that NHRA enforcement procedures were not working. In response to these findings, President Bill Clinton's administration announced the 1998 Nursing Home Initiative. This Initiative proposed a series of steps designed to improve enforcement of nursing home quality standards that were then adopted by HCFA. These included altering the timing of nursing home inspections to include both weekends and evenings as well as weekdays, providing more frequent inspectors of previous violators, imposing immediate sanctions on nursing homes found guilty of a second offense involving violations that harm residents, allowing states to impose monetary penalties on violators, and not lifting sanctions against offenders until an onsite visit verifies that they are now complying with federal regulations. The result of these efforts was increased federal spending to ensure that states are providing adequate survey and certification, raising the amount budgeted for these activities from $290 million in 1998 to $359 million in 2000.

Congressional Hearings on Nursing Home Abuse

Following the California study and the announcement of the 1998 Nursing Home Initiative, GAO and HCFA conducted additional research that included nursing homes nationwide. In September 2000, a Senate Committee on Aging held a hearing on the outcomes of the Nursing Home Initiatives which revealed that the Initiatives had resulted in improvements to state survey and federal oversight procedures, including increases in the number of surveyors, improved tracking of complaints, new methods to detect serious deficiencies, and improved organization of nursing home oversight activities (http://research.aarp.org/health/fs83_reform.html). However, additional hearings on nursing home quality held by the Senate Committee on Aging in 1999 and 2000 revealed that nursing home abuse remained a serious problem. These hearings revealed that nationwide, 27% of nursing homes were cited with violations causing actual harm to residents or placing them at risk of death or serious injury; another 43% were cited for violations that created a potential for more than minimal harm. These hearings also revealed flaws in the surveys; significant problems were often missed, such as pressure sores, malnutrition, and dehydration. In some cases, the nursing homes were cited because a member of the nursing staff committed acts of abuse against residents such as beatings, sexual abuse, and verbal abuse (Abuse of Residents Is a Major Problem in U.S. Nursing Homes Prepared for Rep. Henry A. Waxman Minority Staff Special Investigations Division Committee on Government Reform U.S. House of Representatives July 30, 2001. http://www.house.gov/reform/min/pdfs/pdf_inves/pdf_nursing_abuse_rep.pdf).

The Senate Committee found that if residents or family members made formal complaints, these were uninvestigated for weeks or months; the filing of complaints was also discouraged by the states. Even if serious deficiencies were found, there was inadequate enforcement so that the nursing homes involved did not correct the problems. Finally the majority (54%) of nursing homes were understaffed, putting residents at increased risk of hospitalization for avoidable causes, pressure sores, and significant weight loss.

2002 Nursing Home Quality Initiative

In November 2002, the federal government initiated the National Nursing Home Quality Initiative, a program intended to help consumers find the highest quality nursing homes. The Initiative combined new information for consumers about the quality of care provided in individual nursing homes with resources available to nursing homes to improve the quality of care in their facilities. The Initiative consists of continuing efforts to regulate and enforce standards of care in nursing homes, provision of improved consumer information on the quality of care in each nursing home, making available community-based quality improvement programs, and collaborating with nursing homes to help them improve their quality. Assistance is provided by what are called Quality Improvement Organizations (QIOs), government contractors offering improvement assistance to skilled nursing facilities. The initiative also includes the training of volunteers to serve as ombudspersons to help families and residents on a daily basis find nursing homes that provide the highest possible quality of care and giving consumers tools they need to make an informed, educated decision on selecting a nursing home.

2007 GAO Report

In 2007, the GAO issued a major report analyzing the effectiveness of the online reporting system based on data from 63 nursing homes in California, Michigan, Pennsylvania, and Texas, institutions that had a history of serious compliance problems. From this analysis the GAO concluded that efforts to strengthen federal enforcement of sanctions have not been effective. For example, nursing homes that are cited for harming or abusing residents can be sanctioned through fines, the assignment of monitors, temporary management, or even termination from their sources of federal and state financing. However, when violations are found to occur, the institutions are often given some type of leeway, either in terms of the amount they are penalized or how long they are given before being required to pay the penalty. Many homes showed a "yo-yo" pattern in which they made changes in order to comply with regulations only to slide back temporarily until they were sanctioned again. Residents continue to suffer abusive treatment because the fundamental problems are not corrected (Government Accountability Office, 2007).

CHARACTERISTICS AND NEEDS OF NURSING HOMES AND THEIR RESIDENTS

Although there is a relatively small percentage overall of people 65 and older living in nursing homes, the percentage of older adults who are institutionalized increases dramatically with age, rising from 1.1% for persons 65 to 74 years to 4.7% for persons 75 to 84 years and 18.2% for persons 85+ (Administration on Aging, 2003).

Nearly two-thirds (66%) of nursing homes in the United States fall into the category of "for-profit" facilities, meaning that they seek to have their revenue exceed their expenses. Non-profit facilities, which includes primarily those run by religious organizations, constitute the second largest group (28.1%), and government-owned facilities, primarily those run by the Veterans Administration, compose the remainder (6%). Therefore, most nursing homes are run like a business with the goal of making a profit. Related to this issue is the payment mode of residents. When nursing homes have more private pay patients, they are able to provide better care because the rates for these patients are higher than the reimbursement rates that facilities receive from governmental subsidies.

Information about nursing homes and nursing home residents comes from the On-line Survey, Certification, and Reporting system

TABLE 12.1
Patterns of Nursing Home Abuses

Examples of Deficiencies Causing Harm to Residents by State

	Deficiency History	Enforcement History	Current Status
California Home			
• A resident choked to death when the suction machines that should have been maintained in working order did not have the requisite parts. Indeed, during an unannounced inspection 2 days following the death of this resident, it was noted that there were no functional suction machines in the facility.	• 173 D-level or higher deficiencies • Cycled in and out of compliance 4 times	• DPNA (142 days) • CMP ($193,780) • Mandatory termination imposed (4 times) • Discretionary termination imposed (0 times)	In operation as of November 2006.
Michigan Home			
• The facility failed to provide proper respiratory treatment and care for a resident, resulting in the resident's hospitalization for acute respiratory failure. • During an inspection, several residents' pressure sores were observed to be untreated. For example, one resident had two areas of dead tissue on his feet. The facility acknowledged that the resident should have been wearing protective heel pads when in bed, and yet his bare feet were uncovered, both heels rested directly on the mattress, and he was not wearing heel protectors, which were lying nearby.	• 95 D-level or higher deficiencies • Cycled in and out of compliance 7 times	• DPNA (58 days) • CMP ($40,970) • Mandatory termination imposed (7 times) • Discretionary termination imposed (0 times)	In operation as of November 2006.
Pennsylvania Home			
• "Resident eloped and was found on the courtyard froze (sic) to death." • "A resident was found to have bruises on the inner thighs and arms and appeared to be a victim of abuse. The staff did not report this to the local police and bathed resident prior to assessment for sexual abuse."	• 159 D-level or higher deficiencies, fiscal years 2000–2004 • Cycled in and out of compliance 4 times	• DPNA (229 days) • CMPs ($47,700) • Mandatory termination imposed (6 times) • Discretionary termination imposed (0 times)	Closed January 2004. Reason for closure: voluntary-merger/closure.

A "D-level" deficiency involves the potential for cases of more than minimal harm to the resident. A "DPNA" refers to denial of payment of Medicare or Medicaid for newly admitted patients and a "CMP" is a mandatory payment. This table shows both the lack of sufficient enforcement and the "yo-yo" pattern in which homes cycle in and out of compliance.
Source: Government Accountability Office, 2007.

FIGURE 12.4

Rate of Nursing Home Residence

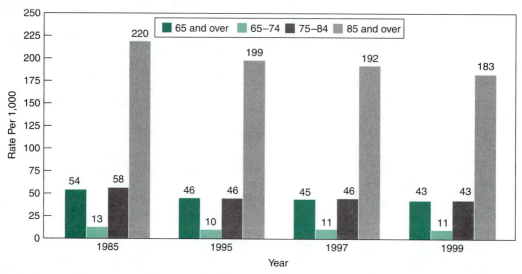

Rate of nursing home residence among people age 65 and over, by age group for the years 1985, 1995, 1997, and 1999.

Source: National Center for Health Statistics, 2006.

(OSCAR). The OSCAR system has information from the state surveys of all certified nursing facilities in the United States, which are entered into a uniform database. Surveyors assess both the process and the outcomes of nursing home care in 15 major areas. Each of these areas has specific regulations, which state surveyors review to determine whether facilities have met the standards. Where a facility fails to meet a standard, a deficiency or citation is given. The deficiencies are given for problems that can result in a negative impact on the health and safety of residents.

Home health agencies are required to submit data on their effectiveness using the Outcomes Assessment and Information Set (OASIS), mandated for use by Medicare-certified home health agencies.

Characteristics of Residents

The most common primary diagnosis of nursing home residents when admitted to a nursing home is cardiovascular disease. However, the greatest form of disability is loss of cognitive skills associated with Alzheimer's disease (Schultz et al., 2002). Given that Alzheimer's disease is found in nearly half of all nursing home residents (43% in 2001), this means that difficulties in carrying out daily living skills are a significant problem among nursing home residents. In fact, over 50% of nursing home residents are chairbound, meaning that they are restricted to a wheelchair. Despite the large number of residents with Alzheimer's disease, only 5.4% of nursing homes have special care units devoted specifically to their care (Harrington, Carrillo, & LaCava, 2006).

Mood and anxiety disorders are present in nearly 20% of all older adults living in these settings (Sahyoun et al., 2001). Being depressed places an individual at greater risk for being admitted to a nursing home over and above having chronic physical illnesses (Harris & Cooper, 2006). Over half

(54.7%) of residents receive psychotropic medications, which includes antidepressants, antianxiety drugs, sedatives and hypnotics, and antipsychotics (Harrington et al., 2006). Although these medications have the potential to be abused if they are given to control and sedate residents, there is no evidence that this is happening in nursing homes (Wunderlich et al., 2001). Health care staff seem to be increasingly sensitive to the need to treat appropriately psychological symptoms such as depression in residents.

As of 2001, about two-thirds (67%) of residents have their nursing home expenses paid for by Medicaid, about one-quarter (23.3%) pay for nursing homes themselves through their own funds or other forms of insurance, and the remainder (9.8%) have their nursing home expenses paid for by Medicare (Harrington et al., 2006).

Nursing Home Deficiencies

As the U.S. government attempts to improve the quality of care provided to nursing homes, monitoring continues on a yearly basis through the listing of deficiencies as reported to OSCAR. In the years between 1999 and 2005, there was a decrease in the quality of nursing home care as indicated by the number and percent of facilities with no deficiencies (Harrington et al., 2006). In 2005 the average number of deficiencies varied substantially across the states. Nursing home in

FIGURE 12.5
Top Ten Nursing Home Deficiencies in 2005

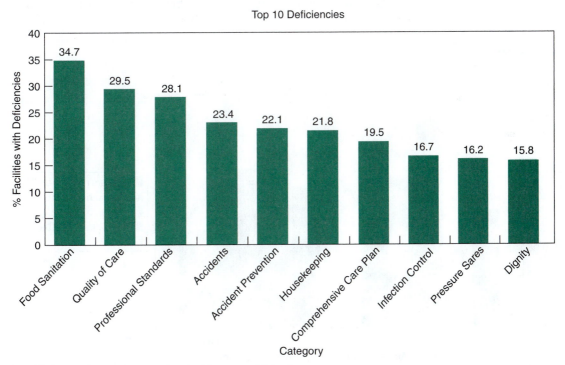

Percent of facilities in the United States with each of the top ten deficiencies.
Source: Harrington, Carrillo, & LaCava, 2006.

the nation's capital, The District of Columbia had the highest number of deficiencies (15). The state with the best record is Oregon, which had 25% of its nursing homes having no deficiencies, and among those which did, the average number of deficiencies was 5.4.

Deficiencies that cause harm or immediate jeopardy to residents are considered the most serious of all. Nursing homes are cited when they have one or more of these as determined by OSCAR. In 2005, 17% of all nursing homes in the United States were cited for one of these deficiencies. The state of Connecticut was cited as having the highest record of poor accident prevention (46.7% of all facilities) but the District of Columbia had the highest number of accidents (70% of all facilities) (Harrington et al., 2006).

Food Sanitation.   Proper sanitation must be ensured in storing, preparing, distributing, and serving food to prevent the spread of foodborne illnesses. Nursing homes that fail to provide proper sanitation of food place residents at risk of food poisoning and the spread of disease and infection. As the most frequently occurring deficiency in 2005, found in over one-third of nursing homes, there are clear ramifications for the health and well-being of residents.

Restraints.   Restraints are defined as mechanical devices, materials, or equipment that restrict freedom of movement or normal access to one's body. A nursing home deficiency is listed if restraints are used for the purposes of discipline or convenience and not required to treat the resident's medical symptoms. The use of restraints on a regular basis can cause decreased muscle tone and increased likelihood of falls, incontinence, pressure ulcers, depression, confusion and mental deterioration. Once again, the District of Columbia topped the list of states, with 35% of facilities cited for failures in this area.

FIGURE 12.6
Racial Differences in Use of Restraints

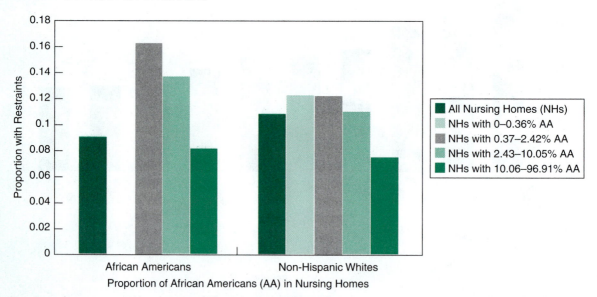

Restraint use by race group and by proportion of African Americans in nursing homes.
Source: Miller, Papandonatos, Fennell, & Mor, 2006.

A physical therapist assists this woman in regaining her mobility. Being treated with dignity and respect is an important contributor to a nursing home resident's satisfaction with care.

Nursing homes seem to vary in their use of restraints by characteristic of resident. In one study of nursing homes in New York state, researchers found that African Americans living in nursing homes with a high percentage of white residents were more likely to be placed in restraints than those living in homes that were largely African American (Miller, Papandonatos, Fennell, & Mor, 2006).

Dignity, Respect, and Privacy. Nursing homes are rated for deficiencies in the area of dignity and respect if they fail to provide care that treats residents as individuals, allowing them to feel that their particular needs are being met. Care that is provided with dignity and respect includes helping residents to maintain their personal hygiene, dress properly, eat without needing to be fed, receive privacy, be listened to, and be communicated with in a respectful manner. Although after a peak of 17.3% of all facilities reporting this deficiency in 2001, the percent dropped off with 15.8% of facilities in 2005 being cited for this problem. Hawaii actually had the highest number of nursing homes (51.3%) with this deficiency.

Housekeeping. Maintenance of a safe and clean environment is a basic job of nursing homes, as a way of protecting residents from disease, infection, and harm due to accidents. In 2005, 21.8% of nursing homes in the United States were cited for deficiencies in the area of housekeeping. All of the facilities in Washington, D.C., were cited for housekeeping deficiencies; West Virginia had the best record with only 5% of nursing homes failing to meet adequate standards.

Nursing Staff, Services, and Programs. Facilities must have sufficient nursing staff to provide nursing and related services to attain or maintain the highest practicable physical, mental, and psychosocial well-being of residents. Total nursing hours provided by registered nurses, licensed practical nurses, and nurses aides averages 3.5 hours per resident day in 2005, with almost 90% of all help provided by nursing assistants.

Related to nursing services is the provision of activities that meet the interests and needs of the residents in terms of their physical, emotional, and social well-being. Nursing homes nationwide received relatively good scores on this count, with only 6.7% being rated for deficiencies in this area in 2005. However, 25% of the nursing homes in Hawaii failed to meet the criterion for adequate activities.

Incontinence. An area in which more efforts are needed for intervention involves incontinence. Over one-half (54%) of all nursing home residents have urinary incontinence, that is, they are unable to control the elimination of urine. However, only 5.8% of residents were involved in bladder training programs, which are behavioral methods designed to assist residents to gain and maintain bladder control (pelvic exercises and frequent toileting). Bowel incontinence, which involves lack of ability to control the elimination of feces at least once a week, affects 43% of nursing home residents.

Training programs exist that are designed to help residents gain and maintain continence through use of diet, fluids, and regular schedules. However, these were available to only 3.3% of residents in 2005 (Harrington et al., 2006). Clearly, the socially appropriate regulation of one's bodily functions is an important need that if unmet, can detract from the quality of an individual's life as well as the quality of the life of the staff. Worsening continence is one of the top reasons that older residents of nursing homes become socially disengaged, a finding that makes sense when you think about the embarrassment that it can cause (Dubeau, Simon, & Morris, 2006).

PSYCHOLOGICAL ISSUES IN LONG-TERM CARE

Just as you wish to control certain aspects of your environment, residents of nursing homes also have the need to perceive that they can control what goes on around them. Even though residents may not have actual control, the perception that they do can help to ease the stress of having to make adjustments to the institutional environment. Residents who feel that they can have mastery over at least some aspects of life in the institution feel less anxious and depressed, experiencing less of the stress that so often accompanies moving from their own homes to the institution. Their adaptation can further be facilitated if they feel that they have support in this adaptation process (Keister, 2006).

The psychosocial needs of residents and strategies that can be implemented to enhance the quality of life in nursing homes became a focus of OBRA 1987. Unfortunately, change is slow to come about. Researchers still believe that nursing homes in the United States had not, at least as

of the late 1990s, made significant changes in the freedom of choice afforded to residents on a day to day basis (Kane et al., 1997). In terms of the rhythm of life in the average nursing home, although deficiencies in activities exist in less than 10% of nursing homes, there still remains a good deal of room for improvement. A study of the daily life of residents conducted in 2002 revealed that, as was the case in the 1960s, residents spend almost two-thirds of the time in their room, doing nothing at all (Ice, 2002). Thus, for many residents, there are simply not enough activities in the average nursing home (Martin, Hancock et al., 2002).

Models of Adaptation

Theoretical models attempting to provide insight into the adaptation of the individual to the institutional environment of a long-term care facility began to develop in the 1970s with the increasing attention in gerontology on ecological approaches to the aging process. Of particular concern in an applied sense are the avoidable disturbances in behavior that can be prevented by appropriate attention to the needs of the individual within the particular setting. A seemingly irresolvable problem, however, in the provision of institutional care is that it is necessary to attempt to satisfy the needs of the "average" resident, and as is true for many averages, the average resident is a hypothetical construct. To put this in very concrete terms, consider the issue of temperature control. For some residents, an ambient temperature of 68 degrees is extremely pleasant, and for others, 76 is the ideal place to set the thermostat. An institution must regulate the temperature of the entire building, however. In attempting to please the average resident, the administrator would need to adjust the temperature to the mean of these two numbers, which would be 72. Neither resident will find this temperature to be a comfortable one, yet on

ASSESS YOURSELF: How Much Control Do You Need over Your Environment?

Although you may not think of yourself as living in an institution, if you are in a college dormitory or any kind of residence hall or group living situation, your life can be affected in ways similar to those of older adults living in nursing homes, assisted living facilities, or extended care facilities. Keeping this in mind, answer the questions below and think about how you would feel if you were in a nursing home:

1. When it comes to having my privacy:
   A. I prefer to keep to myself but I don't mind sharing my living space with others.
   B. I greatly enjoy sharing my living space with others.
   C. I would do almost anything to avoid having to share my living space with others.

2. Having other people around who make a lot of noise:
   A. interferes greatly with my ability to relax.
   B. doesn't bother me particularly.
   C. helps me to feel better adjusted.

3. When the people around me are messy, I:
   A. feel as though I have to clean up after them.
   B. don't really care one way or the other.
   C. feel as though it would take a lot to be messier than I am.

4. In deciding how hot or cold my living space should be, I:
   A. definitely want to set my own levels of temperature control.
   B. don't mind if it is a bit hot or a bit cold.
   C. want to try to accommodate others around me.

5. Sharing a bathroom with someone else is something that I:
   A. very much dislike.
   B. don't mind one way or the other.
   C. very much prefer.

6. My sleeping habits as far as when I go to bed or wake up are something that I:
   A. want to control myself rather than have controlled by others.
   B. don't give much thought to and can go with the flow.
   C. am comfortable having my roommates decide.

7. When it comes to decorating my living space, I:
   A. am just as happy having someone else make the decisions.
   B. want to be able to express my own unique style.
   C. have no thoughts about how I want my place to look.

TABLE 12.2
Decision-Making in Long-Term Care

Vignette A: Bedtimes

Suppose you are interested in going to bed late in the evening, although most people go to bed early. Who do you want to decide what time you go to bed?

Vignette B: Medications

Suppose you are in pain, and there are two kinds of medications you can take. One medication will make you very sleepy but will work better for your pain. The other medication will keep you alert but will work less well for your pain. Who do you want to decide which medication you should take?

Vignette C: Room Transfer

Suppose you are told that the staff want to move you to another room in this same facility. Who do you want to make the decision about whether you should move?

Vignette D: Advance Directives

You may have heard about arrangements that people can make, *in advance*, about what medical procedures they do or do not want at the end of their lives. Who do you want to make the decision about what medical procedures you will receive in the days of your life, if the decision were to be made today?

Residents of a long-term care facility were asked to indicate whether they would want to make the choice alone, by staff, or both in situations described in these vignettes.
Source: Funk, 2004.

the "average" it is the correct level. Researchers are continuing to test new ways of quantifying the physical environment, a process that ultimately may translate into more effective ways to maximize the comfort levels of residents (Sloane et al., 2002).

In addition to understanding the role of the physical environment in adaptation, it is also important to recognize the psychosocial needs of residents. In one interview study of residents in Victoria, British Columbia nursing homes, scenarios were presented of vignettes that involved making decisions such as what time to go to bed, what medicines to take, whether to move to a different room, and deciding what type of end-of-life care to receive. Older adults with more years of education and a greater number of chronic illnesses were likely to state that they wished to be able to make these choices rather than have the decisions made for them by nursing home staff (Funk, 2004).

Examples such as these could be used to determine the preferences of residents for control over their situations rather than to assume that they either want to make the decisions themselves or have the decisions made for them.

Empirical interest in the institutionalization process has dwindled somewhat from the 1970s, when several teams of researchers were actively investigating environmental models and aging. However, one of these models offers some useful concepts for predicting how well people will adapt to an institutional setting. This model, the **competence-press model** (Lawton & Nahemow, 1973), predicts an optimal level of adjustment that institutionalized persons will experience on the basis of their levels of competence (physical and psychological) compared with the demands or "press" of the environment.

As shown in Figure 12.7, there is a funnel-shaped relationship between competence and press according to this model. In the middle of

FIGURE 12.7
Competence-Press Model of Adaptation

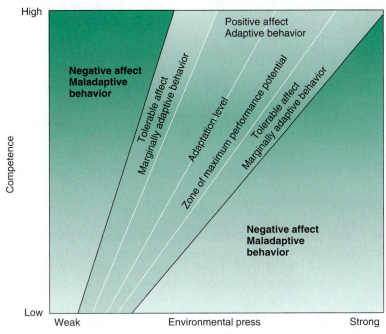

According to the competence-press model, optimal adaptation occurs when there is a match between the abilities of the individual ("competence") and the demands of the environment ("press").

Source: Lawton & Nahemow, 1973.

the funnel is optimal adjustment, which occurs when there is an approximate match between an individual's abilities and the environment's demands. A small degree of discrepancy is acceptable, but when the mismatch goes outside this range, the individual will experience negative affect and maladaptive behaviors. For example, the intellectually competent older resident (high competence) will do well in a setting in which autonomous decisions are expected (high press), but a person with a significant cognitive impairment will adapt maximally when the environment is very structured (low press).

By considering the interaction between the individual and the environment of the institution, the competence-press model avoids making sweeping generalizations about whether institutions should attempt to provide either high levels or low levels of stimulation and demands. The model also allows room for multiple dimensions of competence and press to be considered when evaluating older adults (Lichtenburg, MacNeill, Lysack, & Neufeld, 2003). Competence may be defined in terms of physiological or psychological characteristics. The social factors in this model, namely, the level of press in the environment, may also be conceptualized among multiple dimensions, along which the individual is expected to make adaptations to a different cultural milieu within the institution. Financial pressure may also be seen as a form of press, as individuals with fewer economic resources have fewer alternatives when they are not satisfied with their placement.

"What do you think?"   12-4

How does the competence-press model respond to individual differences among residents?

Environments outside of nursing homes can also be thought of as presenting stress that can impair the older adult's adaptation. For example, neighborhoods that are regarded as unsafe can create stress and ultimately increase the individual's risk of chronic illness. In one study of over 10,000 older people, living in neighborhoods that were more stressful was associated with an increased rate of cardiovascular disease, particularly among whites (Diez Roux, Borrell, Haan, Jackson, & Schultz, 2004). Conversely, living in an environment that people perceive as unsafe can harm their physical and mental health. In an investigation of over 9,400 women in their 70s living in Australia, a sense of belonging to the neighborhood was related to higher scores on measures of physical and psychological symptoms (Young, Russell, & Powers, 2004).

Suggestions for Improving Institutional Care

Clearly the environment plays an important role in affecting our health, both inside and outside the institutional environment. Within the institutional setting, the implications of the competence-press model are that the needs of individuals should be met to the extent possible. Innovations in nursing home care are being developed with this as a goal. For example, bathing, a situation that can be distressing when conducted in a way that embarrasses or exposes the resident, can be treated in a more individualized manner, making it a less aversive experience (Camp, Cohen-Mansfield, & Capezuti, 2002).

Nurses' aides, who manage many of the daily living activities of residents, can be taught to use behavioral methods to help residents maintain self-care and, hence, independence (Burgio et al., 2002). Such interventions can also benefit staff-resident relationships. Since satisfaction with treatment by staff is such a significant component of satisfaction with the institution (Chou, Boldy, & Lee, 2002), any intervention that maximizes positive interactions between staff and residents is bound to have a favorable impact on the sense of well-being experienced by residents.

New models for nursing home design attempt to break up monotony to create more of a feel of a community or neighborhood. Nursing stations are removed from view, allowing residents and staff to share lounges. Hallways have alcoves that can store medicine carts and nursing stations.

Other models of change stress new ways of allocating staff to meeting the care needs of residents. In one such model, rather than basing staff assignments on the completion of specific tasks for all residents (bathing, changing dressings, administering medications), staff were assigned to meet all the needs of a particular group of residents. Although such a system increases the staffing requirements, overall the institutions reduced their expenses in the areas of restraints and antipsychotic medications. Hospitalization rates, staff turnover, and success in rehabilitation also improved as did the satisfaction that residents expressed about their care. Another improvement involves the use of a team approach to providing mental health services. When staff work as a multidisciplinary team, residents receive better services; at the same time, staff are more informed and perform more effectively in their jobs (Bartels, Moak, & Dums, 2002).

In conclusion, the concerns of institutionalized older adults are of great importance to individuals and to their families, many of whom are involved in helping to make long-term care decisions for their older relatives. The dignity and self-respect of the resident, which is fortunately now being regulated by state and federal certification standards, can best be addressed by multidimensional approaches that take into account personal and contextual factors. Interventions based on these approaches will ultimately lead to a higher quality of life for those who must spend their last days or months in the care of another.

SUMMARY

1. A wide range of treatment sites is available specifically designed for older adults such as nursing homes and residential care facilities. The percentage of older adults in these treatment sites with cognitive deficits is relatively high. Increasing attention is being given to home health care. Other residential sites include special housing that is designed for older adults.

2. Medicare is designed to provide hospital insurance and supplemental medical insurance. Other forms of insurance attached to Medicare are becoming increasingly available to older adults. Medicaid is intended to reduce the burden of health care costs among those who are in need of help in payment for medical services, but individuals receiving this assistance must "spend down" to eliminate their assets. The cost of Medicare is expected to skyrocket over the coming decades, and will lead to bankruptcy of the Social Security Trust fund unless preventive measures are taken.

3. The rights of nursing home residents became protected with passage of the Nursing Home Reform Act in 1987. Since passage of this legislation, complaints about nursing home care have decreased. However, problems in areas such as food sanitation remain a concern as does the use of restraint as a means of controlling resident behavior. Care in nursing homes is an area needing continued monitoring, as was evident by the findings obtained in the 2002 General Accountability Office report on nursing home abuse and more recently by the 2007 General Accountability Office's review of the enforcement of violations in nursing home standards.

4. Psychological issues in long-term care focus on the provision of an adequate environment that will maximally meet the needs of residents. The competence-press model proposes an ideal relationship between how demanding an environment is and the abilities of the resident to meet those demands. The environment of neighborhoods in which older adults live is also becoming a concern of researchers who are attempting to understand the relationship between well-being and feelings of safety and security in the residents of these neighborhoods.

CHAPTER 13

Death and Dying

"*Because I could not stop for death — He kindly stopped for me.*"
Emily Dickinson
(1830–1886)

For many of us, the concept of death is as fascinating as it is frightening. By definition, it remains the great unknown; even those individuals who have had so-called near-death experiences cannot claim with certainty that what happened to them is an accurate prediction of what is to come in the future.

If you are in good health, you may not give your own death much thought. However, those who live until the years of later adulthood may find themselves prone to consider their mortality on a more frequent basis. Even if they do not give attention to the existential questions of their own mortality, they are faced with the need to make practical arrangements such as planning the funeral or finalizing the will. Perhaps what most people wish for is to live as long as possible in as healthy a state as possible and to experience a death that will be quick and relatively painless. This concept is one we will return to at several points in this and the next chapter. Another theme relating to death is the desire to leave something of oneself behind and to have made an impact on other people's lives.

As we shall see many times throughout this chapter, death has a social meaning as well as a personal meaning to the individual. For example, after a person's death, the meaning of that death shifts from something that was thought about by the individual to something that is thought about by others. When a person dies prematurely, for example, for many years to come the person may be thought of in terms of that early death, particularly when the death is due to sudden illness or an accident. The meaning that death gives to the life that was lived is another dimension to an already very complicated and multifaceted process.

TECHNICAL PERSPECTIVES ON DEATH

From a medical and legal perspective, the term **death** is defined as the point when there is irreversible cessation of circulatory and respiratory functions, or when all structures of the brain have ceased to function (Commission for the Study of Ethical Problems in Medicine and Biomedical and Behavioral Research, 1981). The term **dying** refers to the period during which the organism loses its vitality. Determination of the point of death has become more complicated over the course of the past three decades, however, since the advent of intensive care. It is possible to keep a person who is brain dead alive almost indefinitely on life support systems such as artificial respirators and heart pumps.

The term "brain death" refers to the permanent absence of all brain functions, including those of the brain stem. Brain-dead patients have lost all brain-stem reflexes, cranial-nerve, and cortical functions. Detailed clinical criteria for the diagnosis of brain death have been outlined by the Royal College of Physicians, UK (1998) and elsewhere (President's Commission, 1981; American Academy of Pediatrics, 1987).

Medical Aspects of Death

Although the death experience varies from person to person, there are some commonalities in the physical changes shown by a person who will die within a few hours or days. The symptoms that death is imminent include being asleep most of the time, being disoriented, breathing irregularly, having visual and auditory hallucinations, being less able to see, producing less urine, and having mottled skin, cool hands and feet, an overly warm trunk, and excessive secretions of bodily fluids (Gavrin & Chapman, 1995). An older adult who is close to death is likely to be unable to walk or eat, has difficulty recognizing family members, is in constant pain, and feels that breathing is difficult. A common syndrome observed at the end of life is the **anorexia-cachexia syndrome**, which involves a loss of appetite (anorexia) and atrophy of muscle mass (cachexia). The majority of cancer patients experience cachexia, and it is also found commonly in patients who have AIDS and dementia. In addition to the symptoms already mentioned, patients who are dying are likely to experience nausea, difficulty swallowing, bowel problems, dry mouth, and the accumulation of liquid in the abdomen which leads to bloating. Anxiety, depression, confusion, and dementia are also common psychological symptoms experienced at the end of life (Field, Cassel, and Committee on Care at the End of Life 1997).

Obviously the symptoms experienced by dying individuals involve pain and suffering, not only for the patients themselves but also indirectly for their family members. However, those who work with the dying observe that against this backdrop, the final period of life can also involve emotional and spiritual growth (Field et al., 1997). As will be seen later, the notion of "acceptance" as the final stage of dying implies an ability to transcend these painful physical symptoms.

The cause of an individual's death must be verified by a coroner or medical examiner, who must code the cause or causes of death, either through external examination or an autopsy. The cause of death information must then be recorded on a death certificate. The coding system in use throughout the world is the World Health Organization International Classification of Diseases, Tenth Revision (ICD-10), which went into effect in 1999.

In many cases, the cause of death may be established on the basis of the individual's symptoms prior to death, particularly if the death occurred while the individual was under medical supervision. However, in other cases,

ASSESS YOURSELF: Planning Your Funeral

Although this may seem like a morbid topic, increasingly, people are planning their own funerals so they can exert control over the way their bodies are handled and, perhaps more importantly, their lives are memorialized. Please answer the following questions keeping these issues in mind.

1. After I die, I want my organs:
   A. to be donated, if possible.
   B. not to be donated under any circumstances.

2. With regard to a funeral home, I:
   A. know which funeral home I would use.
   B. do not know which funeral home I would use.

3. The ceremony should last:
   A. one hour or more.
   B. less than one hour.

4. With regard to who would speak at my funeral, I:
   A. know who I would wish to have speak.
   B. do not know who I would wish to have speak.

5. I want my body to be:
   A. displayed in an open casket.
   B. not displayed in an open casket.

6. At my funeral, I would like to have:
   A. readings and music.
   B. readings only.
   C. music only.
   D. no readings or music.

7. Whether or not my body is on view, I:
   A. know what I want to wear, including clothes and jewelry.
   B. do not know what I want to wear.

8. If people want to honor me, I would prefer that they:
   A. buy flowers.
   B. do not buy flowers, but donate to my favorite charity.

9. I would prefer:
   A. cremation.
   B. burial.

10. Taking this survey makes me feel:
    A. uncomfortable because I would rather not think about these issues.
    B. good that I am thinking about these issues.
    C. neither uncomfortable nor comfortable.

FIGURE 13.1

Autopsies Performed by Age Group

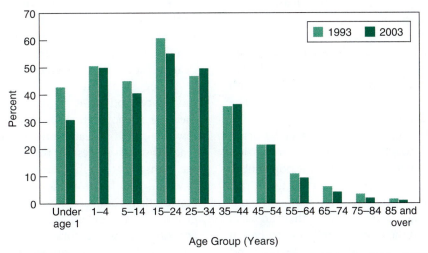

Percentage of deaths for which autopsies were reported, by age groups: 47 states and the District of Columbia, 1993 and 2003.

Source: Hoyert, Kung, & Xu, 2007.

the cause of death can only be performed by autopsy, a medical procedure in which the body is opened and the internal organs and structures are examined. Laboratory tests may also be performed to determine the conditions present in the body prior to death. An autopsy may be performed for research or educational purposes if the pathologist wishes to relate specific symptoms present in life to conditions that can only be determined after death. For example, death from an Alzheimer's disease-related cell is one case in which an autopsy may be performed for this reason. Permission of the next of kin is needed both to perform the autopsy and to determine what materials, if any, are to be retained from the body. Variants of these procedures may need to be employed if the death occurred due to an accident involving multiple fatalities or if there was a disaster involving hundreds or thousands of deaths. There are actually race, age, and sex variations in the likelihood that a death will be followed up by an autopsy, with the highest rates of autopsies occurring for men between the ages

of 15 to 24 in the Northeast, most often dying in emergency rooms or being pronounced dead on arrival (Hoyert, Kung, & Xu, 2007).

Mortality Facts and Figures

Although based on statistics derived from death, **mortality data** provide a fascinating picture of the factors that influence the course of human life. In some ways, mortality can be regarded as the ultimate dependent variable in the study of physical and behavioral aspects of health because unlike rating scales, there is no question about its validity. In the majority of cases, death statistics provide clear numbers that indicate the outcomes of particular environmental conditions or disease processes. However, mortality data are not always 100% clear. There may be some question about the validity of cause of death information as well as debate about the point at which death occurs, as in the case of people who have been on life support machines for prolonged periods.

Mortality rates are calculated based on deaths per 100,000 estimated population in a specified group of people. **Age-specific death rates**, are the number of deaths per 100,000 of the particular age group in question. The **age-adjusted death rate** is used to compare relative mortality risk across groups and over time taking into account the fact that death rates are higher in increasingly older groups. The age-adjusted death rate is calculated by obtaining the weighted averages of the age-specific death rates, with the weights reflecting the proportion of individuals in that age group in the population. In this way, the average age-adjusted death rate takes into account the fact that, although older people have higher death rates, they are also less prevalent in the population. For example, in 2003 the death rate for individuals 85 years and older was 14,593 per 100,000 in the population (nearly three times the rate for those 75 to 79). However, people in the 85 and older age group are only about 1.6% of the U.S. population. By correcting the high death rate in the over-85 age group for their small representation in the population, death rates for the entire population are not be overestimated.

Improvements in public health are measured in terms of age-adjusted mortality rates, such that the lower this rate, the healthier is the population. Within this context, it is considered desirable that not only will people live to be older before they die, but that they will experience less disability prior to their death. This concept, referred to as **compression of morbidity**, appears to be occurring within the U.S. population as a whole (Manton, Corder, & Stallard, 1997). Consistent with the preventive theme of this book, healthy lifestyles were found in one 12-year longitudinal study to be related to a shorter period of disability prior to death. Participants were divided into three groups on the basis of their lifestyles at the start of the study. The risk-factor-free group (no smoking, high physical activity, normal weight) maintained close to zero disability scores near

zero for over a decade prior to their death. The groups with two or more unhealthy factors had higher levels of disability, with large increases in the year and a half before their death. Those with moderate risk were able to remain relatively healthy until just three months prior to their death (Hubert, Bloch, Oehlert, & Fries, 2002).

Along similar lines as the compression of morbidity notion, it would be considered a measure of a population's health to have relatively low age-specific death rates until the point is reached which represents the limit to the human life span, now thought of as about age 120 years. It would also be desirable for these rates to be consistent across race, sex, and socioeconomic groups. To the extent that there are variations according to these factors, a population would be considered to have inequities in conditions that foster adequate disease prevention and health care.

In 2004, there were 2,397,615 deaths in the United States, which is translated into a crude death rate of 816.5 per 100,000 population (Miniño, Heron, Smith, & Kochanek, 2006). This number is substantially lower than the death rate in 1900, which was about 1,720 per 100,000. As shown in Figure 13.2, since 1960 age-adjusted mortality has dropped substantially. Although death rates are decreasing, discrepancies exist within specific subgroups. In the case of gender, women have lower mortality rates than men. The age-adjusted mortality rate in 2004 was 955.7 for males and 679.2 for females. There are also disparities in mortality rates between whites (786.3) and blacks (1,027.3), meaning that the average risk for the black population is 33% higher than for whites.

There are significant variations in death rates by marital status and education, with marriage and higher levels of education serving a protective function (Cooper, Harris, & McGready, 2002). Marital status is related to mortality rate such that those who are never married have nearly twice the age-adjusted rate of death compared

FIGURE 13.2

Crude and Age-Adjusted Mortality Rates: United States, 1960–2004

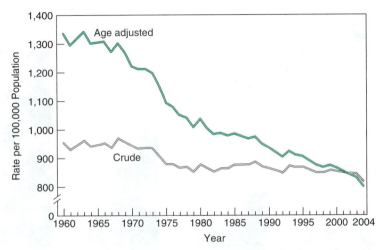

Crude rates and age-adjusted rates of mortality. Age-adjusted rates take into account the fact that there are fewer older adults in the population, but they are more likely to die.

Source: http://www.cdc.gov/nchs/products/pubs/pubd/hestats/finaldeaths04/figure-1.png

with those who were ever married. This disparity between the never married and those who have been married is greater in males than in females. Educational status is also related to mortality rate, as can be seen in Figure 13.3 At all age groups, those with a college education or better have lower mortality rates.

There is a well-established relationship between social status and mortality (Adler et al., 1994). It has been known since the mid-nineteenth century that men in laboring and trade occupations have higher death rates than those of the professional class (Macintyre, 1997). People in lower socioeconomic classes are also more likely to suffer from communicable diseases, exposure to lead, and work-related injuries (Pamuk, Makuc, Heck, Reuben, & Lochner, 1998). Not only the level of occupation but the pattern of jobs held throughout adulthood are related to mortality rates. The risk of mortality is lower in men who move up from manual to professional or managerial level occupations (House, Kessler, Herzog, & Mero, 1990; Moore

& Hayward, 1990). Furthermore, men who hold a string of unrelated jobs have higher rates of early mortality than those with stable career progressions (Pavalko, Elder, & Clipp, 1993).

Although at one time the disparity in death rates was considered to be due to poorer sanitation, nutrition, and housing, current explanations focus on psychosocial factors as well. Stress is an important part of this equation. Workers in jobs who lack control over the pace and direction of what they do with their time (as is true in an assembly-line or migrant farming job) are at higher risk of dying from cardiovascular disease. In a 25-year follow-up study of over 12,500 male workers (aged 25 to 74), it was found that being exposed to even five years of assembly-line work increased the risk of dying from heart disease. Workers who participated in this type of work for the full period of the study had an 83% higher mortality risk than would be expected on the basis of their age (Johnson, Stewart, Hall, Fredlund, & Theorell, 1996).

FIGURE 13.3

Death Rates by Education, United States, 2003

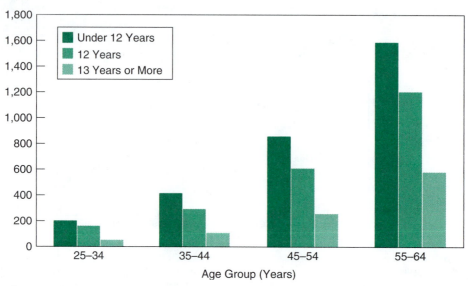

Death rates by education and age group per 100,000 in the population.

Source: Hoyert, Heron, Murphy, & Kung, 2006.

Income is also related to mortality throughout adulthood. For example, 45-year-olds with the highest incomes can expect to live three to seven years longer than those with the lowest incomes. An eight-year follow-up of over 3,600 adults showed that people from the low- and moderate-income levels had a higher rate of mortality than those from the more affluent sectors of society. This finding held even when controlling for differences among the income groups in health risk behaviors as well as age, sex, race, urbanicity, and education (Lantz et al., 1998). It is known that income is related to cigarette smoking prevalence. People with incomes below the poverty level are almost twice as likely to smoke as are men in the highest income groups (Schoenborn, Vickerie, & Barnes, 2003).

However, differences between income groups in health risk behaviors are not sufficient to explain differences in mortality rates. Rather than look toward explanations of social class and income differences in mortality as a function of personal choices made by individuals to control their health, researchers suggest that the influences are far more pervasive, relating to lifelong exposure to social inequality. Such inequality incorporates a host of factors, including exposure to environmental health hazards, inequalities in health care, lack of social support, loss of a sense of mastery and control, chronic exposure to discrimination, and an impoverished childhood. Rather than focus on changing behaviors at the level of the individual, more widespread changes are necessary to reduce inequities in the social structure (Lantz et al., 1998).

In addition to differences by social status, there are differences in mortality in the United States between blacks and whites. The discrepancy in mortality rates had been on the decrease through the early 1980s, after which it soared to record levels, particularly for males.

The mortality increase was due to a differential rise in HIV, homicide, and heart disease among black men. From 1993 to 2003, the differential once again took a 25% turn downward primarily due to mortality improvements between the ages of 15 to 49 years among blacks. Declines in HIV deaths and deaths due to homicide and unintentional injuries were the major causes for this downward trend. Unfortunately, gaps still remain in hypertension, heart disease, and colorectal cancer. Higher death rates due to nephritis (inflammation of the kidney) and diabetes also take a toll on the mortality of blacks (Harper, Lynch, Burris, & Davey Smith, 2007).

Mortality rates throughout the world declined steadily throughout the twentieth century, beginning in European countries and eventually spreading to other continents. Improvements in nutrition, sanitation, and water supply associated with higher income levels are regarded as major reasons for the decline in mortality rates, but improvements in health care are also significant factors. Exceptions to this trend may be found in the parts of Africa affected by AIDS and among adult males in central and eastern Europe. In general, however, over four out of ten deaths in developing countries are due to infectious diseases. In developed countries, almost half the deaths that occur are due to diseases of the circulatory system (American Heart Association, 2003). Mortality rates are disproportionately high among the poor in countries throughout the world as well as within the United States. Across all countries studied by the World Health Organization, the poor are over four times as likely to die between the ages of 15 and 59 as are the nonpoor.

CULTURAL PERSPECTIVES

From the biological and medical perspectives, death is an event that can be defined entirely by a set of physical changes within the body's cells. By contrast, from a sociocultural perspective, the important features of death are the interpretations that a society or culture places on the processes through which life ends. Awareness of the end of life is a uniquely (so we think) human characteristic, as is the ability to endow this event with meaning. That meaning, in turn, is seen as a social creation that reflects the prevailing philosophy, economics, and family structure of a culture. According to the sociocultural perspective, people learn the social meaning of death from the language, arts, and death-related rituals of their cultures. A culture's **death ethos**, or prevailing philosophy of death, can be inferred from funeral rituals, treatment of those who are dying, belief in the presence of ghosts, belief in an afterlife, the extent to which death topics are taboo, the language used to describe death (through euphemisms such as "passed away"), and the representation of death in the arts. Death may be viewed as sacred or profane, as an unwanted extinction of life or a welcome release from worldly existence (Atchley, 2000).

Throughout the course of Western history, remarkable alterations in cultural meanings and rituals have been attached to the process of death and to the disposition of dead bodies. Perhaps the most well known of all death rituals were those practiced by the ancient Egyptians. They believed that a new, eternal life awaited the dead and that the body had to be preserved through mummification in order to make it the permanent home for the spirit of the deceased. The mummies were buried in elaborate tombs, where they were decorated and surrounded by valued possessions. Family members would visit the tombs to bring offers of food to sustain the dead in the afterlife. It was once thought that only kings and wealthy nobles were mummified, but it is now known that even ordinary people preserved their dead, though in a humbler manner than was true of nobility. Furthermore, although the Egyptian mummies are the most well known, they were by no means the only ones to exist, as was found in an investigation of the mummies in the Andean mountains of Peru.

Cultural views within Western society toward death and the dead have undergone many shifts from ancient times to the present (Aries, 1974; 1981). For many centuries until the early Middle Ages, death was considered "tame," accepted as a natural part of life, and neither to be avoided nor exalted. Beginning in the Middle Ages, however, death began to be viewed as an end to the self, as people examined its personal meaning. The view of death as a time of final reckoning with God began to evolve, and people attached significance to personal tombs and epitaphs. The rise of scientific thinking and models led, in the 1700s, to a view of death as remote—a punishment or break with life, to be avoided or denied. By the 1800s, with the rise of romanticism, death became glorified, and it was considered noble to die for a cause (the "beautiful death"), as many people had in the revolutions in America and Europe. However, entry into the twentieth century brought in the period known as "invisible death," involving the denial of death and medicalization of the dying process. People put their faith in science, which in turn took control over the dying individual. Rather than being a shared experience with others, death and mourning became private. In the large scheme of the universe of scientific discoveries, the death of an individual began to be seen as inconsequential.

Contemporary American attitudes toward death reflect this history but are also shaped by and reflect a complex mixture of media images, religious and cultural traditions, and health care practices. The media treatment of death is often sensationalistic, as shown in cases when many people die at once in a bombing, mass murder, plane crash, or earthquake. In some cases, treatment of news stories involving massive loss of life, as occurred with the deaths due to the terrorist attacks on the World Trade Center on September 11, 2001, or the Southeast Asia tsunami of December 2004, attempts to bring the losses to human proportions by focusing on the families of those who died. Similarly, the death of one famous person in a fatal accident may preoccupy the American or European media for weeks, as was the case in the deaths of Princess Diana and John F. Kennedy Jr. Horror stories may also be presented in the media coverage of people with terminal illness such as the case of Terry Schiavo, the Florida woman who existed in a on life support machines for 15 years before her husband

Egyptian mummies provide us with an understanding of views of death in the ancient world.

At this funeral procession in Iraq, mourners carry the coffin through the streets.

finally was able to order that all interventions be stopped. Other stories are of people whose terminal care brings a family to the brink of poverty because their health insurance does not cover hospital costs. Death may also be presented in sentimentalized ways as when a loving wife and mother is depicted as being torn from her husband and children or when two young lovers are parted in an untimely way. These images represent the worst fears that people have about their own death— that it will come tragically and prematurely or that it will follow a long, agonizing, painful, and expensive process.

The religious background of many Americans provides some comfort in the face of these frightening images, through teachings that emphasize the existence of an afterlife and the belief that human events occur because of some higher purpose. The loss of a loved one, particularly when it occurs "prematurely" (i.e., before old age), may be seen as a test of one's faith. The grieving comfort themselves with the knowledge that they will be reunited in heaven with the deceased where they will spend eternity together. Bereaved individuals may also seek solace in the belief or perception that they can sense the presence of departed loved ones. Another belief in which

people may find comfort is that death is a blessed relief from a world of trouble and pain. As the bereaved or terminally ill attempt to come to grips with the ending of a life, they rely on these beliefs to make sense out of the death or achieve some kind of understanding of its meaning.

Changes in health care interact with these cultural images, both in terms of how and where death occurs. Because the age of dying has increased from 1900 to the present, death has increasingly become associated with later life. At the same time, death has become institutionalized and "invisible" (Aries, 1974) as it has moved from the home to the hospital. People no longer are witness to the physical death of another, and therefore it is not as much a part of daily life as in years past (DeSpelder & Strickland, 1999). As death has become removed from the everyday world, it has acquired more fear and mystery. Furthermore, instead of developing our own personal meanings, we are at the mercy of whatever images of death we see in the media.

Fear of death and dying within contemporary Western society is thought to be linked not only to changes in the timing and location of death but also to our fear of aging and growing old. The desire to stop or slow the aging process is evident throughout advertisements of everything from wrinkle creams to exercise machines, and America is often thought of as a youth-oriented culture, despite the aging of the Baby Boomers. Cultural depictions of death seem inextricably linked to fear of loss of capacity, attractiveness, and social relevance. Both reflect an unwillingness, which is perhaps part of the American tradition, to accept the limits imposed by the biological facts of aging and death (Field et al., 1997). We also fear the process of **social death**, through which we would be treated as nonpersons by family or health care workers as we are left to spend their final months or years in the hospital or nursing home. Another perspective on fear of death is based on **Terror Management Theory** (Solomon, Greenberg, & Pyszczynski, 1991). According to this social-psychological perspective, people regard with panic and dread the thought of the finitude of their lives. They engage in defensive mechanisms to protect themselves from the anxiety and threats to self-esteem that this awareness produces.

The development of increasingly sophisticated medical technology has in many ways complicated these already complex issues. Physicians can now keep people alive under far less tenable circumstances than in the past, and they can restore life to a person who has, temporarily, ceased to breathe or sustain a heartbeat. Issues of organ and tissue transplants further cloud the boundary between life and death. Related trends in attitudes toward death emphasize the quality of the death experience and the fear of enduring a prolonged period of terminal decline. **Death with dignity**, the idea that death should not involve extreme physical dependency or loss of control of bodily functions, emerged from the desire of patients and their families to avoid a lengthy and protracted dying process (Humphrey, 1991). The next seemingly logical step to follow, initiated by Dr. Jack Kevorkian

(1991), was to make it possible for a terminally ill patient to complete suicide, a process referred to as **physician-assisted suicide**. Similar in intent is euthanasia, which involves the direct killing of a patient by a physician who administers a lethal injection. Social movements that advocated these measures were instrumental in stimulating the medical community to establish guidelines and practices for the care of the terminally ill at the end of life (see below). However, in terms of cultural attitudes, they reflect the dread that many in our society feel about losing our ability to control this most important aspect of life.

THE DYING PROCESS

Death is an event that marks the end of the process of dying, the period during which an organism loses its viability. During the period of dying, the individual is thought to be likely to die within a few days to several months. People with terminal illnesses that last for years may not be thought of as "dying" because their deaths are not as predictable. Most discussions of dying refer to individuals whose deaths are expected to occur within a period of days to months, although individuals with life-threatening illnesses would also be considered in a sense as "dying" (Field et al., 1997).

There are many variations in the dying process, a concept captured by the term **dying trajectory**, or the rate of decline in functioning prior to death (Glaser & Strauss, 1968). There are two major features of a dying trajectory—duration and shape. Those who die suddenly function normally and then drop precipitously. These would be people with no prior knowledge of illness, as in a victim of sudden cardiac failure, or people who die in accidents. The second and third trajectories include individuals who have advance warning of a terminal illness and who experience

FIGURE 13.4
Dying Trajectories

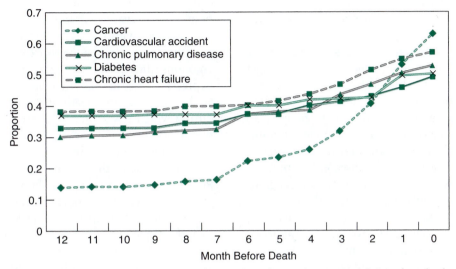

Adjusted proportion of people with trouble getting in and out of bed or chair, showing the more rapid decline of people who are dying from cancer.

Source: Teno, Weitzen, Fennell, & Mor, 2001.

a lingering period of loss of function. A steady downward trajectory applies to people whose disease causes them to undergo a steady and predictable decline such as what happens to many people who die of cancer (see Figure 13.4). Other people go through a generally downward course that is marked by a series of sharp drops. Eventually their death occurs during a crisis related to their illness or to another fatal cause during which their functional abilities suddenly decrease (Teno, Weitzen, Fennell, & Mor, 2001).

Other individuals may be at increased risk of dying, though technically they do not have a terminal disease. One set consists of individuals in their 80s or older who are in good health but have limited physical reserves. They may die from complications associated with an acute condition such as influenza or a broken hip due to a fall. In other cases, people whose organ systems are gradually deteriorating may slowly lose the ability to care for themselves while at the same time developing an illness such as renal failure or pneumonia that eventually causes them to die. The immediate cause of death may be the illness, but it has occurred against a backdrop of general loss of function.

Stages of Dying

Amid the growing institutionalization of death and the attempts by the medical establishment to prolong life, a small book published in 1969 was to alter permanently Western attitudes toward and treatment of the dying. This book, by Elisabeth Kübler-Ross (Kübler-Ross, 1969), called *On Death and Dying*, described five **stages of dying** considered to occur universally among terminally ill patients. These stages of dying have since become part of the cultural mystique surrounding the dying process, even as professionals challenge both the specific stages and the notion of stages at all.

The five stages of dying, according to Kübler-Ross, are as follows. The first stage, denial, describes the patient's reaction to having been informed that he or she has a terminal illness. The individual simply refuses to accept the diagnosis. The second stage, anger, is the reaction the patient has to the news, which is now no longer denied. The individual feels cheated or robbed of the opportunity to live and is furious with the powers that are causing this to happen. In bargaining, the third stage, the patient attempts to strike a deal with God or whatever force is seen as responsible for the disease. Examples of bargaining would be offering to attend religious services on a regular basis if given the chance to live longer, if not recover. People in this stage may "ask" to be allowed to live until an important upcoming event such as the marriage of a child. Fourth comes depression and sense of loss, as the inevitability of the disease's progress is acknowledged. Finally the individual reaches the fifth stage of acceptance, during which the finality of the disease is no longer fought or regretted. As death approaches, it is regarded as a natural end state and perhaps even a release from pain and suffering.

The critical point that Kübler-Ross attempted to make in her writing is that to reach acceptance

of a fatal illness, the dying person must be allowed to talk openly with family members and health care workers. Rather than hide the diagnosis or pretend that everything will be all right, those who interact with the dying individual need to give that person a chance to express the many emotions that surface, ranging from anger to depression. Recall that this book was written at the height of the death as "invisible" period during which it was just as likely as not that a physician would not share the diagnosis of cancer with a patient and family.

Unfortunately the original views of Kübler-Ross became distorted as the book's popularity grew. The five stages began to be interpreted as a series of steps that must be followed with each dying patient. If a patient refused to engage in "bargaining," for instance, then it must mean something was wrong with the way that person was working through the stages. Critics of this approach pointed out that there could be many variations in the dying process that the five-stage model ignored. For example, not everyone would either live long enough or have the ability to reach acceptance. Furthermore, people could fluctuate in the order through which they progressed through the stages. Another point is that Kübler-Ross was writing about relatively

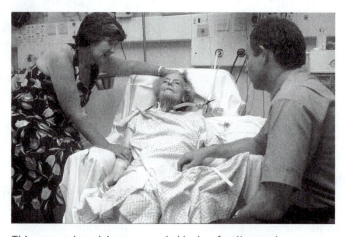

This women lays dying surrounded by her family members.

young patients, and denial may very well have been a natural reaction to the news of their impending death. For older individuals, denial may not be the first reaction, or it may not occur at all. The Kübler-Ross formulation also ignores other emotions that dying individuals may experience, such as curiosity, hope, relief, and apathy. As with many events that take place during life, the dying process is highly individualized and may take many different forms depending on the individual's personality, life history, cultural background, age, and specific nature of the illness. Finally, and perhaps most crucial, is the fact that researchers have never been able to establish the existence of the stages among dying individuals.

Psychological Perspectives on the Dying Process

Rather than proposing that dying individuals go through specific stages as they prepare for their final moments, others have suggested that as the end of life approaches, we attempt to make sense out of the past patterns of our lives. According to Marshall (1980), we engage in these processes when we begin to understand that our life is finite. Such an understanding might be arrived at when a person is diagnosed as having a terminal illness. Another process that occurs more generally, however, is the **awareness of finitude**, which is reached when an individual passes the age when parents or, perhaps, siblings, have died. For example, if a person's father died at the age of 66, when this individual reaches that age, a kind of counting-down process begins. The individual anticipates the end of life and understands that life really will end.

Having passed the age of awareness of finitude, individuals then embark on a process called **legitimization of biography** in which they attempt to gain perspective on their past life events. They attempt to see what they have done

as having meaning, and they prepare the "story" of their lives by which they will be remembered in the minds of others. Some individuals may put their memoirs in writing, while others achieve an internal reckoning in which they evaluate their contributions as well as their shortcomings.

Personality also plays a role in influencing feelings about death and dying. In a study of older adults ranging from 60 to 100 years of age researchers found that it was those people who believed in fate, chance, or luck as determining what happens to them who had higher self-esteem. As predicted by Terror Management Theory, people with higher self-esteem, in turn, were less likely to fear death as an end to the self (Cicirelli, 2002).

The notion that the end of life, or awareness of life's end, triggers an intense period of self-evaluation is also an important component of Erikson's concept of ego integrity, as described in Chapter 8. Erikson emphasized that during this period of life, individuals deal with mortality and questions related to the ending of their existence by attempting to place their lives into perspective. Butler (1974) specifically referred to this process as the **life review**, a time of taking stock through reminiscence or a mental reliving of events from the long-ago past. Presumably, this process may occur at any age, as the dying individual attempts to achieve a peaceful resolution with past mistakes and events that can no longer be made up for or changed. As pointed out in Chapter 11, life review therapy may be useful for older adults who might not spontaneously engage in this potentially important process.

ISSUES IN END-OF-LIFE CARE

Improvements in medical technology along with changes in attitudes toward death and dying have led, within the past two decades, to radical alterations in the approach to the terminally ill.

On the one hand, clinicians have become far more sensitive to the emotional and physical needs of dying patients, leading to an examination and reworking of some of the standard approaches to end-of-life care. On the other hand, legislation and social movements that advocate for the rights of dying patients have argued for greater autonomy and decision making. These efforts attempt to establish as part of medical treatment a role for patients to participate actively not only in the course of their care, but also its ending. Many of these issues involve legal and ethical considerations as well as those that are strictly medical.

Advance Directives and the Patient Self-Determination Act

On December 1, 1991, a federal bill known as the **Patient Self-Determination Act (PSDA)** (passed one year earlier) went into effect in all organizations receiving Medicare or Medicaid. This legislation guarantees the right of all competent adults to write an **advance directive (AD)** to participate in and direct their own health care decisions, and to accept or refuse treatment. The PSDA was passed in response to growing recognition of the burden placed on the dying and their families by advances in medical technology that make it possible to prolong life through artificial means. Prior to becoming ill, an individual can put in writing his or her wishes regarding end-of-life treatment. Furthermore, the PSDA mandated that health care professionals receive education themselves as well as provide information to patients about ADs upon their admission to the hospital. The existence of an AD must be documented in the medical record. Each state was permitted to establish and define its own legislation concerning advance directives, but the basic federal requirements had to be met in all Medicare- and Medicaid-funded facilities in order for them to continue to receive funding.

In an AD (also called a living will), individuals are asked to consider a number of issues regarding the end of their lives. These include what their preferences would be for medical interventions, whether they would trust another person ("proxy") to act on their behalf, and whether they have a specific desire for (or opposition to) any particular medical interventions. They are also encouraged to discuss their desires with family, their physicians, and other health care providers. Having considered these issues, people can then make legally binding arrangements which state that they shall not be sustained by artificial life support if they are no longer able to make that decision themselves. Protection against abuse of the process is provided by various safeguards such as requirements for witnesses and the determination of a terminal condition by more than one physician. In addition to documenting the patient's wishes, the PSDA was intended to ensure more active involvement in planning and treatment by patients and to uphold the principles of respect for their dignity and autonomy.

Research on the End of Life

At the same time that the PSDA legislation was passed, a landmark study was underway to document the experience of patients in medical settings at the end of life. The Study to Understand Prognoses and Preferences for Outcomes and Risks of Treatments (SUPPORT) data both on the final days of dying patients and on the impact of attempts to improve treatment of dying patients through education of health personnel. For two separate two-year periods (1989–1991 and 1992–1994), SUPPORT enrolled all patients who met the study-entry criteria of being in the advanced stages of diseases such as cancer, acute respiratory failure, multiple organ system failure, chronic obstructive pulmonary disease, congestive heart failure, and cirrhosis of the liver. It was expected that about half of the people who enrolled in the study would die within a six-month period after entry (Lynn et al., 1997). Along with SUPPORT, another sample ("HELP") was enrolled of persons 80 years of age and older who were hospitalized in one of four of the centers. This sample was included to make it possible to study the experience of hospitalized persons at advanced ages.

The first set of findings from the SUPPORT and HELP samples concerned the proportion of deaths that occurred in hospitals, nursing homes, hospices, and homes. The majority of patients in SUPPORT stated that they preferred to die at home; nonetheless, most of the deaths occurred in the hospital (Pritchard et al., 1998). Furthermore, the percentage of SUPPORT patients who died in the hospital varied by more than double across the five hospitals in the study (from 29 to 66%). The primary factor accounting for the probability of a patient dying in the hospital rather than at home was the availability of hospital beds. The probability of dying at home was lower in regions that had more nursing homes and hospices. Patient preferences, clinical condition, and socioeconomic status did not predict place of death. Interestingly, in the Canadian Study of Health and Aging, a large-scale investigation of predictors of mortality, institutionalization was associated with a higher risk of dying within the next five years, even after accounting for other relevant factors (Østbye, Steenhuis, Wolfson, Walton, & Hill, 1999).

The second major finding of SUPPORT was documentation of the physical and psychological characteristics of dying persons through interviews with family members. During the last three days of life, approximately 40% of patients who were conscious were reported to have been in severe pain. More than half of those who died from a serious illness had great difficulty breathing (dyspnea), and about one-quarter were severely confused. Nearly 80% of all patients

experienced fatigue. As you might imagine, these physical symptoms caused great discomfort, as was reported by almost three-quarters of the family members of dying patients (Lynn et al., 1997). Even more distressing, however, was the fact that the patients suffering the most severe pain and psychological symptoms (confusion, depression, and anxiety) were most dissatisfied with the level of pain control provided to them. Dissatisfaction with the level of pain control also varied by hospital, physician specialty, and income, with those having lower incomes reporting the most dissatisfaction (Desbiens et al., 1996). Sadly, even after training designed to provide patients, families, physicians, and nurses with information about pain management strategies, no improvements were noted in the experience of pain control among those patients who participated in this intervention (Desbiens et al., 1996). Apparently aggressive pain management is needed far earlier in the process than within the last few months or days of life (Field et al., 1997).

Not only were dying patients uncomfortable, but their care did not match their preferences. Here the distinction was between aggressive measures taken to prolong life in contrast with **palliative care**, which provides comfort care through measures such as pain control. The provision of aggressive care in cases where patients express a preference for comfort only is referred to in the end-of-life literature as **overtreatment** (Field et al., 1997). The majority of patients in SUPPORT preferred to receive palliative rather than aggressive care, but from 3 to 17% (depending on diagnosis) were given life-sustaining treatments regardless of their preferences. These life-sustaining treatments included resuscitation attempts, being placed on a ventilator, or having a feeding tube inserted into the stomach. Overall, over half of the patients had one of these life-sustaining treatments within the three days before they died (Lynn et al., 1997). Furthermore, in contrast to aggressive life-sustaining procedures, no clear guidelines were provided for those who received palliative care (Goodlin, Winzelberg, Teno, Whedon, & Lynn, 1998).

In the case of patients with colorectal cancer specifically (who tended to be in the most pain), it appeared that physicians and patients had difficulty communicating with each other about prognosis and treatment preferences (Haidet et al., 1998). Related studies were conducted under the auspices of SUPPORT on patients hospitalized with exacerbation of severe heart failure. As in the larger study, physicians in the majority of cases did not accurately perceive the preferences of their patients for resuscitation (Krumholz et al., 1998).

The most critical aspect of SUPPORT was investigation of the effectiveness of the PSDA, the legislation that created the requirement of ADs. The two periods of testing (1989–1991 and 1992–1994) coincided with the two years before and the two years immediately after implementation of PSDA. Of the 9,105 patients in the study, 4,301 were enrolled in the early period and 4,804 in the second period. The patients studied in the second period were divided into two groups: an intervention group (2,652 patients) and a control group (2,152 patients) (Teno et al., 1997). The intervention consisted of communication by nurses of detailed information on the prognoses and preferences of patients, which was intended to promote discussions about the course of their care. However, the intervention failed to lead to changes in the frequency of discussions about treatment preferences between physicians and patients. The intervention had no effects on other aspects of end-of-life care, including those identified as most important in the experience of dying patients, such as pain control and overtreatment.

Another aspect of SUPPORT was investigation of the **do not resuscitate (DNR) order**, a document placed in a patient's chart specifying the individual's desire not to be resuscitated if he or she should suffer a cardiac or respiratory arrest (a DNR may be part of an AD). The physician places this order with the consent of the patient or patient surrogate. In SUPPORT, investigators conducted an analysis of patients' preferences for cardiopulmonary resuscitation, severity of illness, and time to the first DNR order. Although DNR orders were issued sooner for patients who had requested a DNR order, only about one-half of the patients who preferred not to be resuscitated actually had DNR orders written. Furthermore DNR orders were more likely to be issued for patients with poorer prognoses. However, the age of the patient also appeared to play a role in the determination of when an order was placed. Those who were over the age of 75 years were more likely to have a DNR written for them regardless of their prognosis (Hakim et al., 1996).

In a subsequent investigation within SUPPORT, the methods of resuscitation examined were expanded to include withholding of ventilator support, surgery, and dialysis according to age, prognosis, and patient preferences. Again, age was associated with the decision to withhold life-sustaining treatment. In addition, physicians were more likely to underestimate the preferences for life-sustaining care among older patients (Hamel et al., 1996). Misunderstandings about patient preferences are more likely to arise when the patients are older because physicians assume that they would prefer not to be revived. Physicians also are less willing to take measures to keep patients alive who have dementia, whether or not the patients have an AD (Richardson, Sullivan, Hill, & Yu, 2007). The presence of a health care proxy, however, someone who is able to monitor and speak for the patient, can increase the chances that the dying individual's wishes will be respected (Fins et al., 1999). However, this proxy must be carefully chosen as one who will in fact represent the patient's wishes accurately (Fowler, Coppola, & Teno, 1999; Tsevat et al., 1998).

TABLE 13.1
Experiences of Dying Patients

Length of terminal phase		
> 48 h	4 (16%)	
24– < 48 h	12 (48%)	
< 24 h	5 (20%)	
Unknown	2 (8%)	
Sudden death	2 (8%)	
Discussion with family		
Yes	18 (78%)	
No		
DNR order		
Yes	21 (84%)	
No[a]	4 (16%)	
Survival after DNR order		
Median (inter-quartile range)	3 days (2.0, 5.5)	
Documented symptoms		
Dyspnoea	13 (52%)	
Pain	6 (24%)	
Agitation	6 (24%)	
Nausea/vomiting	4 (16%)	
Pharyngeal secretions	3 (12%)	
Prescription of treatment for		
symptom control	Yes	No
Dyspnea (n = 13)	9 (69%)	4 (21%)
Pain (n = 6)	3 (50%)	3 (50%)
Agitation (n = 6)	2 (33%)	4 (67%)
Nausea/vomiting (n = 4)	1 (25%)	3 (75%)
Pharyngeal secretions (n = 3)	2 (67%)	1 (33%)
Referred to palliative care team		
Yes	2 (8%)	
No	23 (92%)	

Details of end-of-life care in sample of patients dying in the hospital.
Source: Twomey, McDowell, & Corcoran, 2007.

The findings of SUPPORT continue to be confirmed in subsequent studies that document further the continued need to monitor the experience of dying patients. In addition, studies show that there continues to remain lack of coordination among health care providers, poor communication with dying patients, and failure to alleviate pain in terminally ill individuals. ADs are still not provided, leading to the feelings among the bereaved family that there was poor communication and that overly aggressive care was provided (Teno, Gruneir, Schwartz, Nanda,

& Wetle, 2007). Even when advance directives are written, their language may be vague and inconsistent (Happ et al., 2002). Adding to these problems is the fact that the majority of patients prefer not to think or talk about end-of-life issues (Klinkenberg, Willems, Onwuteaka-Philipsen, Deeg, & van der Wal, 2004).

The prevalence of chronic pain is estimated to occur in 45 to 80 percent of nursing home residents (Wunderlich, Kohler, & Committee on Improving Quality in Long-Term Care, 2001). Yet, adequate pain medication is not provided to alleviate this suffering (Twomey, McDowell, & Corcoran, 2007). In addition to pain, fatigue is a significant symptom that interferes with the dying person's quality of life, even in home palliative care (Husain et al., 2007). Other researchers have identified racial disparities in the presence of DNRs and living wills, with African Americans and Hispanics less likely to have advance care plan documents in their medical files (Degenholtz, Arnold, Meisel, & Lave, 2002). Similar cultural barriers were identified in studies on HIV-infected adults; physicians were less likely to communicate with African-American and Latino patients about end-of-life issues compared with white patients (Wenger et al., 2001).

There may also be cross-cultural variations in the provision of care at the end of life. In one intensive study on the experience of dying patients in Spain. Nearly half of families of patients dying from dementia and heart failure, reported that the symptoms such as pain were not adequately controlled in the last day before death and less than one-fifth received some form of spiritual support. However, unlike some of the data from American studies, there was a fairly high percentage (approximately two-thirds) of families who felt satisfied with the information they received (Formiga et al., 2007).

Some hopeful signs that the treatment of the dying is going to improve exist, however, even in the United States where care has lagged behind that of other countries. One team of investigators has developed the notion of "peaceful awareness," a state in which dying patients are aware that they have a terminal illness but are at peace with this knowledge. In a multisite study of dying patients, the researchers identified 18% of patients who fit these criteria for peaceful awareness. In comparing them to patients who did not have this characteristic, ratings of the overall quality of their death made by caregivers were significantly higher than for patients who were either not aware nor at peace (Ray et al., 2006).

Physician-Assisted Suicide and Euthanasia

Requesting an order for DNR and writing a living will are steps patients take to avoid prolonging life in the event that their bodily functions spontaneously cease to operate. These measures are taken as protection against the likelihood that the individual loses the capacity to make a conscious decision about allowing life to end naturally. In physician-assisted suicide (PAS), individuals make the conscious decision, while they are still able to do so, that they want their lives to end before dying becomes a protracted process. Similarly in **euthanasia**, although the physician's action causes death, the intent is to prevent the suffering associated with a prolonged ending of life.

A strongly vocal proponent of physician-assisted suicide was Dr. Jack Kevorkian. In 1956 he was dubbed "Dr. Death," not because he assisted a patient's suicide, but because he published a journal article in which he discussed his efforts to photograph the eyes of dying patients. Throughout the 1980s he published numerous articles on euthanasia, and by 1989 he had built a "suicide machine" which he then used in 1990 on his first patient, a 54-year-old woman with Alzheimer's disease. Throughout the 1990s he conducted a series of over 100 assisted suicides. In a highly controversial televised segment on the program *60 Minutes*, aired in November 1998, Kevorkian ended the life of a 52-year old Michigan man suffering from a terminal neurological disease. In this case Kevorkian administered the lethal dose, so the death was technically euthanasia, not assisted suicide. This action led to Kevorkian's arrest and subsequent conviction on second-degree murder charges. In 2007, Kevorkian was released from prison after serving eight years of a 10- to 25-year sentence.

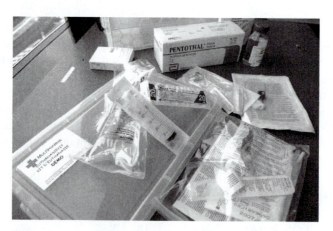

Shown here are medications used in physician-assisted suicide.

One state in the U.S. has legalized physician-assisted suicide. The Oregon Death with Dignity Act (OWDA), enacted in 1997, specifies that a physician may prescribe lethal medication to hasten death for competent, terminally ill persons who voluntarily request it (Oregon Death with Dignity Act, 2 Ore. Rev. Stat. Sec. 127.800-127.897). Patients must wait 15 days from the request, but the law does not require that the patient seek mental health interventions or notification of family. Since its passage 292 patients have died under the terms of the legislation (http://oregon.gov/DHS/ph/pas/faqs.shtml). The most common requests for assisted suicide between the years of 1998 and 2004 were loss of autonomy, diminished ability to participate in activities that enhance the quality of life, and loss of dignity (Charatan, 2006). In January 2006, the Supreme Court upheld the Oregon law, which had been challenged by the administration of President George W. Bush, who had attempted to prosecute physicians for violating the Federal Substances Control Act.

To put this into context, directives specifying the withholding or withdrawal of life-extending medical treatment represent voluntary passive euthanasia. This procedure is legal in all states, whereas physician-assisted suicide is legal only in Oregon. Voluntary active euthanasia, which is a request for the physician to end the life of terminally ill patients, is legal in such European countries as Switzerland, the Netherlands and Belgium.

Those who favor physician-assisted suicide (or active euthanasia) and who support measures such as the Oregon Death with Dignity Law regard as essential the individual's right to make the decision, the need to relieve suffering, and fears that life can be extended beyond the point when it has meaning. A study in the Netherlands, found that taking into account the dying individual's wishes to die with dignity is perhaps the most important component of this process (Georges et al., 2007).

Those who oppose physician-assisted suicide regard as primary the physician's ethical code to "do no harm" and do not wish to present options to patients that they do not find morally acceptable (Curlin, Lawrence, Chin, & Lantos, 2007). Opponents also are concerned with abuse or misuse and the belief that life-and-death decisions fall in the province of religion. Furthermore, the status of being "terminally ill" may be unclear because the definition of what is terminal cannot be supported reliably by data (Lynn, 1996). Other arguments against assisted suicide are that

Scott Rice, whose wife used Oregon's assisted suicide law to end her life, holds up a sketch of the supreme Court hearings.

personal growth may occur even in the last stages of dying (Byock, 1993).

Surveys conducted to determine the extent to which measures such as the Oregon DWDA are seen favorably show some variations in attitudes toward physician-assistance. In Oregon the large majority of psychologists were in favor of the DWDA, both in terms of supporting its enactment (78%) and in terms of stating that they would consider physician-assisted suicide for themselves (Fenn & Ganzini, 1999). Physicians (31%), however, are far less likely to support the enactment of such legislation (Duberstein et al., 1995). Although an important ethical question, practically speaking, there has been little in the way of change in Oregon in response to this law, because relatively a small number of terminally ill patients have chosen to end their lives in this manner (Hedberg, Hopkins, & Kohn, 2003).

One of the strongest arguments against physician-assisted suicide is based on evidence that the decision by the terminally ill individual to end life may be based on lack of appropriate care of dying individuals. Those dying patients who are suicidal may have treatable psychological symptoms that, when addressed properly, lead them to regain the will to live. There is tremendous variation even on a day-to-day basis in feelings about assisted suicide (Pacheco, Hershberger, Markert, & Kumar, 2003). People who make this decision may be suicidal because they are depressed, anxious, or in pain. When the source of their symptoms is identified and treatment is attempted, the desire to die wanes (Bascom & Tolle, 2002); the individual may be grateful for having additional time to live (Hendin, 1999).

Suggestions for End-of-Life Care

Clearly, those who are dying wish to have their preferences respected with regard to the way they end their lives. Because there is no one scenario that best describes the type of ending that they envision, individuals must be given the opportunity to make the choice that best fits their values and desires (Vig, Davenport, & Pearlman, 2002). Unfortunately, this is generally not the case; in part because dying patients are often not able to express their wishes. One suggestion to overcome this obstacle to respecting the individual's autonomy is to reconstruct the patient's wishes from documents or relatives (Sullivan, 2002).

There may also be problems stemming from differences in cultural values between health care workers and patients. For example, interviews with Chinese older adults living in Canada revealed a lack of acceptance of advance directives due to differences in values between Confucianist, Buddhist, and Taoist religions and those of Western medicine (Bowman & Singer, 2001). It is therefore necessary to understand the patient's cultural background when providing end-of-life care (Crawley, Marshall, Lo, & Koenig, 2002). Options should, if possible, be discussed with family members (Haley et al., 2002; Hickman, 2002).

Another problem is the lack of coordination within long-term care facilities in the decision-making process used to initiate end-of-life care. Nursing home staff often have not developed procedures to communicate either among themselves or with patients to determine at what point in the resident's illness palliative care should begin (Travis et al., 2002). As with the provision of good nursing home care, an interdisciplinary approach can help to overcome the problems of lack of coordination and communication among health care workers (Connor, Egan, Kwilosz, Larson, & Reese, 2002).

Increasingly, the provision of end-of-life care designed to meet the needs of the individual patient is the domain of a facility known as a **hospice** (Ganzini et al., 2001). The term hospice is ordinarily used to refer to a site or program that provides medical and supportive services for dying patients and their families and friends (Field et al., 1997). Within the hospice environment, the needs of dying patients are attended to with regard to their needs for physical comfort, psychological and social support, and the opportunity to express and have their spiritual needs met. The care is palliative, focusing on controlling pain and other symptoms, and it is likely to take place within the home. Hospice care was introduced in the 1960s, with the goal of alleviating the pain, nausea, confusion, and sleep disturbances experienced by cancer patients within their last months of life. The first well-known hospice was St. Christopher's in London, which opened in 1967. The hospice movement spread to the United States in the 1970s. In 1982, hospice benefits were made available to persons on Medicare who had a life expectancy of less than six months.

When asked to provide their perspectives on the desired aspects of end-of-life care, patients describe concerns very similar to those that are addressed within the hospice framework. These needs include obtaining adequate pain control and symptom management, avoiding an extended period of dying, achieving a sense of personal control, relieving the burden they place on others, and strengthening ties with those who are close to them (Kelly et al., 2002).

In 1997, the American Medical Association approved a set of guidelines to establish quality care for individuals at the end of life. These included providing patients with the opportunity to discuss and plan for end-of-life care, assurance that attempts will be made to provide comfort and respect the patient's end-of-life wishes, assurance of dignity, and attention to the individual's goals. These rights also include minimizing the burden to the family and assisting the bereaved through the stages of mourning and adjustment. There is some indication that efforts such as this are improving the quality

of care provided to terminally ill patients. A 1996 survey of over 1,000 physicians studied 20 years earlier reported an increase in the willingness of these physicians to discuss issues related to end-of-life care (Dickinson, Tournier, & Still, 1999). Moreover, medical schools are increasingly incorporating palliative care into their curriculums (Dickinson, 2002).

The report of the Committee on the Care at the End of Life sponsored by the Institute of Medicine recommended attending to the practical needs of patients as a crucial component of care (Field et al., 1997). They proposed assisting the patient and family in obtaining home health services, making changes in the home to accommodate the patient, and providing help with routine daily tasks such as shopping. Attending to these practical needs may also involve a variety of other people in the patient's social network. Neighbors can provide help with daily tasks, employers can allow for flexible work schedules of caregivers, and groceries and pharmacies can provide delivery services. In general, the community can be supportive in alleviating some of the stress encountered by caregivers in adjusting to the need to care for a terminally ill relative. Furthermore the comfort provided to the patient can carry over to meeting other psychological needs. In the course of providing for the concerns of everyday life, the patient also feels cared for in a larger sense.

As physicians, psychologists, and other health care workers entering the field are given education in end-of-life care, we may hope that there will be improvement in the near future in communication with dying patients and alleviation of their symptoms (Block & Billings, 2005). Programs in the United States, Canada, Sweden, and the United Kingdom are benefiting from knowledge about the dying trajectory, adjusting approaches to end-of-life care to the nature of the patient's needs, rhythms, and situations (Dy & Lynn, 2007).

BEREAVEMENT

Bereavement is the process during which we attempt to overcome the death of another person with whom there we had a relationship. The bereavement process may occur at any point in life. However, it is more likely to take place in later adulthood when people have an increased risk of losing spouse, siblings, friends, colleagues, and other peers.

The physical and psychological symptoms associated with bereavement are particularly severe in the first year following loss. The physical symptoms can include shortness of breath, frequent sighing, tightness in the chest, feelings of emptiness, loss of energy and strength, and digestive disturbances. In some cases, the individual may be vulnerable to physical illness due to the reduced effectiveness of the immune system, which is sensitive to stress. The emotional reactions to bereavement include anger, depression, anxiety, sleep disturbances, and preoccupation with thoughts of the deceased. Other problems associated with bereavement include impairments in attention and memory, a desire to withdraw from social activities, and increased risk of accidents. The symptoms of bereavement, as difficult as they are, nevertheless appear to subside greatly in most of us after a period of one year.

Death of a Spouse

The death of a spouse is regarded as one of the most stressful events of life, and for many older adults, widowhood involves the loss of a relationship that may have lasted as long as 50 years or more (see also Chapter 9). Among the many ramifications of widowhood are loss of an attachment figure, interruption of the plans and hopes invested in the relationship, and construction of a new identity in accordance with the reality of being single (Field, Nichols, Holen, & Horowitz, 1999). People who are widowed are at higher risk of developing depression and anxiety disorders (Onrust & Cuijpers, 2006). They may experience symptoms such as sensing the presence, dreaming about, and having hallucinations or illusions of seeing or hearing the deceased (Lindstrom, 1995; LoConto, 1998). These feelings of grief over the loss of the spouse may persist for as long as two and a half years (Ott & Lueger, 2002). Indeed, as pointed out in Chapter 9, widows may continue to think about the spouse and even have "conversations" with the deceased on a weekly basis for as long as 35 years or more (Carnelley, Wortman, Bolger, & Burke, 2006).

A number of factors may affect the extent to which an individual experiences adverse effects of widowhood. One set of factors has to do with the bereaved individual's personality. A major prospective study of over 200 individuals who were tested before they became widowed, and followed for 18 months after they became widowed, identified five patterns of bereavement: common grief, chronic grief, chronic depression, improvement during bereavement, and resilience (Bonanno et al., 2002). In common grief, the individual experiences an initial increase in depression that diminishes over time. This pattern is actually relatively infrequent. More likely to occur is resilient grief, in which the bereaved shows little or no distress following the loss. Two additional patterns distinguish grief from depression. In chronic grief, the individual experiences high levels of both depression and grief within 6 months after the loss, and the grief does not subside over time. In chronic depression, the bereaved suffers from high levels of depression prior to and after the loss.

In addition to measuring marital conflict, Bonanno and his co-investigators examined the coping resources, interpersonal dependency, personality traits (based on the Five Factor Model), religiosity, world views, and social support of the widows. People with high levels of interpersonal dependency (including dependence on their spouses) were most likely to show the

FIGURE 13.5
Patterns of Grief in Widowhood

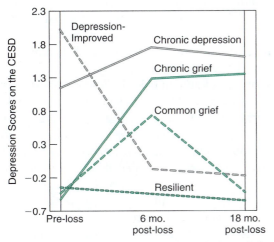

Depression scores for the five bereavement groups before and after the loss of the spouse.

Source: Bonanno et al., 2002.

chronic grief pattern. Those who showed the pattern of resilience were most accepting of death and were more likely to agree with the notion that the world is "just" (i.e., that people "get" what they "deserve"). Studies such as these underscore the notion that bereavement is not a unitary process and that there are multiple factors influencing reactions to the loss of a spouse.

Age is another individual difference factor predicting reactions to widowhood. It is well established by now that younger widows suffer more negative consequences of widowhood, including more severe deterioration of health and higher mortality rates (Stroebe, Stroebe, Gergen, & Gergen, 1981; Stroebe & Stroebe, 1987). One reason for the differing effects of widowhood on younger and older spouses may be the expectedness of the death. Older spouses are more prepared for the death of the partner, a fact that is particularly true for women, who are likely to be younger than their husbands. However, being able to anticipate the death is not necessarily the key factor in accounting for the age difference in reactions to widowhood. Anticipatory grief may heighten rather than reduce the grief that follows the spouse's death (Gilliland & Fleming, 1998). Younger widows may benefit somewhat more from the forewarning given to them by an anticipated death because they may be better able to withstand the caregiving process.

Difficult emotional responses may follow the death of a spouse due to illnesses such as cancer and Alzheimer's disease that involved marked physical and mental deterioration and placed extensive burden on the caregivers (Ferrario, Cardillo, Vicario, Balzarini, & Zotti, 2004). Relief from the pressures of caregiving can lead to alleviation of symptoms of depression and stress present during the spouse's dying months or years (Bonanno, Wortman, & Nesse, 2004).

Men appear to experience greater stress following the death of their wives than women upon the death of their husbands (Stroebe, 2001)(see also Chapter 9). Widowers are at greater mortality risk within the first six months after bereavement than are widows, with a mortality rate estimated in one study to be 12 times higher for men than women for those over 75 years of age (Gallagher-Thompson, Futterman, Farberow, Thompson, & Peterson, 1993). This sex difference in reactions to bereavement does not appear to be due to the greater social support that women experience as widows (Stroebe, Stroebe, & Abakoumkin, 1999). Men are more likely to remarry, but women are more likely to form new friendships, particularly with neighbors (Lamme, Dykstra, & Broese Van Groenou, 1996). It is possible that social support plays a greater role in the adaptation of women to widowhood, but for men (particularly current cohorts) a more relevant factor is the availability of practical support in performing household tasks (Gass, 1989).

A **dual-process model of stress and coping** has been proposed to account for the multiple changes that occur following the loss of a spouse (Stroebe & Schut, 1999). According to this model, the stress experienced following the loss of a partner can be divided into two broad categories. The first, the emotional category, includes the sadness directly associated with the loss of the loved one as attachment figure. The second category includes the set of life changes that accompany the loss, including moving from an identity as being a part of a couple to the identity of being a single person. For example, becoming a "widow" can lead to social isolation when a woman's friends were all friends of the couple. This model states that the bereaved must deal with both components of loss. If they focus on one to the exclusion or neglect of the other, they will have a much more difficult and lengthy period of readjustment. The model postulates that dealing with both the direct emotional consequences of loss and concurrently occurring life changes is essential for adjustment to loss and that preoccupation with one of these aspects, to the neglect of the other, slows down this process.

The dual processes involved in coping with the stress of bereavement are known as the "loss" and "restoration" dimensions. The loss dimension involves coping with the emotional pain of not having the attachment figure present. Coping with the secondary stress of changes in daily life and identity is the restoration dimension. Health adjustment is promoted by alternating between the two forms of coping. At times it is best to confront the emotional loss of the partner; at other times, it is most advantageous to avoid confronting these emotions and instead attempting to manage the secondary consequences of loss (Stroebe, Schut, & Stroebe, 2005).

Death of Other Family Members

The loss of an adult child is perhaps the most distressing and devastating of all forms of bereavement. The grief a parent experiences over a child's death is highly intense and is associated with increased risk of depression, guilt, and health complaints. The distress of a parent who loses a child may also be associated with feelings of helplessness, insecurity, and isolation. In addition, for older adults, the individual experiences the very practical loss of a central supportive figure in life (McKiernan, 1996). Loss of an adult child also violates the individual's normative expectations that a parent dies before the children. Consequently, the depression and deterioration of health experienced after a child's death may persist unabated for a decade, if not longer (de Vries, Davis, Wortman, & Lehman, 1997). Although these feelings may never be completely overcome, bereaved parents eventually seem to be able to find a sense of meaning and purpose in life, particularly through connections with other people and the feeling of connection with the lost child (Wheeler, 2001).

In the death of a grandchild, the emotional pain of the older individual is intensified by that shared with the child's parents. Feelings of guilt over being alive while one's grandchild is not may accompany the emotional devastation over the child's loss (Fry, 1997). The suffering of grandparents may be especially pronounced when they were involved in raising the child, as was documented for grandmothers of children killed in the Oklahoma City bombing of 1995. However, at least for these grandmothers, formation of a sense of community and use of each other for support can help foster resilience even in the face of this profound loss (Allen, Whittlesey, Pfefferbaum, & Ondersma, 1999).

Compared with the death of a child or grandchild, the death of a parent is a far more normative event of adult life. Nevertheless, this experience can cause psychological distress and a deterioration of health status (Umberson & Chen, 1994). The death of a parent can also lead to increased marital conflict, particularly when the loss is of a father (Umberson, 1995). In general daughters are more negatively affected by parental death than are sons who, in turn, tend to be more accepting of the loss (Moss, Resch, & Moss, 1997).

Although somewhat normative as well, the deaths of siblings and friends are also sources of distress in later adulthood. The death of a brother in particular may bring not only emotional pain but increased financial hardship (Hays, Gold, & Peiper, 1997). For those who suffer the loss of friends, in addition to feelings of grief there may be an increased incentive to develop new relationships, including closer relations with other friends and relatives (Roberto & Stanis, 1994).

Certain losses that occur in adulthood fall outside the category of family and friends but may be painful nevertheless. Individuals whose job places them in situations where they work with dying persons may experience severe anxiety symptoms that interfere with their daily lives and ability to perform their jobs. For example, not only survivors but also the recovery workers in a disaster site experience lingering symptoms of trauma that proved resistant to treatment (Tucker, Pfefferbaum, Nixon, & Foy, 1999). These are common reactions.

Theories of Bereavement

Until relatively recently, conventional and professional wisdom regarding bereavement was based on the assumption that the survivor must "work through" the death of the deceased. According to this view, the individual must experience a period of mourning, but after that, it is time to move on and seek new relationships and attachments. In part, this view was based on the assumption within psychodynamic theory that to resolve grief normally, emotional bonds to the loved one must be broken (Bowlby, 1980). However, a new view of bereavement is taking shape. It is recognized that expressions of continuing attachment are potentially adaptive in providing

the individual with a sense of continuity in the face of loss (Kastenbaum, 1999). This view, which is held within contemporary non-Western cultures such as the Japanese and Egyptian Muslim cultures, was also strongly maintained by nineteenth-century romanticists. Furthermore, though not necessarily advocated by the professional community, continued attachment to the deceased remains a part of the experience of bereaved individuals (Stroebe, Gergen, Gergen, & Stroebe, 1992).

Feelings of continued attachment to the deceased may be expressed in several of the behaviors noted earlier as "symptoms" of bereavement. For example, the sense of the spouse's presence helps maintain the feeling that the spouse is watching over or guiding the individual. Another form of attachment is to maintain the spouse's possessions because of their symbolic value. Comfort may also come from keeping alive the memories of the deceased spouse. Rather than abandoning all these forms of attachment to the spouse, part of successful adaptation seems to involve moving away from the concrete reminders of the deceased (possessions) to the more abstract ties that involve thoughts and memories (Field, Gal-Oz, & Bonanno, 2003). Such forms of coping may help the individual acknowledge and accept the death while making the transition to a new, single identity. Mastery over the loss may then occur, even as the deceased spouse remains an active mental presence. According to this view, the normal response to grief involves living with rather than "getting over it."

As we have seen in this chapter, we can all learn from the experience of people as they cope with death, dying, and bereavement. In particular, older adults have a remarkable ability to manage with the fear of death that causes younger people to react with anxiety and efforts at denial. It may be the ability to move ahead without losing memory for the departed individuals in one's life that long-lived individuals possess and make it possible for them to survive repeated losses in later adulthood. These individuals have developed ways of integrating the pain of multiple losses into their lives and can take their lives in positive new directions (Kastenbaum, 1999). In the future, this process may be made that much less painful by the understanding among mental health professionals of the need to retain rather than abandon the emotional ties of attachment.

SUMMARY

1. Death is defined as the point of irreversible loss of bodily functions, although this state may be difficult to determine as a result of the advent of life support systems which can keep people alive on life-support. At the end of life, individuals experience a number of physical changes, many of which are physically uncomfortable in addition to involving a great deal of pain.

2. Mortality data provide insight into the variations by age, sex, and race in the causes of death. Younger adults are more likely to die from accidents and older adults from heart disease. Variations exist, however, within age, race, and sex groups reflecting sociocultural factors in lifestyles and risk factors. Mortality rates are decreasing around the world, primarily because of a decrease in infant mortality. However, mortality reductions vary according to the level of a country's economic development. The poor are disproportionately more likely to die in all countries around the world, particularly where there is inadequate health care.

3. A culture's death ethos is reflected in the traditions established by that culture in funeral rituals, belief in the afterlife, and the language used to describe death. Western attitudes toward death have undergone major shifts throughout history. Contemporary American attitudes regard death in a sensationalistic way, but there is a predominant tendency to institutionalize death and make it "invisible." The death with dignity movement has attempted to promote the idea that the individual should have control over the conditions of death. The dying process may occur through one of several dying trajectories, or rate of decline in functioning prior to death.

4. Issues in end-of-life care focus on the extent to which dying patients can exert control over their medical care. As a result of the Patient Self Determination Act, individuals can establish advance directives that indicate whether they wish to extend their lives through artificial means prior to needing to make this decision. The SUPPORT study on end-of-life care revealed a number of serious weaknesses in the medical care of dying patients in the United States. Many were in pain, felt their preference for palliative care was not respected, and did not believe that they had an adequate opportunity to discuss their preferences with their health care providers. Physician-assisted suicide is a controversial issue that is now legal in the state of Oregon. Hospices are settings that provide medical and supportive services for dying patients, allowing them to receive personal attention and maintain contact with family.

5. Bereavement is the process of mourning the loss of a close person. The death of a spouse is the most severe loss an individual can experience, but the death of other family members, especially children, causes extreme and long-lasting distress. In the past, theories of grief resolution focused on the need to "work through" a death. Current views are emphasizing an alternative in which the bereaved are more accepting of the sad feelings accompanying the loss.

CHAPTER 14

Successful Aging
and Creativity

"Grow old along with me! The best is yet to be."

Robert Browning
(1812–1889)

Many of us assume that the personal and social losses associated with this period of life lead to an inevitable deterioration of well-being and adjustment. Yet survival into the later years of adulthood requires that, in fact, the individual can negotiate the many threats presented to living a long life. These include the threats of dying from accident, illness, and violent acts. Because they have managed to avoid these threats to their existence and personal happiness, there may be some special quality about increasingly older individuals that can account, in part, for their having reached advanced old age.

In this final chapter, we will have the opportunity to explore the topics of psychological growth and creativity in the later adult years. The concept of "survival" as applied to old age fails to capture the additional element present in the lives of successful agers—namely, the ability to achieve heightened levels of personal expression and happiness. As we look at **successful aging**, it is these inspirational qualities that can guide and sustain our own optimism and hope about our future adult years.

THEORETICAL PERSPECTIVES ON SUCCESSFUL AGING

The study of successful aging is, in part, an attempt by theorists and researchers to identify and understand the factors that contribute to the ability of the older individual to survive. However, as noted above, the study of successful aging goes beyond the question of survival. Successful aging involves the additional quality of enhancing the healthy spirit and sense of joy in life seen in older adults who seem to transcend physical limitations. In many ways, successful aging is synonymous with "mental health" in that the qualities thought to be desirable for optimal adaptation, such as a positive outlook and greater self-understanding, are also part of the criteria for successful aging. The fact that these qualities are achieved in later adulthood, thought to be a time of loss and perhaps a diminution of energy, is regarded as placing this type of mental health into a special category of adaptive phenomena.

"What do you think?" | **14-1**

Do you know people who exemplify successful aging? What are their characteristics?

A model of successful aging based on a major research effort in the United States known as the MacArthur Foundation Study of Aging in America, incorporates three interactive components (Rowe & Kahn, 1998). The absence of disease and the disability associated with disease is the first component, which includes not being ill but also not having the risk factors that will increase the chances of disease and disability. The second component is maintaining high cognitive and physical function, which gives the individual the potential to be active and competent. The third component, called "engagement with life," refers to involvement in productive activity and involvement with other people.

Subsequent research has built on this model and continues to emphasize the point that although in order to age successfully you have to "not die" (as pointed out in Chapter 1),

there are additional elements involving multiple dimensions of functioning. These dimensions include adaptive processes that allow the older individual to compensate effectively for a variety of challenges to mental and physical health. Using criteria derived roughly from the Rowe and Kahn definition, it appears that over one-third of older adults on average meet these criteria, although some studies have identified as many as 95% fitting the definition of successful agers (Depp & Jeste, 2006).

Social support and the involvement of others are also crucial factors in successful aging (Reichstadt, Depp, Palinkas, Folsom, & Jeste, 2007). For example, an investigation of Australian elders pointed to the importance of involvement with family in helping individuals cope with stressful life circumstances (Kissane & McLaren, 2006).

When discussing successful aging, people have a tendency to view the happy and productive older person as an anomaly. This productive older person has managed to avoid the expected state of gloom and despair we think is a normal accompaniment to the aging process. The implicit assumption is that aging inevitably brings about depression and despair, so when people do not show these qualities, they must be truly special. However, as we have seen elsewhere in this book, most older people do not become depressed, and personality development in middle and later adulthood appears to be in the positive direction of greater adaptiveness. Cognitive functioning is also preserved in the majority of older adults. As shown in one study of Italian centenarians, over half (54%) had either no or slight impairments (Motta, Bennati, Ferlito, Malaguarnera, & Motta, 2005).

One reason that the successful ager is thought of as the miraculous exception rather than the rule is that many theorists, researchers, and laypeople believe in the **social indicator model** (Mroczek & Kolarz, 1998). According to this model, demographic and social structural variables, such as age, gender, marital status, and income account for individual differences in levels of well-being. Because by demographic standards older individuals are in a disadvantaged position on these indices they should therefore have lower feelings of happiness. When someone is able to avoid becoming depressed by the potentially disturbing circumstances of poor health, widowhood, and low income, then that person seems deserving of some kind of special recognition.

As judged solely by the standards of being able to avoid the despair brought about by lower status on important social indicators, however, there would in fact be many successful agers. The majority of older adults maintain relatively high levels of well-being, a phenomenon referred to as the **paradox of well-being** (Mroczek & Kolarz,

1998). Despite their objective difficulties, people in later life feel good about themselves and their situations. Successful aging, then, appears to be the norm rather than the exception. The large majority rate themselves as "very" or "pretty" happy (Mroczek & Kolarz, 1998). As shown in Figure 14.1, most older adults also rate their physical health as good to excellent even though, objectively, we know that aging is associated with a number of chronic conditions.

Findings from countries around the world support this positive image of aging as a time of increased feelings of satisfaction (Diener & Suh, 1998). Regardless of age, most people report having a positive evaluation of themselves and their lives (Diener, 1998).

Clearly, however, people of all ages vary in their levels of happiness and well-being, and

FIGURE 14.1

Percentages of Older Adults Who Reported Having Good to Excellent Health—United States, 2002–2004

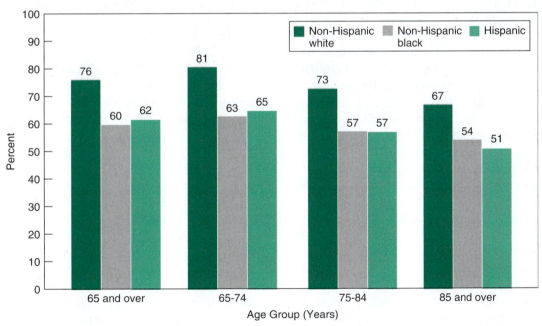

Despite the fact that most older adults have at least one chronic health condition, the fact that the large majority rate their health as good to excellent suggests that older adults are able to maintain a positive view of life.

Source: http://www.agingstats.gov/agingstatsdotnet/Main_Site/Data/2006_Documents/slides/OA_2006.ppt.

not everyone can be equally optimistic about his or her life situation. It is for this reason that research within the successful aging framework has focused on refining the concept of well-being and studying in depth its correlates in middle and later adulthood.

SUBJECTIVE WELL-BEING

The variable studied within the psychology of adult development and aging most closely related to the notion of successful aging is **subjective well-being**. In a general sense, subjective well-being refers to an individual's overall sense of happiness. For research purposes, however, the concept is divided into three components: positive affect, negative affect, and **life satisfaction**, or the cognitive evaluation of one's life circumstances (Diener, 1998).

Perhaps the most extensive recent investigation of the factors contributing to subjective well-being in middle adulthood was the Midlife in the United States Survey (MIDUS) carried out within the context of the MacArthur Study of Successful Midlife Development. The MIDUS sample was made up of over 2,700 participants, who were asked to complete mail and phone surveys focusing on issues of middle and later adulthood. The surveys were completed in 1995 through early 1996. The ages of the participants ranged from 25 to 74 years, with an average of 46, placing the sample squarely within midlife. The findings of the MIDUS study were consistent in many ways with earlier data in that the older adults in the sample emerged as successful agers, at least as judged in terms of their ratings of affect (Mroczek & Kolarz, 1998). However, personality also played a role. Extraverted men throughout adulthood in the MIDUS study had higher levels of well-being, a finding that points to the importance of considering longstanding

dispositional factors as influences on well-being throughout life.

The notion that well-being reflects personality traits is known as the **set point perspective**. According to this view, biologically determined temperament sets the boundaries for the levels of well-being we experience throughout life. For example people high in self-esteem in childhood tend to have higher self-esteem throughout life (Robins & Trzesniewski, 2005). Extraverts have an advantage over introverts according to this viewpoint, for people high on the trait of extraversion tend to view the world in a more positive light, regardless of actual circumstances. Furthermore it is possible that extraverted people, because of their sunny natures, have more success in their dealings with others and, therefore, a stronger objective basis for their optimism. A large scale longitudinal investigation of U.S. veterans supported this view, in that men high in extraversion tended to have consistently high life satisfaction throughout the adult years (Mroczek & Spiro, 2005).

However, of greater interest to researchers are the psychological mechanisms that people use to reach higher levels of well-being than their objective circumstances would warrant. Simple **adaptation** or habituation is one of these theorized psychological mechanisms that people may use to maintain high well-being in the face of objectively negative circumstances. Through adaptation, we learn to live at a certain level of health, income, or discomfort in our situations as we adjust our daily lives to fit the constraints presented to us (Easterlin, 2006). The kind of negative life events that we may experience within the course of our ordinary lives (deaths of relatives, divorce of self or parents, loss of job) may even be adapted to through a kind of habituation process even though each of us may have higher or lower set points (Diener, Lucas, & Scollon, 2006).

| *"What do you think?"* | **14-2** |

Are people who feel good about themselves despite objective limitations better off than people who are realists? Why or why not?

The extent to which our experiences are consistent with our goals provides another source of the basis for subjective well-being (Austin & Vancouver, 1996). If we are able to achieve or make progress toward reaching our goals, we will feel better about ourselves and our experiences. Furthermore, we will be more satisfied with our objective situations in life if we see these as potentially contributing to the achievement of our goals (Diener & Fujita, 1995). For example you might live in a cramped and uncomfortable student apartment while in graduate school if this is seen as facilitating your long-term educational goal of obtaining an advanced degree.

There are life-span components to goal setting as well. Longitudinal data from a study of gifted individuals revealed that people who set high goals for themselves in midlife were the most likely to have high goals in later adulthood, particularly if they valued having a rich cultural life and contributing to society (Holahan & Chapman, 2002).

On a more active level, we may alter our views of our life circumstances through problem-focused and emotion-focused coping strategies. Although the objective nature of our life circumstances must be taken into account (Diener, Oishi, & Lucas, 2003), coping accounts for the way that we interpret these circumstances. For example, in one study of community-dwelling older adults, those in good physical condition with few depressive symptoms were better able to withstand stressful life events such as personal illness and death or illness of a friend or family member (Hardy, Concato, &

Gill, 2004). Religion also plays a role in adapting to difficult life circumstances, serving as another important coping resource for many older adults (Van Ness & Larson, 2002). Finally, cultures and nations vary in their norms or expectations for experiencing emotions. For example, people in China have the lowest frequency and intensity of both positive and negative emotions compared to people living in the United States, Australia, and Taiwan (Eid & Diener, 2001).

Another active adaptational process is **social comparison**, through which we look at the situations of others who are more unfortunate than we are, and comfort ourselves with the thought that things could be worse (Michalos, 1985). In the face of threat, such as death from cancer, people manage to maintain a positive outlook by regarding themselves as having adjusted better than have others to the disease (Helgeson & Taylor, 1993). Similarly, older individuals may use social comparison to help negotiate potentially stressful transitions, such as having to relocate their place of residence (Kwan, Love, Ryff, & Essex, 2003). Regulation of affect, through processes described in socioemotional selectivity theory, is another mechanism that people may use to maintain a positive outlook on life, particularly in later adulthood. Changes in the ability to regulate affect and alterations in the nature of relationships with others may provide a concrete basis for improved feelings of well-being in later life (Mroczek & Kolarz, 1998). Both a change in perspective and in the focus of their emotional investment accounts for the ability of older adults to experience high levels of well-being. In other words, older adults manage to find ways to maximize their feelings of happiness by focusing on the positive features of their relationships.

Positive relationships contribute to well-being in other ways as well. Among older adults, those who feel that they have high levels of social support are most likely to have higher feelings of subjective well-being and a more positive evaluation of their quality of life (Bowling, Banister, Sutton, Evans, & Windsor, 2002). It is not only the number of people in their social network, but also the quality of social support that can help older people feel more satisfied with their lives (Berg, Hassing, McClearn, & Johansson, 2006). Think of how this process applies in your own life; by having others regard you positively, it is likely that you will develop enhanced sense of self-esteem, which in turn has positive effects on your subjective health, which in turn enhances your well-being, and so on. Interestingly, even physical performance factors, such as measures of gait (walking), may be improved by the social support that can make people feel better about themselves (Kim & Nesselroade, 2002). The specific aspect of self-esteem involved in these processes is the sense that you are valued by others (Bailis & Chipperfield, 2002). Older adults who value social participation tend to maintain a consistent level of activity over time, as long as their health permits, and they tend to become involved in a variety of activities, including participation in politics (Bukov, Maas, & Lampert, 2002).

Thus, social support and relationships with others have an influence on feelings of well-being by reinforcing the view that you are valued. At the same time, being concerned about family and having a sense of responsibility for your children and other family members seems to have additional adaptive value. In one investigation of Australians ranging from 61 to 95 years of age, sense of belonging and concern about family predicted high scores on a measure assessing reasons for living (Kissane & McLaren, 2006).

At a less empirical level, Erikson captured some of the creative qualities of the process of successful aging in the book *Vital Involvement in Old Age* (Erikson, Erikson, & Kivnick, 1986). The book analyzes interviews conducted on 29 participants in the Berkeley Growth Study who had been studied from birth and were in their 80s at the time of the study. Erikson and his collaborators identified people who had risen above the infirmities and limitations of aging. For example, one woman, an "inveterate reader," had become blind. Rather than give up her goal of reading, she switched to books on tape. This woman also felt free to "act on impulse" in the area of cooking: "If I want to bake a cake during the day, I just do it" (Erikson et al., 1986, p. 193). The story of this woman, like that of others in the sample, demonstrated that "although impairment and a certain degree of disability may be inevitable in old age, handicap and its deleterious effects on psychosocial well-being need not necessarily follow" (Erikson et al., 1986, p. 194). Not all the people in the sample shared this determination to overcome adversity. The key factor seemed to be an ability to define oneself independently of age- or illness-based limitations.

Finally, identity processes may provide a means of maintaining high levels of well-being in the face of less than satisfactory circumstances. Through identity assimilation, people may place a positive interpretation on what might otherwise cause them to feel that they are not accomplishing their desired objectives. The process of the **life story**, through which we develop a narrative view of our lives that emphasizes the positive, is an example of identity assimilation as it alters the way that we interpret events that might otherwise detract from our self-esteem (Whitbourne, Sneed, & Skultety, 2002). For instance, older psychiatric patients in one study were found to minimize or even deny the fact that they had spent a significant part of their lives within the hospital (Whitbourne & Sherry, 1991). The sense of subjective well-being is maintained as people manage to portray their identity in a positive light, even when their actual experiences would support less favorable interpretations.

PRODUCTIVITY AND CREATIVITY

Although many strategies people use to enhance their well-being involve an active process of reinterpreting their experiences, there is still a reactive focus to the subjective well-being literature. Within this framework, older individuals are seen as finding ways to adjust their experiences or their views of their experiences so that they are able to maintain a positive overall outlook. However, this literature does not necessarily address the extent to which people seek out new experiences and encounters that will move them beyond their current levels of well-being and accomplishments. Successful aging must surely involve more than maintaining a positive outlook on life, even as that life becomes potentially more stressful. To tackle this issue, it is necessary to go beyond some of the traditional social psychological literature on aging and move into the areas of productivity and creativity in adulthood.

The Relationship between Age and Creativity: Early Studies

Creativity is conventionally thought of as the ability to produce a notable or extraordinary piece of work. It is judged by a group of experts relative to a particular time period as having novelty, an impact on society, and an element of surprise. For almost two centuries, researchers and theorists have been interested in the question of whether aging is associated with changes in creativity as measured by the production of creative works. Examples of illustrious creative figures who continued to remain productive in old age, such as Michelangelo (1475–1564), challenge the stereotyped notion that youth is prime time for the expression of genius. The first empirical investigation of this question was conducted by Quetelet (1835/1968), who attempted to determine the quality of plays written by French playwrights over the course of the adult years.

The most extensive early investigation into the question of age and productivity was conducted by Lehman in his 1953 book *Age and Achievement* (Lehman, 1953). Lehman analyzed the production by age of creative works in all fields from the sciences to the arts. His analysis included both the number of works produced and their quality, but his main focus was on works that had significant impact in their fields. The major conclusion to emerge from Lehman's study was that the peak of productivity in the adult years tends to occur prior to the age of 40, often between 30 and 35. However, the age period corresponding to a creative peak, in terms of quality and quantity, varies by discipline. The graphs for three of these disciplines are shown in Figure 14.2. The vertical axis represents the percentage of total works completed by an individual in the five-year intervals shown on the horizontal axis. In other words, the graph shows the percentage of an individual's total works completed within each five-year age span. A peak corresponds to the five-year period when the majority of a person's works were completed. The data points represent averages for all individuals whose works were analyzed by age.

Lehman concluded from his data that earlier peaks are reached in the sciences and in fields in which success was dependent on intellectual imagination and physical ability. This phenomenon was later to be dubbed with the name the "Planck hypothesis" (Dietrich, 2004) after the scientist Max Planck, and refers to the tendency of younger scientists to have more innovative ideas.

As observed by Lehman, increasingly later peaks are reached in fields that rely on experience and diplomacy. The writing of "best books" by authors falls in between these extremes, for success in literature involves imagination, discipline, and the philosophical perspectives gained from experience. A more detailed portrayal of the age peaks in various disciplines showing these

FIGURE 14.2
Age and Production in Three Disciplines

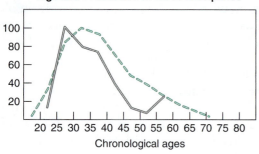

Age and Production in Three Disciplines

(a) Age versus production in chemistry. Solid line – 52 of the greatest chemical discoveries by 46 men now deceased. Broken line – 903 contributions of lesser average merit by 244 chemists now deceased.

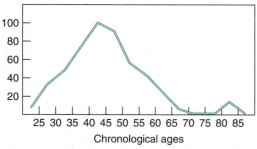

(b) Age versus production of 224 "best books" by 101 authors.

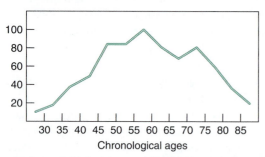

(c) Ages of chief ministers of England from 930 to 1950.

Source: Lehman, 1953.

relationships more clearly is given in Table 14.1. Although in general the ages increase in moving from the top to the bottom of the table, there is an exception for movie actresses, who have an earlier peak age than actors, a fact that is almost certainly still true today.

TABLE 14.1
Peak Ages by Field

Field	Peak Age
Athletics (tennis, baseball)	25–29
Chemistry	26–30
Mathematics	30–34
Physics	30–34
Practical inventions	30–34
Orchestral music	35–39
Psychology	30–39
Chess championships	29–33
Philosophy	35–39
Music	35–39
Art (oil paintings)	32–36
Best books	40–44
Movie actors (best paid)	30–34
Movie actresses (best paid)	23–27
College presidents	50–54
United States presidents	55–59
Foreign ambassadors	60–64
Senators	60–64
Supreme Court justices	70–74
Speakers of the House	70–74
Popes	82–92

Source: Lehman, 1953.

The next major investigation conducted on age and creativity was conducted by Dennis (1966), who examined the total output, regardless of the quality of work, by contributors to seven domains within the arts and sciences. As can be seen from Figure 14.3, although there is a rather steep decline after the peak age in the arts, and somewhat less so in the sciences, productivity in terms of scholarship is maintained at a steady rate throughout later adulthood, with even a slight peak in the 60s. Dennis attempted to compensate for the differential ages that creators lived to be, (which would obviously cut down on productivity in the later years), by limiting his sample to people who lived to be at least 80 years old. Furthermore, unlike Lehman, who factored the impact of a work into his age curves, Dennis did not attempt to evaluate the quality of a contribution. Instead, Dennis relied entirely on counts of published or produced works.

This studies by Lehman and Dennis can be summarized as showing a rapid increase in creative output that reaches a career peak in the late 30s or early 40s, after which a steady decline begins. The peak and rate of decline vary by

FIGURE 14.3

Age and Productivity by Discipline as Judged by Dennis (1966)

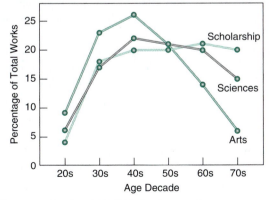

Percentage of total works by field of endeavor and age.

Source: Simonton, 1990.

discipline, but the decline occurs nevertheless. Based on this research, one would have to argue that creative productivity is unlikely to be a component of successful aging.

Fortunately, the pessimistic interpretation of the early literature may not tell the whole story. Even Lehman (1953), noted that "older thinkers" produced many great achievements. Figure 14.4, for example, shows the production of great works of art, and as is evident, there is an upturn in the 70s for "best" paintings. This apparent increase is in part a function of the fact that fewer individuals are alive at these ages. Those who are producing works of art represent a select portion of the population of artists who probably always were productive, a point that we will return to later. Although the tip of the peak is not as pronounced as in the earlier years, it nevertheless represents the work of some exceptionally talented older artists.

Similar trends toward late-life upturns can also be found in other disciplines within Lehman's investigation, including mathematics, physics, astronomy, medicine, philosophy, music, and poetry. What might seem to be a striking omission is Ludwig van Beethoven, who produced some of his greatest work at the end of his life, including his renowned late string quartets. However, because he died at the age of 56, his late-career accomplishments would not be considered within discussions of late-life productivity. Similarly, the amazingly prolific Wolfgang Mozart died at the age of 35. These examples illustrate some of the problems of conducting this type of research because important figures who die at a younger age but who might have remained productive had they lived longer are not counted.

A related problem with the simple counts or percentages of creative works as a function of age is that the works of all productive individuals lose their distinctness when curves representing the average are drawn. This problem is called the

FIGURE 14.4
Production of Works of Art by Age

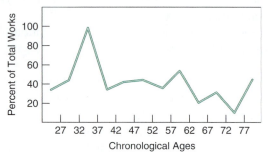

"Best paintings" by age of artist.
Source: Lehman, 1953.

even in midlife are obscured when his work is collapsed with those of others.

"What do you think?"   **14-3**

What is the difference between evaluating a person's creativity by number of works produced versus quality of works produced?

compositional fallacy and refers to the fact that when the productivity rates per time period are averaged across the careers of several individuals, the summary curve that results does not describe the productivity of any of the individuals in that group (Simonton, 1997).

Let us return to the example of composer Ludwig von Beethoven, who was productive up until his death at age 56. Another composer with lesser or more short-lived talents may have stopped producing new works much earlier, at the age of 35 or 40. However, if you average the two productivity rates for the age of 50, Beethoven's productivity will be underestimated and the other composer's will be overestimated. Another aspect to this problem is the fact that Beethoven died before reaching his sixtieth birthday. Therefore, a person who most likely would have remained a highly productive individual is no longer in the population of composers after that point. Consequently, his personal creativity will not be reflected in the statistics on creativity in later life.

The averaging of productive achievements across individuals results in a biased estimate of the age-creativity relationship. Beethoven was a highly productive individual whose abilities

Simonton's Model of Age and Creative Productivity

The types of problems just described in research on age and creative achievement led one of the more innovative scholars on this topic to develop a model of late-life productivity that proves to be relatively insensitive to these methodological problems. Simonton (1997) came up with a mathematical model in which he relates age to creative productivity, controlling for individual differences in creative potential, age, and the nature of an individual's field of endeavor. He developed this model through mathematical analyses of the previous data collected by Lehman, Dennis, and others.

Simonton's model of creative productivity is based on three assumptions (Simonton, 1998b). First of all, individuals vary in what he calls the initial creative potential, which is a hypothetical count of the total number of works that someone would be able to produce in a life span with no upper limits. It can also be thought of as the number of original ideas that a given individual could ever theoretically produce. A person with a high creative potential might produce thousands of works of art during his or her career, but a person with low creative potential may produce ten, twenty, or perhaps just one (a "one hit wonder").

The second assumption of Simonton's model is that the individual's creative potential is translated into concrete products (e.g., compositions, scientific articles) through a two-step process.

TABLE 14.2
Well-Known Historical Late-Life Creative Older Adults

Name	Field	Age at contribution	Contribution
Giovanni Bellini, 1430–1516	Art	83	Altarpiece in San Giovanni Cristostomo, Venice
Anton Bruckner, 1824–1896	Music	70	*Ninth Symphony*
Michelangelo Buonaroti, 1475–1564	Art	89	*Pieta Rondanini*
Miguel de Cervantes, 1547–1616	Literature	68	*Don Quixote* (2nd part)
Benjamin Franklin, 1706–1790	Invention	78	Bifocals
Sir John Floyer, 1649–1734	Medicine	75	First medical text on geriatrics
Galileo Galilei, 1564–1642	Mechanics	74	Dialogues on mechanics
Johann Wolfgang von Goethe, 1749–1832	Literature	80	*Faust* (2nd part)
Thomas Hardy, 1840–1928	Poetry	88	*Winter Words* (posthumous)
Victor Hugo (1802–1885)	Poetry	75	"The Art of Being a Grandfather"
Alexander Humboldt, 1769–1859	Cosmology	78	Cosmos
Samuel Johnson, 1792–1868	Biography	72	*Lives of the English Poets*
Andrea Mantegna, 1431–1506	Painting	70	Parnassus
Gioacchino Rossini, 1792–1868	Music	72	Petite Messe solemnelle
Herbert Spencer, 1820–1903	Philosophy	76	*System of Philosophy*
John Stephens, 1749–1838	Invention	76	First American built locomotive
Alfred Tennyson, 1809–1892	Literature	80	Crossing the Bar
Giuseppe Verde, 1813–1901	Music	80	*Falstaff*
Wilhelm Wundt, 1832–1920	Psychology	82–88	*Social Psychology* (2nd edition)

Source: Lehman, 1953.

One component of this process is ideation, the production of ideas for new products. The second component of the process is elaboration, which is the laborious process of transforming ideas into actual products. It is one thing to have an idea, and another to translate it into something that you can see, hear, or ponder.

The productivity of an individual, then, is a function of creative potential (which he called "m"), ideation rate ("a"), and elaboration rate

("b"). To determine a person's creativity, all three factors must be considered.

A key aspect of Simonton's model is that the productivity of an individual is defined on the basis of **career age**, which is the age at which an individual begins to embark on his or her career (Simonton, 1988). Prior to Simonton, researchers in this area based their theories on chronological age. As a result, they failed to take into account the fact that people begin their careers at different ages. In calculating peak age of productivity, the age at which a person embarks on a career must be accounted for to control for the fact that some people may be past their prime when others are just beginning theirs.

Variations may also occur in the extent of an individual's creative potential. Even within the same domain of creative activity, people vary in their ability to produce creative works (again, think of Beethoven). A very productive individual will have a different career trajectory than one who is more limited in the ability to produce novel ideas. Simonton modeled several variations in productivity according to age based on the three points in the career of a creative individual that seemed to matter the most. These are the first contribution, the "best" contribution (as judged by such factors as critical reviews), and the last contribution.

The age of first contribution corresponds to the age at which the first work of high quality is produced. This is the point that signifies the beginning of the individual's career. Let us look at the case of the long-lived artist Pablo Picasso (1881–1973), one of the most famous artists of all time. His first work was produced at the very young age of 10 years. The "best" contribution might be more subjective, but would represent the work that received the greatest acclaim. Many people regard Picasso's *Guernica* as his best work. The last work that Picasso completed was during the year of his death, 1973, so the end of his career corresponds to the end of his life. His last works still received critical acclaim, unlike some artists, whose last productions have very little noteworthy value.

Now, let us turn to Simonton's model. The ages of first, best, and last creative productions are predicted within the model on the basis of age of career onset and degree of creative potential. The higher the person's creative potential, the longer will be the spread between first and last works.

The top graphs in Figure 14.5 show people who have an early career onset age, meaning that they have their first significant production at the actual age of 20. A person with high creative potential will show a rapid growth in productivity to the age of best contribution and will maintain relatively high productivity until late in both career and actual ages. The bottom two graphs are of individuals with a late onset career, with a first contribution at age 30. These individuals will peak later and continue to produce until a later actual age than those with an early onset. Individuals who begin early reach their peak early and achieve their last significant production at an earlier age than those who begin later.

However, as you can also see from these curves, artists (such as Picasso) with higher creative potential will remain more productive throughout their careers than will those with lower potential, regardless of when they produce their first important work. Those with higher creative potential will also achieve a significant production relatively earlier in their careers than those with lower potential. Those with higher creative potential also achieve their last important creative landmark at a later age than do those with lower potential.

The next question that might seem important is whether quality of creative productivity has any connection to quantity. According to the **equal odds rule**, there is a positive relationship between quality and quantity of work. Those who produce more output are more likely to score a "hit" or success than are those who produce fewer works (in sports this is referred to as the principle that "if you don't shoot you can't score"). An implication of this principle is the notion that people are most likely to produce their best work during their peak period of productivity on the basis of probability alone.

Returning to the question of the relationship between age and creative output, Simonton's model places the greatest emphasis not on actual age but on career age. Productivity in later life will be higher among people who began their careers at a later age and so will the age of

FIGURE 14.5
Productivity and Career Age

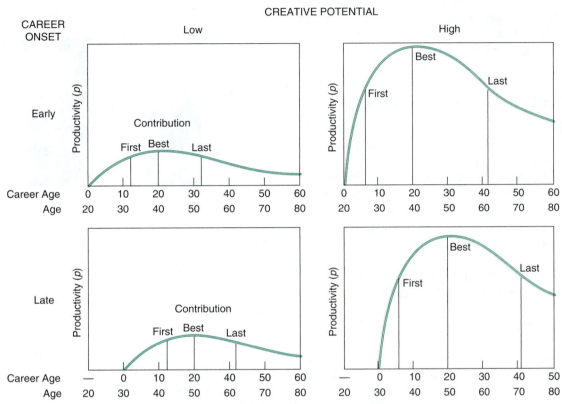

In these curves, four models of productivity are shown based on creative potential as low or high and career onset as early or late.

Source: Simonton, 1997.

best work. However, people with high creative potential are more likely to have a high rate of productivity both early and late in their careers. There will be as long as a 20-year span between best and last work for highly creative people compared with the 10-year span for the less creative. Some individuals with very low creative potential may produce only one significant work, which is their first, best, and last contribution (the one-hit wonder, again).

Even though later life may be associated with a drop from the time of peak productivity, Simonton's model allows for the possibility of

highly productive and creative older individuals. Going back to Table 14.2, some of these individuals began their careers at relatively late ages. Anton Bruckner, for example, wrote his first symphony at the age of 42 and his first masterpiece at the age of 50. A late career peak would also be reached by an individual who changed fields in midcareer, which resets the career clock back to zero. Other people excelled in later life in fields with relatively late peaks such as history and philosophy. Remember that artists and composers with a high degree of creative potential will also have longer careers than do those who have less potential. Verdi composed his first operatic masterpiece at the age of 29 and his last at the age of 80. He also fits the equal odds rule, with a relatively high probability of creating a masterwork because he continued to produce a large number of pieces of music.

The Neuroscience of Creativity

Having examined the statistics on age and creativity, we turn now to a completely different approach. Underlying our creative impulses are brain mechanisms responsible for generating new ideas. Learning and memory involve consolidating our experiences, but coming up with new insights involves generating thoughts that no one has had before. Researchers exploring the neurological basis of creativity have focused on the prefrontal cortex, the last structure of the brain to develop both in evolution and development, not reaching full maturity until the early 20s. Some scientists believe that this is the part of the brain responsible for generating new ideas. Our creativity is likely to be highest when our prefrontal cortex has sufficiently matured so that we are able to be flexible but at the same time have had sufficient training in our area of expertise so that we can put that flexibility to good use (Dietrich, 2004). Presumably, this happy coincidence occurs about 20 years into the career, when most people are midlife (Feist, 2006).

The right hemisphere of the cortex seems to play a particularly important function in supporting creativity throughout life. In one intriguing investigation of the brain correlates of creative thought, participants were hooked up to an electroencephalograph (EEG) asked to provide accounts of what might have led to unusual situations (such as "Person A is lying, Person B is sitting, and Person C is standing"—how would you explain this?). They were instructed to press a button when they had an idea. Subsequently, they rated the originality

FIGURE 14.6
Brain Correlates of Creativity

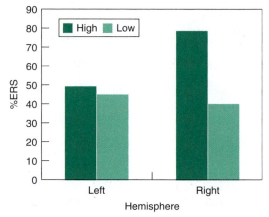

Activity of right and left hemisphere on EEG during production of thoughts rated as high or low in creativity. ERS is a measure of activation.

Source: Grabner, Fink, & Neubauer, 2007.

of their own ideas, allowing the researchers to compare brainwave activity during original and unoriginal thoughts. Greater patterns of activation were observed in the EEGs from the right hemisphere when participants were creating more highly original thoughts (Grabner, Fink, & Neubauer, 2007).

We might hope someday that similar research on aging might help scientists understand more about brain function and creativity in older adults.

Characteristics of Last Works

Until we know more about the neuroscience of aging and creativity, we must go back to examining the creative products of older artists, composers, writers, and scientists. Researchers in this area have found that these works possess special qualities not observed in the work of younger persons. One important quality is the ability to criticize their own work. An intensive study of Beethoven's letters and notes from conversations with others showed that as he aged, he was able to make more "accurate" assessments of the quality of his works, as judged by the frequency with which his works were subsequently performed and recorded (Kozbelt, 2007). Some insight into his thinking can be found in the movie "Copying Beethoven."

A second distinctive characteristic of last works is the **old age style** (Lindauer, 1998). This refers to an approach to one's art that eliminates the fine details and instead presents the essence of the work's intended meaning. The work becomes less objective and focused on formal perfection and instead more subjective. In a painting, for example, the artist may simplify the image by eliminating details closely tied to accurate renditions of objects and people. A sculptor may concentrate more on the form and underlying emotion of the piece rather than on representing each and every detail.

The emergence of an old age style can be seen in the works of many artists in addition to Michelangelo, including Rembrandt, Renoir, Matisse, Degas, Georgia O'Keeffe, and Picasso. Critics have noted that the older artist paints with a larger brushstroke, so that each packs a larger emotional punch. Instead of the painstakingly crafted renderings that a younger artist may produce, the older artist stands back and concentrates on form and meaning.

The artist Henri Matisse referred to this change in his style as a "distillation of form. I now

The "old age style" in Michelangelo's two pietas (1475–1564) work can be seen in these two pietas. The St. Peter's Pieta (left) is carefully crafted, lavish in detail, and serene; the Rondanini Pieta (right) is roughly carved and portrays a far less peaceful image. In fact, the Rondanini is a fragment, destroyed partly by Michelangelo's own hand shortly before he died.

keep only the sign which suffices, necessary for its existence in its own form, for the composition as I conceive it" (Brill, 1967, p.40). The cover illustration on this book shows the "essence" of a snail; it was completed the year before he died (see http://tate.org.uk/imap/pages/animated/cutout/matisse/snail.htm).

Another excellent example of the old age style is provided by the work of Michelangelo, whose two Pietas, produced in youth and old age, contrast sharply in their style and emotional tone. Some critics actually regard the late Pieta as more emotionally charged and hence effective than the iconic one that resides in the Vatican (see photo).

Another characteristic is the choice of theme related to aging or death. This is not to say that the work has become morbid or depressing, but that it presents the reality of the artist's life and impending death in a manner that may have particular clarity and a strong impact on the viewer. These features of old age style are by no means universal, however, for some artists may continue to paint with the attention to detail and refinement shown in their earlier work without their making a transition to this more reflective and emotionally stronger approach.

The old age style may also be seen in a writer's work, as it becomes more reflective, introspective, and subjective (Lubart & Sternberg, 1998). Characters in literature may be portrayed more realistically but also with greater empathy, and they come to take on greater complexity and a sense of timelessness (Adams-Price, 1998).

Related to old-age style is the **swan song phenomenon**, a brief renewal of creativity that can stimulate the creation of new works and a new style of work (Simonton, 1989). Musical compositions that reflect the swan song phenomenon are characterized by shorter main themes and simpler melodies than the prior works of the composer. As a result, they are strong and evocative and tend to be easy to remember.

This Picasso painting ("The Young Painter" 1972) provides a vivid illustration of the old age style. Note the simplicity of line and form.

Simonton considers the best example of the swan song to be "Lachrymosa," from Mozart's last work, the *Requiem in D minor*. Although Mozart was young when he died, he knew that his death was imminent and fittingly wrote a piece of music intended to honor the dead. Centuries later, this melody was to be the music played in the funeral scene of the movie, *Amadeus*, while Mozart's body is buried in a pauper's grave outside of Vienna.

As in Mozart's case, the resurgence of creativity that stimulates the swan song may come about with the composer's awareness of increased closeness to death. With the approach of their death, composers may strip away some of their professional and personal ties and focus with renewed vigor on composing a piece of music for the ages. These works often become some of the most successful that the composers produce,

Wolfgang Amadeus Mozart on his deathbed. During his final weeks of life, he composed "Requiem in D Minor," a masterful work that contained Lachrymosa, one of the most haunting examples of the swan song.

and thus in many ways may grant the composer a certain immortality. The swan song phenomenon is perhaps a special case of the old age style because it also implies a certain simplicity and paring away of distractions and details.

A third feature of the old age style is observed primarily among scientists and academicians. They shift their creative products away from innovation and discovery and instead become oriented toward integration and synthesis of existing knowledge. The aging scientist may become more involved in the writing of texts and integrative review articles rather than producing new scientific articles. In some cases, they may decide to focus their subject matter on studies of aging, as was true for B. F. Skinner toward the end of his life (Skinner & Vaughan, 1983) and apparently for Sir John Floyer, who wrote the first geriatrics text in the early 1700s when he was 75 years old. A shift to age-related concerns may also be apparent in a person's research or practical inventions, as was the case for Benjamin Franklin, who invented bifocals when he himself was 78 years old, actually well past the age when most people start to need them.

The old age style may be stimulated by proximity to death, a desire to leave behind a legacy, or perhaps age-related changes or health problems. Beethoven became deaf in his later years, and his musical style also changed. For example, in his late string quartets, he became more expressive and less bound by conventional forms. Blindness forced changes in the painting of a number of well-known older artists, including Georgia O'Keeffe, Mary Cassatt, Edgar Degas, and Claude Monet. Henri Matisse suffered from stomach cancer and was confined to a wheelchair at the end of his life. Despite these severe limitations, these artists continued to produce great works until or nearly until their last years of life.

In the case of the artist Monet, cataracts caused changes not only in the clarity of his vision but in his ability to see colors. You are most likely familiar with Monet's water lilies. When he developed cataracts, he was literally unable to see the colors on the canvas that he knew appeared in nature. Even special glasses (colored yellow) could not correct this defect, and it was not until he was successfully treated with cataract surgery at the age of 85 that his color vision was restored. His final work, an enormous series of water lilies, was installed in a Paris museum after his death. The colors in these final paintings were as vibrant as they had been in his earlier work. In 1908, he wrote, "These landscapes of water and reflections have become an obsession, it is beyond the stength of an old man, and yet I want to succeed in portraying what I feel. I have destroyed some, I have started all over again, and I hope that something will emerge from so much effort" (http://boutique.museeguimet.fr/produits/details/CU600090).

Similarly, unable to paint due to the discomfort of his illness, Matisse changed his medium to paper sculptures, which have since become some of the classic instances of this master's life contributions. In another creative medium, the poet William Carlos Williams suffered a stroke in his 60s, after which he became severely depressed. Following treatment for depression, he went on to produce some of his greatest works, including the Pulitzer Prize–winning *Pictures from Bruegel*, published when he was 79 (Cohen, 1998b).

The limitations caused by physical and sensory age-related changes suffered by some of these artists were not necessarily met with equanimity. Michelangelo, for example, attempted to destroy his last Pieta, and it was saved only through the efforts of his apprentices. Similarly Monet destroyed many of the canvases he produced during the years he suffered from cataracts. Picasso's Self-Portrait "Facing Death" (see photo) portrays the man, who refuses to accept his own physical aging. Georgia O'Keeffe, who lived to the age of 98, was similarly frustrated with her inability to see in her last decade of life, and her need to change mediums from painting to sculpture and pottery because she could no longer see the canvas. Nevertheless, all of these individuals lived very long lives, and despite their personal frustrations, found ways to express their creative potential right up until the very end.

Sociocultural Variations

These models of successful aging and creativity are useful and inspiring, but one important shortcoming is that they fail to take sufficient account of sociocultural context. Socioeconomically and racially disadvantaged individuals have a much lower chance of ever reaching old age, much less "successful" old age, as traditionally defined within psychology or the arts. Certain sectors of the population, particularly minorities from low-income backgrounds, do not have the opportunity to achieve good health and full expression of their innate abilities. Everyone we have talked about up to now came from a relatively advantaged background. Older African Americans in their daily lives use religion as a coping mechanism for surviving discrimination, poor living conditions, and demoralization (Taylor & Chatters, 1991). However, this does not negate the fact that education and income remain lower among blacks in the United States and that even a college education does not protect a person from career discrimination, as noted in Chapter 10.

A second critical fact in analyses of successful aging regards the definition of eminence as used in studies of aging and creativity. Women are far less likely than would be expected on the basis of chance to appear in lists of the creative and productive at any age. However, it is only within the area of children's literature that Lehman (1953) listed women as constituting anywhere near 50% of the notable contributors. A total of only 20 women were listed in the Lehman work as "worthy of mention" (p. 91).

The second group who receives little, if any, mention in analysis of productivity is African Americans. In fact, Simonton (1998a) explored the question of whether assessments of creative output among historical figures would show evidence of bias against this group. He examined whether African Americans who had achieved recognition within reference works specific to black scholarship would also be mentioned in reference works of the white majority culture. Although there was considerable convergence between the minority and majority reference works, one-fifth of African Americans who had achieved eminence in the minority reference works were not mentioned in any of the majority indices of eminence. Furthermore, certain areas of accomplishment within black culture were not recognized within the majority reference works, including law, education, religion, classical music, and the sciences. White reference works gave higher ratings to African Americans in the fields of athletics, and jazz and blues music, but African American sources gave greater recognition to those who achieved eminence in the civil rights movement.

These differential patterns of recognition, though against a backdrop of closer than expected similarities between minority and white reference works, point to differential opportunities that affect an individual's ability to achieve career recognition, if not personal fulfillment. Clearly differences in educational opportunities as well as cultural values play a role in determining the ultimate achievements of people from nonmajority backgrounds. Those who do manage to break through cultural barriers are likely to receive considerable recognition within their own as well as the majority culture. Some examples are Jackie Robinson, who was the first African American to play major league baseball; Booker T. Washington, the first black to receive an honorary degree from Harvard; and William Grant Still, the first black to conduct a major symphony orchestra and to have his own composition performed by a major American orchestra. These "famous firsts" seem particularly important within African American reference works of eminence because they attest to the ability of highly talented and persistent individuals to overcome the effects of discrimination. That their work has until recently been overlooked in studies of aging and creativity limits the generalizability of current models of successful aging.

SUCCESSFUL AGING: FINAL PERSPECTIVES

People in later life appear not only to manage to feel satisfied with their lives but also to be able to achieve new forms of creative expression. Many scientists, artists, writers, and political leaders have produced notable contributions in their later adult years. The accomplishments of these unusual individuals adds to the literature on subjective well-being as well as the framework proposed by Erikson and colleagues of "vital involvement" to add support to the concept of successful aging.

As was shown in the analysis of Simonton's model of creative productivity, people who begin their careers with a high degree of creative potential are likely to maintain higher creative output well into their 60s, 70s, and beyond. Where does this creative potential come from? In part, as we saw earlier, the level of talent needed to sustain such a long and productive career may have a neurological basis (Dietrich, 2004). Personality may also play a role. There is evidence from an unusual 45-year longitudinal study of men orginally tested as graduate students that the personality qualities of openness and flexibility predict creativity and success in later adulthood. Those men with the highest numbers of awards and notable publications at age 72 were higher on scales of tolerance and psychological-mindedness at age 27 (Feist & Barron, 2003).

"What do you think?"   **14-4**

How is productivity measured in "ordinary" people at the end of life?

ASSESS YOURSELF: Age Busters

An "Age Buster" is a person who has managed to overcome the odds that age will make him or her socially and professionally obsolete. Although you don't have to be famous to be an age buster in terms of your own personal feelings of productivity and satisfaction, researchers such as Simonton, Dennis, and Lehman looked at well-known scientists, artists, musicians, and other prominent historical figures. For this survey you are going to identify the people you think are Age Busters. I have identified my choices (and those of my students) in Table 14.3.

Please indicate your Number One choice for an Age Buster:

_____

Now answer the following questions about this person.

1. Why did you choose this person?
   A. I personally admire him or her even though he or she is not well known.
   B. He or she is an important media figure and receives a great deal of attention.
   C. He or she makes outstanding contributions to society.
   D. He or she makes outstanding contributions to the arts.

2. How do you think age affects the way you view a celebrity?
   A. I rarely consider a celebrity's age when I think about him or her.
   B. I take into account the celebrity's age when I think about him or her.
   C. The celebrity's age is the most important feature about him or her.

3. How do you think Age Busters are viewed in the media?
   A. They are treated favorably as highly unusual and not at all like their age peers.
   B. They are regarded similarly as are other older adults; no better or no worse.
   C. They are treated unfavorably compared to other older adults.

4. Do you think that there has been a change in the way Age Busters are regarded by society?
   A. Yes, I think they are regarded more favorably than was true in the past.
   B. No, I do not think there has been a change.
   C. Yes, I think they are regarded much less favorably than was true in the past.

5. In the future, I think that Age Busters will be treated:
   A. Much more negatively than they are now.
   B. About the same as they are now.
   C. Much more positively than they are now.

Moving beyond the unusual contributions of highly creative individuals, we can see creativity as a process that can characterize ordinary people as well. Creativity can be thought of as a process of personality development in which we develop a completely open mind to new experiences and are able to enjoy and appreciate the finer nuances of life.

For the ordinary individual who does not achieve lasting fame, then, the process of successful aging may involve the creative process of constructing a personal narrative or life story

TABLE 14.3
"Age Busters" in Current Times

Field	Name, Year of Birth (and Death), and Age, if Alive in 2007	Accomplishment
National and international figures	Jesse Jackson (1941–) age 65	Spokesperson for civil rights
	Sen. Edward Kennedy (1932–) age 75	Senator from Massachusetts, Chair of the Senate Committee on Health, Education, Labor, and Pensions
	Henry Kissinger (1923–) age 83	Active in public service
	Mother Teresa (1910–1997)	Head of Missionaries of Charity until death at age 87
	Pope John Paul II (1920–2005)	Active as head of Catholic Church until death at age 84
	Strom Thurmond (1902–2003)	United States Senator until death at 100
	Jesse Helms (1921–)	United States Senator until age 81
	Queen Elizabeth II (1926–) age 81	Active monarch and world figure
	Bob Dole (1923–) age 83	Ran for United States President at age 74
	Rosa Parks (1913–2005)	Received United States Presidential Medal of Freedom in 1996 at age of 83
Science and exploration	Jacques Cousteau (1910–1997)	Active in sea exploration until death at 87
	Roy Walford (1924–2004)	Continued his research on the caloric restriction hypothesis until death at age 79 of ALS
	John Glenn (1921–) age 85	Flew on Shuttle Mission at age 77, oldest person to fly in space
Leading ladies	Helen Mirren (1945–) age 61	Received Academy Award at age 61
	Susan Sarandon (1946–) age 60	Continues to star in movies
	Diane Keaton (1946–) age 61	Continues to star in movies
	Dame Judy Dench (1934–) age 72	Won Academy Award at age 72
	Katharine Hepburn (1907–2003)	Won 3 Academy Awards after the age of 60
	Bette Davis (1908–1999)	Active in movies until age 78

TABLE 14.3 *(Continued)*
"Age Busters" in Current Times

Field	Name, Year of Birth (and Death), and Age, if Alive in 2007	Accomplishment
Leading men	Sir John Gielgud (1904–2000)	Gave his final performance as Merlin at age 94
	Sir Alec Guinness (1914–2000)	Received fifth Academy Award nomination at age 75
	Jack Nicholson (1937–) age 70	Continues to star in movies
	Sean Connery (1930–) age 76	Continues to star in movies
	Walter Matthau (1920–2000)	One-half of the *Grumpy Old Men*
	Jack Lemmon (1925–2001)	The other half of the *Grumpy Old Men*
	Morgan Freeman (1937–) age 69	Won first Academy Award at age 67
Comedians	George Burns (1886–1986)	Continued to appear in movies until age 98; won Academy Award at age 80
	Groucho Marx (1890–1977)	Appeared in movies and on television until age 86
	Bill Cosby (1937–) age 69	Performs in comedy and speaking engagements
Aging rockers and divas	Mick Jagger (1943–) age 63	Performs with Rolling Stones
	Keith Richards (1943–) age 63	Performs with Rolling Stones
	Sir Paul McCartney (1942–) age 64	Performs on solo tours
	Madonna (1958–) age 48	Performs on solo tours
	Bette Midler (1945–) age 61	Maintains active singing and acting career
	Cher (1946–) age 60	Performs on solo tours
	Tina Turner (1939–) age 67	Performs on solo tours
	Barbra Streisand (1942–) age 65	Performs on solo tours
	Aretha Franklin (1942–) age 65	Performs on solo tours
Popular musicians and singers	Duke Ellington (1899–1974)	Composed over 2,000 songs
	Frank Sinatra (1915–1998)	Performed until death at age 82
	Tony Bennett (1926–) age 80	Won Grammy Award at age 80

(Continued Overleaf)

TABLE 14.3 *(Continued)*

"Age Busters" in Current Times

Field	Name, Year of Birth (and Death), and Age, if Alive in 2007	Accomplishment
Television actors and personalities	William Shatner (1931–) age 76	Stars on *Boston Legal;* won Emmy at age 74
	Regis Philbin (1931–) age 75	Hosts TV morning show
	Barbara Walters (1929–) age 77	Hosts *The View*
	Fred Rogers (1928–2003)	Hosted *Mr. Rogers* until death at age 74
	Julia Child (1912–2004)	Appeared on her show, *The French Chef* until death at age 91
	Joan Rivers (1933–) age 73	Appears on awards ceremonies and other TV shows
	Bob Barker (1923–) age 83	Held a weekly TV job continuously for 50 years
Writers and poets	Agatha Christie (1890–1976)	Wrote last novel at age 73
	John Updike (1932–) age 75	Wrote over 60 novels
	Betty Friedan (1921–2006)	Feminist author, published last book at age 79
	Maya Angelou (1928–) age 79	Writes poetry, won a Grammy at age 65
Movie directors and actors	Clint Eastwood (1930–) age 76	Won Academy Award for Best Director at age 74
	Woody Allen (1935–) age 71	Directs and appears in movies
	Alfred Hitchcock (1899–1980)	Directed last film at age 77
Artists	Georgia O'Keeffe (1887–1986)	Produced sculpture until age 99 after becoming blind
	Pablo Picasso (1881–1973)	Produced great masterworks until death at age 91
	Henri Matisse (1869–1964)	Produced collages until age 84 after becoming ill
	Claude Monet (1840–1926)	Painted his last water lilies at age 86
	Philip Johnson (1906–2005)	Architect, completed last work at age 90
	Grandma Moses (1860–1961)	Paint until death at age 101
Exercise guru	Jack LaLanne (1914–) age 92	Educates the public about value of exercise and healthy eating

(Luborsky, 1998). This narrative will involve a complex negotiation of cultural (Luborsky & McMullen, 1999) and personal forces (Whitbourne, 1985). Cultural forces shape the parameters we use to evaluate ourselves and by which we are evaluated by others. Furthermore these forces set the parameters for the opportunities that we have to achieve our goals.

Part of a "successful" life narrative may involve coming to grips with the recognition of how cultural constraints have affected the individual's ability to realize the hopes and dreams of youth. Yet, we must also strive to transcend these constrictions and arrive at a personal sense of meaning in life that rises above the boundaries of culture and time.

SUMMARY

1. The process of successful aging involves being able to overcome the threats to physical and psychological well-being presented by the aging process. However, in addition to "survival," successful aging involves the ability to become engaged with life in terms of both relationships and productive activity. Subjective well-being, a component of successful aging, is higher in older adults, a phenomenon referred to as the paradox of well-being. There are several possible mechanisms through which higher subjective well-being is achieved, including adaptation, goal achievement, coping mechanisms, social comparison, and the use of identity assimilation in forming a life story.

2. Research on productivity and creativity has involved attempts to determine whether older individuals are more or less able to maintain the quality and quantity of works produced when younger. Variations by discipline were

observed in early studies in which peak ages were reached earlier for areas in which imagination and physical ability are required. However, the findings of various authors indicated overall declines after peaks reached in young adulthood. In some cases, upturns were noted in the productivity of individuals living until the 70s and beyond among exceptionally talented older persons. Many achievements have also been produced by people in advanced old age. This area of research is hampered by the fact that some individuals who may have maintained their productivity do not live until old age. Furthermore, average productivity rates do not take into account the individual variations shown in the quality and quantity of works. Simonton's model of creative productivity describes the relationship between age and production of creative works using a mathematical formula that incorporates creative potential, ideation, and elaboration based on the career age of an individual rather than chronological age. In this model, highly productive individuals begin early and maintain a high production rate long into their careers. Those who are more productive are also more likely to produce works of high quality.

3. The old age style characterizes the works of older artists and musicians. One component of the old age style is simplification of detail and increasing subjectivity. The swan song is a related phenomenon, referring to the tendency of composers to produce very simple themes in their last works. Among scientists and academicians, the old age style refers to a tendency to synthesize, producing works such as texts and reviews that integrate existing knowledge. The old age style may be a reaction to increasing proximity to death or to the presence of age-related changes or

health problems. Age Busters also maintain their productivity throughout life.

4. For individuals who do not achieve lasting fame through their work, the expression of creativity may come about through the construction of a personal narrative. In this process, the individual comes to grips with the accomplishments and failures of his or her life and arrives at a personal sense of meaning.

GLOSSARY

Accommodation: process in Piagetian theory in which individuals change their existing mental structures to incorporate information from experiences.

Activity theory: proposal that it is harmful to the well-being of older adults to force them out of productive social roles.

Adaptation: psychological mechanisms that individuals may use to maintain high well-being in the face of objectively negative circumstances.

Adrenopause: age-related decline in dehydroepiandros-terone (DHEA).

Advance directive (AD): specification of the patient's desire to participate in and direct their own healthcare decisions, and to accept or refuse treatment.

Aerobic capacity: the maximum amount of oxygen that can be delivered through the blood.

Affective evaluation theory: theory proposing that positive and negative emotions at work should be considered as influences on our satisfaction.

Age-adjusted death rates: mortality statistic calculated by obtaining the weighted averages of the age-specific death rates, with the weights reflecting the proportion of individuals in that age group in the population.

Age-complexity hypothesis: proposal that due to slowing of central processes in the nervous system, age differences increase with increasing complexity of the task.

Age Discrimination in Employment Act (ADEA): federal law initially passed in 1967 to prohibit discrimination against workers on the basis of age; later expanded to prohibit mandatory retirement except in selected occupations.

Ageism: a set of beliefs, attitudes, social institutions, and acts that denigrate individuals or groups based on their chronological age.

Age-related macular degeneration: progressive form of blindness in which there is a destruction of the photoreceptors located in the central region of the retina known as the macula.

Age-specific death rates: the number of deaths per 100,000 of the particular age group.

Agoraphobia: the fear of being trapped or stranded during a panic attack.

Alzheimer's disease: the most common form of dementia.

Amnesia: profound memory loss.

Amyloid: generic name for protein fragments that collect together in a specific way to form insoluble deposits.

Amyloid cascade hypothesis: proposal that the formation of amyloid plaques causes the death of neurons in Alzheimer's disease.

Amyloid plaque: collection of dead and dying neurons surrounding a central core amyloid.

Amyloid precursor protein (APP): protein manufactured by neurons that plays a role in their growth and communication with each other, and perhaps contributes to the repair of injured brain cells.

Androgenetic alopecia: condition in which the hair follicles stop producing the long, thick pigmented, hair leading ultimately to baldness.

Andropause: age-related decline in the male sex hormone testosterone.

Anorexia-cachexia syndrome: condition at the end of life which involves a loss of appetite (anorexia) and atrophy of muscle mass (cachexia).

Anorexia of aging: condition involving inadequate energy intake.

Anterograde amnesia: inability to learn new information.

Anticholinesterase treatment: known as THA or tetrahydroaminoacridine, blocks the action of the enzyme cholinesterase, which destroys acetylcholine.

Anxiety disorders: psychological disorders in which the major symptom is that of excessive anxiety.

Apolipoprotein E (ApoE) gene: gene located on chromosome 19 that controls the production of ApoE, a protein that carries blood cholesterol throughout the body.

Apoptosis: the process of cell death.

APP gene: gene located on chromosome 21 that appears to control the production of the protein that generates beta-amyloid.

Archival research: a method of research in which investigators use existing resources that contain data relevant to a question about aging.

Arteriosclerosis: a general term for the thickening and hardening of arteries.

Assessment: evaluation of the psychological, physiological, and social factors that are potentially affecting the individual's current state of functioning.

Atherogenesis: the process that stimulates and accelerates atherosclerosis.

Atherosclerosis: a form of cardiovascular disease in which fat and other substances accumulate within the arteries at an abnormally high rate and substantially reduce the width of the arteries.

Attention: ability to focus or concentrate on a portion of experience while ignoring other features of experience, to be able to shift that focus as demanded by the situation, and to be able to coordinate information from multiple sources.

Attentional resources: proposal that older adults have a limited amount of energy available for cognitive operations because of reductions in central nervous system capacity.

Autobiographical memory: recall of information from one's own past.

Awareness of finitude: point at which an individual passes the age when parents or, perhaps, siblings, have died.

Baby Boomers: generation who currently are between the ages of 35 and 54 years old, born between 1945 and 1965.

Balance theory of wisdom: view of wisdom as the ability to balance the various components of intelligence outlined in the theory and apply them to problems involving the common good, or welfare of others.

Behavioral approach to marital interactions: approach that emphasizes the actual behaviors that partners engage in with each other during marital interactions as an influence on marital stability and quality.

Bereavement: the process in which an individual attempts to overcome the death of another person with whom there was a relationship.

Biological age: the age of the individual based on the quality of functioning of the individual's organ systems.

Biopsychosocial perspective: a view of development as a complex interaction of biological, psychosocial, and social processes.

Bipolar disorder: Mood disorder characterized by the experience of manic episodes.

Blended families (also called reconstituted families): families in which the parents were not originally married to each other in which there are children and stepchildren of one or both parents.

Body Mass Index (BMI): an index of body fat, calculated as weight in kilograms divided by (height in meters) squared.

Boundaryless career: a career that does not follow a set pathway.

Bridge employment: employment in one job while officially retired from another job.

Brinley plot: graph in which reaction times of older adults are plotted against reaction times of younger adults.

Caloric restriction hypothesis: the view that restriction of caloric intake is the key to prolonging life.

Cardiac output: the amount of blood that the heart pumps per minute.

Career age: the age at which an individual begins to embark on his or her career.

Caregiver burden: the stress that these people experience in the daily management of their afflicted relative.

Caregivers: family members most likely to be the ones providing care for the patient, and in particular, wives and daughters.

Caregiving: the provision of aid in daily living activities to an infirm older adult, often a relative.

Case report: a method of research in which an in-depth analysis is provided of particular individuals.

Caspase: enzyme that destroys neurons.

Cataract: clouding that has developed in the normally clear crystalline lens of the eye, resulting in blurred or distorted vision because the image cannot be focused clearly onto the retina.

Centenarians: people over the age of 100 years.

Cerebrovascular accident: (also known as a stroke or brain attack) an acute condition in which an artery leading to the brain bursts or is clogged by a blood clot or other particle.

Chromosomes: distinct, physically separate units of coiled threads of deoxyribonucleic acid (DNA) and associated protein molecules.

Chronic obstructive pulmonary disease (COPD): respiratory disorder composed primarily of two related diseases, chronic emphysema and chronic bronchitis.

Circadian rhythm: daily variation in various bodily functions.

Climacteric: gradual winding down of reproductive ability.

Clinical geropsychology: specialty used primarily in applied settings such as hospitals, clinics, and long-term institutions.

Clinical interview: assessment method in which the clinician asks questions of the client to establish insight into the client's psychological processes.

Cognition: study of the abilities to learn, remember, solve problems, and become knowledgeable about the world.

Cognitive-behavioral treatment: form of psychotherapy in which the client is encouraged to develop new behaviors and constructive ways of thinking about the self.

Cognitive evaluation theory: the view that financial incentives cause employees to feel less self-determination and psychological investment in their jobs.

Cognitive restructuring: form of cognitive therapy in which the individual is encouraged to develop greater tolerance toward negative experiences and not make sweeping overgeneralizations.

Cognitive self theories: theories proposing that individuals view the events in their lives from the standpoint of the relevance of these events to the self.

Cognitive therapy: form of psychotherapy in which the clinician attempts to change the client's maladaptive emotions and ways of coping with difficult situations by changing the client's thoughts.

Cohabitation effect: greater likelihood of divorce among couples who cohabitated before marriage.

Cohort: variable in developmental research used to signify the general era in which a person was born.

Collagen: substance found throughout the body, which makes up about one-third of all bodily proteins.

Communication predicament model: model in which the use of patronizing speech (elderspeak) constrains the older person from being able to participate fully in conversations with others.

Competence-press model: proposal that there is an optimal level of adjustment which institutionalized persons will experience on the basis of their levels of competence compared to the demands or "press" of the environment.

Compositional fallacy: the fact that when the productivity rates per time period are averaged across the careers of several individuals, the summary curve that results does not describe the productivity of any of the individuals in that group.

Compression of morbidity: concept referring to the desirable state in which people live to be older before they die and also experience less disability prior to their death.

Congestive heart failure (or heart failure): a condition in which the heart is unable to pump enough blood to meet the needs of the body's other organs.

Congruence: "fit" between a person's RIASEC type and that of the occupation within Holland's vocational development theory.

Conscientious-Conformist stage: in Loevinger's theory, period when individuals begin to gain a "conscience," or internal set of rules of right and wrong, and start to gain self-awareness as well as understanding of the needs and thoughts of other people.

Context processing deficiency: proposal that aging affects the ability to take the context of information into account when making judgments in situations such as the sustained attention task.

Contextual influences on development: the effects of social processes on changes within the individual.

Contingency management: form of behavioral treatment in which a specific desirable outcome is made dependent (or "contingent" upon) the performance of a specific behavior.

Continuing care retirement community (CCRC): a housing community that provides different levels of care based on the residents' needs.

Continuity theory: proposal that older adults will suffer a loss of well-being and negative effects of being excluded from social roles if this exclusion goes against their will.

Continuity theory of retirement: proposal that retirement does not lead to serious disruptions in the individual's sense of identity, social connections, or feelings of productivity.

Coping: the process used to manage stress.

Coronary artery disease (or coronary heart disease): a form of cardiovascular disease in which there is a lack of blood supply to the arteries that feed the heart muscle.

Correlational design: research design in which the relationship is observed between two or more variables.

Cross-sectional: developmental research design in which people of different ages are compared at the same point of measurement.

Crystallized intelligence (Gc): the acquisition of specific skills and information acquired through familiarity with the language, knowledge, and conventions of one's culture.

Day care center: form of community treatment in which individuals receive supervised meals and activities on a daily basis.

Death: the point when there is irreversible cessation of circulatory and respiratory functions, or when all structures of the brain have ceased to function.

Death ethos: a culture's prevailing philosophy of death.

Death with dignity: the idea that death should not involve extreme physical dependency or loss of control of bodily functions.

Debriefing: providing a research participant with information about the study's real purpose, after the participation has ended.

Defense mechanisms: in psychodynamic theory, unconscious strategies intended to protect the conscious mind from knowing the improper urges of the unconscious mind, which include a wide range of socially unacceptable behaviors.

Delirium: an acute state in which the individual experiences a disturbance in consciousness and attention; cognitive disorder characterized by temporary but acute confusion that can be caused by diseases of the heart and lung, infection, or malnutrition.

Delirium, dementia, and amnestic disorders: disorders involving significant loss of cognitive functioning as the result of neurological dysfunction or medical illness.

Dementia: clinical condition in which the individual experiences a loss of cognitive function severe enough to interfere with normal daily activities and social relationships.

Dependent variable: the variable on which people are observed to differ.

Depressive disorders: mood disorders characterized primarily by periods of intense sadness.

Developmental schism: an emotional gap created between parents and their children.

Developmental science: term replacing "developmental psychology" to reflect the need to take a broad, interdisciplinary approach to understanding patterns of change in life.

Diabetes: a disease caused by a defect in the process of metabolizing glucose.

Diagnostic and Statistical Manual-Fourth Edition-Text Revision or DSM-IV-TR: psychiatric manual published by the American Psychiatric Association.

Dialectical thinking: an interest in and appreciation for debate, arguments, and counterarguments.

Disengagement theory: proposal that there is an optimal relationship between the older individual and society—one in which the older person retreats from active involvement in social roles.

Dispositional affectivity: the general dimension of a person's affective responding.

Divided attention: task in which the individual is given information from two input sources (same as dual task).

Divorce proneness: characteristic of divorced people to be more likely to consider divorce as an option when their marriage is not going smoothly.

DNA (deoxyribonucleic acid): the basic unit of genetics that carries inherited information and that controls the functioning of the cell.

Doing gender: the process of enacting traditional gender roles.

Do not resuscitate (DNR) order: a document placed in a patient's hospital chart specifying the individual's desire not to be resuscitated if he or she should suffer a cardiac or respiratory arrest.

Dual-process model of stress and coping: a model of bereavement proposing that there are two processes involved in bereavement; the first with regard to loss of the attachment figure and the second with regard to loss of role and identity.

Dual task: task in which the individual is given information from two input sources (same as divided attention).

Dying: the period during which an organism loses its viability.

Dying trajectory: the rate of decline in functioning prior to death.

Dysphoria: sad mood.

Dysthermia: conditions in which the individual shows excessive raising of body temperature (hyperthermia) or excessive lowering of body temperature (hypothermia).

Early-onset familial Alzheimer's disease: form of Alzheimer's disease that begins in middle adulthood and shows an inherited pattern.

Ecological perspective: theoretical model emphasizing that changes occur throughout life in the relations between the individual and multiple levels of the environment.

Ego: in psychodynamic theory, structure in personality that, according to Freud's theory, is most accessible to conscious awareness, performs the rational, executive functions of mind, and organizes the individual's activities so that important goals can be attained. In Erikson's theory, the self.

Ego Integrity versus Despair: stage in Erikson's psychosocial development theory in which the individual attempts to establish a sense of acceptance and integration.

Ego psychology: framework of theorists whose conceptualizations of personality revolve around the role of the ego in actively directing behavior.

Elastase: enzyme that breaks down the elastin found in lung tissue.

Elder abuse: actions taken directly against an older adult through the inflicting of physical or psychological harm.

Elderspeak: a simplified speech pattern directed at older adults who presumably are unable to understand adult language.

Electroconvulsive therapy (ECT): somatic treatment in which an electric current is applied through electrodes attached across the head.

Emotional intelligence: the ability to understand and regulate one's emotions.

Empty nest: the departure of children from the home.

Epigenetic principle: the principle in Erikson's theory which states that each stage unfolds from the previous stage.

Episodic memory: memory for events ("episodes"), which can include the recall of material presented in a memory experiment such as a word list.

Equal odds rule: the fact that there is a positive relationship between quality and quantity of work.

Equilibrium: state in Piagetian theory through which individuals are able to interpret their experiences through a consistent framework but are able to change this framework when it no longer is helpful in organizing experiences.

Equity theory: proposal that relationships continue when the partners feel they are contributing equal benefits.

Erectile dysfunction: a condition in which a man is unable to achieve an erection sustainable for intercourse.

Ethnicity: the cultural background of an individual, reflecting the predominant values, attitudes, and expectations in which the individual has been raised.

Euthanasia: the direct killing of a patient by a physician who administers a lethal injection.

Experimental design: a research method in which an independent variable is manipulated and scores are then measured on the dependent variable. Involves random assignment of respondents to treatment and control groups.

Explicit memory: recall of information that the individual has consciously or deliberately attempted to recall.

Extrinsic factors: features that accompany a job that may also be found in other jobs.

Filial anxiety: the idea that one might be forced to take on the role of parent to the parent.

Filial maturity: the identification of the adult child with the parent.

Filial obligation (or filial piety): the feeling that one is obligated to take care of aging parents should this become necessary.

Five Factor Model (also called "Big Five"): theory intended to capture all the essential characteristics of personality described in other trait theories.

Fluid intelligence (Gf): the individual's innate abilities to carry out higher-level cognitive operations involving the integration, analysis, and synthesis of new information.

Focus group: a meeting of a group of respondents oriented around a particular topic of interest.

Formal operations: the ability of adolescents and adults to use logic and abstract symbols in arriving at solutions to complex problems.

Free radical: molecular fragment that seeks to bind to other molecules.

Friendship styles: friendship patterns in adulthood based on individual differences in approaches toward friends.

Fronterotemporal dementia: dementia that attacks specifically the frontal lobes of the brain and is reflected in personality changes such as apathy, lack of inhibition, obsessiveness, and loss of judgment.

Gender: the individual's identification as being male or female.

Gender gap: difference between the salaries of men and women.

Gene: a functional unit of a DNA molecule carrying a particular set of instructions for producing a specific protein or other molecules needed by the body's cells.

General slowing hypothesis: proposal that the age-related increase in reaction time reflects a general decline of information processing speed within the aging nervous system.

Generalized anxiety disorder: Anxiety disorder in which a person feels an overall sense of uneasiness and concern but without having a particular focus.

Generativity versus Stagnation: stage in Erikson's psychosocial development theory in which the individual focuses on the issues of procreation, productivity, and creativity.

Geriatric continuing day treatment: program in which clients attend a day treatment program three days a week but are encouraged to live independently during the remaining days of the week.

Geriatric partial hospital: treatment site in which daily outpatient therapy is provided with intensive, structured multidisciplinary services to older persons who have recently been discharged from a psychiatric hospital.

Gerontology: the scientific study of the aging process.

Geropsychology: applications of the field of gerontology to the psychological treatment of older adults.

Glaucoma: a group of conditions in which the optic nerve is damaged, causing loss of visual function.

Glucocorticoid cascade hypothesis: proposal that aging causes dangerous increases in cortisol levels affecting immune response, fat deposits, and cognition.

Gompertz equation: a function that expresses the relationship between age of the organism and age of death.

Hierarchical linear modeling: a method used for longitudinal studies in which individual patterns of change are investigated rather than simply comparing mean scores.

High-density lipoproteins (HDLs): the plasma lipid transport mechanism responsible for carrying lipids from the peripheral tissues to the liver where they are excreted or synthesized into bile acids.

Holland's vocational development theory: proposal by Holland that vocational aspirations and interests are the expression of an individual's personality.

Home health services: services provided to older adults who are ill or disabled but are able to maintain an independent life in the community.

Hormone: chemical messenger produced by the endocrine system.

Hormone replacement therapy (HRT): therapeutic administration of lower doses of estrogen than in ERT, along with progestin to reduce the cancer risk associated with ERT.

Hospice: a site or program that provides medical and supportive services for dying patients and their families and friends.

Humanistic or client-centered therapy: form of psychotherapy in which the emphasis is on helping the individual gain greater self-acceptance and ultimately achieve fuller expression of the true or underlying self.

Hypertension: blood pressure that is chronically greater than or equal to the value of 140 mm Hg systolic pressure and 90 mm Hg diastolic pressure.

Identity: a composite of the individual's self-representations in biological, psychological, and social domains.

Identity accommodation: the process through which changes occur in the individual's view of the self.

Identity Achievement versus Identity Diffusion: stage in Erikson's psychosocial development theory in which the individual attempts to establish a sense of self.

Identity assimilation: the process through which individuals interpret new experiences relevant to the self in terms of their existing self-schemas or identities.

Identity process theory: theoretical perspective describing interactions between the individual and experiences.

Immune senescence: term used to refer to features of the aging immune system.

Impaired aging: processes that result from diseases that do not occur in all individuals.

Implicit memory: recall of information acquired unintentionally.

Independent variable: the variable that explains or "causes" the range of scores in the dependent variable.

Information processing: perspective in psychology in which cognitive functioning of humans is regarded as comparable to the functioning of a computer.

Informed consent: written agreement to participate in research based on knowing what that participation will involve.

Inhibitory deficit hypothesis: proposal that aging involves a reduction in the cognitive resources available for controlling or inhibiting attention.

Interactionist model: view that genetics and environments interact in complex ways and that the individual actively participates in his or her development through reciprocal relations with the environment.

Intergenerational solidarity model: model proposing six dimensions that characterize the cohesiveness of adult child-parent relationships.

Interindividual differences: differences between individuals in developmental processes.

Intermediate care facility: treatment site in which health-related services are provided to individuals who do not require hospital or skilled nursing facility care but do require institutional care above the level of room and board.

Interpersonal therapy (IPT): form of psychotherapy integrating cognitive methods with a focus on social factors that contribute to psychological disturbance.

Intimacy versus Isolation: stage in Erikson's psychosocial development theory in which the individual attempts to establish an intimate relationship with another adult.

Intra-individual differences (also called multidirectionality of development): differences within individuals in developmental processes.

Intrinsic factors: aspects of a job inherent in the work itself.

Korsakoff syndrome: a form of dementia that occurs when there is a deficiency of vitamin B_1 (thiamine).

Labor force: all civilians in the over-16 population who are living outside of institutions and who have or are actively seeking employment.

Laboratory study: a research method in which participants are tested in a systematic fashion using standardized procedures.

Late-onset depression: mild or moderate depression that first appears after the age of 60.

Late-onset familial Alzheimer's disease: inherited form of Alzheimer's disease that starts at the age of 60 or 65 years.

Late-onset schizophrenia: form of schizophrenia that can occur among adults over the age of 45 years.

Legitimization of biography: process in which older or dying individuals attempt to gain perspective on the events in their past lives.

Lewy bodies: tiny spherical structures consisting of deposits of protein found in dying nerve cells in damaged regions deep within the brains of people with Parkinson's disease.

Life course perspective: theoretical model in social gerontology that emphasizes the importance of age-based norms, roles, and attitudes as influences that shape events throughout development.

Life expectancy: the average number of years of life remaining to the people born within a similar period of time.

Life review: a time of taking stock through reminiscence or a mental reliving of events from the long-ago past.

Life review therapy: psychological intervention intended to help an older adult rework past experiences with the goal of gaining greater acceptance of previous life events.

Life satisfaction: the cognitive evaluation of one's life circumstances.

Life-span perspective: the understanding of development as continuous from childhood through old age.

Life story: process through which individuals develop a narrative view of their lives that emphasizes the positive.

Life structure: basic pattern or design of an individual's life at a particular point in time.

Living will or advance directive (AD): written statement by an individual concerning preferred treatment should he or she require medical or surgical treatment to prolong life.

Logistic regression: method in which researchers test the likelihood of an individual receiving a score on a discrete yes-no variable.

Longitudinal: developmental research design in which the same people are compared at different ages.

Long-term memory: repository of information that is held for a period of time ranging from several minutes to a lifetime.

Manic episode: period during which an individual feels unduly elated, grandiose, expansive, and energetic.

Marriage: legally sanctioned union between a man and a woman as traditionally defined.

Maturation hypothesis: proposal that the Cluster B or "immature" personality types (borderline, histrionic, narcissistic, and antisocial) improve or at least are more treatable in older adults.

Mechanics of intelligence: cognitive operations of speed, working memory, and fluid intelligence.

Mechanistic model: view in which "nurture" or the environment is regarded as the prime mover in development.

Medicaid: a federal and state matching entitlement program that pays for medical assistance for certain individuals and families with low incomes and resources.

Medicare: Title XVIII of the Social Security Act entitled Health Insurance for the Aged and Disabled.

Medicare Part A (Hospital Insurance or HI): coverage of inpatient hospitalization and related services.

Medicare Part B (Supplementary Medical Insurance (SMI): medical benefits to individuals age 65 and over with payment of a monthly premium.

Medicare Part C (Medicare + Choice program): additional medical insurance available for purchase through Medicare.

Medicare Part D: subsidy for prescription drug privileges.

Memantine: Alzheimer's disease medication that operates on the glumatate system.

Memory contollability: beliefs about the effects of the aging process on memory.

Menopause: the point in a woman's life when menstruation stops permanently.

Metabolic syndrome: a clinical condition involving high levels of abdominal obesity, abnormal levels of blood cholesterol, hypertension, insulin resistance, high triglycerides, high levels of C-reactive proteins in the blood, and the presence of coronary plaques.

Midlife crisis: term that originated in the early 1970s as a description of the radical changes in personality that supposedly accompanied entry into the midpoint of life.

Mild cognitive impairment (MCI): a subtle loss of memory and learning abilities.

Mixed anxiety-depressive disorder: disorder in which the individual experiences recurrent or persistent dysphoria along with at least four symptoms of anxiety disorders; changes in personality that are theorized to accompany entry into the midpoint of life (age 40–45).

Mood disorders: psychological disorders involving abnormalities in the individual's experience of emotion.

Mortality data: statistics derived from death.

Most efficient design: framework originated by Schaie to organize the collection of sequential data.

Motivational crowding out: the idea that extrinsic rewards crowd out intrinsic satisfaction.

Multidimensionality: the principle that there are multiple processes in development.

Multidirectionality of development: the principle that not all systems develop at the same rate within the person—some functions may show positive changes and others negative changes over time; Even within the same function, the same individual may show gains in one area, losses in another, and stability in yet a third domain.

Multi-infarct dementia or MID: most common form of vascular dementia, caused by transient ischemic attacks.

Multiple regression analysis: multivariate correlational research design in which a set of variables are used to predict scores on another variable.

Multiple threshold model: theoretical perspective proposing that personal recognition of aging occurs in a stepwise process across the years of adulthood.

Multivariate correlational design: research design that involves the analysis of relationships among multiple variables.

Mutations: alterations in genes that lead to changes in their functions.

Myocardial infarction: acute form of cardiovascular disease that occurs when the blood supply to part of the heart muscle (the myocardium) is severely reduced or blocked.

Need complementary hypothesis: the proposal that people seek and are more satisfied with marital partners who are the opposite of themselves.

NEO Personality Inventory-Revised (NEO-PI-R): chief measure used to assess an individual's personality according to the Five Factor Model.

Neurofibrillary tangles: tangled fibers within neurons.

Neuroleptics: medications intended to reduce psychotic symptoms by altering dopamine activity.

Neuronal fallout model: view of the aging nervous system as involving progressive loss of brain tissue across the adult years noticeable by the age of 30.

Niche-picking: the notion that a child's genetically based abilities lead that child to select certain activities which further enhance the development of those abilities.

Nonnormative influences: random, chance factors that occur due to a combination of coincidence, the impact of earlier decisions on later events, and relationships with other people.

Normal aging: changes built into the hard wiring of the organism that occur more or less in all individuals (although at different rates) and are distinct from those changes associated with disease.

Normal-pressure hydrocephalus: reversible form of dementia that can cause cognitive impairment, dementia, urinary incontinence, and difficulty in walking.

Normative age-graded influences: the influences on life that are linked to chronological age and associated with a society's expectations for people of a given age.

Normative history-graded influences: influences that transcend the individual's life and are associated with changes in a given culture or geopolitical unit as a whole.

Nursing home: a residence that provides a room, meals, skilled nursing and rehabilitative care, medical services, and protective supervision.

Nursing Home Reform Act: U.S. federal legislation passed in 1987 which mandated that facilities must meet physical standards, provide adequate professional staffing and services, and maintain policies governing the administrative and medical procedures of the nursing facility.

Observational method: a research method in which conclusions are drawn about behavior through careful and systematic examination in particular settings.

Obsessive-compulsive disorder: a form of anxiety disorder in which individuals suffer from obsessions (repetitive thoughts) and compulsions (repetitive behaviors).

Occupational Information Network (O*NET): online interactive national database of occupations intended for purposes of job classification, training, and vocational counseling.

Occupational reinforcement patterns (ORPs): the work values and needs likely to be reinforced or satisfied by a particular occupation.

Old age style: an approach to one's art that eliminates the fine details and instead presents the essence of the work's intended meaning.

Old-old: portion of the over-65 population ages 75 to 84.

Oldest-old: portion of the over-65 population ages 85 and older.

Optimal aging (also called "successful aging"): avoidance of changes that would otherwise occur with age through preventative and compensatory stratagies.

Orderly careers: occupations held by an individual that are logically connected.

Organismic model: view in which "nature" or genetics is regarded as the prime mover in development.

Osteoarthritis: a painful, degenerative joint disease that often involves the hips, knees, neck, lower back, or the small joints of the hands.

Osteoporosis: loss of bone mineral content of more than 2.5 standard deviations below the mean of young white, non-Hispanic women.

Overtreatment: the provision of aggressive care in cases where terminally ill patients express a preference for comfort only.

Palliative care: comfort care to dying individuals through measures such as pain control.

Panic disorder: anxiety disorder involving the experience of panic attacks.

Paradox of well-being: proposal that despite their objective difficulties, people in later life feel good about themselves and their situations.

Parkinson's disease: progressive neurological disorder causing motor disturbances, including tremors (shaking at rest), speech impediments, slowing of movement, muscular rigidity, shuffling gait, and postural instability or the inability to maintain balance.

Patient Self-Determination Act (PSDA): legislation affecting all organizations receiving Medicare or Medicaid guaranteeing the right of all competent adults to write a living will or advance directive (AD).

Perimenopause: three- to five-year span during which women gradually lose their reproductive ability.

Peripheral ties: friendships that persist but are not characterized by a high degree of closeness.

Persistent vegetative state: condition in which the subcortical areas of the brain remain intact and therefore are able to regulate basic bodily functions, including sleep-wake cycles, but the individual lacks conscious awareness.

Personal aging: changes occurring over time within the individual, also referred to as ontogenetic change.

Personality disorders: disorders thought to reflect a disturbance within the basic personality structure of the individual.

Perspective: a proposal that presents a position or set of ideas to account for a set of processes; less formal than a theory.

Photoaging: age changes caused by exposure to the sun's harmful radiation.

Physician-assisted suicide: situation in which a physician provides the means for a terminally ill patient to complete suicide.

Pick's disease: form of dementia that involves severe atrophy of the frontal and temporal lobes.

Plasticity: the proposal that the course of development may be altered depending on the nature of the specific interactions of the individual in the environment.

Plasticity model: view of the aging nervous system which proposes that although some neurons die, the remaining ones continue to develop.

Plateauing: the attainment of a point in one's career where further hierarchical advancement is unlikely.

Polypharmacy: condition in which the individual takes multiple drugs, sometimes without knowledge of the physician.

Possible selves: views of the self that guide the choice and pursuit of future endeavors.

Postformal operations: proposed stage following formal operations referring to the way that adults structure their thinking over and beyond that of the adolescent.

Post-traumatic stress disorder (PTSD): anxiety disorder in which an individual suffers prolonged effects of exposure to a traumatic experience.

Pragmatics of intelligence: application of a person's abilities to the solution of real-life problems.

Presbycusis: age-related hearing loss due to degenerative changes in the cochlea or auditory nerve leading from the cochlea to the brain.

Presbyopia: age-related change in the eye involving loss of accommodative power of the crystalline lens resulting in loss of the ability to focus on near objects.

Presenilin genes (PS1 and PS2): PS1 gene, a gene that is located on chromosome 14 and accounts for up to 50 to 80% of early-onset cases; PS2 gene, a gene that is located on chromosome 1 and accounts for a much smaller percentage of early-onset familial Alzheimer's disease.

Primary aging (also called normal aging): age-related changes that are universal, intrinsic, and progressive.

Primary mental abilities: factors in intelligence proposed by Thurstone incorporating verbal meaning, word fluency, number, spatial relations, memory, perceptual speed, and general reasoning.

Primary Mental Abilities (PMA) test: test of five primary mental abilities that is the basis for the Seattle Longitudinal Study data.

Procedural memory: knowledge of how to perform certain activities.

Prospective memory: recall of events to be performed in the future.

Protean career: a career in which the person has determination over his or her career path.

Proximal social relational level: level of interaction in the ecological perspective involving the individual's relationships with significant others, peers, and nuclear families.

Pseudodementia: cognitive symptoms of depression that appear to be dementia.

Psychodynamic psychotherapy: form of psychotherapy in which the clinician focuses on unconscious processes, such as conflicts, defense mechanisms, dreams, and issues based on early relationships with parents.

Psychological age: the age of the individual based on psychological measures such as intelligence, memory, and learning ability.

Psychological disorder: a condition that significantly alters the individual's adaptation.

Psychomotor speed: amount of time it takes a person to process a signal, prepare a response, and then execute that response.

Psychopathy: a set of traits thought to lie at the core of antisocial personality disorder.

Psychosocial: term used by Erikson to refer to developmental processes that involve a combination of psychological and social forces.

Psychotherapeutic medications: substances that by their chemical nature alter the individual's brain structure or function.

Quasi-experimental: a research method in which groups are compared on predetermined characteristics.

Race: a biological term for classifications within species based on physical and structural characteristics.

Reaction time: time calculated for an individual to study a stimulus array and then respond when that stimulus array takes a certain form.

Reciprocal nature of development: the principle that people both influence and are influenced by the events in their lives.

Recycling: process in which workers change their main field of career activity part way into occupational life and reexperience the early career development stages.

Reliability: the consistency of a measurement procedure.

Religion: an individual's identification with an organized belief system.

Remote memory: recall of information from the distant past.

Replicative senescence: the loss of the ability to reproduce.

Reserve capacity: additional abilities possessed by older adults that are normally untapped.

Residential care facility: treatment site that provides 24-hour supportive care services and supervision to individuals not requiring skilled nursing care.

Resource model: proposal that adaptation even to difficult retirement transitions can be facilitated by having sufficient biological, psychological, and social resources.

Retirement: the withdrawal of an individual in later life from the labor force.

Retirement self-efficacy: a person's belief that he or she will be able to make a smooth and satisfactory adjustment to retirement.

Retrograde amnesia: inability to remember events from the past.

Reversible dementias: loss of cognitive functioning due to the presence of a medical condition that affects but does not destroy brain tissue.

RIASEC model: Holland's vocational development theory which proposes that there are six facets of vocational interests and environments-Realistic (R), Investigative (I), Artistic (A), Social(S), Enterprising (E), and Conventional (C).

Role reversal: discredited belief that parents and their adult children switch responsibilities.

Role strain: model proposing that work and family involvement are inversely related, so that the higher the person's involvement in his or her work role, the lower the individual's involvement in the family.

Role theory: proposal that normative expectations for behavior provide a major source of fulfillment because they integrate the individual with society.

Sandwich generation: popular term used to refer to women with aging parents needing help and children living in the home.

Sarcopenia: progressive loss of muscle mass.

Schema: term used by Piaget to refer to the individual's existing mental structures.

Schizophrenia: severe form of psychopathology involving a wide range of unusual symptoms affecting thought, language, motivation, and the expression of emotion.

Secondary aging (also called impaired aging): changes in later life that are due to disease.

Secondary mental abilities: the broad constructs that underlie specific abilities.

Secretases: enzymes that snip proteins such amyloid precursor protein.

Selective Estrogen Replacement Modulator (SERM): therapeutic administration of estrogen with more targeted effects than ERT.

Selective optimization with compensation: the principle that adults attempt to preserve and maximize the abilities that are of central importance and put less effort into maintaining those that are not.

Self-determination theory: view that intrinsic motivation plays a central role in occupational satisfaction but that certain forms of extrinsic motivation can also have intrinsic components.

Self-Directed Search (SDS): self-administered and self-scored test based on Holland's vocational development theory.

Semantic memory: equivalent to "knowledge" and includes the words and definitions of words found in one's vocabulary or storehouse of historical facts.

Sequential designs: developmental research design in which the researcher conducts a sequence of cross-sectional or longitudinal studies.

Set point perspective: proposal that biologically determined temperament sets the boundaries for the levels of well-being an individual experiences throughout life.

Similarity hypothesis: the proposal that similarity and perceived similarity predict interpersonal attraction.

Skilled nursing facility: treatment site that provides the most intensive nursing care available outside of a hospital.

Skip generation family: family in which children are living with grandparents and no parents are present.

Sleep apnea: condition in which the individual experiences a particular form of snoring in which a partial obstruction in the back of the throat restricts airflow during inhalation.

Social age: the age of the individual based on occupying certain social roles, including family, work, and possibly community roles.

Social aging: changes in people that occur along with or perhaps as the result of historical change.

Social clock: the normative expectations for the ages at which major life events should occur.

Social-cognitive: form of psychotherapy involving attempts to raise a client's sense of self-efficacy by enabling the client to have steplike increments in success at completing a previously unattainable goal.

Social comparison: process through which individuals look at the situations of others who are more unfortunate than they are and comfort themselves with the thought that things could be worse.

Social death: situation in which the dying are treated as nonpersons by family or health care workers as they are left to spend their final months or years in the hospital or nursing home.

Social exchange theory: proposal that relationships continue when partners perceive that the rewards of remaining in the relationship outweigh the rewards associated with alternatives.

Social indicator model: proposal that demographic and social structural variables account for individual differences in levels of well-being.

Social phobia: a form of anxiety disorder that applies to situations in which people must perform some action in front of others.

Social Security Act: law passed by Congress in 1935 that provided retirement income for older adults.

Sociocultural level: level of interaction in the ecological perspective involving relations with the larger social institutions of educational, public policy, governmental, and economic systems.

Socioeconomic status (or social class): an index of a person's position in society based on level of education and level of occupation.

Socioemotional selectivity theory: proposition that, throughout adulthood, individuals reduce the range of their relationships to maximize social and emotional gains and minimize risks.

Somatopause of aging: age-related decline in the somatotrophic axis (GH and IGF-1) of the endocrine system.

Source memory (source monitoring): recall of where information was heard or seen.

Specific phobia: an irrational fear of a particular object or situation.

Spillover model: proposal regarding work and family roles that attitudes and behaviors from one role carry over into the other.

Sporadic Alzheimer's disease: nonfamilial Alzheimer's disease.

Stages of dying: denial, anger, bargaining, depression, and acceptance.

Stereotype threat: our tendency to perform in ways consistent with negative stereotypes of the group to which we belong.

Strong Vocational Interest Inventory (SVII): test in which respondents indicate their preferences for occupations, topics of study, activities, and types of people.

Structural equation modeling: multivariate correlational research in which a set of relationships among variables are tested to determine whether the variables provide a good fit to the data.

Subdural haematoma: blood clot that creates pressure on brain tissue.

Subject attrition: loss of respondents over time in a longitudinal study.

Subjective well-being: psychological state composed of positive affect, negative affect, and life satisfaction.

Subsidized senior housing: form of housing provided for individuals with low to moderate incomes.

Successful aging: term used to reflect the ability of an older person to adapt to the aging process.

Successful intelligence: the ability to achieve success in life according to one's personal standards and in the framework of one's sociocultural context.

Supercentenarians: people over the age of 110 years.

Super's self-concept theory: proposal that career development is a process driven by the individual's desire to achieve full realization of his or her self-concept in work that will allow the self-concept to be expressed.

Survey: a research method that involves asking people to provide answers to structured questions, with the intention of generalizing to larger populations.

Sustained attention: measure in which efficient performance depends on the ability to make a quick response even after a long delay of waiting for the target to appear.

Swan song phenomenon: a brief renewal of creativity that can stimulate the creation of new works and a new style of work.

Systematic desensitization: form of behavioral treatment in which a client is taught to replace an unwanted response (such as fear) with a desirable response (such as relaxation).

Tau: protein that seems to play a role in maintaining the stability of the microtubules which form the internal support structure of the axons.

Telomere: the terminal region or tail of a chromosome that is made up of DNA but that contains no genetic information.

Terror Management Theory: social-psychological perspective proposing that people regard the thought of the finitude of their lives with panic and dread.

Testing the limits: method developed by Baltes and his coworkers to determine how much the performance of older adults can be increased through training.

Theory of multiple intelligences: proposal that there are eight independent categories of intelligence, each of which can contribute to an individual's ability to adapt to the world.

Time of measurement: the year or period in which testing has occurred.

Tinnitus: condition in which the individual perceives sounds in the head or ear (such as a ringing noise) when there is no external source for it.

Trait: a stable, enduring attribute that characterizes one element of an individual's personality.

Transient ischemic attack (TIA) (also called a mini-stroke): a condition caused by the development of clots in the cerebral arteries.

Transition to parenthood: the period in which a first child is born to the parents.

Triarchic theory of intelligence: proposal that there are three aspects to intelligence: componential, experiential, and contextual.

Two-factor theory: theory of work motivation developed by Herzberg proposing that the intrinsic features of a job are motivators and the extrinsic features of a job are hygiene factors.

Type A behavior pattern: a collection of traits thought to increase a person's risk of developing cardiovascular disease.

Validity: the extent to which a test measures what it is supposed to measure.

Vascular dementia: progressive loss of cognitive functioning that occurs as the result of damage to the arteries supplying the brain.

Vertigo: a sense of movement when the body is actually at rest, usually the sense that one is spinning.

Vocation: pursuit of an occupation.

Vocational satisfaction: the extent to which the worker has positive views of the job or aspects of a job.

Wechsler Adult Intelligence Scale: test of intelligence with Verbal and Performance scales.

Wernicke's disease: an acute condition involving delirium, eye movement disturbances, difficulties maintaining balance and movement, and deterioration of nerves to the hands and feet.

White matter hyperintensities: abnormalities in the brain thought to be made up of parts of deteriorating neurons.

Widowhood effect: the fact that there is a greater probability of death in those who have become widowed.

Wisdom: as defined by Baltes, a form of expert knowledge in the pragmatics of life.

Working memory: system that keeps information temporarily available and active while the information is being used in other cognitive tasks.

Young-old: portion of the over-65 population ages 65 to 74.

REFERENCES

Aartsen, M. J., Smits, C. H., van Tilburg, T., Knipscheer, K. C., & Deeg, D. J. (2002). Activity in older adults: Cause or consequence of cognitive functioning? A longitudinal study on everyday activities and cognitive performance in older adults. *Journals of Gerontology Psychological Sciences 57B*, P153–162.

Aartsen, M. J., Van Tilburg, T., Smits, C. H., Comijs, H. C., & Knipscheer, K. C. (2005). Does widowhood affect memory performance of older persons? *Psychological Medicine, 35*, 217–226.

Abeles, N., Cooley, S., Deitch, I., Harper, M. S., Hinrichsen, G., Lopez, M., & Molinari, V. (1997). *What practitioners should know about working with older adults*. Washington, DC: American Psychological Association.

Abrams, R. C., & Horowitz, S. V. (1999). Personality disorders after age 50: A meta-analytic review of the literature. In E. Rosowsky, R. C. Abrams & R. A. Zweig (Eds.), *Personality disorders in older adults: Emerging issues in diagnosis and treatment* (pp. 55–68). Mahweh, NJ: Lawrence Erlbaum.

Acacio, B. D., Stanczyk, F. Z., Mullin, P., Saadat, P., Jafarian, N., & Sokol, R. Z. (2004). Pharmacokinetics of dehydroepiandrosterone and its metabolites after long-term daily oral administration to healthy young men. *Fertility and Sterility, 81*, 595–604.

Achem, S. R., & Devault, K. R. (2005). Dysphagia in aging. *Journal of Clinical Gastroenterology, 39*, 357–371.

Achenbaum, W. A. (1978). *Old age in the new land The American experience since 1970*. Baltimore: Johns Hopkins University Press.

Adams, R. G., & Blieszner, R. (1994). An integrative conceptual framework for friendship research. *Journal of Social and Personal Relationships, 11*, 163–184.

Adams, R. G., & Blieszner, R. (1995). Midlife friendship patterns. In N. Vanzetti & S. Duck (Eds.), *A lifetime of relationships* (pp. 336–363). San Francisco: Brooks/Cole.

Adams-Price, C. (1998). Aging, writing, and creativity. In C. Adams-Price (Ed.), *Creativity and successful aging: Theoretical and empirical approaches* (pp. 289–310). New York: Springer.

Adler, N. E., Boyce, T., Chesney, M. A., Cohen, S., Folkman, S., Kahn, R. L., & Syme, S. L. (1994). Socioeconomic status and health: The challenge of the gradient. *American Psychologist, 49*, 15–24.

Administration on Aging (2006). A profile of older Americans: 2005. Washington, DC: U.S. Department of Health and Human Services.

Administration on Aging (2003). A profile of older Americans: 2002. Washington, DC: U.S. Department of Health and Human Services.

Agronick, G. S., & Duncan, L. E. (1998). Personality and social change: Individual differences, life path, and importance attributed to the women's movement: A longitudinal analysis. *Journal of Personality and Social Psychology, 74*, 1545–1555.

Ahluwalia, N. (2004). Aging, nutrition and immune function. *Journal of Nutrition, Health, and Aging, 8*, 2–6.

Ainsworth, M., Blehar, M., Waters, E., & Wall, S. (1978). *Patterns of attachment: A psychological study of the strange situation*. Hillsdale, NJ: Erlbaum.

Ajani, U. A., Ford, E. S., & McGuire, L. C. (2006). Distribution of lifestyle and emerging risk factors by 10-year risk for coronary heart disease. *European Journal of Cardiovascular Prevention and Rehabilitation, 13*, 745–752.

Aldwin, C. M., & Gilmer, D. F. (1999). Health and optimal aging. In J. C. Cavanaugh & S. K. Whitbourne (Eds.), *Gerontology: Interdisciplinary perspectives* (pp. 123–154). New York: Oxford University Press.

Alexopoulos, G. S., Buckwalter, K., Olin, J., Martinez, R., Wainscott, C., & Krishnan, K. R. (2002). Comorbidity of late life depression: an opportunity for research on mechanisms and treatment. *Biological Psychiatry, 52*, 543–558.

Allaire, J. C., & Marsiske, M. (2002). Well- and ill-defined measures of everyday cognition: Relationship to older adults' intellectual ability and functional status. *Psychology and Aging, 17,* 101–115.

Allen, J. R., Whittlesey, S., Pfefferbaum, B., & Ondersma, M. L. (1999). Community and coping of mothers and grandmothers of children killed in a human-caused disaster. *Psychiatric Annals, 29,* 85–91.

Allen, K. R., Blieszner, R., & Roberto, K. A. (2000). Families in the middle and later years: A review and critique of research in the 1990s. *Journal of Marriage and the Family, 62,* 911–926.

Allen, K. R., & Walker, A. J. (2000). Qualitative research. In C. Hendrick & S. S. Hendrick (Eds.), *Close relationships* (pp. 19–30). Thousand Oaks, CA: Sage Publications.

Allman, D., & Miller, J. P. (2005). B cell development and receptor diversity during aging. *Current Opinion in Immunology, 17,* 463–467.

Aloia, J. F., Vaswani, A., Feuerman, M., Mikhail, M., & Ma, R. (2000). Differences in skeletal and muscle mass with aging in black and white women. *American Journal of Physiology—Endocrinology & Metabolism, 278,* E1153–1157.

Amato, P. R. (2000). The consequences of divorce for adults and children. *Journal of Marriage and the Family, 62,* 511–521.

Amato, P. R., & Afifi, T. D. (2006). Feeling caught between parents: Adult children's relations with parents and subjective well-being. *Journal of Marriage and the Family, 68,* 222–235.

American Academy of Pediatrics Task Force on Brain Death in Chindren. Report of a special task force: guidelines for determination of brain death in children. (1987). *Pediatrics, 80,* 298–300.

American Cancer Society (2007). *Cancer facts and figures 2007.* Atlanta, GA: American Cancer Society.

American Heart Association (2003). *International Cardiovascular Disease Statistics.* http://www.americanheart.org.

American Psychiatric Association (2000). *DSM-IV: Diagnostic and Statistical Manual of Mental Disorders Text Revision.* Washington, DC: American Psychiatric Association.

American Psychological Association (2003). *Ethical principles of psychologists and code of conduct,* from http://www.apa.org/ethics/code2002.html#8_02.

American Psychological Association (2004). Guidelines for psychological practice with older adults. *American Psychologist, 59,* 336–265.

Amore, M., Tagariello, P., Laterza, C., & Savoia, E. M. (2007). Beyond nosography of depression in elderly. *Archives of Gerontology and Geriatrics, 44 Suppl 1,* 13–22.

An, J. S., & Cooney, T. M. (2006). Psychological well-being in mid to late life: The role of generativity development and parent-child relationships across the lifespan. *International Journal of Behavioral Development, 30,* 410–421.

Ancoli-Israel, S., & Cooke, J. R. (2005). Prevalence and comorbidity of insomnia and effect on functioning in elderly populations. *Journal of the American Geriatrics Society, 53,* S264–271.

Andreoletti, C., Veratti, B. W., & Lachman, M. E. (2006). Age differences in the relationship between anxiety and recall. *Aging and Mental Health, 10,* 265–271.

Andrew, M. K., Freter, S. H., & Rockwood, K. (2006). Prevalence and outcomes of delirium in community and non-acute care settings in people without dementia: A report from the Canadian Study of Health and Aging. *BMC Medicine, 4,* 15.

Ardelt, M. (2000). Still stable after all these years? Personality stability theory revisited. *Social Psychology Quarterly, 63,* 392–405.

Ardelt, M. (2004). Wisdom as expert knowledge system: A critical review of a contemporary operationalization of an ancient concept. *Human Development, 47,* 257–285.

Arean, P. A., & Ayalon, L. (2005). Assessment and treatment of depressed older adults in primary care. *Clinical Psychology: Science and Practice, 12,* 321–335.

Aries, P. (1974). *Western attitudes toward death: From the middle ages to the present.* Baltimore: Johns Hopkins University Press.

Aries, P. (1981). *The hour of our death.* New York: Alfred A. Knopf.

Armstrong-Stassen, M. (2001). Reactions of older employees to organizational downsizing: The role of gender, job level, and time. *Journal of Gerontology: Psychological Sciences, 56B,* P234–P243.

Arnett, J. J. (2000). Emerging adulthood: A theory of development from the late teens through the twenties. *American Psychologist, 55,* 469–480.

Arnold, J. T., Le, H., McFann, K. K., & Blackman, M. R. (2005). Comparative effects of DHEA vs. testosterone, dihydrotestosterone, and estradiol on proliferation and gene expression in human LNCaP prostate cancer cells. *American Journal of Physiology: Endocrinology and Metabolism, 288,* E573–E584.

Artistico, D., Cervone, D., & Pezzuti, L. (2003). Perceived self-efficacy and everyday problem solving among young and older adults. *Psychology and Aging, 18,* 68–79.

Atchley, R. C. (1989). A continuity theory of normal aging. *The Gerontologist, 29,* 183–190.

Atchley, R. C. (2000). *Social forces and aging* (9th ed.). Belmont, CA: Wadsworth Thomson Learning.

Augat, P., & Schorlemmer, S. (2006). The role of cortical bone and its microstructure in bone strength. *Age and Ageing, 35 Supplement 2,* ii27–ii31.

Austin, J. T., & Vancouver, J. F. (1996). Goal constructs in psychology: Structure, process, and content. *Psychological Bulletin, 120,* 338–375.

Avery, N. C., & Bailey, A. J. (2005). Enzymic and non-enzymic cross-linking mechanisms in relation to turnover of collagen: relevance to aging and exercise. *Scandinavian Journal of Medicine and Science in Sports, 15,* 231–240.

Ayers, C. R., Sorrell, J. T., Thorp, S. R., & Wetherell, J. L. (2007). Evidence-based psychological treatments for late-life anxiety. *Psychology and Aging, 22,* 8–17.

Babb, T. G., Rodarte, J. R. (2000). Mechanism of reduced maximal expiratory flow with aging. *Journal of Applied Physiology, 89,* 505–511.

Baddeley, A. (2003). Working memory: Looking back and looking forward. *Nature Reviews Neuroscience, 4,* 829–839.

Baheiraei, A., Pocock, N. A., Eisman, J. A., Nguyen, N. D., & Nguyen, T. V. (2005). Bone mineral density, body mass index and cigarette smoking among Iranian women: implications for prevention. *BMC Musculoskeletal Disorders, 6,* 34.

Bailis, D. S., & Chipperfield, J. G. (2002). Compensating for losses in perceived personal control over health: a role for collective self-esteem in healthy aging. *Journals of Gerontology: Psychological Sciences, 57B,* P531–539.

Ball, K., Berch, D. B., Helmers, K. F., Jobe, J. B., Leveck, M. D., Marsiske, M., Morris, J. N. Rebok, G. W., Smith, D. M., Tennstedt, S. L., Unverzagt, F. W., & Willis, S. L., (2002). Effects of cognitive training interventions with older adults: A randomized controlled trial. *Journal of the American Medical Association, 288,* 2271–2281.

Baltes, P. B. (1979). Life-span developmental psychology: Some converging observations on history and theory. In P. B. Baltes & O. G. Brim Jr. (Eds.), *Life-span development and behavior* (Vol. 2, pp. 255–279). New York: Academic Press.

Baltes, P. B., & Baltes, M. M. (1990). Psychological perspectives on successful aging: A model of selective optimization with compensation. In P. B. Baltes & M. M. Baltes (Eds.), *Successful aging: Perspectives from the behavioral sciences* (pp. 1–34). New York: Cambridge University Press.

Baltes, P. B., & Graf, P. (1996). Psychological aspects of aging: Facts and frontiers. In D. Magnusson (Ed.), *The lifespan development of individuals: Behavioral, neurobiological, and psychosocial perspectives* (pp. 427–460). New York: Cambridge University Press.

Baltes, P. B., & Kliegl, R. (1992). Further testing of limits of cognitive plasticity: Negative age differences in a mnemonic skill are robust. *Developmental Psychology, 28,* 121–125.

Baltes, P. B., & Schaie, K. W. (1976). On the plasticity of intelligence in adulthood and old age: Where Horn and Donaldson fail. *American Psychologist, 31,* 720–725.

Baltes, P. B., & Staudinger, U. M. (2000). Wisdom. A metaheuristic (pragmatic) to orchestrate mind and virtue toward excellence. *American Psychologist, 55,* 122–136.

Baltes, P. B., Staudinger, U. M., Maercker, A., & Smith, J. (1995). People nominated as wise: A comparative study of wisdom-related knowledge. *Psychology and Aging, 10,* 155–166.

Banks, J., Marmot, M., Oldfield, Z., & Smith, J. P. (2006). Disease and disadvantage in the United States and in England. *Journal of the American Medical Association, 295,* 2037–2045.

Baran, X. Y., & Young, R. C. (2006). Bipolar and depressive types of schizoaffective disorder in old age. *American Journal of Geriatric Psychiatry, 14,* 382–383.

Barbaste, M., Berke, B., Dumas, M., Soulet, S., Delaunay, J. C., Castagnino, C., Arnaudinaud, V., Cheze, C., Vercauterer, J. (2002). Dietary antioxidants, peroxidation and cardiovascular risks. *Journal of Nutrition Health and Aging, 6,* 209–223.

Barbour, K. A., & Blumenthal, J. A. (2005). Exercise training and depression in older adults. *Neurobiology of Aging, 26 Supplement 1,* 119–123.

Barefoot, J. C., Mortensen, E. L., Helms, M. J., Avlund, K., & Schroll, M. (2001). A longitudinal study of gender differences in depressive symptoms from age 50 to 80. *Psychology and Aging, 16,* 342–345.

Barnow, S., Linden, M., & Freyberger, H. J. (2004). The relation between suicidal feelings and mental disorders in the elderly: Results from the Berlin Aging Study (BASE). *Psychological Medicine, 34,* 741–746.

Bartels, S. J., Moak, G. S., & Dums, A. R. (2002). Models of mental health services in nursing homes: A review of the literature. *Psychiatric Services, 53,* 1390–1396.

Bartels, S. J., & Mueser, K. T. (1999). Severe mental illness in older adults: Schizophrenia and other late-life psychoses. In M. A. Smyer & S. H. Qualls (Eds.), *Aging and mental health* (pp. 182–207). Malden, MA: Blackwell.

Bartholomew, K., & Horowitz, L. M. (1991). Attachment styles among young adults: A test of a four-category model. *Journal of Personality and Social Psychology, 61*, 226–244.

Bartzokis, G., Beckson, M., Lu, P. H., Nuechterlein, K. H., Edwards, N., & Mintz, J. (2001). Age-related changes in frontal and temporal lobe volumes in men: A magnetic resonance imaging study. *Archives of General Psychiatry, 58*, 461–465.

Bascom, P. B., & Tolle, S. W. (2002). Responding to requests for physician-assisted suicide: "These are uncharted waters for both of us." *Journal of the American Medical Association, 288*, 91–98.

Basseches, M. (1984). *Dialectical thinking and adult development.* Norwood, NJ: Ablex.

Bassett-Jones, N., & Lloyd, G. C. (2005). Does Herzberg's motivation theory have staying power? *Journal of Management Development, 24*, 929–943.

Baumeister, R. F. (1996). Self-regulation and ego threat: Motivated cognition, self deception, and destructive goal setting. In P. M. Gollwitzer & J. A. Bargh (Eds.), *The psychology of action: Linking cognition and motivation to behavior* (pp. 27–47). New York: Guilford Press.

Baumeister, R. F. (1997). Identity, self-concept, and self-esteem: The self lost and found. In R. Hogan, J. A. Johnson & S. R. Briggs (Eds.), *Handbook of personality psychology* (pp. 681–710). San Diego, CA: Academic Press.

Baumeister, R. F., Bratslavsky, E., Finkenauer, C., & Vohs, K. D. (2001). Bad is stronger than good. *Review of General Psychology, 54*, 323–370.

Baur, J. A., Pearson, K. J., Price, N. L., Jamieson, H. A., Lerin, C., Kalra, A., Prabhu, V. V., Allard, J. S., Lopez-Lluch, G., Lewis, K., Pistell, P. J., Poosala, S., Becker, K. G., Boss, O., Gwinn, D., Wang, M., Ramaswamy, S., Fishbein, K. W., Spencer, R. G., Lakatta, E. G., Le Couteur, D., Shaw, R. J., Navas, P., Puigserver, P., Ingram, D. K., de Cabo, R., & Sinclair, D. A. (2006). Resveratrol improves health and survival of mice on a high-calorie diet. *Nature, 444*, 337–342.

Bazzano, L. A. (2006). The high cost of not consuming fruits and vegetables. *Journal of the American Dietetic Association, 106*, 1364–1368.

Bechtold, M., Palmer, J., Valtos, J., Iasiello, C., & Sowers, J. (2006). Metabolic syndrome in the elderly. *Current Diabetes Reports, 6*, 64–71.

Bedford, V. H., Volling, B. L., & Avioli, P. S. (2000). Positive consequences of sibling conflict in childhood and adulthood. *International Journal of Aging & Human Development, 51*, 53–69.

Beekman, A. T.., Bremmer, M. A., Deeg, D. J., van Balkom, A. J., Smit, J. H., de Beurs, E., van Dyck, R., & van Tilburg, W. (1998). Anxiety disorders in later life: A report from the Longitudinal Aging Study Amsterdam. *International Journal of Geriatric Psychiatry, 13*, 717–726.

Beekman, A. T., Geerlings, S. W., Deeg, D. J., Smit, J. H., Schoevers, R. S., de Beurs, E., Braam, A. W., Penninx, B. W., & van Tilburg, W. (2002). The natural history of late-life depression: A 6-year prospective study in the community. *Archives of General Psychiatry, 59*, 605–611.

Beer, K. R. (2006). Comparative evaluation of the safety and efficacy of botulinum toxin type A and topical creams for treating moderate-to-severe glabellar rhytids. *Dermatological Surgery, 32*, 184–197.

Beeri, M. S., Schmeidler, J., Sano, M., Wang, J., Lally, R., Grossman, H., & Silverman, J. M. (2006). Age, gender, and education norms on the CERAD neuropsychological battery in the oldest old. *Neurology, 67*, 1006–1010.

Beier, M. E., & Ackerman, P. L. (2001). Current-events knowledge in adults: An investigation of age, intelligence, and nonability determinants. *Psychology and Aging, 16*, 615–628.

Beier, M. E., & Ackerman, P. L. (2005). Age, ability, and the role of prior knowledge on the acquisition of new domain knowledge: Promising results in a real-world learning environment. *Psychology and Aging, 20*, 341–355.

Belleville, S., Gilbert, B., Fontaine, F., Gagnon, L., Ménard, É. & Gauthier, S. (2006). Improvement of episodic memory in persons with mild cognitive impairment and healthy older adults: Evidence from a cognitive intervention program. *Dementia and Geriatric Cognitive Disorders, 22*, 486–499.

Bellipanni, G., Bianchi, P., Pierpaoli, W., Bulian, D., & Ilyia, E. (2001). Effects of melatonin in perimenopausal and menopausal women: A randomized and placebo controlled study. *Experimental Gerontology, 36*, 297–310.

Bengston, V. L. (2001). Beyond the nuclear family: The increasing importance of multigenerational bonds. *Journal of Marriage and the Family, 63*, 1–16.

Bengtson, V. L., & Schrader, S. S. (1982). Parent-child relations. In D. J. Mangen & W. A. Peterson (Eds.), *Research instruments in social gerontology, Vol 2* (pp. 115–185). Minneapolis: University of Minnesota Press.

Benloucif, S., Green, K., L'Hermite-Baleriaux, M., Weintraub, S., Wolfe, L. F., & Zee, P. C. (2006). Responsiveness of the aging circadian clock to light. *Neurobiology of Aging, 27*, 1870–1879.

Bennett, D. A., Schneider, J. A., Tang, Y., Arnold, S. E., & Wilson, R. S. (2006). The effect of social networks on the relation between Alzheimer's disease pathology and level of cognitive function in old people: A longitudinal cohort study. *Lancet Neurology, 5,* 406–412.

Bennett, K. M. (2005). Psychological wellbeing in later life: The longitudinal effects of marriage, widowhood and marital status change. *International Journal of Geriatric Psychiatry, 20,* 280–284.

Bennett, K. M. (2006). Does marital status and marital status change predict physical health in older adults? *Psychogical Medicine, 36,* 1313–1320.

Bennett, K. M., Smith, P. T., & Hughes, G. M. (2005). Coping, depressive feelings and gender differences in late life widowhood. *Aging and Mental Health, 9,* 348–353.

Berg, A. I., Hassing, L. B., McClearn, G. E., & Johansson, B. (2006). What matters for life satisfaction in the oldest-old? *Aging and Mental Health, 10,* 257–264.

Berntsen, D., & Rubin, D. C. (2002). Emotionally charged autobiography memories across the life span: The recall of happy, sad, traumatic and involuntary memories. *Psychology and Aging, 17,* 636–652.

Bharucha, A. E., & Camilleri, M. (2001). Functional abdominal pain in the elderly. *Gastroenterological Clinics of North America, 30,* 517–529.

Bherer, L., Kramer, A. F., Peterson, M. S., Colcombe, S., Erickson, K., & Becic, E. (2006). Testing the limits of cognitive plasticity in older adults: Application to attentional control. *Acta Psychologica (Amsterdam), 123,* 261–278.

Bieman-Copland, S., & Ryan, E. B. (2001). Social perceptions of failures in memory monitoring. *Psychology and Aging, 16,* 357–361.

Binstock, R. H. (1999). Public policy issues. In J. C. Cavanaugh & S. K. Whitbourne (Eds.), *Gerontology: Interdisciplinary perspectives* (pp. 414–447). New York: Oxford University Press.

Bittman, M., England, P., Sayer, L., Folbre, N., & Matheson, G. (2003). When does gender trump money? Bargaining and time in household work. *American Journal of Sociology, 109,* 186–214.

Blanchet, S., Belleville, S., & Peretz, I. (2006). Episodic encoding in normal aging: Attentional resources hypothesis extended to musical material. *Aging, Neuropsychology, and Cognition, 13,* 490–502.

Blazer, D., George, L. K., & Hughes, D. (1991). The epidemiology of anxiety disorders: An age comparison. In C. Salzman & B. D. Lebowitz (Eds.), *Anxiety in the Elderly: Treatment and Research* (pp. 17–30). Berlin: Springer-Verlag.

Blazer, D. G. (1999). Depression. In W. R. Hazzard, J. P. Blass, J. W. H. Ettinger, D. B. Halter & J. G. Ouslander

(Eds.), *Principles of geriatric medicine and gerontology* (4th ed., pp. 1331–1339). New York: McGraw-Hill.

Blenkner, M. (1963). Social work and family relations in later life with some thoughts on filial maturity. In E. Shanas & G. F. Streib (Eds.), *Social structure and the family: Generational relations* (pp. 46–59). Englewood Cliffs, NJ: Prentice-Hall.

Blieszner, R. (2006). A lifetime of caring: Dimensions and dynamics in late-life close relationships. *Personal Relationships, 13,* 1–18.

Block, J. (1995). A contrarian view of the five-factor approach to personality description. *Psychological Bulletin, 117,* 187–215.

Block, S. D., & Billings, J. A. (2005). Learning from the dying. *New England Journal of Medicine, 353,* 1313–1315.

Boling, M. C., Bolgla, L. A., Mattacola, C. G., Uhl, T. L., & Hosey, R. G. (2006). Outcomes of a weight-bearing rehabilitation program for patients diagnosed with patellofemoral pain syndrome. *Archives of Physical Medicine and Rehabilitation, 87,* 1428–1435.

Boll, T., Ferring, D., & Filipp, S. H. (2003). Perceived parental differential treatment in middle adulthood: Curvilinear relations with individuals' experienced relationship quality to sibling and parents. *Journal of Family Psychology, 17,* 472–487.

Bonanno, G. A., Wortman, C. B., Lehman, D. R., Tweed, R. G., Haring, M., Sonnega, J., Carr, D., & Neese, R. M et al. (2002). Resilience to loss and chronic grief: A prospective study from preloss to 18-months postloss. *Journal of Personality and Social Psychology, 83,* 1150–1164.

Bonanno, G. A., Wortman, C. B., & Nesse, R. M. (2004). Prospective patterns of resilience and maladjustment during widowhood. *Psychology and Aging, 19,* 260–271.

Bonnefond, A., Härmä, M., Hakola, T., Sallinen, M., Kandolin, I., & Virkkala, J. (2006). Interaction of age with shift-related sleep-wakefulness, sleepiness, performance, and social life. *Experimental Aging Research, 32,* 185–208.

Bord, S., Ireland, D. C., Beavan, S. R., & Compston, J. E. (2003). The effects of estrogen on osteoprotegerin, RANKL, and estrogen receptor expression in human osteoblasts. *Bone, 32,* 136–141.

Bortz, W. M. (2005). Biological basis of determinants of health. *American Journal of Public Health, 95,* 389–392.

Botwinick, J. (1977). Intellectual abilities. In J. E. Birren & K. W. Schaie (Eds.), *Handbook of the psychology of aging* (pp. 580–605). New York: Van Nostrand Reinhold.

Bouchard, T. J. J. (2004). Genetic influence on human psychological traits: A survey. *Current Directions in Psychological Science, 13,* 148–151.

Boudreau, J. W., Boswell, W. R., & Judge, T. A. (2001). Effects of personality on executive career success in the United States and Europe. *Journal of Vocational Behavior, 58,* 53–81.

Bowlby, J. (1969). *Attachment and loss: Attachment.* New York: Basic Books.

Bowlby, J. (1973). *Attachment and loss: Separation, anxiety and anger.* New York: Basic Books.

Bowlby, J. (1980). *Attachment and loss*: Vol. 3. *Loss: Sadness and depression.* London: Hogarth.

Bowling, A., Banister, D., Sutton, S., Evans, O., & Windsor, J. (2002). A multidimensional model of the quality of life in older age. *Aging and Mental Health, 6,* 355–371.

Bowling, N. A., Beehr, T. A., & Lepisto, L. R. (2006). Beyond job satisfaction: A five-year prospective analysis of the dispositional approach to work attitudes. *Journal of Vocational Behavior, 69,* 315–330.

Bowman, K. W., & Singer, P. A. (2001). Chinese seniors' perspectives on end-of-life decisions. *Social Science and Medicine, 53,* 455–464.

Bowman, R. E. (2005). Stress-induced changes in spatial memory are sexually differentiated and vary across the lifespan. *Journal of Neuroendocrinology, 17,* 526–535.

Bowman, T. S., Sesso, H. D., & Gaziano, J. M. (2006). Effect of age on blood pressure parameters and risk of cardiovascular death in men. *American Journal of Hypertension, 19,* 47–52.

Boyle, S. H., Jackson, W. G., & Suarez, E. C. (2007). Hostility, anger, and depression predict increases in C3 over a 10-year period. *Brain, Behavior, and Immunity, 21,* 816–823.

Bradbury, T. N., Fincham, F. D., & Beach, S. R. H. (2000). Research on the nature and determinants of marital satisfaction: A decade in review. *Journal of Marriage and the Family, 62,* 964–980.

Braitman, K. A., Kirley, B. B., Chaudhary, N. K., & Ferguson, S. A. (2006). *Factors leading to older drivers' intersection crashes.* Arlington, VA: Insurance Institute for Highway Safety.

Bramlett, M. D., & Mosher, W. D. (2002). Cohabitation, marriage, divorce, and remarriage in the United States. *National Center for Health Statistics. Vital and Health Statistics* 23 (22).

Braver, T. S., & Barch, D. M. (2002). A theory of cognitive control, aging cognition, and neuromodulation. *Neuroscience and Biobehavioral Reviews, 26,* 809–817.

Brenes, G. A., Kritschesky, S. B., Mehta, K. M., Yaffe, K., Simonsick, E. M., Ayonayon, H. N., Rosano, C., Rubin, S. M.,

Satterfield, S., & Penninx, B. W. (2007). Scared to death: Results from the Health, Aging, and Body Composition Study. *American Journal of Geriatric Psychiatry, 15,* 262–265.

Brennan, P. L., Schutte, K. K., & Moos, R. H. (2006). Long-term patterns and predictors of successful stressor resolution in later life. *International Journal of Stress Management, 13,* 253–272.

Brickman, A. M., Zimmerman, M. E., Paul, R. H., Grieve, S. M., Tate, D. F., Cohen, R. A., Williams, L. M., Clark, C. R., & Gordon, E. (2006). Regional white matter and neuropsychological functioning across the adult lifespan. *Biological Psychiatry, 60,* 444–453.

Brill, F. (1967). *Matisse.* London: Paul Hamlyn.

Brim, O. G. Jr. (1976). Theories of the male mid-life crisis. *The Counseling Psychologist, 6,* 2–9.

Brink, J. M., & McDowd, J. M. (1999). Aging and selective attention: An issue of complexity or multiple mechanisms? *Journal of Gerontology: Psychological Sciences, 54B,* P30–P33.

Briones, T. L. (2006). Environment, physical activity, and neurogenesis: Implications for prevention and treatment of Alzheimer's disease. *Current Alzheimer Research, 3,* 49–54.

Briscoe, J. P., Hall, D. T., & Frautschy DeMuth, R. L. (2006). Protean and boundaryless careers: An empirical exploration. *Journal of Vocational Behavior, 69,* 30–47.

Broach, K., Joseph, K. M., & Schroeder, D. J. (2003). *Pilot age and accident reports 3: An analysis of professional air transport pilot accident rates by age.* Oklahoma City, OK: Civil Aeromedical Institute.

Brody, E. M. (1981). "Women in the middle" and family help to older people. *The Gerontologist, 21,* 471–479.

Bronfenbrenner, U. (1979). *The ecology of human development.* Cambridge MA: Harvard University Press.

Bronfenbrenner, U. (1995). Developmental ecology through space and time: A future perspective. In P. Moen, G. H. J. Elder & K. Luscher (Eds.), *Examining lives in context: Perspectives on the ecology of human development* (pp. 619–647). Washington DC: American Psychological Association.

Bronfenbrenner, U. (2001). Human development, bioecological theory of. In N. J. Smelser & P. B. Baltes (Eds.), *International encyclopedia of the social and behavioral sciences* (pp. 6963–6970). New York: Elsevier.

Bronfenbrenner, U., & Ceci, S. J. (1994). Nature-nurture reconceptualized in developmental perspective: A bioecological model. *Psychological Review, 101,* 568–586.

Brooke, L., & Taylor, P. (2005). Older workers and employment: Managing age relations. *Ageing and Society, 25,* 415–429.

Brookmeyer, R., Corrada, M. M., Curriero, F. C., & Kawas, C. (2002). Survival following a diagnosis of Alzheimer disease. *Archives of Neurology, 59,* 1764–1767.

Brookmeyer, R., & Kawas, C. (1998). Projections of Alzheimer's Disease in the United States and the public health impact of delaying disease onset. *American Journal of Public Health, 88,* 1337–1342.

Brower, K. J., & Hall, J. M. (2001). Effects of age and alcoholism on sleep: A controlled study. *Journal of Studies on Alcohol, 62,* 335–343.

Brown, L. A., Gage, W. H., Polych, M. A., Sleik, R. J., & Winder, T. R. (2002). Central set influences on gait. Age-dependent effects of postural threat. *Experimental Brain Research, 145,* 286–296.

Bruce, M. L. (2002). Psychosocial risk factors for depressive disorders in late life. *Biological Psychiatry, 52,* 175–184.

Bruck, C. S., & Allen, T. D. (2003). The relationship between big five personality traits, negative affectivity, type A behavior, and work-family conflict. *Journal of Vocational Behavior, 63,* 457–472.

Brummett, B. H., Babyak, M. A., Williams, R. B., Barefoot, J. C., Costa, P. T., & Siegler, I. C. (2006). NEO personality domains and gender predict levels and trends in body mass index over 14 years during midlife. *Journal of Research in Personality, 40,* 222–236.

Bugg, J. M., DeLosh, E. L., & Clegg, B. A. (2006). Physical activity moderates time-of-day differences in older adults' working memory performance. *Experimental Aging Research, 32,* 431–446.

Bukov, A., Maas, I., & Lampert, T. (2002). Social participation in very old age: Cross-sectional and longitudinal findings from BASE. Berlin Aging Study. *Journal of Gerontology: Psychological Sciences 57B,* P510–517.

Bureau of Labor Statistics (2006). *Nonfatal occupational injuries and illnesses requiring days away from work, 2005* (No. USDL 06-1982).

Burgess, W., Liu, Q., Zhou, J., Tang, Q., Ozawa, A., VanHoy, R., Arkins, S., Dantzer, R., & Kelley, K. W. (1999). The immune-endocrine loop during aging: Role of growth hormone and insulin-like growth factor-I. *Neuroimmunomodulation, 6,* 56–68.

Burgio, L. D., Stevens, A., Burgio, K. L., Roth, D. L., Paul, P., & Gerstle, J. (2002). Teaching and maintaining behavior management skills in the nursing home. *The Gerontologist, 42,* 487–496.

Burke, D. M., & Mackay, D. G. (1997). Memory, language, and ageing. *Philosophical Transactions of the Royal Society of London—Series B: Biological Sciences, 352,* 1845–1856.

Burke, S. N., & Barnes, C. A. (2006). Neural plasticity in the ageing brain. *Nature Reviews Neuroscience, 7,* 30–40.

Burns, N. R., Bryan, J., & Nettelbeck, T. (2006). Ginkgo biloba: No robust effect on cognitive abilities or mood in healthy young or older adults. *Human Psychopharmacology: Clinical and Experimental, 21,* 27–37.

Burton, C. L., Strauss, E., Hultsch, D. F., & Hunter, M. A. (2006). Cognitive functioning and everyday problem solving in older adults. *Clinical Neuropsychology, 20,* 432–452.

Burton, C. L., Strauss, E., Hultsch, D. F., Moll, A., & Hunter, M. A. (2006). Intraindividual variability as a marker of neurological dysfunction: A comparison of Alzheimer's disease and Parkinson's disease. *Journal of Clinical and Experimental Neuropsychology, 28,* 67–83.

Butler, K. M., McDaniel, M. A., Dornburg, C. C., Price, A. L., & Roediger, H. L. I. (2004). Age differences in veridical and false recall are not inevitable: The role of frontal lobe function. *Psychonomic Bulletin and Review, 11,* 921–925.

Butler, R. (1974). Successful aging and the role of life review. *Journal of the American Geriatrics Society, 22,* 529–535.

Byles, J., Young, A., Furuya, H., & Parkinson, L. (2006). A drink to healthy aging: The association between older women's use of alcohol and their health-related quality of life. *Journal of the American Geriatric Society, 54,* 1341–1347.

Byock, I. R. (1993). Consciously walking the fine line: Thoughts on a hospice response to assisted suicide and euthanasia. *Journal of Palliative Care, 9,* 25–28.

Caggiano, D. M., Jiang, Y., & Parasuraman, R. (2006). Aging and repetition priming for targets and distracters in a working memory task. *Aging, Neuropsychology, and Cognition, 13,* 552–573.

Callahan, C. M., Boustani, M. A., Unverzagt, F. W., Austrom, M. G., Damush, T. M., Perkins, A. J., Fultz, B. A., Hui, S. L., Counsell, S. R., & Hendrie, H. C. (2006). Effectiveness of collaborative care for older adults with Alzheimer disease in primary care: A randomized controlled trial. *Journal of the American Medical Association, 295,* 2148–2157.

Calle, E. E., Rodriguez, C., Walker-Thurmond, K., & Thun, M. J. (2003). Overweight, obesity, and mortality from cancer in a prospectively studied cohort of U.S. adults. *New England Journal of Medicine, 348,* 1625–1638.

Calvaresi, E., & Bryan, J. (2001). B vitamins, cognition, and aging: A review. *Journal of Gerontology: Psychological Sciences 56B,* P327–P339.

Camp, C. J., Cohen-Mansfield, J., & Capezuti, E. A. (2002). Use of nonpharmacologic interventions among nursing home residents with dementia. *Psychiatric Services, 53,* 1397–1404.

Canadian Institutes of Health Research (2006). Heart disease. http://www.cihr-irsc.gc.ca/e/32627.html

Cao, J. J., Wronski, T. J., Iwaniec, U., Phleger, L., Kurimoto, P., Boudignon, B., & Halloran, B. P. (2005). Aging increases stromal/osteoblastic cell-induced osteoclastogenesis and alters the osteoclast precursor pool in the mouse. *Journal of Bone and Mineral Research*, 20, 1659–1668.

Caputo, R. K. (2002). Adult daughters as parental caregivers: Rational actors versus rational agents. *Journal of Family and Economic Issues*, 23, 27–50.

Carnelley, K. B., Wortman, C. B., Bolger, N., & Burke, C. T. (2006). The time course of grief reactions to spousal loss: Evidence from a national probability sample. *Journal of Personality and Social Psychology*, 91, 476–492.

Carnevale, V., Scillitani, A., Vecci, E., D'Erasmo, E., Romagnoli, E., Paglia, F., Pepe, J., Baldini, V., Santori, C., De Geronimo, S., & Minisola, S. (2005). Dehydroepiandrosterone sulfate and bone resorption rate as reflected by serum levels of C-terminal telopeptide of type I collagen: A study in healthy men. *Journal of Endocrinological Investigation*, 28, 102–105.

Carson, P. J., Nichol, K. L., O'Brien, J., Hilo, P., & Janoff, E. N. (2000). Immune function and vaccine responses in healthy advanced elderly patients. *Archives of Internal Medicine*, 160, 2017–2024.

Carstensen, L. L. (1987). Age-related changes in social activity. In L. L. Carstensen & B. A. Edelstein (Eds.), *Handbook of clinical gerontology* (pp. 222–237). Elmsford, Pergamon Press.

Carstensen, L. L., Gross, J. J., & Fung, H. H. (1997). The social context of emotion. *Annual Review of Gerontology and Geriatrics*, 17, 325–352.

Carstensen, L. L., Isaacowitz, D. M., & Charles, S. T. (1999). Taking time seriously: A theory of socioemotional selectivity. *American Psychologist*, 54, 165–181.

Carstensen, L. L., & Turk-Charles, S. (1994). The salience of emotion across the adult life span. *Psychology and Aging*, 9, 259–264.

Caruso, C., Candore, G., Colonna Romano, G., Lio, D., Bonafe, M., Valensin, S., Franceshi, C. (2000). HLA, aging, and longevity: A critical reappraisal. *Human Immunology*, 61, 942–949.

Casper, M. L., Barnett, E., Williams, I., Halverson, J., Braham, V., & Greenlund, K. (2003). *The atlas of stroke mortality: Racial, ethnic, and geographic disparities in the United States, 1st ed.* Atlanta, GA: U.S. Department of Health and Human Services, CDC.

Caspi, A., & Roberts, B. W. (2001). Target article: Personality development across the life course: The argument for change and continuity. *Psychological Inquiry*, 12, 49–66.

Castillo, E. M., Goodman-Gruen, D., Kritz-Silverstein, D., Morton, D. J., Wingard, D. L., & Barrett-Connor, E. (2003). Sarcopenia in elderly men and women: The Rancho Bernardo study. *American Journal of Preventive Medicine*, 25, 226–231; *Erratum American Journal of Preventive Medicine*, (2004) 227, 2265–2265.

Cattell, R. B. (1963). Theory of fluid and crystallized intelligence: A critical experiment. *Journal of Educational Psychology*, 54, 1–22.

Cattell, R. B. (1971). *Abilities: Their structure, growth, and action*. Boston: Houghton Mifflin.

Cauley, J. A., Lui, L. Y., Stone, K. L., Hillier, T. A., Zmuda, J. M., Hochberg, M., Beck, T. J., & Ensrud, K. E. (2005). Longitudinal study of changes in hip bone mineral density in Caucasian and African-American women. *Journal of the American Geriatrics Society*, 53, 183–189.

Cavan, R. S., Burgess, E. W., Havighurst, R. J., & Goldhamer, H. (1949). *Personal adjustment in old age*. Chicago: Science Research Associates.

Cavanaugh, J. C. (1989). The importance of awareness in memory aging. In L. W. Poon, D. C. Rubin & B. A. Wilson (Eds.), *Everyday cognition in adulthood and late life* (pp. 416–436). Cambridge: Cambridge University Press.

Center for Medicare and Medicaid Services (2007). *National health expenditure amounts, and annual percent change by type of expenditure: Calendar years 2001–2016.*

Centers for Disease Control and Prevention (2003a). Diabetes: Deadly, disabling, and on the rise. http://www.cdc.gov/ncdphp/publications/aag/ddt.htm

Centers for Disease Control and Prevention (2003b). *Health United States 2002*. Washington, DC: Department of Health and Human Services.

Centers for Disease Control and Prevention (2006). *Health United States 2006*. Washington, DC: Department of Health and Human Services.

Centers for Disease Control and Prevention (2007a). Trends in health and aging. http://www.cdc.gov/nchs/agingact.htm

Centers for Disease Control and Prevention (2007b). Prevalence of Stroke—United States, 2005. *Morbidity and Mortality Weekly Report*, 56, 469–474.

Chakravarthy, U., Augood, C., Bentham, G. C., de Jong, P. T., Rahu, M., Seland, J., Soubrane, G., Tomazzoli, L., Topouzis, F., Vingerling, J. R., Vioque, J., Young, I. S., & Fletcher, A. E. (2007). Cigarette smoking and age-related macular degeneration in the EUREYE Study, *Ophthalmology*, *114*, 1157–1163.

Chandola, T., Brunner, E., & Marmot, M. (2006). Chronic stress at work and the metabolic syndrome: Prospective study. *British Medical Journal*, *332*, 521–525.

Chandra, R. K. (2004). Impact of nutritional status and nutrient supplements on immune responses and incidence of infection in older individuals. *Ageing Research Reviews*, *3*, 91–104.

Charatan, F. (2006). US Supreme Court upholds Oregon's Death with Dignity Act. *British Medical Journal*, *332*, 195.

Charles, S. T., Reynolds, C. A., & Gatz, M. (2001). Age-related differences and change in positive and negative affect over 23 years. *Journal of Personality and Social Psychology*, *80*, 136–151.

Charlson, M., & Peterson, J. C. (2002). Medical comorbidity and late life depression: What is known and what are the unmet needs? *Biological Psychiatry*, *52*, 226–235.

Charlton, R. A., Morris, R. G., Nitkunan, A., & Markus, H. S. (2006). The cognitive profiles of CADASIL and sporadic small vessel disease. *Neurology*, *66*, 1523–1526.

Charney, D. S., Reynolds, C. F., 3rd, Lewis, L., Lebowitz, B. D., Sunderland, T., Alexopoulos, G. S., Blazer, D. G., Katz, I. R., Meyers, B. S., Arean, P. A., Borson, S., Brown, C., Bruce, M. L., Callahan, C. M., Charlson, M. E., Conwell, Y., Cuthbert, B. N., Devanand, D. P., Gibson, M. J., Gottlieb, G. L., Krishnan, K. R., Laden, S. K., Lyketsos, C. G., Mulsant, B. H., Niederehe, G., Olin, J. T., Oslin, D. W., Pearson, J., Persky, T., Pollock, B. G., Raetzman, S., Reynolds, M., Salzman, C., Schulz, R., Schwenk, T. L., Scolnick, E., Unutzer, J., Weissman, M. M., & Young, R. C. (2003). Depression and Bipolar Support Alliance consensus statement on the unmet needs in diagnosis and treatment of mood disorders in late life. *Archives of General Psychiatry*, *60*, 664–672.

Chen, J. S., Cameron, I. D., Cumming, R. G., Lord, S. R., March, L. M., Sambrook, P. N., Simpson, J. M., & Seibel, M. J. (2006). Effect of age-related chronic immobility on markers of bone turnover. *Journal of Bone and Mineral Research*, *21*, 324–331.

Cherkas, L. F., Aviv, A., Valdes, A. M., Hunkin, J. L., Gardner, J. P., Surdulescu, G. L., Kimura, M., & Spector, T. D. (2006). The effects of social status on biological aging as measured by white-blood-cell telomere length. *Aging Cell*,. *5*, 361–365.

Cheung, N., & Wong, T. Y. (2007). Obesity and eye diseases. *Survey of Ophthalmology*, *52*, 180–195.

Chiu, C. J., Milton, R. C., Gensler, G., & Taylor, A. (2006). Dietary carbohydrate intake and glycemic index in relation to cortical and nuclear lens opacities in the Age-Related Eye Disease Study. *American Journal of Clinical Nutrition*, *83*, 1177–1184.

Chodosh, J., Kado, D. M., Seeman, T. E., & Karlamangla, A. S. (2007). Depressive symptoms as a predictor of cognitive decline: MacArthur Studies of Successful Aging. *American Journal of Geriatric Psychiatry*, *15*, 406–415.

Chou, S.-C., Boldy, D. P., & Lee, A. H. (2002). Resident satisfaction and its components in residential aged care. *The Gerontologist*, *42*, 188–198.

Christensen, U., Stovring, N., Schultz-Larsen, K., Schroll, M., & Avlund, K. (2006). Functional ability at age 75: Is there an impact of physical inactivity from middle age to early old age? *Scandinavian Journal of Medicine and Science in Sports*, *16*, 245–251.

Christiansen, S. L., & Palkovitz, R. (2001). Why the "good provider" role still matters: Providing as a form of paternal involvement. *Journal of Family Issues*, *22*, 84–106.

Cicirelli, V. C. (1982). Sibling influence throughout the lifespan. In M. E. Lamb & B. Sutton-Smith (Eds.), *Sibling relationships: Their nature and significance across the lifespan* (pp. 267–284). Hillsdale, NJ: Erlbaum.

Cicirelli, V. G. (1988). A measure of filial anxiety regarding anticipated care of elderly parents. *The Gerontologist*, *28*, 478–482.

Cicirelli, V. G. (2002). Fear of death in older adults: Predictions from terror management theory. *Journal of Gerontology Psychological Sciences*, *57B*, P358–P366.

Clark, A., Ostwald, A., & Warr, P. (1996). Is job satisfaction U-shaped in age? *Journal of Occupational and Organizational Psychology*, *69*, 57–81.

Clark, R., Anderson, N. B., Clark, V. R., & Williams, D. R. (1999). Racism as a stressor for African Americans: A biopsychosocial model. *American Psychologist*, *54*, 805–816.

Clarke, S. (1995). *Advance report of final divorce statistics, 1989 and 1990* (Vol. 43, No. 9, Suppl.). Hyattsville, MD: National Center for Health Statistics.

CME Institute of Physicians Postgraduate Press (2006). New paradigms in the treatment of Alzheimer's disease. *Journal of Clinical Psychiatry*, *67*, 2002–2013.

Cohan, C. L., & Kleinbaum, S. (2002). Toward a greater understanding of the cohabitation effect: Premarital cohabitation and marital communication. *Journal of Marriage and the Family*, *64*, 180–192.

Cohen, A., Houck, P. R., Szanto, K., Dew, M. A., Gilman, S. E., & Reynolds, C. F., 3rd. (2006). Social inequalities in response to antidepressant treatment in older adults. *Archives of General Psychiatry*, *63*, 50–56.

Cohen, C. I., Magai, C., Yaffee, R., Huangthaisong, P., & Walcott-Brown, L. (2006). The prevalence of phobia and its associated factors in a multiracial aging urban population. *American Journal of Geriatric Psychiatry, 14*, 507–514.

Cohen, G. (1996). Memory and learning in normal aging. In R. T. Woods (Ed.), *Handbook of the Clinical Psychology of Ageing* (pp. 43–58). London: Wiley.

Cohen, G. (1998a). The effects of aging on autobiographical memory. In P. Thompson & D. J. Herrmann (Eds.), *Autobiographical memory: Theoretical and applied perspectives* (pp. 105–123). Mahwah NJ: Lawrence Erlbaum.

Cohen, G. D. (1998b). Creativity and aging: Ramifications for research, practice, and policy. *Geriatrics, 53 (Suppl. 1)*, S4–S8.

Cohn, L. D., & Westenberg, P. M. (2004). Intelligence and maturity: Meta-analytic evidence for the incremental and discriminant validity of Loevinger's measure of ego development. *Journal of Personality and Social Psychology, 86*, 760–772.

Colcombe, S. J., Erickson, K. I., Scalf, P. E., Kim, J. S., Prakash, R., McAuley, E., Elavsky, S., Marquez, D. X., Hu, L., & Kramer, A. F. (2006). Aerobic exercise training increases brain volume in aging humans. *Journal of Gerontology: Medical Sciences, 61A*, 1166–1170.

Colliver, J. D., Compton, W. M., Gfroerer, J. C., & Condon, T. (2006). Projecting drug use among aging Baby Boomers in 2020. *Annals of Epidemiology, 16*, 257–265.

Coltrane, S. (2000). Research on household labor: Modeling and measuring the social embeddedness of routine family work. *Journal of Marriage and the Family, 62*, 1208–1233.

Commission for the Study of Ethical Problems in Medicine and Biomedical and Behavioral Research (1981). *Defining death.* Washington, DC: U.S. Government Printing Office.

Committee on National Statistics (2003). *Elder mistreatment: Abuse, neglect, and exploitation in an aging America.* Washington, DC: National Academies Press.

Commons, M., Richards, F., & Armon, C. (Eds.). (1984). *Beyond formal operations: Late adolescent and adult cognitive development.* New York: Praeger.

Conley, K., Amara, C., Jubrias, S., & Marcinek, D. (2006). Mitochondrial function, fiber types and aging: New insights from human muscle in vivo. *Experimental Physiology, 92*, 333–339.

Connidis, I. A. (1992). Life transitions and the adult sibling tie: A qualitative study. *Journal of Marriage and the Family, 54*, 972–982.

Connor, S. R., Egan, K. A., Kwilosz, D. M., Larson, D. G., & Reese, D. J. (2002). Interdisciplinary approaches to assisting with end-of-life care and decision making. *American Behavioral Scientist, 46*, 340–356.

Consedine, N. S., Magai, C., Cohen, C. I., & Gillespie, M. (2002). Ethnic variation in the impact of negative affect and emotion inhibition on the health of older adults. *Journal of Gerontology: Psychological Sciences, 57*, P396–408.

Constantinople, A. (1969). An Eriksonian measure of personality development in college students. *Developmental Psychology, 1*, 357–372.

Conwell, Y., Duberstein, P. R., & Caine, E. D. (2002). Risk factors for suicide in later life. *Biological Psychiatry, 52*, 193–204.

Cooke, L. P. (2006). "Doing" gender in context: Household bargaining and risk of divorce in Germany and the United States. *American Journal of Sociology, 112*, 442–472.

Cooper, J. K., Harris, Y., & McGready, J. (2002). Sadness predicts death in older people. *Journal of Aging and Health, 14*, 509–526.

Corder, R., Mullen, W., Khan, N. Q., Marks, S. C., Wood, E. G., Carrier, M. J., & Crozier, A, (2006). Oenology: Red wine procyanidins and vascular health. *Nature, 444*, 566.

Costa, P. T., Jr., & McCrae, R. R. (1992). *Revised NEO Personality Inventory (NEO-PI-R) and NEO Five-Factor Inventory (NEO-FFI) professional manual.* Odessa FL: Psychological Assessment Resources.

Costa, P. T. J., Herbst, J. H., McCrae, R. R., & Siegler, I. C. (2000). Personality at midlife: Stability, intrinsic maturation, and response to life events. *Assessment, 7*, 365–378.

Costa, P. T. J., & McCrae, R. R. (1978). Objective personality assessment. In M. Storandt, I. C. Siegler & M. F. Elias (Eds.), *The clinical psychology of aging* (pp. 119–143). New York: Plenum.

Cowgill, D. O., & Holmes, L. D. (1972). *Aging and modernization.* New York: Appleton-Century-Crofts.

Cramer, P. (2003). Personality change in later adulthood is predicted by defense mechanism use in early adulthood. *Journal of Research in Personality, 37*, 76–104.

Crawford, S., & Channon, S. (2002). Dissociation between performance on abstract tests of executive function and problem solving in real-life-type situations in normal aging. *Aging and Mental Health, 6*, 12–21.

Crawley, L. M., Marshall, P. A., Lo, B., & Koenig, B. A. (2002). Strategies for culturally effective end-of-life care. *Annals of Internal Medicine, 136*, 673–679.

Cropanzano, R., Rupp, D. E., & Byrne, Z. S. (2003). The relationship of emotional exhaustion to work attitudes, job performance, and organizational citizenship behaviors. *Journal of Applied Psychology, 88*, 160–169.

Crosnoe, R., & Elder, G. H., Jr. (2002). Life course transitions, the generational stake, and grandparent-grandchild relationships. *Journal of Marriage and the Family, 64,* 1089–1096.

Cuddy, A. J. C., Norton, M. I., & Fiske, S. T. (2005). This old stereotype: The pervasiveness and persistence of the elderly stereotype. *Journal of Social Issues, 61,* 267–285.

Cumming, E., & Henry, W. E. (1961). *Growing old: The process of disengagement.* New York: Basic Books.

Curlin, F. A., Lawrence, R. E., Chin, M. H., & Lantos, J. D. (2007). Religion, conscience, and controversial clinical practices. *New England Journal of Medicine, 356,* 593–600.

Curran, M., Hazen, N., Jacobvitz, D., & Sasaki, T. (2006). How representations of the parental marriage predict marital emotional attunement during the transition to parenthood. *Journal of Family Psychology, 20,* 477–484.

Daly, M. C., & Bound, J. (1996). Worker adaptation and employer accommodation following the onset of a health impairment. *Journal of Gerontology: Social Sciences, 51B,* S53–S60.

Damush, T. M., Stump, T. E., & Clark, D. O. (2002). Body-mass index and 4-year change in health-related quality of life. *Journal of Aging and Health, 14,* 195–210.

Dasilva, K. A., Aubert, I., & McLaurin, J. (2006). Vaccine development for Alzheimer's disease. *Current Pharmaceutical Design, 12,* 4283–4293.

Davidson, P. S. R., Cook, S. P., & Glisky, E. L. (2006). Flashbulb memories for September 11th can be preserved in older adults. *Aging, Neuropsychology, and Cognition, 13,* 196–206.

Davignon, J., & Leiter, L. A. (2005). Ongoing clinical trials of the pleiotropic effects of statins. *Vascular Health and Risk Management, 1,* 29–40.

Davis, H. P., Trussell, L. H., & Klebe, K. J. (2001). A ten-year longitudinal examination of repetition priming, incidental recall, free recall, and recognition in young and elderly. *Brain and Cognition, 46,* 99–104.

Davis, M. A. (2003). Factors related to bridge employment participation among private sector early retirees. *Journal of Vocational Behavior, 63,* 55–71.

Dawis, R. V. (1996). Vocational psychology, vocational adjustment, and the workforce: Some familiar and unanticipated consequences. *Psychology, Public Policy, and Law, 2,* 229–248.

Dawis, R. V., & Lofquist, L. H. (1984). *A psychological theory of work adjustment.* Minneapolis: University of Minnesota Press.

Dawson-Hughes, B., Heaney, R. P., Holick, M. F., Lips, P., Meunier, P. J., & Vieth, R. (2005). Estimates of optimal vitamin D status. *Osteoporosis International, 16,* 713–716.

Deary, I. J., & Der, G. (2005). Reaction time, age, and cognitive ability: Longitudinal findings from age 16 to 63 years in representative population samples. *Aging, Neuropsychology, and Cognition, 12,* 187–215.

Deci, E. L., & Ryan, R. M. (1985). *Intrinsic motivation and self-determination in human behavior.* New York: Plenum.

Degenholtz, H. B., Arnold, R. A., Meisel, A., & Lave, J. R. (2002). Persistence of racial disparities in advance care plan documents among nursing home residents. *Journal of the American Geriatrics Society, 50,* 378–381.

DeGroot, D. W., & Kenney, W. L. (2007). Impaired defense of core temperature in aged humans during mild cold stress. *American Journal of Physiology: Regulatory, Integrative, and Comparative Physiology, 292,* R103–R108.

de Jong, P. T. (2006). Age-related macular degeneration. *New England Journal of Medicine, 355,* 1474–1485.

DeLamater, J. D., & Sill, M. (2005). Sexual desire in later life. *Journal of Sex Research, 42,* 138–149.

Delano-Wood, L., & Abeles, N. (2005). Late-life depression: Detection, risk reduction, and somatic intervention. *Clinical Psychology: Science and Practice, 12,* 207–217.

Delgoulet, C., & Marquie, J. C. (2002). Age differences in learning maintenance skills: A field study. *Experimental Aging Research, 28,* 25–37.

DeLorey, D. S., & Babb, T. G. (1999). Progressive mechanical ventilatory constraints with aging. *American Journal of Respiratory and Critical Care in Medicine, 160,* 169–177.

Dennerstein, L., Dudley, E., & Guthrie, J. (2002). Empty nest or revolving door? A prospective study of women's quality of life in midlife during the phase of children leaving and re-entering the home. *Psychological Medicine, 32,* 545–550.

Dennis, W. (1966). Creative productivity between the ages of 20 and 80 years. *Journal of Gerontology, 21,* 1–8.

U.S Department of Health and Human Services (1999). *Mental health: A report of the Surgeon General.* Bethesda, MD: U.S. Public Health Service.

Depp, C. A., & Jeste, D. V. (2006). Definitions and predictors of successful aging: A comprehensive review of larger quantitative studies. *American Journal of Geriatric Psychiatry, 14,* 6–20.

De Raedt, R., & Ponjaert-Kristoffersen, I. (2006). Self-serving appraisal as a cognitive coping strategy to deal with age-related limitations: An empirical study with elderly adults in a real-life stressful situation. *Aging and Mental Health, 10,* 195–203.

Desai, P., Reidy, A., & Minassian, D. C. (1999). Profile of patients presenting for cataract surgery in the UK: National data collection. *British Journal of Ophthalmology, 83*, 893–896.

Desbiens, N. A., Wu, A. W., Broste, S. K., Wenger, N. S., Connors, A. F., Jr., Lynn, J., Yasui, Y., Phillips, R. S., & Fulkerson, W. (1996). Pain and satisfaction with pain control in seriously ill hospitalized adults: Findings from the SUPPORT research investigations. For the SUPPORT investigators. Study to Understand Prognoses and Preferences for Outcomes and Risks of Treatment. *Critical Care Medicine, 24*, 1953–1961.

DeSpelder, L. A., & Strickland, A. L. (1999). *The last dance: Encountering death and dying* (5th ed.). Mountain View, CA: Mayfield Publishing.

de Vries, B., Davis, C. G., Wortman, C. B., & Lehman, D. R. (1997). Long-term psychological and somatic consequences of later life parental bereavement. *Omega—Journal of Death and Dying, 35*, 97–117.

Devine, A., Dick, I. M., Islam, A. F., Dhaliwal, S. S., & Prince, R. L. (2005). Protein consumption is an important predictor of lower limb bone mass in elderly women. *American Journal of Clinical Nutrition, 81*, 1423–1428.

Di Bonito, P., Di Fraia, L., Di Gennaro, L., Vitale, A., Lapenta, M., Scala, A., Iardino, M. R., Cusati, B., Attino, L., & Capaldo, B. (2007). Impact of impaired fasting glucose and other metabolic factors on cognitive function in elderly people. *Nutrition, Metabolism, and Cardiovascular Diseases 17*, 203–208.

Diab, T., Condon, K. W., Burr, D. B., & Vashishth, D. (2006). Age-related change in the damage morphology of human cortical bone and its role in bone fragility. *Bone, 38*, 427–431.

Dickin, D. C., Brown, L. A., & Doan, J. B. (2006). Age-dependent differences in the time course of postural control during sensory perturbations. *Aging Clinical and Experimental Research, 18*, 94–99.

Dickinson, G. E. (2002). A quarter century of end-of-life issues in U.S. medical schools. *Death Studies, 26*, 635–646.

Dickinson, G. E., Tournier, R. E., & Still, B. J. (1999). Twenty years beyond medical school: Physicians' attitudes toward death and terminally ill patients. *Archives of Internal Medicine, 159*, 1741–1744.

Diefenbach, G. J., Hopko, D. R., Feigon, S., Stanley, M. A., Novy, D. M., Beck, J. G., & Averill, P. M. (2003). 'Minor GAD': Characteristics of subsyndromal GAD in older adults. *Behaviour Research and Therapy, 41*, 481–487.

Diehl, M., Coyle, N., & Labouvie-Vief, G. (1996). Age and sex differences in coping and defense across the life span. *Psychology and Aging, 11*, 127–139.

Diener, E. (1998). Subjective well-being: Three decades of progress. *Psychological Bulletin, 125*, 276–302.

Diener, E., & Fujita, F. (1995). Resources, personal strivings, and subjective well-being: A nomothetic and idiographic approach. *Journal of Personality and Social Psychology, 68*, 926–935.

Diener, E., Lucas, R. E., & Scollon, C. N. (2006). Beyond the hedonic treadmill: Revising the adaptation theory of well-being. *American Psychologist, 61*, 305–314.

Diener, E., Oishi, S., & Lucas, R. E. (2003). Personality, culture, and subjective well-being: Emotional and cognitive evaluations of life. *Annual Review of Psychology, 54*, 403–425.

Diener, E., & Suh, E. (1998). Age and subjective well-being: An international analysis. In K. W. Schaie & M. P. Lawton (Eds.), *Annual review of gerontology and geriatrics.* Vol. *17: Focus on emotion and adult development* (pp. 304–324). New York: Springer.

Dietrich, A. (2004). The cognitive neuroscience of creativity. *Psychonomic Bulletin and Review, 11*, 1011–1026.

Diez, J. J., & Iglesias, P. (2004). Spontaneous subclinical hypothyroidism in patients older than 55 years: An analysis of natural course and risk factors for the development of overt thyroid failure. *Journal of Clinical Endocrinology and Metabolism, 89*, 4890–4897.

Diez Roux, A. V., Borrell, L. N., Haan, M., Jackson, S. A., & Schultz, R. (2004). Neighbourhood environments and mortality in an elderly cohort: results from the cardiovascular health study. *Journal of Epidemiology and Community Health, 58*, 917–923.

Di Francesco, V., Fantin, F., Omizzolo, F., Residon, L. Bissoli, L., Bosello, L., & Zamboni, M. (2007). The anorexia of aging. *Digestive Diseases, 25*, 129–137.

DiNardo, P. A., & Barlow, D. H. (1988). *Anxiety Disorders Interview Schedule-Revised (ADIS-R)*. Albany, NY: Graywind Publications.

Ding, C., Cicuttini, F., Scott, F., Cooley, H., & Jones, G. (2005). Association between age and knee structural change: A cross sectional MRI based study. *Annals of the Rheumatic Diseases, 64*, 549–555.

Ding, J., Kritchevsky, S. B., Newman, A. B., Taafee, D. R., Nicklas, B. J., Visser, M., Lee, J. S., Nevitt, M., Tylavsky, F. A., Rubin, S. M., Pahor, M., & Harris, T. B. (2007). Effects of birth cohort and age on body composition in a sample of community-based elderly. *American Journal of Clinical Nutrition, 85*, 405–410.

Dionne, C. E., Dunn, K. M., & Croft, P. R. (2006). Does back pain prevalence really decrease with increasing age? A systematic review. *Age and Ageing, 35,* 229–234.

Dirks, A. J., & Leeuwenburgh, C. (2006a). Caloric restriction in humans: Potential pitfalls and health concerns. *Mechanisms of Ageing and Development, 127,* 1–7.

Dirks, A. J., & Leeuwenburgh, C. (2006b). Tumor necrosis factor alpha signaling in skeletal muscle: Effects of age and caloric restriction. *Journal of Nutritional Biochemistry, 17,* 501–508.

Dishman, R. K., Berthoud, H. R., Booth, F. W., Cotman, C. W., Edgerton, V. R., Fleshner, M. R., Gandevia, S. C., Gomez-Pinilla, F., Greenwood, B. N., Hillman, C. H., Kramer, A. F., Levin, B. E., Moran, T. H., Russo-Neustadt, A. A., Salamone, J. D., Van Hoomissen, J. D., Wade, C. E., York, D. A., & Zigmond, M. J. (2006). Neurobiology of exercise. *Obesity (Silver Spring), 14,* 345–356.

Dixon, R. A., & Hultsch, D. F. (1999). Intelligence and cognitive potential in late life. In J. C. Cavanaugh & S. K. Whitbourne (Eds.), *Gerontology: Interdisciplinary perspectives* (pp. 213–237). New York: Oxford University Press.

Dodson, C. S., Bawa, S., & Slotnick, S. D. (2007). Aging, source memory, and misrecollections. *Journal of Experimental Psychology: Learning, Memory, and Cognition, 33,* 169–181.

Dombrovski, A. Y., & Mulsant, B. H. (2007). The evidence for electroconvulsive therapy (ECT) in the treatment of severe late-life depression. ECT: The preferred treatment for severe depression in late life. *International Psychogeriatrics, 19,* 10–14, 27–35; discussion 24–16.

Donohue, R. (2006). Person-environment congruence in relation to career change and career persistence. *Journal of Vocational Behavior, 68,* 504–515.

Dorfman, L. T. (1989). Retirement preparation and retirement satisfaction in the rural elderly. *The Journal of Applied Gerontology, 8,* 432–450.

Drentea, P. (2002). Retirement and mental health. *Journal of Aging and Health, 14,* 167–194.

Drew, L. M., & Smith, P. K. (2002). Implications for grandparents when they lose contact with their grandchildren: Divorce, family feud, and geographical separation. *Journal of Mental Health and Aging, 8,* 95–119.

Dreyer, H. C., & Volpi, E. (2005). Role of protein and amino acids in the pathophysiology and treatment of sarcopenia. *Journal of the American College of Nutrition, 24,* 140S–145S.

Drozdowski, L., & Thomson, A. B. (2006). Aging and the intestine. *World Journal of Gastroenterology, 12,* 7578–7584.

Dubeau, C. E., Simon, S. E., & Morris, J. N. (2006). The effect of urinary incontinence on quality of life in older nursing home residents. *Journal of the American Geriatrics Society, 54,* 1325–1333.

Duberstein, P. R., & Conwell, Y. (1997). Personality disorders and completed suicide: A methodological and conceptual review. *Clinical Psychology: Science and Practice, 4,* 359–376.

Duberstein, P. R., & Conwell, Y. (2000). Suicide. In S. K. Whitbourne (Ed.), *Psychopathology in later life* (pp. 245–276). New York: Wiley.

Duner, A., & Nordstrom, M. (2005). Intentions and strategies among elderly people: Coping in everyday life. *Journal of Aging Studies, 19,* 437–451.

Dy, S., & Lynn, J. (2007). Getting services right for those sick enough to die. *British Medical Journal, 334,* 511–513.

Dye, J. (2005). *Fertility of American Women: June 2004.* Washington, DC: U.S. Bureau of the Census.

Easterlin, R. A. (2006). Life cycle happiness and its sources: Intersections of psychology, economics, and demography. *Journal of Economic Psychology, 27,* 463–482.

Edelstein, B., Martin, R. R., & McKee, D. R. (2000). Assessment of older adult psychopathology. In S. K. Whitbourne (Ed.), *Psychopathology in later life* (pp. 61–88). New York: Wiley.

Eid, M., & Diener, E. (2001). Norms for experiencing emotions in different cultures: Inter- and intranational differences. *Journal of Personality and Social Psychology, 81,* 869–885.

Elder, G. H. Jr., Shanahan, M., & Clipp, E. C. (1994). When war comes to men's lives: Life course patterns in family, work, and health. *Psychology and Aging, 9,* 5–16.

Elias, M. F., Elias, P. K., Sullivan, L. M., Wolf, P. A., & D'Agostino, R. B. (2005). Obesity, diabetes and cognitive deficit: The Framingham Heart Study. *Neurobiology of Aging, 26 Suppl 1,* 11–16.

Eliasson, L., Birkhed, D., Osterberg, T., & Carlen, A. (2006). Minor salivary gland secretion rates and immunoglobulin A in adults and the elderly. *European Journal of Oral Sciences, 114,* 494–499.

Ellis, A. (1998). Flora: A case of severe depression and treatment with rational emotive behavior therapy. In R. P. Halgin & S. K. Whitbourne (Eds.), *A casebook in abnormal psychology: From the files of experts* (pp. 166–181). New York: Oxford University Press.

Elwert, F. & Christakis, N. A. (2006). Widowhood and race. *American Sociological Review, 71,* 16–41.

Emaus, N., Berntsen, G. K., Joakimsen, R., & Fonnebo, V. (2006). Longitudinal changes in forearm bone mineral density in women and men aged 45–84 years: The

Tromso Study, a population-based study. *American Journal of Epidemiology, 163*, 441–449.

Engelke, K., Kemmler, W., Lauber, D., Beeskow, C., Pintag, R., & Kalender, W. A. (2006). Exercise maintains bone density at spine and hip EFOPS: A 3-year longitudinal study in early postmenopausal women. *Osteoporosis International, 17*, 133–142.

Engels, G. I., Duijsens, I. J., Haringsma, R., & van Putten, C. M. (2003). Personality disorders in the elderly compared to four younger age groups: A cross-sectional study of community residents and mental health patients. *Journal of Personality Disorders, 17*, 447–459.

Enserink, M. (1998). First Alzheimer's disease confirmed. *Science, 279*, 2037.

Erdem, N., & Chu, F. M. (2006). Management of overactive bladder and urge urinary incontinence in the elderly patient. *American Journal of Medicine, 119*, 29–36.

Erikson, E. H. (1959). Identity and the life cycle: Selected papers. *Psychological Issues Monograph, 1*, 1–177.

Erikson, E. H. (1963). *Childhood and society* (2d ed.). New York: Norton.

Erikson, E. H., Erikson, J. M., & Kivnick, H. Q. (1986). *Vital involvement in old age*. New York: W.W. Norton.

Espay, A. J., Mandybur, G. T., & Revilla, F. J. (2006). Surgical treatment of movement disorders. *Clinics in Geriatric Medicine, 22*, 813–825, vi.

Espino, D. V., Lichtenstein, M. J., Palmer, R. F., & Hazuda, H. P. (2004). Evaluation of the mini-mental state examination's internal consistency in a community-based sample of Mexican-American and European-American elders: Results from the San Antonio Longitudinal Study of Aging. *Journal of the American Geriatrics Society, 52*, 822–827.

Ettington, D. R. (1998). Successful career plateauing. *Journal of Vocational Behavior, 52*, 72–88.

Evrard, M. (2002). Ageing and lexical access to common and proper names in picture naming. *Brain and Language, 81*, 174–179.

Fallico, F., Siciliano, L., & Yip, F. (2005). Hypothermia-related deaths—United States, 2003-2004. *Morbidity and Mortality Weekly Report, 54*, 173–175.

Farrell, M. P., & Rosenberg, S. D. (1981). *Men at midlife*. Boston: Auburn House.

Farrimond, S., Knight, R. G., & Titov, N. (2006). The effects of aging on remembering intentions: Performance on a simulated shopping task. *Applied Cognitive Psychology, 20*, 533–555.

Federal Interagency Forum on Aging-Related Statistics (2006). 2006 Older American update: Key indicators of wellness. http://agingstats.gov/Agingstatsdotnet/Main_Site/Data/Data_2006.aspx.

Federmeier, K. D., McLennan, D. B., De Ochoa, E., & Kutas, M. (2002). The impact of semantic memory organization and sentence context information on spoken language processing by younger and older adults: an ERP study. *Psychophysiology, 39*, 133–146.

Feist, G. J. (2006). How development and personality influence scientific thought, interest, and achievement. *Review of General Psychology, 10*, 163–182.

Feist, G. J., & Barron, F. X. (2003). Predicting creativity from early to late adulthood: Intellect, potential, and personality. *Journal of Research in Personality, 37*, 62–88.

Feldman, D. C. (1994). The decision to retire early: A review and conceptualization. *Academy of Management Review, 19*, 285–311.

Feldman, H. A., Longcope, C., Derby, C. A., Johannes, C. B., Araujo, A. B., Coviello, A. D., Bremner, W. J., & McKinlay, J. B. (2002). Age trends in the level of serum testosterone and other hormones in middle-aged men: Longitudinal results from the Massachusetts male aging study. *Journal of Clinical Endocrinology and Metabolism, 87*, 589–598.

Fenn, D. S., & Ganzini, L. (1999). Attitudes of Oregon psychologists toward physician-assisted suicide and the Oregon Death With Dignity Act. *Professional Psychology: Research and Practice, 30*, 235–244.

Fernandes, M. A., Pacurar, A., Moscovitch, M., & Grady, C. (2006). Neural correlates of auditory recognition under full and divided attention in younger and older adults. *Neuropsychologia, 44*, 2452–2464.

Ferrari, A. U., Radaelli, A., & Centola, M. (2003). Invited review: Aging and the cardiovascular system. *Journal of Applied Physiology, 95*, 2591–2597.

Ferrari, S. L., & Rizzoli, R. (2005). Gene variants for osteoporosis and their pleiotropic effects in aging. *Molecular Aspects of Medicine, 26*, 145–167.

Ferrario, S. R., Cardillo, V., Vicario, F., Balzarini, E., & Zotti, A. M. (2004). Advanced cancer at home: Caregiving and bereavement. *Palliative Medicine, 18*, 129–136.

Ferraro, F. R. (2002). *Minority and cross-cultural aspects of neuropsychological assessment*. Bristol, PA: Swets and Zeitlinger.

Ferraro, K. F., & Farmer, M. M. (1996). Double jeopardy, aging as leveler, or persistent health inequality? A longitudinal analysis of white and black Americans. *Journal of Gerontology: Social Sciences, 51*, S319–328.

Field, A. E., Colditz, G. A., Willett, W. C., Longcope, C., & McKinlay, J. B. (1994). The relation of smoking, age, relative weight, and dietary intake to serum adrenal steroids, sex hormones, and sex hormone-binding globulin in middle-aged men. *Journal of Clinical Endocrinology and Metabolism, 79*, 1310–1316.

Field, M. J., Cassel, C. K., & Committee on Care at the End of Life (1997). *Approaching death: Improving care at the end of life, Institute of Medicine, Division of Health Care Services*. Washington, DC: National Academy Press.

Field, N. P., Gal-Oz, E., & Bonanno, G. A. (2003). Continuing bonds and adjustment at 5 years after the death of a spouse. *Journal of Consulting and Clinical Psychology, 71*, 110–117.

Field, N. P., Nichols, C., Holen, A., & Horowitz, M. J. (1999). The relation of continuing attachment to adjustment in conjugal bereavement. *Journal of Consulting and Clinical Psychology, 67*, 212–218.

Fields, J., & Casper, L. M. (2001). *America's family and living arrangements: Population characteristics March 2000. Current Population Reports, P20–537*. Washington, DC: U.S. Census Bureau.

Fields, J., O'Connell, M., & Downs, B. (2006). Grandparents in the United States, 2001. Paper presented at the annual meeting of the American Sociological Association, Montreal Convention Center, Montreal, Quebec, Canada, August 10, 2006.

Fiksenbaum, L. M., Greenglass, E. R., & Eaton, J. (2006). Perceived social support, hassles, and coping among the elderly. *Journal of Applied Gerontology, 25*, 17–30.

Fingerman, K. L. (1996). Sources of tension in the aging mother and adult daughter relationship. *Psychology and Aging, 11*, 591–606.

Fingerman, K. L. (2001). *Aging mothers and their adult daughters: A study in mixed emotions*. New York: Springer.

Fingerman, K. L., & Griffiths, P. C. (1999). Seasons greetings: Adults' social contacts at the holiday season. *Psychology and Aging, 14*, 192–205.

Fingerman, K. L., Hay, E. L., & Birditt, K. S. (2004). The best of ties, the worst of ties: Close, problematic, and ambivalent social relationships. *Journal of Marriage and the Family, 66*, 792–808.

Fins, J. J., Miller, F. G., Acres, C. A., Bacchetta, M. D., Huzzard, L. L., & Rapkin, B. D. (1999). End-of-life decision-making in the hospital: Current practice and future prospects. *Journal of Pain and Symptom Management, 17*, 6–15.

First, M. B., Spitzer, R. L., Gibbon, M., & Williams, J. B. W. (1997). *SCID-I/P (for DSM-IV) Patient Edition Structured Clinical Interview for DSM-IV Axis I Disorders, Research Version, Patient/Non-patient Edition. (SCID-I/P)*. New York: Biometrics Research, New York State Psychiatric Institute.

Fisher, C. D. (2002). Antecedents and consequences of real-time affective reactions at work. *Motivation and Emotion, 26*, 3–30.

Fisher, W. A., Rosen, R. C., Eardley, I., Sand, M., & Goldstein, I. (2005). Sexual experience of female partners of men with erectile dysfunction: The female experience of men's attitudes to life events and sexuality (FEMALES) study. *Journal of Sexual Medicine, 2*, 675–684.

Fitzpatrick, T. R., Spiro, A., III, Kressin, R; Greene, E., & Bosse, R. (2001). Leisure activities, stress, and health among bereaved and non-bereaved elderly men: The Normative Aging Study. *Omega: Journal of Death & Dying, 43*, 217–245.

Flint, A. J., & Rifat, S. L. (1997). Anxious depression in elderly patients. Response to antidepressant treatment. *American Journal of Geriatric Psychiatry, 5*, 107–115.

Floyd, F. J., & Wasner, G. H. (1994). Social exchange, equity, and commitment: Structural equation modeling of dating relationships. *Journal of Family Psychology, 8*, 55–73.

Foley, D. J., Vitiello, M. V., Bliwise, D. L., Ancoli-Israel, S., Monjan, A. A., & Walsh, J. K. (2007). Frequent napping is associated with excessive daytime sleepiness, depression, pain, and nocturia in older adults: Findings from the National Sleep Foundation "2003 Sleep in America" Poll. *American Journal of Geriatric Psychiatry, 15*, 344–350.

Folstein, M. F., Folstein, S. E., & McHugh, P. R. (1975). Mini-Mental State: A practical method for grading the cognitive state of patients for the clinician. *Journal of Psychiatric Research, 12*, 189–198.

Folwell, A. L., Chung, L. C., Nussbaum, J. F., Bethea, L. S., & Grant, J. A. (1997). Differential accounts of closeness in older adult sibling relationships. *Journal of Social and Personal Relationships, 14*, 843–849.

Ford, D. H., & Lerner, R. M. (Eds.). (1992). *Developmental systems theory: An integrative approach*. Newbury Park, CA: Sage.

Forde, C. G., Cantau, B., Delahunty, C. M., & Elsner, R. J. (2002). Interactions between texture and trigeminal stimulus in a liquid food system: Effects on elderly consumers preferences. *Journal of Nutrition Health and Aging, 6*, 130–133.

Formiga, F., Olmedo, C., Lopez-Soto, A., Navarro, M., Culla, A., & Pujol, R. N. (2007). Dying in hospital of terminal heart failure or severe dementia: The circumstances associated with death and the opinions of caregivers. *Palliative Medicine, 21,* 35–40.

Forsmo, S., Langhammer, A., Forsen, L., & Schei, B. (2005). Forearm bone mineral density in an unselected population of 2,779 men and women—the HUNT Study, Norway. *Osteoporosis International, 16,* 562–567.

Fowler, F. J. Jr., Coppola, K. M., & Teno, J. M. (1999). Methodological challenges for measuring quality of care at the end of life. *Journal of Pain and Symptom Management, 17,* 114–119.

Fraley, R. C., & Roberts, B. W. (2005). Patterns of continuity: A dynamic model for conceptualizing the stability of individual differences in psychological constructs across the life course. *Psychological Review, 112,* 60–74.

Franceschi, C., Capri, M., Monti, D., Giunta, S., Olivieri, F., Sevini, F., Panourgia, M. P., Invidia, L., Celani, L., Scurti, M., Cevenini, E., Castellani, G. C., & Salvioli, S. (2007). Inflammaging and anti-inflammaging: A systemic perspective on aging and longevity emerged from studies in humans. *Mechanisms of Ageing and Development, 128,* 92–105.

Fraser, J., Maticka-Tyndale, E., & Smylie, L. (2004). Sexuality of Canadian women at midlife. *Canadian Journal of Human Sexuality, 13,* 171–188.

Frazier, L. D., Johnson, P. M., Gonzalez, G. K., & Kafka, C. L. (2002). Psychosocial influences on possible selves: A comparison of three cohorts of older adults. *International Journal of Behavioral Development, 26,* 308–317.

Friedman, H. S., Tucker, J. S., Schwartz, J. E., Martin, L. R., Tomlinson-Keasey, C., Wingard, D. L., & Criqui, M. H. (1995). Childhood conscientiousness and longevity: Health behaviors and cause of death. *Journal of Personality and Social Psychology, 68,* 696–703.

Friedman, M., & Rosenman, R. H. (1974). *Type A behavior and your heart.* New York: Knopf.

Fry, P. S. (1997). Grandparent's reactions to the death of a grandchild: An exploratory factor analytic study. *Omega— Journal of Death and Dying, 35,* 119–140.

Fuiano, G., Sund, S., Mazza, G., Rosa, M., Caglioti, A., Gallo, G., Natale, G., Andreucci, M., Memoli, B., De Nicola, L., & Conte, G. (2001). Renal hemodynamic response to maximal vasodilating stimulus in healthy older subjects. *Kidney International, 59,* 1052–1058.

Fultz, N. H., Jenkins, K. R., Ostbye, T., Taylor, D. H. J., Kabeto, M. U., & Langa, K. M. (2005). The impact of own and spouse's urinary incontinence on depressive symptoms. *Social Science and Medicine, 60,* 2537–2548.

Funk, L. M. (2004). Who wants to be involved? Decision-making preferences among residents of long-term care facilities. *Canadian Journal of Aging, 23,* 47–58.

Gagne, M., & Deci, E. L. (2005). Self-determination theory and work motivation. *Journal of Organizational Behavior, 26,* 331–362.

Gagnon, M., Hersen, M., Kabacoff, R. L., & Van Hasselt, V. B. (1999). Interpersonal and psychological correlates of marital dissatisfaction in late life: A review. *Clinical Psychology Review, 19,* 359–378.

Gallagher-Thompson, D., Futterman, A., Farberow, N., Thompson, L. W., & Peterson, J. (1993). The impact of spousal bereavement on older widows and widowers. In M. S. Stroebe, W. Stroebe & R. O. Hansson (Eds.), *Handbook of bereavement.* Cambridge: Cambridge University Press.

Gallo, J. J., Rebok, G. W., Tennsted, S., Wadley, V. G., & Horgas, A. (2003). Linking depressive symptoms and functional disability in late life. *Aging and Mental Health, 7,* 469–480.

Gallo, L. C., & Matthews, K. A. (2003). Understanding the association between socioeconomic status and physical health: do negative emotions play a role? *Psychological Bulletin, 129,* 10–51.

Gallo, W. T., Bradley, E. H., Dubin, J. A., Jones, R. N., Falba, T. A., Teng, H. M., & Kasl, S. V. (2006). The persistence of depressive symptoms in older workers who experience involuntary job loss: Results from the health and retirement survey. *Journal of Gerontology: Social Sciences, 61B,* S221–S228.

Galper, D. I., Trivedi, M. H., Barlow, C. E., Dunn, A. L., & Kampert, J. B. (2006). Inverse association between physical inactivity and mental health in men and women. *Medicine and Science in Sports and Exercise, 38,* 173–178.

Galvan, V., Gorostiza, O. F., Banwait, S., Ataie, M., Logvinova, A. V., Sitaraman, S., Carlson, E., Sagi, S. A., Chevallier, N., Jin, K., Greenberg, D. A., & Bredesen, D. E. (2006). Reversal of Alzheimer's-like pathology and behavior in human APP transgenic mice by mutation of Asp664. *Proceedings of the National Academies of Sciences of the United States of America, 103,* 7130–7135.

Gans, D., & Silverstein, M. (2006). Norms of filial responsibility for aging parents across time and generations. *Journal of Marriage and the Family, 68,* 961–976.

Ganzini, L., Nelson, H. D., Lee, M. A., Kraemer, D. F., Schmidt, T. A., & Delorit, M. A. (2001). Oregon physicians' attitudes about and experiences with end-of-life care since passage of the Oregon Death With Dignity Act. *Journal of the American Medical Association, 285,* 2363–2369.

Garden, S. E., Phillips, L. H., & MacPherson, S. E. (2001). Midlife aging, open-ended planning, and laboratory measures of executive function. *Neuropsychology, 15,* 472–482.

Gardner, H. (1983). *Frames of mind: The theory of multiple intelligences.* New York: Basic Books.

Gardner, H. (1993). *Multiple intelligences: The theory in practice.* New York: Basic Books.

Gass, K. A. (1989). Appraisal, coping, and resources: Markers associated with the health of aged widows and widowers. In D. A. Lund (Ed.), *Older bereaved spouses: Research and practical applications* (pp. 79–94). New York: Hemisphere.

Gaunt, R. (2006). Couple similarity and marital satisfaction: Are similar spouses happier? *Journal of Personality, 74,* 1401–1420.

Gavrin, J., & Chapman, C. R. (1995). Clinical management of dying patients. *Western Journal of Medicine, 163,* 268–277.

Geal-Dor, M., Goldstein, A., Kamenir, Y., & Babkoff, H. (2006). The effect of aging on event-related potentials and behavioral responses: Comparison of tonal, phonologic and semantic targets. *Clinical Neurophysiology, 117,* 1974–1989.

Gee, S., & Baillie, J. (1999). Happily ever after? An exploration of retirement expectations. *Educational Gerontology, 25,* 109–128.

Geerlings, S. W., Beekman, A. T., Deeg, D. J., Twisk, J. W., & Van Tilburg, W. (2002). Duration and severity of depression predict mortality in older adults in the community. *Psychological Medicine, 32,* 609–618.

Gendell, M., & Siegel, J. S. (1996). Trends in retirement age in the United States, 1995–1993, by sex and race. *Journal of Gerontology: Social Sciences, 51,* S132–139.

Georges, J. J., Onwuteaka-Philipsen, B. D., Muller, M. T., Van Der Wal, G., Van Der Heide, A., & Van Der Maas, P. J. (2007). Relatives' perspective on the terminally ill patients who died after euthanasia or physician-assisted suicide: A retrospective cross-sectional interview study in the Netherlands. *Death Studies, 31,* 1–15.

Geserick, C., & Blasco, M. A. (2006). Novel roles for telomerase in aging. *Mechanisms of Ageing and Development, 127,* 579–583.

Geurts, S. A. E., Kompier, M. A. J., Roxburgh, S., & Houtman, I. L. D. (2003). Does work-home interference mediate the relationship between workload and well-being? *Journal of Vocational Behavior, 63,* 532–559.

Ghisella, P., & Lindenberger, U. (2005). Exploring structural dynamics within and between sensory and intellectual functioning in old and very old age: Longitudinal data from the Berlin Aging Study. *Intelligence, 33,* 555–587.

Giannantonio, C. M., & Hurley-Hanson, A. E. (2006). Applying image norms across Super's career development stages. *The Career Development Quarterly, 54,* 318–330.

Giannoulis, M. G., Sonksen, P. H., Umpleby, M., Breen, L., Pentecost, C., Whyte, M., McMillan, C. V., Bradley, C., & Martin, F. C. (2006). The effects of growth hormone and/or testosterone in healthy elderly men: A randomized controlled trial. *Journal of Clinical Endocrinology and Metabolism, 91,* 477–484.

Gildengers, A. G., Houck, P. R., Mulsant, B. H., Pollock, B. G., Mazumdar, S., Miller, M. D., Dew, M. A., Frank, E., Kupfer, D. J., & Reynolds, C. F., 3rd. (2002). Course and rate of antidepressant response in the very old. *Journal of Affective Disorders, 69,* 177–184.

Gill, S. C., Butterworth, P., Rodgers, B., Anstey, K. J., Villamill, E., & Melzer, D. (2006). Mental health and the timing of mens's retirement. *Social Psychiatry and Psychiatric Epidemiology, 41,* 933–954.

Gilliland, G., & Fleming, S. (1998). A comparison of spousal anticipatory grief and conventional grief. *Death Studies, 22,* 541–569.

Giunta, S. (2006). Is inflammaging an auto[innate]immunity subclinical syndrome? *Immunity and Ageing, 3,* 12.

Glaser, B. G., & Strauss, A. L. (1968). *Time for dying.* Chicago: Aldine.

Glaser, R. (2005). Stress-associated immune dysregulation and its importance for human health: A personal history of psychoneuroimmunology. *Brain, Behavior, and Immunity, 19,* 3–11.

Glass, J. C. Jr., & Kilpatrick, B. B. (1998). Gender comparisons of Baby Boomers and financial preparation for retirement. *Educational Gerontology, 24,* 719–745.

Goedert, M., & Spillantini, M. G. (2006). A century of Alzheimer's disease. *Science, 314,* 777–781.

Gold, D. T. (1989). Sibling relationships in old age: A typology. *International Journal of Aging and Human Development, 28,* 37–51.

Goldberg, A. E., & Sayer, A. (2006). Lesbian couples' relationship quality across the transition to parenthood. *Journal of Marriage and the Family, 68,* 87–100.

Goldstein, I. (2004). Epidemiology of erectile dysfunction. *Sexuality and Disability, 22,* 113–120.

Goldstein, I., Young, J. M., Fischer, J., Bangerter, K., Segerson, T., & Taylor, T. (2003). Vardenafil, a new phosphodiesterase type 5 inhibitor, in the treatment of erectile dysfunction in men with diabetes: A multicenter double-blind placebo-controlled fixed-dose study. *Diabetes Care, 26,* 777–783.

Golier, J. A., Harvey, P. D., Legge, J., & Yehuda, R. (2006). Memory performance in older trauma survivors: Implications for the longitudinal course of PTSD. *Annals of the New York Academy of Science, 1071*, 54–66.

Goodlin, S. J., Winzelberg, G. S., Teno, J. M., Whedon, M., & Lynn, J. (1998). Death in the hospital. *Archives of Internal Medicine, 158*, 1570–1572.

Gottfredson, G. D. (2002). Interests, aspirations, self-estimates, and the Self-Directed Search. *Journal of Career Assessment, 10*, 200–208.

Gottman, J., Coan, J., Carrere, S., & Swanson, C. (1998). Predicting marital happiness and stability from newlywed interactions. *Journal of Marriage and the Family, 60*, 5–22.

Gottman, J. M., & Driver, J. L. (2005). Dysfunctional marital conflict and everyday marital interaction. *Journal of Divorce and Remarriage, 43*, 63–78.

Gottman, J. M., & Levenson, R. W. (2000). The timing of divorce: Predicting when a couple will divorce over a 14-year period. *Journal of Marriage and the Family, 62*, 737–745.

Gottman, J. M., & Levenson, R. W. (2002). A two-factor model for predicting when a couple will divorce: Exploratory analyses using 14-year longitudinal data. *Family Process, 41*, 83–96.

Gould, R. L. (1978). *Transformations: Growth and change in adult life*. New York: Simon and Schuster.

Gournellis, R., Lykouras, L., Fortos, A., Oulis, P., Roumbos, V., & Christodoulou, G. N. (2001). Psychotic (delusional) major depression in late life: A clinical study. *International Journal of Geriatric Psychiatry, 16*, 1085–1091.

Government Accountability Office (2007). *Efforts to strengthen federal enforcement have not deterred some homes from repeatedly harming residents*. Washington, DC: Government Accountability Office.

Graakjaer, J., Londono-Vallejo, J. A., Christensen, K., & Kolvraa, S. (2006). The pattern of chromosome-specific variations in telomere length in humans shows signs of heritability and is maintained through life. *Annals of the New York Academy of Science, 1067*, 311–316.

Grabner, R. H., Fink, A., & Neubauer, A. C. (2007). Brain correlates of self-rated originality of ideas: Evidence from event-related power and phase-locking changes in the EEG. *Behavioral Neuroscience, 121*, 224–230.

Graham, C., Arthur, A., & Howard, R. (2002). The social functioning of older adults with schizophrenia. *Aging and Mental Health, 6*, 149–152.

Graham, K., & Vidal-Zeballos, D. (1998). Analyses of use of tranquilizers and sleeping pills across five surveys of the same population (1985–1991): The relationship with gender, age

and use of other substances. *Social Science and Medicine, 46*, 381–395.

Grant, B. S., Harford, T. C., Dawson, D. A., Chou, P., Dufour, M., & Pickering, R. (1995). Prevalence of DSM-IV alcohol abuse and dependence, United States, 1992. *Alcohol Health and Research World, 18*, 243–248.

Greenberg, S. (2006). *A profile of older Americans: 2005*. U.S. Department of Health and Human Services.

Greenhaus, J. H., Collins, K. M., & Shaw, J. D. (2003). The relation between work-family balance and quality of life. *Journal of Vocational Behavior, 63*, 510–531.

Greenhaus, J. H., & Powell, G. N. (2006). When work and family are allies: A theory of work-family enrichment. *Academy of Management Review, 31*, 72–92.

Greenwood, C. E., & Winocur, G. (2005). High-fat diets, insulin resistance and declining cognitive function. *Neurobiology of Aging, 26* Supplement 1, 42–45.

Greif, G. L. (1995). Single fathers with custody following separation and divorce. *Marriage and Family Review, 20*, 213–231.

Grodstein, F., Manson, J. E., & Stampfer, M. J. (2006). Hormone therapy and coronary heart disease: The role of time since menopause and age at hormone initiation. *Journal of Womens Health (Larchmont), 15*, 35–44.

Grossman, M., Cooke, A., DeVita, C., Alsop, D., Detre, J., Chen, W., & Gee, J, (2002). Age-related changes in working memory during sentence comprehension: An fMRI study. *Neuroimage, 15*, 302–317.

Grote, N. K., Clark, M. S., & Moore, A. (2004). Perceptions of injustice in family work: The role of psychological distress. *Journal of Family Psychology, 18*, 480–492.

Grote, N. K., Naylor, K. E., & Clark, M. S. (2002). Perceiving the division of family work to be unfair: Do social comparisons, enjoyment, and competence matter? *Journal of Family Psychology, 16*, 510–522.

Grzywacz, J. G., & Marks, N. F. (2000). Reconceptualizing the work-family interface: An ecological perspective on the correlates of positive and negative spillover between work and family. *Journal of Occupational Health Psychology, 5*, 111–126.

Gubin, D. G., Gubin, G. D., Waterhouse, J., & Weinert, D. (2006). The circadian body temperature rhythm in the elderly: Effect of single daily melatonin dosing. *Chronobiology International, 23*, 639–658.

Guidelines for the determination of death: Report of the medical consultants on the diagnosis of death to the President's commission for the study of ethical problems in medicine and biomedical and behavioural research. (1981). *Journal of the American Medical Association, 246*, 2184–2186.

Guinot, C., Malvy, D. J., Ambroisine, L., Latreille, J., Mauger, E., Tenenhaus, M., Morizot, F., Lopez, S., Le Fur, I., & Tschachler, E. (2002). Relative contribution of intrinsic vs extrinsic factors to skin aging as determined by a validated skin age score. *Archives of Dermatology, 138*, 1454–1160.

Gurland, B. J., Cross, P. S., & Katz, S. (1996). Epidemiological perspectives on opportunities for treatment of depression. *American Journal of Geriatric Psychiatry, 4 (Suppl. 1)*, S7–S13.

Hagestad, G. O., & Neugarten, B. L. (1985). Age and the life course. In R. H. Binstock & E. Shanas (Eds.), *Handbook of aging and the social sciences* (pp. 35–61). New York: Van Nostrand Reinhold.

Haidet, P., Hamel, M. B., Davis, R. B., Wenger, N., Reding, D., Kussin, P. S., Conners, A. F., Jr., Lynn, J., Weeks, J. C., & Phillips, R. S. (1998). Outcomes, preferences for resuscitation, and physician-patient communication among patients with metastatic colorectal cancer. SUPPORT Investigators. Study to Understand Prognoses and Preferences for Outcomes and Risks of Treatments. *American Journal of Medicine, 105*, 222–229.

Hakim, R. B., Teno, J. M., Harrell, F. E., Jr., Knaus, W. A., Wenger, N., Phillips, R. S., Layde, P., Califf, R., Connors, A. F., Jr., & Lynn, J. (1996). Factors associated with do-not-resuscitate orders: patients' preferences, prognoses, and physicians' judgements. SUPPORT Investigators. Study to Understand Prognoses and Preferences for Outcomes and Risks of Treatment. *Annals of Internal Medicine. 125*, 284–293.

Halevy, A., & Brody, B. (1993). Brain death: Reconciling definitions, criteria, and tests. *Annals of Internal Medicine, 119*, 519–525.

Haley, W. E., Allen, R. S., Reynolds, S., Chen, H., Burton, A., & Gallagher-Thompson, D. (2002). Family issues in end-of-life decision making and end-of-life care. *American Behavioral Scientist, 46*, 284–298.

Halgin, R. P., & Whitbourne, S. K. (2005). *Abnormal psychology: Clinical perspectives on psychological disorders* (5th ed.). New York: McGraw-Hill.

Hamel, M. B., Phillips, R. S., Teno, J. M., Lynn, J., Galanos, A. N., Davis, R. B., Connors, A. F., Jr., Oye, R. K., Desbiens, N., Reding, D. J., & Goldman, L. (1996). Seriously ill hospitalized adults: do we spend less on older patients? Support Investigators. Study to Understand Prognoses and Preference for Outcomes and Risks of Treatments. *Journal of the American Geriatrics Society, 44*, 1043–1048.

Hamilton, M. (1959). The assessment of anxiety states by rating. *British Journal of Medical Psychology, 32*, 50–55.

Hamilton, M. (1967). Development of a rating scale for primary depressive illness. *British Journal of Social and Clinical Psychology, 6*, 278–296.

Hanke, T. A., & Tiberio, D. (2006). Lateral rhythmic unipedal stepping in younger, middle-aged, and older adults. *Journal of Geriatric Physical Therapy, 29*, 22–27.

Happ, M. B., Capezuti, E., Strumpf, N. E., Wagner, L., Cunningham, S., Evans, L., & Maislin, G. (2002). Advance care planning and end-of-life care for hospitalized nursing home residents. *Journal of the American Geriatrics Society, 50*, 829–835.

Hardy, J. (2006). Alzheimer's disease: The amyloid cascade hypothesis: An update and reappraisal. *Journal of Alzheimers Disease, 9*, 151–153.

Hardy, J., & Selkoe, D. J. (2002). The amyloid hypothesis of Alzheimer's disease: Progress and problems on the road to therapeutics. *Science, 297*, 353–356.

Hardy, M. A., & Quadagno, J. (1995). Satisfaction with early retirement: Making choices in the auto industry. *Journal of Gerontology: Social Sciences, 50B*, S217–S228.

Hardy, S. E., Concato, J., & Gill, T. M. (2004). Resilience of community-dwelling older persons. *Journal of the American Geriatrics Society, 52*, 257–262.

Hare, R. D. (1997). *Hare Psychopathy Checklist-Revised (PCL-R)*. Odessa, FL: Personality Assessment Resources.

Harman, D. (2006). Alzheimer's disease pathogenesis: Role of aging. *Annals of the New York Academy of Sciences, 1067*, 454–460.

Harmon, L. W., Hansen, J. C., Borgen, F. H., & Hammer, A. L. (1994). *Strong Interest Inventory applications and technical guide*. Palo Alto, CA: Consulting Psychologists Press.

Harms, C. A. (2006). Does gender affect pulmonary function and exercise capacity? *Respiratory Physiology and Neurobiology, 151*, 124–131.

Harper, S., Lynch, J., Burris, S., & Davey Smith, G. (2007). Trends in the black-white life expectancy gap in the United States, 1983–2003. *Journal of the American Medical Association, 297*, 1224–1232.

Harpur, T. J., Hart, S. D., & Hare, R. D. (2002). Personality of the psychopath. In P. T. Costa, Jr., & T. A. Widiger (Eds.), *Personality disorders and the five-factor model of personality* (2nd Ed.) (pp. 299–324). Washington, DC: American Psychological Association.

Harrington, C., Carrillo, H., & LaCava, C. (2006). Nursing facilities, staffing, residents, and facility deficiencies, 1999 through 2005. Department of Social and Behavioral Sciences University of California San Francisco, CA.

Harris, Y., & Cooper, J. K. (2006). Depressive symptoms in older people predict nursing home admission. *Journal of the American Geriatrics Society, 54*, 593–597.

Harrison, P. M., & Beck, A. J. (2005). Prisoners in 2004. *Bureau of Justice Statistics Bulletin, NCJ 210677.*

Hartley, A. A. (1992). Attention. In F. I. M. Craik & T. A. Salthouse (Eds.), *The handbook of aging and cognition* (pp. 3–50). Hillsdale, NJ: Erlbaum.

Hartup, W. W., & Stevens, N. (1997). Friendships and adaptation in the life course. *Psychological Bulletin, 121*, 355–370.

Hartvigsen, J., Frederiksen, H., & Christensen, K. (2006). Back and neck pain in seniors—prevalence and impact. *European Spine Journal, 15*, 802–806.

Harwood, D. G., Sultzer, D. L., & Wheatley, M. V. (2000). Impaired insight in Alzheimer disease: Association with cognitive deficits, psychiatric symptoms, and behavioral disturbances. *Neuropsychiatry, Neuropsychology, and Behavioral Neurology, 13*, 83–88.

Harwood, J., & Lin, M.-C. (2000). Affiliation, pride, exchange, and distance in grandparents' accounts of relationships with their college-aged grandchildren. *Journal of Communication, 50*, 31–47.

Harwood, K., McLean, N., & Durkin, K. (2007). First-time mothers' expectations of parenthood: What happens when optimistic expectations are not matched by later experiences? *Developmental Psychology, 43*, 1–12.

Hasher, L., Goldstein, F., & May, C. (2005). It's about time: Circadian rhythms, memory and aging. In C. Izawa & N. Ohta (Eds.), *Human learning and memory: Advances in theory and application* (Vol. 18, pp. 179–186). Mahwah, NJ: Lawrence Erlbaum Associates.

Hasher, L., Zacks, R. T., & May. C. P. (1999). Inhibitory control, circadian arousal, and age. In D. Gopher & A. Koriat (Eds.), *Attention and performance, XVII, Cognitive regulation of performance: Interaction of theory and application* (pp. 653–675). Cambridge, MA: MIT Press.

Hayflick, L. (1994). *How and why we age.* New York: Ballantine Books.

Hayflick, L., & Moorhead, P. S. (1961). The serial cultivation of human diploid cell strains. *Experimental Cell Research, 25*, 585–621.

Hays, J., Ockene, J. K., Brunner, R. L., Kotchen, J. M., Manson, J. E., Patterson, R. E., Aragaki, A. K., Shumaker, S. A., Brzyski, R. G., LaCroix, A. Z., Granek, I. A., & Valanis, B. G. (2003). Effects of estrogen plus progestin on health-related quality of life. *New England Journal of Medicine, 348*, 1839–1854.

Hays, J. C., Gold, D. T., & Peiper, C. F. (1997). Sibling bereavement in late life. *Omega—Journal of Death & Dying, 35*, 25–42.

Hays, N. P., & Roberts, S. B. (2006). The anorexia of aging in humans. *Physiology and Behavior, 88*, 257–266.

He, W., Sangupta, M., Velkoff, V. A., & DeBarros, K. A. (2005). *65 + in the United States: 2005. Current Population Reports Special Studies. U.S. Census Bureau, Current Population Reports, P23–209.* Washington, DC: U.S. Government Printing Office.

Heaton, J. P., & Morales, A. (2001). Andropause—A multisystem disease. *Canadian Journal of Urology, 8*, 1213–1222.

Hedberg, K., Hopkins, D., & Kohn, M. (2003). Five years of legal physician-assisted suicide in Oregon. *New England Journal of Medicine, 348*, 961–964.

Hedden, T., & Gabrieli, J. D. (2004). Insights into the ageing mind: A view from cognitive neuroscience. *Nature Review Neuroscience, 5*, 87–96.

Hedden, T., & Park, D. (2001). Aging and interference in verbal working memory. *Psychology and Aging, 16*, 666–681.

Hedden, T., & Yoon, C. (2006). Individual differences in executive processing predict susceptibility to interference in verbal working memory. *Neuropsychology, 20*, 511–528.

Heffner, K. L., Loving, T. J., Kiecolt-Glaser, J. K., Himawan, L. K., Glaser, R., & Malarkey, W. B. (2006). Older spouses' cortisol responses to marital conflict: Associations with demand/withdraw communication patterns. *Journal of Behavioral Medicine, 29*, 317–325.

Heisel, M. J. (2006). Suicide and its prevention among older adults. *Canadian Journal of Psychiatry, 51*, 143–154.

Helgeson, V. S., & Taylor, S. E. (1993). Social comparisons and adjustment among cardiac patients. *Journal of Applied Social Psychology, 23*, 1171–1195.

Helson, R. (1967). Personality characteristics and developmental history of creative college women. *Genetic Psychology Monographs, 76*, 205–256.

Helson, R., & Moane, G. (1987). Personality change in women from college to midlife. *Journal of Personality and Social Psychology, 53*, 176–186.

Helson, R., & Soto, C. J. (2005). Up and down in middle age: Monotonic and nonmonotonic changes in roles, status, and personality. *Journal of Personality and Social Psychology, 89*, 194–204.

Helson, R., & Srivastava, S. (2001). Three paths of adult development: Conservers, seekers, and achievers. *Journal of Personality and Social Psychology, 80*, 995–1010.

Helson, R., & Wink, P. (1992). Personality change in women from the early 40s to the early 50s. *Psychology and Aging, 7,* 46–55.

Helzner, E. P., Cauley, J. A., Pratt, S. R., Wisniewski, S. R., Zmuda, J. M., Talbott, E. O., de Rekeneire, N., Harris, T. B., Rubin, S. M., Simonsick, E. M., Tylavsky, F. A., & Newman, A. B. (2005). Race and sex differences in age-related hearing loss: The Health, Aging and Body Composition Study. *Journal of the American Geriatrics Society, 53,* 2119–2127.

Henderson, V. W. (2006). Estrogen-containing hormone therapy and Alzheimer's disease risk: Understanding discrepant inferences from observational and experimental research. *Neuroscience, 138,* 1031–1039.

Hendin, H. (1999). Suicide, assisted suicide, and medical illness. *Journal of Clinical Psychiatry, 60,* 2.

Henry, J. D., & Phillips, L. H. (2006). Covariates of production and perseveration on tests of phonemic, semantic and alternating fluency in normal aging. *Aging, Neuropsychology and Cognition, 13,* 529–551.

Hermann, M., & Berger, P. (2001). Hormonal changes in aging men: A therapeutic indication? *Experimental Gerontology, 36,* 1075–1082.

Heron, M. P., & Smith, B. L. (2007). Deaths: Leading causes for 2003. *National Vital Statistics Reports 55, no. 10.*

Herzberg, F., Mausner, B., & Snyderman, B. B. (1959). *The motivation to work.* New York: Wiley.

Hess, T. M., Auman, C., Colcombe, S. J., & Rahhal, T. A. (2003). The impact of stereotype threat on age differences in memory performance. *Journal of Gerontology: Psychological Sciences, 58B,* P3–P11.

Hess, T. M., & Hinson, J. T. (2006). Age-related variation in the influences of aging stereotypes on memory in adulthood. *Psychology and Aging, 21,* 621–625.

Hetherington, E. M., & Kelly, J. (2002). *For better or for worse: Divorce reconsidered.* New York: W.W. Norton.

Hetherington, M., & Henderson, S. H. (1997). Fathers in step families. In M. E. Lamb (Ed.) *The role of the father in child development* (pp. 212–226). New York: John Wiley.

Hickman, S. E. (2002). Improving communication near the end of life. *American Behavioral Scientist, 46,* 252–267.

Hillman, J., & Stricker, G. (2002). A call for psychotherapy integration in work with older adult patients. *Journal of Psychotherapy Integration, 12,* 395–405.

Hinrichsen, G. A., & Dick-Siskin, L. P. (2000). Psychotherapy with older adults. In S. K. Whitbourne (Ed.), *Psychopathology in later life* (pp. 323–353). New York: Wiley.

Hofland, B. F., Willis, S. L., & Baltes, P. B. (1980). Fluid performance in the elderly: Intraindividual variability and conditions of assessment. *Journal of Educational Psychology, 73,* 573–586.

Holahan, C. J., Moos, R. H., Holahan, C. K., Brennan, P. L., & Schutte, K. K. (2005). Stress generation, avoidance coping, and depressive Symptoms: A 10-year model. *Journal of Consulting and Clinical Psychology, 73,* 658–666.

Holahan, C. K., & Chapman, J. R. (2002). Longitudinal predictors of proactive goals and activity participation at age 80. *Journal of Gerontology: Psychological Sciences, 57B* P418–P425.

Holland, J. L. (1994). *The Self-Directed Search.* Odessa, FL: Psychological Assessment Resources.

Holland, J. L. (1997). *Making vocational choices: A theory of vocational personalities and work environments* (3d ed.). Odessa, FL: Psychological Assessment Resources.

Hollenberg, M., Yang, J., Haight, T. J., & Tager, I. B. (2006). Longitudinal changes in aerobic capacity: Implications for concepts of aging. *Journal of Gerontology: Biological Sciences and Medical Sciences, 61A,* 851–858.

Hooker, K., & Kaus, C. R. (1994). Health-related possible selves in young and middle adulthood. *Psychology and Aging, 9,* 126–133.

Hootman, J. M., & Helmick, C. G. (2006). Projection of US prevalence of arthritis and associated activity limitation. *Arthritis and Rheumatism, 54,* 226–229.

Horn, J. L. (1970). Organization of data on life-span development of human abilities. In L. R. Goulet & P. B. Baltes (Eds.), *Life-span developmental psychology: Theory and research* (Vol. 1, pp. 211–256). New York: Academic Press.

Horn, J. L., & Cattell, R. B. (1966). Refinement and test of the theory of fluid and crystallized intelligence. *Journal of Educational Psychology, 57,* 253–270.

Horstmann, T., Maschmann, J., Mayer, F., Heitkamp, H. C., Handel, M., & Dickhuth, H. H. (1999). The influence of age on isokinetic torque of the upper and lower leg musculature in sedentary men. *International Journal of Sports Medicine, 20,* 362–367.

House, J. S., Kessler, R. C., Herzog, A. R., & Mero, R. P. (1990). Age, socioeconomic status, and health. *Milbank Quarterly, 68,* 383–411.

House, J. S., Landis, K. R., & Umberson, D. (1988). Social relationships and health. *Science, 241,* 540–545.

Howes, R. M. (2006). The free radical fantasy: A panoply of paradoxes. *Annals of the New York Academy of Science, 1067,* 22–26.

Hoyert, D. L., Heron, M. P., Murphy, S. L., & Kung, H.-C. (2006). Deaths: Final data for 2003. *National Vital Statistics Reports, 54,* 13.

Hoyert, D. L., Kung, H.-C., & Xu, J. (2007). Autopsy patterns in 2003. *National Center for Health Statistics, 20 (32)*.

Hoyle, R. H. (Ed.). (1995). *Structural equation modeling: Concepts, issues, and applications*. Thousand Oaks, CA: Sage.

Hsu, Y. H., Venners, S. A., Terwedow, H. A., Feng, Y., Niu, T., Li, Z., Laird, N., Brain, J. D., Cummings, S. R., Bouxsein, M. L., Rosen, C. J., & Xu, X. (2006). Relation of body composition, fat mass, and serum lipids to osteoporotic fractures and bone mineral density in Chinese men and women. *American Journal of Clinical Nutrition, 83*, 146–154.

Hubert, H. B., Bloch, D. A., Oehlert, J. W., & Fries, J. F. (2002). Lifestyle habits and compression of morbidity. *Journal of Gerontology: Medical Sciences, 57A*, M347–M351.

Hughes, V. A., Frontera, W. R., Wood, M., Evans, W. J., Dallal, G. E., Roubenoff, R., & Fiatarone Singh, M. A. (2001). Longitudinal muscle strength changes in older adults: Influence of muscle mass, physical activity, and health. *Journal of Gerontology: Biological Sciences, 56A*, B209–B217.

Hummert, M. L., Shaner, J. L., Garstka, T. A., & Henry, C. (1998). Communication with older adults: The influence of age stereotypes, context and communicator age. *Human Communication Research, 25*, 124–151.

Humphrey, D. (1991). *Final exit: The practicalities of self-deliverance and assisted suicide for the dying*. Eugene OR: Hemlock Society.

Hunter, G. R., McCarthy, J. P., & Bamman, M. M. (2004). Effects of resistance training on older adults, *Sports Medicine, 34*, 329–348.

Hurd, Clarke L. (2006). Older women and sexuality: Experiences in marital relationships across the life course. *Canadian Journal of Aging, 25*, 129–140.

Husain, A. F., Stewarts, K., Arseneault, R., Moineddin, R., Cellarius, F., Librach, L., & Dudgeon, D. (2007). Women experience higher levels of fatigue than men at the end of life: A longitudinal home palliative care study. *Journal of Pain and Symptom Management, 33*, 389–387.

Hy, L. X., & Keller, D. M. (2000). Prevalence of AD among whites: A summary by levels of severity. *Neurology, 55*, 198–204.

Hyun, D. H., Emerson, S. S., Jo, D. G., Mattson, M. P., & de Cabo, R. (2006). Calorie restriction up-regulates the plasma membrane redox system in brain cells and suppresses oxidative stress during aging. *Proceedings of the National Academies of Science U S A, 103*, 19908–19912.

Ice, G. H. (2002). Daily life in a nursing home: Has it changed in 25 years? *Journal of Aging Studies, 16*, 345–359.

Ingersoll-Dayton, B., Neal, M. B., Ha, J.-H., & Hammer, L. B. (2003). Redressing inequity in parent care among siblings. *Journal of Marriage and the Family, 65*, 201–212.

Isaacowitz, D. M., Wadlinger, H. A., Goren, D., & Wilson, H. R. (2006). Selective preference in visual fixation away from negative images in old age? An eye-tracking study. *Psychology and Aging, 21*, 40–48.

Ishida, K., Sato, Y., Katayama, K., & Miyamura, M. (2000). Initial ventilatory and circulatory responses to dynamic exercise are slowed in the elderly. *Journal of Applied Physiology, 89*, 1771–1777.

Jacoby, L. L., & Rhodes, M. G. (2006). False remembering in the aged. *Current Directions in Psychological Science, 15*, 49–53.

Jagust, W., Gitcho, A., Sun, F., Kuczynski, B., Mungas, D., & Haan, M. (2006). Brain imaging evidence of preclinical Alzheimer's disease in normal aging. *Annals of Neurology, 59*, 673–681.

Jakes, R. W., Day, N. E., Patel, B., Khaw, K. T., Oakes, S., Luben, R., Welch, A., Bingham, S., & Wareham, N. J. (2002). Physical inactivity is associated with lower forced expiratory volume in 1 second: European Prospective Investigation into Cancer-Norfolk Prospective Population Study. *American Journal of Epidemiology, 156*, 139–147.

James, H. S. J. (2005). Why did you do that? An economic examination of the effect of extrinsic compensation on intrinsic motivation and performance. *Journal of Economic Psychology, 26*, 549–566.

James, L. E., & MacKay, D. G. (2007). New age-linked asymmetries: Aging and the processing of familiar versus novel language on the input versus output side. *Psychology and Aging, 22*, 94–103.

Jang, Y. S., Hwang, C. H., Shin, J. Y., Bae, W. Y., & Kim, L. S. (2006). Age-related changes on the morphology of the otoconia. *Laryngoscope, 116*, 996–1001.

Jaques, E. (1965). Death and the mid-life crisis. *International Journal of Psychoanalysis, 46*, 502–514.

Jastrzembski, T. S., Charness, N., & Vasyukova, C. (2006). Expertise and age effects on knowledge activation in chess. *Psychology and Aging, 21*, 401–405.

Jeste, D. V., Lohr, J. B., Eastham, J. H., Rockwell, E., & Caligiuri, M. P. (1998). Adverse neurobiological effects of long-term use of neuroleptics: Human and animal studies. *Journal of Psychiatric Research, 32*, 201–214.

Jeste, D. V., Symonds, L. L., Harris, M. J., Paulsen, J. S., Palmer, B. W., & Heaton, R. K. (1997). Nondementia nonpraecox dementia praecox? Late onset schizophrenia. *American Journal of Geriatric Psychiatry, 5*, 302–317.

Johnson, E. J., & Schaefer, E. J. (2006). Potential role of dietary n-3 fatty acids in the prevention of dementia and macular degeneration. *American Journal of Clinical Nutrition*, *83*, 1494S–1498S.

Johnson, J., Stewart, W., Hall, E., Fredlund, P., & Theorell, T. (1996). Long-term psychosocial work environment and cardiovascular mortality among Swedish men. *American Journal of Public Health*, *86*, 324–331.

Johnson, T., & Dye, J. (2005). *Indicators of marriage and fertility in the United States from the American Community Survey: 2000 to 2003*. Washington, D.C.: U.S. Bureau of the Census.

Jorm, A. F., Windsor, T. D., Dear, K. B., Anstey, K. J., Christensen, H., & Rodgers, B. (2005). Age group differences in psychological distress: the role of psychosocial risk factors that vary with age. *Psychological Medicine*, *35*, 1253–1263.

Judge, T. A., Heller, D., & Mount, M. K. (2002). Five-factor model of personality and job satisfaction: A meta-analysis. *Journal of Applied Psychology*, *87*, 530–541.

Kalimo, R., Taris, T. W., & Schaufeli, W. B. (2003). The effects of past and anticipated future downsizing on survivor well-being: An equity perspective. *Journal of Occupational Health Psychology*, *8*, 91–109.

Kalmijn, M. (2003). Shared friendship networks and the life course: An analysis of survey data on married and cohabiting couples. *Social Networks*, *25*, 231–249.

Kamel, N. S., & Gammack, J. K. (2006). Insomnia in the elderly: Cause, approach, and treatment. *American Journal of Medicine*, *119*, 463–469.

Kamimoto, L. A., Easton, A. N., Maurice, E., Husten, C. G., & Macera, C. A. (1999). Surveillance for five health risks among older adults—United States, 1993–1997. *Morbidity and Mortality Weekly Reports*, *48*(SS08), 89–130.

Kane, R. A., Caplan, A. L., Urv-Wong, E. K., Freeman, I. C., Aroskar, M. A., & Finch, M. (1997). Everyday matters in the lives of nursing home residents: Wish for and perception of choice and control. *Journal of the American Geriatrics Society*, *45*, 1086–1093.

Kanfer, R., & Ackerman, P. L. (2004). Aging, adult development, and work motivation. *Academy of Management Review*, *29*, 440–458.

Kannus, P., Uusi-Rasi, K., Palvanen, M., & Parkkari, J. (2005). Non-pharmacological means to prevent fractures among older adults. *Annals of Medicine*, *37*, 303–310.

Karakelides, H., & Sreekumaran Nair, K. (2005). Sarcopenia of aging and its metabolic impact. *Current Topics in Developmental Biology*, *68*, 123–148.

Karney, B., & Bradbury, T. (1997). Neuroticism, marital interaction, and the trajectory of marital satisfaction. *Journal of Personality and Social Psychology*, *72*, 1075–1092.

Karpansalo, M., Kauhanen, J., Lakka, T. A., Manninen, P., Kaplan, G. A., & Salonen, J. T. (2004). Depression and early retirement: Prospective population based study in middle aged men. *Journal of Epidemiology and Community Health*, *59*, 70–74.

Kastenbaum, R. (1999). Dying and bereavement. In J. C. Cavanaugh & S. K. Whitbourne (Eds.), *Gerontology: An interdisciplinary perspective* (pp. 155–185). New York: Oxford.

Kasthurirangan, S., & Glasser, A. (2006). Age related changes in accommodative dynamics in humans. *Vision Research*, *46*, 1507–1519.

Katzel, L. I., Sorkin, J. D., & Fleg, J. L. (2001). A comparison of longitudinal changes in aerobic fitness in older endurance athletes and sedentary men. *Journal of the American Geriatrics, Society*, *49*, 1657–1664.

Kaufman, A. S. (2001). WAIS-III IQs, Horn's theory, and generational changes from young adulthood to old age. *Intelligence*, *29*, 131–167.

Kaufman, A. S., Kaufman, J. L., McLean, J. E., & Reynolds, C. R. (1991). Is the pattern of intellectual growth and decline across the adult life span different for men and women? *Journal of Clinical Psychology*, *47*, 801–812.

Kawas, C., Gray, S., Brookmeyer, R., Fozard, J., & Zonderman, A. (2000). Age-specific incidence rates of Alzheimer's disease: The Baltimore Longitudinal Study of Aging. *Neurology*, *54*, 2072–2077.

Kay, E. J., Harris, R. M., Voros, R. S., Hillman, D. J., Hyland, D. T., & Deimler, J. D. (1994). *Age 60 study, part III: Consolidated database experiments final report*. Washington, DC: Federal Aviation Administration (NTIS No. DOT/FAA/AM-94/22).

Keefe, J. M., & Fancey, P. J. (2002). Work and eldercare: Reciprocity between older mothers and their employed daughters. *Canadian Journal on Aging*, *21*, 229–241.

Keefe, S. E., Padilla, A. M., & Carlos, M. L. (1979). The Mexican-American extended family as an emotional support system. *Human Organization*, *38*, 144–152.

Keister, K. J. (2006). Predictors of self-assessed health, anxiety, and depressive symptoms in nursing home residents at week 1 postrelocation. *Journal of Aging and Health*, *18*, 722–742.

Keith, S. J., Regier, D. A., & Rae, D. S. (1991). Schizophrenic disorders. In L. N. Robins & D. A. Regier (Eds.), *Psychiatric disorders in America* (pp. 33–52). New York: Free Press.

Keles, I., Aydin, G., Basar, M. M., Hayran, M., Atalar, E., Orkun, S., & Batislam, E, (2006). Endogenous sex steroids and bone mineral density in healthy men. *Joint Bone Spine*, 73, 80–85.

Kelly, B., Burnett, P., Pelusi, D., Badger, S., Varghese, F., & Robertson, M. (2002). Terminally ill cancer patients' wish to hasten death. *Palliative Medicine*, 16, 339–345.

Kemper, S. (1992). Language and aging. In F. I. M. Craik & T. A. Salthouse (Eds.), *The handbook of aging and cognition* (pp. 213–270). Hillsdale NJ: Erlbaum.

Kemper, S., Greiner, L. H., Marquis, J. G., Prenovost, K., & Mitzner, T. L. (2001). Language decline across the life span: Findings from the Nun Study. *Psychology and Aging*, 16, 227–239.

Kemper, S., Marquis, J., & Thompson, M. (2001). Longitudinal change in language production: Effects of aging and dementia on grammatical complexity and propositional content. *Psychology and Aging*, 16, 600–614.

Kemper, S., & Sumner, A. (2001). The structure of verbal abilities in young and older adults. *Psychology and Aging*, 16, 312–322.

Kerby, D. S., & Ragan, K. M. (2002). Activity interests and Holland's RIASEC system in older adults. *International Journal of Aging and Human Development*, 55, 117–139.

Kessel, L., Jorgensen, T., Glumer, C., & Larsen, M. (2006). Early lens aging is accelerated in subjects with a high risk of ischemic heart disease: An epidemiologic study. *BMC Ophthalmology*, 6, 16.

Kessler, R. C., Berglund, P., Demler, O., Jin, R., Koretz, D., Merikangas, K. R., Rush, A. J., Walters, E. E., & Wang, P. S. (2003). The epidemiology of major depressive disorders: results from the National Comorbidity Survey Replication (NCS-R). *Journal of the American Medical Association*, 289, 3095–3105.

Kessler, R. C., Berglund, P., Demler, O., Jin, R., Merikangas, K. R., & Walters, E. E. (2005). Lifetime prevalence and age-of-onset distributions of DSM-IV disorders in the National Comorbidity Survey Replication. *Archives of General Psychiatry*, 62, 593–602.

Kessler, R. C., Berglund, P. A., Glantz, M. D., Koretz, D. S., Merikangas, R. R., Walters, E. E., & Zaslavsky, A. M. (2004). Estimating the prevalence and correlates of serious mental illness in community epidemiological surveys. In R. W. Manderscheid & M. J. Henderson (Eds.), *Mental health: United States, 2002* (pp. 155–164). Rockville MD: U.S. Department of Health and Human Services.

Kessler, R. C., McGonagle, K. A., Zhao, S., Nelson, C. B., Hughes, M., Eshleman, S., Wittchen, H.-U., & Kendler, K. S. (1994). Lifetime and 12-month prevalence of *DSM-III-R* psychiatric disorders in the United States: Results from the National Comorbidity Survey. *Archives of General Psychiatry*, 51, 8–19.

Kessler, R. C., Stein, M. B., & Berglund, P. (1998). Social phobia subtypes in the National Comorbidity Survey. *American Journal of Psychiatry*, 155, 613–619.

Kevorkian, J. (1991). *Prescription—medicide: The goodness of planned death*. Buffalo, NY: Prometheus Books.

Khosla, S., Melton, L. J. 3rd, Achenbach, S. J., Oberg, A. L., & Riggs, B. L. (2006). Hormonal and biochemical determinants of trabecular microstructure at the ultradistal radius in women and men. *Journal of Clinical Endocrinology and Metabolism*, 91, 885–891.

Kiecolt-Glaser, J. K., & Glaser, R. (2002). Depression and immune function: Central pathways to morbidity and mortality. *Journal of Psychosomatic Research*, 53, 873–876.

Kieffer, K. M., Schinka, J. A., & Curtiss, G. (2004). Person-environment congruence and personality domains in the prediction of job performance and work quality. *Journal of Counseling Psychology*, 51, 168–177.

Kim, J. E., & Moen, P. (2001). Is retirement good or bad for subjective well-being? *Current Directions in Psychological Science*, 10, 83–86.

Kim, J. E., & Nesselroade, J. R. (2002). Relationships among social support, self-concept, and wellbeing of older adults: A study of process using dynamic factor models. *International Journal of Behavioral Development*, 27, 49–63.

King, D. A., & Markus, H. E. (2000). Mood disorders in older adults. In S. K. Whitbourne (Ed.), *Psychopathology in later life* (pp. 141–172). New York: Wiley.

Kinsella, K., & Veloff, V. A. (2001). *U.S. Census Bureau, Series P95/01-1. An aging world: 2001*. Washington, DC: U.S. Department of Health and Human Services.

Kissane, M., & McLaren, S. (2006). Sense of belonging as a predictor of reasons for living in older adults. *Death Studies*, 30, 243–258.

Kite, M. E., & Wagner, L. S. (2002). Attitudes toward older adults. In T. D. Nelson (Ed.), *Ageism: Stereotyping and prejudice against older persons*. (pp. 129–161): The MIT Press.

Klass, M., Baudry, S., & Duchateau, J. (2006). Voluntary activation during maximal contraction with advancing age: A brief review. *European Journal of Applied Physiology*.

Klemmack, D. L., Roff, L. L., Parker, M. W., Koenig, H. G., Sawyer, P., & Allman, R. M. (2007). A cluster analysis typology of religiousness/spirituality among older adults. *Research on Aging*, 29, 163–183.

Klerman, E. B., Duffy, J. F., Dijk, D. J., & Czeisler, C. A. (2001). Circadian phase resetting in older people by ocular bright light exposure. *Journal of Investigative Medicine, 49,* 30–40.

Klinkenberg, M., Willems, D. L., Onwuteaka-Philipsen, B. D., Deeg, D. J., & van der Wal, G. (2004). Preferences in end-of-life care of older persons: After-death interviews with proxy respondents. *Social Science and Medicine, 59,* 2467–2477.

Klysner, R., Bent-Hansen, J., Hansen, H. L., Lunde, M., Pleidrup, E., Poulsen, D. L., Andersen, M., & Petersen, H. E. (2002). Efficacy of citalopram in the prevention of recurrent depression in elderly patients: Placebo-controlled study of maintenance therapy. *British Journal of Psychiatry, 181,* 29–35.

Knight, S., Bermingham, M. A., & Mahajan, D. (1999). Regular non-vigorous physical activity and cholesterol levels in the elderly. *Gerontology, 45,* 213–219.

Knoester, C., & Eggebeen, D. J. (2006). The effects of the transition to parenthood and subsequent children on men's well-being and social participation. *Journal of Family Issues, 27,* 1532–1560.

Knopman, D. S., Parisi, J. E., Salviati, A., Floriach-Robert, M., Boeve, B. F., Ivnik, R. J., Smith, G. E., Dickson, D. W., Johnson, K. A., Peterson, L. E., McDonald, W. C., Braak, H., & Petersen, R. C. (2003). Neuropathology of cognitively normal elderly. *Journal of Neuropathology and Experimental Neurology, 62,* 1087–1095.

Koropeckyj-Cox, T. (2002). Beyond parental status: Psychological well-being in middle and old age. *Journal of Marriage and the Family, 64,* 957–971.

Kosek, D. J., Kim, J.-S., Petrella, J. K., Cross, J. M., & Bamman, M. M. (2006). Efficacy of 3 days/wk resistance training on myofiber hypertrophy and myogenic mechanisms in young vs. older adults. *Journal of Applied Physiology, 101,* 531–544.

Kosloski, K., Ekerdt, D., & DeViney, S. (2001). The role of job-related rewards in retirement planning. *Journal of Gerontology: Psychological Sciences, 56B,* P160–P169.

Koster, A., Bosma, H., Kempen, G. I., Penninx, B. W., Beekman, A. T., Deeg, D. J., & van Eijk, J. T. (2006). Socioeconomic differences in incident depression in older adults: The role of psychosocial factors, physical health status, and behavioral factors. *Journal of Psychosomatic Research, 61,* 619–627.

Kostka, T. (2005). Quadriceps maximal power and optimal shortening velocity in 335 men aged 23–88 years. *European Journal of Applied Physiology, 95,* 140–145.

Kozbelt, A. (2007). A quantitative analysis of Beethoven as self-critic: Implications for psychological theories of musical creativity. *Psychology of Music, 35,* 144–168.

Kramer, A. F., Boot, W. R., McCarley, J. S., Peterson, M. S., Colcombe, A., & Scialfa, C. T. (2006). Aging, memory and visual search. *Acta Psychologica, 122,* 288–304.

Kramer, A. F., Colcombe, S. J., McAuley, E., Scalf, P. E., & Erickson, K. I. (2005). Fitness, aging and neurocognitive function. *Neurobiology of Aging, 26 Suppl 1,* 124–127.

Krause, K. H. (2007). Aging: A revisited theory based on free radicals generated by NOX family NADPH oxidases. *Experimental Gerontology 42,* 256–262.

Kreider, R. M. (2005a). *Living arrangements of children: 2001.* Washington, DC: U.S. Bureau of the Census.

Kreider, R. M. (2005b). *Number, timing, and duration of marriages: 2001.* Washington, DC: U.S. Bureau of the Census.

Kril, J. J., Patel, S., Harding, A. J., & Halliday, G. M. (2002). Neuron loss from the hippocampus of Alzheimer's disease exceeds extracellular neurofibrillary tangle formation. *Acta Neuropathologica (Berlin), 103,* 370–376.

Kripke, D. F., Garfinkel, L., Wingard, D. L., Klauber, M. R., & Marler, M. R. (2002). Mortality associated with sleep duration and insomnia. *Archives of General Psychiatry, 59,* 131–136.

Krumholz, H. M., Butler, J., Miller, J., Vaccarino, V., Williams, C. S., Mendes de Leon, C. F., Seeman, T. E., Kasl, S. V., & Berkman, L. F. (1998). Prognostic importance of emotional support for elderly patients hospitalized with heart failure. *Circulation, 97,* 958–964.

Kübler-Ross, E. (1969). *On death and dying.* New York: MacMillan.

Kubo, N., Kato, A., & Nakamura, K. (2006). Deterioration of planning ability with age in Japanese monkeys (Macaca fuscata). *Journal of Comparative Psychology, 120,* 449–455.

Kubzansky, L. D., Cole, S. R., Kawachi, I., Vokonas, P., & Sparrow, D. (2006). Shared and unique contributions of anger, anxiety, and depression to coronary heart disease: A prospective study in the Normative Aging Study. *Annals of Behavioral Medicine, 31,* 21–29.

Kubzansky, L. D., Koenen, K. C., Spiro, A. 3rd, Vokonas, P. S., & Sparrow, D. (2007). Prospective study of posttraumatic stress disorder symptoms and coronary heart disease in the Normative Aging Study. *Archives of General Psychiatry, 64,* 109–116.

Kudielka, B. M., Schmidt-Reinwald, A. K., Hellhammer, D. H., Schurmeyer, T., & Kirschbaum, C. (2000). Psychosocial stress and HPA functioning: No evidence for a reduced resilience in healthy elderly men. *Stress, 3,* 229–240.

Kunzmann, U., & Grühn, D. (2005). Age differences in emotional reactivity: The sample case of sadness. *Psychology and Aging, 20*, 47–59.

Kuzuya, M., Ando, F., Iguchi, A., & Shimokata, H. (2006). Effect of smoking habit on age-related changes in serum lipids: A cross-sectional and longitudinal analysis in a large Japanese cohort. *Atherosclerosis, 185*, 183–190.

Kwan, C. M., Love, G. D., Ryff, C. D., & Essex, M. J. (2003). The role of self-enhancing evaluations in a successful life transition. *Psychology and Aging, 18*, 3–12.

Kyle, U. G., Gremion, G., Genton, L., Slosman, D. O., Golay, A., & Pichard, C. (2001). Physical activity and fat-free and fat mass by bioelectrical impedance in 3853 adults. *Medicine and Science in Sports and Exercise, 33*, 576–584.

Labouvie-Vief, G., & Medler, M. (2002). Affect optimization and affect complexity: Modes and styles of regulation in adulthood. *Psychology and Aging, 17*, 571–588.

Lachman, M. E. (2004). Development in midlife. *Annual Review of Psychology, 55*, 305–331.

Lachman, M. E. (2006). Perceived control over aging-related declines. *Current Directions in Psychological Science, 15*, 282–286.

Lachman, M. E., & Andreoletti, C. (2006). Strategy use mediates the relationship between control beliefs and memory performance for middle-aged and older adults. *Journal of Gerontology: Psychological Sciences, 61B*, P88–P94.

Lachman, M. E., Andreoletti, C., & Pearman, A. (2006). Memory control beliefs: How are they related to age, strategy use and memory improvement? *Social Cognition, 24*, 359–385.

Lachman, M. E., Neupert, S. D., Bertrand, R., & Jette, A. M. (2006). The effects of strength training on memory in older adults. *Journal of Aging and Physical Activity, 14*, 59–73.

Lachman, M. E., Weaver, S. L., Bandura, M., Elliott, E., & Lewkowicz, C. J. (1992). Improving memory and control beliefs through cognitive restructuring and self-generated strategies. *Journal of Gerontology: Psychological Sciences, 47B*, P293–P299.

Lachs, M. S., Williams, C. S., O'Brien, S., Pillemer, K. A., & Charlson, M. E. (1998). The mortality of elder mistreatment. *Journal of the American Medical Association, 280*, 428–432.

Lamme, S., Dykstra, P. A., & Broese Van Groenou, M. I. (1996). Rebuilding the network: New relationships in widowhood. *Personal Relationships, 3*, 337–349.

Lang, F. R., & Carstensen, L. L. (1994). Close emotional relationships in late life: Further support for proactive aging in the social domain. *Psychology and Aging, 9*, 315–324.

Lang, F. R., & Carstensen, L. L. (2002). Time counts: Future time perspective, goals, and social relationships. *Psychology and Aging, 17*, 125–139.

Lantz, P. M., House, J. S., Lepkowski, J. M., Williams, D. R., Mero, R. P., & Chen, J. (1998). Socioeconomic factors, health behaviors, and mortality: Results from a nationally representative prospective study of U.S. adults. *Journal of the American Medical Association, 279*, 1703–1708.

Lau, A. W., & Gallagher-Thompson, D. (2002). Ethnic minority older adults in clinical and research programs: Issues and recommendations. *Behavior Therapist, 25*, 10–11.

Laub, J. H., & Vaillant, G. E. (2000). Delinquency and mortality: A 50-year follow-up study of 1,000 delinquent and nondelinquent boys. *American Journal of Psychiatry, 157*, 96–102.

Lavender, A. P., & Nosaka, K. (2007). Fluctuations of isometric force after eccentric exercise of the elbow flexors of young, middle-aged, and old men. *European Journal of Applied Physiology.*

Lawlor, D. A., Martin, R. M., Gunnell, D., Galobardes, B., Ebrahmin, S., Sandhu, J., Ben-Shlomo, Y., McCarron, P., & Davey Smith, G. (2006). Association of body mass index measured in childhood, adolescence, and young adulthood with risk of ischemic heart disease and stroke: findings from 3 historical cohort studies. *American Journal of Clinical Nutrition, 83*, 767–773.

Lawrence, J., & Leyva, J., (2006). Randomized, controlled, six-month trial of yoga in healthy seniors: Effects on cognition and quality of life. *Alternative Therapies in Health and Medicine, 12*, 40–47.

Lawton, M. P., & Nahemow, L. (1973). Ecology and the aging process. In C. Eisdorfer & M. P. Lawton (Eds.), *The psychology of adult development and aging*. Washington, DC: American Psychological Association.

Lease, S. H. (1998). Annual review, 1993–1997: Work attitudes and outcomes. *Journal of Vocational Behavior, 53*, 154–183.

Lee, G. R., & Bulanda, J. R. (2005). Change and consistency in the relation of marital status to personal happiness. *Marriage and Family Review, 38*, 69–84.

Lee, M. S., Lee, K. H., Sin, H. S., Um, S. J., Kim, J. W., & Koh, B. K. (2006). A newly synthesized photostable retinol derivative (retinyl N-formyl aspartamate) for photodamaged skin: profilometric evaluation of 24-week study. *Journal of the American Academy of Dermatology, 55*, 220–224.

Lehman, H. C. (1953). *Age and achievement*. Princeton, NJ: Princeton University Press.

Lenze, E. J., Munin, M. C., Skidmore, E. R., Dew, M. A., Rogers, J. C., Whyte, E. M., Quear, T., Begley, A., & Reynolds, C. F., 3rd. (2007). Onset of depression in elderly persons after hip feature: Implications for prevention and early interventio n of late-life depression. *Journal of the American Geriatrics Society, 55,* 81–86.

Leonardelli, G. J., Hermann, A. D., Lynch, M. E., & Arkin, R. M. (2003). The shape of self-evaluation: Implicit theories of intelligence and judgments of intellectual ability. *Journal of Research in Personality, 37,* 141–168.

Lerner, R. M., (1995). Developing individuals within changing contexts: Implications of developmental contextualism for human development, research, policy, and programs. In T. J. Kindermann & J. Valsiner (Eds.), *Development of person-context relations* (pp. 13–37). Hillsdale, NJ: Lawrence Erlbaum.

Lerner, R. M. (2003). What are SES effects effects of? A developmental systems perspective. In M. H. Bornstein & R. H. Bradley (Eds.), *Socioeconomic status, parenting, and child development.* Mahwah, NJ: Lawrence Erlbaum Associates.

Letenneur, L., Proust-Lima, C., Le George, A., Dartigues, J. F., & Barberger-Gateau, P. (2007). Flavonoid intake and cognitive decline over a 10-year period. *American Journal of Epidemiology, 165,* 1364–1371.

Lethbridge-Cejku, M., Rose, D., & Vickerie, J. (2006). Summary health statistics for U.S.Adults: National Health Interview Survey, 2004. *National Center for Health Statistics Vital Health Statistics, 10* (228).

Leveille, S. G. (2004). Musculoskeletal aging. *Current Opinions in Rheumatology, 16,* 114–118.

Levey, A., Lah, J., Goldstein, F., Steenland, K., & Bliwise, D. (2006). Mild cognitive impairment: An opportunity to identify patients at high risk for progression to Alzheimer's disease. *Clinical Therapeutics, 28,* 991–1001.

Levinson, D. J., Darrow, C. N., Klein, E. B., Levinson, M. H., & McKee, B. (1978). *The seasons of a man's life.* New York: Alfred A. Knopf.

Levinson, D. J., & Levinson, J. D. (1996). *The seasons of a woman's life.* New York: Knopf.

Levy, B. R., Slade, M. D., Kunkel, S. R., & Kasl, S. V. (2002). Longevity increased by positive self-perceptions of aging. *Journal of Personality and Social Psychology, 83,* 261–270.

Li, G., Cherrier, M. M., Tsuang, D. W., Petrie, E. C., Colasurdo, E. A., Craft, S., Schellenberg, G. D., Peskind, E. R., Raskind, M. A., & Wilkinson, C. W. (2006). Salivary cortisol and memory function in human aging. *Neurobiology of Aging, 27,* 1705–1714.

Lichtenburg, P. A., MacNeill, S. E., Lysack, C. L. B., Adam L, & Neufeld, S. W. (2003). Predicting discharge and long-term outcome patterns for frail elders. *Rehabilitation Psychology, 48,* 37–43.

Licht-Strunk, E., van der Windt, D. A., van Marwijk, H. W., de Haan, M., & Beekman, A. T. (2007). The prognosis of depression in older patients in general practice and the community. A systematic review. *Family Practice, 24,* 168–180.

Lindauer, M. S. (1998). Artists, art, and arts activities: What do they tell us about aging? In C. Adams-Price (Ed.), *Creativity and successful aging: Theoretical and empirical approaches* (pp. 237–250). New York: Springer.

Lindstrom, T. C. (1995). Experiencing the presence of the dead: Discrepancies in "the sensing experience" and their psychological concomitants. *Omega—Journal of Death and Dying,* 11–21

Lipton, S. A. (2006). Paradigm shift in neuroprotection by NMDA receptor blockade: Memantine and beyond. *Nature Reviews: Drug Discovery, 5,* 160–170.

LoConto, D. G. (1998). Death and dreams: A sociological approach to grieving and identity. *Omega—Journal of Death & Dying, 37,* 171–185

Loevinger, J. (1976). *Ego development: Conceptions and theories.* San Francisco: Jossey-Bass.

Lohr, J. B., Alder, M., Flynn, K., Harris, M. J., & McAdams, L. A. (1997). Minor physical anomalies in older patients with late-onset schizophrenia, early-onset schizophrenia, depression, and Alzheimer's disease. *American Journal of Geriatric Psychiatry, 5,* 318–323.

Lombardi, G., Tauchmanova, L., Di Somma, C., Musella, T., Rota, F., Savanelli, M. C., & Colao, A. (2005). Somatopause: Dismetabolic and bone effects. *Journal of Endocrinological Investigation, 28,* 36–42.

Longcope, C., Feldman, H. A., McKinlay, J. B., & Araujo, A. B. (2000). Diet and sex hormone-binding globulin. *Journal of Clinical Endocrinology and Metabolism, 85,* 293–296.

Lott, L. A., Schneck, M. E., Haegerstrom-Portnoy, G., Brabyn, J. A., Gildengorin, G. L., & West, C. G. (2001). Reading performance in older adults with good acuity. *Optometry Vision Science, 78,* 316–324.

Lovasi, G. S., Lemaitre, R. N., Siscovick, D. S., Dublin, S., Bis, J. C., Lumley, T., Heckbert, S. R., Smith, N. L., & Psaty, B. M. (2007). Amount of leisure-time physical activity and risk of nonfatal myocardial infarction. *Annuals of Epidemiology, 17,* 410–416.

Low, K. S. D., Yoon, M., Roberts, B. W., & Rounds, J. (2005). The stability of vocational interests from early adolescence to middle adulthood: A quantitative review of longitudinal studies. *Psychological Bulletin, 131,* 713–737.

Lubart, T. I., & Sternberg, R. J. (1998). Life span creativity: An investment theory approach. In C. Adams-Price (Ed.), *Creativity and successful aging: Theoretical and empirical approaches* (pp. 21–41). New York: Springer.

Luber, G. E., & Sanchez, C. A. (2006). Heat-related deaths—United States, 1999–2003. *Morbidity and Mortality Weekly Report, 55,* 796–798.

Luborsky, M. R. (1998). Creative challenges and the construction of meaningful life narratives. In C. Adams-Price (Ed.), *Creativity and successful aging: Theoretical and empirical approaches* (pp. 311–337). New York: Springer.

Luborsky, M. R., & McMullen, C. K. (1999). Culture and aging. In J. C. Cavanaugh & S. K. Whitbourne (Eds.), *Gerontology: Interdisciplinary perspectives* (pp. 65–90). New York: Oxford University Press.

Lucas, R. E., Clark, A. E., Georgellis, Y., & Diener, E. (2003). Reexamining adaptation and the set point model of happiness: Reactions to changes in marital status. *Journal of Personality and Social Psychology, 84,* 527–539.

Luckenhoff, C. E., & Carstensen, L. L. (2007). Aging, emotion, and health-related decision strategies: Motivational manipulations can reduce age differences. *Psychology and Aging, 22,* 134–146.

Luoh, M. C., & Herzog, A. R. (2002a). Individual consequences of volunteer and paid work in old age: Health and mortality. *Journal of Health and Social Behavior, 43,* 490–509.

Luoh, M.-C., & Herzog, A. R. (2002b). Individual consequences of volunteer and paid work in old age: Health and mortality. *Journal of Health and Social Behavior, 43,* 490–509.

Lupien, S., Lecours, A. R., Schwartz, G., Sharma, S., Hauger, R. L., Meaney, M. J., & Nair, N. P. (1996). Longitudinal study of basal cortisol levels in healthy elderly subjects: Evidence for subgroups. *Neurobiology of Aging, 17,* 95–105.

Lupsakko, T., Mantyjarvi, M., Kautiainen, H., & Sulkava, R. (2002). Combined hearing and visual impairment and depression in a population aged 75 years and older. *International Journal of Geriatric Psychiatry, 17,* 808–813.

Lutgendorf, S. K., Russell, D., Ullrich, P., Harris, T. B., & Wallace, R. (2004). Religious participation, interleukin-6, and mortality in older adults. *Health Psychology, 23,* 465–475.

Lynn, J. (1996). Caring at the end of our lives. *New England Journal of Medicine, 335,* 201–202.

Lynn, J., Teno, J. M., Phillips, R. S., Wu, A. W., Desbiens, N., Harrold, J., Claessens, M. T., Wenger, N., Kreling, B., &

Connors, A. F., Jr. (1997). Perceptions by family members of the dying experience of older and seriously ill patients. SUPPORT Investigators. Study to Understand Prognoses and Preferences for Ourcomes and Risks of Treatments. *Annals of Internal Medicine, 126,* 97–106.

Lyons, H. Z., & O'Brien, K. M. (2006). The role of person-environment fit in the job satisfaction and tenure intentions of African American employees. *Journal of Counseling Psychology, 53,* 387–396.

Macintyre, S. (1997). The Black report and beyond: What are the issues? *Social Science and Medicine, 44,* 723–745.

Mackay, J., & Mensah, G. A. (2006). *The atlas of heart disease and stroke*: World Health Organization and Centers for Disease Control and Prevention.

Madden, D. J. (2001). Speed and timing of behavioural processes. In J. E. Birren & K. W. Schaie (Eds.), *Handbook of the psychology of aging* (5th ed., pp. 288–312). San Diego, CA: Academic Press.

Magai, C., Consedine, N. S., Gillespie, M., O'Neal, C., & Vilker, R. (2004). The differential roles of early emotion socialization and adult attachment in adult emotional experience: Testing a mediator hypothesis. *Attachment and Human Development, 6,* 389–417.

Magai, C., Consedine, N. S., Krivoshekova, Y. S., Kudadjie-Gyamfi, E., & McPherson, R. (2006). Emotion experience and expression across the adult life span: Insights from a multimodal assessment study. *Psychology and Aging, 21,* 303–317.

Magnusson, D. (Ed.). (1996). *The lifespan development of individuals: Behavioral, neurobiological, and psychosocial perspectives: A synthesis.* New York: Cambridge University Press.

Mahlberg, R., Tilmann, A., Salewski, L., & Kunz, D. (2006). Normative data on the daily profile of urinary 6-sulfatoxymelatonin in healthy subjects between the ages of 20 and 84. *Psychoneuroendocrinology, 31,* 634–641.

Malhi, G. S., Mitchell, P. B., & Salim, S. (2003). Bipolar depression: Management options. *CNS Drugs, 17,* 9–25.

Malmstrom, T., & LaVoie, D. J. (2002). Age differences in inhibition of schema-activated distractors. *Experimental Aging Research, 28,* 281–298.

Mancini, A. D., & Bonanno, G. A. (2006). Marital closeness, functional disability, and adjustment in late life. *Psychology and Aging, 21,* 600–610.

Manning, J. S. (2003). Difficult-to-treat depressions: a primary care perspective. *Journal of Clinical Psychiatry, 64 Supplement 1,* 24–31.

Mannino, D. M., Homa, D. M., Akinbami, L. J., Ford, E. S., & Redd, S. C. (2002). Chronic Obstructive Pulmonary Disease surveillance—United States, 1971–2000. *Morbidity and Mortality Weekly Report, 51*, No. SS–6.

Manton, K. G., Corder, L., & Stallard, E. (1997). Chronic disability trends in elderly United States populations: 1982–1994. *Proceedings of the National Academy of Sciences, USA, 94*, 2593–2598.

Manzoli, L., Villari, P., M Pirone, G., & Boccia, A. (2007). Marital status and mortality in the elderly: A systematic review and meta-analysis. *Social Science & Medicine, 64*, 77–94.

Marcell, T. J. (2003). Sarcopenia: Causes, consequences, and preventions. *Journal of Gerontology Medical Sciences, 58A*, M911–M916.

Marcus, B. H., Williams, D. M., Dubbert, P. M., Sallis, J. F., King, A. C., Yancey, A. K., Franklin, B. A., Buchner, D., Daniels, S. R., & Claytor, R. P. (2006). Physical activity intervention studies: What we know and what we need to know: A scientific statement form the American Heart Association Council on Nutrition, Physical Activity, and Metabolism (Subcommittee on Physical Activity); Council on Cardiovascular Disease in the Young; and the Interdisciplinary Working Group on Quality of Care and Outcomes Research. *Circulation, 114*, 2739–2752.

Markman, H., & Hahlweg, K. (1993). The prediction and prevention of marital distress. *Clinical Psychology Review, 13*, 29–43.

Markus, H., & Nurius, P. (1986). Possible selves. *American Psychologist, 41*, 954–969.

Maron, B. J., Araujo, C. G., Thompson, P. D., Fletcher, G. F., de Luna, A. B., Fleg, J. L., Pelliccia, A., Balady, G. J., Furlanello, F., Van Camp, S. P., Elosua, R., Chaitman, B. R., & Bazzarre, T. L. (2001). Recommendations for preparticipation screening and the assessment of cardiovascular disease in masters athletes: An advisory for healthcare professionals from the working groups of the World Heart Federation, the International Federation of Sports Medicine, and the American Heart Association Committee on Exercise, Cardiac Rehabilitation, and Prevention. *Circulation, 103*, 327–334.

Marshall, V. W. (1980). *Last chapters: A sociology of aging and dying.* Monterey, CA: Brooks-Cole.

Marsiglio, W. (1992). Stepfathers with minor children living at home: Parenting perceptions and relationship quality. *Journal of Family Issues, 13*, 195–214.

Marsiglio, W., Amato, P., Day, R. D., & Lamb, M. E. (2002). Scholarship on fatherhood in the 1990s and beyond. *Journal of Marriage and the Family, 62*, 1173–1191.

Marsiske, M., & Margrett, J. A. (2006). Everyday problem solving and decision making. In J. E. Birren & K. W. Schaire (Eds.), *Handbook of the psychology of aging* (pp. 315–342): Elsevier.

Martens, A., Greenberg, J., Schimel, J., & Landau, M. J. (2004). Ageism and death: Effects of mortality salience and perceived similarity to elders on reactions to elderly people. *Personality and Social Psychology Bulletin, 30*, 1524–1536.

Martin, J. A., Hamilton, B. E., Sutton, P. D., Ventura, S. J., Menaker, F., & Kirmeyer, S. (2006). Births: Final data for 2004. *National Vital Statistics Reports, 55* (1).

Martin, L. R., Friedman, H. S., Tucker, J. S., Tomlinson-Keasey, C., Criqui, M. H., & Schwartz, J. E. (2002). A life course perspective on childhood cheerfulness and its relation to mortality risk. *Personality & Social Psychology Bulletin, 28*, 1155–1165.

Martin, M. D., Hancock, G. A., Richardson, B., Simmons, P., Katona, C., Mullan, E., & Orrell, M. (2002). An evaluation of needs in elderly continuing-care settings. *International Psychogeriatrics, 14*, 379–388.

Martire, L. M., Stephens, M. A. P., & Townsend, A. L. (1998). Emotional support and well-being of midlife women: Role-specific mastery as a mediational mechanism. *Psychology and Aging, 13*, 396–404.

Masayesva, B. G., Mambo, E., Taylor, R. J., Goloubeva, O. G., Zhou, S., Cohen, Y., Minhas, K., Koch, W., Sciubba, J., Alberg, A. J., Sidransky, D., & Califano, J. (2006). Mitochondrial DNA contest increase in response to cigarette smoking. *Cancer Epidemiology Biomarkers and Prevention, 15*, 19–24.

Mast, B. T., Fitzgerald, J., Steinberg, J., MacNeill, S. E., & Lichtenberg, P. A. (2001). Effective screening for Alzheimer's disease among older African Americans. *Clinical Neuropsychologist*, 196–202.

Mast, B. T., MacNeill, S. E., & Lichtenberg, P. A. (2002). A MIMIC model approach to research in geriatric neuropsychology: The case of vascular dementia. *Aging, Neuropsychology, & Cognition, 9*, 21–37.

Masunaga, H., & Horn, J. (2000). Characterizing mature human intelligence: Expertise development. *Learning & Individual Differences, 12*, 5–33.

Matthews, L., Wickrama, K., & Conger, R. (1996). Predicting marital instability from spouse and observer reports of marital interaction. *Journal of Marriage and the Family, 58*, 641–655.

Matthews, S. H. (1986). *Friendships through the life course.* Beverly Hills, CA: Sage.

Maurer, T. J. (2001). Career-relevant learning and development, worker age, and beliefs about self-efficacy for development. *Journal of Management, 27*, 123–140.

Mayhew, P. M., Thomas, C. D., Clement, J. G., Loveridge, N., Beck, T. J., Bonfield, W., Burgoyne, C. J., & Reeve, J. (2005). Relation between age, femoral neck cortical stability, and hip fracture risk. *Lancet, 366*, 129–135.

McArdle, J. J., Ferrer-Caja, E., Hamagami, F., & Woodcock, R. W. (2002). Comparative longitudinal structural analyses of the growth and decline of multiple intellectual abilities over the life span. *Developmental Psychology, 38*, 115–142.

McArdle, J. J., & Hamagami, F. (2006). Longitudinal tests of dynamic hypotheses on intellectual abilities measured over sixty years. In C. S. Bergeman & S. M. Boker (Eds.), *Methodological issues in aging research.* (pp. 43–98): Mahweh, NJ: Lawrence Erlbaum.

McAuley, E., Marquez, D. X., Jerome, G. J., Blissmer, B., & Katula, J. (2002). Physical activity and physique anxiety in older adults: Fitness, and efficacy influences. *Aging and Mental Health, 6*, 222–230.

McCabe, L., Cairney, J., Veldhuizen, S., Herrmann, N., & Streiner, D. L. (2006). Prevalence and correlates of agoraphobia in older adults. *American Journal of Geriatric Psychiatry, 14*, 515–522.

McCrae, R. R. (2002). The maturation of personality psychology: Adult personality development and psychological well-being. *Journal of Research in Personality, 36*, 307–317.

McCrae, R. R., & Costa, P. T. J. (2003). *Personality in adulthood: A five-factor theory perspective.* (2d ed.) New York: Guilford.

McDaniel, M. A., & Snell, A. F. (1999). Holland's theory and occupational information. *Journal of Vocational Behavior, 55*, 74–85.

McDonald-Miszczak, L., Hertzog, C., & Hultsch, D. F. (1995). Stability and accuracy of metamemory in adulthood and aging: A longitudinal analysis. *Psychology and Aging, 10*, 553–564.

McGue, M., & Christensen, K. (2002). The heritability of level and rate-of-change in cognitive functioning in Danish twins aged 70 years and older. *Experimental Aging Research, 28*, 435–451.

McKeith, I. G. (2006). Consensus guidelines for the clinical and pathologic diagnosis of dementia with Lewy bodies (DLB): Report of the Consortium on DLB International Workshop. *Journal of Alzheimers' Disease, 9*, 417–423.

McKhann, G., Drachman, D., Folstein, M., Katzman, R., Price, D., & Stadlan, E. M. (1984). Clinical diagnosis of Alzheimer's Disease: Report of the NINCDS-ADRDA Work Group under the auspices of Department of Health and Human Services Task Force on Alzheimer's Disease. *Neurology, 34*, 939–944.

McKiernan, F. (1996). Bereavement and attitudes toward death. In R. T. Woods (Ed.), *Handbook of the clinical psychology of ageing* (pp. 159–182). Chichester, England: Wiley.

Meeks, S. (2000). Schizophrenia and related disorders. In S. K. Whitbourne (Ed.), *Psychopathology in later life* (pp. 189–215). New York: Wiley.

Mehta, K. M., Yaffe, K., Brenes, G. A., Newman, A. B., Shorr, R. I., Simonsick, E. M., Ayonayon, H. N., Rubin, S. M., & Covinsky, K. E. (2007). Anxiety symptoms and decline in physical function over 5 years in the health, aging and body composition study. *Journal of the American Geriatrics Society, 55*, 265–270.

Mellstrom, D., Johnell, O., Ljunggren, O., Eriksson, A. L., Lorentzon, M., Mallmin, H., Holmberg, A., Redlund-Johnell, I., Orwoll, E., & Ohlsson, C. (2006). Free testosterone is an independent predictor of BMD and prevalent fractures in elderly men: MrOS Sweden. *Journal of Bone and Mineral Research, 21*, 529–535.

Michalos, A. C. (1985). Multiple discrepancies theory (MDT). *Social Indicators Research, 16*, 347–413.

Mickelson, K. D., Kessler, R. C., & Shaver, P. R. (1997). Adult attachment in a nationally representative sample. *Journal of Personality and Social Psychology, 73*, 1092–1106.

Miller, P. J. E., Niehuis, S., & Huston, T. L. (2006). Positive illusions in marital relationships: A 13-year longitudinal study. *Personality and Social Psychology Bulletin, 32*, 1579–1594.

Miller, S. C., Papandonatos, G., Fennell, M., & Mor, V. (2006). Facility and county effects on racial differences in nursing home quality indicators. *Social Science and Medicine, 63*, 3046–3059.

Milton, R. C., Sperduto, R. D., Clemons, T. E., & Ferris, F. L. 3rd. (2006). Centrum use and progression of age-related cataract in the Age-Related Eye Disease Study: A propensity score approach. AREDS report No. 21. *Ophthalmology, 113*, 1264–1270.

Min, H., Montecino-Rodriguez, E., & Dorshkind, K. (2005). Effects of aging on early B- and T-cell development. *Immunological Reviews, 205*, 7–17.

Miner-Rubino, K., Winter, D. G., & Stewart, A. J. (2004). Gender, social class, and the subjective experience of aging: Self-perceived personality change from early adulthood to late midlife. *Personality and Social Psychology Bulletin, 30*, 1599–1610.

Miniño, A. M., Heron, M., Smith, B. L., & Kochanek, K. D. (2006). Deaths: Final data for 2004. Health E-Stats. Released November 24, 2006.

Mireles, D. E., & Charness, N. (2002). Computational explorations of the influence of structured knowledge on age-related cognitive decline. *Psychology and Aging, 17*, 245–259.

Mitchell, A. J., & Subramaniam, H. (2005). Prognosis of depression in old age compared to middle age: A systematic review of comparative studies. *American Journal of Psychiatry, 162*, 1588–1601.

Moen, P. (1996). A life course perspective on retirement, gender, and well-being. *Journal of Occupational Health Psychology, 1*, 131–144.

Moen, P., Kim, J. E., & Hofmeister, H. (2001). Couples' work/retirement transitions, gender, and marital quality. *Social Psychology Quarterly, 64*, 55–71.

Moffat, S. D., Elkins, W., & Resnick, S. M. (2006). Age differences in the neural systems supporting human allocentric spatial navigation. *Neurobiology of Aging, 27*, 965–972.

Mohlman, J., & Price, R. (2006). Recognizing and treating late-life generalized anxiety disorder: Distinguishing features and psychosocial treatment. *Expert Reviews in Neurotherapy, 6*, 1439–1445.

Montero-Odasso, M., & Duque, G. (2005). Vitamin D in the aging musculoskeletal system: An authentic strength preserving hormone. *Molecular Aspects of Medicine, 26*, 203–219.

Moore, D. E., & Hayward, M. D. (1990). Occupational careers and mortality of elderly men. *Demography, 27*, 31–53.

Moore, P. J., Adler, N. E., Williams, D. R., & Jackson, J. S. (2002). Socioeconomic status and health: The role of sleep. *Psychosomatic Medicine, 64*, 337–344.

Moorman, S. M., Booth, A., & Fingerman, K. L. (2006). Women's romantic relationships after widowhood. *Journal of Family Issues, 27*, 1281–1304.

Moos, R. H., Schutte, K., Brennan, P., & Moos, B. S. (2004). Ten-year patterns of alcohol consumption and drinking problems among older women and men. *Addiction, 99*, 829–838.

Morais, J. A., Chevalier, S., & Gougeon, R. (2006). Protein turnover and requirements in the healthy and frail elderly. *Journal of Nutrition, Health and Aging, 10*, 272–283.

Morgan, W. K., & Reger, R. B. (2000). Rise and fall of the FEV(1). *Chest, 118*, 1639–1644.

Morris, M. C., Evans, D. A., Tangney, C. C., Bienias, J. L., & Wilson, R. S. (2005). Fish consumption and cognitive decline with age in a large community study. *Archives of Neurology, 62*, 1849–1853.

Morrow, D. G., Menard, W. E., Stine-Morrow, E. A., Teller, T., & Bryant, D. (2001). The influence of expertise and task factors on age differences in pilot communication. *Psychology and Aging, 16*, 31–46.

Morse, C. I., Thom, J. M., Reeves, N. D., Birch, K. M., & Narici, M. V. (2005). In vivo physiological cross-sectional area and specific force are reduced in the gastrocnemius of elderly men. *Journal of Applied Physiology, 99*, 1050–1055.

Morse, J. Q., & Lynch, T. R. (2004). A preliminary investigation of self-reported personality disorders in late life: Prevalence, predictors of depressive severity, and clinical correlates. *Aging and Mental Health, 8*, 307–315.

Moss, M. S., Resch, N., & Moss, S. Z. (1997). The role of gender in middle-age children's responses to parent death. *Omega—Journal of Death & Dying, 35*, 43–65.

Motta, M., Bennati, E., Ferlito, L., Malaguarnera, M., & Motta, L. (2005). Successful aging in centenarians: Myths and reality. *Archives of Gerontology and Geriatrics, 40*, 241–251.

Mottram, P. G., Wilson, K. C., Ashworth, L., & Abou-Saleh, M. (2002). The clinical profile of older patients' response to antidepressants—an open trial of sertraline. *International Journal of Geriatric Psychiatry, 17*, 574–578.

Mount, M. K., Barrick, M. R., Scullen, S. M., & Rounds, J. (2005). Higher-order dimensions of the big five personality traits and the big six vocational interest types. *Personnel Psychology, 58*, 447–478.

Mroczek, D. K., & Kolarz, C. M. (1998). The effect of age on positive and negative affect: A developmental perspective on happiness. *Journal of Personality and Social Psychology, 75*, 1333–1349.

Mroczek, D. K., & Spiro, A. 3rd. (2005). Change in life satisfaction during adulthood: Findings from the Veterans Affairs Normative Aging Study. *Journal of Personality and Social Psychology, 88*, 189–202.

Mroczek, D. K., Spiro, A. 3rd., & Griffin, P. W. (2006). Personality and aging. In J. E. Birren & K. W. Schaie (Eds.), *Handbook of the psychology of aging* (pp. 363–377). London: Elsevier.

Muchinsky, P. (1999). Application of Holland's theory in industrial and organizational settings. *Journal of Vocational Behavior, 55*, 127–125.

Mueller, M. M., Wilhelm, B., & Elder, G. H. Jr. (2002). Variations in grandparenting. *Research on Aging, 24*, 360–388.

Mukesh, B. N., Le, A., Dimitrov, P. N., Ahmed, S., Taylor, H. R., & McCarty, C. A. (2006). Development of cataract and associated risk factors: The Visual Impairment Project. *Archives of Ophthalmology*, *124*, 79–85.

Munson, M. L. (1999). Characteristics of elderly home health care users: Data from the 1996 National Home and Hospice Care Survey. *Advance Data from Vital and Health Statistics of the Centers for Disease Control and Prevention*, Number 309, December 22, 1999.

Murphy, C., Schubert, C. R., Cruickshanks, K. J., Klein, B. E., Klein, R., & Nondahl, D. M. (2002). Prevalence of olfactory impairment in older adults. *Journal of the American Medical Association*, *288*, 2307–2312.

Murphy, D. R., Daneman, M., & Schneider, B. A. (2006). Why do older adults have difficulty following conversations? *Psychology and Aging*, *21*, 49–61.

Mutran, E. J., Reitzes, D. C., & Fernandez, M. E. (1997). Factors that influence attitudes toward retirement. *Research on Aging*, *19*, 251–273.

Nadien, M. B. (2006). Factors that influence abusive interactions between aging women and their caregivers. *Annals of the New York Academy of Sciences*, *1087*, 158–169.

Nakanishi, N., Suzuki, K., & Tatara, K. (2003). Alcohol consumption and risk for development of impaired fasting glucose or Type 2 diabetes in middle-aged Japanese men. *Diabetes Care*, *26*, 48–54.

Narici, M. V., & Maganaris, C. N. (2006). Adaptability of elderly human muscles and tendons to increased loading. *Journal of Anatomy*, *208*, 433–443.

National Center for Health Statistics (2006). National Nursing Home Survey (NNHS). http://www.cdc.gov/nchs/about/major/nnhsd/Facilitytables.htm

National Highway Traffic Safety Administration (2005). Traffic Safety Facts. Insurance Institute for Highway Safety and Highway Loss Data Institute (2007). *Fatality facts 2005: Teenagers*.

National Institute on Alcohol Abuse and Alcoholism (1998). Alcohol and aging. *Alcohol Alert*, *40*.

National Institute for Mental Health (2005). Depression: What every woman should know. http://www.nimh.nih.gov/publicat/NIMHdepwomenknows.pdf.

Nelson, E. A., & Dannefer, D. (1992). Aged heterogeneity: Fact or fiction? The fate of diversity in gerontological research. *Gerontologist*, *32*, 17–23.

Ness, J., Aronow, W. S., & Beck, G. (2006). Menopausal symptoms after cessation of hormone replacement therapy. *Maturitas*, *53*, 356–361.

Neugarten, B. L., & Weinstein, K. K. (1964). The changing American grandparent. *Journal of Marriage and the Family*, *26*, 199–204.

Neupert, S. D., Almeida, D. M., Mroczek, D. K., & Spiro, A. 3rd. (2006). Daily stressors and memory failures in a naturalistic setting: Findings from the VA Normative Aging Study. *Psychology and Aging*, *21*, 424–429.

Newson, R. S., & Kemps, E. B. (2006). Cardiorespiratory fitness as a predictor of successful cognitive ageing. *Journal of Clinical and Experimental Neuropsychology: Section A, Neuropsychology, Development, and Cognition*, *28*, 949–967.

Ng, T. W. H., & Feldman, D. C. (2007). Organizational embeddedness and occupational embeddedness across career stages. *Journal of Vocational Behavior*, *70*, 336–351.

Nikitin, N. P., Loh, P. H., de Silva, R., Witte, K. K., Lukaschuk, E. I., Parker, A., Farnsworth, T. A., Alamgir, F. M., Clark, A. L., & Cleland, J. G. (2006). Left ventricular morphology, global and longitudinal function in normal older individuals: A cardiac magnetic resonance study. *International Journal of Cardiology*, *108*, 76–83.

Niklas, C. D., & Dormann, C. (2005). The impact of affect on job satisfaction. *European Journal of Work and Organizational Psychology*, *14*, 367–388.

Nordahl, C. W., Ranganath, C., Yonelinas, A. P., Decarli, C., Fletcher, E., & Jagust, W. J. (2006). White matter changes compromise prefrontal cortex function in healthy elderly individuals. *Journal of Cognitve Neuroscience*, *18*, 418–429.

Norton, C. (2004). Behavioral management of fecal incontinence in adults. *Gastroenterology*, *126*, S64–S70.

Norton, P., & Brubaker, L. (2006). Urinary incontinence in women. *Lancet*, *367*, 57–67.

O'Brien, L. T., & Hummert, M. L. (2006). Memory performance of late middle-aged adults: Contrasting self-stereotyping and stereotype threat accounts of assimilation to age stereotypes. *Social Cognition*, *24*, 338–358.

O'Donovan, D., Hausken, T., Lei, Y., Russo, A., Keogh, J., Horowitz, M., & Jones, K. L. (2005). Effect on aging on transpyloric flow, gastric emptying, and intragastric distribution in healthy humans—impact on glycemia. *Digestive Diseases and Sciences*, *50*, 671–676.

Office of Applied Studies (2006). Suicidal thoughts, suicide attempts, major depressive episode, and substance use among adults. Substance Abuse and Mental Health Services Administration. *Results from the 2005 National Survey on Drug Use and Health: National Findings (Office of Applied Studies, NSDUH Series H-30, DHHS Publication No. SMA 06-4194)*. Rockville, MD. http://oas.samhsa.gov/2k6/suicide/suicide.pdf.

O'Hanlon, L., Kemper, S., & Wilcox, K. A. (2005). Aging, encoding, and word retrieval: Distinguishing phonological and memory processes. *Experimental Aging Research*, *31*, 149–171.

Oken, B. S., Zajdel, D., Kishiyama, S., Flegal, K., Dehen, C., Haas, M., Kraemer, D. F. Lawrence, J., & Leyva, J. (2006). Randomized, controlled, six-month trial of yoga in healthy seniors: Effects on cognition and quality of life. *Alternative Therapies in Health and Medicine*, *12*, 40–47.

Okereke, O., Kang, J. H., Ma, J., Hankinson, S. E., Pollak, M. N., & Grodstein, F. (2007). Plasma IGF-I levels and cognitive performance in older women. *Neurobiology of Aging*, *28*, 135–142.

ONeill, C., Jamison, J., McCulloch, D., & Smith, D. (2001). Age-related macular degeneration: Cost-of-illness issues. *Drugs and Aging*, *18*, 233–241.

Ong, A. D., Bergeman, C. S., Bisconti, T. L., & Wallace, K. A. (2006). Psychological resilience, positive emotions, and successful adaptation to stress in later life. *Journal of Personality and Social Psychology*, *91*, 730–749.

Onrust, S. A., & Cuijpers, P. (2006). Mood and anxiety disorders in widowhood: A systematic review. *Aging and Mental Health*, *10*, 327–334.

Organization for Economic Co-operation and Development (2007). *Table 1321. Percentage of the Adult Population Considered to be Obese*. http://www.oecd.org.

Oslin, D. W., Datto, C. J., Kallan, M. J., Katz, I. R., Edell, W. S., & TenHave, T. (2002). Association between medical comorbidity and treatment outcomes in late-life depression. *Journal of the American Geriatrics Society*, *50*, 823–828.

Østbye, T., Steenhuis, R., Wolfson, C., Walton, R., & Hill, G. (1999). Predictors of five-year mortality in older Canadians: The Canadian Study of Health and Aging. *Journal of the American Geriatrics Society*, *47*, 1249–1254.

Otsuka, Y., Osaka, N., Morishita, M., Kondo, H., & Osaka, M. (2006). Decreased activation of anterior cingulate cortex in the working memory of the elderly. *Neuroreport*, *17*, 1479–1482.

Otsuki, T., Maeda, S., Kesen, Y., Yokoyama, N., Tanabe, T., Sugawara, J., Miyauchi, T., Kuno, S., Ajisaka, R., & Matsuda, M. (2006). Age-related reduction of systemic arterial compliance induces excessive myocardial oxygen consumption during sub-maximal exercise. *Hypertension Research*, *29*, 65–73.

Ott, C. H., & Lueger, R. J. (2002). Patterns of change in mental health status during the first two years of spousal bereavement. *Death Studies*, *26*, 387–411.

Owsley, C., McGwin, G. Jr., Phillips, J. M., McNeal, S. F., & Stalvey, B. T. (2004). Impact of an educational program on the safety of high-risk, visually impaired, older drivers. *American Journal of Preventive Medicine*, *26*, 222–229.

Pacheco, J., Hershberger, P. J., Markert, R. J., & Kumar, G. (2003). A longitudinal study of attitudes toward physician-assisted suicide and euthanasia among patients with noncurable malignancy. *American Journal of Hospital Palliative Care*, *20*, 99–104.

Packer, D. J., & Chasteen, A. L. (2006). Looking to the future: How possible aged selves influence prejudice toward older adults. *Social Cognition*, *24*, 218–247.

Paley, B., Cox, M. J., Kanoy, K. W., Harter, K. S., Burchinal, M., & Margand, N. A. (2005). Adult attachment and marital interaction as predictors of whole family interactions during the transition to parenthood. *Journal of Family Psychology*, *19*, 420–429.

Palmer, B. W., Heaton, R. K., Gladsjo, J. A., Evans, J. D., Patterson, T. L., Golshan, S., & Jeste, D. V. (2002). Heterogeneity in functional status among older outpatients with schizophrenia: Employment history, living situation, and driving, *Schizophrenia Research*, *55*, 205–215.

Pamuk, E., Makuc, D., Heck, K., Reuben, C., & Lochner, K. (1998). *Socioeconomic status and health chartbook. Health, United States, 1998*. Hyattsville, MD: National Center for Health Statistics.

Patient Self-Determination Act, 42 USC 1395cc, 1396(a) (1994)

Patterson, T. L., McKibbin, C., Taylor, M., Goldman, S., Davila-Fraga, W., Bucardo, J., & Jeste, D. V. (2003). Functional Adaptation Skills Training (FAST): A Pilot Psychosocial Intervention Study in Middle-Aged and Older Patients with Chronic Psychotic Disorders. *American Journal of Geriatric Psychiatry*, *11*, 17–23.

Patterson, T. L., Shaw, W., Semple, S. J., Moscona, S., Harris, M. J., Kaplan, R. M., Grant, I., & Jeste, D. V. (1997). Health-related quality of life in order patients with schizophrenia and other psychoses: Relationships among psychosocial and psychiatric factors. *International Journal of Geriatric Psychiatry*, *12*, 452–461.

Pavalko, E. K., Elder, G. H., & Clipp, E. C. (1993). Work lives and longevity: Insights from a life course perspective. *Journal of Health and Social Behavior*, *34*, 363–380.

Paxton, J. L., Barch, D. M., Storandt, M., & Braver, T. S. (2006). Effects of environmental support and strategy training on older adults' use of context. *Psychology and Aging*, *21*, 499–509.

Pegula, S., Marsh, S. M., & Jackson, L. L. (2007). Fatal occupational injuries—United States, 2005. *Morbidity and Mortality Weekly Report, 56, No. 13,* 297–301.

Peplau, L. A., & Fingerhut, A. W. (2007). The close relationships of lesbians and gay men. *Annual Review of Psychology, 58,* 405–424.

Perls, T. T., Reisman, N. R., & Olshansky, S. J. (2005). Provision or distribution of growth hormone for "antiaging": Clinical and legal issues. *Journal of the American Medical Association, 294,* 2086–2090.

Perren, S., Von Wyl, A., Bürgin, D., Simoni, H., & Von Klitzing, K. (2005). Intergenerational transmission of marital quality across the transition to parenthood. *Family Process, 44,* 441–459.

Perrig-Chiello, P., & Haöflinger, F. (2005). Aging parents and their middle-aged children: Demographic and psychosocial challenges. *European Journal of Ageing, 2,* 183–191.

Perruccio, A. V., Badley, E. M., & Trope, G. E. (2007). Self-reported glaucoma in Canada: Findings from population-based surveys, 1994–2003. *Canadian Journal of Ophthalmology, 42,* 219–226.

Persson, G. R., Persson, R. E., MacEntee, C. I., Wyatt, C. C., Hollender, L. G., & Kiyak, H. A. (2003). Periodontitis and perceived risk for periodontitis in elders with evidence of depression. *Journal of Clinical Periodontology, 30,* 691–696.

Persson, J., Nyberg, L., Lind, J., Larsson, A., Nilson, L. G., Ingvar, M., & Buckner, R. L. (2006). Structure-function correlates of cognitive decline in aging. *Cerebral Cortex, 16,* 907–915.

Petersen, R. C. (2004). Mild cognitive impairment as a diagnostic entity. *Journal of Internal Medicine, 256,* 183–194.

Petersen, R. C., et al. (2006). Neuropathologic features of amnestic mild cognitive impairment. *Archives of Neurology, 63,* 665–672.

Pfirrmann, C. W., Metzdorf, A., Elfering, A., Hodler, J., & Boos, N. (2006). Effect of aging and degeneration on disc volume and shape: A quantitative study in asymptomatic volunteers. *Journal of Orthopedics Research, 24,* 1086–1094.

Pfisterer, M. H., Griffiths, D. J., Schaefer, W., & Resnick, N. M. (2006). The effect of age on lower urinary tract function: A study in women. *Journal of the American Geriatrics Society, 54,* 405–412.

Phillips, J. A., & Sweeney, M. M. (2005). Premarital cohabitation and marital disruption among white, black, and Mexican American women. *Journal of Marriage and the Family, 67,* 296–314.

Pinilla, F. G. (2006). The impact of diet and exercise on brain plasticity and disease. *Nutrition and Health, 18,* 277–284.

Pinson-Millburn, N. M., Fabian, E. S., Schlossberg, N. K., & Pyle, M. (1996). Grandparents raising grandchildren. *Journal of Counseling and Development, 74,* 548–554.

Piolino, P., Desgranges, B., Benali, K., & Eustache, F. (2002). Episodic and semantic remote autobiographical memory in ageing. *Memory, 10,* 239–257.

Piolino, P., Desgranges, B., Clarys, D., Guillery-Girard, B., Taconnat, L., Isingrini, M., & Eustache, F. (2006). Autobiographical memory, autonoetic consciousness, and self-perspective in aging. *Psychology and Aging, 21,* 510–525.

Plaut, V. C., Markus, H. R., & Lachman, M. E. (2003). Place matters: Consensual features and regional variation in American well-being and self. *Journal of Personality and Social Psychology, 83,* 160–184.

Pleis, J. R., & Lethbridge-Cejku, M. (2006). Summary health statistics for U.S. adults: National Health Interview Survey, 2005, *10*(232).

Plemons, J. K., Willis, S. L., & Baltes, P. B. (1978). Modifiability of fluid intelligence in aging: A short-term longitudinal training approach. *Journal of Gerontology, 33,* 224–231.

Pongchaiyakul, C., Nguyen, T. V., Kosulwat, V., Rojroongwasinkul, N., Charoenkiatkul, S., & Rajatanavin, R. (2005). Effect of urbanization on bone mineral density: A Thai epidemiological study. *BMC Musculoskeletal Disorders, 6,* 5.

Popenoe, D., & Whitehead, B. D. (1999). *The state of our unions: The social health of marriage in America.* New Brunswick, NJ: Rutgers University National Marriage Project.

Portin, R., Saarijaervi, S., Joukamaa, M., & Salokangas, R. K. R. (1995). Education, gender and cognitive performance in a 62-year-old normal population: Results from the Turva Project. *Psychological Medicine, 25,* 1295–1298.

Pratt, L. A., Dey, A. N., & Cohen, A. J. (2007). Characteristics of adults with serious psychological distress as measured by the K6 Scale: United States, 2001–04. *Advance Data from Vital and Health Statistics, No. 382,* March 30, 2007.

Previti, D., & Amato, P. R. (2003). Why stay married? Rewards, barriers, and marital stability. *Journal of Marriage and Family, 65,* 561–573.

Previti, D., & Amato, P. R. (2004). Is infidelity a cause or a consequence of poor marital quality? *Journal of Social and Personal Relationships, 21,* 217–230.

Prinz, P. N., Bailey, S. L., & Woods, D. L. (2000). Sleep impairments in healthy seniors: Roles of stress, cortisol, and interleukin-1 beta. *Chronobiology International, 17,* 391–404.

Pritchard, R. S., Fisher, E. S., Teno, J. M., Sharp, S. M., Reding, D. J., Knaus, W. A., Wennberg, J. E., &

Lynn, J. (1998). Influence of patient preferences and local health system characteristics on the place of death. SUPPORT Investigators. Study of Understand Prognoses and Preferences for Risks and Outcomes of Treatment. *Journal of the American Geriatrics Society, 46,* 1242–1250.

Pruchno, R. A., & McKenney, D. (2002). Psychological well-being of black and white grandmothers raising grandchildren: Examination of a two-factor model. *Journal of Gerontology: Psychological Sciences, 57B,* P444–P452.

Pulkki-Raback, L., Elovainio, M., Kivimaki, M., Raitakari, O. T., & Keltikangas-Jarvinen, L. (2005). Temperament in childhood predicts body mass in adulthood: The Cardiovascular Risk in Young Finns Study. *Health Psychology, 24,* 307–315.

Qualls, S. H., Segal, D. L., Norman, S. N., George, & Gallagher-Thompson, D. (2002). Psychologists in practice with older adults: Current patterns, sources of training, and need for continuing education. *Professional Psychology: Research and Practice, 33,* 435–442.

Quetelet, A. (1835/1968). *A treatise on man and the development of his faculties.* New York: Franklin.

Raabe, B., Frese, M., & Beehr, T. A. (2007). Action regulation theory and career self-management. *Journal of Vocational Behavior, 70,* 297–311.

Rabe, J. H., Mamelak, A. J., McElgunn, P. J., Morison, W. L., & Sauder, D. N. (2006). Photoaging: Mechanisms and repair. *Journal of the American Academy of Dermatology, 55,* 1–19.

Raguso, C. A., Kyle, U., Kossovsky, M., Roynette, C., Paolini-Giacobino, A., Hans, D., Genton, L., & Pichard, C. (2006). A 3-year longitudinal study on body composition changes in the elderly: Role of physical exercise. *Clinical Nutrition, 25,* 573–580.

Rahhal, T. A., Colcombe, S. J., & Hasher, L. (2001). Instructional manipulations and age differences in memory: Now you see them, now you don't. *Psychology and Aging, 16,* 697–706.

Ram, N., Rabbitt, P., Stollery, B., & Nesselroade, J. R. (2005). Cognitive performance inconsistency: Intraindividual change and variability. *Psychology and Aging, 20,* 623–633.

Raudenbush, S. W., & Bryk, A. S. (2002). *Hierarchical linear models: Applications and data analysis methods,* (2d ed.) Newbury Park, CA: Sage.

Ravaglia, G., Forti, P., Maioli, F., Pratelli, L., Vettori, C., Bastagli, L., Mariani, E., Facchini, A., & Cucinotta, D. (2001). Regular moderate intensity physical activity and blood concentrations of endogenous anabolic hormones and thyroid hormones in aging men. *Mechanisms of Ageing and Development, 122,* 191–203.

Rawson, N. E. (2006). Olfactory loss in aging. *Science of Aging Knowledge Environment, 2006,* pe6.

Ray, A., Block, S. D., Friedlander, R. J., Zhang, B., Maciejewski, P. K., & Prigerson, H. G. (2006). Peaceful awareness in patients with advanced cancer. *Journal of Palliative Medicine, 9,* 1359–1368.

Raz, N., & Rodrigue, K. M. (2006). Differential aging of the brain: Patterns, cognitive correlates and modifiers. *Neuroscience and Biobehavioral Reviews, 30,* 730–748.

Reardon, J. Z., Lareau, S. C., & ZuWallack, R. (2006). Functional status and quality of life in chronic obstructive pulmonary disease. *American Journal of Medicine, 119,* 32–37.

Reeves, N. D., Narici, M. V., & Maganaris, C. N. (2006). Myotendinous plasticity to ageing and resistance exercise in humans. *Experimental Physiology, 91,* 483–498.

Reichstadt, J., Depp, C. A., Palinkas, L. A., Folsom, D. P., & Jeste, D. V. (2007). Building blocks of successful aging: A focus group study of older adults' perceived contributors to successful aging. *American Journal of Geriatric Psychiatry, 15,* 194–201.

Rexbye, H., Petersen, I., Johansens, M., Klitkou, L., Jeune, B., & Christensen, K. (2006). Influence of environmental factors on facial ageing. *Age and Ageing, 35,* 110–115.

Reynolds, C. A., Finkel, D., Gatz, M., & Pedersen, N. L. (2002). Sources of influence on rate of cognitive change over time in Swedish twins: An application of latent growth models. *Experimental Aging Research, 28,* 407–433.

Reynolds, C. F. I., Frank, E., Perel, J. M., Imber, S. D., Cornes, C., Miller, M. D., Mazumdar, S., Houck, P. R., Dew, M. A., Stack, J. A., Pollock, B. G., & Kupfer, D. J. (1999). Nortriptyline and interpersonal psychotherapy as maintenance therapies for recurrent major depression: A randomized controlled trial in patients older than 59 years. *Journal of the American Medical Association, 281,* 39–45.

Reynolds, K., Lewis, L. B., Nolen, J. D. L., Kinney, G. L., Sathya, B., & He, J. (2003). Alcohol consumption and risk of stroke: A meta-analysis. *Journal of the American Medical Association, 289,* 579–588.

Richardson, S. S., Sullivan, G., Hill, A., & Yu, W. (2007). Use of aggressive medical treatments near the end of life: Differences between patients with and without dementia. *Health Services Research, 42,* 183–200.

Riedel, B., & Lichstein, K. (2000). Insomnia in older adults. In S. K. Whitbourne (Ed.), *Psychopathology in later life* (pp. 299–322). New York: Wiley.

Riggs, K. M., Lachman, M. E., & Wingfield, A. (1997). Taking charge of remembering: Locus of control and older adults' memory for speech. *Experimental Aging Research, 23*, 237–256.

Riordan, C. M., Griffith, R. W., & Weatherly, E. W. (2003). Age and work-related outcomes: The moderating effects of status characteristics. *Journal of Applied Social Psychology, 33*, 37–57.

Roberson, E. D., & Mucke, L. (2006). 100 years and counting: Prospects for defeating Alzheimer's disease. *Science, 314*, 781–784.

Roberto, K. A., & Stanis, P. I. (1994). Reactions of older women to the death of their close friends. *Omega—Journal of Death and Dying, 29*, 17–27.

Roberto, K. A., & Stroes, J. (1992). Grandchildren and grandparents: Roles, influences, and relationships. *International Journal of Aging and Human Development, 34*, 227–239.

Roberts, B. W., & DelVecchio, W. F. (2000). The rank-order consistency of personality traits from childhood to old age: A quantitative review of longitudinal studies. *Psychological Bulletin, 126*, 3–25.

Robins, L. R., & Regier, D. A. (1991). *Psychiatric disorders in America*. New York: Free Press.

Robins, R. W., & Trzesniewski, K. H. (2005). Self-esteem development across the lifespan. *Current Directions in Psychological Science, 14*, 158–162.

Ronnlund, M., & Nilsson, L.-G. (2006). Adult life-span patterns in WAIS-R Block Design performance: Cross-sectional versus longitudinal age gradients longitudinal age gradients and relations to demographic factors. *Intelligence 34*, 63–78.

Rosamond, W., Flegal, K., Friday, G., Furie, K., Go, A., Greenlund, K., Haase, N., Ho, M., Howard, V., Kissela, B., Kittner, S., Lloyd-Jones, D., McDermott, M., Meigs, J., Moy, C., Nichol, G., O'Donnell, C. J., Roger, V., Rumsfeld, J., Sorlie, P., Steinberger, J., Thom, T., Wasserthiel-Smoller, S., & Hong, Y. (2007). Heart disease and stroke statistics—2007 update: a report from the American Heart Association Statistics Committee and Stroke Statistics Subcommittee. *Circulation, 115*, e69–171.

Rosenberg, S. D., Rosenberg, H. J., & Farrell, M. P. (1999). The midlife crisis revisited. In J. D. Reid & S. L. Willis (Eds.), *Life in the middle: Psychological and social development in middle age* (pp. 25–45). San Diego: Academic Press.

Rossow, J. E., Anderson, G. L., Prentice, R. L., Lacroix, A. Z., Kooperberg, C., Stefanick, M. L., Jackson, R. D., Beresford, S. A., Howard, B. V., Johnson, K. C., Kotchen, J. M., & Ockene, J. (2002). Risks and benefits of estrogen plus progestin in healthy postmenopausal women: Principal results from the Women's Health Initiative randomized controlled trial. *Journal of the American Medical Association, 288*, 321–333.

Rottinghaus, P. J., Coon, K. L., Gaffey, A. R., & Zytowski, D. G. (2007). Thirty-year stability and predictive validity of vocational interests. *Journal of Career Assessment, 15*, 5–22.

Rowe, G., Valderrama, S., Hasher, L., & Lenartowicz, A. (2006). Attentional disregulation: A benefit for implicit memory. *Psychology and Aging, 21*, 826–830.

Rowe, J. W., & Kahn, R. L. (1998). *Successful aging*. New York: Pantheon Books.

Roy, M. L., & Cairns, A. P. (2007). *Federal budget estimates for the year 2008*. Washington, D.C.: U.S. Department of Commerce Bureau of Economic Analysis.

Royal College of Physicians (1998). A code of practice for the diagnosis of brain stem death. National Health Service Department of Health. http://WWW.dh.gov.uk/en/Publicationsandstatistics/Publications/PublicationsPolicyAndGuidance/DH 4009696.

Rubin, D. C., Rahhal, T. A., & Poon, L. W. (1998). Things learned in early adulthood are remembered best. *Memory and Cognition, 26*, 3–19.

Rupp, D. E., Vodanovich, S. J., & Crede, M. (2006). Age bias in the workplace: The impact of ageism and causal attributions. *Journal of Applied Social Psychology, 36*, 1337–1364.

Ruschena, D., Mullen, P. E., Burgess, P., Cordner, S. M., Barry-Walsh, J., Drummer, O. H., Palmer, S., Browne, C., & Wallace, C. (1998). Sudden death in psychiatric patients. *British Journal of Psychiatry, 172*, 331–336.

Rush, B. K., Barch, D. M., & Braver, T. S. (2006). Accounting for cognitive aging: Context processing, inhibition or processing speed? *Aging, Neuropsychology, and Cognition, 13*, 588–610.

Russell-Aulet, M., Dimaraki, E. V., Jaffe, C. A., DeMott-Friberg, R., & Barkan, A. L. (2001). Aging-related growth hormone (GH) decrease is a selective hypothalamic GH-releasing hormone pulse amplitude mediated phenomenon. *Journal of Gerontology: Medical Sciences, 56A*, M124–129.

Ryan, C. M. (2005). Diabetes, aging, and cognitive decline. *Neurobiology of Aging, 26 Supplement 1*, 21–25.

Ryan, E. B., Hummert, M. L., & Boich, L. H. (1995). Communication predicaments of aging: Patronizing behavior toward older adults. *Journal of Language and Social Psychology, 14*, 144–166.

Ryan, E. B., & See, S. K. (1993). Age-based beliefs about memory changes for self and others across adulthood. *Journal of Gerontology: Psychological Sciences, 48*, P199–P201.

Ryder, K. M.. Shorr, R. I., Bush, A. J., Kritchevsky, S. B., Harris, T., Stone, K., Cauley, J., & Tylavsky, F. A. (2005). Magnesium intake from food and supplements is associated with bone mineral density in healthy older white subjects. *Journal of the American Geriatrics Society, 53*, 1875–1180.

Sacher, G. A. (1977). Life table modification and life prolongation. In C. E. Finch & L. Hayflick (Eds.), *Handbook of the biology of aging* (pp. 582–638). New York: Van Nostrand Reinhold.

Saczynski, J. S., Willis, S. L., & Schaie, K. W. (2002). Strategy use in reasoning training with older adults. *Aging, Neuropsychology, & Cognition., 9*, 48–60.

Sadavoy, J., & LeClair, J. K. (1997). Treatment of anxiety disorders in late life. *Canadian Journal of Psychiatry, 42*, 28–34.

Sahyoun, N. R., Pratt, L. A., Lentzner, H., Dey, A., & Robinson, K. N. (2001). *The changing profile of nursing home residents: 1985–1997*. Aging Trends; No. 4. Hyattsville, Maryland: National Center for Health Statistics.

Salari, S. M., & Rich, M. (2001). Social and environmental infantilization of aged persons: Observations in two adult day care centers. *International Journal of Aging and Human Development, 52*, 115–134.

Salmela-Aro, K., Nurmi, J.-E., Saisto, T., & Halmesmaeki, E. (2001). Goal reconstruction and depressive symptoms during the transition to motherhood: Evidence from two cross-lagged longitudinal studies. *Journal of Personality & Social Psychology, 81*, 1144–1159.

Salthouse, T. A. (1996). The processing-speed theory of adult age differences in cognition. *Psychological Review, 103*, 403–428.

Salthouse, T. A. (2001). Structural models of the relations between age and measures of cognitive functioning. *Intelligence, 29*, 93–115.

Salthouse, T. A., & Ferrer-Caja, E. (2003). What needs to be explained to account for age-related effects on multiple cognitive variables? *Psychology and Aging, 18*, 91–110.

Salzman, C. (1992). *Clinical geriatric psychopharmacology* (2d ed.). Baltimore: Williams & Wilkins.

Samelson, E. J., Hannan, M. T., Zhang, Y., Genant, H. K., Felson, D. T., & Kiel, D. P. (2006). Incidence and risk factors for vertebral fracture in women and men: 25-year follow-up results from the population-based Framingham study. *Journal of Bone and Mineral Research, 21*, 1207–1214.

Samuels, J., Eaton, W. W., Bienvenu, O. J. I., Brown, C., Costa, P. T., Jr, & Nestadt, G. (2002). Prevalence and correlates of personality disorders in a community sample. *British Journal of Psychiatry, 180*, 536–542.

Sasson, Y., Zohar, J., Chopra, M., Lustig, M., Iancu, I., & Hendler, T. (1997). Epidemiology of obsessive–compulsive disorder: A world view. *Journal of Clinical Psychiatry, 12*, 7–10.

Satre, D. D., Knight, B. G., & David, S. (2006). Cognitive-behavioral interventions with older adults: Integrating clinical and gerontological research. *Professional Psychology: Research and Practice, 37*, 489–498.

Scandura, T. A., & Lankau, M. J. (1997). Relationships of gender, family responsibility and flexible work hours to organizational commitment and job satisfaction. *Journal of Organizational Behavior, 18*, 377–391.

Scarmeas, N., Stern, Y., Mayeux, R., & Luchsinger, J. A. (2006). Mediterranean diet, Alzheimer disease, and vascular mediation. *Archives of Neurology, 63*, 1709–1717.

Scarr, S., & McCartney, K. (1983). How people make their own environments: A theory of genotype → environment effects. *Child Development, 54*, 424–435.

Schaie, K. W. (1965). A general model for the study of developmental change. *Psychological Bulletin, 64*, 92–107.

Schaie, K. W. (1994). The course of adult intellectual development. *American Psychologist, 49*, 304–313.

Schaie, K. W. (1996). Intellectual development in adulthood. In J. E. Birren, K. W. Schaie, R. P. Abeles, M. Gatz & T. A. Salthouse (Eds.), *Handbook of the psychology of aging* (4th ed.) (pp. 266–286). San Diego, CA: Academic Press.

Schaie, K. W. (2005). *Developmental influences on adult intelligence: The Seattle Longitudinal Study*. New York: Oxford University Press.

Schaie, K. W., Nguyen, H. T., Willis, S. L., Dutta, R., & Yue, G. A. (2001). Environmental factors as a conceptual framework for examining cognitive performance in Chinese adults. *International Journal of Behavioral Development, 25*, 193–202.

Schaie, K. W., Willis, S. L., & Caskie, G. I. (2004). The Seattle Longitudinal Study: Relationship between personality and cognition. *Aging, Neuropsychology and Cognition, 11*, 304–324.

Schaie, K. W., & Zanjani, F. A. K. (2006). Intellectual development across adulthood. In C. Hoare (Ed.), *Handbook of adult development and learning.* (pp. 99–122). New York: Oxford University Press.

Scheff, S. W., & Price, D. A. (2006). Alzheimer's disease-related alterations in synaptic density: Neocortex and hippocampus. *Journal of Alzheimers' Disease, 9*, 101–115.

Schellenberg, G. D. (2006). Early Alzheimer's disease genetics. *Journal of Alzheimers Disease, 9*, 367–372.

Schiltz, K., Szentkuti, A., Guderian, S., Kaufmann, J., Munte, T. F., Heinze, H. J., & Düzel, E. (2006). Relationship between hippocampal structure and memory function in elderly humans. *Journal of Cognitive Neuroscience, 18,* 990–1003.

Schirmer, L. L., & Lopez, F. G. (2001). Probing the social support and work strain relationship among adult workers: Contributions of adult attachment orientations. *Journal of Vocational Behavior, 59,* 17–33.

Schmidt, P. J., Murphy, J. H., Haq, N., Rubinow, D. R., & Danaceau, M. A. (2004). Stressful life events, personal losses, and perimenopause-related depression. *Archives of Womens Mental Health, 7,* 19–26.

Schoenborn, C. A., Vickerie, J. L., & Barnes, P. M. (2003). *Cigarette smoking behavior of adults: United States, 1997–98.* Hyattsville, MD: National Center for Health Statistics.

Schoenhofen, E. A., Wyszynski, D. F., Andersen, S., Pennington, J., Young, R., Terry, D. F., & Perls, T. T. (2006). Characteristics of 32 supercentenarians. *Journal of the American Geriatrics Society, 54,* 1237–1240.

Schoevers, R. A., Smit, F., Deeg, D. J., Cuijpers, P., Dekker, J., Van Jilburg, W., & Beekman, A. T. (2006). Prevention of late-life depression in primary care: Do we know where to begin? *American Journal of Psychiatry, 163,* 1611–1621.

Schooler, C., & Mulatu, M. S. (2001). The reciprocal effects of leisure time activities and intellectual functioning in older people: A longitudinal analysis. *Psychology and Aging, 16,* 466–482.

Schooler, C., Mulatu, M. S., & Oates, G. (1999). The continuing effects of substantively complex work on the intellectual functioning of older workers. *Psychology and Aging, 14,* 483–506.

Schroeder, D. H., & Salthouse, T. A. (2004). Age-related effects on cognition between 20 and 50 years of age. *Personality and Individual Differences, 36,* 393–404.

Schulberg, H. C., Post, E. P., Raue, P. J., Have, T. T., Miller, M., & Bruce, M. L. (2007). Treating late-life depression with interpersonal psychotherapy in the primary care sector. *International Journal of Geriatic Psychiatry, 22,* 106–114.

Schulman, C., & Lunenfeld, B. (2002). The ageing male. *World Journal of Urology, 20,* 4–10.

Schultz, S. K., Ellingrod, V. L., Moser, D. J., Kutschner, E., Turvey, C., & Arndt, S. (2002). The influence of cognitive impairment and psychiatric symptoms on daily functioning in nursing facilities: A longitudinal study. *Annals of Clinical Psychiatry, 14,* 209–213.

Schwarz, B., Trommsdorff, G., Albert, I., & Mayer, B. (2005). Adult parent-child relationships: Relationship quality, support, and reciprocity. *Applied Psychology: An International Review, 54,* 396–417.

Scogin, F., Floyd, M., & Forde, J. (2000). Anxiety in older adults. In S. K. Whitbourne (Ed.), *Psychopathology in later life* (pp. 117–140). New York: Wiley.

Scollon, C. N., & Diener, E. (2006). Love, work, and changes in extraversion and neuroticism over time. *Journal of Personality and Social Psychology, 91,* 1152–1165.

Seeman, E., & Delmas, P. D. (2006). Bone quality—The material and structural basis of bone strength and fragility. *New England Journal of Medicine, 354,* 2250–2261.

Segal, D. L., Coolidge, F. L., & Rosowsky, E. (2000). Personality disorders. In S. K. Whitbourne (Ed.), *Psychopathology in later life* (pp. 89–116). New York: Wiley.

Segal, D. L., Hook, J. N., & Coolidge, F. L. (2001). Personality dysfunction, coping styles, and clinical symptoms in younger and older adults. *Journal of Clinical Geropsychology, 7,* 201–212.

Seibert, S. E., & Kraimer, M. L. (2001). The Five-Factor Model of personality and career success. *Journal of Vocational Behavior, 58,* 1–21.

Seidman, S. N. (2006). Normative hypogonadism and depression: Does "andropause" exist? *International Journal of Impotence Research, 18,* 415–422.

Selkoe, D. J. (2006). The ups and downs of Abeta. *Nature Medicine, 12,* 758–759; discussion 759.

Semple, S. J., Patterson, T. L., Shaw, W. S., Grant, I., Moscona, S., & Jeste, D. V. (1999). Self-perceived interpersonal competence in older schizophrenia patients: The role of patient characteristics and psychosocial factors. *Acta Psychiatrica Scandinavica, 100,* 126–135.

Serra-Majem, L., Roman, B., & Estruch, R. (2006). Scientific evidence of interventions using the Mediterranean diet: A systematic review. *Nutrition Reviews, 64,* S27–S47.

Serste, T., & Bourgeois, N. (2006). Ageing and the liver. *Acta Gastro-enterologica Belgium, 69,* 296–298.

Shackelford, T. K., Schmitt, D. P., & Buss, D. M. (2005). Mate preferences of married persons in the newlywed year and three years later. *Cognition and Emotion, 19,* 1262–1270.

Shaver, P. R., & Mikulincer, M. (2004). Attachment in the later years: A commentary. *Attachment and Human Development, 6,* 451–464.

Shaver, P. R., & Mikulincer, M. (2005). Attachment theory and research: Resurrection of the psychodynamic approach to personality. *Journal of Research in Personality, 39,* 22–45.

Sheehy, G. (1974). *Passages: Predictable passages of adult life.* New York: Dutton.

Sherwin, B. B. (2006). Estrogen and cognitive aging in women. *Neuroscience, 138,* 1021–1026.

Shin, J. S., Hong, A., Solomon, M. J., & Lee, C. S. (2006). The role of telomeres and telomerase in the pathology of human cancer and aging. *Pathology, 38,* 103–113.

Shumway-Cook, A., Guralnik, J. M., Phillips, C. L., Coppin, A. K., Ciol, M. A., Bandinelli, S., & Ferrucci, L. (2007). Age-associated declines in complex walking task performance: The Walking InCHIANTI toolkit. *Journal of the American Geriatrics Society, 55,* 58–65.

Siebert, D. C., Mutran, E. J., & Reitzes, D. C. (2002). Friendship and social support: The importance of role identity to aging adults. *Social Work, 44,* 522–533.

Siegler, I. C., Bastian, L. A., Steffens, D. C., Bosworth, H. B., & Costa, P. T. (2002). Behavioral medicine and aging. *Journal of Consulting and Clinical Psychology, 70,* 843–851.

Sigurdsson, G., Aspelund, T., Chang, M., Jonsdottir, B., Sigurdsson, S., Eiriksdottir, G., Gudmundsson, A., Harris, T. B., Gudnason, V., & Lang, T. F. (2006). Increasing Sex Difference in bone strength in old age: The Age, Gene/Environment Susceptibility-Reykjavik study (AGESREYKJAVIK). *Bone, 39,* 644–651.

Silverstein, M., & Bengtson, V. L. (1997). Intergenerational solidarity and the structure of adult child-parent relationships in American families. *American Journal of Sociology, 103,* 429–460.

Silverstein, M., Conroy, S. J., Wang, H., Giarrusso, R., & Bengtson, V. L. (2002). Reciprocity in parent-child relations over the adult life course. *Journal of Gerontology: Social Sciences, 57B,* S3–S13.

Silverstein, M., Gans, D., & Yang, F. M. (2006). Intergenerational support to aging parents: The role of norms and needs. *Journal of Family Issues, 27,* 1068–1084.

Silverstein, M., & Parker, M. G. (2002). Leisure activities and quality of life among the oldest old in Sweden. *Research on Aging, 24,* 528–547.

Simmons, T., & O'Connell, M. (2003). *Married-couple and unmarried-partner households: 2000,* http://www.census .gov/prod/2003pubs/censr-5.pdf.

Simoni-Wastila, L., & Yang, H. K. (2006). Psychoactive drug abuse in older adults. *American Journal of Geriatric Pharmacotherapy, 4,* 380–394.

Simonton, D. K. (1988). Age and outstanding achievement: What do we know after a century of research? *Psychological Bulletin, 104,* 251–267.

Simonton, D. K. (1989). The swan-song phenomenon: Last-works effects for 172 classical composers. *Psychology and Aging, 4,* 42–47.

Simonton, D. K. (1997). Creative productivity: A predictive and explanatory model of career trajectories and landmarks. *Psychological Review, 104,* 66–89.

Simonton, D. K. (1998a). Achieved eminence in minority and majority cultures: Convergence versus divergence in the assessments of 294 African Americans. *Journal of Personality and Social Psychology, 74,* 804–817.

Simonton, D. K. (1998b). Career paths and creative lives: A theoretical perspective on late-life potential. In C. Adams-Price (Ed.), *Creativity and successful aging: Theoretical and empirical approaches* (pp. 3–18). New York: Springer.

Simpson, J. A., & Rholes, W. S. (2002). Attachment orientations, marriage, and the transition to parenthood. *Journal of Research in Personality, 36,* 622–628.

Singley, S., & Hynes, K. (2005). Transitions to parenthood: Work-family policies, gender, and the couple context. *Gender and Society, 19,* 376–397.

Sinnott, J. D. (1998). Career paths and creative lives: A theoretical perspective on late-life potential. In C. Adams-Price (Ed.), *Creativity and successful aging: Theoretical and empirical approaches* (pp. 43–72). New York: Springer.

Sjögren, M., & Andersen, C. (2006). Frontotemporal dementia—A brief review. *Mechanisms of Ageing and Development, 127,* 180–187.

Skinner, B. F., & Vaughan, M. E. (1983). *Enjoy old age: A practical guide.* New York: W. W. Norton.

Skultety, K. M., & Whitbourne, S. K. (2004). Gender differences in identity processes and self-esteem in middle and later adulthood. *Journal of Women and Aging, 16,* 175–188.

Sliwinski, M. J., & Hall, C. B. (1998). Constraints on general slowing: A meta-analysis using hierarchical linear models with random coefficients. *Psychology and Aging, 13,* 164–175.

Sliwinski, M. J., Smyth. J. M., Hofer, S. M., & Stawski, R. S. (2006). Intraindividual coupling of daily stress and cognition. *Psychology and Aging, 21,* 545–557.

Sliwinski, M. J., Stawski, R. S., Hall, C. B., Katz, M., Verghese, J., & Lipton, R. (2006). Distinguishing preterminal and terminal cognitive decline. *European Psychologist, 11,* 172–181.

Sloane, P. D., Mitchell, C. M., Weisman, G., Zimmerman, S., Foley, K. M., Lynn, M., Calkins, M., Lawton, M. P., Teresi, J., Grant, L., Lindeman, D., & Montgomery, R. (2002). The Therapeutic Environment Screening Survey for Nursing Homes (TESS-NH): An observational instrument for assessing the physical environment of institutional settings for persons with dementia. *Journal of Gerontology: Social Sciences, 57B*, S69–S78.

Sluiter, J. K. (2006). High-demand jobs: Age-related diversity in work ability? *Applied Ergonomics, 37*, 429–440.

Smith, C. D., Walton, A., Loveland, A. D., Umberger, G. H., Kryscio, R. J., & Gash, D. M. (2005). Memories that last in old age: Motor skill learning and memory preservation. *Neurobiology of Aging, 26*, 883–890.

Smith, J., & Freund, A. M. (2002). The dynamics of possible selves in old age. *Journal of Gerontology: Psychological Sciences 57B*, P492–P500.

Smith, S. C., Jr. (2007). Multiple risk factors for cardiovascular disease and diabetes mellitus. *American Journal of Medicine, 120*, S3–S11.

Sneed, J. R., Kasen, S., & Cohen, P. (2007). Early-life risk factors for late-onset depression. *International Journal of Geriatric Psychiatry, 22*, 663–667.

Sneed, J. R., & Whitbourne, S. K. (2003). Identity processing and self-consciousness in middle and later adulthood. *Journal of Gerontology: Psychological Sciences, 58B*, P313–P319.

Social Security Trust Fund Report (2007), http://www.ssa .gov/OACT/TR/TR07/Index.html.

Sohal, R. S. (2002). Role of oxidative stress and protein oxidation in the aging process. *Free Radical Biology and Medicine, 33*, 37–44.

Solano, N. H., & Whitbourne, S. K. (2001). Coping with schizophrenia: Patterns in later adulthood. *International Journal of Aging and Human Development, 53*, 1–10.

Soldz, S., & Vaillant, G. E. (1999). The Big Five personality traits and the life course: A 45-year longitudinal study. *Journal of Research in Personality, 33*, 208–232.

Solomon, S., Greenberg, J. & Pyszczynski, T. (1991). A terror management theory of social behavior: the psychological functions of self-esteem and cultural worldviews. In M. P. Zanna (Ed.), *Advances in experimental social psychology* (Vol. 24, pp. 93–159). Orlando, FL: Academic Press.

Solomon, Z., & Mikulincer, M. (2006). Trajectories of PTSD: A 20-year longitudinal study. *American Journal of Psychiatry, 163*, 659–666.

Sonnenberg, C. M., Beekman, A. T., Deeg, D. J., & Van Tilburg, W. (2003). Drug treatment in depressed elderly in the Dutch community. *International Journal of Geriatric Psychiatry, 18*, 99–104.

Spearman, C. (1904). "General intelligence": Objectively determined and measured. *American Journal of Psychology, 15*, 201–292.

Spearman, C. (1927). *The abilities of man.* New York: Macmillan.

Spindler, H., & Pedersen, S. S. (2005). Posttraumatic stress disorder in the wake of heart disease: Prevalence, risk factors, and future research directions. *Psychosomatic Medicine, 67*, 715–723.

Sprecher, S. (1988). Investment model, equity, and social support determinants of relationship commitment. *Social Psychology Quarterly, 51*, 318–328.

Sprung, J., Gajic, O., & Warner, D. O. (2006). Review article: Age related alterations in respiratory function—anesthetic considerations: [Article de synthese: Les modifications de fonction respiratoire liees a l'age—considerations anesthesiques]. *Canadian Journal of Anaesthesiology, 53*, 1244–1257.

Squire, L. R. (1989). On the course of forgetting in very long term memory. *Journal of Experimental Psychology: Learning, Memory, and Cognition, 15*, 241–245.

Stanley, S. M., Amato, P. R., Johnson, C. A., & Markman, H. J. (2006). Premarital education, marital quality, and marital stability: Findings from a large, random household survey. *Journal of Family Psychology, 20*, 117–126.

Stanley, S. M., Rhoades, G. K., & Markman, H. J. (2006). Sliding versus deciding: Inertia and the premarital cohabitation effect. *Family Relations: Interdisciplinary Journal of Applied Family Studies, 55*, 499–509.

Stanley, S. M., Whitton, S. W., & Markman, H. J. (2004). Maybe I do: Interpersonal commitment levels and premarital or non-marital cohabitation. *Journal of Family Issues, 25*, 496–519.

Starr, J. M., Deary, I. J., Fox, H. C., & Whalley, L. J. (2007). Smoking and cognitive change from age 11 to 66 years: A confirmatory investigation. *Addictive Behaviors, 32*, 63–68.

Statistics, Bureau of Labor (2006). *Nonfatal occupational injuries and illnesses requiring days away from work, 2005* (No. USDL 06–1982).

Staudinger, U. M., & Kunzmann, U. (2005). Positive adult personality development: Adjustment and/or growth? *European Psychologist, 10*, 320–329.

Staudinger, U. M., Marsiske, M., & Baltes, P. B. (1995). Resilience and reserve capacity in later adulthood: Potentials and limits of development across the life span. In D. Cicchetti & D. J. Cohen (Eds.), *Developmental psychopathology* (Vol. 2: Risk, disorder, and adaptation, pp. 801–847). New York: Wiley.

Staudinger, U. M., Smith, J., & Baltes, P. B. (1993). Wisdom-related knowledge in a life review task: age differences and role of professional specialization. *Psychology and Aging, 7*, 271–281.

Steele, C. M., Spencer, S. J., & Aronson, J. (2002). Contending with group image: The psychology of stereotype and social identity threat. In M. P. Zanna (Ed.), *Advances in experimental social psychology* (Vol. 34, pp. 379–440). San Diego, CA: Academic Press.

Stefanick, M. L., Anderson, G. L., Margolis, K. L., Hendrix, S. L., Rodabough, R. J., Paskett, E. D., Lane, D. S., Hubbell, F. A., Assaf, A. R., Sarto, G. E., Schenken, R. S., Yasmeen, S., Lessin, L., & Chlebowski, R. T., (2006). Effects of conjugated equine estrogens on breast cancer and mammography screening in postmenopausal women with hysterectomy. *Journal of the American Medical Association. 295*, 1647–1657.

Stengel, B., Couchoud, C., Cenee, S., & Hemon, D. (2000). Age, blood pressure and smoking effects on chronic renal failure in primary glomerular nephropathies. *Kidney International, 57*, 2519–2526.

Sternberg, R. J. (1985). *Beyond IQ: A triarchic theory of human intelligence*. New York: Cambridge University Press.

Sternberg, R. J. (1998). A balance theory of wisdom. *Review of General Psychology, 3*, 347–365.

Sternberg, R. J. (1999). The theory of successful intelligence. *Review of General Psychology, 3*, 292–316.

Sterns, H. L., & Gray, J. H. (1999). Work, leisure, and retirement. In J. C. Cavanaugh & S. K. Whitbourne (Eds.), *Gerontology: Interdisciplinary perspectives* (pp. 355–390). New York: Oxford University Press.

Steunenberg, B., Beekman, A. T., Deeg, D. J., Bremmer, M. A., & Kerkhof, A. J. (2007). Mastery and neuroticism predict recovery of depression in later life. *American Journal of Geriatric Psychiatry, 15*, 234–242.

Stevens, J. A., Ryan, G., & Kresnow, M. (2006). Fatalities and injuries from falls among older adults—United States, 1993–2003 and 2001–2005. *Morbidity and Mortality Weekly Report, 55*(45), 1221–1224.

Stimpson, J. P., Kuo, Y. F., Ray, L. A., Raji, M. A., & Peek, M. K. (2007). Risk of mortality related to widowhood in older Mexican Americans. *Annals of Epidemiology, 17*, 313–319.

Stine-Morrow, E. A., Milinder, L., Pullara, O., & Herman, B. (2001). Patterns of resource allocation are reliable among younger and older readers. *Psychology and Aging, 16*, 69–84.

Stine-Morrow, E. A. L., & Miller, L. M. S. (1999). Basic cognitive processes. In J. C. Cavanaugh & S. K. Whitbourne (Eds.), *Gerontology: Interdisciplinary perspectives* (pp. 186–212). New York: Oxford University Press.

Stoppe, A., Louza, M., Rosa, M., Gil, G., & Rigonatti, S. (2006). Fixed high-dose electroconvulsive therapy in the elderly with depression: A double-blind, randomized comparison of efficacy and tolerability between unilateral and bilateral electrode placement. *Journal of ECT, 22*, 92–99.

Strasser, A., Skalicky, M., & Viidik, A. (2006). Impact of moderate physical exercise—in comparison with dietary restrictions—on age-associated decline in cell-mediated immunity of Sprague-Dawley rats. *Aging Clinical and Experimental Research, 18*, 179–186.

Strenk, S. A., Strenk, L. M., & Koretz, J. F. (2005). The mechanism of presbyopia. *Progress in Retinal and Eye Research, 24*, 379–393.

Stroebe, M. (2001). Gender differences in adjustment to bereavement: An empirical and theoretical review. *Review of General Psychology, 5*, 62–83.

Stroebe, M., Gergen, M. M., Gergen, K. J., & Stroebe, W. (1992). Broken hearts or broken bonds: Love and death in historical perspective. *American Psychologist, 47*, 1205–1212.

Stroebe, M., & Schut, H. (1999). The dual process model of coping with bereavement: Rationale and description. *Death Studies, 23*, 197–224.

Stroebe, M. S., Stroebe, W., Gergen, K. J., & Gergen, M. (1981). The broken heart: Reality or myth. *Omega, 12*, 87–105.

Stroebe, W., Schut, H., & Stroebe, M. S. (2005). Grief work, disclosure and counseling: Do they help the bereaved? *Clinical Psychology Review, 25*, 395–414.

Stroebe, W., & Stroebe, M. S. (1987). *Bereavement and health: The psychological and physical consequences of partner loss*. Cambridge, England: Cambridge University Press.

Stroebe, W., Stroebe, M. S., & Abakoumkin, G. (1999). Does differential social support cause sex differences in bereavement outcome? *Journal of Community and Applied Social Psychology, 9*, 1–12.

Strotmeyer, E. S., Cauley, J. A., Schwartz, A. V., Nevitt, M. C., Resnick, H. E., Bauer, D. C., Tylavsky, F. A., de Rekeneire, N., Harris, T. B., & Newman, A. B. (2005). Nontraumatic fracture risk with diabetes mellitus and impaired fasting glucose in older white and black adults: The Health, Aging, and Body Composition Study. *Archives of Internal Medicine, 165*, 1612–1617.

Subak, L. L., Quesenberry, C. P., Posner, S. F., Cattolica, E., & Soghikian, K. (2002). The effect of behavioral therapy on urinary incontinence: A randomized controlled trial. *Obstetrics and Gynecology, 100*, 72–78.

Subramaniam, H., Dennis, M. S., & Byrne, E. J. (2006). The role of vascular risk factors in late onset bipolar disorder. *International Journal of Geriatric Psychiatry.*

Substance Abuse and Mental Health Services Administration (2006). *Results from the 2005 National Survey on Drug Use and Health: National Findings (Office of Applied Studies, NSDUH Series H-30*, DHHS Publication No. SMA 06–4194). Rockville, MD.

Sullivan, M. D. (2002). The illusion of patient choice in end-of-life decisions. *American Journal of Geriatric Psychiatry, 10*, 365–372.

Suominen, H. (2006). Muscle training for bone strength. *Aging Clinical and Experimental Research, 18*, 85–93.

Super, D. E. (1957). *The psychology of careers*. New York: Harper.

Super, D. E. (1990). A life span, life-space approach to career development. In D. Brown & L. Brooks (Eds.), *Career choice and development* (2d ed.). San Francisco: Jossey-Bass.

Sweeney, M. M., & Cancian, M. (2004). The changing importance of white women's economic prospects for assortative mating. *Journal of Marriage and the Family, 66*, 1015–1028.

Sweeper, S., & Halford, K. (2006). Assessing adult adjustment to relationship separation: The Psychological Adjustment to Separation Test (PAST). *Journal of Family Psychology, 20*, 632–640.

Szanto, K., Mulsant, B. H., Houck, P. R., Dew, M. A., Dombrovski, A., Pollock, B. G., & Reynolds, C. F., 3rd. (2007). Emergence, persistence, and resolution of suicidal ideation during treatment of depression in old age. *Journal of Affective Disorders, 98*, 153–161.

Takahashi, K., Takahashi, H. E., Nakadaira, H., & Yamamoto, M. (2006). Different changes of quantity due to aging in the psoas major and quadriceps femoris muscles in women. *Journal of Musculoskeletal and Neuronal Interactions, 6*, 201–205.

Talaga, J. A., & Beehr, T. A. (1995). Are there gender differences in predicting retirement decisions? *Journal of Applied Psychology, 80*, 16–28.

Talbot, L. A., Fleg, J. L., & Metter, E. J. (2003). Secular trends in leisure-time physical activity in men and women across four decades. *Preventive Medicine, 37*, 52–60.

Tanaka, H., & Seals, D. R. (2003). Invited review: Dynamic exercise performance in Masters athletes: Insight into the effects of primary human aging on physiological functional capacity. *Journal of Applied Physiology, 95*, 2152–2162.

Taylor, J. L., Kennedy, Q., Noda, A., & Yesavage, J. A. (2007). Pilot age and expertise predict flight simulator performance: A 3-year longitudinal study. *Neurology, 68*, 648–654.

Taylor, R. J., & Chatters, L. M. (1991). Non-organizational religious participation among elderly blacks. *Journal of Gerontology: Social Sciences, 46*, 103–111.

Taylor-Piliae, R. E., Haskell, W. L., Stotts, N. A., & Froelicher, E. S. (2006). Improvement in balance, strength, and flexibility after 12 weeks of Tai chi exercise in ethnic Chinese adults with cardiovascular disease risk factors. *Alternative Therapies in Health and Medicine, 12*, 50–58.

Teaster, P. B., Dugar, T. A., Mendiondo, M., Abner, E. L., Cecil, K. A., & Otto, J. M. (2006). *The 2004 Survey of State Adult Protective Services: Abuse of adults 60 years of age and older*. Washington, D.C.: National Center on Elder Abuse.

Teno, J., Lynn, J., Connors, A. F., Jr., Wenger, N., Phillips, R. S., Alzola, C., Murphy, D. P., Desbiens, N., & Knaus, W. A. (1997). The illusion of end-of-life resource savings with advance directives. SUPPORT Investigators. Study to Understand Prognoses and Preferences for Outcomes and Risks of Treatment. *Journal of the American Geriatrics Society, 45*, 513–518.

Teno, J. M., Gruneir, A., Schwartz, Z., Nanda, A., & Wetle, T. (2007). Association between advance directives and quality of end-of-life care: A national study. *Journal of the American Geriatrics Society, 55*, 189–194.

Teno, J. M., Weitzen, S., Fennell, M. L., & Mor, V. (2001). Dying trajectory in the last year of life: Does cancer trajectory fit other diseases? *Journal of Palliative Medicine, 4*, 457–464.

Tenover, J. L. (2000). Experience with testosterone replacement in the elderly. *Mayo Clinics Proceedings, 75 Supplement*, S77–S81.

Tentori, K., Osherson, D., Hasher, L., & May, C. (2001). Wisdom and aging: Irrational preferences in college students but not older adults. *Cognition, 81*, B87–B96.

Teri, L. (1994). Behavioral treatment of depression in patients with dementia. *Alzheimer's Disease and Associated Disorders, 8*, 66–74.

Terracciano, A., & Costa, P. T. Jr. (2004). Smoking and the five-factor model of personality. *Addiction, 99*, 472–481.

Terracciano, A., Costa, P. T. Jr. & McCrae, R. R. (2006). Personality plasticity after age 30. *Personality and Social Psychology Bulletin, 32*, 999–1009.

Terracciano, A., McCrae, R. R., Brant, L. J., & Costa, P. T. Jr. (2005). Hierarchical linear modeling analyses of the NEO-PI-R Scales in the Baltimore Longitudinal Study of Aging. *Psychology and Aging, 20*, 493–506.

Tharyan, P. (2007). The evidence for electroconvulsive therapy (ECT) in the treatment of severe late-life depression. ECT for depressed elderly: What is the evidence and is the evidence enough? *International Psychogeriatrics*, *19*, 19–23, 27–35; discussion 24–26.

Thomas, A. K., & Bulevich, J. B. (2006). Effective cue utilization reduces memory errors in older adults. *Psychology and Aging*, *21*, 379–389.

Thornton, W. J. L., & Dumke, H. A. (2005). Age differences in everyday problem-solving and decision-making effectiveness: A meta-analytic review. *Psychology and Aging*, *20*, 85–99.

Thurstone, L. L. (1938). *Primary mental abilities*. Chicago: University of Chicago Press.

Tinetti, M. E., Baker, D., Gallo, W. T., Nanda, A., Charpentier, P., & O'Leary, J. (2002). Evaluation of restorative care vs usual care for older adults receiving an acute episode of home care. *Journal of the American Medical Association*, *287*, 2098–2105.

Titone, D. A., Koh, C. K., Kjelgaard, M. M., Bruce, S., Speer, S. R., & Wingfield, A. (2006). Age-related impairments in the revision of syntactic misanalyses: Effects of prosody. *Language and Speech*, *49*, 75–99.

Tolin, D. F., Robison, J. T., Gaztambide, S., & Blank, K. (2005). Anxiety disorders in older Puerto Rican primary care patients. *American Journal of Geriatrc Psychiatry*, *13*, 150–156.

Tomita, T., & Iwatsubo, T. (2006). Gamma-secretase as a therapeutic target for treatment of Alzheimer's disease. *Current Pharmaceutical Design*, *12*, 661–670.

Townsend, J., Adamo, M., & Haist, F. (2006). Changing channels: an fMRI study of aging and cross-modal attention shifts. *Neuroimage*, *31*, 1682–1692.

Travis, S. S., Bernard, M., Dixon, S., McAuley, W. J., Loving, G., & McClanahan, L. (2002). Obstacles to palliation and end-of-life care in a long-term care facility. *The Gerontologist*, *42*, 342–349.

Trifunovic, A. (2006). Mitochondrial DNA and ageing. *Biochimica et Biophysica Acta*, *1757*, 611–617.

Troll, L. E. (1985). The contingencies of grandparenting. In V. L. Bengston & J. F. Robertson (Eds.), *Grandparenthood* (pp. 135–149). Beverly Hills, CA: Sage.

Tsai, S. P., Wendt, J. K., Donnelly, R. P., de Jong, G., & Ahmed, F. S. (2005). Age at retirement and long term survival of an industrial population: Prospective cohort study. *British Medical Journal*, *331*, 995.

Tsevat, J., Dawson, N. V., Wu, A. W., Lynn, J., Soukup, J. R., Cook, E. F., Vidaillet, H., & Phillips, R. S., (1998). Health values of hospitalized patients 80 years or older. HELP Investigators. Hospitalized Elderly Longitudinal Project. *Journal of the American Medical Association*, *279*, 371–375.

Tucker, P., Pfefferbaum, B., Nixon, S. J., & Foy, D. W. (1999). Trauma and recovery among adults highly exposed to a community disaster. *Psychiatric Annals*, *29*, 78–83.

Turcotte, M. (2006). Parents with adult children living at home. *Canadian Social Trends*, 11–14.

Turgeon, J. L., Carr, M. C., Maki, P. M., Mendelsohn, M. E., & Wise, P. M. (2006). Complex actions of sex steroids in adipose tissue, the cardiovascular system, and brain: Insights from basic science and clinical studies. *Endocrine Review*, *27*, 575–605.

Turvey, C. L., Conwell, Y., Jones, M. P., Phillips, C., Simonsick, E., Pearson, J. L., & Wallace, R. (2002). Risk factors for late-life suicide: A prospective, community-based study. *American Journal of Geriatric Psychiatry*, *10*, 398–406.

Twomey, F., McDowell, D. K., & Corcoran, G. D. (2007). End-of-life care for older patients dying in an acute general hospital—Can we do better? *Age and Ageing.*, *36*, 462–464.

Tyagi, S., Thomas, C. A., Hayashi, Y., & Chancellor, M. B. (2006). The overactive bladder: Epidemiology and morbidity. *Urological Clinics of North America*, *33*, 433–438, vii.

Uchino, B. N., Berg, C. A., Smith, T. W., Pearce, G., & Skinner, M. (2006). Age-related differences in ambulatory blood pressure during daily stress: Evidence for greater blood pressure reactivity with age. *Psychology and Aging*, *21*, 231–239.

Umberson, D. (1995). Marriage as support or strain: Marital quality following the death of a parent. *Journal of Marriage and the Family*, *57*, 709–723.

Umberson, D., & Chen, M. D. (1994). Effects of a parent's death on adult children: Relationship salience and reaction to loss. *American Sociological Review*, *59*, 152–168.

U.S. Bureau of the Census (1998). *Statistical abstract of the United States*. Washington, D.C.: U.S. Bureau of the Census.

U.S. Bureau of the Census (2001). AD-1. Young adults living at home: 1960 to Present. Washington, D.C.: U.S. Bureau of the Census.

U.S. Bureau of the Census (2006a). *America's families and living arrangements: 2005*. Washington, D.C.: U.S. Bureau of the Census.

U.S. Bureau of the Census (2006b). *Educational attainment in 2004*. Washington, D.C.: U.S. Bureau of the Census.

U.S. Bureau of the Census (2006c). Facts for Features. Washington, D.C.: U.S. Bureau of the Census.

U.S. Bureau of the Census (2007a). American Community Survey 2003 Data Profile. Washington, D.C.: U.S. Bureau of the Census.

U.S. Bureau of the Census, (2007b). American Community Survey 2005 Data Profile. Washington, D.C.: U.S. Bureau of the Census.

U.S. Bureau of the Census (2007c). B12007. Median Age at First Marriage—Universe: Population 15 to 54 Years. Washington, D.C.: U.S. Bureau of the Census.

U.S. Bureau of the Census (2007d). Current Population Surveys. Washington, D.C.: U.S. Bureau of the Census.

U.S. Bureau of the Census (2007e). National population estimates. Washington, D.C.: U.S. Bureau of the Census.

U.S. Bureau of the Census (2007f). Statistical Abstract of the United States, Table 274. Washington, D.C.: U.S. Bureau of the Census.

U.S. Bureau of the Census (2007g). Statistical Abstract of the United States: Table 294. Washington, D.C.: U.S. Bureau of the Census.

U.S. Bureau of the Census (2007h). Statistical Abstract of the United States, Table 608. Washington, D.C.: U.S. Bureau of the Census.

U.S. Bureau of the Census. (2007i). U.S. Interim Projections by Age, Sex, Race, and Hispanic Origin. Washington, D.C.: U.S. Bureau of the Census.

U.S. Cancer Statistics Working Group (2005). United States Cancer Statistics: 1999–2002 Incidence and Mortality Web-based Report Version. Atlanta: Department of Health and Human Services, Centers for Disease Control and Prevention, and National Cancer Institute.

U.S. Cancer Statistics Working Group (2006). *United States Cancer Statistics: 2003 Incidence and Mortality*. Atlanta: U.S. Department of Health and Human Services, Centers for Disease Control and Prevention and National Cancer Institute.

U.S. Department of Health and Human Services (1999). *Mental health: A report of the Surgeon General*. Bethesda, MD: U.S. Public Health Service.

U.S. Department of Health and Human Services (2004). *Bone health and osteoporosis: A report of the surgeon general*. Rockville, MD: U.S. Department of Health and Human Services, Office of the Surgeon General.

Vaillant, G. E. (1977). *Adaptation to life*. Boston: Little, Brown.

Vaillant, G. E. (1993). *The wisdom of the ego*. Cambridge MA: Harvard University Press.

Vaillant, G. E. (2000). Adaptive mental mechanisms: Their role in a positive psychology. *American Psychologist, 55,* 89–98.

Vaillant, G. E. (2003). A 60-year follow-up of alcoholic men. *Addiction, 98,* 1043–1051.

Vaillant, G. E., DiRago, A. C., & Mukamal, K. (2006). Natural history of male psychological health, XV: Retirement satisfaction. *American Journal of Psychiatry, 163,* 682–688.

Valentijn, S. A. M., Hill, R. D., Van Hooren, S. A. H., Bosma, H., Van Boxtel, M. P. J., Jolles, J., & Ponds, R. W. H. M. (2006). Memory self-efficacy predicts memory performance: Results from a 6-year follow-up study. *Psychology and Aging, 21,* 165–172.

van den Beld, A. W., Bots, M. L., Janssen, J. A., Pols, H. A., Lamberts, S. W., & Grobbee, D. E. (2003). Endogenous hormones and carotid atherosclerosis in elderly men. *American Journal of Epidemiology, 157,* 25–31.

Van Egeren, L. A. (2004). The development of the coparenting relationship over the transition to parenthood. *Infant Mental Health Journal, 25,* 453–477.

Van Gaalen, R. I., & Dykstra, P. A. (2006). Solidarity and conflict between adult children and parents: A latent class analysis. *Journal of Marriage and the Family, 68,* 947–960.

Van Manen, K.-J., & Whitbourne, S. K. (1997). Psychosocial development and life experiences in adulthood: A 22-year sequential study. *Psychology and Aging, 12,* 239–246.

Van Ness, P. H., & Larson, D. B. (2002). Religion, senescence, and mental health: The end of life is not the end of hope. *American Journal of Geriatric Psychiatry, 10,* 386–397.

Van Someren, E. J., Lijzenga, C., Mirmiran, M., & Swaab, D. F. (1997). Long-term fitness training improves the circadian rest-activity rhythm in healthy elderly males. *Journal of Biological Rhythms, 12,* 146–156.

Van Volkom, M. (2006). Sibling relationships in middle and older adulthood: A review of the literature. *Marriage and Family Review, 40,* 151–170.

van Zelst, W., de Beurs, E., & Smit, J. H. (2003). Effects of the September 11th attacks on symptoms of PTSD on community-dwelling older persons in the Netherlands. *International Journal of Geriatric Psychiatry, 18,* 190.

Vance, D. E., Roenker, D. L., Cissell, G. M., Edwards, J. D., Wadley, V. G., & Ball, K. K. (2006). Predictors of driving exposure and avoidance in a field study of older drivers from the state of Maryland. *Accident Analysis and Prevention, 38,* 823–831.

Vandewater, E. A., Ostrove, J. M., & Stewart, A. J. (1997). Predicting women's well-being in midlife: the importance of personality development and social role involvements. *Journal of Personality and Social Psychology, 72,* 1147–1160.

Vasdev, S., Gill, V., & Singal, P. K. (2006). Beneficial effect of low ethanol intake on the cardiovascular system:

Possible biochemical mechanisms. *Vascular Health and Risk Management, 2*, 263–276.

Vassar, R., Bennett, B. D., Babu-Khan, S., Kahn, S., Mendiaz, E. A., Denis, P., Teplow, D. B., Ross, S., Amarante, P., Loeloff, R., Luo, Y., Fisher, S., Fuller, J., Edenson, S., Lile, J., Jarosinski, M. A., Biere, A. L., Curran, E., Burgess, T., Louis, J.-C., Collins, F., Treanor, J., Rogers, G., & Citron, M. (1999). Beta-secretase cleavage of Alzheimer's amyloid precursor protein by the transmembrane aspartic protease BACE. *Science, 288*, 735–740.

Velkoff, V. A., & Lawson, V. A. (1998). *Gender and aging: Caregiving* (No. IB/98–3). Washington, DC: U.S. Department of Commerce.

Verhaeghen, P., Steitz, D. W., Sliwinski, M. J., & Cerella, J. (2003). Aging and dual-task performance: A meta-analysis. *Psychology and Aging, 18*, 443–460.

Verhaeghen, P., Vandenbroucke, A., & Dierckx, V. (1998). Growing slower and less accurate: Adult age differences in time-accuracy functions for recall and recognition from episodic memory. *Experimental Aging Research, 24*, 3–19.

Vermeulen, A. (2000). Andropause. *Maturitas, 34*, 5–15.

Vermeulen, A., Goemaere, S., & Kaufman, J. M. (1999). Testosterone, body composition and aging. *Journal of Endocrinological Investigation, 22*, 110–116.

Verquer, M. L., Beehr, T. A., & Wagner, S. H. (2003). A meta-analysis of relations between person-organization fit and work attitudes. *Journal of Vocational Behavior, 63*, 473–489.

Vig, E. K., Davenport, N. A., & Pearlman, R. A. (2002). Good deaths, bad deaths, and preferences for the end of life: A qualitative study of geriatric outpatients. *Journal of the American Geriatrics Society, 50*, 1541–1548.

Vitale, S., Cotch, M. F., & Sperduto, R. D. (2006). Prevalence of visual impairment in the United States. *Journal of the American Medical Association, 295*, 2158–2163.

von Muhlen, D., Laughlin, G. A., Kritz-Silverstein, D., & Barrett-Connor, E. (2007). The Dehydroepiandrosterone And WellNess (DAWN) study: Research design and methods. *Contemporary Clinical Trials, 28*, 153–168.

Wagg, A., Wyndaele, J. J., & Sieber, P. (2006). Efficacy and tolerability of solifenacin in elderly subjects with overactive bladder syndrome: A pooled analysis. *American Journal of Geriatric Pharmacotherapy, 4*, 14–24.

Walford, R. L., Mock, D., Verdery, R., & MacCallum, T. (2002). Calorie restriction in biosphere 2: Alterations in physiologic, hematologic, hormonal, and biochemical parameters in humans restricted for a 2-year period. *Journal of Gerontology: Biological Sciences, 57A*, B211–B224.

Walster, E., Walster, G. W., & Berscheid, E. (1978). *Equity: Theory and research*. Boston: Allyn & Bacon.

Wang, M. (2007). Profiling retirees in the retirement transition and adjustment process: Examining the longitudinal change patterns of retirees' psychological well-being. *Journal of Applied Psychology, 92*, 455–474.

Wang, Q. S., Tian, L., Huang, Y. L., Qin, S., He, L. Q., & Zhou, J. N. (2002). Olfactory identification and apolipoprotein E epsilon 4 allele in mild cognitive impairment. *Brain Research, 951*, 77–81.

Wannamethee, S. G., Shaper, A. G., & Whincup, P. H. (2005). Body fat distribution, body composition, and respiratory function in elderly men. *American Journal of Clinical Nutrition, 82*, 996–1003.

Warr, P. (1994). Age and employment. In H. C. Triandis, M. D. Dunnette & L. M. Hough (Eds.), *Handbook of industrial and organizational psychology* (pp. 485–550). Palo Alto, CA: Consulting Psychologists Press.

Warr, P., Butcher, V., Robertson, I., & Callinan, M. (2004). Older people's well-being as a function of employment, retirement, environmental characteristics and role preference. *British Journal of Psychology, 95*, 297–324.

Wayne, J. H., Randel, A. E., & Stevens, J. (2006). The role of identity and work-family support in work-family enrichment and its work-related consequences. *Journal of Vocational Behavior, 69*, 445–461.

Webster, B. H., & Bishaw, A. (2006). *Income, earnings, and poverty data from the 2005 American Community Survey*. Washington, DC: U.S. Bureau of the Census.

Wegge, J., von Dick, R., Fisher, G. K., West, M. A., & Dawson, J. F. (2006). A test of basic assumptions of Affective Events Theory (AET) in call centre work. *British Journal of Management, 17*, 237–254.

Weiner, D. K., Rudy, T. E., Morrow, L., Slaboda, J., & Lieber, S. (2006). The relationship between pain, neuropsychological performance, and physical function in community-dwelling older adults with chronic low back pain. *Pain Medicine, 7*, 60–70.

Weiss, A., & Costa, P. T. Jr. (2005). Domain and facet personality predictors of all-cause mortality among Medicare patients aged 65 to 100. *Psychosomatic Medicine, 67*, 724–733.

Weissel, M. (2006). Disturbances of thyroid function in the elderly. *Wiener Klinisch Wochenschrift: The Middle European Journal of Medicine, 118*, 16–20.

Weissman, M. M., Bland, R. C., Canino, G. J., Faravelli, C., Greenwald, S., Hwu, H. G., Joyce, P. R., Karam, E. G., Lee, C. K., Lellouch, J., Lepine, J. P., Newman, S. C.,

Oakley-Browne, M. A., Rubio-Stipec, M., Wells, J. E., Wickramaratne, P. J., Wittchen, H. U., & Yeh, E. K. (1997). The cross-national epidemioloty of panic disorder. *Archives of General Psychiatry, 54,* 305–309.

Weltman, A., Weltmen, J. Y., Roy, C. P., Wideman, L., Patrie, J., Evans, W. S., & Veldhuis, J. D. (2006). Growth hormone response to graded exercise intensities is attenuated and the gender difference abolished in older adults. *Journal of Applied Physiology, 100,* 1623–1629.

Wenger, N. S., Kanouse, D. E., Collins, R. L., Liu, H., Schuster, M. A., Gifford, A. L., Bozzette, S. A., & Shapiro, M. F. (2001). End-of-life discussions and preferences among persons with HIV. *Journal of the American Medical Association, 285,* 2880–2887.

Werner, P., Buchbinder, E., Lowenstein, A., & Livni, T. (2005). Mediation across generations: A tri-generational perspective. *Journal of Aging Studies, 19,* 489–502.

West, R., & Schwarb, H. (2006). The influence of aging and frontal function on the neural correlates of regulative and evaluative aspects of cognitive control. *Neuropsychology, 20,* 468–481.

Wetherell, J. L., Reynolds, C. A., & Gatz, M. P., Nancy L. (2002). Anxiety, cognitive performance, and cognitive decline in normal aging. *Journal of Gerontology: Psychological Sciences, 57B,* P246–P255.

Wethington, E. (2000). Expecting stress: Americans and the "midlife crisis." *Motivation and Emotion, 24,* 85–103.

Wheeler, I. (2001). Parental bereavement: The crisis of meaning. *Death Studies, 25,* 51–66.

Whisman, M. A., Uebelacker, L. A., Tolejko, N., Chatav, Y., & McKelvie, M. (2006). Marital discord and well-being in older adults: Is the association confounded by personality? *Psychology and Aging, 21,* 626–631.

Whitbourne, S. K. (1985). The life-span construct as a model of adaptation in adulthood. In J. E. Birren & K. W. Schaie (Eds.), *Handbook of the psychology of aging* (2d ed., pp. 594–618). NewYork: Van Nostrand Reinhold.

Whitbourne, S. K. (1986a). *Adult development.* New York: Praeger.

Whitbourne, S. K. (1986b). *The me I know: A study of adult identity.* New York: Springer-Verlag.

Whitbourne, S. K. (2002). *The aging individual: Physical and psychological perspectives* (2d ed.). New York: Springer.

Whitbourne, S. K. (in press). The search for fulfillment: Life paths in adulthood. New York: Ballantine Books.

Whitbourne, S. K., & Collins, K. C. (1998). Identity and physical changes in later adulthood: Theoretical and clinical implications. *Psychotherapy, 35,* 519–530.

Whitbourne, S. K., & Connolly, L. A. (1999). The developing self in midlife. In J. D. Reid & S. L. Willis (Eds.), *Life in the middle: Psychological and social development in middle age* (pp. 25–45). San Diego: Academic Press.

Whitbourne, S. K., Culgin, S., & Cassidy, E. (1995). Evaluation of infantilizing intonation and content of speech directed at the aged. *International Journal of Aging and Human Development, 41,* 107–114.

Whitbourne, S. K., & Sherry, M. S. (1991). Subjective perceptions of the life span in chronic mental patients. *International Journal of Aging and Human Development, 33,* 65–73.

Whitbourne, S. K., & Sneed, J. R. (2002). The paradox of well-being, identity processes, and stereotype threat: Ageism and its potential relationships to the self in later life. In T. D. Nelson (Ed.), *Ageism: Stereotyping and prejudice against older persons.* (pp. 247–273): MIT Press.

Whitbourne, S. K., Sneed, J. R., & Skultety, K. M. (2002). Identity processes in adulthood: Theoretical and methodological challenges. *Identity, 2,* 29–45.

Whitbourne, S. K., & van Manen, K.-J. (1996). Age differences and correlates of identity status from college through middle adulthood. *Journal of Adult Development, 3,* 59–70.

Whitbourne, S. K., & Waterman, A. S. (1979). Psychosocial development in young adulthood: Age and cohort comparisons. *Developmental Psychology, 15,* 373–378.

Whitbourne, S. K., & Willis, S. L. (Eds.). (2006). *The baby boomers grow up: Contemporary perspectives on midlife.* Mahwah, NJ: Lawrence Erlbaum.

Whitbourne, S. K., & Wills, K.-J. (1993). Psychological issues in institutional care of the aged. In S. B. Goldsmith (Ed.), *Long-term care administration handbook* (pp. 19–32). Gaithersburg, MD: Aspen.

Whitbourne, S. K., Zuschlag, M. K., Elliot, L. B., & Waterman, A. S. (1992). Psychosocial development in adulthood: A 22-year sequential study. *Journal of Personality and Social Psychology, 63,* 260–271.

Whitfield, K. E., Allaire, J. C., & Wiggins, S. A. (2004). Relationships among health factors and everyday problem solving in African Americans. *Health Psychology, 23,* 641–644.

Wickremaratchi, M. M., & Llewelyn, J. G. (2006). Effects of ageing on touch. *Postgraduate Medical Journal, 82,* 301–304.

Wieser, M. J., Muhlberger, A., Kenntner-Mabiala, R., & Pauli, P. (2006). Is emotion processing affected by advancing age? An event-related brain potential study. *Brain Research, 1096,* 138–147.

Wiggs, C. L., Weisberg, J., & Martin, A. (2006). Repetition priming across the adult lifespan—The long and short of it. *Aging, Neuropsychology and Cognition, 13,* 308–325.

Wilcox, S., Evenson, K. R., Aragaki, A., Wassertheil Smoller, S., Mouton, C. P., & Loevinger, B. L. (2003). The effects of widowhood on physical and mental health, health behaviors, and health outcomes: The Women's Health Initiative. *Health Psychology, 22,* 513–522.

Wilkins, C. H., Sheline, Y. I., Roe, C. M., Birge, S. J., & Morris, J. C. (2006). Vitamin D deficiency is associated with low mood and worse cognitive performance in older adults. *American Journal of Geriatric Psychiatry, 14,* 1032–1040.

Williams, K., & Dunne-Bryant, A. (2006). Divorce and adult psychological well-being: Clarifying the role of gender and child age. *Journal of Marriage and the Family, 68,* 1178–1196.

Willis, S. L., Blieszner, R., & Baltes, P. B. (1981). Intellectual training research in aging: Modification of performance on the fluid ability of figural relations. *Journal of Educational Psychology, 73,* 41–50.

Willis, S. L., & Marsiske, M. (1997). *Everyday problems test.*

Willis, S. L., Tennstedt, S. L., Marsiske, M., Ball, K., Elias, J., Koepke, K. M., Morris, J. N., Rebok, G. W., Unverzagt, F. W., Stoddard, A. M., & Wright, E. (2006). Long-term effects of cognitive training on everyday functional outcomes in older adults. *Journal of the American Medical Association, 296,* 2805–2814.

Wilson, M. N. (1986). The black extended family: An analytical consideration. *Developmental Psychology, 22,* 246–258.

Wilson, R. S., Arnold, S. E., Tang, Y., & Bennett, D. A. (2006). Odor identification and decline in different cognitive domains in old age. *Neuroepidemiology, 26,* 61–67.

Wilson, R. S., Mendes De Leon, C. F., Barnes, L. L., Schneider, J. A., Bienias, J. L., Evans, D. A., & Bennett, D. A. (2002). Participation in cognitively stimulating activities and risk of incident Alzheimer disease. *Journal of the American Medical Association, 287,* 742–748.

Winch, R. F. (1958). *Mate selection: A study of complementary needs.* New York: Harper & Row.

Wingfield, A., & Kahana, M. J. (2002). The dynamics of memory retrieval in older adulthood. *Canadian Journal of Experimental Psychology, 56,* 187–199.

Wittchen, H. U., Zhao, S., Kessler, R. C., & Eaton, W. W. (1994). DSM-III-R generalized anxiety disorder in the National Comorbidity Survey. *Archives of General Psychiatry, 51,* 355–364.

Womack, C. J., Harris, D. L., Katzel, L. I., Hagberg, J. M., Bleecker, E. R., & Goldberg, A. P. (2000). Weight loss, not aerobic exercise, improves pulmonary function in older obese men. *Journal of Gerontology: Medical Sciences, 55A,* M453–457.

Woo, J. S., Derleth, C., Stratton, J. R., & Levy, W. C. (2006). The influence of age, gender, and training on exercise efficiency. *Journal of the American College of Cardiology, 47,* 1049–1057.

World Health Organization (1997). *Composite International Diagnostic Interview (CIDI).* http://www.hcp.med.harvard.edu/wmhcidi/.

World Health Organization (2001). The World Health Report 2001. Mental health: New understanding, new hope, from http://www.who.int/whr2001/2001/main/en/index.htm.

World Health Organization (2002). *World Health Report: 2002.* Geneva, Switzerland: World Health Organization.

Wrosch, C., Schulz, R., & Heckhausen, J. (2002). Health stresses and depressive symptomatology in the elderly: The importance of health engagement control strategies. *Health Psychology, 21,* 340–348.

Wunderlich, G. S., Kohler, P. O., & Committee on Improving Quality in Long-Term Care, Division of Health Care Services, Institute of Medicine (Eds.). (2001). *Improving the quality of long-term care.* Washington, DC: National Academies Press.

Wyatt, C. M., Kim, M. C., & Winston, J. A. (2006). Therapy insight: How changes in renal function with increasing age affect cardiovascular drug prescribing. *Nature Clinical Practice: Cardiovascular Medicine, 3,* 102–109.

Yamamoto, Y., Uede, K., Yonei, N., Kishioka, A., Ohtani, T., & Furukawa, F. (2006). Effects of alpha-hydroxy acids on the human skin of Japanese subjects: The rationale for chemical peeling. *Journal of Dermatology, 33,* 16–22.

Yan, E., & So-Kum, T. C. (2001). Prevalence and psychological impact of Chinese elder abuse. *Journal of Interpersonal Violence, 16,* 1158–1174.

Yang, Y. (2006). How does functional disability affect depressive symptoms in late life? The role of perceived social support and psychological resources. *Journal of Health and Social Behavior, 47,* 355–372.

Yesavage, J. A., Brink, T. L., Rose, T. L., Lum, O., Huang, V., Adey, M., & Leirer, V. O. (1982). Development and validation of a geriatric depression screening scale: A preliminary report. *Journal of Psychiatric Research, 17,* 37–49.

Yong, H. H. (2006). Can attitudes of stoicism and cautiousness explain observed age-related variation in levels of self-rated pain, mood disturbance and functional interference in chronic pain patients? *European Journal of Pain, 10,* 399–407.

Young, A. F., Russell, A., & Powers, J. R. (2004). The sense of belonging to a neighbourhood: Can it be measured and is it related to health and well being in older women? *Social Science and Medicine, 59*, 2627–2637.

Zalaquett, C. P., & Stens, A. N. (2006). Psychosocial treatments for major depression and dysthymia in older adults: A review of the literature. *Journal of Counseling and Development, 84*, 192–201.

Zanetti, M. V., Cordeiro, Q., & Busatto, G. F. (2007). Late onset bipolar disorder associated with white matter hyperintensities: A pathophysiological hypothesis. *Progress in Neuropsychopharmacology and Biological Psychiatry, 31*, 551–556.

Zarit, S. H., Reever, K. E., & Bach-Peterson, J. (1980). Relatives of the impaired elderly: Correlates of feelings of burden. *The Gerontologist, 20*, 649–655.

Zarit, S. H., & Zarit, J. M. (1998). *Mental disorders in older adults: Fundamentals of assessment and treatment.* New York: Guilford.

Zeiss, A. M., & Steffan, A. (1996). Behavioral and cognitive-behavioral treatments: An overview of social learning. In S. H. Zarit & B. G. Knight (Eds.), *A guide to psychotherapy and aging* (pp. 35–60). Washington D.C.: American Psychological Association.

Zelinski, E. M., & Burnight, K. P. (1997). Sixteen-year longitudinal and time lag changes in memory and cognition in older adults. *Psychology and Aging, 12*, 503–513.

Zhang, F., & Labouvie-Vief, G. (2004). Stability and fluctuation in adult attachment style over a 6-year period. *Attachment & Human Development, 6*, 419–437.

Zhang, S. M., Manson, J. E., Rexrode, K. M., Cook, N. R., Buring, J. E., & Lee, I. M. (2006). Use of oral conjugated estrogen alone and risk of breast cancer. *American Journal of Epidemiology, 165*, 524–529.

Zimprich, D., & Martin, M. (2002). Can longitudinal changes in processing speed explain longitudinal age changes in fluid intelligence? *Psychology and Aging, 17*, 690–695.

Zmuda, J. M., Cauley, J. A., Kriska, A., Glynn, N. W., Gutai, J. P., & Kuller, L. H. (1997). Longitudinal relation between endogenous testosterone and cardiovascular disease risk factors in middle-aged men. A 13-year follow-up of former Multiple Risk Factor Intervention Trial participants. *American Journal of Epidemiology, 146*, 609–617.

PHOTO CREDITS

NAME INDEX

451